This book shows King James VI and I, of Scotland and England, in an unaccustomed light. Long regarded as inept, pedantic, and whimsical, James is shown here as an astute and far-sighted statesman whose reign was focused on achieving a permanent union between his two kingdoms and a peaceful and stable community of nations throughout Europe.

James sought closer relations among the major Christian churches – English, Calvinist, Lutheran, Roman Catholic, and Greek Orthodox – out of the conviction that they shared a common heritage and as a way of easing tensions in an era of recurring religious wars. As a result of these efforts and of British diplomacy wherever conflicts arose, James helped to secure and maintain a European-wide peace during most of his reign as king of Great Britain. In the major international crisis of his career, the outbreak of the Thirty Years' War, he worked tirelessly to try to reconcile the warring parties, despite opposition to his efforts at home and abroad, and came closer to succeeding than historians have recognized. James was a European by education and instinct, and he made Britain a major and constructive force in the international relations of his day.

Cambridge Studies in Early Modern British History

KING JAMES VI AND I
AND THE REUNION OF CHRISTENDOM

Cambridge Studies in Early Modern British History

Series editors

ANTHONY FLETCHER
Professor of History, University of Essex

JOHN GUY
Professor of Modern History, University of St Andrews

and JOHN MORRILL
Reader in Early Modern History, University of Cambridge, and Vice-Master of Selwyn College

This is a series of monographs and studies covering many aspects of the history of the British Isles between the late fifteenth and the early eighteenth century. It includes the work of established scholars and pioneering work by a new generation of scholars. It includes both reviews and revisions of major topics and books, which open up new historical terrain or which reveal startling new perspectives on familiar subjects. All the volumes set detailed research into our broader perspectives and the books are intended for the use of students as well as of their teachers.

For a list of titles in the series, see end of book.

KING JAMES VI
AND I
AND THE REUNION
OF CHRISTENDOM

W. B. PATTERSON

University of the South
Sewanee, Tennessee

CAMBRIDGE
UNIVERSITY PRESS

PUBLISHED BY THE PRESS SYNDICATE OF THE UNIVERSITY OF CAMBRIDGE
The Pitt Building, Trumpington Street, Cambridge CB2 1RP, United Kingdom

CAMBRIDGE UNIVERSITY PRESS
The Edinburgh Building, Cambridge, CB2 2RU, United Kingdom
40 West 20th Street, New York, NY 10011–4211, USA
10 Stamford Road, Oakleigh, Melbourne 3166, Australia

First published 1997

Printed in the United Kingdom at the University Press, Cambridge

Typeset in Sabon 10/12 [CE]

A catalogue record for this book is available from the British Library

Library of Congress Cataloguing in Publication data
Patterson, W. B. (William Brown), 1930–
King James VI and I and the reunion of Christendom / W. B. Patterson.
p.   cm. – (Cambridge studies in early modern British history)
Includes bibliographical references and index.
ISBN 0 521 41805 4
1. Great Britain – History – James I, 1603–1625.
2. Great Britain – Church history – 17th century.
3. Great Britain – Foreign relations – 1603–1625.
4. Scotland – History – James VI, 1567–1625.
5. James I, King of England, 1566–1625. 6. Thirty Years' War, 1618–1648.
7. Church history – 17th century.
I. Title. II. Series.
DA391.P38 1997
941.06'1–dc21   96–49359 CIP

ISBN 0 521 41805 4 hardback

CONTENTS

PREFACE

This book describes the efforts of King James VI and I to achieve a religious reconciliation among Christians of many persuasions – English Protestants, Lutherans, Calvinists, Roman Catholics, and Greek Orthodox. James saw religious reconciliation as the key to a stable and peaceful Christendom at a time when religious disputes exacerbated the conflicts among states. Despite the mistrust and opposition some of his efforts generated, they brought significant benefits to Britain and the continent.

While this is a study centered on James's ecumenical and irenic ideas and activities – not a political biography, nor a church history of his reign, nor an account of his foreign policy – it is broadly conceived. The book deals with the whole course of James's reign in Scotland and England in order to show how his vision of a reunited Christendom arose, how it developed in the context of domestic and foreign events, what various statesmen, scholars, and theologians contributed to it, and how he applied that vision to specific political and religious problems. The onset of a European war in the last part of James's reign thwarted his hopes for achieving a lasting peace, but in that crisis he came closer to attaining his objectives than is generally recognized. This book puts several aspects of James's reign in a new perspective: his foreign policy, his relations with the papacy, his part in the controversy over the Oath of Allegiance, his friendship with leading European intellectuals, his interest in the Greek East, his close relations with leaders of Protestant churches abroad, and his peace diplomacy in the early years of the Thirty Years' War. The resulting picture of James – very different from the one which prevailed until quite recently – is of a shrewd, determined, flexible, and resourceful political leader who had a coherent plan for religious pacification aimed at resolving urgent problems in the wake of the Reformation and Counter-Reformation.

I have been fortunate in having received generous support for my research and writing, including a Short-Term Fellowship at the Folger Shakespeare Library in Washington in the autumn of 1975, a semester in residence at the Institute for Research in the Humanities at the University of

Wisconsin–Madison in the winter and spring of 1976, and a National Endowment for the Humanities Fellowship at the Newberry Library in Chicago in 1979–1980. The Committee for Faculty Research and the Dean of the Faculty at Davidson College, North Carolina, made it possible for me to spend parts of several summers in the 1970s in Rome, Geneva, Paris, and Oxford, and the Joint Faculties' Research Grants Committee and the Fund for Faculty Development at the University of the South provided similar support for parts of several summers in the 1980s and early 1990s in London and Oxford. The Conant Fund administered by the Board for Theological Education of the Episcopal Church awarded me a fellowship for the 1992–1993 academic year, which I spent at the University of Virginia. It is a great pleasure to acknowledge the help and encouragement of the staffs at the libraries and archives at which most of my research has been carried out: the E. H. Little Library at Davidson College; the Jessie Ball duPont Library and the Library of the School of Theology at the University of the South; the Alderman Library at the University of Virginia; the Memorial Library at the University of Wisconsin–Madison; the Folger Shakespeare Library in Washington; the Newberry Library in Chicago; the Bodleian Library and the Exeter College Library in Oxford; the Cambridge University Library and the Sidney Sussex College Library in Cambridge; the British Library, the Public Record Office, and the Lambeth Palace Library in London; the National Library of Scotland in Edinburgh; the Bibliothèque Nationale and the Bibliothèque de l'Arsenal in Paris; the Bibliothèque Publique et Universitaire in Geneva; the Bibliothèque de la Faculté de Théologie Protestante in Montpellier; and the Vatican Library and Secret Archives in Rome. Special thanks are due to Sue Armentrout, Interlibrary Loan Librarian at the University of the South, for having obtained hundreds of books and articles for my use.

Most of the writing of the final draft of this book was done at the University of Virginia in 1992–1993, where I held a Mellon Appalachian Fellowship. I am immensely grateful to the Andrew W. Mellon Foundation, which funded the Appalachian Fellowship, and the Faculty Scholars Program at the University of Kentucky in Lexington which awarded the fellowship to me and administered it. Alice Brown, Director of the Faculty Scholars Program, and Robin Weinstein, Extension Coordinator, provided practical assistance throughout the year. Alexander Sedgwick, Dean of the Graduate School of Arts of Sciences at the University of Virginia, and Melvyn P. Leffler, Chair, and other members of the History Department were extremely hospitable. Most important for my project, Martin J. Havran, my mentor at the University of Virginia, devoted many hours to conversations with me, which were immensely beneficial. I read papers based on drafts of two chapters to the Medieval Circle, chaired by Everett

U. Crosby, and the History Department Workshop, chaired by Duane J. Osheim, where I received many helpful criticisms and suggestions.

Over the long period of gestation this book has required, I have benefited from the advice and encouragement of a large number of scholars. They include George H. Williams, Christopher Hill, the late Sir Geoffrey Elton, David L. Clark, Patrick Collinson, Simon Adams, Frederick Shriver, Georgianna Ziegler, Andreas Tillyrides, John Barkley, Ruzica Popovitch, James K. Cameron, Robert W. Henderson, Robert Kingdon, Hugh Trevor-Roper, Baron Dacre of Glanton, Donna B. Hamilton, Sir John Elliott, Brian G. Armstrong, Stephen Foster, John Tedeschi, Mark A. Kishlansky, John Booty, John Platt, Francis Edwards, Kevin Sharpe, Margo Todd, Peter Lake, Kenneth Fincham, Dewey D. Wallace, Jr., David Underdown, Glynne Wickham, Guy F. Lytle, III, Anthony Milton, Thomas F. Mayer, Francis C. Oakley, Arthur P. Monahan, W. Speed Hill, David Norbrook, Colin Davey, George Core, and Susan J. Ridyard. Among the many students who have helped me in a variety of ways, I am especially grateful to Charles Skinner, Paul Gallis, Martin Grey, Robert Bryan, William Eskridge, Robert Campany, Russell Snapp, Carleton Cunningham, Lisa Frost Phillips, Robert Ingram, Benjamin Stone, and Kevin Sparrow. In preparing the final typescript, Sherry Cardwell, Word Processor in Print Services at the University of the South, has been unfailingly professional and sympathetic.

Three historians were especially helpful to me as I wrote my final draft. John Morrill, Jenny Wormald, and Martin J. Havran read every chapter with their accustomed good humor and critical acumen. They saved me from many errors and started me on many fruitful lines of inquiry. The final shape of the book owes a great deal to their counsel, for which I am extremely grateful. Of course, the final result is my own responsibility, including any remaining errors and all idiosyncratic judgements.

I have received permission from the following to reprint parts of my earlier articles and chapters in collections of essays: Ecclesiastical History Society for "King James I's Call for an Ecumenical Council," *Studies in Church History*, VII (1971), "The Peregrinations of Marco Antonio de Dominis, 1616–24," ibid., XV (1978), "Educating the Greeks: Anglican Scholarships for Greek Orthodox Students in the Early Seventeenth Century," ibid., XVII (1981), "King James I and the Protestant Cause in the Crisis of 1618–22," ibid., XVIII (1982), and "Pierre Du Moulin's Quest for Protestant Unity, 1613–18," ibid., XXXII (1996); *Harvard Theological Review* for "James I and the Huguenot Synod of Tonneins of 1614," 65 (1972) – copyright 1972 by the President and Fellows of Harvard College; and Cowley Publications for "The Synod of Dort and the Early Stuart Church," in Donald S. Armentrout, ed., *This Sacred History: Anglican Reflections for John Booty* (1990). Some of the discussion of conciliarism is presented in expanded form in my article, "Hooker on Ecumenical Relations: Conciliarism in the English Reformation," in A. S. McGrade, ed., *Richard Hooker and the Construction of Christian Community* (Tempe, Ariz.: Medieval & Renaissance Texts & Studies, 1997), published by the Arizona Center for Medieval and Renaissance Studies at Arizona State University.

My wife Evelyn Byrd Patterson has been my closest collaborator and most valuable critic since I began this project more than two decades ago. I deeply cherish her continuing encouragement.

ABBREVIATIONS

BL	British Library
BN	Bibliothèque Nationale
Bodl.	Bodleian Library, Oxford
HMSO	Her/His Majesty's Stationery Office
PRO	Public Record Office
SP	State Papers
Vat. Arch.	Vatican Secret Archives

A NOTE ON DATING AND QUOTATIONS
FROM MANUSCRIPTS

Britain followed the Julian calendar during the late sixteenth and early seventeenth centuries, while most other countries in western Europe followed the Gregorian calendar. The Julian calendar was ten days behind the Gregorian calendar. In addition, the new year in Britain began on March 25, the Feast of the Annunciation, rather than January 1. For all British documents, including the despatches of ambassadors abroad, I have kept the Julian or old style of dating, except that I have made the new year begin on January 1. Other documents bear the original date, which can be assumed to be according to the Gregorian or new style of dating. In presenting quotations from manuscripts written in English, I have preserved as far as possible the original spelling, capitalization, and punctuation.

1

Scottish reconciler

On December 31, 1603, Jacques-Auguste de Thou, president of the Parlement of Paris and royal librarian to Henry IV of France, wrote a congratulatory letter to King James VI of Scotland who had recently ascended the English throne. De Thou's purpose, apart from celebrating the close joining of the French, Scottish, and English royal houses in James's lineage, was to present the monarch with a copy of his recently published book.[1] This was the first volume of the *Historia sui temporis*, a work which was soon to be regarded as one of the authoritative histories of the tumultuous events in France and Europe in the second half of the sixteenth century.[2] Henry IV, said de Thou, had urged him to send the British king a copy, and he had generously said that it should be inscribed to James. De Thou's letter specifically asked James, who was now cultivating new friendships and taking on new duties, to promote "the concord of the Church with common consent," rather than limiting himself to establishing peace within his own borders.[3]

Religious reconciliation, particularly in France, had long been one of de Thou's major concerns. Brought up and educated during the French religious wars, he had intended at one time to enter the priesthood of the Roman Catholic Church, but he had become, instead, a lawyer active in public life and had served as a counsellor to both Henry III and Henry

---

[1] Paris, BN MS. DuPuy 409, fol. 38; MS. Dupuy 632, fol. 2. De Thou evidently entrusted the delivery of the letter and the book to Christophe de Harlay, comte de Beaumont, the French ambassador in England. Beaumont reported on their favorable reception by the king in a letter to de Thou on March 10, 1604. MS. Dupuy 632, fols. 5–5 verso.

[2] James W. Thompson, *A History of Historical Writing*, 2 vols. (New York: Macmillan, 1942), vol. I, pp. 569–570; A. G. Dickens and John M. Tonkin, *The Reformation in Historical Thought* (Cambridge, Mass.: Harvard University Press, 1985), p. 72; Samuel Kinser, *The Works of Jacques-Auguste de Thou* (The Hague: Martinus Nijhoff, 1966), pp. 1–3.

[3] BN MS. Dupuy 409, fols. 3–38 verso; MS. Dupuy 632, fol. 2. For parallels between James's views and those of Gallican spokesmen like de Thou, see J. H. M. Salmon, "Gallicanism and Anglicanism in the Age of the Counter-Reformation," in his *Renaissance and Revolt: Essays in the Intellectual and Social History of Early Modern France* (Cambridge: Cambridge University Press, 1987), pp. 155–188.

1

IV.[4] While president of the Parlement of Paris, the central law court of France, he had helped to negotiate the Edict of Nantes, which guaranteed French Protestants a large measure of religious freedom and brought more than three decades of civil war to an end.[5] His history of this period, written in Latin so as not to inflame popular feelings, traced the efforts of moderate political and religious leaders to find a solution to the conflicts rending the social fabric of the nation. In his dedication of the history to Henry IV, written in 1601, de Thou paid tribute to the efforts of the French king in bringing about a judicious religious settlement. Differences over religion, he noted in the dedication, had provoked continuous warfare in the Christian world for the better part of a century.[6] "Flames, exile, and proscriptions" had done more to irritate than to heal afflictions of the spirit.[7] Persecution had only strengthened resistance and inspired dissidents to greater efforts.[8] What was needed was to draw together "by moderate conversations and by pacific conferences" those who otherwise seemed bent on confrontation and violence.[9] Using specific examples, de Thou endeavored to show that princes who "preferred sweetness to the force of arms for terminating wars of religion, even on disadvantageous terms, have acted prudently and in conformity with the maxims of the ancient Church."[10] It was for this challenging task of religious reconciliation that de Thou's letter and book sought to recruit James, a monarch

[4] Corrado Vivanti, *Lotta politica e pace religiosa in Francia fra Cinque e Seicento* (Turin: Einaudi, 1963), pp. 292–324.

[5] N. M. Sutherland, *The Huguenot Struggle for Recognition* (New Haven: Yale University Press, 1980), pp. 321–332; Roland Mousnier, *The Assassination of Henry IV: The Tyrannicide Problem and the Consolidation of the French Absolute Monarchy in the Early Seventeenth Century*, trans. Joan Spencer (London: Faber and Faber, 1973), pp. 143–151.

[6] De Thou's book appeared as *Historiarum sui temporis, pars prima* (Paris: Mamertus Patissonus, 1604). The preface was translated into French by Jean Hotman de Villiers and was published in Paris in 1604. The edition used here is Jacques-Auguste de Thou, *Histoire universelle*, 11 vols. (The Hague: Henri Scheurleer, 1740), vol. I, pp. xxxix–lxii. The reference is to page xli.

[7] Ibid., pp. xli–xlii.   [8] Ibid., p. xliii.   [9] Ibid.

[10] Ibid., p. xlvii. For Henry's efforts to achieve a religious reconciliation in France, see Mousnier, *Assassination of Henry IV*, pp. 138–183; Vivanti, *Lotta politica e pace religiosa*, pp. 189–291; W. B. Patterson, "Henry IV and the Huguenot Appeal for a Return to Poissy," in Derek Baker, ed., *Schism, Heresy and Religious Protest* (Cambridge: Cambridge University Press, 1972), Studies in Church History, IX, pp. 247–257, and "Jean de Serres and the Politics of Religious Pacification, 1594–8," in Derek Baker, ed., *Church, Society and Politics* (Oxford: Basil Blackwell, 1975), Studies in Church History, XII, pp. 223–244; David Buisseret, *Henry IV* (London: Allen and Unwin, 1984), pp. 28–29, 44–50, 70–74; Mark Greengrass, *France in the Age of Henri IV: The Struggle for Stability* (London: Longman, 1984), pp. 58–87; and Ronald S. Love, "Winning the Catholics: Henri IV and the Religious Dilemma in August 1589," *Canadian Journal of History*, 24 (December, 1989), 361–379. For Henry's conversion to Roman Catholicism and the religious, political, and cultural circumstances surrounding the event, see Michael Wolfe, *The Conversion of Henri IV: Politics, Power, and Religious Belief in Early Modern France* (Cambridge, Mass.: Harvard University Press, 1993).

who now reigned over three nations in the British Isles and could significantly influence European religious and political affairs.

If de Thou's audacious request that James commit himself to the cause of Christian unity is surprising, the king's reply is equally so. In his letter from Westminster on March 4, 1604, James thanked de Thou for his letter and book, and declared that he took in good part de Thou's exhortation that he participate in "the union of the Church" by helping to compose "the differences which prevail in Religion."[11] He assured de Thou that he was not only well disposed to this enterprise but wholeheartedly committed to it. James declared that he had never been "of a sectarian spirit nor resistant to the well-being of Christendom."[12] He wished, moreover, "that all Princes and Potentates were touched by the same inclination and desire" as he. James's hope was "to achieve and manage a work so worthy and important to that good conclusion, [namely] to the solace and universal peace of Christendom."[13] The king thereby pledged to be an active participant in a movement aimed at bringing about a new era of religious peace and concord in Europe. This exchange of letters between a Catholic historian and jurist, closely associated with the king of France, and a Protestant king, brought up as a Calvinist in Scotland and now the Supreme Governor of the Church of England, is striking in the concern both men showed for a religious peace beyond their own national borders. Neither de Thou nor James was content to see religious issues dealt with only on one side of the English Channel. Both felt that religious differences posed a serious threat to the Europe of which their countries were a part; both believed that a broader, more permanent settlement was urgently needed. Their letters speak of the concord of the Church, not the churches, and they stress the well-being of Christendom. Neither man, moreover, was simply using polite and well-modulated phrases without any intention of acting in accordance with his stated convictions. De Thou made Paris a center of irenic activity by his scholarship and by his correspondence with statesmen, scholars, and religious leaders.[14] James devoted a great deal of his time for more than two decades on the English throne to the task he had agreed to help carry out –

---

[11] BN MS. Dupuy 409, fol. 39; MS. Dupuy 632, fol. 3.
[12] BN MS. Dupuy 409, fol. 39; MS. Dupuy 632, fol. 3.
[13] BN MS. Dupuy 409, fol. 39; MS. Dupuy 632, fol. 3.
[14] BN MS. Dupuy 632 contains letters to de Thou thanking him for his book from Frederick, Elector Palatine, in Heidelberg, December 10, 1606 (fol. 7); Cardinal François de Joyeuse in Rome, January 29, 1604 (fol. 11); Philippe Canaye, sieur de Fresnes in Venice, March 10, 1604 (fol. 49); Joseph della Scala [Scaliger] in Leyden, March 13, 1604 (fol. 53); George Michael Lingelsheim in Heidelberg, October 1604 (fol. 66); and William Camden in London, May 1605 (fol. 101). Canaye commented that he believed that God had chosen such means as de Thou described for calming the clamors in church and state; he noted the exclusivist claims of Roman Catholicism towards the Reformed Churches and of the Reformed Churches towards the Anabaptists, and the need for charity by all (fols. 49

indeed, he had already begun this work through diplomatic channels, as de Thou was probably aware.[15]

James's concern for church unity on an international scale – reaching across denominational as well as national boundaries – became evident at the time of his accession in England. But it had been shaped and developed in Scotland, where he had been king for thirty-five of his thirty-six years before coming to England and where he had been personally responsible for the government for almost two decades. In a period of civil war and violent upheavals in Scotland, he had had ample opportunity to witness the divisive effects religion could have on the social and political life of his own nation. He had reflected upon the larger questions of the ruler's authority and responsibility in the religious as well as in the political sphere.

James was born on June 19, 1566, in the midst of a political and religious upheaval threatening the government of his mother, Mary Queen of Scots; and he was crowned king a little over a year later as one event in a rebellion aimed at ousting her from the throne and securing the Scottish Reformation on a permanent basis.[16] A civil war ensued between adherents of the queen and those of the infant king that continued until the surrender of Edinburgh Castle in 1573, when James was nearly seven years old. Some of James's earliest memories must have been of events during these years of religious and political turmoil, even though he was cared for by the earl and countess of Mar in the relative safety of Stirling Castle, and the government was in

verso–50). De Thou's thought and activities are described in Vivanti, *Lotta politica e pace religiosa*, pp. 292–324, 357–362, and *passim*.

[15] See below, chapter 2. De Thou kept in touch with events in England through Ambassador Beaumont, a family connection. BN MS. Dupuy 819, fols. 83–93, and MS. Dupuy 830, fols. 33–51, contain Beaumont's letters to de Thou, 1603–1604. For de Thou's subsequent relations with James, see H. R. Trevor-Roper, *Queen Elizabeth's First Historian: William Camden and the Beginnings of English 'Civil History'* (London: Jonathan Cape, 1971), pp. 12–17.

[16] Scholarly treatments of James's life and career in Scotland include Jenny Wormald, *Court, Kirk and Community: Scotland, 1470–1625* (London: Edward Arnold, 1981), pp. 143–190; W. Croft Dickinson, *Scotland: From the Earliest Times to 1603*, third edition, revised by Archibald A. M. Duncan (Oxford: Clarendon Press, 1977), pp. 365–401; Jennifer M. Brown, "Scottish Politics, 1567–1625," in Alan G. R. Smith, ed., *The Reign of James VI and I* (London: Macmillan, 1973), pp. 22–39; and Gordon Donaldson, *Scotland: James V to James VII* (Edinburgh: Oliver & Boyd, 1965), pp. 157–275. Maurice Lee, Jr., *John Maitland of Thirlestane and the Foundation of the Stewart Despotism in Scotland* (Princeton: Princeton University Press, 1959) says a great deal about James as well as his able minister. See also Maurice Lee, Jr., *Great Britain's Solomon: James VI and I in His Three Kingdoms* (Urbana: University of Illinois Press, 1990), esp. pp. 1–92. The still standard biography of James, D. Harris Willson, *King James VI and I* (New York: Henry Holt, 1956), treats the king's reign in Scotland in some detail on pp. 13–137. Among older works, T. J. Henderson, *James I and VI* (Paris and London: Goupil, 1904), pp. 1–169, is of special interest on Scotland. For a contemporary life by an unknown author, see *The Historie and Life of King James the Sext*, ed. Thomas Thomson (Edinburgh: Bannatyne Club, 1825).

the hands of regents who spent most of their time elsewhere.[17] But the fate of the regents themselves brought home to him the harsh facts of Scottish public life. His mother's half-brother, James Stewart, earl of Moray, the first regent, was killed in 1570 by a member of a family closely allied with his mother's party. The second regent, Matthew Stewart, earl of Lennox, James's paternal grandfather, was killed in Stirling by raiders from the queen's garrison in Edinburgh. John Erskine, earl of Mar, James's guardian, who served as the third regent for only a year, died a natural death. But the fourth regent, James Douglas, earl of Morton, whose firm control of the government lasted for a half-dozen years beginning in 1572, was eventually beheaded in 1581 for complicity in the murder of James's father, Henry, Lord Darnley, many years earlier.[18]

This lurid spectacle of political intrigue and violence may seem to have more to do with Scotland's propensity for feuding than with religion. But the parties that formed as a result of Mary's forced abdication had a great deal to do with the Protestant Reformation which had been approved by Parliament in the summer of 1560, during an interval between the death of the queen mother and regent, Mary of Guise, and the return to Scotland from France of her daughter Mary Queen of Scots.[19] Though Mary Queen of Scots had not attempted a Catholic restoration, neither had she ratified the legislation of 1560, and she had continued to attend mass in her own chapel. Her marriage to a Catholic, her cousin Darnley, and the birth of their son James seemed to threaten the future of Protestantism as well as the political prospects and material well-being of the supporters of the Refor-mation. Religion was a key element in the uprising against Mary Queen of Scots and in the formation of parties around her and around her infant son.[20]

Even after the king's party captured Edinburgh Castle with the help of English forces, and the future of Protestantism in Scotland seemed assured, parties with a religious as well as political orientation struggled to control the young king and to dominate his government. After Morton had been toppled from power in March 1578 by his political enemies, he managed to regain much of his influence over the king by joining in a plot with the

---

17 Willson, *King James VI and I*, pp. 19–27; Henderson, *James I and VI*, pp. 6–11. The violent and often treacherous actions of the civil war are described in *Historie and Life of King James the Sext*, pp. 74–145.
18 Donaldson, *Scotland: James V to James VII*, pp. 163–173.
19 Wormald, *Court, Kirk and Community*, pp. 95–102.
20 Dickinson, *Scotland: From the Earliest Times to 1603*, pp. 347–361. The complexities of these factions are made clear in Jenny Wormald, *Mary Queen of Scots: A Study in Failure* (London: George Philip, 1988), pp. 129–176. For the uneven pace of the Reformation, see Ian B. Cowan, *The Scottish Reformation: Church and Society in Sixteenth Century Scotland* (London: Weidenfeld and Nicolson, 1982), esp. pp. 115–120, 159–181.

young earl of Mar to take custody of the king at Stirling.[21] This grim example was to be imitated by other powerful figures who either kidnapped James or made audacious attempts to do so. In order to end the personal ascendancy over the king by his cousin Esmé Stuart, duke of Lennox, suspected of furthering pro-Catholic and pro-French activities, a group of Protestant nobles seized James in the Ruthven Raid in 1582 and kept him in confinement for ten months. James escaped, taking refuge with a group of conservative magnates, several of them Catholics.[22] Again, in 1585, a group of Protestant lords rose in arms, with the support of England, to force the removal of the king's leading minister, James Stewart, earl of Arran, whose policies were inimical to their interests and to the Scottish Kirk. In the 1590s, further attempts to seize the king – James then being a young man in his twenties – were made by his cousin Francis Stewart, earl of Bothwell, who for a time championed the cause of Protestants outraged by the actions of rebellious Catholic lords. As late as 1600, in a mysterious episode known as the Gowrie conspiracy, involving the same family with strong Protestant ties that had been involved in the Ruthven Raid, John Ruthven, earl of Gowrie, and his brother Alexander, master of Ruthven, both suspected of plotting to seize the king, were slain by followers of James.[23]

Religion was not, of course, the only element – or necessarily the most important element – in these and other threats and acts of violence in James's years at the head of the Scottish government. For better or worse, government in Scotland was intensely personal, even at the national level, and personal and familial loyalties as well as animosities played an important part in the political life of the nation.[24] But Scotland was also undergoing a momentous change as the result of the Reformation in 1560. Institutional forms were disappearing, worship had been drastically altered in some places, a reversal in foreign alliances was taking place, and social and moral values were being redefined. Powerful elements in society favored or opposed these changes and acted accordingly.[25] The crown had com-

[21] Donaldson, *Scotland: James V to James VII*, pp. 171–172. John Erskine, earl of Mar, wrested control of the king from his uncle Alexander Erskine, "who had succeeded his brother, the Regent Mar, as keeper of the king's person" (p. 171).

[22] Willson, *King James VI and I*, pp. 42–47; Donaldson, *Scotland: James V to James VII*, pp. 178–180, 187. Leaders of the Ruthven faction included William Ruthven, earl of Gowrie; Sir Thomas Lyon of Baldukie, master of Glamis; and Archibald Douglas, earl of Angus. Esmé Stuart (or Stewart), the only son of John, the third son of the third earl of Lennox, was brought up in France from an early age. Matthew Stewart, the fourth earl of Lennox, an older brother of John's, was James VI's paternal grandfather as well as the second regent. Esmé was thus a first cousin of James's father, Lord Darnley.

[23] Willson, *King James VI and I*, pp. 126–130; Donaldson, *Scotland: James V to James VII*, pp. 203–204; *Historie and Life of King James the Sext*, pp. 375–376.

[24] Brown, "Scottish Politics, 1567–1625," in Smith, *The Reign of James VI and I*, pp. 22–39; Wormald, *Court, Kirk and Community*, pp. 151–155.

[25] Dickinson, *Scotland: From the Earliest Times to 1603*, pp. 313–345; Wormald, *Court, Kirk*

paratively slender resources with which to maintain order and to extend, even in a modest way, the rule of law. Religious differences, dating from the middle decades of the century, when Protestant teachings and practices began to supplant those of Catholicism in many lowland areas, tended to exacerbate other sources of conflict and to make actions of an irresponsible and lawless kind seem morally acceptable. James's awareness of the uses to which differences in religion could be put was no doubt one reason that he, like Henry IV of France, became intensely interested in ways in which these differences could be peacefully resolved.

A special problem for James and for Scotland was the unfinished character of the Scottish Reformation during his reign, a circumstance which had led to serious disagreements among Protestants, especially on the subject of polity. The Reformed Kirk took shape in the 1560s, after Parliament had repudiated the jurisdiction of the pope, forbidden the mass, and approved a new confession of faith. This legislation had not been approved by Mary, though she had allowed its provisions to take effect and had, in the spring of 1567, accepted an Act of Parliament which affirmed the state of religion as it had existed from the time of her return to Scotland. The three fundamental religious acts of 1560 were finally reenacted by Parliament in December 1567, after James's accession.[26] In the meantime, the new Church had grown up alongside the shadow of the old, since those who held ecclesiastical offices were not dispossessed, though they found it difficult or impossible to carry out their spiritual functions. It was not until 1573, at the end of the civil war, that a systematic attempt was made to remove from office those clergymen who did not adhere to the teachings of the Scots Confession.[27] In the meantime, some of the provisions of the first Book of Discipline, drawn up by a group of ministers associated with John Knox in 1560–61, had been put into effect, including the holding of a General Assembly of the Kirk as the highest institution of ecclesiastical government. A major obstacle to the implementation of the book's provisions for education and charity was that it called for the use of all ecclesiastical revenues, and many of these were in lay hands.[28] The Book of Discipline had recognized the need for officials who would oversee local

---

and Community, pp. 75–121; J. H. S. Burleigh, *A Church History of Scotland* (London: Oxford University Press, 1960), pp. 117–187.

[26] Wormald, *Mary Queen of Scots: A Study in Failure*, pp. 103, 107–110, 120, 162–163; William Croft Dickinson, Gordon Donaldson, and Isabel A. Milne, eds., *A Source Book of Scottish History*, 3 vols. (Edinburgh: Thomas Nelson, 1958–1961), vol. II, pp. 185–187; vol. III, p. 3. For the full texts of these documents, see Thomas Thomson and C. Innes, eds., *The Acts of the Parliaments of Scotland*, 12 vols. (Edinburgh: Published by Royal Command, 1814–1875), vol. II, pp. 525–535, 548–549, and vol. III, pp. 36–37.

[27] Burleigh, *Church History of Scotland*, p. 194.

[28] James K. Cameron, *First Book of Discipline* (Edinburgh: Saint Andrew Press, 1972), pp. 3–14.

churches, supervise the establishment of new ones, and ensure that only qualified persons would serve as ministers. It specified that such officials, called superintendents, would be in charge of areas whose boundaries were intended to reflect the geographical configurations of the country.[29] In the early 1560s five superintendents and three bishops who conformed to the new religious settlement had begun their work. Despite the existence of this system, the government under Morton replaced it with another, by appointing Protestants to bishoprics held by Catholics, as they became vacant. The jurisdictional problems with the surviving superintendents were mostly resolved, but the new bishops earned the sarcastic name of "tulchans" for their willingness to allow revenues from their offices to be used for pensions or other political purposes.[30]

The opponents of episcopacy found an influential spokesman in Andrew Melville, recently returned from several years of study in Geneva, who helped to draw up a second Book of Discipline. This book described a system of polity by ecclesiastical councils from the local to the national level without any reference to bishops.[31] Though the book received the approval of the General Assembly in 1578, it was not immediately approved by Parliament. The result was that two systems of polity existed simultaneously in the late 1570s and early 1580s. One was that of bishops, with jurisdiction over the dioceses of the pre-Reformation Church. The other was that of kirk sessions and presbyteries, associations of ministers and elders which were linked to the higher councils or "courts" of provincial synods and the General Assembly of the whole Kirk.[32] James had, perforce, to grapple with a problem which threatened the unity and stability of the established Church. When the Melvillian system was accepted by the Assembly,

[29] Cameron, *First Book of Discipline*, pp. 20–75, 115–128. For discussion of this system and its significance, see Gordon Donaldson, *The Scottish Reformation* (Cambridge: Cambridge University Press, 1960), pp. 59–66, 102–129. For a contemporary description by a defender of episcopacy in the Scottish Church, see John Spottiswoode, *The History of the Church of Scotland* [first published 1655], ed. M. Russell, 3 vols. (Edinburgh: Oliver & Boyd, 1851), vol. I, pp. 325, 331–345, 371–372.

[30] Burleigh, *Church History of Scotland*, pp. 192–196; Donaldson, *Scottish Reformation*, pp. 159–173, 194–195; James Melville, *The Autobiography and Diary*, ed. Robert Pitcairn (Edinburgh: Wodrow Society, 1842), p. 31. As Burleigh explains, the bishops "were popularly derided as 'Tulchan,' the name given to straw-stuffed calf skins which country folk used to induce their cows to give milk more freely!" (p. 196). Such inroads on episcopal revenues by the government had been commonplace in pre-Reformation Scotland and were familiar in the Elizabethan Church of England.

[31] For Melville's part in drafting the book, which had over thirty authors, see James Kirk, ed., *The Second Book of Discipline* (Edinburgh: Saint Andrew Press, 1980), pp. 46–56. For a treatment of Scottish ecclesiastical polity seen as essentially presbyterian from 1560, see James Kirk, "'The Polities of the Best Reformed Kirks': Scottish Achievements and English Aspirations in Church Government after the Reformation: A Revision Article," *Scottish Historical Review*, 59 (1980), 22–53.

[32] Donaldson, *Scottish Reformation*, pp. 203–210.

however, he was not yet twelve years old, and the first steps that were taken to counter it were more the work of his leading ministers than they were his own. Under Arran's influence, the "Black Acts" of 1584 were passed, calling upon the bishops to set their dioceses in order and declaring the king supreme over the spiritual as well as the temporal estates.[33] This action was undermined by the Act of Annexation of 1587, passed under the influence of John Maitland of Thirlestane, the king's leading minister, which appropriated most of the properties of the bishops to the crown, severely weakening their position and lowering them in public esteem. Maitland had been a Marian and was suspected of Catholic leanings by some of the more extreme Protestants. But he saw clear advantages in maintaining close ties with the Kirk.[34] Meanwhile presbyteries continued to spread across the country and, in 1592, their dominance was recognized by a parliamentary act confirming the existing presbyterian system and in effect approving the major features of the second Book of Discipline.[35]

It might seem that the problem of polity had been solved for James as well as for the Kirk, so that all he needed to do was to accept the decisions made in 1592. But in fact this arrangement presented several practical difficulties, and it was, in addition, personally distasteful to the king. For one thing, it did not provide adequate representation of the Church in Parliament, where the clergy had traditionally constituted one of the three estates and had helped to counterbalance the influence of the nobility. For another, the system of presbyteries was not complete, especially in less populous areas, and the assembly found it necessary to appoint commissioners to exercise oversight where it was needed.[36] More importantly James had reason to be apprehensive about a system of ecclesiastical polity in which the crown did not play a central part. He was made acutely aware of this in a conversation with Andrew Melville in 1596 in which the theologian elaborated on the presbyterian theory of the two kingdoms by saying that in addition to the kingdom of which James was head, there was

Christ Jesus, and his kingdome the kirk, whose subject King James the Sixt is, and of whose kingdome [he is] not a king, nor a head, nor a lord, but a member; and they whom Christ has called, and commanded to watch over his kirk, and governe his spirituall kingdome, have sufficient power of him, and authoritie so to doe, both together and severallie, the which no Christian king nor prince sould controll and

[33] Dickinson, Donaldson, and Milne, *Source Book of Scottish History*, vol. III, pp. 39–43.
[34] Lee, *John Maitland of Thirlestane*, pp. 136–144; Gordon Donaldson, "The Scottish Church, 1567–1625," in Smith, *Reign of James VI and I*, p. 49.
[35] Dickinson, Donaldson, and Milne, *Source Book of Scottish History*, vol. III, pp. 47–49; Kirk, *Second Book of Discipline*, pp. 152–154; Lee, *John Maitland of Thirlestane*, pp. 248–250.
[36] Donaldson, *Scottish Reformation*, pp. 218–225. Donaldson argues that practical considerations were James's main concern.

discharge, but fortifie and assist, otherwise, not faithfull subjects, nor members of Christ.[37]

It was this theory, rooted in the theology of the Protestant Reformers and in formularies and pronouncements of the Kirk, which lay behind the distinction between ecclesiastical and civil authority in the second Book of Discipline: "the ministeris exerce not the civil jurisdictioun, bot teaches the magistrat how it sould be exercit according to the word."[38] James was not willing to subordinate the civil authority to the Kirk in the way this theory prescribed. Nor did he enjoy the hectoring to which he and members of his government were exposed from pulpits in Edinburgh and elsewhere. For his own part, he felt a deep responsibility for the Church which the theory and the polity of the second Book of Discipline seemed to deny.

Consequently the king took steps, in the late 1590s, to reshape the polity of the Church, make its voice heard in a regular way in the councils of government, and link it more closely to the crown. In this campaign, which had all the appearances of being well thought out in advance, James made use of the power given to the crown in the ecclesiastical legislation of 1584 and 1592 to determine the time and place of the meetings of the General Assembly of the Scottish Kirk.[39] Beginning in 1597 he deliberately scheduled most of its meetings in places that the more conservative ministers from the north of Scotland could easily reach and away from Edinburgh and St. Andrews, where members of the party of Melville were numerous. He also exercised a good deal of personal influence over the members by attending meetings and lobbying for the measures he wanted.[40] In May 1597 at Dundee, he persuaded the assembly to create a commission to confer with him about matters of concern to the Kirk between assembly meetings. By

---

[37] David Calderwood, *The History of the Kirk of Scotland*, ed. Thomas Thomson, 8 vols. (Edinburgh: Wodrow Society, 1842–1849), vol. V, p. 440. Andrew Melville's nephew James describes this incident, which he witnessed, in detail in *The Autobiography and Diary*, ed. Pitcairn, pp. 369–371. For a similar expression of this theory by Melville in 1595, see Calderwood, *History of the Kirk*, vol. V, p. 378.

[38] Kirk, *Second Book of Discipline*, pp. 171–172. For a detailed rationale for the theory, showing its theological antecedents in Scotland and on the continent, see James Kirk, *Patterns of Reform: Continuity and Change in the Reformation Kirk* (Edinburgh: T. & T. Clark, 1989), pp. 232–279. For a critique of the "two kingdoms" theory in light of medieval and Reformation relations between the civil and religious authorities in Scotland, see Gordon Donaldson, *Scottish Church History* (Edinburgh: Scottish Academic Press, 1985), pp. 220–238.

[39] Burleigh, *Church History of Scotland*, pp. 202, 204. Maurice Lee, Jr., in his "James VI and the Revival of Episcopacy in Scotland: 1596–1600," *Church History*, 43, 1 (March 1974), pp. 50–64, argues that James did not plan the restoration of bishops from an earlier time, as both of the contemporary church historians, David Calderwood, the presbyterian, and John Spottiswoode, the episcopalian, believed. Rather, writes Lee, "it was not until the summer of 1600 that he definitively made up his mind" (p. 51).

[40] Lee, "James VI and the Revival of Episcopacy in Scotland: 1596–1600," pp. 55–60.

December 1597 this commission, most of whose members were favorably inclined to the king, had petitioned that ministers be named to represent the Kirk in Parliament. In the same month, Parliament approved the naming by the king of ministers who would sit as prelates, though this would not affect their role in ecclesiastical affairs.[41]

The changes that followed led gradually but inexorably towards an episcopal system. In March 1598, at Dundee, the General Assembly responded to James's speech on behalf of parliamentary representation from the Kirk by approving a proposal for such representation. At an ecclesiastical convention at Falkland in July 1598, further suggestions were made that the king pick the names of these representatives from a list supplied by the General Assembly and that the representatives report to the assembly annually.[42] What James had in mind, however, is suggested by his *Basilikon Doron*, probably written in the summer or autumn of 1598, where he advised his son Henry, the heir to the throne, to support "godly, learned and modest men of the ministerie," so as to counter the influence of those "fierie spirited men," who maintained the doctrine of parity of ministers while calumniating and plotting against the king. By advancing the former "to Bishoprickes and Benefices," James wrote, "yee shall not onely banish their conceited paritie, ... which can neither stand with the order of the Church, nor the peace of a commonweale and well ruled Monarchie: but ye shall also reestablish the olde institution of three Estates in Parliament."[43]

The implementation of James's plan began in October 1600, when, with the support of the commissioners, he appointed ministers to the bishoprics of Aberdeen, Caithness, and Ross. They sat in Parliament and served as visitors to churches in their dioceses as directed by the General Assembly. By the summer of 1603 James had appointed two other bishops.[44] By these steps, an episcopal polity gradually emerged which was linked to the existing presbyterian system while preserving the role of the General Assembly as the supervisor of the bishops as well as the rest of the Kirk. In

[41] Dickinson, Donaldson, and Milne, *Source Book of Scottish History*, vol. III, pp. 53–54; Thomson and Innes, *Acts of the Parliaments*, vol. IV, pp. 130–131.

[42] Lee, "James VI and the Revival of Episcopacy in Scotland: 1596–1600," p. 61.

[43] Charles H. McIlwain, ed., *The Political Works of James I* (New York: Russell and Russell, 1965 – first published in 1918), pp. 23–24. James's Βασιλικον Δωρον, published in 1599 and 1603, is generally known as *Basilikon Doron*; the text followed here is that edited by McIlwain. For James's project to restore episcopacy in the context of Scottish religious and political history, see David George Mullan, *Episcopacy in Scotland: The History of an Idea, 1560–1638* (Edinburgh: John Donald, 1986), pp. 74–113. The extent and significance of James's insistence that bishops be understood as one of the three estates is analyzed in Michael Mendle, *Dangerous Positions: Mixed Government, the Estates of the Realm, and the Making of the Answer to the XIX Propositions* (University, Ala.: University of Alabama Press, 1985), pp. 3, 21–26, 73–113.

[44] Donaldson, "The Scottish Church, 1567–1625," in Smith, *The Reign of James VI and I*, p. 51; Burleigh, *A Church History of Scotland*, p. 206.

1606 James restored the endowments of the bishops, whose duties now included serving as moderators of presbyteries and provincial synods. To complete the project, in 1610, three Scottish bishops were brought to England to be consecrated by three English bishops, thus restoring to the Scottish episcopate the historic or apostolic succession that had been lost in Scotland but maintained in the Church of England.[45] The resulting polity combined presbyterian and episcopal forms of government.

These arrangements, though far from complete at the time James left Scotland for England, gave him an authority in the Church of Scotland analogous to that enjoyed by English monarchs in the Church of England.[46] They were consistent with parliamentary legislation in 1573 and 1584 which affirmed the king's supreme authority over all estates spiritual as well as temporal.[47] They also preserved a very real continuity with the past, since the resulting episcopal polity was close to the system of superintendents described by the original reformers in the first Book of Discipline and even to the proposals for a reinvigorated episcopacy set forth by Catholic reformers in Scotland in the 1540s and 1550s.[48] While there was a good deal of opposition to bishops, the system seems to have been acceptable to a majority of the members of the Kirk, perhaps because the changes involved were gradual and because they little affected the pattern of life developing in

---

[45] Dickinson, Donaldson, and Milne, *Source Book of Scottish History*, vol. III, pp. 55–61; Donaldson, *Scotland: James V to James VII*, pp. 205–207; Walter Roland Foster, *The Church before the Covenants: The Church of Scotland, 1596–1638* (Edinburgh: Scottish Academic Press, 1975), pp. 12–31; and George I. R. McMahon, "The Scottish Episcopate, 1600–1638," Ph.D. thesis, University of Birmingham, 1972, pp. 13–35. The Scottish bishops who were brought to London in 1610 were not consecrated by the archbishops of Canterbury and York, which might imply their subjection to the English Church, but by the bishops of Bath, Ely, and London. For the character of the Jacobean episcopate in Scotland – moderate, conciliatory, and Calvinist – see Jenny Wormald, "No Bishop, No King: The Scottish Jacobean Episcopate, 1600–1625," in *Miscellanea Historiae Ecclesiasticae*, VIII, ed. Bernard Vogler (Brussels: Nauwelaerts, 1987), pp. 259–267. Episcopal authority was reinforced by Courts of High Commission on the English model. See George I. R. McMahon, "The Scottish Courts of High Commission, 1610–38," *Records of the Scottish Church History Society*, 15, 3 (1965), 193–209.

[46] For the royal supremacy in England, see Claire Cross, "Churchmen and the Royal Supremacy," in Felicity Heal and Rosemary O'Day, eds., *Church and Society in England: Henry VIII to James I* (London: Macmillan, 1977), pp. 15–34; Henry Chadwick, "Royal Ecclesiastical Supremacy," in Brendan Bradshaw and Eamon Duffy, eds., *Humanism, Reform and the Reformation: The Career of Bishop John Fisher* (Cambridge: Cambridge University Press, 1989), pp. 169–203, and Leo F. Solt, *Church and State in Early Modern England, 1509–1640* (New York: Oxford University Press, 1990), pp. 8–30.

[47] Dickinson, Donaldson, and Milne, *Source Book of Scottish History*, vol. III, pp. 15, 40; Mullan, *Episcopacy in Scotland*, pp. 17–53.

[48] See Donaldson, *Scottish Reformation*, pp. 33–35. It was also close to the compromise proposed by ministers and councillors in 1586, combining elements of the presbyterian and episcopal systems; the General Assembly was unwilling, at that time, to put the compromise into practice. Dickinson, Donaldson, and Milne, *Source Book of Scottish History*, vol. III, pp. 43–48.

the local churches.[49] The king, as the one who appointed the bishops, was thus restored to a central position in the Scottish Church, which, at the same time, remained largely self-governing through its own representative institutions.

From the late 1580s to the late 1590s there was a recurring fear of Roman Catholicism in Scotland, coupled with a sense of apprehension occasionally resembling panic over Spanish designs in northern Europe. These apprehensions complicated James's efforts to reconcile religious and political factions in his kingdom. In 1586, the same year in which Mary Queen of Scots wrote from her involuntary confinement at Chartley Hall in England to the young Catholic Anthony Babington, giving her support to a plan to depose Queen Elizabeth with the help of foreign troops,[50] it was discovered that several Scottish lords were in communication with Spain. George Gordon, earl of Huntly, Robert, Lord Maxwell, and Lord Claud Hamilton asked for material support from Spain, as they did again in early 1588 in association with the Jesuit William Crichton.[51] Such intrigues were bound to be alarming to those who knew of them or suspected them in the era of Spain's ambitious attempt to launch an invasion of the British Isles. Even in the winter after the failure of the "Invincible" Armada of July and August 1588, Huntly, with the support of George Hay, earl of Errol, a recent convert to Catholicism, and David Lindsay, earl of Crawford, as well as Maxwell and Hamilton, promised the duke of Parma their assistance if he invaded England.[52] The Armada of 1588, as everyone knew, was not likely to be the last of King Philip II's military efforts in the vicinity of Scotland. Not only was Parma's Spanish army intensifying its efforts to subdue the rebellious Dutch, but the duke invaded northern France in support of the Catholic League in the year following Henry IV's accession in 1589. Meanwhile Spain was rebuilding its fleet for an invasion of England.[53] The actions of Huntly and the other Catholic lords were, in this

[49] Donaldson, *Scotland: James V to James VII*, pp. 202, 205–208. Lee, in *John Maitland of Thirlestane*, argues, on the other hand, that the restoration of episcopacy, reversing a key policy of Maitland, was "probably the most serious error of policy James ever made as king of Scotland . . . Episcopacy was desperately unpopular with the earnest presbyterians; it was popular with nobody" (p. 294). See also Mullan, *Episcopacy in Scotland*, pp. 114–135.
[50] Antonia Fraser, *Mary Queen of Scots* (London: Weidenfeld and Nicolson, 1969), pp. 475–500.
[51] Donaldson, *Scotland: James V to James VII*, p. 185.
[52] Ibid., pp. 189–190; Lee, *John Maitland of Thirlestane*, pp. 181–183; Henderson, *James I and VI*, pp. 108–110.
[53] J. H. Elliott, *Europe Divided, 1559–1598* (New York: Harper & Row, 1969), pp. 339–350; R. B. Wernham, *After the Armada: Elizabethan England and the Struggle for Western Europe, 1588–1595* (Oxford: Clarendon Press, 1984), pp. 23–47, 83–84, 96–97, 122–130, 181–206.

context, bound to seem subversive both to the state and to the established Protestant religion in Scotland.

Yet in these very years Huntly seemed to advance steadily in James's favor. After the fall of Arran at the end of 1585, Huntly and Crawford had become members of the council. Following Mary's execution in England in 1587, for which Patrick, master of Gray, the Scottish ambassador, received a great deal of the blame, much of Gray's property at Dunfermline was given to Huntly.[54] In July 1588, Huntly married the daughter of Esmé Stuart, with whom James had been on close personal terms, and for the rest of the year he was the king's favorite courtier. It was only after the arrival in Scotland in February 1589 of the incriminating letters to Parma that Huntly was dismissed as captain of the guard and briefly imprisoned.[55] During the next spring, when Huntly, Errol, and Crawford were reported to be assembling troops for a march on Edinburgh, the king advanced against them at Brig of Dee, near Aberdeen. Huntly and Crawford were given the light punishment of a few months' confinement.[56]

In 1592, following James's marriage to Anne of Denmark, which involved an extended stay at the Danish court, Huntly and his associates renewed their treasonable communications. At the end of the year, a packet of papers was discovered in the possession of George Ker, a Catholic soon to sail for Spain, which implicated Huntly, Errol, the young William Douglas, earl of Angus, and Sir Patrick Gordon of Auchindoun in a plan to give their support to a Spanish invasion. Blank sheets of paper signed by these four were presumably to be filled in with details of the help they would provide.[57] The discovery of these "Spanish Blanks" only strengthened the popular hostility against Huntly who, in the previous February, while he was resident at court, had treacherously murdered the young and "bonnie" earl of Moray, the son-in-law of the first regent of James's reign.[58] The murder by Huntly of the head of a rival northern family was a crime for which the king was apparently unwilling or unable to bring him to justice. But because of the recently discovered letters, James felt compelled in February 1593 to pursue Huntly in a short and inconclusive campaign. James's concern over the misdeeds of the Catholic lords seemed markedly

---

[54] Donaldson, *Scotland: James V to James VII*, p. 187; Lee, *John Maitland of Thirlestane*, pp. 113–114.

[55] Lee, *John Maitland of Thirlestane*, pp. 183–185.

[56] Donaldson, *Scotland: James V to James VII*, pp. 189.

[57] Donaldson, *Scotland: James V to James VII*, pp. 189–190; Lee, *John Maitland of Thirlestane*, pp. 256–258; *Historie and Life of King James the Sext*, pp. 257–269. Angus, who had only recently become earl, had reversed the staunchly Protestant tradition of his family.

[58] Dickinson, *Scotland: From the Earliest Times to 1603*, pp. 385–387; *Historie and Life of King James the Sext*, pp. 247–248.

less serious than over those of the earl of Bothwell, who had attempted to seize the king at the end of 1591 and again in June 1592, and who succeeded in a daring coup in late July 1593, which put Bothwell in control of the court until early September.[59]

During the ensuing months, the leaders of the Kirk were much less disposed to leniency towards the Catholic lords than the king. In late September 1593, the synod of Fife excommunicated Huntly, Errol, Angus, and Alexander, Lord Home, captain of the guard, in accordance with provisions adopted in the previous year to force Roman Catholics to accept the religion established by law. In October, commissioners of the Kirk presented the king with a petition which spoke of "the present daynger, wharein the kirk of God, the Kings Majesties awin person, and the haill commonweill standis into," if the excommunicated lords, described as heads of "all the papistis in Scotland," were not brought to justice.[60]

The steps by which the Catholic lords were disgraced and exiled took a year and a half, and the dénouement of this struggle was not at all what the leaders of the Kirk might have expected. By an Act of Abolition in late November 1593, Parliament decreed that everyone in the kingdom would be required to accept the established religion by the next February 1 or else go into exile. The act specified that the three earls, along with Gordon of Auchindoun, "sall not be accusit of the cryme thay war summonit for, foundit upoun the blancs, bot the same to remain aboleist and in oblevioun."[61] Huntly was to send away his uncle, James Gordon, a Jesuit, and Errol to do the same with William Ogilvie, a Jesuit. This offer was not accepted, however, with the result that in May 1594 Parliament declared the earls traitors. Meanwhile Bothwell had conducted his final raid against the king, who had repulsed the attack with the aid of the citizens of Edinburgh.[62] James conducted an extensive campaign against the earls in the autumn, burning the houses of Huntly and Errol, and commissioning Ludovick Stuart, duke of Lennox – the son of Esmé Stuart – to pursue their followers.[63] In February 1595, both Huntly and Errol went into exile, followed in April by Bothwell, who had ended up on the side of the

---

[59] Lee, *John Maitland of Thirlestane*, pp. 234–236, 252, 261–264.

[60] *Historie and Life of King James the Sext*, pp. 284–286. For the provision for excommunicating those who professed the "Romayne religion," see p. 256. The author – or one of the authors – of the contemporary *Historie* must have been a member of the group of commissioners from the Kirk who presented the petition to the king; he uses the pronouns "our" and "us" in his account of their interview at court.

[61] *Historie and Life of King James the Sext*, p. 294.

[62] Donaldson, *Scotland: James V to James VII*, p. 191; *Historie and Life of King James the Sext*, pp. 304–306.

[63] *Historie and Life of King James the Sext*, pp. 342–344. The earl of Argyll, acting as the king's lieutenant, had tried, unsuccessfully, to subdue Huntly's forces in early October; Sir Patrick Gordon of Auchindoun, on Huntly's side, was killed in the fighting (p. 342).

Catholics. But Huntly and Errol, unlike Bothwell, returned to Scotland in June 1596.[64]

The return of Huntly and Errol, coupled with the appointment in the same year of a council of eight financial officials at court, chaired by Alexander Seton, a suspected Catholic, helped to provoke outspoken criticism of the king and the government in the pulpit and in the General Assembly. After a riot in Edinburgh in December 1596, which involved demands for the ouster of Seton and two other members of the government, James began a series of moves that restored royal influence in the government of the Kirk.[65] By May 1597, the General Assembly had decided to lift the excommunication of the earls if they would follow strict procedures for showing their repentance and their commitment to the Protestant faith. They agreed to do so and were received into the established Church. In November the forfeiture of their property was lifted by Parliament.[66] So complete was their seeming rehabilitation that in 1599, when only seven copies of James's *Basilikon Doron*, giving advice to his young son, were printed and distributed, three of them went to the formerly Catholic earls, Angus, Errol, and Huntly.[67] Roman Catholicism in Scotland no longer seemed a political threat.

James's leniency towards the Catholic earls was difficult for most of his subjects to understand, especially since his own religious faith was, from all indications, resolutely Protestant. Separated from his Catholic mother and father in the first few months of his life, he had been brought up in a Protestant environment by the earl and countess of Mar. From the age of

[64] Donaldson, *Scotland: James V to James VII*, p. 193; *Historie and Life of King James the Sext*, p. 344. Bothwell remained abroad, where he died in Naples in 1612.

[65] Donaldson, *Scotland: James V to James VII*, p. 217; Lee, "King James's Popish Chancellor," in Ian B. Cowan and Duncan Shaw, eds., *The Renaissance and Reformation in Scotland: Essays in Honour of Gordon Donaldson* (Edinburgh: Scottish Academic Press, 1983), pp. 170–174; Lee, "James VI and the Revival of Episcopacy in Scotland, 1596–1600," pp. 53–54.

[66] Lee, "James VI and the Revival of Episcopacy in Scotland, 1596–1600," p. 56; Donaldson, *Scotland: James V to James VII*, pp. 193–194.

[67] James Craigie, ed., *The Basilicon Doron of King James VI*, 2 vols. (Edinburgh: Scottish Text Society, 1944–1950), vol. II, p. 7. Angus, who had apparently not gone into exile, was reconciled to the Kirk in 1597; he was excommunicated in 1603 and retired to France in the following year. Errol's reconciliation did not last; he was excommunicated in 1603. Huntly, whose rise to favor was marked by his becoming a marquis in 1599, was an undependable convert. Under suspicion for being insincere in his renunciation of Rome, he was received by the archbishop of Canterbury in 1612 and absolved by the General Assembly in 1616. Nevertheless, he apparently died as a Catholic in 1636. T. F. Henderson in *Dictionary of National Biography*, 22 vols. (London: Oxford University Press, 1959–1960), vol. VIII, p. 189; Gordon Donaldson and Robert S. Morpeth, *Who's Who in Scottish History* (Oxford: Blackwell, 1973), p. 102; Jenny Wormald, " 'Princes' and the Regions in the Scottish Reformation," in Norman Macdougall, ed., *Church, Politics and Society: Scotland, 1408–1929* (Edinburgh: John Donald, 1983), p. 78.

four he was tutored by the renowned scholar and poet, George Buchanan, whose faith was conventionally Calvinist, and by the younger and more amiable Peter Young, who had studied at Geneva under Theodore Beza, Calvin's associate and successor.[68] In 1581, when Esmé Stuart was a controversial visitor, James asked John Craig, an eminent minister and associate of the late John Knox, to draw up an unambiguous statement of Protestant principles by which he and other members of the court could clearly distinguish their views from those of the Church of Rome. The result was the King's or Negative Confession, signed by James and the rest of the court. It affirmed "the trew Christian Faith" as revealed in the preaching of the gospel, and rejected "all contrare Religion and Doctrine; but chiefly all kynde of *Papistrie* in generall and particular headis."[69] James's understanding and appreciation of the Scottish Kirk, moreover, was expressed in forthright terms to the General Assembly in 1590, when he called it "the sincerest kirk in the world."[70] The theology to which James adhered was, as might be expected, that of the Scottish Reformers of the early years of his reign. James himself wrote and published, in 1588 and 1589, two meditations on scripture that vividly expressed his theological convictions. His *Frvitfvll Meditation* on Revelation 20: 7–10, written in 1588, the year of the Armada, to rally his countrymen against attack, developed the view that Christendom had long suffered from the rule of "the Antichrist and his Clergie."[71] This rule had largely overcome "the sincere preaching of the Gospel, the true use of the Sacraments, which are seales and pledges of the promises contained therein, and lawfull exercise of Christian discipline."[72] Despite the Antichrist's joining forces with the kings of the earth, however, "victorie shall he not have, and shame and confusion shalbe his."[73] The stronger those forces became, "the faster approacheth their wracke, and the day of our delivery."[74] As to whether the pope bore the marks of the Antichrist, James asked bluntly: "Doeth he not vsurpe Christ his office, calling himselfe vniuersall Bishop and head of the Church? Blasphemeth he not, in denying vs to be saved by the imputation of Christ his righteousness? Hath . . . hee not so fully ruled ouer the world these many hundreth yeeres,

[68] Willson, *King James VI and I*, pp. 19–25.
[69] G. D. Henderson, ed., *Scots Confession, 1560 (Confessio Scoticana) and Negative Confession, 1580 (Confessio Negativa)* (Edinburgh: Church of Scotland, 1937), pp. 26–30, 103–105. For the historical circumstances, see Spottiswoode, *History of the Church of Scotland*, vol. II, pp. 267–268.
[70] Calderwood, *History of the Kirk of Scotland*, ed. Thomson, vol. V, p. 106.
[71] James I, *Frvitfvll Meditation, Containing a Plaine and Easie Exposition, or Laying Open of the vii. viii. ix. and x. Verses of the 20. Chapter of the Revelation, in Forme and Maner of a Sermon* [first published in Edinburgh, 1588] in *The Workes of the Most High and Mightie Prince, Iames by the Grace of God, King of Great Britaine, France and Ireland, Defender of the Faith*, ed. James Montague (London: Robert Barker and John Bill, 1616), p. 74.
[72] James VI, *Frvitfvll Meditation*, p. 74.   [73] Ibid., p. 78.   [74] Ibid., p. 80.

as to the fire went hee, whosoever hee was, that durst deny any part of his vsurped supremacie?"[75]

In James's *Meditation* on I Chronicles 15: 25–29, the king gave thanks for his country's dramatic deliverance from the Armada. When King David had vanquished the Philistines, he brought "the Arke of the Lordes covenant to his house in great triumph and gladnesse, accompanied with the sound of musicall Instruments."[76] David himself danced and rejoiced in a way which offended his wife, Michal. James defended "dancing, plaiing and such like actions" as matters indifferent in themselves and "good or evill according to their vse, and intention of the vser."[77] In any case, it was the religious response of the heart that mattered. He invited his countrymen to join him in bringing in the Ark by receiving the Gospel and by reforming themselves "as becomes regenerate Christians."[78] Christ is the source of salvation, James reminded his readers. Christians are saved through faith, as a result of which they strive to live in conformity with God's will.[79] Despite his own religious faith and that of most of his countrymen, there were, nevertheless, important reasons why James did not want to alienate the Catholic "interest" in Scotland.[80] For one thing, he depended on members of the nobility, including members of traditionally Catholic families who had served his mother, to help control extensive areas of the north and west. For another, he wanted to avoid forcing prominent Catholics into alliances with France or Spain, with the potential such alliances had for fomenting civil war. He was also eager to avoid a papal sentence of excommunication and deposition, such as that which had caused many difficulties for Queen Elizabeth in England. There were also personal reasons. The earl and countess of Huntly, for example, were very much his protégés. He must also have hesitated to condemn the Catholic lords for being in communication with Catholic powers abroad when he himself had been in communication with Spain, the papacy, the Guises (his French cousins), and even the duke of Parma. [81]

But there were important positive reasons, too. James seldom lost sight of long-range objectives, and in this case the objective was reconciliation. Reconciling those who were at enmity by reason of traditional rivalries,

[75] Ibid., p. 78.
[76] James VI, *A Meditation vppon the xxv. xxvi. xxvii. xxviii. and xxix. Verses of the XV. Chapter of the First Booke of the Chronicles of the Kings* [first published in Edinburgh, 1589] (London: Felix Norton, 1603), sig. A$_5$ verso.
[77] Ibid., sig. B$_4$ verso.   [78] Ibid., sig. B$_8$.   [79] Ibid., sig. B$_5$.
[80] See Donaldson, *Scotland: James V to James VII*, pp. 188–194; Lee, *John Maitland of Thirlestane*, pp. 273–283. For the continuing adherence to Catholicism by many members of the nobility in this period, see Wormald, "'Princes' and the Regions in the Scottish Reformation," pp. 65–84, and Keith M. Brown, "The Nobility of Jacobean Scotland, 1567–1625," in Jenny Wormald, ed., *Scotland Revisited* (London: Collins & Brown, 1991), pp. 61–72, esp. pp. 67–68.
[81] Lee, *John Maitland of Thirlestane*, p. 182; Willson, *King James VI and I*, p. 51.

conflicts, and feuds had been very much a part of his political program since the mid-1580s. In 1587, just before his twenty-first birthday, he had sought, somewhat naively, to resolve the disagreements between such traditional enemies as the master of Glamis and the earl of Crawford, and the earl of Angus and the earl of Montrose, by inviting them to a banquet and then having them take hands and walk in procession, two by two, from Holyroodhouse to the Market Cross in Edinburgh through apparently approving crowds.[82] He also attempted a resolution of conflicts at the end of 1595 in Edinburgh, when those who were seriously at odds, especially the border families, the Maxwells and the Johnstons, were invited to court to be reconciled.[83] The reconciliation of a significant number of Catholic lords to the court and to the Kirk was probably his most conspicuously successful effort, even if their religious conversion was only temporary and superficial. Furthermore, their example among their numerous kin over large areas of the country remote from the Protestant southeast was likely to be as effective as any number of newly established local churches. Throughout the 1590s James's hope for the future was fixed on the prospect of being Elizabeth's successor on the English throne. He not only wanted to avoid generating opposition to his accession on the part of Scottish and English Catholics and on the part of the Catholic powers abroad; he also wanted their support.[84] Consequently Catholics were, for the most part, admonished and exhorted in Scotland rather than persecuted, and James managed to stay on good terms with France, Spain, and the Spanish Netherlands, as well as with the Protestant states that were now Scotland's more natural allies.

But these considerations do not explain the number of Catholics or suspected Catholics who frequented his court in the 1580s and 1590s or were given his active encouragement. They included his cousin and boon companion, Esmé Stuart; the trio of earls – Huntly, Errol, and Angus; Alexander Seton, head of the group of ministers known as the Octavians; James Elphinstone and Thomas Hamilton, both Octavians; Alexander, Lord Home, chief of the guard; Patrick, master of Gray, a favorite courtier who became a diplomat; James Beaton, Catholic archbishop of Glasgow, an agent of his mother's whom James used as a diplomat in France; John Leslie, Catholic bishop of Ross, and William Chisholm, Catholic bishop of Dunblane, whose fortunes the king restored; and Alexander Montgomerie, the leading court poet.[85] Not only were Catholics or suspected Catholics

---

[82] *Historie and Life of King James the Sext*, p. 229.
[83] Ibid., p. 356.
[84] Willson, *King James VI and I*, pp. 143–149.
[85] Donaldson, *Scotland: James V to James VII*, p. 189; Wormald, *Court, Kirk and Community*, p. 189.

prominent at court and in his government in this period, but several of them, notably Seton, Elphinstone, and Hamilton, were key members of his Scottish administration after James became king of England.[86] It seems fair to say that, at least compared to many of his Protestant contemporaries, James found Roman Catholics congenial, perhaps because of their association with his mother and her party, perhaps because of their cosmopolitan interests and experiences, or perhaps because he liked to discuss and debate theological issues with them. It also seems reasonable to surmise that he hoped, by bringing the conservative, traditionally Catholic, formerly Marian elements of Scottish society into the Kirk, that he would help to moderate the influence there of the ultra-Protestants or those whom he called "Puritans," by analogy with the English party.[87]

In any case, by the end of the 1590s, there was no longer an active, politically involved group of Catholics in Scotland, and the presbyterian party of Melville was declining in power and on the defensive. Most of the major conflicts among the nobility had been resolved or were in abeyance. The crown was independent of the factions which had sought to control it and had sufficient support to be largely free from the threat of a seizure of power. The established Church was being reconstructed in such a way that it was clearly subject to royal control. The country was enjoying a long peace which helped to encourage the growth of the economy. This achievement invites comparison with the more celebrated achievements of Henry IV of France and Elizabeth I of England. Both France and England were largely secure, unified, and stable monarchies by the end of the sixteenth century, after France had been wracked by a generation of civil and religious war and after England had endured the threat of invasion and the disruptive activities of religious extremists of the left and right. What is remarkable about James's achievement, in contrast to those of Henry and Elizabeth, is how much he was able to achieve with so little physical force. Henry fought a long and bitter war against the French Catholic League. Elizabeth's government imprisoned and executed significant numbers of Roman Catholics and radical Protestants. James, on the other hand, worked patiently and resourcefully with only an occasional use of coercion. This partly resulted from the relative weakness and poverty of the crown; it was partly in recognition of the fact that, in many cases, the territorial magnates had larger numbers of kinsmen, retainers, and allies than he could easily put into the field. But, mainly, it was a matter of temperament and strategy. In

[86] Lee, "King James's Popish Chancellor," pp. 171–176; Donaldson, *Scotland: James V–James VII*, pp. 217–221; Lee, *Government by Pen: Scotland under James VI and I* (Urbana: University of Illinois Press, 1980).

[87] McIlwain, *Political Works of James I*, pp. 23–24; Donaldson, *Scotland: James V to James VII*, p. 220.

the recurrent crises of the 1580s and 1590s, James allowed the Catholic lords and the extreme Protestants in Edinburgh and the other burghs to play themselves out, ultimately allowing them to discredit themselves by their disruptive activities. He was then ready to receive back those who became moderates and were receptive to his leadership. By this means the crown grew steadily in reputation as a symbol of unity, and the court became a center of constructive political activity.[88]

It was in the confidence inspired by the events of the later 1590s that James wrote his first two treatises on government. In them can be seen the development not only of a theory of monarchy by divine right but of a view of the Church and the monarch's responsibility for its welfare.

In *The Trew Law of Free Monarchies*, published in 1598, James undertook to teach his countrymen the mutual obligations between subjects and their sovereign.[89] Ignorance of these principles – or adherence to contrary principles – had "procured the wracke and ouerthrow of sundry flourishing Common-wealths."[90] Scotland, especially, needed such instruction: "no Commonwealth, that euer hath bene since the beginning, hath had greater need of the trew knowledge of this ground, then this our so long disordered, and distracted Common-wealth hath."[91] James patterned his theory of the monarchy on the scriptures, especially Old Testament passages concerning kingship; on the history of Scotland; and on what he called the law of nature. According to I and II Samuel, I and II Kings, I and II Chronicles, the book of the prophet Jeremiah, certain of the Psalms, and St. Paul's Epistle to the Romans, kings had the duty of administering justice, establishing good laws and seeing that they were obeyed, serving "*as a good Pastour, to goe out and in before his people,*" and procuring peace.[92] "Kings are called Gods by the propheticall King *Dauid*," wrote James, "because they sit vpon God his Throne in the earth, and haue the [ac]count of their administration to giue vnto him."[93] The king's duties were similarly, though more specifically, spelled out in the coronation oath reflecting the development of

[88] Donaldson, *Scotland: James V to James VII*, pp. 212–237; Wormald, *Court, Kirk and Community*, pp. 150–159. Scottish Catholics were, in any case, almost chronically unable to act in concert or in accordance with a clearly formulated strategy. See Wormald, "'Princes' and the Regions in the Scottish Reformation," pp. 76–77, and William Forbes-Leith, ed., *Narratives of Scottish Catholics under Mary Stuart and James VI* (London: Thomas Baker, 1889), pp. 128–274.

[89] James VI, *The Trew Law of Free Monarchies: or, The Reciprock and Mvtvall Duetie betwixt a Free King, and His Naturall Subjects* (Edinburgh, 1598) – the book was published anonymously. It was subsequently published in London by T. C. in 1603 "according to the copie printed in Edenburgh." The text followed here is that in McIlwain, *Political Works of James I*, pp. 53–70. See also Johann P. Sommerville, ed., *King James VI and I: Political Writings* (Cambridge: Cambridge University Press, 1994), pp. 62–84.

[90] James VI, *Trew Law*, pp. 53–54.   [91] Ibid., p. 54.

[92] Ibid., p. 55. The italicized words refer to I Samuel 8: 20.

[93] Ibid., pp. 54–55. This sentence refers to Psalm 82: 6.

the institution in Scottish history. The oath committed the king "to maintaine the Religion presently professed within their countrie, according to their lawes, whereby it is established, and to punish all those that should presse to alter, or disturbe the profession thereof."[94] In his care and concern for his subjects and in his exercise of authority over them, the king acted as a father whose "chiefe ioy ought to be in procuring his childrens welfare."[95] This, James asserted, was according to the law of nature. He made clear that, in this conception of monarchy, the king was ordained for his people and not the people for him.

In return, James argued, the people owed their lawful and Christian king such obedience "as to Gods Lieutenant in earth, obeying his commands in all thing, except directly against God, as the commands of Gods Minister, acknowledging him a Iudge set by God ouer them, hauing power to iudge them, but to be iudged onely by God, whom to onely hee must give count of his iudgement."[96] In Scotland, he claimed, kings owed the nature of their authority in government to the special circumstances of the nation's early history. When the country was still thinly inhabited it had been conquered by King Fergus of Ireland. Fergus and his successors were thereby made masters of the land and all of its inhabitants. Kings were thereafter "the authors and makers of the Lawes, and not the Lawes of the kings."[97] Not only did kings precede Parliaments, but the king's approval was, to James's own time, necessary to give the force of law to any parliamentary statute. Though it was thus clear, James argued, "that the king is aboue the law," yet a good king would always conform to the law, since it was, after all, his own.[98] He was, indeed, bound morally, religiously, and pragmatically to keep it. At the same time his subjects had no more right to control, rebel against, or displace their legitimate king than vassals had to act in such a way against their liege-lords. Returning to the image of the family, James argued that the title *Pater patriae*, commonly given to kings, expressed the king's duty to promote his subjects' welfare and their duty to respect and obey him.[99]

James denied that a contract between the king and his people was contained in or implied by the coronation oath, but he agreed that "a king at his coronation, or at the entry to his kingdome, willingly promiseth to his people, to discharge honorably and trewely the office giuen him by God ouer them."[100] If the king should fail to keep his promises, the judge of his actions was God, not the people. "It followes therefore of necessitie, that God must first giue sentence vpon the King that breaketh, before the people can thinke themselues freed of their oath."[101] A complete breakdown of the

94 Ibid., p. 55.   95 Ibid., p. 56.   96 Ibid., p. 61.   97 Ibid., p. 62.
98 Ibid., p. 63.   99 Ibid., pp. 64–65.   100 Ibid., p. 68.   101 Ibid.

relationship between the king and his subjects would still not justify him in seeking to destroy them nor them in seeking to overthrow him. The people remain duty-bound not only to their particular king but to his "lawfull heires and posterity."[102] This did not mean, however, that wicked kings would escape divine judgement, even in this life: "*Ioues* thunderclaps light oftner and sorer upon the high & stately oakes, then on the low and supple willow trees."[103]

James was attempting to refute theories of resistance and contract that had grown up in France during the civil wars there, in Germany and Switzerland among English exiles during the reign of Mary Tudor, and in Scotland itself.[104] The chief Scottish exponent of this point of view was, in fact, George Buchanan, James's childhood tutor who had, all too strenuously, attempted to instill his principles into the young king's mind. Perhaps because of that circumstance, Buchanan's *De jure regni apud Scotos*, or "The Powers of the Crown in Scotland," was the work James's *Trew Law* most directly contradicted.[105] Buchanan's treatise was evidently written in the aftermath of the successful attempt to force James's mother Mary Queen of Scots off the throne – an action in which Buchanan was very much involved. The treatise was dedicated to James when it was eventually published in 1579. The king, then twelve years old, was still under his teacher's care and would remain so for the next few years. Buchanan's theory, developed in an imaginary dialogue with Thomas Maitland, a brother of Sir William Maitland of Lethington, a key though not unwavering supporter of Mary Queen of Scots, stressed that kings owed their

[102] Ibid., p. 69.   [103] Ibid., p. 70.
[104] J. W. Allen, *A History of Political Thought in the Sixteenth Century*, revised edition (London: Methuen, 1957), pp. 103–120, 302–342; J. H. M. Salmon, *The French Religious Wars in English Political Thought* (Oxford: Clarendon Press, 1959); Quentin Skinner, *The Foundations of Modern Political Thought*, 2 vols. (Cambridge: Cambridge University Press, 1978), vol. II, pp. 189–238, 302–348; J. H. Burns, "The Political Ideas of the Scottish Reformation," *Aberdeen University Review*, 36 (1955–1956), 251–268; and Lee, *Great Britain's Solomon*, pp. 81–86.
[105] Buchanan published his *De jure regni apud Scotos* in 1579, though it had been, he said, written some years before. The text followed here is George Buchanan, *The Powers of the Crown in Scotland*, ed. and trans. Charles F. Arrowood (Austin: University of Texas Press, 1949). Commentaries, in addition to those cited above, include J. H. Burns, "The Political Ideas of George Buchanan," *Scottish Historical Review*, 30 (1951), 60–68; H. R. Trevor-Roper, "George Buchanan and the Ancient Scottish Constitution," *English Historical Review*, Supplement 3 (1966), 1–53; Skinner, *Foundations*, vol. II, pp. 339–348; I. D. McFarlane, *Buchanan* (London: Duckworth, 1981), pp. 320–354, 392–421; Roger A. Mason, "Rex Stoicus: George Buchanan, James VI and the Scottish Polity," in John Dwyer, Roger A. Mason, and Alexander Murdoch, eds., *New Perspectives on the Politics and Culture of Early Modern Scotland* (Edinburgh: John Donald, 1982), pp. 9–33; and Jenny Wormald, "Resistance and Regicide in Sixteenth-Century Scotland: The Execution of Mary Queen of Scots," *Majestas*, 1 (1993), 67–87.

political authority to the people over whom they ruled.[106] Limitations, expressed in law, were placed by the people on kings to curtail their excesses. Laws were enacted not by kings alone but jointly with representatives of the people in a public proceeding.[107] Nor were kings the sole interpreters of the laws, since the laws would then serve as little restraint. Kings who abused their powers by becoming tyrants could be called to account by their subjects, imprisoned, exiled, or put to death.[108] Such actions had frequently occurred in Scottish history, Buchanan argued. Indeed, he devoted many years to composing a *Historia* to support the theory developed here.[109] When Maitland asked what would happen if an accused king would not submit to a trial, Buchanan answered that "robbers who are so powerful that they cannot be dealt with by the ordinary process of law are pursued as in a war with force of arms."[110] To Maitland's objection that subjects are sworn to obey their king, Buchanan answered that there is "a mutual compact between king and citizens" and that the one who "first withdraws from the covenant" breaks the agreement.[111] Tyrants, he argued, were to be regarded "as the most savage of all monsters."[112] From James's point of view, Buchanan's theory was a formula for civil war and chaos of a kind from which Scotland, under his leadership, was just emerging. It was also, he felt, based on a misunderstanding of Scottish history as well as the country's political institutions.

James's other treatise, *Basilikon Doron*, was published in only seven copies in 1599.[113] Though intended for his son alone, inaccurate copies were soon in circulation, making it necessary to publish another edition in 1603 with a preface explaining some of the more contentious passages. The fact that the book was originally intended for a small circle, not the general public, probably accounts for the king's occasional use of more pungent and outspoken language than he used in the first treatise. James began by describing the king's duty to God, in the course of which he stated the key

[106] Buchanan, *Powers of the Crown*, p. 52.   [107] Ibid., pp. 56–58, 70.
[108] Ibid., pp. 117, 123–124, 131.
[109] Ibid., pp. 100–103; McFarlane, *Buchanan*, pp. 416–440. Buchanan's *Rerum Scoticarum Historia* was published in Edinburgh in 1582.
[110] Buchanan, *Powers of the Crown*, p. 142.   [111] Ibid.
[112] Ibid., p. 145.
[113] James VI, βασιλικον Δώρον: *Devided into Three Bookes* (Edinburgh: R. Waldegrave, 1599). A critical edition with commentary is provided in Craigie, ed., *Basilicon Doron*, 2 vols. Seven copies were printed so that key individuals – Queen Anne, Adam Newton (the prince's schoolmaster), the three so-called Catholic earls, Angus, Huntly, and Errol, and the marquis of Hamilton – could have copies to share with the prince, then five years old, if the need arose. The first public edition, βασιλικον Δώρον: *or, His Maiesties Instructions to His Dearest Sonne Henry the Prince* (Edinburgh: R. Waldegrave, 1603), is a considerably revised version. It was also published in London by John Norton in 1603. The text used here for the book generally known as *Basilikon Doron* is that in McIlwain, *Political Works of James I*, pp. 3–52.

components of his own religious faith, which he invited his son to follow. His religion was based on "the plaine words of the Scripture, without the which all points of Religion are superfluous, as any thing contrary to the same is abomination."[114] Salvation he understood as the result of Christ's sacrifice apprehended by faith, not the result of works. Faith was "*the free gift of God*," and was nourished by prayer.[115] With reference to the Church, he warned the young prince to avoid two extremes: "the one, to beleeue with the Papists, the Churches authority, better then your owne knowledge; the other, to leane with the Anabaptists, to your owne conceits and dreamed reuelations."[116]

In describing the king's civic duties, James warned that Parliament, "the honourablest and highest iudgement in the land (as being the Kings head Court)," could become the "in-iustest Iudgement-seat that may be," if it were made to serve the interests of particular men.[117] He therefore advised his son to "hold no Parliaments, but for necessitie of new Lawes, which would be but seldome: for few Lawes and well put in execution, are best in a well ruled common-weale."[118] Among crimes requiring the strictest sanctions he cited "the false and vnreuerent writing or speaking of malicious men against your Parents and Predecessors."[119] His reference here was to his own unhappy experience: "For besides the iudgments of God, that with my eyes I haue seene fall vpon all them that were chiefe traitours to my parents, I may iustly affirme, I neuer found yet a constant biding by me in all my straites, by any that were of perfite aage in my parents dayes, but onely by such as constantly bode by them; I meane specially by them that serued the Queen my mother."[120]

Consideration of his mother's reign evidently led James to consider the way in which the Scottish Reformation had occurred. He had no doubt that it was the pride, ambition, and avarice of the old Church which had brought about its downfall. But in the process "many things were inordinately done by a popular tumult and rebellion," with the result that the traditional polity of the Church was destroyed and the Reformation lacked a "Princes order."[121] James said that "some fierie spirited men in the ministerie" then got a considerable popular following, began to think about a "Democraticke forme of gouernment," and resolved to remain active in politics.[122] They had been involved in every faction James had known since his youth. They overshadowed and intimidated the "learned, godly, and modest" ministers.[123] James warned his son against such "Puritanes," describing them as "verie pestes in the Church and Common-weale, whom

---

[114] James VI, *Basilikon Doron*, p. 13.
[115] Ibid., p. 15. The italicized words refer to Philippians 1: 29.   [116] Ibid., p. 17.
[117] Ibid., p. 19.   [118] Ibid., p. 20.   [119] Ibid., p. 21.   [120] Ibid.
[121] Ibid., p. 23.   [122] Ibid.   [123] Ibid.

no deserts can oblige, neither oathes or promises bind, breathing nothing but sedition and calumnies, aspiring without measure, railing without reason, and making their own imaginations (without any warrant of the word) the square of their conscience."[124] The best antidote for their poison was to advance "the godly, learned and modest men of the ministerie," of whom there were many, to benefices and bishoprics.[125]

Underlying the discussion of religion was James's vision of the Church as one which would foster moral behavior, peace in the commonwealth, and true learning. The king had much of the responsibility for seeing that the Church developed in this way. He called upon the prince to be

a louing nourish-father to the Church, seeing all the Churches within your dominions planted with good Pastors, the Schooles (the seminarie of the Church) maintained, the doctrine and discipline preserued in puritie, according to Gods word, a sufficient prouision for their sustentation, a comely order in their policie, pride punished, humilitie aduanced, and they so to reuerence their superiors, and their flockes them, as the flourishing of your Church in pietie, peace, and learning, may be one of the chiefe points of your earthly glory.[126]

Just as the prince was to be wary of the "vaine Puritane," so he was to be of "proude Papall Bishops."[127] Against fractious clergy he was to proceed only on "good ground and warrant," but without much debate.[128] No meetings or conventions of clergy were to be held without his "knowledge and permission."[129]

A clue to James's view of his own role in the Church is to be found in a comment on clothing suitable for a king, where he urges modest dress in keeping with the religious nature of his position: "Be also moderate in your raiment . . . not ouer lightly like a Candie souldier or a vaine young Courtier; nor yet ouer grauely, like a Minister . . . as your office is likewise mixed, betwixt the Ecclesiasticall and civill estate: For a King is not *mere laicus*, as both the Papists and the Anabaptists would haue him, to the which error also the Puritanes incline ouer farre."[130] By "not a mere layman," James no doubt meant to point both to his constitutional responsibility for the Church and to the sacred character of the monarchy itself.

---

[124] Ibid., pp. 23–24. James defended his description of Puritans in the Preface to the 1603 edition where he spoke of "such brain-sicke and headie Preachers their disciples and followers" as persons who put their particular beliefs – especially on polity – above king, people, and law (p. 7).

[125] James VI, *Basilikon Doron*, p. 24.   [126] Ibid.   [127] Ibid.

[128] Ibid., p. 39.   [129] Ibid.

[130] Ibid., p. 45. Not surprisingly, this was one of the passages which gave offence to the party of Melville in the Kirk. From this passage came one of the propositions in the list of "Anglo-pisco-papisticall Conclusions" attributed to James and circulated in 1598. Craigie, *Basilicon Doron*, vol. II, p. 10.

As many writers have found, it is easy to parody James's divine-right political theories, even using his own language to do so, and to represent his political views as, fundamentally, an expression of his own vanity. Even commentators who take his views seriously are likely to misconstrue them by examining them in an English context and by relating them almost exclusively to the issue of relations between the English crown and Parliament.[131] Yet it is clear that James's theories were developed largely in Scotland to assert the authority of the Scottish crown and to defend it against the threat of Calvinist aggrandizement, as represented by the presbyterian polity of Andrew Melville and the radical political ideology of George Buchanan.[132] He was also very much aware of the threat posed by militant Roman Catholicism at home and abroad. To combat such threats, James, like his contemporary Jean Bodin, the foremost political writer of the day, stressed the need for a sovereign power and argued persuasively for a strong monarchy as the most effective form of government. James, however,

[131] For treatments of James's political thought largely in an English context, see McIlwain, introduction to *Political Works of James I*, pp. xv–cxi; J. W. Allen, *English Political Thought, 1603–1644* (London: Methuen, 1938), pp. 3–12; Francis D. Wormuth, *The Royal Prerogative, 1603–1649: A Study in English Political and Constitutional Ideas* (Ithaca: Cornell University Press, 1939), pp. 83–93; Margaret A. Judson, *The Crisis of the Constitution: An Essay in Constitutional and Political Thought in England, 1603–1645* (New York: Octagon, 1964 – first published, 1949), pp. 17–27; W. H. Greenleaf, *Order, Empiricism and Politics: Two Traditions of English Political Thought* (London: Oxford University Press, 1964), pp. 58–67; J. P. Sommerville, *Politics and Ideology in England, 1603–1640* (London: Longman, 1986), pp. 9–50. Two recent articles come to sharply different conclusions about the extent to which James, in England, should be considered an absolutist in his political theory: J. P. Sommerville, "James I and the Divine Right of Kings: English Politics and Continental Theory," in Linda Levy Peck, ed., *The Mental World of the Jacobean Court* (Cambridge: Cambridge University Press, 1991), pp. 55–70, and Paul Christianson, "Royal and Parliamentary Voices on the Ancient Constitution, c. 1604–1621," in the same collection, pp. 71–95.
[132] Commentaries which discuss the Scottish intellectual and political setting include: Helena M. Chew, "King James I," in J. J. C. Hearnshaw, ed., *The Social and Political Ideas of Some Great Thinkers of the Sixteenth and Seventeenth Centuries* (New York: Barnes and Noble, 1949 – first published, 1926), pp. 105–129; Craigie, ed., *Basilicon Doron*, vol. II, pp. 1–38, 74–87; Gerhard A. Ritter, "Divine Right und Prärogative der englischen Könige, 1603–1640," *Historische Zeitschrift*, 196 (1963), 584–624; Lorenzo d'Avack, *La ragione dei re: il pensiero politico di Giacomo I* (Milan: A. Giuffrè, 1974), pp. 12–97; Arthur H. Williamson, *Scottish National Consciousness in the Age of James VI: The Apocalypse, the Union and the Shaping of Scotland's Public Culture* (Edinburgh: John Donald, 1979), pp. 39–53; Mason, "Rex Stoicus: George Buchanan, James VI and the Scottish Polity," pp. 9–33; Jenny Wormald, "James VI and I, *Basilikon Doron* and *The Trew Law of Free Monarchies*: The Scottish Context and the English Translation," in Peck, *The Mental World of the Jacobean Court*, pp. 36–54; Sommerville, introduction to *King James VI and I: Political Writings*, pp. xv–xix, xxviii; and Rebecca W. Bushnell, "George Buchanan, James VI and Neo-Classicism," pp. 91–111, Roger A. Mason, "George Buchanan, James VI and the Presbyterians," pp. 112–137, and J. H. Burns, "George Buchanan and the Anti-Monarchomachs," pp. 138–158, in Roger A. Mason, ed., *Scots and Britons: Scottish Political Thought and the Union of 1603* (Cambridge: Cambridge University Press, 1994).

had received a theological as well as a classical education and was considerably less secular in orientation than Bodin. He thus developed a distinctly religious view, drawing both from the medieval theory of divine-right monarchy and the Protestant conception of the Godly Prince.[133] But, in forging his own statement of monarchy by divine right, he did not contrive something artificial for the needs of the moment. All the evidence suggests that when James spoke of himself as divinely appointed and as ultimately responsible to God and God alone, he was expressing a deeply held conviction about his kingly vocation.

Reduced to its essentials, the theory was a plea for the independence of the state, free from rival ecclesiastical jurisdictions, and for the exercise of a central power within the state adequate for the administration of justice and the maintenance of peace and order. James's theory, one of the most cogent contemporary statements of a body of doctrines and attitudes which was to dominate the first half of the seventeenth century,[134] was an important step,

[133] John Neville Figgis, *The Divine Right of Kings*, introduction by G. R. Elton (New York: Harper & Row, 1965 – the first edition of Figgis's book was published in 1896), pp. vii–xxxviii, 1–16, 81–176, 256–266. See also, for the relation between James's thought and medieval constitutional and legal theories: Francis Oakley, "Jacobean Political Theology: The Absolute and Ordinary Powers of the King," *Journal of the History of Ideas*, 29 (1968), 323–346, "The 'Hidden' and 'Revealed' Wills of James I: More Political Theology," *Studia Gratiana*, 15 (1972), 363–375, and *Omnipotence, Covenant, and Order: An Excursion in the History of Ideas from Abelard to Leibnitz* (Ithaca: Cornell University Press, 1984), pp. 94–118. For Bodin, see Julian H. Franklin, *Jean Bodin and the Rise of Absolutist Theory* (Cambridge: Cambridge University Press, 1973), esp. pp. 54–69. For parallels between James's political thought and Bodin's, see d'Avack, *La ragione dei re: il pensiero politico di Giacomo I*, pp. 26, 53, 91–92. James's acquaintance with Bodin is suggested not only by the content of his political theory but by the fact that his library contained Bodin's *Les six livres de la république*. See George F. Warner, ed., "The Library of James VI, 1573–1583, from a Manuscript in the Hand of Peter Young, His Tutor," *Publications of the Scottish History Society*, 15 (1893), p. xlii. For the Protestant conception of the Godly Prince, see, for its expression in Lutheranism, W. D. J. Cargill Thompson, *The Political Thought of Martin Luther*, ed. Philip Broadhead (Sussex: Harvester Press, 1984), pp. 36–78, 144–154; in Calvinism, John T. McNeill, "John Calvin on Civil Government," in George L. Hunt, ed., *Calvinism and the Political Order* (Philadelphia: Westminster Press, 1965), pp. 23–45; in Anglicanism, Norman Sykes, *Old Priest and New Presbyter* (Cambridge: Cambridge University Press, 1956), pp. 1–29, and Edward O. Smith, Jr., *Crown and Commonwealth: A Study in the Official Elizabethan Doctrine of the Prince* (Philadelphia: American Philosophical Society, 1976), pp. 5–30. In Scotland, the idea of the Godly Prince is stated in unqualified terms in Article 24 of the Scots Confession of 1560. See W. Ian P. Hazlett, "The Scots Confession of 1560: Context, Complexion and Critique," *Archiv für Reformationsgeschichte*, 78 (1987), pp. 315–317.

[134] Cf. R. W. K. Hinton, "Government and Liberty under James I," *Cambridge Historical Journal*, 11 (1953–1955), pp. 48–64; W. H. Greenleaf, "James I and the Divine Right of Kings," *Political Studies*, 5 (1957), 36–48; James Daly, "The Idea of Absolute Monarchy in Seventeenth-Century England," *Historical Journal*, 21 (1978), 227–250, and *Cosmic Harmony and Political Thinking in Early Stuart England* (Philadelphia: American Philosophical Society, 1979), pp. 9–13, 21–31; David Wootton, ed., *Divine Right and Democracy: An Anthology of Political Thinking and Writing in Stuart England* (Harmondsworth: Penguin, 1986), pp. 9–19, 22–38, 91–109; and J. H. M. Salmon, "Catholic Resistance

ideologically, towards the modern conception of the world community as made up of autonomous, sovereign states. At the same time, as James's actions repeatedly showed, he was deeply concerned about the Christendom whose unity had been shattered by the Reformation and Counter-Reformation and whose peace was constantly being threatened or violated, portending disaster for his own kingdom as well as for the other states of Europe.

In the winter of 1589–1590, when James was in Denmark to celebrate his wedding to Princess Anne and then to await fair weather for their voyage to Scotland, he discussed with Danish statesmen and diplomats a project for a European peace.[135] Once home, James sent ambassadors to Denmark to use the opportunity of the wedding of Anne's older sister Elizabeth to the duke of Brunswick to further the project with the electors of Saxony and Brandenburg and the dukes of Brunswick, Mecklenburg, Pomerania, and Holstein, as well as the king of Denmark. At the heart of James's concern was the series of international conflicts in which the king of Spain, the queen of England, and the king of France were all involved. James's instructions to his ambassadors expressed the wish that "a nombre of Princes weill affected to Christian peax and trew religioun, wolde be commoun resolutioun direct a joinct legatioun of a few persones authorized and instructed from thame all to the said Princes of Englande France and Spayne" to encourage them to make peace.[136] The project died, partly through lack of support from the northern princes. But James in his own foreign policy continued to stress close relations with countries nearby: England, France, the Netherlands, and Denmark. After 1589, he remained at peace with Spain. Characteristically, when negotiations got under way for peace between England and Spain, following James's accession to the English throne, he expressed the wish that "all the States and Princes of Christendom" might be included.[137]

Theory, Ultramontanism, and the Royalist Response, 1580–1620," in J. H. Burns, ed., *The Cambridge History of Political Thought, 1450–1700* (Cambridge: Cambridge University Press, 1991), pp. 219–253, esp. pp. 244–253. For the divine-right theory of Hadrian Saravia, a late sixteenth-century writer who helped to create a favorable climate in England for ideas such as James's, see J. P. Sommerville, "Richard Hooker, Hadrian Saravia, and the Advent of the Divine Right of Kings," *History of Political Thought*, 4, 2 (Summer 1983), 229–245.

135 Helen Georgia Stafford, *James VI of Scotland and the Throne of England* (New York: Appleton-Century, 1940), pp. 125–131.

136 Annie I. Cameron and Robert S. Rait, eds., *The Warrender Papers*, 2 vols. (Edinburgh: Scottish History Society, 1931–1932), vol. II, p. 135. The full text of the instructions for Colonel Stewart and John Skene, June 9, 1590, are printed on pp. 133–141.

137 M. S. Giuseppi, ed., *Calendar of the Manuscripts of the Most Hon. the Marquess of Salisbury, Preserved at Hatfield House*, part XVI (London: HMSO, 1933), pp. 225–226. James's international approach had sound historical precedents. For the European role played by Scottish monarchs in the fifteenth and sixteenth centuries, see Wormald, *Mary Queen of Scots*, pp. 22–42.

Despite what his enemies on both religious and political extremes might assert, James did not exaggerate when he wrote to de Thou in March 1604 that he had never been "of a sectarian spirit nor resistant to the well-being of Christendom."[138] He had brought peace to a country in which civil wars and violent feudal conflicts had long been rife, had curbed the excesses – as he saw them – of the more extreme elements within the Church of Scotland, had pacified or subdued the leaders of the Roman Catholic faction, and had begun a reorganization of the established Church aimed at giving the monarchy a decisive voice in its affairs. His concern for peace extended far beyond Scotland to the major continental powers. By the time James left Scotland in the spring of 1603 – and certainly by the time he received de Thou's letter – he believed that it was his vocation to extend the work of religious reconciliation not just to England but to the rest of Europe.

[138] BN MS. Dupuy 409, fol. 39; MS. Dupuy 632, fol. 3.

2

Call for an ecumenical council

When James VI of Scotland came to the English throne as James I in 1603, he looked upon this event as one of enormous significance and promise, both for himself and for his two kingdoms. In his proclamation of October 1604, in which he declared his title to be king of Great Britain, he called attention to "the blessed Union, or rather Reuniting of these two mightie, famous, and ancient Kingdomes of England and Scotland, under one Imperiall Crowne."[1] The two kingdoms, he observed, shared an island which "within it selfe hath almost none but imaginarie bounds of separation . . . making the whole a little world within it selfe."[2] Its inhabitants shared "A communitie of Language, the principall meanes of Civil societie, An unitie of Religion, the chiefest band of heartie Union, and the surest knot of lasting Peace."[3] Even the ancient laws of the two kingdoms were marked by "a greater affinitie and concurrence" than existed between those "of any other two Nations."[4] This union, brought about not by conquest but by James's descent from the ancient royal lines of both kingdoms, would join the energies and talents of two "mightie Nations" that had been "ever from their first separation continually in blood against each other."[5] James intended the result to be the perpetuation of the era of peace existing between England and Scotland, peace which had begun with his own reign in the north and was a decisive step towards a complete political and constitutional union.[6] He also saw an exciting opportunity ahead for securing a broader European peace.

---

[1] James F. Larkin and Paul L. Hughes, eds., *Stuart Royal Proclamations*, 2 vols. (Oxford: Clarendon Press, 1973–1983), vol. I: *Royal Proclamations of King James I, 1603–1625*, p. 95. For commentary on the origins of this title, see S. T. Bindoff, "The Stuarts and Their Styles," *English Historical Review*, 60 (1945), 192–216, and Denys Hay, *Europe: The Emergence of an Idea*, revised edition (Edinburgh: Edinburgh University Press, 1968), appendix, "The Use of the Term 'Great Britain' in the Middle Ages," pp. 128–144.

[2] Larkin and Hughes, *Stuart Royal Proclamations*, vol. I, p. 95.

[3] Ibid.   [4] Ibid.   [5] Ibid.

[6] For this Union, initially frustrated in the Parliament of 1604–1610, but finally achieved in the Act of Union of 1707, see David Harris Willson, "King James I and Anglo-Scottish Unity," in William Appleton Aiken and Basil Duke Henning, eds., *Conflict in Stuart England: Essays in*

The kingdom of England, long ruled by Queen Elizabeth I, a strong-willed sovereign, much heralded in her own time,[7] was not without serious problems. The prolonged Anglo-Spanish conflict had plunged the government deeply into debt and had produced a climate of war-weariness within all ranks of society. Religious tensions, which had reached their heights in the 1570s and 1580s with the growth of Puritanism and the threat of aggressive Catholic action supported from abroad, had been significantly reduced, but a legacy of bitterness and frustration among religious dissi-

Honour of Wallace Notestein (London: Jonathan Cape, 1960), pp. 41–55; Gordon Donaldson, "Foundations of Anglo-Scottish Union," in S. T. Bindoff, J. Hurstfield, and C. H. Williams, eds., *Elizabethan Government and Society: Essays Presented to Sir John Neale* (London: Athlone Press, 1961), pp. 282–314; Wallace Notestein, *The House of Commons 1604–1610* (New Haven: Yale University Press, 1971), pp. 1–2, 78–85, 127, 211–254; Brian P. Levack, *The Formation of the British State: England, Scotland, and the Union, 1603–1707* (Oxford: Clarendon Press, 1987); Bruce Galloway, *The Union of England and Scotland, 1603–1608* (Edinburgh: John Donald, 1986); Keith M. Brown, *Kingdom or Province? Scotland and the Regal Union, 1603–1715* (New York: St. Martin's Press, 1992). Neil Cuddy has shown how the Privy Council and the Privy Chamber were reorganized by James to represent the Union, though the entourage of the Bedchamber, the innermost circle at court, long remained exclusively Scottish: "Anglo-Scottish Union and the Court of James I, 1603–1625," *Transactions of the Royal Historical Society*, fifth series, 39 (1989), 107–124. For the theological and political roots of James's vision of a united Britain which had a European role to play in the cause of peace and the Protestant faith, see Arthur H. Williamson, *Scottish National Consciousness in the Age of James VI: The Apocalypse, the Union and the Shaping of Scotland's Public Culture* (Edinburgh: John Donald, 1979), esp. pp. 12–18, 39–52, 97–106, and "Scotland, Antichrist and the Invention of Great Britain," in John Dwyer, ed., *New Perspectives on the Politics and Culture of Early Modern Scotland* (Edinburgh: John Donald, 1982), pp. 34–58; Roger A. Mason, "Scotching the Brut: Politics, History and National Myth in Sixteenth-Century Britain," in Roger A. Mason, ed., *Scotland and England, 1286–1815* (Edinburgh: John Donald, 1987), pp. 60–84, and Marcus Merriman, "James Henrisoun and 'Great Britain': British Union and the Scottish Commonweal," in the same collection, pp. 85–112; Roger A. Mason, ed., *Scots and Britons: Scottish Political Thought and the Union of 1603* (Cambridge: Cambridge University Press, 1994); Conrad Russell, "The Anglo-Scottish Union 1603–1643: A Success?" in Anthony Fletcher and Peter Roberts, eds., *Religion, Culture and Society in Early Modern Britain: Essays in Honour of Patrick Collinson* (Cambridge: Cambridge University Press, 1994), pp. 238–256; Jenny Wormald, "James VI, James I and the Identity of Britain," in Brendan Bradshaw and John Morrill, eds., *The British Problem, c. 1534–1707: State Formation in the Atlantic Archipelago* (Basingstoke: Macmillan, 1996), pp. 148–171. For conflicting concepts of the Union in the seventeenth century and afterwards, see Jenny Wormald, "The Creation of Britain: Multiple Kingdoms or Core and Colonies?" *Transactions of the Royal Historical Society*, 6th series, 2 (1992), 175–194.

[7] For the political achievements of Elizabeth's reign, see, especially, Wallace T. MacCaffrey, *The Shaping of the Elizabethan Regime* (Princeton: Princeton University Press, 1968), *Queen Elizabeth and the Making of Policy, 1572–1588* (Princeton: Princeton University Press, 1981), *Elizabeth I: War and Politics, 1588–1603* (Princeton: Princeton University Press, 1992), and *Elizabeth I* (London: Edward Arnold, 1993). J. E. Neale, *Elizabeth I and Her Parliaments*, 2 vols. (London: Jonathan Cape, 1953–1957), and G. R. Elton, ed., *The Tudor Constitution*, second edition (Cambridge: Cambridge University Press, 1982) are important for understanding the Elizabethan political and constitutional system. The opening chapters of Neale's study of Elizabeth's Parliaments have been corrected and revised by Norman L. Jones, *Faith by Statute: Parliament and the Settlement of Religion, 1559* (London: Royal

dents of all sorts remained. Elizabeth's court had been the scene of intense personal rivalries for several decades and had recently been caught up in a factional dispute resulting in an abortive *coup d'état* by the earl of Essex and his supporters. Relations between the crown and Parliament had begun to sour over monopolies and other issues, and relations between the central government and local governments were strained by the need for tax revenues to support the war. Social problems included vagabondage and crime, exacerbated by unemployment and rising prices. There was continuing, stubborn resistance to English rule in Ireland, which meant a serious drain on English as well as Irish resources and an open invitation to foreign powers to intervene in the conflict there. Despite friendly relations on the official level between England and Scotland, there was a widespread suspicion in England of almost all things Scottish.[8]

England was involved in a European struggle involving some of its nearest neighbors on the European continent. Since the 1520s there had been a continuous struggle for dominance between the Habsburg powers in Spain and Austria on the one hand and France on the other. In the last half-century that struggle had become entangled in the revolt of the Netherlands against Spain and in the civil and religious wars within

Historical Society, 1982), while G. R. Elton's *The Parliament of England, 1559–1581* (Cambridge: Cambridge University Press, 1986) successfully challenges many of Neale's judgements. The Elizabethan era is critically assessed by Christopher Haigh, ed., *The Reign of Elizabeth I* (London: Macmillan, 1984). See also Haigh's revisionist study, *Elizabeth I* (London: Longman, 1988). The "cult of Elizabeth" is treated by Elkin Calhoun Wilson, *England's Eliza* (Cambridge, Mass.: Harvard University Press, 1934); Frances A. Yates, *Astraea: The Imperial Theme in the Sixteenth Century* (London: Routledge and Kegan Paul, 1975); Roy Strong, *The Cult of Elizabeth: Elizabethan Portraiture and Pageantry* (London: Thames and Hudson, 1977); John N. King, "Queen Elizabeth I: Representations of the Virgin Queen," *Renaissance Quarterly*, 43, 1 (Spring 1990), 30–74; and Susan Frye, *Elizabeth I: The Competition for Representation* (New York: Oxford University Press, 1993).

[8] See R. B. Wernham, *After the Armada: Elizabethan England and the Struggle for Western Europe, 1588–1595* (Oxford: Clarendon Press, 1984), esp. pp. 555–568, and *The Making of Elizabethan Foreign Policy, 1558–1603* (Berkeley: University of California Press, 1980); Patrick Collinson, *The Elizabethan Puritan Movement* (London: Jonathan Cape, 1967), pp. 168–416; Arnold Oskar Meyer, *England and the Catholic Church under Queen Elizabeth*, trans. J. R. McKee, introduction by John Bossy (New York: Barnes & Noble, 1967); Adrian Morey, *The Catholic Subjects of Elizabeth I* (London: George Allen and Unwin, 1978), pp. 59–95; Simon Adams, "Favourites and Factions at the Elizabethan Court," in Ronald G. Asch and Adolf M. Birke, eds., *Princes, Patronage, and the Nobility: The Court at the Beginning of the Modern Age, c. 1450–1650* (Oxford: Oxford University Press for the German Historical Institute, 1991), pp. 265–287; Thomas M. Coakley, "Robert Cecil in Power: Elizabethan Politics in Two Reigns," in Howard S. Reinmuth, Jr., ed., *Early Stuart Studies: Essays in Honor of David Harris Willson* (Minneapolis: University of Minnesota Press, 1970), pp. 64–94; Penry Williams, *The Tudor Regime*, corrected impression (Oxford: Clarendon Press, 1981); and John Guy, *Tudor England* (Oxford: Oxford University Press, 1988), pp. 379–407, 437–458.

France.[9] Though France and Spain had made peace in 1598, the war between the northern provinces of the Netherlands and Spain continued, and Europe seemed ready at any moment to be ignited in another conflict of continental proportions. As the internecine conflicts in the Netherlands, in Germany, and in France demonstrated, the most volatile and intractable issue in this era of ideological conflict was religion.[10]

The evidence of his actions over the next two decades shows that James recognized and addressed these problems, drawing upon a wealth of political experience which derived from his difficult but ultimately successful reign in Scotland. One theme which ran through James's policies, especially those aimed at achieving stability and peace among the nations of Europe, was the need to effect a settlement of major religious disputes. Until comparatively recently, historians have not seen James as a reconciler of religious differences.[11] Yet there is considerable evidence from the first years of his reign in England – the very period of the Hampton Court Conference, which was long seen as an exhibition of royal intolerance – that James was actively interested in reconciling religious differences both at home and

[9] See J. H. Elliott, *Europe Divided, 1559–1598* (New York: Harper & Row, 1968); Geoffrey Parker, *The Dutch Revolt* (London: Allen Lane, 1977), esp. pp. 109–110, 148, 191–192, 216–221; N. M. Sutherland, *Princes, Politics and Religion, 1547–1589* (London: Hambledon Press, 1984), esp. pp. 73–112, 183–206. Peter Clark, ed., *The European Crisis of the 1590s: Essays in Comparative History* (London: George Allen and Unwin, 1985), esp. pp. 3–66, shows how economic problems in England and on the continent coincided with and exacerbated the crisis brought on by prolonged warfare.

[10] For the bloody conflicts between Roman Catholics and Protestants in this era, see Erwin Iserloh, Joseph Glazik, and Hubert Jedin, *Reformation and Counter Reformation* (New York: Crossroad, 1990), pp. 265–300, 511–534, 615–623; Marvin R. O'Connell, *The Counter Reformation, 1559–1610* (New York: Harper and Row, 1974), pp. 119–172, 207–306; *The New Cambridge Modern History*, vol. III: *The Counter-Reformation and Price Revolution*, ed. R. B. Wernham (Cambridge: Cambridge University Press, 1968), pp. 234–318, and vol. IV: *The Decline of Spain and the Thirty Years War, 1609–48/59*, ed. J. P. Cooper (Cambridge: Cambridge University Press, 1970), pp. 260–384; Michel Pernot, *Les guerres de religion en France, 1559–1598* (Paris: Sedes, 1987); and Euan Cameron, *The European Reformation* (Oxford: Clarendon Press, 1991), pp. 339–360.

[11] For James's efforts to reconcile religious differences in Scotland, the work of Gordon Donaldson is essential. See, especially, his *Scotland: James V to James VII* (Edinburgh: Oliver & Boyd, 1965), pp. 157–291. A new way of looking at the Hampton Court Conference, seeing James as a peacemaker between the Puritans and the bishops, was set forth by Mark H. Curtis in his article "Hampton Court Conference and Its Aftermath," *History*, 46 (1961), 1–16. My own article, "King James I's Call for an Ecumenical Council," in G. J. Cuming, ed., *Councils and Assemblies* (Cambridge: Cambridge University Press, 1971), Studies in Church History, VII, pp. 267–275, showed that James sought a general council as a means of achieving Christian unity. More recently, Jenny Wormald has described James as willing to assess opposing arguments and even engage in debate as a way of mediating between different religious and political positions. See her article, "James VI and I: Two Kings or One?" *History*, 68 (June 1983), 187–209. Kenneth Fincham and Peter Lake see James as conciliatory about religious differences out of a concern to achieve stability, peace, and a large measure of religious unity. See their article, "The Ecclesiastical Policy of King James I," *Journal of British Studies*, 24, 2 (April 1985), 169–207.

abroad. Surviving documents in the Public Record Office, the British Library, and the Vatican Archives reveal, moreover, that he had a plan for attaining this objective, the essential feature of which was a proposal that an ecumenical council be convened, representing both Rome and the major Reformation traditions.[12]

James referred publicly to this plan in his speech to the first Parliament of his reign, on March 19, 1604. In this speech, in which he expressed his gratitude for the friendly reception so far given him in England, he talked at length about the blessings of peace. His coming had brought peace abroad, in that the war with Spain had been ended.[13] He had also brought peace at home, in that in him were combined the royal lines of Lancaster and York, and of England and Scotland, which circumstance, he hoped, would mean the end of internal wars in the island.[14] He also talked about religious peace. He affirmed in the strongest terms his commitment to the religious faith "publikely allowed, and by the Law maintained" in England, while distinguishing his views sharply from those of Puritans and Roman Catholics.[15] Yet of the Puritans he said that they "doe not so farre differ from vs in points of Religion, as in their confused forme of Policie and Paritie."[16] Concerning Roman Catholics, he said:

I acknowledge the Romane Church to be our Mother Church, although defiled with some infirmities and corruptions, as the Iews were when they crucified Christ: And as I am none enemie to the life of a sicke man, because I would haue his bodie purged of ill humours; no more am I enemie to their Church, because I would haue them reforme their errors, not wishing the downethrowing of the Temple, but that it might be purged and cleansed from corruption: otherwise how can they wish vs to enter, if their house be not first made cleane?[17]

---

[12] Scattered references to this plan may be found in Samuel R. Gardiner, *History of England from the Accession of James I to the Outbreak of the Civil War, 1603–1642*, 10 vols. (London: Longman, 1884), vol. I, pp. 202–203, 220–221; Ludwig von Pastor, *The History of the Popes from the Close of the Middle Ages*, 40 vols. (St. Louis: Herder, 1891–1954), vol. XXIV, p. 78; and D. Harris Willson, *King James VI and I* (New York: Henry Holt, 1956), pp. 219–220. Early seventeenth-century documents which discuss James's plan are cited in the appropriate places below.

[13] Charles H. McIlwain, ed., *The Political Works of James I* (Cambridge, Mass.: Harvard University Press, 1918), p. 270. For comments on this speech and James's frequently uneasy relations with Parliament, see Notestein, *House of Commons, 1604–1610*, pp. 14–23, and 60–63.

[14] *Political Works of James I*, pp. 271–273.   [15] Ibid., p. 274.   [16] Ibid.

[17] Ibid. The language is reminiscent of that of a letter which James wrote to Cecil before his accession in England, in which he said of Roman Catholics: "I ame so farre from any intention of persecution, as I proteste to God I reuerence thaire churche as oure mother churche, althoch clogged with many infirmities and corruptions, besydes that I did euer holde persecution as one of the infallible notes of a false churche." He also commented: "I did euer hate alyke both extremities in any cace, only allowing the middes for uertue, as my booke nou laitely published doeth plainly appeare" – an evident reference to *Basilikon Doron*. John Bruce, ed., *Correspondence of King James VI of Scotland with Sir Robert Cecil*

James then expressed the wish that the differences between the churches might be reconciled, and he pledged his willingness to help effect such a reconciliation. "I could wish from my heart," he said,

that it would please God to make me one of the members of such a generall Christian vnion in Religion, as laying wilfulnesse aside on both hands, wee might meete in the middest, which is the Center and perfection of all things. For if they [the Roman Catholics] would leaue, and be ashamed of such new and gross Corruptions of theirs, as themselves cannot maintaine, nor denie to bee worthy of reformation, I would for mine owne part be content to meete them in the mid-way, so that all nouelties might be renounced on either side. For as my faith is the Trew, Ancient Catholike and Apostolike faith, grounded vpon the Scriptures and expresse word of God: so will I euer yeeld all reverence to antiquitie in the points of Ecclesiasticall pollicy; and by that meanes shall I euer with Gods grace keepe my selfe from either being an hereticke in Faith, or schismatick in matters of Pollicie.[18]

It was this "generall Christian vnion" that James evidently hoped to effect by means of an ecumenical council. At the time he made this declaration to Parliament he had already communicated his desire for such a council through diplomatic channels which led to the papacy.

James had been proclaimed king on the death of Elizabeth I on March 24, 1603, though his coronation had not taken place until July 25. On May 8, 1603, the Venetian secretary in England, Giovanni Carlo Scaramelli, had a conference with Edward Bruce, Lord Kinloss, a Scot who was a member of the English Privy Council, which touched on religious affairs. Lord Kinloss informed Scaramelli that the king was deeply grateful to Pope Clement VIII, "and spoke of him as truly Clement," because, though he had been urged to do so by other princes, the pope had not excommunicated him.[19] He added that the Catholics in England had little to fear from James: "as long as the Catholics remain quiet and decently hidden they will neither be hunted nor persecuted."[20] Scaramelli replied that many people expected much more from James, namely that "his Majesty sooner or later would restore the Kingdom of England to the Roman cult."[21] To this Lord Kinloss answered emphatically, if not altogether unambiguously, "No! beyond a doubt this will never happen; our bow which hitherto had two strings will have but one for the future, for he who wishes for the peaceable enjoyment of a kingdom must take care how he changes the religion of it, the smallest suspicion of such a thing is too serious a matter in a people firmly rooted in

and Others in England during the Reign of Queen Elizabeth (London: Camden Society, 1861), pp. 37, 36.
[18] *Political Works of James I*, pp. 275–276.
[19] *Calendar of State Papers and Manuscripts, Relating to English Affairs, Existing in the Archives and Collections of Venice, and in Other Libraries of Northern Italy*, 40 vols. (London: PRO, 1864–1947), vol. X, p. 21.
[20] Ibid., pp. 21–22.
[21] Ibid., p. 22.

one faith."[22] The reference to the bow and strings must mean, when it is considered along with the evidence of James's earlier negotiations with the papacy,[23] that whereas he had formerly played for the support of both Catholics and Protestants in England in his claim for the throne, he would henceforth rely upon the political support of the Protestants alone.

Lord Kinloss then disclosed James's plan for an ecumenical council, for which the king felt he could galvanize considerable support in northern Europe.

True it is that if the Pope wished to summon a General Council, which, according to the ancient usage, should be superior to all Churches, all doctrine, all Princes, secular and ecclesiastic, none excepted, my master, upon whom, as they will soon find out, depend in this and in other matters, Denmark, Sweden, Norway, the Free Cities of the Empire and the States [of the Netherlands] as though upon an Emperor, would be extremely willing to take the lead and to prove himself the warm supporter of so great a benefit to Christendom. Beyond a doubt abuses would be removed on all hands, and a sound decision would put an end, perhaps for ever, to the discords in the Christian faith, nor would his Majesty think he could act more nobly than to be the first to offer complete obedience to Council's decrees.[24]

James thus proposed that the papacy take the initiative of calling a council which, it was hoped, would secure the religious peace of Christendom. At the end of September the Venetian secretary found James wholeheartedly behind the plan, though there were aspects of the plan, as the Venetian understood it, about which the papacy might well have been apprehensive. Writing from Oxford on September 28, 1603, Scaramelli reported to the Doge and Senate that the king showed "a growing desire for the assembly of a free Council to discuss the basis of religion and the question of Papal authority."[25]

Meanwhile, in a conversation with the French ambassador to England,

[22] Ibid.
[23] For James's negotiations with Clement VIII, see Arnold Oskar Meyer, "Clemens VIII. und Jakob I. von England," *Quellen und Forschungen aus italienischen Archiven und Bibliotheken*, 7, 2 (1904), 268–306; G. F. Warner, "James VI and Rome," *English Historical Review*, 20 (1905), 124–127; A. W. Ward, "James VI and the Papacy," *Scottish Historical Review*, 2 (1905), 249–252; J. Martin, "Clément VIII et Jacques Stuart," *Revue d'histoire diplomatique*, 25 (1911), 279–307; and Helen Georgia Stafford, *James VI of Scotland and the Throne of England* (New York: Appleton-Century, 1940), pp. 232–246. For artistic expressions of Clement's policies aimed at religious peace, see Jack Freiberg, "Clement VIII, the Lateran, and Christian Concord," in Marilyn Aronberg Lavin, ed., *IL 60: Essays Honoring Irving Lavin on His Sixtieth Birthday* (New York: Italica Press, 1990), pp. 167–190.
[24] *Calendar of State Papers*, Venetian, vol. X, p. 22. As Franklin Le Van Baumer points out in "The Conception of Christendom in Renaissance England," *Journal of the History of Ideas*, 6, 2 (April 1945), 131–156, the word Christendom implied a degree of cultural and religious unity even in the era of the Reformation and the Counter-Reformation. In using this term, James reminded his contemporaries of a unity which needed to be recovered and preserved.
[25] *Calendar of State Papers*, Venetian, vol. X, p. 98.

Christophe de Harlay, comte de Beaumont, on July 23, 1603, James had spoken in some detail about his hopes for a general or ecumenical council, a project which he evidently hoped the French king would support. Henry IV had, after all, proposed a council himself in the 1580s and 1590s as a means of ending the religious conflicts within France.[26] The setting for James's remarks was a frank exchange of views about religion and the powers of the papacy following a hunt which the king and the ambassador had enjoyed together.[27] Beaumont assured James that if he would return to the Church from which he "had been snatched away from his youth," Henry IV would support him with advice and influence and that Pope Clement VIII would use this as a means of achieving "the Union and the reformation of the said Church in Christendom."[28] James replied that he was "not at all a heretic, that is to say one refusing to recognize the truth, that he was no Puritan nor even less separated from the Church."[29] He considered hierarchy "essential" to the Church, and the pope, "the first Bishop in it, President and Moderator in Council, but not head or superior."[30] There were, he observed, ceremonies "and other things indifferent" which were matters of dispute among Christians, as well as disagreements about matters of faith. He took a broadly tolerant view of the first and "entrusted the decision" on the second to "the decree of a general Council well and legitimately assembled in a neutral place and with free access and made up of persons of honor, of virtue and of learning."[31] In order to secure such a council, the king promised that "he would ask all his friends to commit their word and authority with his."[32] Without such a resolution, James argued, the diversity of religious opinions which had "spread across all nations" would be a continuing occasion of wars fomented by ambitious princes and sometimes abetted even by the popes themselves "in order to better establish their grandeur."[33] Unless this religious dissension were resolved by means of a general council, James saw "no way to hope for peace in the Church

---

[26] Raoul Patry, *Philippe du Plessis-Mornay: un huguenot homme d'état (1549–1623)* (Paris: Fischbacher, 1933), pp. 53–54, 105–106, 114, 155–156, 177–178, 194–196, 238–240; W. B. Patterson, "Henry IV and the Huguenot Appeal for a Return to Poissy," in Derek Baker, ed., *Schism, Heresy and Religious Protest* (Cambridge: Cambridge University Press, 1972), Studies in Church History, IX, pp. 247–257; Jean-Pierre Babelon, *Henri IV* (Paris: Fayard, 1982), pp. 456–458, 557–560; Mark Greengrass, "The Public Context of the Abjuration of Henri IV," in Keith Cameron, ed., *From Valois to Bourbon: Dynasty, State and Society in Early Modern France* (Exeter: University of Exeter, 1989), pp. 107–126.

[27] BL MS. King's 123: *Dépêches de Messire Christophe de Harlay, comte de Beaumont*, 1603, fol. 321 verso. For a commentary on this conversation, see P. Laffleur de Kermaingant, *Mission de Christophe de Harlay, Comte de Beaumont (1602–1605): l'ambassade de France en Angleterre sous Henri IV* (Paris: Firmin-Didot, 1895), pp. 137–138.

[28] BL Kings 123, fols. 325 verso–326.   [29] Ibid., fol. 326.

[30] Ibid., fols. 326–326 verso.   [31] Ibid., fol. 326 verso.

[32] Ibid.   [33] Ibid., fol. 327.

without which he held it as impossible consequently that that of Christendom would ever be firm and assured."[34]

In this same conversation Beaumont replied that, without the urging of the French king and his allies, the pope would never agree "to convene a free Council in order to see put to hazard the titles of his authority for which his predecessors have struggled for so long."[35] Beaumont believed that when he could assure his king that James was ready to return to the Church, the time would then be appropriate to approach the papacy about the means to be employed, knowing that one of James's "greatest ambitions" was "to promote the peace, and the union of the Church."[36] In answer to Beaumont's letter reporting this conversation, Henry IV wrote to his ambassador from Rouen on August 15: "You can say to him that I will always be very glad and happy to support and assist the good desire that he has told you he has to procure and advance the peace of the Church by the same means that he has proposed to you believing like him that that of Christendom will never be firm and assured so long as the discord in religion is such as we see at present."[37] Henry IV thus gave his moral support to James in the project of convening a general council for the sake of a secure peace in Christendom.

James also approached the papacy more directly on the subject of a council. While in Scotland, James and Anne of Denmark, his queen, had been in touch with Pope Clement VIII through secret emissaries who sought to win the favor of the pope as well as of several Catholic heads of state.[38] The king's intentions were evidently to prepare for his peaceful accession in England by preventing invasions or civil wars on behalf of rival candidates and plots against his life by zealous Catholics. The effect of these missions, however, was to raise in the minds of Catholic leaders abroad the possibility of James's conversion. In the last months of 1601 or the early months of 1602, Clement received a message from an emissary sent by Queen Anne in which she stated her allegiance to the Roman faith and assured the pope of James's good will towards his Catholic subjects.[39] In reply, in the summer

---

[34] Ibid.   [35] Ibid., fol. 327 verso.

[36] Ibid., fol. 328.   [37] BL Kings 124, fol. 39 verso.

[38] Meyer, "Clemens VIII. und Jakob I.," 268–306; Warner, "James VI and Rome," 124–127; Thomas Graves Law, ed., "Documents Illustrating Catholic Policy in the Reign of James VI," *Miscellany of the Scottish History Society*, 1 (1893), 1–70; J. D. Mackie, "A Secret Agent of James VI," *Scottish Historical Review*, 9 (1912), 376–386; J. D. Mackie, "The Secret Diplomacy of King James VI. in Italy Prior to His Accession to the English Throne," *Scottish Historical Review*, 21 (1924), 267–282; J. D. Mackie, *Negotiations between King James VI. and I. and Ferdinand I., Grand Duke of Tuscany* (London: Oxford University Press for St. Andrews University, 1927), pp. iii–xxiii, 7–11, 44–45.

[39] Meyer, "Clemens VIII. und Jakob I.," 279–280, 301–303. For the evidence for Anne's Catholicism, see Albert J. Loomie, "King James I's Catholic Consort," *Huntington Library Quarterly*, 34 (1971), 303–316. The foundation for her conversion to Catholicism from

of 1602, Clement sent a letter and a verbal message to James. In the message, conveyed by Sir James Lindsay, a Scottish Catholic who was returning to his native land, the pope promised James support in his claim to the English throne. In return, James was to grant the request made in the letter, that the heir to the throne, Prince Henry, be brought up in the Roman Catholic faith.[40] Lindsay was prevented for some time by illness from returning with James's answer. The king therefore undertook to send an answer by way of his ambassador in Paris, Sir Thomas Parry, who was to communicate it to the papal nuncio, Monsignor Innocenzo del Bufalo, bishop of Camerino. Parry and del Bufalo had developed a professional relationship in the summer of 1603, and the nuncio had offered to be an intermediary between James and Pope Clement. Along with the letter, James sent a copy of the instructions given to Lindsay for his diplomatic journey back to Rome. The letter to Parry was sent in early November 1603,[41] by which time, of course, James had acceded without incident to the English throne.

In these instructions James declined, with some asperity, the suggestion that the prince be brought up as a Roman Catholic. It was contrary to the very laws of nature, he declared, for a son to be instructed in a faith different from that in which his father had been imbued since infancy. The heir to the throne, moreover, must be acceptable in this respect to his people.[42] The king recognized, however, that some of his subjects were of a different mind than he on matters of religion. For his Roman Catholic subjects he wished justice, peace, and tranquillity, as long as they did not pose a danger to the realm. He then introduced a proposal for a council to settle the controver-

Lutheranism in about 1600 seems to have come with her association with the countess of Huntly in the early 1590s. Her Catholicism was apparently a moderate, undogmatic kind which did not prevent her from attending Protestant services with her husband. According to Scaramelli, the Venetian ambassador, she did not, however, receive communion at James's coronation in England.

[40] Meyer, "Clemens VIII. und Jakob I.," 282–283, 304–305. See also Gardiner, *History of England*, vol. I, pp. 97–98.

[41] See the Latin version of the letter in [Hugh Tootell,] *Dodd's Church History of England from the Commencement of the Sixteenth Century to the Revolution in 1688*, ed. M. A. Tierney, 5 vols. (London: Charles Dolman, 1839–1843), vol. IV, pp. lxvi–lxxi. For the date and an English version of the letter, see M. S. Giuseppi, ed., *Calendar of the Manuscripts of the Most Hon. the Marquess of Salisbury, Preserved at Hatfield House,* part XV (London: HMSO, 1930), pp. 299–302. Copies of the Latin instructions to Lindsay, sent by James I to Parry on November 6, 1603, are preserved in the PRO, London, State Papers, France, 78, vol. 50, fols. 86–89, 90–94. The role of the papal nuncio in Paris as a diplomatic link between the English government and the papacy is analyzed in Bernard Barbiche, "La nonciature de France et les affaires d'Angleterre au début du XVIIe siècle," *Bibliothèque de l'Ecole des Chartes,* 125 (1967), 399–429. See also Bernard Barbiche, ed., *Correspondance du nonce en France: Innocenzo del Bufalo, Evêque de Camerino (1601–1604)* (Rome: Presses de l'Université Grégorienne, 1964), pp. 87–102.

[42] [Tootell,] *Dodd's Church History*, vol. IV, p. lxx.

sies in religion which divided his countrymen as well as Christians throughout Europe:

And would that (which has always been in our prayers) this course be entered upon, and care be taken, by means of a General Council, justly and legitimately declared and assembled, by which all contentions and controversies could be settled and composed: whence it would be clear in the case of each doctrine what would be agreeable to antiquity, to the first and purer times of the Christian Church, [and] what was born from and sprang from the inventions of men not long ago.[43]

Just as he opposed such innovations by inner conviction, James favored the practices and doctrines of primitive Christianity: "whatever has been received from ancient times in the Church, and confirmed by the authority of the divine word, these things we think ought to be preserved and observed most religiously."[44] He added to this proposal an expression of his own desire for a common service of worship:

we think nothing is to be more earnestly wished for, and we should approve nothing more willingly, than divine worship which is common and uniform in all things, not thoroughly defiled by the corruptions of men, nor repugnant to the divine laws; from which the Church may receive the most joyful fruits of peace and tranquillity, and may acquire strength to repulse and carry the war to the finish against the common and most dangerous enemy of God and of all Christians.[45]

James's daring suggestion for a common service of worship was evidently intended to provide an experience through which Christians could gradually recapture the unity which had been lost.

A papal response soon came. In a collection of documents in the Vatican Archives entitled "A Brief Narrative of What Was Treated between His Holiness and the King of England," there is a paraphrase of the instructions which James had sent.[46] The king is reported to have stated that he intended to "distinguish the peaceful Catholics from the factious and troublemaking ones." Peaceful Catholics would be permitted to live without any interference. "But," James was said to have added, "we do especially desire a general council to be called, so that this division can be composed in a most Christian manner, and a restoration can take place, and also in this matter we would wish that the state of the early Church be agreed upon as the pattern by all contenders."[47] According to the same documents, this information arrived in Rome towards the end of December and was the basis of a response by Cardinal Pietro Aldobrandini, the nephew of the pope, in a letter to del Bufalo, the nuncio in Paris. "Concerning a general council," the cardinal wrote, "it cannot yet be arranged" for several

---

[43] Ibid., p. lxxi.   [44] Ibid.   [45] Ibid.
[46] Rome, Vat. Arch., Miscellanea Armadio III, 44, fols. 227 verso–228 verso. The instructions were received in Paris by the nuncio on November 17, 1603 (fol. 227 verso).
[47] Vat. Arch., Misc. Arm. III, 44, fol. 229 verso.

reasons. Some of the issues in dispute had already been dealt with in councils, especially the Council of Trent, "where safe conduct was granted to the Protestants," to enable them to attend. It would be difficult to discuss issues with the Protestants, since they did not agree among themselves. An ecumenical council would also require the support of the Catholic princes. Questions about who would call it, who would preside, and how voting would take place would have to be resolved. On these and other matters, there should be further discussions, until such time as the wishes of the pope were known.[48] The cardinal added that he was willing to go to extraordinary lengths, including the shedding of his own blood, to lead the king into the fold of the Church.[49]

Also included in this collection is a letter from the cardinal dated January 12, 1604, reporting the response of the pope. A copy was sent by the nuncio to the English ambassador in Paris exactly a month later.[50] Clement observed that if the king were willing to recognize the truth, "ways would not be lacking to be able to make contact with him" without convening a "great Council."[51] Many general councils, ancient and modern, had already been held, which had only confirmed the truth of the Roman Church's faith. As a result of these councils, where all doubts and questions concerning the faith had been resolved, many emperors and kings had submitted "to their holy doctrine."[52] Issues in dispute had been settled in this manner by the Council of Trent. The pope recalled the example of King Henry IV of France, who, before he became a Catholic, had also wished to have a council called, but who came to recognize the truth without such means.[53] Faith was the gift of God, and the pope prayed continually to God on behalf of the English king.[54]

The contrast between Clement's and James's hopes can clearly be seen in the diplomatic errand undertaken in 1603 by the English adventurer Sir Anthony Standen. Standen, whose diplomatic and military career before James's accession had included service on behalf of Philip II of Spain, Ferdinand, grand duke of Tuscany, and the earl of Essex, as well as William Cecil, Lord Burghley, left in the early summer of 1603 on a tour of Catholic countries, evidently on James's behalf.[55] After visiting France, Lorraine, and Venice, he wound up in Tuscany, in September, and from there made

---

[48] Ibid.   [49] Ibid.
[50] Ibid., fols. 240–241. This letter is in Latin. For an Italian version of the letter from Aldobrandini to del Bufalo, dated December 29, 1603, see Barbiche, ed., *Correspondance du nonce en France: Innocenzo del Bufalo*, pp. 637–639.
[51] Vat. Arch., Misc. Arm. III, 44, fol. 240 verso.
[52] Ibid.   [53] Ibid., fol. 241.   [54] Ibid.
[55] L. Hicks, "The Embassy of Sir Anthony Standen in 1603," part I, *Recusant History*, 5 (1959/1960), 91–127; Part II, *Recusant History*, 5 (1959/1960), 184–188. See also Meyer, "Clemens VIII. und Jakob I.," pp. 292–293.

contact through an English exile with the papacy. Clement VIII was delighted to have a chance to enlist the aid of one of James's subjects in his effort to convert the king. Accordingly the pope sent a message of goodwill along with relics, rosaries, and other devotional objects to Queen Anne, to sustain her faith and apparently to encourage her to extend her religious influence over her husband and children.[56] But when Standen finally reached the English court in late January 1604, the gifts he brought created a scandal. As Sir Robert Cecil described the situation in his letter to Ambassador Parry at Paris on January 24, 1604, the king

> can not but thinke it very preposterous, for the Pope to serve himself by so improper a meane for his Majesty's conversion, whose fayth is grounded upon the true foundation of Gods holy word, without possibility to be shaken by any of those opinions which are annexed to the corruption of superstitious Ceremonies, the continuation whereof is no small touch, to the gravity of the Popes judgement, who should rather seeke, by a generall Counsaill to cleanse and purge all sydes of such absurdities, then so to continue them, to the end that by such an unity the schisme in the Church might be taken away and abolished.[57]

To James, the objects sent to the queen were the very symbols of the superstitions and corruptions which a general council would be expected to eliminate. They were, accordingly, sent back to Rome via the nuncio in Paris, while Standen, for his indiscretions, was sent to the Tower of London.[58]

Meanwhile pressing domestic matters involving religious dissension demanded James's attention. The Hampton Court Conference, held in January 1604, was convened at least partly to deal with issues raised by Protestant nonconformists or Puritans in the Millenary Petition and in other petitions which had come to the king since the beginning of his reign in England. The issues covered a wide range of topics: the use of the sign of the cross in the service of baptism and the giving of a ring in the marriage service; the need for a preaching ministry; clergy who held more than one benefice; and the use of excommunication by lay officials.[59] James declared

---

[56] Hicks, "Embassy," Part II, *Recusant History*, 5 (1959/1960), 188–194; part III, *Recusant History*, 6 (1961/1962), 163–165.

[57] PRO SP 78/51, fols. 13 verso–14. Cecil also asked Parry to let the nuncio know, on the basis of Queen Anne's word, that "although when she was in Scotland, she mislyked many of those precise opinions, which were maintayned by most of those Churches, yet for matters of her fayth, she never was tyed, to the Romish assertions" (fol. 13 verso). See also Hicks, "Embassy," part IV, *Recusant History*, 7 (1963/1964), 54–55.

[58] Hicks, "Embassy," part IV, 50. Standen's indiscretions included exchanging letters with the Jesuit Robert Parsons in Rome. Parsons was considered at the English court as a major opponent of James's government. After being moved to the Marshalsea prison, Standen was released in 1605. He was in Rome by March 1606, where he lived the rest of his life on a small pension from the pope (pp. 65, 80 note).

[59] For the text of the Millenary Petition, see J. P. Kenyon, ed., *The Stuart Constitution, 1603–1688: Documents and Commentary*, second edition (Cambridge: Cambridge Univer-

in a "Proclamation Concerning Such as Seditiously Seeke Reformation in Church Matters" on October 24, 1603, that he was persuaded that the "constitution and doctrine" of the Church of England were "agreeable to Gods word, and neere to the condition of the Primitive Church," yet experience had shown that the passage of time brought corruptions even to the Church Militant.[60] In order to free the Church of England from any scandals which undermined its effectiveness or diminished its reputation, he had asked for "a meeting to be had before our selfe and our counsell, of divers of the Bishops and other learned men" to ascertain the state of the Church and to correct any evident faults or abuses.[61] Because of "sicknesse reigning in many places of our kingdome," the time for this meeting was set ahead for some point after Christmas.[62]

The conference was long seen as an expression of James's intransigence on key religious issues and of his intolerant attitude towards the Puritans.[63] Only in the last thirty years has this view been challenged and modified.[64] The traditional view was largely the result of the most widely circulated account, that of William Barlow, a participant who wrote and published his narrative with the encouragement of Richard Bancroft, bishop of London and soon to be John Whitgift's successor as archbishop of Canterbury. Barlow's *Svmme and Svbstance of the Conference* is not only very sympathetic to the defenders of the established Church but is the source of several intemperate remarks attributed to the king. For example, it was Barlow who reported that at the end of the second day of the conference James said of the Puritan spokesmen "as hee was going to his inner Chamber": "If this bee al . . . that they haue to say, I shall make them conforme themselues, or

sity Press, 1986), pp. 117–119. Other petitions are described in Patrick Collinson, *The Elizabethan Puritan Movement* (London: Jonathan Cape, 1967), pp. 452–454.
[60] Larkin and Hughes, *Stuart Royal Proclamations*, vol. I, p. 61.
[61] Ibid., p. 62.   [62] Ibid.
[63] See, for example, Gardiner, *History of England*, vol. I, pp. 153–158; Roland G. Usher, *The Reconstruction of the English Church*, 2 vols. (New York: Appleton, 1910), vol. I, pp. 310–333; Charles Williams, *James I* (London: Arthur Barker, 1934), pp. 184–192; Willson, *King James VI and I*, pp. 201–209; William McElwee, *The Wisest Fool in Christendom: The Reign of King James I and VI* (London: Faber and Faber, 1958), pp. 136–140; G. P. V. Akrigg, *Jacobean Pageant, or, The Court of King James I* (Cambridge, Mass.: Harvard University Press, 1962), pp. 304–307.
[64] Curtis, "Hampton Court Conference and Its Aftermath," began the process of revision. For recent treatments which modify the traditional view, see Frederick Shriver, "Hampton Court Re-visited: James I and the Puritans," *Journal of Ecclesiastical History*, 30, 1 (January 1982), 48–71; Patrick Collinson, "The Jacobean Religious Settlement: The Hampton Court Conference," in Howard Tomlinson, ed., *Before the Civil War: Essays on Early Stuart Politics and Government* (London: Macmillan, 1983), pp. 27–51; and Nicholas Tyacke, *Anti-Calvinists: The Rise of English Arminianism, c. 1590–1640* (Oxford: Clarendon Press, 1987), pp. 9–28.

I wil harrie them out of the land, or else doe worse."[65] Barlow makes the Puritan case appear weak, and he represents James as being generally in agreement with the bishops. But Barlow's is not the only contemporary account. There are more than half a dozen others, some brief, to be sure, but others extensive; they represent a spectrum of viewpoints.[66] If all the extant accounts are considered, a different picture from that given by Barlow emerges.

It is evident that on the first day of the conference, Saturday, January 14, 1604, when James met with some of the leading bishops and cathedral deans along with his Privy Council, he sought as much as anything else to become better acquainted with the Church of England and to pose questions to the bishops which he not only felt certain the Puritan spokesmen would ask but which he wanted to have answered to his own satisfaction. Bancroft chose his ground carefully in defending confirmation and absolution to a king brought up and educated in the Reformed Church of Scotland. In both cases Bancroft claimed the support of antiquity and of "master Calvin."[67] James wanted to proceed with the conference and was willing to make changes in the English Church where they seemed warranted. According to accounts sympathetic to the Puritans, three of the bishops – John Whitgift, archbishop of Canterbury, Thomas Bilson, bishop of Winchester, and Bancroft – went down on their knees to implore the king not to alter anything in the government or worship of the Church. James responded that "there was no state either Ecclesiasticall or Civill whereunto in

65 William Barlow, The Svmme and Svbstance of the Conference, Which It Pleased His Excellent Maiestie to Have with the Lords, Bishops, and Other of His Clergie (at Which the Most of the Lordes of the Councell Were Present) in His Maiesties Priuy–Chamber, at Hampton Court, Ianuary 14, 1603; Whereunto Are Added, Some Copies, (Scattered Abroad,) Vnsauory, and Vntrue (London: Mathew Law, 1604), p. 83.
66 There are three other accounts appended to Barlow's narrative, which represent James as more opposed to existing practices of the Church of England during the first day of the conference and which tend to be hostile to the bishops. See Barlow, Svmme and Svbstance of the Conference, sigs. P_1–P_2 verso, A_3–A_3 verso, and Usher, Reconstruction, vol. II, appendix III, pp. 338–341. Usher also provides texts of "The Bishopps Proceedings and Opinions Towching Those Things Which Were Comitted to Theire Consideracon" (BL, Additional MS. 28571, fols. 187–192), pp. 331–335; "An Anonymous Account in Favour of the Bishops, Hampton Court Conference" (Cambridge University Library, Baker MS. M. m. l. 45, fols. 155–157), pp. 335–338; and a Puritan account which begins, "A declaration of the conference had before the kings most excellent Majesty" (BL, Harleian MS. 828, fol. 32), pp. 341–354. See also Edward Cardwell, A History of Conferences and Other Proceedings Connected with the Revision of the Book of Common Prayer, third edition (Oxford: Oxford University Press, 1849), "King James to some person unknown in Scotland," pp. 160–161; "A letter written from court by Toby Matthew, bishop of Durham, to Hutton, archbishop of York," pp. 161–166; and "A letter from Patrick Galloway to the presbytery of Edinburgh, concerning the conference," pp. 212–217. See also James Montague's account in Ralph Winwood, Memorials of Affairs of State in the Reigns of Queen Elizabeth and King James I, ed. Edmund Sawyer, 3 vols. (London: T. Ward, 1725), vol. II, pp. 13–16.
67 Barlow, Svmme and Svbstance of the Conference, pp. 11, 13.

40 yeares some corruptions might not creepe."[68] The king engaged energetically in discussion for some four hours, "to his good satisfaction," reported Bishop Tobias Matthew of Durham, "in all such objections as he propounded."[69]

On the second day, Monday, January 16, four Puritan spokesmen – John Reynolds, president of Corpus Christi College, Oxford, Laurence Chaderton, master of Emmanuel College, Cambridge, John Knewstubs, fellow of St. John's College, Cambridge, and Thomas Sparke, rector of Bletchley, Buckinghamshire – were brought in to present their own arguments.[70] To the occasional discomfort and even dismay of the two bishops present, Bancroft and Bilson, the king discussed a wide range of issues with them and promised to consider changes, many of a minor nature, in the liturgy and practices of the Church. In response to Reynolds's request that those who were ordained be such "as were able to instructe the people, and were [of] unblameable life," James outlined a program whereby the Church might be better supplied with learned and able ministers.[71] On two extremely important matters he and Reynolds proved to be in entire agreement. James accepted Reynolds's suggestion that there be one uniform catechism in the realm, with adequate definition of baptism and the Lord's Supper.[72] He responded equally favorably to Reynolds's suggestion that there be a new translation of the Bible.[73] James agreed that the translation should be "consonant to the originall Greeke and Hebrew and set forth without note, for that some of them [other translations] enforce a sence further then the texte will beare."[74] His fundamental concerns in the project were peace and unity. As Barlow reported: "Whereupon his Highnesse wished, that some especiall pains should be taken in that behalf for one vniforme translation . . . and this to be done by the best learned in both the Vniuersities, after them to be reuiewed by the Bishops, and the chiefe learned of the Church; from them to be presented to the Priuy Councell; and

---

[68] Usher, *Reconstruction*, vol. II, pp. 341–342; also 338, 339. See also Cardwell, *History of Conferences*, p. 213.

[69] Cardwell, *History of Conferences*, p. 163.

[70] Usher, *Reconstruction*, vol. II, pp. 337–338. According to this account, the Puritan group also included Patrick Galloway, a Scot serving as royal chaplain, who was "silent in all thinges" (p. 337), and Richard Field, another royal chaplain, who "went in with the Puritans" but "never spake but once, and that altogether ageinst them" (p. 338).

[71] Usher, *Reconstruction*, vol. II, pp. 346–347. See also Cardwell, *History of Conferences*, p. 216.

[72] Usher, *Reconstruction*, vol. II, p. 345.   [73] Ibid., pp. 336, 345.

[74] Ibid., p. 345. The king disliked the Geneva translation of the Bible, which most Puritans used, partly because of its marginal notes, which expressed political as well as religious ideas. See Thomas Fuller, *The Church-History of Britain* (London: John Williams, 1655), Bk. X, p. 14.

lastly to bee ratified by his Royall authority; and so this whole Church to be bound vnto it, and none other."[75]

Only on the subject of discipline did James become exasperated with the Puritans. When Reynolds called for a system of councils beginning with the local pastors, proceeding to annual synods under the bishop's direction, then to synods of the province and the nation, the king saw in this the outline of a presbyterian system such as that in Scotland, which, Barlow quoted him as saying, "as wel agreeth with a Monarchy, as God, and the Deuill."[76] Even so, a Puritan account states that James assured the Puritans that while only the bishops would govern the Church and handle excommunications, they would be "assisted with the deanes and grauest preachers."[77] This went some way towards meeting the Puritans' concerns.

On the third day, Wednesday, January 18, James spoke to the bishops, deans, and privy councillors at length about the results of the discussions, and to a group of civil lawyers about the proceedings of the ecclesiastical courts. The changes to be made were referred to committees of councillors and bishops to be appointed following the conference.[78] When the Puritan spokesmen were brought in, the king urged all present to work together in a spirit of moderation, mutual forebearance, and unity, "thereupon," as a Puritan account stated, "exhorting the ministers to carrie themselves duetifull towards their Bishops; and the Bishops to deale fauorable with them, and more gently than euer they had don before."[79] Some of the Puritan requests were refused, and some of those which the king agreed to were not carried out or were carried out only in part.[80] But the new translation of the scriptures was undertaken in accordance with the king's instructions and proved to be one of the great achievements of James's reign. Six companies of scholars, whose number included several from both

[75] Barlow, *Svmme and Svbstance of the Conference*, p. 46.
[76] Ibid., p. 79. See also Usher, *Reconstruction*, vol. II, pp. 351–352.
[77] Usher, *Reconstruction*, p. 347. See also Winwood, *Memorials*, vol. II, p. 14.
[78] Barlow, *Svmme and Svbstance of the Conference*, p. 96. For the implementation of reforms and the enforcement of conformity in the dioceses of Ely, Bath and Wells, and Chichester, see K. C. Fincham, "Ramifications of the Hampton Court Conference in the Dioceses, 1603–1609," *Journal of Ecclesiastical History*, 36, 2 (April 1985), 208–227.
[79] Usher, *Reconstruction*, vol. II, p. 353. The same account adds that later in the same session, "the king moued the Bishops that they shoold take heede and deal gently and fauorably with their brethren, and not when they were gon to use fire and sword and make a vacuum lest the Deuill enter in" (p. 353). See also, for a similar expression of views by the king: Winwood, *Memorials*, vol. II, p. 15.
[80] For lists of things to be reformed, see Cardwell, *History of Conferences*, pp. 214–216; Winwood, *Memorials*, vol. II, pp. 15–16. Episcopal visitation articles in 1605–1609 and James's own instructions to the bishops in 1610–1611 show that efforts were made to effect reforms by such measures as curbing pluralism and encouraging preaching; see Kenneth Fincham, ed., *Visitation Articles and Injunctions of the Early Stuart Church* (London: Church of England Record Society, 1994), vol. I, pp. xxv, 4–99.

groups at Hampton Court – Lancelot Andrewes, John Overall, and William Barlow from among the deans, Chaderton and Reynolds from among the Puritans – produced a translation which virtually all English Protestants came to treasure.[81] The seventeenth-century church historian Thomas Fuller said of the translators "as also of that Gracious King that employed them": "Wheresoever the Bible shall be preached or read in the whole world, there shall also this that they have done be told in memoriall of them."[82]

The Hampton Court Conference was, in the light of all the evidence available, very much in keeping with the king's call for an ecumenical council at the beginning of his reign in England. The king aimed to find a middle ground between two widely separated groups in the English Church. He undertook to identify what needed to be reformed and to assign responsibility for making appropriate changes. Above all, he sought to find a basis – through a revised Prayer Book, an expanded catechism, and a new translation of the Bible – for a genuine religious unity among his subjects. Commentators on the conference often seem preoccupied with the question of who won – the bishops or the Puritans? Actually, neither party did. The king was looking for a compromise which the two parties would find acceptable. To a large extent, he succeeded. As the voluminous literature on Puritanism in England in the early seventeenth century indicates, the religious outlook called Puritan certainly did not disappear in the years which followed. But the Elizabethan Puritan movement, with its clearly defined agenda of organizational and liturgical changes which it was determined to effect in the established Church, finally came to an end. For the most part, its adherents sought other, less militant ways of achieving reforms through the rest of James's reign.[83]

[81] Fuller, *Church-History*, Bk. X, pp. 44–47. See also, for the organization of the project and the principles which the translators followed: Alfred W. Pollard, ed., *Records of the English Bible: The Documents Relating to the Translation and Publication of the Bible in English, 1525–1611* (London: Oxford University Press, 1911), pp. 331–377; Ward Allen, ed., *Translating for King James: Being a True Copy of the Only Notes Made by a Translator of King James's Bible, the Authorized Version, as the Final Committee of Review Revised the Translation of Romans through Revelation at Stationers' Hall in London in 1610–1611, Taken by the Reverend John Bois* (Nashville: Vanderbilt University Press, 1969), pp. vii–x, 3–34; and Ward Allen and Edward C. Jacobs, eds., *The Coming of the King James Gospels: A Collation of the Translators' Work-in-Progress* (Fayetteville: University of Arkansas Press, 1995), pp. 3–57. Informative studies include: David Daiches, *The King James Version of the English Bible: An Account of the Development and Sources of the English Bible of 1611 with Special Reference to the Hebrew Tradition* (Chicago: University of Chicago Press, 1941); A. C. Partridge, *English Biblical Translation* (London: André Deutsch, 1973), pp. 105–158; and F. F. Bruce, *History of the Bible in English from the Earliest Versions*, third edition (New York: Oxford University Press, 1978), pp. 96–112.
[82] Fuller, *Church-History*, Bk. X, p. 59 (an adaptation of Mark 14: 9).
[83] For the changes in the Puritan movement after 1604, see Collinson, *The Elizabethan Puritan Movement*, pp. 448–467, and *English Puritanism* (London: Historical Association, 1987), pp. 23–39; Peter Lake, *Moderate Puritans and the Elizabethan Church* (Cambridge: Cam-

If James's program of seeking peace and unity in the Church of England did not work perfectly or succeed permanently, it resolved some rancorous domestic problems which had long disturbed the country. The principles the king followed in attempting to secure religious peace at home between 1603 and 1605 were very much in keeping with those he followed in his diplomacy abroad.

In late February 1604, about the time that James probably heard about the initial response to his proposal in Rome, he announced his hopes for a council in a proclamation in England. In this edict he took stern measures against all "Jesuits, Seminaries, and other Priests whatsoever, having Ordination from any authoritie by the Lawes of this Realme prohibited."[84] A draft of this proclamation was drawn up in July 1603, after a plot to seize the king, organized by William Watson, a Catholic priest, had been exposed and the conspirators jailed. At their trial in November, testimony damaging to the Jesuits, suggesting widespread plotting against the king, had been given.[85] By getting in touch with James through the English ambassador, the nuncio in Paris aimed, in part, to assure the king that the pope was making every effort to discourage such treasonable efforts by Catholics. By February 22, 1604, however, James was ready to move to drive all Catholic priests abroad, giving them in the proclamation a deadline of March 19, the

bridge University Press, 1982), pp. 243–292; and Patrick McGrath, *Papists and Puritans under Elizabeth I* (London: Blandford Press, 1967), pp. 339–363. The rigorous efforts of Archbishop Bancroft to enforce conformity from 1604 to 1610 are described in Usher, *Reconstruction*, vol. I, pp. 334–423, vol. II, pp. 3–49; and Stuart Barton Babbage, *Puritanism and Richard Bancroft* (London: SPCK, 1962), esp. pp. 74–232, 259–293, 323–369. Kenneth Fincham in *Prelate as Pastor: The Episcopate of James I* (Oxford: Clarendon Press, 1990), pp. 212–247, revises downward Babbage's estimates of the number of clergy deprived between 1604 and 1609 and shows that James's policy was aimed at tolerating moderate nonconformity. B. W. Quintrell has shown that much of the initial impetus for securing conformity in the southeast came from the king himself: "The Royal Hunt and the Puritans, 1604–1605," *Journal of Ecclesiastical History*, 31, 1 (January 1980), 41–58. For the survival of Puritanism as an ideology, a way of life, and a network of relationships reaching from England to the Netherlands and to New England, see William Haller, *The Rise of Puritanism: or, The Way to the New Jerusalem as Set Forth in Pulpit and Press from Thomas Cartwright to John Lilburne and John Milton* (New York: Columbia University Press, 1938); Christopher Hill, *Society and Puritanism in Pre-Revolutionary England* (London: Secker and Warburg, 1964); Everett H. Emerson, *English Puritanism from John Hooper to John Milton* (Durham, Duke University Press, 1968); Paul S. Seaver, *The Puritan Lectureships: The Politics of Religious Dissent, 1560–1662* (Stanford: Stanford University Press, 1970); Nicholas Tyacke, *The Fortunes of Puritanism, 1603–1640* (London: Dr. Williams's Trust, 1989); and Stephen Foster, *The Long Argument: English Puritanism and the Shaping of New England Culture, 1570–1700* (Chapel Hill: University of North Carolina Press, 1991).

[84] Larkin and Hughes, *Stuart Royal Proclamations*, vol. I, pp. 70–73.
[85] BL, Hatfield House, Cecil Papers (microfilm), M. 485/20, fols. 74 verso–79. See also Giuseppi, *Calendar of the Manuscripts of the Most Hon. the Marquess of Salisbury*, part XV, p. 346. Watson's plot and its aftermath are described in Gardiner, *History of England*, vol. I, pp. 108–145.

day on which Parliament was to convene, by which they must have departed from the kingdom.[86] The reason given was that their "absolute submission to Forreine Jurisdiction at their first taking of Orders" made them less than fully subject to their king's authority, and endangered the peace of the realm.[87]

The same proclamation acknowledged, however, James's own gratitude to the "now bishop of Rome for his kinde offices and private temporall cariage towards us in many things," which the king intended to return to the pope as one "in state and condition of a Secular Prince."[88] The proclamation ended with a passage on the dangers posed by religious divisions and the benefits which "a generall Councell free and lawfully called" could bring:

> Yet when wee consider and observe the course and claime of that Sea [of Rome], Wee have no reason to imagine, that Princes of our Religion and Profession, can expect any assurance long to continue, unlesse it might be assented by mediation of other Princes Christian, that some good course might be taken (by a generall Councell free and lawfully called) to plucke up those roots of dangers and jealousies which arise for cause of Religion as well betweene Princes and Princes, as betweene them and their Subjects, and to make it manifest that no State or Potentate either hath or can challenge power to dispose of earthly Kingdomes or Monarchies, or to dispense with Subjects obedience to their naturall Soveraignes: In which charitable Action, there is no Prince living, that will be readier then Wee shall be to concurre even to the uttermost of our power, not only out of particular disposition to live peaceably with all States and Princes of Christendome, but because such a setled amitie might (by an union in Religion) be established among Christian Princes, as might enable us all to resist the common Enemie.[89]

The king's public declaration was, therefore, that he wished to settle once and for all the issues of religion which were a source of conflict between and within states, to check for good the papacy's claim to be able to depose rulers, and to achieve a "union in Religion" throughout Christendom.

Thus, by the time James spoke of his wish to be a member of "a generall Christian union in Religion" to Parliament in March 1604, he had communicated his proposal for an ecumenical council to resolve the religious conflicts in Europe to the Venetian and French governments, the papacy, and the nation at large. In the light of these developments it is interesting to note what was reported to the papacy from Catholic sources in 1604 concerning the atmosphere at the English court. As these reports indicate, James's readiness to move towards a religious reconciliation was certainly not unknown there.

On February 10, 1604, del Bufalo, the papal nuncio in Paris, wrote to Cardinal Aldobrandini in Rome, enclosing with his letter two recent letters

---

[86] Larkin and Hughes, *Stuart Royal Proclamations*, vol. I, p. 72.
[87] Ibid., p. 73.   [88] Ibid.   [89] Ibid.

from England reporting on affairs in that country. The author of the enclosed letters, the English Catholic Henry Constable, a poet and formerly a courtier in Elizabeth's reign, had recently returned to England from France, where he had become a pensioner of King Henry IV. Whether or not he was on any kind of official mission is not clear, though he does profess his desire in the first letter to serve his Church, if he does not lack the means of being able to stay at the English court.[90] His acquaintance with James dated from 1589, when he visited Scotland to congratulate the king on his impending marriage. Constable had long wished to win James to his own religious point of view. The first letter, dated January 9, 1604, at Hampton Court, expresses Constable's view that the king is "most benign, and the enemy of persecution," but that nevertheless there cannot be any possibility of an official declaration of religious freedom for Catholics "until such time as His Majesty is personally more convinced than he is at present of the authenticity and good grounds of the Catholic cause."[91] For this purpose it would be highly desirable to send learned persons versed in theological controversies to talk with the king. Constable had, furthermore, some advice for those sent to talk to James. "In what follows," he wrote,

I am simply reporting to your Most Illustrious Lordship the opinion of those who are very well acquainted with the humour and disposition of the king at the present time and who desire, above all else, the good of the Catholic Religion, namely, that those who will speak with His Majesty on behalf of Our Master, should explain at once the intention which His Holiness has of negotiating with the King, in his capacity as the greatest and most able of those Princes who are today separated from the Apostolic See, about the ways and means of uniting the whole of Christendom in one faith and one single true religion.[92]

Since, he added, the king had a great opinion of his own knowledge of theology and deemed himself capable of great things, he would derive a great deal of satisfaction from discussing such a proposal which would, therefore, "be of the utmost value in leading to the aim which we desire."[93]

In a second letter, enclosed by del Bufalo with the first and sent to

[90] PRO, Roman Transcripts, PRO 31/9/88, pp. 1–4. For Henry Constable, see the article by Sidney Lee in the *Dictionary of National Biography*, 22 vols. (London: Oxford University Press, 1959–1960), vol. IV, pp. 959–960; George Wickes, "Henry Constable, Poet and Courtier (1562–1613)," *Biographical Studies*, 2 (1954), 272–300; David Rogers, "The Catholic Moderator: A French Reply to Bellarmine and Its English Author, Henry Constable," *Recusant History*, 5 (1959–1960), 224–235; John Bossy, "A Propos Henry Constable," *Recusant History*, 6 (1961–1962), 228–237; T. G. A. Nelson, "Sir John Harington and Henry Constable," *Recusant History*, 9 (1967–68), 263–264; and G. H. M. Posthumus Meyjes, "L'*Examen pacifique de la doctrine des Huguenots* et son auteur (1589): Henry Constable et la critique," *Lias*, 14 (1987), 1–14. See also Barbiche, ed., *Correspondance du nonce en France: Innocenzo del Bufalo*, pp. 617, 665, 692, 703, 722, 782.
[91] PRO PRO 31/9/88, p. 2.   [92] Ibid., pp. 2–3.   [93] Ibid., p. 3.

Cardinal Aldobrandini, Constable commented on what he saw as favorable opinion in England for such negotiations:

> Meanwhile I have to inform your Lordship that the more I move in the court circle the more I become aware that the most important people at court, and the most learned amongst those who bear the title of Prelate in this kingdom, speak willingly and show themselves desirous of some move towards the reunion of England with the Apostolic See. Many of them have spoken about it with great emotion, and although the details that they have proposed are not such that they may be approved by a Catholic, nonetheless that desire for negotiations for a reunion between His Holiness and the king makes me hope well for the future.[94]

Constable saw the edict against Catholic priests "under the pretense," as he said, "of the undue influence and obedience that they owe the Pope," as an occasion to work for an amicable agreement with the new king.[95] In a letter to del Bufalo of February 26, sent by the nuncio to Cardinal Aldobrandini, he suggested that the king be told that "differences may be brought into accord by means of a General Council, making the king understand the desire that His Holiness has to remove all occasions of jealousy that the Apostolic See should appear to have caused, and to wish to be united with him in this holy desire to seek the Union of Christendom."[96] In the same month, Constable wrote to Charles, the duke of Guise, calling his attention to the passage in James's recent edict in which the king had expressed the wish that "by means of a General Council the occasions of jealousy could be extinguished and the differences which are among Christians on the matter of religion reconciled."[97] Since, Constable said, "the Pope seems slow to respond to these designs," he urged the duke to seek the permission of the French king to come to England to talk to James about this proposal before the convening of Parliament.[98] "The Catholics of England," he reported, desired this "infinitely."[99]

Del Bufalo's letters also give us a vivid picture of James describing aspects of his proposal to the representatives of a Catholic prince. On September 21, 1604, del Bufalo reported to Rome that the duke of Lorraine had sent an embassy to England to speak to James about the status of the Catholics in his kingdom.[100] On their way back to Lorraine from England the duke's

---

[94] Ibid., p. 5. The letter is undated.   [95] Ibid., p. 53.   [96] Ibid.
[97] PRO SP 78/51, fol. 71.   [98] Ibid., fol. 72.
[99] Ibid. Constable was imprisoned in the Tower of London for twelve weeks beginning in April 1604 for views he expressed about the king in letters which were intercepted. Though once again in favor at court for a short time, his political career essentially came to an end. See Wickes, "Henry Constable, Poet and Courtier, 1562–1613," pp. 290–291.
[100] PRO PRO 31/9/88, p. 121; Barbiche, ed., *Correspondance du nonce en France: Innocenzo del Bufalo*, p. 785. The embassy from the duke of Lorraine is mentioned in a communication from Dudley Carleton to John Chamberlain, from London, August 27, 1604. See *Calendar of State Papers, Domestic Series, of the Reign of James I*, ed. Mary Anne Everett Green, 4 vols. (London: Public Record Office, 1857–1859), vol. I, p. 146.

representatives had stopped off in Paris to report to the papal nuncio on their conversations. According to del Bufalo, they reported that James had said repeatedly "that he recognized the Roman Church as the Mother Church, and the Pope as the Universal bishop of the whole Church, with spiritual authority over all, and that he himself would gladly be reunited with the Roman Church and would take three steps in that direction if only the Roman Church would take one."[101] They also reported that James seemed prepared "to believe all that which should be shown him through the Scriptures and through the Holy Fathers of the three centuries after Christ, holding a different opinion of what St. Augustine and St. Bernard wrote from that expressed by Calvin and Luther."[102] As for the treatment of the Catholics, he regretted that Parliament had confirmed the laws against them, but would himself see that no action was taken against Catholics on purely religious grounds.[103] Clement VIII was not impressed by James's comments on religious matters. A note on the back of del Bufalo's letter, apparently in the pope's hand, reads: "These are things which make me doubt that he believes anything."[104]

Another visitor to the English court, the ambassador of Spain, Don Juan de Tassis, who became the count of Villa Mediana, arrived at the end of August 1603 to begin discussing prospects for a formal peace between his country and England.[105] In early October, James, who had ordered hostilities with Spain to cease following his accession in England, made it clear to the ambassador that he wanted peace. Formal negotiations, however, did not get under way until May 1604, when representatives of Spain, the Spanish Netherlands, and England assembled in Somerset House to discuss the terms of agreement. The treaty, bringing a long and costly war to an end, was agreed to by James and Juan de Velasco, duke of Frias, the constable of Castile, whom Philip III had empowered to act on Spain's behalf, in mid-August 1604.[106]

Tassis had been enjoined by his monarch to attempt to secure a toleration for English Catholics or at least a significant mitigation of their lot.[107] This he failed to do, partly because most of the members of Parliament were

---

[101] PRO PRO 31/9/88, pp. 121–122.
[102] Ibid., p. 122.   [103] Ibid.   [104] Ibid.
[105] Albert J. Loomie, *Toleration and Diplomacy: The Religious Issue in Anglo-Spanish Relations, 1603–1605* (Philadelphia: American Philosophical Society, 1963), pp. 12–22. For the preliminaries to this embassy, see Loomie, "Philip III and the Stuart Succession in England, 1600–1603," *Revue belge de philologie et d'histoire*, 43 (1965), 492–514. The negotiations are treated from the perspective of relations with France in Maurice Lee, Jr., *James I and Henry IV: An Essay in English Foreign Policy, 1603–1610* (Urbana: University of Illinois Press, 1970), pp. 17–40.
[106] Loomie, *Toleration and Diplomacy*, pp. 25–30; Gardiner, *History of England*, vol. I, pp. 206–214.
[107] Loomie, *Toleration and Diplomacy*, pp. 5, 12–13, 25–27.

opposed to any relaxation of the penal laws against Catholics. The constable's memorandum to Philip, written from Bordeaux on his return from England on November 22, 1604, nevertheless struck an optimistic note about the king's attitude towards Roman Catholics. James was "a princely friend of learning, gentle, literate, attentive to the practice of virtue and well disposed to the affairs of Spain," wrote the constable.[108] Despite his profession of the Protestant faith, the king "calls the Catholic religion the ancient and true mother, but will maintain that it has abuses."[109] He "confers offices and honours on persons who are held to be Catholics, a thing never permitted in the days of the Queen."[110] Executions were not being carried out as before; fines against Catholics were not being collected. In the Privy Council, he observed, there were Catholics as well as Protestants, though only a few of the former had declared the fact.[111] In general "there is a growing expectation [among Catholics] that this realm is moving to change for the better."[112]

The constable also urged that James's proposal concerning a general council be carefully considered. "That the establishment of religion and the destruction of error in England may be begun," wrote the constable, "I say that, although this question of a Council is to be left to the prudent discretion of his Holiness who ought to be the first to consider it, still since their request is sincere, it appears to be important, even if all their beliefs have been already debated and decided in previous councils, they are anxious and sincere in their demand and have the approval of a large part of the Catholics, many of whom are wavering over certain articles."[113] He added, when discussing James's religion: "I have read on more than one occasion that he will remain willing to grasp the true light of the gospel, and that he keeps seeking a Council along with a large portion of the Catholics of the realm."[114]

At the end of 1604, over a year after James had sent word to the papal nuncio in Paris that Sir James Lindsay would be returning to Rome with an

---

[108] Albert J. Loomie, ed., *Spain and the Jacobean Catholics*, 2 vols. (London: Catholic Record Society, 1973–1978), vol. I, p. 42.

[109] Ibid., p. 43.   [110] Ibid.   [111] Ibid.

[112] Ibid. Before arriving in England, Tassis received a report, evidently drawn up in the spring of 1603, listing those at the English court who were Catholic or pro-Catholic. It was drawn up by Robert Spiller, an associate of the Jesuit priest Henry Garnet. The list includes Lord Buckhurst (soon to be earl of Dorset); Baron Mountjoy (soon to be earl of Devonshire); Sir John Fortescue; Edward Wotton; and the earls of Worcester, Northumberland, Cumberland, and Southampton. Loomie, ed., *Spain and the Jacobean Catholics*, vol. I, pp. 1–8. Those at court whom Tassis found particularly sympathetic to his proposals included the earls of Dorset, Devonshire, Nottingham, Cumberland, Suffolk, and Worcester; Lord Home; Lord Kinloss; Lord Ramsay; Sir Thomas Lake and Sir James Lindsay. Loomie, *Toleration and Diplomacy*, pp. 31–35.

[113] Loomie, ed., *Spain and the Jacobean Catholics*, vol. I, pp. 41–42.

[114] Ibid., p. 43.

answer to the pope's message carried by Lindsay in 1602, the Scottish envoy was at last well enough to set out. Cecil, now viscount Cranborne, sent to the recently appointed ambassador extraordinary in Paris, Ludovick Stuart, duke of Lennox, a copy of Lindsay's instructions. According to this communication, dated January 1605, Lindsay was to reply to the pope on the king's behalf that James "was resolute in his [religious] profession, both out of knowledge and conscience, and he would be, untill he might see more sufficient warrant, then ever yet he could read or hear of to the contrary."[115] Yet, lest this seem to proceed from an obdurate heart, the king added that it was his resolution, "and so he had often made publick profession," "that he would never refuse any conference in any generall Councill, which should be lawfully called by the consent of all the Princes of Europe, for the pacification of all those contentions which make them all lesse able to resist the common enemy of the same."[116]

Lindsay's message was interpreted in Rome as an encouraging sign of James's willingness to consider the claims of the Roman faith.[117] On January 6, 1605, Bernardus Paulinus, papal datary, wrote to James to express his pleasure over Lindsay's arrival and to assure the king of the pope's goodwill and affection. He offered to assist in any way with James's plans.[118] Cardinal Aldobrandini wrote in a similar vein on January 23, expressing also his desire to be united in the faith with the king on the basis of "the singular virtue handed down by the pious and most renowned queen your mother," Mary Queen of Scots.[119] In his own letter to James on January 23, Lindsay reported that the pope had called together a congregation of twelve cardinals to confer about "what was meetest to his Holines to doe in that which concerned your Matie and your dominions."[120] It was, he said, the first such congregation assembled to consult about England in forty-six years. Among the matters discussed was whether to send to James "a Legate, a Nuncio, or some saecular gentleman."[121] Lindsay wrote to Cranborne that when he expressed reservations to Cardinal Aldobrandini about the congregation and the suspicions it might breed among the king's subjects and his allies abroad, the cardinal explained that "the Pope could not do otherwise, seeing the wholle Embassadours that had bene in England

---

[115] PRO SP 78/52, fol. 31 verso. Ludovick Stuart, second duke of Lennox, was the eldest son of Esmé, the first duke. Like his father, he had been high in James's favor in Scotland. Lennox was sent to declare James's friendship and affection to the French king in response to such expressions from France on his accession. PRO SP 78/51, fols. 328–331 verso, and 336.

[116] PRO SP 78/52, fol. 31 verso. See also Stafford, *James VI of Scotland and the Throne of England*, pp. 247–248.

[117] Meyer, "Clemens VIII. und Jakob I. von England," pp. 294–300.

[118] PRO SP, Italian States and Rome, 85/3, fol. 28.

[119] Ibid., fol. 44.   [120] Ibid., fol. 46.   [121] Ibid.

employed by Catholique Princes had shewen by their relations here of his Ma[ties] vertue, prudence and literature and how that there was no cause to despaire, but sometyme he might be made to acknowledge the Catholique Church."[122] On February 5, the day before he planned to leave Rome, Lindsay wrote to James that the pope himself prayed for two hours every night "for your Ma[tie], the Quene, and your Children, and for the conversion of your Ma[tie], and your dominions."[123]

As Cranborne wrote to Lennox in January, it seemed evident to the king that Lindsay, back among his fellow Catholics, had seriously misrepresented his mission.[124] For the sake of winning favor among his papal hosts, he had exaggerated James's receptivity to initiatives aimed at the king's conversion, while assuring his English superiors that he had exercised caution and restraint. Meanwhile, in France, the English ambassador continued to press for a council. In June 1604 Parry had urged del Bufalo, who had been recalled to Rome and elevated to the rank of cardinal, to work in his new surroundings for the convening of a general council.[125] On January 3, 1605, he reported to Cranborne that del Bufalo was a member of the congregation discussing English affairs. Parry had spoken to the newly arrived nuncio in Paris, Maffeo Barberini, archbishop of Nazareth, on this subject. Parry reminded Barberini that a proposal had been made to the pope for "a free and lawful General Counsel, for publick reformation of errors, and reducing of Christendom to unite."[126] He expressed the hope that the pope and cardinals would be "inclyned therto."[127] The nuncio replied that results from such overtures were not to be despaired of.[128]

Not surprisingly, in view of his first reaction to the conciliar initiatives of King James, Clement VIII did not move towards unity on the terms which James proposed. The king described the reception his proposal for a council received in an interview with Zorzi Giustinian, the Venetian ambassador in England, reported to the Doge and Senate on June 14, 1606: "Pope Clement VIII invited me to join the Roman Church. I replied that if they would resolve the various difficulties in a general Council, legitimately convened, I would submit myself to its decisions. What do you think he answered? – just look at the zeal of the Vicar of Christ – why, he said, 'The king of

---

[122] Ibid., fol. 48. Dated January 23, 1605.   [123] Ibid., fol. 50.

[124] PRO SP 78/52, fol. 25 verso. Dated January 1605. These suspicions are described as widespread in a letter to Lindsay from his fellow Scot, Sir James Sempill, dated July 1605. PRO SP 85/3, fols. 72–75. Lindsay had announced his intention to go from Rome to Spain to "give that King thankes for many favours, w[ch] it hath pleased his Ma[tie] to shew me." PRO SP 85/3, fol. 42.

[125] PRO PRO 31/9/88, fol. 91. Reported in a letter of del Bufalo to Cardinal Aldobrandino, dated June 29, 1604. Cf. Barbiche, ed., *Correspondance du nonce en France: Innocenzo del Bufalo*, p. 743.

[126] PRO SP 78/52, fol. 2. The new nuncio was eventually to become Pope Urban VIII.

[127] PRO SP 78/52. fol. 2.   [128] Ibid.

England need not speak of Councils; I won't hear of one. If he will not come in by any other means things may stand as they are.' "[129] To judge from the tone of James's comments, the passage of time had not rendered him any the less outraged.

James's call for an ecumenical council, reiterated over the course of his first two and a half years as king of England, owes a great deal to the ecclesiological theories of the conciliar movement which flourished in the fourteenth and fifteenth centuries. A succession of thinkers, including Dietrich of Niem, Pierre d'Ailly, Jean Gerson, Francesco Zabarella, and Nicholas of Cusa, whose teachings provided the basis for the Councils of Constance and Basel, argued for the supremacy of the general council over the pope and for the centrality of the general council in the governance of the Church.[130] The general council was understood as representing the whole body of Christians and as the appropriate institution for dealing with problems of heresy and schism threatening the unity of the Church. The Council of Constance, for example, resolved the problem of the Great Schism between rival lines of popes, called for a reform of the Church "in head and members," and prescribed a mechanism for convening general councils at regular intervals.[131] Conciliar thought, moreover, did not end

[129] *Calendar of State Papers*, Venetian, vol. X, p. 360. Clement VIII died early in March 1605.
[130] E. F. Jacob, *Essays in the Conciliar Epoch*, third edition (Manchester: Manchester University Press, 1963), pp. 1–43; Francis Oakley, *The Political Thought of Pierre d'Ailly: The Voluntarist Tradition* (New Haven: Yale University Press, 1964); Louis B. Pascoe, *Jean Gerson: Principles of Church Reform* (Leiden: Brill, 1973); Thomas E. Morrisey, "Franciscus Zabarella (1360–1417): Papacy, Community and Limitations upon Authority," in Guy Fitch Lytle, ed., *Reform and Authority in the Medieval and Reformation Church* (Washington: Catholic University of America Press, 1981), pp. 37–54; Mirimichi Watanabe, *The Political Ideas of Nicholas of Cusa with Special Reference to His De Concordantia Catholica* (Geneva: Droz, 1963); Nicholas of Cusa, *The Catholic Concordance*, ed. and trans. Paul E. Sigmund (Cambridge: Cambridge University Press, 1991). For the origins of conciliarism in the interpretation of canon law, see Brian Tierney, *Foundations of the Conciliar Theory: The Contribution of the Medieval Canonists from Gratian to the Great Schism* (Cambridge: Cambridge University Press, 1955). For the development of conciliarism in the era of the Council of Basel, see Antony Black, *Monarchy and Community: Political Ideas in the Later Conciliar Controversy, 1430–1450* (Cambridge: Cambridge University Press, 1970), and *Council and Commune: The Conciliar Movement and the Fifteenth Century Heritage* (London: Burns and Oates, 1979). For an analysis of conciliar scholarship over several decades, see Francis Oakley, "Natural Law, the *Corpus Mysticum*, and Consent in Conciliar Thought from John of Paris to Matthias Ugonius," *Speculum*, 56, 4 (October 1981), 786–810.
[131] Brian Tierney, "Hermeneutics and History: The Problem of *Haec Sancta*," in T. A. Sandquist and M. R. Powicke, eds., *Essays in Medieval History Presented to Bertie Wilkinson* (Toronto: University of Toronto Press, 1969), pp. 354–370; Thomas E. Morrisey, "The Decree 'Haec Sancta' and Cardinal Zabarella: His Role in Its Formulation and Interpretation," *Annuarium Historiae Conciliorum*, 10 (1978), 145–176; C. M. D. Crowder, ed., *Unity, Heresy and Reform, 1378–1460: The Conciliar Response to the Great Schism* (London: Edward Arnold, 1977), pp. 11–24, 82–83, 128–129; and Paul de Vooght, "Le conciliarisme aux conciles de Constance et de Bâle," in Bernard Botte, H. S.

with the fifteenth century, and it influenced both Protestantism and Roman Catholicism.[132] James no doubt drew some of his ideas from writers in the conciliar era, but he probably drew them initially from writers who were more nearly contemporary with him.

Scotland had a flourishing conciliar tradition which went back to the 1430s, nurtured by contacts between the Scottish universities and the University of Paris, the traditional home of conciliar theory. In the early sixteenth century, John Major (or Mair), a brilliant teacher who influenced a generation of students at the University of Paris, as well as at Glasgow and St. Andrews in his native Scotland, was one of the leading conciliar theorists in Europe.[133] According to his views, the general council was the institution which, in extraordinary circumstances, took appropriate steps to provide for the Church's well-being; its authority, though exercised only in special

Alivisatas, and R. Aubet, *Le concile et les conciles: contribution à l'histoire de la vie conciliare de l'Eglise*, ed. O. Rousseau (Paris: Editions de Chevetogne, 1960), pp. 143–181, esp. pp. 146–162, and *Les pouvoirs du concile et l'autorité du pape au Concile de Constance: le décret Haec Sancta Synodus du 6 avril 1415* (Paris: Editions du Cerf, 1965).

[132] Hubert Jedin, *A History of the Council of Trent*, trans. Ernest Graf, 2 vols. (London: Nelson, 1957–1961), vol. I, pp. 32–138, and *passim*; Heiko A. Oberman, Daniel E. Zerfoss, and William J. Courtenay, "The Twilight of the Conciliar Era," introduction to their edition of Gabriel Biel, *Defensorium Obedientiae Apostolicae et Alia Documenta* (Cambridge, Mass.: Harvard University Press, 1968), pp. 3–59; Walter Ullmann, "Julius II and the Schismatic Cardinals," in Derek Baker, ed., *Schism, Heresy and Religious Protest* (Cambridge: Cambridge University Press, 1972), Studies in Church History, IX, pp. 177–193; Thomas F. Mayer, "Marco Mantova: A Bronze Age Conciliarist," *Annuarium Historiae Conciliorum*, 16 (1984), 385–408; W. B. Patterson "The Idea of Renewal in Girolamo Aleander's Conciliar Thought," in Derek Baker, ed., *Renaissance and Renewal in Christian History* (Oxford: Blackwell, 1977), Studies in Church History, XIV, pp. 175–186; Jaroslav Pelikan, *Obedient Rebels: Catholic Substance and Protestant Principle in Luther's Reformation* (New York: Harper and Row, 1964), pp. 54–76; Theodore W. Casteel, "Calvin and Trent: Calvin's Reaction to the Council of Trent in the Context of His Conciliar Thought," *Harvard Theological Review*, 53 (1970), 91–117; Paul Avis, *Anglicanism and the Christian Church: Theological Resources in Historical Perspective* (Edinburgh: T. & T. Clark, 1989), pp. 32–44; and Hermann Josef Sieben, *Die katholische Konzilsidee von der Reformation bis zur Aufklärung* (Paderborn: F. Schöningh, 1988), esp. pp. 13–273.

[133] For Major's life and career, see J. Durkan, "John Major: After 400 Years," *Innes Review*, 1 (1950), 131–139; J. H. Burns, "New Light on John Major," *Innes Review*, 5 (1954), 83–100; James Durkan and James Kirk, *The University of Glasgow, 1451–1577* (Glasgow: University of Glasgow Press, 1977), pp. 155–165, 206–207, 239–240: James K. Farge, *Biographical Register of Paris Doctors of Theology, 1500–1536* (Toronto: Pontifical Institute of Mediaeval Studies, 1980), pp. 304–311, and *Orthodoxy and Reform in Early Reformation France: The Faculty of Theology of Paris, 1500–1543* (Leiden: E. J. Brill, 1985), pp. 14, 72–73, 100–104, 179–180. For Scottish conciliarism, see J. H. Baxter, "Four 'New' Medieval Scottish Authors," *Scottish Historical Review*, 25 (1928), 90–97; James H. Burns, "John Ireland and 'The Meroure of Wysodome,'" *Innes Review*, 6, 2 (Autumn 1955), 77–98, *Scottish Churchmen and the Council of Basle* (Glasgow: Burns, 1962), and "The Conciliarist Tradition in Scotland," *Scottish Historical Review*, 42 (October 1963), 89–104.

cases, exceeded that of the pope.[134] Among Major's many Scottish students, both in Scotland and in France, was George Buchanan, who was later to become James's tutor. Buchanan's view of general councils, as expressed in 1550 to the Lisbon Inquisition, was that papal supremacy was "subject to the proviso that the Pope himself, was under the power of a council."[135] About the same time, in Scotland, John Hamilton, archbishop of St. Andrews, issued his *Catechism* in 1552 as a summary of Catholic doctrine. He claimed for its teachings that in controversial points it was "agrend to the decisiouns and determinatiouns of general counsallis, lauchfully gaderit in the halye spreit for the corroboratioun of our faith."[136] The *Catechism* does not specifically mention the teaching office of the papacy, but it expounds upon the importance of general councils as the means by which the sense of the scriptures, the articles of belief, and other matters were determined and declared. General councils, according to Hamilton, were "gaderit togidder and concludit be the inspiratioun of the haly spirit, quhame the father eternall and our salviour Jesus Christ his natural sone hais gevin to the kirk to be ledar, techar, and direckar of the same kirk, in all matteris concerning our catholike faith and gud maneris of the christin peple, quhilk catholike kirk is trewly representit in all general counsellis lauchfully gaderit in the haly spirit."[137]

In the Reformed Scottish Kirk, significant elements of this conciliar theology survived. In the Scots Confession of 1560, ratified by the first Parliament of the infant James VI in 1567, the "chiefe cause of general Councellis" is described as "confutation of heresies, and for giving publick

---

[134] For Major's conciliar thought, see Francis Oakley, "Almain and Major: Conciliar Theory on the Eve of the Reformation," *American Historical Review*, 70, 3 (April 1965), 673–690, "On the Road from Constance to 1688: The Political Thought of John Major and George Buchanan," *The Journal of British Studies*, 1, 2 (May 1962), 1–31, "Conciliarism in the Sixteenth Century: Jacques Almain Again," *Archiv für Reformationsgeschichte*, 68 (1977), 111–131; Quentin Skinner, *The Foundations of Modern Political Thought*, 2 vols. (Cambridge: Cambridge University Press, 1978), vol. I, p. 65, vol. II, pp. 24, 44–47, 65 note, 320–321, 340–348; J. H. Burns, "*Politia Regalis et Optima*: The Political Ideas of John Mair," *History of Political Thought*, 2 (1981–1982), 31–61; James K. Cameron, "The Conciliarism of John Mair: A Note on *A Disputation on the Authority of a Council*," in Diana Wood, ed., *The Church and Sovereignty, c. 590–1918: Essays in Honour of Michael Wilks* (Oxford: Blackwell, 1991), Studies in Church History, Subsidia 9, pp. 429–435; and Arthur P. Monahan, *From Personal Duties towards Personal Rights: Late Medieval and Early Modern Political Thought, 1300–1600* (Montreal and Kingston: McGill–Queen's University Press, 1994), pp. 107–127. For a translation of a part of Major's commentary on St. Matthew in 1518 dealing with general councils, see Matthew Spinka, ed., *Advocates of Reform: From Wyclif to Erasmus* (Philadelphia: Westminster Press, 1953), pp. 175–184 (where the piece is incorrectly dated as 1529).

[135] Quoted in Burns, "The Conciliarist Tradition in Scotland," p. 102.

[136] Thomas Graves Law, ed., *The Catechism of John Hamilton, Archbishop of St. Andrews, 1552* (Oxford: Clarendon Press, 1884), p. 5.

[137] Law, ed., *Catechism of John Hamilton*, p. 47.

confession of their faith to the posteritie following."[138] The other cause was "for gude policie, and ordour to be constitute and observed in the Kirk."[139] But John Knox and the other ministers who drew up the document were also critical of councils in the era of the council assembled by the papacy at Trent: "As we do not rashlie damne that quhilk godly men, assembled together in a generall Councel lawfully gathered, have proponed unto us; so without just examination dare we not receive quhatsoever is obtruded unto men under the name of generall Councelis."[140] The second Book of Discipline, drawn up by reformed ministers under the leadership of Andrew Melville in 1578 and recognized by James VI's government in 1592, represented the general council as a regular part of the Kirk's polity. With reference to the great councils of the ancient period – those which met at Nicaea, Constantinople, Ephesus, and Chalcedon to resolve doctrinal matters in dispute – the second Book of Discipline stated: "Thais assembleis war appointit and callit togidder speciallie quhene an greit sisme or controversie in doctrene did aryse in the kirk and war convocat at command of the godlie emperouris being for the tyme for the avoiding of sismis within the universall kirk of God."[141] Such councils were envisioned as being of more than historical interest. This book cited the general council as the fourth type of assembly, after local, provincial, and national assemblies. Besides the national or General Assembly, "thair is . . . an uther mair generall kynd of assemblie quhilk is of all nationis or of all estaitis of personis within the kirk representing the universall kirk of Chryst quhilk may be callit properlie the generall assemblie or generall counsall of the haill kirk of God."[142]

James certainly knew both the Scots Confession and the second Book of Discipline. Directly or indirectly, he must also have known the contents of Hamilton's *Catechism*. Through his tutor Buchanan he would have been exposed to the conciliar ideas of John Major.

Conciliar ideas, which had been supported at Oxford at the end of the fourteenth century and by English clerics and lay representatives at the Council of Constance,[143] were revived and reformulated in the Church of England in the period of its separation from the jurisdiction of Rome. King Henry VIII appealed to a general council during his campaign to have his marriage annulled and then sought to forestall the council called by Pope

[138] G. D. Henderson, ed., *Scots Confession, 1560 (Confessio Scoticana) and Negative Confession, 1581 (Confessio Negativa)* (Edinburgh: Church of Scotland, 1937), p. 81.
[139] Henderson, *Scots Confession*, p. 81.
[140] Ibid., pp. 79–81.
[141] James Kirk, ed., *The Second Book of Discipline* (Edinburgh: The Saint Andrew Press, 1980), pp. 205–206.
[142] Kirk, ed., *The Second Book of Discipline*, p. 205.
[143] Jacob, *Essays in the Conciliar Era*, pp. 44–84.

Paul III in 1536 for fear that it would take hostile action against him.[144] A series of pamphlets, resolutions, and memoranda in the next two years defined a general council as one convened with the assent of the Christian princes, who were seen as the inheritors of the authority exercised by the ancient emperors in the era of the councils of Nicaea, Constantinople, Ephesus, and Chalcedon.[145] The author of *A Treatise Concernynge General Councilles*, probably the Scottish theologian Alexander Alesius, who worked under the supervision of Thomas Cromwell, Henry's leading minister of state, asserted in 1538 that popes had no power "to somon a generall councill, and to commaunde kynges and princis to assiste theym therin," but that such a council was to be "gathered by kynges and princis . . . to the honour of god . . . and for the mayntenance also of the unitie of faithe in Christis Churche."[146] Archbishop Thomas Cranmer, who contrib-

[144] J. J. Scarisbrick, *Henry VIII* (Berkeley: University of California Press, 1968), pp. 262–263, 286, 291, 293–294, 319, 323, 325, 335–336, 358, 360, 387–388, 397–398.

[145] Stanford E. Lehmberg, *The Later Parliaments of Henry VIII, 1536–1547* (Cambridge: Cambridge University Press, 1977), pp. 37–39; P. A. Sawada, "Two Anonymous Tudor Treatises on the General Council," *Journal of Ecclesiastical History*, 12, 2 (October 1961), 197–214, and "The Abortive Council of Mantua and Henry VIII's *Sententia de Concilio* 1537," *Akademia (Nanzan Gakkai)*, 27 (1960), 1–15; Franklin Le Van Baumer, *The Early Tudor Theory of Kingship* (New Haven: Yale University Press, 1940), pp. 49–56.

[146] *A Treatise Concernynge Generall Councilles, the Byshoppes of Rome, and the Clergy* (London: Thomas Berthelet, 1538), sigs. Biii, Diii–Diii verso. For the authorship of the tract, see Sawada, "Two Anonymous Tudor Treatises," pp. 210–211. Two other tracts, both written in the name of Henry VIII, develop a similar argument: *A Protestation Made for the Mighty and Moste Redoubted Kynge of Englande, etc. and his Hole Counsell and Clergie* (London: Thomas Berthelet, 1537) and *An Epistle of the Moste Myghty & Redoubted Prince Henry the VIII* (London: Thomas Berthelet, 1538). For further evidence of conciliarism at court, see W. Gordon Zeeveld, *Foundations of Tudor Policy* (Cambridge, Mass.: Harvard University Press, 1948), pp. 87–89, 130–135, 150–153; Denys Hay, "Note on More and the General Council," *Moreana*, 15–16 (1967), 249–251; Brian Gogan, *The Common Corps of Christendom: Ecclesiological Themes in the Writings of Sir Thomas More* (Leiden: E. J. Brill, 1982), pp. 289–293, 347–348; Thomas F. Mayer, "Thomas Starkey, an Unknown Conciliarist at the Court of Henry VIII," *Journal of the History of Ideas*, 49, 2 (April–June 1988), 207–227, and *Thomas Starkey and the Commonweal: Humanist Politics and Religion in the Reign of Henry VIII* (Cambridge: Cambridge University Press, 1989), pp. 79–86, 181, 186, 209–210, 224–226, 240, 253, 270–271, 280–281. On the importance of the general council in the development of the theology of the Church of England in the sixteenth and early seventeenth centuries, see Franklin Le Van Baumer, "The Church of England and the Common Corps of Christendom," *Journal of Modern History*, 16 (1944), 1–21; Kenneth J. Woollcombe, "The Authority of the First Four General Councils in the Anglican Communion," *Anglican Theological Review*, 44 (April 1962), 155–181; Stephen Neill, "The Anglican Communion and the Ecumenical Council," in Hans Jochen Margull, ed., *The Councils of the Church: History and Analysis* (Philadelphia: Fortress Press, 1966), pp. 370–390; Stanley Lawrence Greenslade, "The English Reformers and the Councils of the Church," in F. W. Kantzenbach and V. Vajta, eds., *Oecumenica: Annales de Recherche Oecuménique, 1967* (Neuchâtel: Editions Delachaux et Niestlé, 1967), pp. 95–114; Henry Chadwick, "The Status of Ecumenical Councils in Anglican Thought," in David Neiman and Margaret Schatkin, eds., *The Heritage of the Early Church: Essays in Honor of the Very Reverend Georges*

uted significantly to the English understanding of the place of general councils in the 1530s, proposed between 1547 and 1552, during the reign of King Edward VI, that a conference of European Protestant leaders be held in England to resolve the differences which had arisen among the churches of the Reformation.[147] In the Ten Articles of 1536, the first attempt to formulate the faith of the English Church after the decisive parliamentary steps which established its independence from the papacy, the articles of belief are defined with reference to the first four general councils.[148] This was also the case in the Act of Supremacy of 1559, at the beginning of the reign of Elizabeth I.[149]

In March 1561, a nuncio from Pope Pius IV set out for England to invite Queen Elizabeth to send ambassadors to the resummoned Council of Trent. The pope omitted any mention of bishops, and he made clear that the queen would be expected to abide by the council's decisions.[150] Not surprisingly, the Privy Council voted not to admit the nuncio on the grounds that the visit would violate the recently passed act of Supremacy, which repudiated the jurisdiction of the papacy in England. Elizabeth subsequently expressed to Catherine de Medici, queen regent of France, her view that no good was likely to come from a council under the control of the pope. Like many of

Vasilievich Florovsky (Rome: Pont. Institutum Studiorum Orientalium, 1973), pp. 393–408; J. Robert Wright, "The Authority of Chalcedon for Anglicans," in G. R. Evans, ed., *Christian Authority: Essays in Honour of Henry Chadwick* (Oxford: Clarendon Press, 1988), pp. 224–250; Frederick H. Shriver, "Councils, Conferences and Synods," in Stephen Sykes and John Booty, eds., *The Study of Anglicanism* (London: SPCK, 1988), pp. 188–199; Francis Oakley, "Constance, Basel and the Two Pisas: The Conciliarist Legacy in Sixteenth- and Seventeenth–Century England," *Annuarium Historiae Conciliorum*, 26 (1994), 87–118; and W. B. Patterson, "Hooker on Ecumenical Relations: Conciliarism in the English Reformation," in A. S. McGrade, ed., *Richard Hooker and the Construction of Christian Community* (Tempe, Ariz.: Medieval & Renaissance Texts & Studies, 1997), pp. 283–303. The fullest treatment of this subject is Charles John Fenner, "The Concept and Theological Significance of Ecumenical Councils in the Anglican Tradition," Ph.D. thesis, Washington, D.C.: Catholic University of America, 1974.

[147] Thomas Cranmer, *Miscellaneous Writings and Letters*, ed. John Edmund Cox (Cambridge: Cambridge University Press, 1846), pp. 467–468; Hastings Robinson, ed., *Original Letters Relative to the English Reformation, Written during the Reigns of King Henry VIII, King Edward VI, and Queen Mary*, 2 parts (Cambridge: Cambridge University Press, 1846–1847), part I, pp. 17, 21–26; John T. McNeill, *Unitive Protestantism: Its Ecumenical Spirit and Its Persistent Expression*, revised edition (London: Epworth Press, 1964), pp. 229–254. For Cranmer's interest in conciliarism in the 1520s and early 1530s, before his elevation to Canterbury, see Diarmaid MacCulloch, "Two Dons in Politics: Thomas Cranmer and Stephen Gardiner, 1503–1533," *Historical Journal*, 37, 1 (1994), 1–22.

[148] Charles Lloyd, ed., *Formularies of Faith, Set Forth by Authority during the Reign of Henry VIII* (Oxford: Oxford University Press, 1856), p. xviii.

[149] G. R. Elton, ed., *The Tudor Constitution: Documents and Commentary*, second edition (Cambridge: Cambridge University Press, 1982), p. 377.

[150] C. G. Bayne, *Anglo-Roman Relations, 1558–1565* (Oxford: Clarendon Press, 1913), pp. 77–78, 96–99, 270–271.

the German Protestant princes, Elizabeth favored a council independent of the papacy, where the views of Protestants would be heard and Protestant leaders could participate as full members.[151] John Jewel, the official apologist of the Church of England in the early years of Elizabeth's reign, continued a Henrician theme by stressing that the ancient general councils had been assembled by emperors. Their example served for Jewel to discredit the council whose final sessions at Trent took place at the invitation of Pope Pius IV. Inasmuch as the Christian commonwealth was made up of many kingdoms, the task of calling a general council was, he wrote, "the common right of all princes."[152] According to the Thirty-Nine Articles of Religion, the Church of England's official statement of belief, authorized by Convocation in 1563 and by the queen in 1571, "General Councils may not be gathered together without the commandment and will of Princes." The article added that councils "may err, and sometimes have erred."[153] The authority of general councils was, in any case, subject to the primary authority of the scriptures: "things ordained by them as necessary to salvation have neither strength nor authority, unless it may be declared that they be taken out of Holy Scripture."[154]

The most sustained rationale for a general council as a means of achieving Christian unity was provided by Richard Hooker in his *Of the Laws of Ecclesiastical Polity*, the first four books of which were published in 1593. Hooker described general councils as part of God's plan for the Church, in order to provide "lawes of spiritual commerce betweene Christian nations."[155] The use of councils, based on the practice of the apostles

[151] Bayne, *Anglo-Roman Relations, 1558–1565*, pp. 108–116, 145–148, 228–229.

[152] John Jewel, *An Apologie, or Aunswer in Defence of the Church of England, Concerninge the State of Religion Used in the Same* (London: Reginalde Wolfe, 1562), sigs. Niii verso–Piii verso. For discussion of this and other expressions of Jewel's conciliar thought, see W. M. Southgate, *John Jewel and the Problem of Doctrinal Authority* (Cambridge, Mass.: Harvard University Press, 1962), pp. 57–60, 128–134.

[153] B. J. Bicknell, *A Theological Introduction to the Thirty-Nine Articles of the Church of England*, third edition, ed. H. J. Carpenter (London: Longman, 1955), p. 267. For the work of the Convocation in formulating the Thirty-Nine Articles, see William P. Haugaard, *Elizabeth and the English Reformation* (Cambridge: Cambridge University Press, 1968), pp. 233–272.

[154] Bicknell, *Theological Introduction*, pp. 267–268; see also the commentary, pp. 268–272. Article XXI, Of the Authority of General Councils, was omitted from the Articles of Religion adopted by the Protestant Episcopal Church in the U.S.A. in 1801 with the explanation that it was "partly of a local and civil nature" – presumably because of its reference to princes. *The Book of Common Prayer and Administration of the Sacraments and Other Rites and Ceremonies of the Church, Together with the Psalter or Psalms of David, According to the Use of the Episcopal Church* (New York: Church Hymnal Corporation, 1979), p. 872.

[155] Richard Hooker, *Of the Laws of Ecclesiastical Polity* [Books I–V], ed. Georges Edelen and W. Speed Hill, 2 vols. (Cambridge, Mass.: Harvard University Press, 1977), vol. I, p. 109 (Bk. I, ch. 10, sec. 14). For commentary on Hooker's conciliar thought, see Peter Munz, *The Place of Hooker in the History of Thought* (London: Routledge and Kegan Paul,

themselves (Acts 15), was, he argued, continued "throughout the world," until perverted by "ambition and tyrannie."[156] But misuse did not justify disuse. There was now an urgent need "to studie how so gratious a thing may againe be reduced to that first perfection."[157] The purposes which could be served by councils were manifold: to resolve theological issues, settle conflicts over matters indifferent in themselves, heal rifts and schisms, and deal with "matters of politie, order, and regiment."[158] Therefore, he concluded:

I nothing doubt but that Christian men should much better frame them selves to those heavenly preceptes, which our Lorde and Saviour with so great instancie gave as concerning peace and unitie, if we did all concurre in desire to have the use of auncient councels againe renued, rather then these proceedinges continued which either make all contentions endlesse, or bring them to one onely determination and that of all other the worst, which is by sword.[159]

Hooker did not insist upon episcopacy by divine right in his *Laws*, despite his belief that church government by bishops was apostolic and justified by history and practicality. But, in speaking of general councils as instituted by "Gods owne blessed spirit" and as a "divine invention," he gave them the status of an institution by divine right whose revival was urgently needed.[160] This did not mean that matters once decreed by councils could not be altered. The Church always had the power to alter whatever the passage of time had rendered harmful or obsolete.[161] In his *Ivst and Temperate Defence* of Hooker in 1603, William Covel endorsed the "true vse of a generall councell" as a means of restoring soundness to the Roman

1952), pp. 95–99, 106–110; Gunnar Hillerdal, *Reason and Revelation in Richard Hooker* (Lund: CWK Gleerup, 1962), pp. 53–55; Egil Grislis, "The Role of *Consensus* in Richard Hooker's Method of Theological Inquiry," in Robert E. Cushman and Egil Grislis, eds., *The Heritage of Christian Thought: Essays in Honor of Robert Lowry Calhoun* (New York: Harper and Row, 1965), pp. 83–85; Avis, *Anglicanism and the Christian Church,* pp. 23–24, 32–33, 42–44, 47–67; and Patterson, "Hooker on Ecumenical Relations: Conciliarism in the English Reformation," pp. 283–303. The ecumenical aspects of Hooker's thought are dealt with in Olivier Loyer, *L'Anglicanisme de Richard Hooker,* 2 vols. (Paris: Honoré Champion, 1979), vol. II, pp. 524–526, 581–585; Lee W. Gibbs, "Richard Hooker's *Via Media* Doctrine of Justification," *Harvard Theological Review,* 74, 2 (1981), 211–220; H. R. Trevor-Roper, "Richard Hooker and the Church of England," in his *Renaissance Essays* (Chicago: University of Chicago Press, 1985), pp. 103–120; and William P. Haugaard, "Richard Hooker: Evidences of an Ecumenical Vision from a Twentieth-Century Perspective," *Journal of Ecumenical Studies,* 24, 3 (Summer 1987), 427–439.

[156] Hooker, *Laws,* vol. I, p. 109.
[157] Ibid.   [158] Ibid., p. 110.   [159] Ibid.
[160] Ibid., p. 109. For an illuminating discussion of Hooker's views on episcopacy, see Peter Lake, *Anglicans and Puritans? Presbyterianism and English Conformist Thought from Whitgift to Hooker* (London: Unwin Hyman, 1988), pp. 220–225. See also Stanley Archer, "Hooker on Apostolic Succession: The Two Voices," *Sixteenth Century Journal,* 24, 1 (Spring 1993), 67–74.
[161] Hooker, *Laws,* vol. I, p. 340 (Bk. IV, ch. xiv, sec. 5).

Church, which he considered to be, like the Church of England, a part of the visible and Catholic Church.[162]

Two former students of Hooker's at Corpus Christi College, Oxford, George Cranmer, the great-nephew of Archbishop Thomas Cranmer, and Edwin Sandys, the son of Archbishop Edwin Sandys, encouraged Hooker in his writing of the *Laws*. They took their tutor's conciliar ideas seriously and set out in 1593 to tour the continent of Europe to see what basis there might be for religious unity.[163] Sandys's report, entitled *A Relation of the State of Religion*, was finished in Paris in 1599 and then presented to Archbishop John Whitgift; but it was not published until 1605 – and then in an unauthorized edition.[164] He found a great deal of dissension among Protestants and a discouraging degree of intransigence among many Catholics. On the other hand, there seemed to be some persons in all countries who sought to extinguish "these flames of controversie" and to reestablish "some tollerable peace" in the Church.[165] Sandys proposed that a unity between Protestants and Roman Catholics be sought with the following features: "an vniforme Lyturgy, a correspondent forme of Church-government to bee made of the points both should agree in, and to be established vniversally throughout all Christendome . . . [and] all other questions to be confined to the Schooles."[166] This was to be effected "by some generall councell assembled and composed indifferently out of both sides."[167] Sandys was favorably impressed by Pope Clement VIII's apparently sincere desire to "affect the quiet of Christendome," but if he or any group of ministers should stand in the way of this project, then "the Princes of Christendome" should impose their authority.[168] Their aim would be to free their subjects from "those inestimable calamities" brought on by dissensions in religion.[169]

---

[162] William Covel, *A Ivst and Temperate Defence of the Five Books of Ecclesiastical Policie Written by M. Richard Hooker* (London: Clement Knight, 1603), p. 77.

[163] Trevor-Roper, "Richard Hooker and the Church of England," pp. 110–113. See also C. J. Sisson, *The Judicious Marriage of Mr. Hooker and the Birth of The Laws of Ecclesiastical Polity* (Cambridge: Cambridge University Press, 1940), pp. 4, 12, 18, 20, 22, 32, 45, 47, 62, 100, 104, 107; and Joseph Lecler, *Toleration and the Reformation*, 2 vols. (London: Longman, 1960), vol. II, pp. 403–406.

[164] Theodore K. Rabb, "The Editions of Sir Edwin Sandys's *Relation of the State of Religion*," *Huntington Library Quarterly*, 26, 4 (1963), 323–336. The book was suppressed after three editions in 1605 and not published again until 1629. Italian and French translations appeared in 1625 and 1626, respectively. A Dutch translation appeared in 1675.

[165] Edwin Sandys, *A Relation of the State of Religion: And with What Hopes and Policies It Hath Beene Framed, and Is Maintained in the Severall States of These Westerne Parts of the World* (London: Simon Waterson, 1605), sigs. G4 verso, R3–R4, S4 verso.

[166] Ibid., sig. T2.   [167] Ibid.   [168] Ibid., sigs. P1–P2, T2.

[169] Ibid., sig. T2. On the argument and significance of Sandys's book, see Gaetano Cozzi, "Sir Edwin Sandys e la *Relazione dello Stato della Religione*," *Rivista Storica Italiana*, 19 (1967), 1096–1121; and Theodore Rabb, "A Contribution to the Toleration Controversy of the Sixteenth Century: Sandys's 'A Relation of the State of Religion,'" in Anthony

The deep desire of Thomas Cranmer and other leaders of the Church of England for peace and concord across denominational lines was memorably expressed in the prayer "for the whole state of Christes Church militant here in earth" in the liturgy for the Holy Communion. Here the priest prayed to God "to inspire continually the uniuersall churche with the spirite of trueth, unitie, and concorde: And graunt that all they that dooe confess thy holye name, may agree in the trueth of thy holy woord, and liue in unitie and godlye loue."[170] James heard this prayer, with its broad definition of the Church as comprised of all professing Christians, at every celebration of the eucharist in the Chapel Royal and elsewhere in the churches of his new realm.

In coming to England, James found the Scottish conciliar tradition powerfully reinforced by a succession of thinkers in the English Church, especially by Hooker, who envisioned the revival of the ancient practice of holding councils in order to resolve disruptive conflicts among Christians. This was, according to Hooker, a proven way to avoid violence and bloodshed. Did James know Hooker's *Laws of Ecclesiastical Polity?*

James might have heard of Hooker's ideas from Sandys, who accompanied the king on his journey from Scotland. Sandys was well informed on theological issues, having helped Hooker to prepare the *Laws of Ecclesiastical Polity* and underwritten the cost of publication of its first five books.[171] He could have become a valuable ally of James's in the cause of church unity had he and the king not disagreed on basic political and constitutional issues in the first session of the Parliament which began meeting in 1604.[172]

Molho and John A. Tedeschi, eds., *Renaissance Studies in Honor of Hans Baron* (De Kalb: Northern Illinois University Press, 1971), pp. 831–847.

[170] *The First and Second Prayer Books of Edward VI* (London: J. M. Dent, 1910), p. 382. This prayer, a part of the second Prayer Book of Edward VI (1552), chiefly the work of Thomas Cranmer, was included in the Prayer Book of 1559 used during James's reign.

[171] For the tangled history of the publication of Hooker's *Laws*, see Sisson, *The Judicious Marriage of Mr. Hooker and the Birth of The Laws of Ecclesiastical Polity*, pp. 49–108. Sandys helped to plan the work and he offered advice to Hooker during the course of its composition (pp. 45–49).

[172] Conrad Russell, "English Parliaments, 1593–1606: One Epoch or Two?" in D. M. Dean and N. L. Jones, eds., *The Parliaments of Elizabethan England* (Oxford: Blackwell, 1990), pp. 191–213, esp. 207–213; and Theodore K. Rabb, "Sir Edwin Sandys and the Parliament of 1604," *American Historical Review*, 69, 3 (1963–1964), 646–670. For the composition and significance of the *Apology* (1604), an eloquent defense of the Commons's activities drawn up by a committee which included Sandys, see G. R. Elton, "A High Road to Civil War?" in Charles H. Carter, ed., *From the Renaissance to the Counter-Reformation: Essays in Honor of Garrett Mattingly* (New York: Random House, 1965), pp. 325–347; and J. H. Hexter, "The Apology," in Richard Ollard and Pamela Tudor-Craig, eds., *For Veronica Wedgwood These Studies in Seventeenth-Century History* (London: Collins, 1986), pp. 13–44. Elton shows that the *Apology* was never approved by the House of Commons or sent to the king; rather, it was referred back to committee. Hexter stresses the perspicacity and aptness of the document. T. K. Rabb provides a convenient summary of Sandys's career in Richard L. Greaves and Robert Zaller, eds.,

Sandys evidently saw in the king's project of Union between England and Scotland an ominous challenge to the place of Parliament in the English constitution and consequently to the laws and liberties of English subjects. Having emerged in 1604 as an articulate and consistent defender of the House of Commons in its strained relations with the crown, Sandys went on to oppose the king and his ministers on a broad range of issues for the next two decades. Nevertheless, as one thoroughly familiar with Hooker's major work, he could have introduced the king to Hooker's conciliar ideas. Or, of course, James could have discovered them for himself. It would be surprising if a person of his learning and theological interests, one who had long looked forward to the prospect of acceding to the English throne, had not read at least portions of Hooker's work before coming to England.

Izaak Walton – a dubious authority on many biographical matters, to be sure – reported that "at the first coming of King James into this Kingdom," the king asked Archbishop Whitgift about Hooker.[173] On learning that Hooker had died some time before, the king expressed his deep regret "that I shall want the desired happiness of seeing and discoursing with that man, from whose Books I have received such satisfaction."[174] Between Hooker's and James's ideas on the subject of conciliarism there was, in any case, a remarkably close affinity.[175]

James derived his proposal for an ecumenical council from the conciliar tradition, but he did not derive from that tradition the principles which helped to shape the political theories of George Buchanan and a succession of constitutionalist and resistance writers in the sixteenth and seventeenth

---

Biographical Dictionary of British Radicals in the Seventeenth Century, 3 vols. (Brighton: Harvester Press, 1982–1984), vol. III, pp. 141–143. R. C. Munden has pointed out that the misunderstandings and ill-will that developed between the king and the House of Commons in the first four months of the Parliament of 1604 were the result of missteps by privy councillors, members of the two houses, and the king, and that on the question of the Union hostility to the Scots played a major role in the Commons's unfavorable response. See Munden's "James I and 'the growth of mutual distrust': King, Commons, and Reform, 1603–1604," in Kevin Sharpe, ed., *Faction and Parliament: Essays on Early Stuart History* (Oxford: Clarendon Press, 1978), pp. 43–72.

173 Izaak Walton, *Life of Mr. Richard Hooker* [first published, 1665] in Walton, *The Lives of John Donne, Sir Henry Wotton, Richard Hooker, George Herbert & Robert Sanderson*, ed. George Saintsbury (London: Oxford University Press, 1956), p. 212. For Walton's numerous errors and distortions, see Sisson, *The Judicious Marriage of Mr. Hooker and the Birth of The Laws of Ecclesiastical Polity*, pp. x–xii and *passim*, and David Novarr, *The Making of Walton's Lives* (Ithaca: Cornell University Press, 1958), pp. 208–210, 226–297.

174 Walton, *Hooker*, p. 212.

175 James's affinity with Hooker on theological issues is shown in Richard A. Crofts, "The Defence of the Elizabethan Church: Jewel, Hooker, and James I," *Anglican Theological Review*, 54, 1 (January 1972), 20–31. Monahan argues, in *From Personal Duties towards Personal Rights*, pp. 273–293, that James's moderate absolutism was consistent with Hooker's political philosophy.

centuries.[176] The fifteenth-century conciliarists saw the pope as exercising authority delegated to him for the good of the Church, but they believed that final authority in the Church resided in the whole body of the faithful or their representatives gathered in a general council. Thus a general council could, for adequate reasons, depose a pope. Translated into the language of civil polity, this meant for Buchanan that sovereignty lay ultimately with the people, that it was exercised by their representatives in Parliament, that monarch and people were bound by a mutual contract, and that an unjust or tyrannical monarch could be resisted or even overthrown by leaders acting on the people's behalf.[177] James, needless to say, was not a conciliarist in this extended political sense. On the contrary, he was an articulate defender of divine-right monarchy, which he saw as essential to the maintenance of domestic peace and order and to the promotion of the common good.[178] Like Henry IV of France, he was attracted to conciliarism because of its original achievement in resolving religious problems of a seemingly intractable kind. Had not the Council of Constance restored unity to a western Church rent for a generation by the Great Schism? In the councils of the fifteenth century, James no doubt saw a "collective act of medieval Christendom" appropriate to the immense problems of the time.[179] A general council must have seemed to him the only institution capable of restoring religious peace and unity to the Europe of his own day, a Europe torn by competing religious orthodoxies and institutional allegiances.

---

[176] Oakley, "On the Road from Constance to 1688: The Political Thought of John Major and George Buchanan," 1–31, "Almain and Major: Conciliar Theory on the Eve of the Reformation," 673–690, and "Figgis, Constance, and the Divines of Paris," *American Historical Review*, 75, 2 (December 1969), 368–386. Roger A. Mason stresses that Aristotelian and Ciceronian elements are also prominent in Buchanan's thought: "*Rex Stoicus*: George Buchanan, James VI and the Scottish Polity," in John Dwyer, R. A. Mason, and A. Murdoch, eds., *New Perspectives on the Politics and Culture of Early Modern Scotland* (Edinburgh: John Donald, 1982), pp. 9–33. For the use made by Buchanan of the work of the humanist Hector Boece, see H. R. Trevor-Roper, "George Buchanan and the Ancient Scottish Constitution," *English Historical Review*, Supplement 3 (1966), 1–53. For a critique of Buchanan's political theory, see J. H. Burns, "The Political Ideas of George Buchanan," *Scottish Historical Review*, 30 (1951), 60–68. For other discussions of Buchanan's thought, see above, chapter 1.

[177] See George Buchanan, *The Powers of the Crown in Scotland* [*De Jure Regni apud Scotos*], ed. and trans. Charles F. Arrowood (Austin: University of Texas Press, 1949), pp. 70–74, 100–103, 117, 122–131, 146–147.

[178] Jenny Wormald, "James VI and I, *Basilikon Doron* and the *Trew Law of Free Monarchies*: The Scottish Context and the English Translation," in Linda Levy Peck, ed., *The Mental World of the Jacobean Court*, (Cambridge: Cambridge University Press, 1991), pp. 36–54. For other discussions of James's political thought, see chapter 1.

[179] Jacob, *Essays in the Conciliar Epoch*, p. v. For documents relating to Constance, see John Hine Mundy and Kennerly M. Woody, eds., *The Council of Constance: The Unification of the Church*, trans. Louise Ropes Loomis (New York: Columbia University Press, 1961).

The striking feature of James's proposal, when seen in the context of Protestant treatments of general councils – where the stress is on the role of kings and emperors in convening councils – is that he appealed to the pope to convene a council. His repeated references to the legitimate assembly of a council in his communications to Clement VIII would have been understood by the pope as meaning that the council would be convened by the pope and presided over by him or his legate.[180] James evidently recognized that no movement to resolve the religious issues in dispute was likely to have much chance of success without papal leadership and support. In Clement VIII he saw a person imbued with a desire to restore religious harmony in Europe. James also wanted a council broadly representing the religious points of view current in Europe – a more difficult matter for Clement or any other pope to accept. Such a council would have to be very different from the Council of Trent.

James's proposal for an ecumenical council was discussed in September 1605 by the papal nuncio in Flanders, Ottavio Mirto Frangipani, and Thomas Howard, earl of Arundel, who had recently arrived to take charge of the regiment of English volunteers recruited to assist the Spanish Netherlands in its war against the United Provinces to the north. Arundel, a Catholic, had an interview with Frangipani about the penalties imposed on Catholics in England, a conversation which the nuncio reported on September 24, to Scipione Caffarelli, Cardinal Borghese, the secretary of state to the new pope, Paul V.[181] Though the penalties in England were more severe in terms of property than lives, Arundel said, the situation "had never been so intolerable than it was now."[182] One way to alleviate it, he suggested, was to reassure the king that Catholics would be no threat to him and to support James's wish for a "General Council or a particular one in Britain" to ascertain the truth among "so many sects of religion."[183] After this conversation Frangipani sought an opportunity to talk to Sir Thomas Edmondes, the English ambassador in Brussels, about what the nuncio had evidently called "some propositions . . . for the common good of the state

[180] For the reassertion of papal authority over general councils following the councils of the fifteenth century, see Jedin, *History of the Council of Trent*, vol. I, pp. 5–100.
[181] Léon Van der Essen, and Armand Louant, eds., *Correspondance d'Ottavio Mirto Frangipani, premier nonce de Flandre (1596–1606)*, 3 vols. (Rome: Institut historique belge, 1924–42), vol. III, part 2, p. 549.
[182] Van der Essen and Louant, eds., *Correspondance d'Ottavio Mirto Frangipani*, vol. III, part 2, p. 549. As Louant points out in the introduction to vol. III, the nunciature in Flanders was established in 1596 with the aim, among other things, of ascertaining the state of affairs in England. English Catholics were frequent visitors there and could be expected to supply first-hand information (vol. III, part 1, pp. xiii–xxv).
[183] Van der Essen and Louant, eds., *Correspondance d'Ottavio Mirto Frangipani*, vol. III, part 2, p. 550.

of Christendome."[184] Edmondes reported that he had ascertained that the subject would be "a favorable moderation, or rather cessation of the penall statutes" against Catholics in England.[185] In return the pope would bring to an end "all practises of the partie of the Catholickes" against the state.[186] Edmondes thought that the nuncio was likely to use James's conciliar proposal as a way of engaging the king in negotiations: "I have ben tould that the said Nuntio hath ben advised, for the engaging the king into some kinde of Treatie, to presse his Matie upon his offer made in some of his private professions, for desiring that there might be an assemblie of a Generall or Provinciall Councell, for the clearing of the controversies."[187] Edmondes was reluctant to meet with the nuncio, having no instructions to do so, and he asked Cecil, created earl of Salisbury in 1605, to inform him of "his Maties pleasure."[188] There is no evidence of the matter being pursued further. Presumably James or his leading minister was unwilling to use the relaxation of the penal laws as a first step in such discussions.

The most positive response to James's proposal for an ecumenical council came from Spain, though the response was accompanied by diplomatic initiatives which threatened to overshadow it.

James's proposal was evidently discussed at some length in Spain in the summer of 1605. There is a document of Spanish origin in the Vatican Archives, which dates from July or August 1605, entitled "Discourse on the desire which the king of England is said to have to conform to the Catholic Church by means of a Council."[189] The author, Richard Haller, an Austrian Jesuit, commented in this memorandum on reports made by English representatives at the Spanish court that James "is not obstinate in the points of Religion and that while differing in some things he will be inclined to be convinced of the truth by means of a Council."[190] The context of these discussions was, no doubt, the recent peace negotiations with England, which were soon to be ratified by treaty in Spain.[191] Haller was cautious about the king's proposal, observing that it "has always been customary for heretics to cover up their obstinacy with the demand for a

---

[184] PRO SP, Flanders, 77/7, fol. 232 verso. Edmondes's letter to Salisbury is dated September 25, 1605.
[185] Ibid., fol. 232 verso.   [186] Ibid.   [187] Ibid., fol. 233 verso.
[188] Ibid., fol. 233.
[189] Vat. Arch., Fondo Borghese, Ser. III, vol. 68, fols. 182–185.
[190] Ibid., fol. 182.
[191] The ambassador named to secure the official ratification of the Treaty of London in Spain was Charles Howard, earl of Nottingham. Loomie, *Toleration and Diplomacy*, p. 42. His instructions enjoined him to express to Philip III James's ardent desire "to maintaine firmely and inviolably all good correspondency with him, according to the true construction of the Treatie, accounting it one of the greatest blessings that God hath endewed Us withall to be in perfect Peace and amitie with all the Princes and States of Christendome, the conservation whereof shall ever be highly recommended into Us." PRO SP, Spain, 94/12, fol. 173 verso.

council."[192] Furthermore, he argued, most of the theological issues in dispute had already been settled at Trent. Nevertheless, if the pope, the king of Spain, and other princes, "for the regard in which they hold the king of England and his ministers," should proceed with the matter, the readiness of the king to accept its decisions should be ascertained beforehand.[193] So that the reasons for a council should be made clear, these should be declared, together with the articles to be discussed, and sent to the prelates of the Church and to the secular princes.[194]

The discussions in Spain involved the resident English ambassador, Sir Charles Cornwallis. On July 28, 1605 Cornwallis, who had been sent to Spain early in the year, wrote to the earl of Salisbury from Valladolid that "some Projects" were afoot which "were promised to be both pleasing, and profitable" to the English king.[195] What he had at present was "from the retaylours," since the "Merchants themselves [were] now not at home."[196] But "a savour is given me of a will had to immortalize the King, by honoring him with being the meane of reducing to Concord, and good Course the estate both of the Church, and Christianitie."[197] James would also be able to enlarge his dominions or at least increase his financial resources by an alliance with Spain; this would evidently involve helping to resolve the issues between "the king heere, and his subjects our neighboures" – an evident reference to the United Provinces of the Netherlands.[198] Concerning a council, his informants said that

yf the King [of England] hath a will, ther will at his Desyre be graunted a generall Counsayle, and that in the most free, and irrestrayned manner. Therein all things now doubted of, being with greate libertie called in Question, and every Man suffered in publique to deliver his Opinion, much hope they say there is, that by the goodnesse of god some perfect concord may be had in all thinges, or at lest such reformation in most, as may give to men charitable, and trulie relligiouse some good Contentment.[199]

It seems unlikely that a plan for a council could have been drawn up without consultation with the papacy. Cornwallis reported on July 9 that "the Popes Nuncio is dayly heere expected; and that this Pope [the recently elected Paul V] is sayd to be very much affectionate to the King my Master."[200] On July 17, he reported that the nuncio had arrived.[201]

In his letter of July 28, Cornwallis said that he had raised some questions

---

[192] Vat. Arch., Fondo Borghese, Ser. III, vol. 68, fol. 182.
[193] Ibid., fol. 183 verso.   [194] Ibid., fol. 184.
[195] PRO SP, Spain, 94/11, fol. 196. See also Winwood, *Memorials*, vol. II, p. 100. For a brief discussion of this letter in relation to Spanish aims and policies, see Lee, *James I and Henri IV: An Essay in English Foreign Policy, 1603–1610*, pp. 41–45.
[196] PRO SP 94/11, fol. 196.
[197] Ibid.   [198] Ibid.   [199] Ibid.
[200] Ibid., fol. 172.   [201] Ibid., fol. 185.

about how "a Counsayle with such freedome, and libertie" would conduct its business. Who would be "an Indifferent head, or Judg" to preside over its sessions? How would the voting be carried out?[202] If only bishops and abbots were allowed to vote, he observed, then England "and other partes, wher the reformed Relligion is embraced" would be at a serious disadvantage. "Italie, and Fraunce being so full farced with men mytred" would easily carry the day.[203] His informants, all laymen, were not able to answer these questions, though they commented that the model for such a council might be that which "was held by the Apostles at Jerusalem."[204] They also informed Cornwallis that the suggestion for a council "came at first from a Bishop, and an Embassadour resident at this Court."[205]

What seems clear from this letter is that some Spanish officials were prepared to back James's proposal for a council not so much to achieve a broad religious reconciliation but as part of a comprehensive plan to resolve immediate political problems. Though peace had been agreed to between England and Spain, the war went on between the Spanish Netherlands and the United Provinces of the Netherlands, which had been struggling for a generation to win its independence from Spain. The war was not only an enormous financial burden for Spain, but it seemed to be approaching a stalemate, with neither side able to win a decisive victory. The Anglo-Spanish peace did not end English aid for the United Provinces, though it did give the Spanish Netherlands the same opportunity as its antagonists to recruit soldiers in Britain.[206] What the Spanish officials who formulated this plan presumably wanted was a peace in the Netherlands which recognized Spanish sovereignty but gave England some territory or spheres of influence, perhaps in the form of "cautionary" towns of the kind the English already had in certain parts of the United Provinces.[207] There were two other significant parts of the Spanish plan. Henry, the prince of Wales, would be married to the Spanish infanta, and English shipping would be regulated in such a way as not to threaten Spain and its dominions.[208] In return for this

---

[202] Ibid., fol. 196.   [203] Ibid.   [204] Ibid.   [205] Ibid.

[206] See, for the costs of the war and the military situation in the early seventeenth century, Pieter Geyl, *The Revolt of the Netherlands, 1555–1609*, second edition (London: Ernest Benn, 1962), pp. 239–259; and Geoffrey Parker, *The Army of Flanders and the Spanish Road, 1567–1659* (Cambridge: Cambridge University Press, 1972), pp. 16–18, 125–227, 247–251, and *Spain and the Netherlands, 1559–1659: Ten Studies* (London: Fontana, 1979), pp. 44–63, 85–103, and 177–203.

[207] This seems to be the meaning of the phrases, "some good Partes of Those Countryes to be delivered to England," and there would remain "only a caution of such part" to the king of Spain. PRO SP 94/11, fol. 196 verso. The "cautionary towns" were towns in the United Provinces held by England as security for loans made to the government of the northern provinces during their struggle against Spain. See Willson, *King James VI and I*, pp. 275–276 and 349.

[208] PRO SP 94/11, fol. 196 verso.

last concession, the king of Great Britain would receive annually a million ducats or more.[209]

Cornwallis later reported further consultations with Spanish officials and several times asked Salisbury for advice on the projects he had described. His letter of October 11, 1605 brought the news that the plan had the backing of major figures at the Spanish court. The projects, he reported, "have byne heere considered of by the Dukes of Lerma, of Sessa, of Infantado, the Conestable [Constable], the Conde de Myranda, the Conde de Villa Longa, Don Juan de Idiaquer, [and] Secretary Prada," and all except the constable were in favor of them.[210] On October 24, Salisbury responded to what he had heard from Cornwallis in early September about "ouvertures" from Spain for a closer alliance and for "reducing Christendome to a generall peace by his Ma^{ts} meanes." To Salisbury these appeared to be "specious pretences, to engage his Ma^{ty} into a warr, for the reduction of the United Provinces."[211] Meanwhile Cornwallis grew more enthusiastic about the plan, which he had evidently endeavored to shape. On November 19, he wrote: "I have now by gods goodness brought the great busynes to an head, and the same warranted by the most effectuall and powerful means I cold have desyred."[212] Rather than setting down the details in a letter and thus risking a breach of security, he undertook to send his secretary, Walter Hawkesworth, to London to present the plan. Hawkesworth, delayed by illness in leaving Spain, arrived in London at a most inauspicious time – just after the Gunpowder Plot had been exposed. On November 26, even before his secretary was well enough to set out on his journey, Cornwallis received news of a plot that had been planned for execution earlier in the month. He reported that the Spanish king and his whole court were astonished at the news and that the duke of Lerma and half a dozen other nobles had come to him to congratulate him on "the most happie Discoverie of this horrible Treason."[213] When Hawkesworth arrived in London at the end of December, he found the English court preoccupied with the task of bringing the conspirators to justice. Salisbury responded on January 3, 1606 to the Spanish plan as reported by Hawkesworth by saying that the matters dealt with in papers sent by the ambassador and described by his secretary were "of such weight and consequence, as they require advised and mature deliberation."[214] The king, Salisbury said, "hath ben constrained, to deferr the consideration of it, for some few daies, tyll he might wish less

---

[209] Ibid.
[210] PRO SP 94/12, fol. 79. See also Winwood, *Memorials*, vol. II, p. 147.
[211] PRO SP 94/12, fols. 96 verso–97. See also Winwood, *Memorials*, vol. II, p. 147.
[212] PRO SP 94/12, fol. 120. See also Winwood, *Memorials*, vol. II, p. 169.
[213] PRO SP 94/12, fol. 128.
[214] PRO SP 94/13, fol. 1.

distraction, or interruption of other affaires."[215] He nevertheless assured Cornwallis "that no oportunity wilbe omitted to further the same, as soone as tyme and occasion will geve leave, without precipitation, wch is the onely subverter of such propositions."[216]

That the Spanish initiatives did not significantly affect English foreign policy is perhaps not surprising. From Salisbury's point of view, the plan looked like a way to ensure Spain's hegemony in Europe and overseas, while making England a client state. On the other hand, James favored not only a council but peace negotiations between the warring states across the channel.[217] There was thus some basis on which agreement might have been sought. But the Gunpowder Plot, by sharpening the antagonism between Catholics and Protestants in England and on the continent, made cooperation between England and Spain immensely more difficult, especially if it were perceived to be at the expense of the Protestant-controlled United Provinces. The political and ecclesiological theories enunciated by spokesmen on both sides of the Oath of Allegiance controversy, moreover, drove a wedge between James and the papacy, virtually extinguishing the initial hopes the king had entertained for an ecumenical council under the pope's direction.

---

[215] Ibid.

[216] Ibid. When the Spanish initiatives were renewed a year later, there was no mention of a council. See Cornwallis to Salisbury, January 10, 1607, PRO SP 94/13, fols. 127–128 verso.

[217] See James's instructions to Edward Seymour, earl of Hertford, ambassador extraordinary to Brussels, April 9, 1605. PRO SP 77/7, fol. 111 verso.

Oath of Allegiance

The Gunpowder Plot, which King James described to Parliament in late 1605 as an attempt by Roman Catholics to destroy both the place and the persons associated with the passage of "cruell Lawes (as they say) . . . against their Religion," has been controversial ever since James announced its discovery.[1] Though the plotters evidently considered themselves loyal Roman Catholics, the provincial of the Jesuits in England, Henry Garnet, who knew most of them well, disavowed any connection with their activities and denied having given them moral support. Beginning in the middle of the seventeenth century, a theory was advanced, which still has some proponents, that the plot was as much the work of the English government as it was of those who were accused of treason and had as its object, not the restitution of Roman Catholicism in England, but its final extirpation.[2]

---

[1] James I, *His Maiesties Speach in This Last Session of Parliament, as Neere His Very Words as Could Be Gathered at the Instant; Together with a Discourse of the Maner of the Discouery of This Late Intended Treason* (London: Robert Barker, 1605), sig. B$_2$ verso and *passim*. See also the king's proclamations of November 5, 7, and 8, 1605 in James F. Larkin and Paul L. Hughes, eds., *Stuart Royal Proclamations*, 2 vols. (Oxford: Clarendon Press, 1973–1983), vol. I, pp. 123–127. James's *Discourse*, published with his speech to Parliament delivered on November 9, is the basis of the traditional story of the plot as one planned by a small group of Roman Catholics, whose activities were detected and foiled on the very eve of the opening of Parliament on November 5. For the trial of the surviving lay members of the group in January 1606, see *A Trve and Perfect Relation of the Proceedings at the Seuerall Arraignments of the Late Most Barbarous Traitors* (London: Robert Barker, 1606), sigs. A$_3$–N$_3$ verso. Henry Garnet, the only one of three Jesuit priests alleged to have been involved to be apprehended, was found guilty of having knowledge of the plot on March 28. For his trial, see *A Trve and Perfect Relation*, sigs. N$_4$–Eee$_4$ verso. The other two Jesuit priests, John Gerard and Oswald Tesimond, who escaped to the continent, wrote accounts of the plot. For Gerard's, see John Morris, ed., *The Condition of Catholics under James I: Father Gerard's Narrative of the Gunpowder Plot*, second edition (London: Longmans, Green, 1872); for Tesimond's, see Oswald Tesimond, *The Gunpowder Plot: The Narrative of Oswald alias Greenway*, ed. Francis Edwards (London: Folio Society, 1973).

[2] Thomas Fuller stated in 1655 that there was a "posthume report" that King James had been "privie to this Plot all along" and had allowed it to develop until he was able to announce its discovery almost at the last moment. See his *The Church-History of Britain, from the Birth of Jesus Christ, untill the Year M. DC. XLVIII* (London: John Williams, 1655), Bk. X, p. 37. Bishop Godfrey Goodman, writing between 1650 and 1655, espoused another version of this

Recent investigations of the plot, especially of its ideological context, suggest that the attempted destruction of the central government was a serious threat by a handful of discontented men and could have caused immense, though unpredictable, changes in British society. It grew out of a long period of hostility between the see of Rome and the English government.[3]

After the discovery of the Gunpowder Plot, King James modified the conciliatory policy towards his Roman Catholic subjects that he had followed earlier in his reign in England. Even before the plot was uncovered, that policy had been altered after Parliament renewed the Elizabethan penal laws. Now, an aroused public opinion and an increasingly anti-Catholic Parliament demanded a more stringent penal code. One component of that code was an Oath of Allegiance in 1606 which sought to establish the grounds of civil obedience for those who acknowledged the spiritual authority of the papacy. James himself did not give up his vision of a peaceful and united Church at home and abroad which he had unfolded to Parliament at its opening session in 1604. But in defending the Oath of Allegiance, he allowed himself to be drawn into a bitter European-wide

theory, namely, that James's chief minister, the earl of Salisbury, knew all about the plot and allowed it to develop in order to justify repressive measures against Roman Catholics. See Godfrey Goodman, *The Court of King James the First*, ed. John S. Brewer, 2 vols. (London: Richard Bentley, 1839), vol. I, pp. 100–102. Modern writers who accept some version of Goodman's theory include John Gerard, *What Was the Gunpowder Plot? The Traditional Story Tested by Original Evidence* (London: Osgood, McIlvaine, 1897); Hugh Ross Williamson, *The Gunpowder Plot* (London: Faber and Faber, 1951); Francis Edwards, *Guy Fawkes: The Real Story of the Gunpowder Plot?* (London: Rupert Hart-Davies, 1969); Paul Durst, *Intended Treason: What Really Happened in the Gunpowder Plot* (London: W. H. Allen, 1970); and C. Northcote Parkinson, *Gunpowder Treason and Plot* (London: Weidenfeld and Nicolson, 1976). For a view of the plotters as "brave but incompetent idealists," see Joel Hurstfield, "A Retrospect: Gunpowder Plot and the Politics of Dissent," in his *Freedom, Corruption and Government in Elizabethan England* (London: Jonathan Cape, 1973), pp. 327–351.

[3] See, for the care taken by James's government to try to ascertain the truth about the plot in the shortest possible time, Mark Nicholls, *Investigating Gunpowder Plot* (Manchester: Manchester University Press, 1991); also his "Investigating Gunpowder Plot," *Recusant History*, 19, 2 (1988), 124–145. For the likelihood of a massacre of Scots in England following the destruction of Parliament, see Jenny Wormald, "Gunpowder, Treason, and Scots," *Journal of British Studies*, 24, 2 (April 1985), 141–168. For the ideological context of the plot, see Michael L. Carrafiello, "Robert Parsons' Climate of Resistance and the Gunpowder Plot," *Seventeenth Century*, 3 (1988), 115–134. See also Thomas H. Clancy, *Papist Pamphleteers: The Allen–Persons Party and the Political Thought of the Counter-Reformation in England, 1572–1615* (Chicago: Loyola University Press, 1964); Peter Holmes, *Resistance and Compromise: The Political Thought of the Elizabethan Catholics* (Cambridge: Cambridge University Press, 1982); and Julian Lock, " 'Strange Usurped Potentates': Elizabeth I, the Papacy and the Indian Summer of the Medieval Deposing Power," D.Phil. thesis, Oxford University, 1992. See also Antonia Fraser, *The Gunpowder Plot: Terror and Faith in 1605* (London: Weidenfeld, 1996), for the devastation intended by the plotters.

theological controversy. This controversy, which moved from a discussion of the deposing power claimed by the papacy to an examination of fundamental political issues and the doctrines of the Christian faith, did little to assuage the animosities and passions of those on both sides of the Catholic–Protestant divide. Nevertheless, at the very height of the controversy, James and some of his supporters renewed the ecumenical appeal the king had made in the first two and a half years of his reign in England. This time James made his appeal not directly to the papacy but to the civil rulers and states of Europe.

I

The House of Commons began discussing Roman Catholicism in England as soon as its second session of 1605 to 1606 opened on January 21.[4] With the investigation of the Gunpowder Plot still under way, the House focused on the security of the king and the government. As early as February 6 the two houses of Parliament conferred about the provisions under consideration. After further consultations between the two houses and between the houses and spokesmen for the king, two bills were passed at the end of May and became law in June.[5] The first law required that recusants who conformed to the established Church by attending services should "receive the blessed Sacrament of the Lord's Supper" at least once a year or else be subject to a graduated series of fines – £20 the first year, £40 the second, and £60 the third.[6] Those who refused to come to services could be made to pay £20 a month or lose two-thirds of their property at the king's discretion. Anyone who attempted to reconcile any of the king's subjects to "the Pope or See of Rome" was considered to be guilty of high treason.[7] These measures were intended to sap the strength of the Roman Catholic community, even at the expense of making the eucharist, the sacrament of unity, into a weapon of coercion. The same law contained an oath to be required of recusants or those suspected of recusancy "for the better trial how his Majesty's subjects stand affected in point of their loyalty and due obedience."[8]

---

[4] Wallace Notestein, *The House of Commons, 1604–1610* (New Haven: Yale University Press, 1971), pp. 145–146.

[5] Ibid., pp. 151–159; David Harris Willson, ed., *The Parliamentary Diary of Robert Bowyer, 1606–1607* (Minneapolis: University of Minnesota Press, 1931), pp. 19–31, 57, 73, 106–107, 156, 160–163, 170–176, 183–184.

[6] J. R. Tanner, ed., *Constitutional Documents of the Reign of James I, A.D. 1603–1625, with an Historical Commentary* (Cambridge: Cambridge University Press, 1930) – "Act for the Better Discovering and Repressing of Popish Recusants" – p. 86. See also J. P. Kenyon, ed., *The Stuart Constitution, 1603–1688: Documents and Commentary*, second edition (Cambridge: Cambridge University Press, 1986), pp. 168–171, and, for commentary, pp. 165–168.

[7] Tanner, *Constitutional Documents of the Reign of James I*, p. 92.   [8] Ibid., p. 89.

The other law specified that no recusant was to come to the king's residence unless summoned there or to remain within ten miles of London.[9] Nor could recusants practice law or medicine or command troops or a ship in the king's service. Recusants were not allowed to have gunpowder or weapons beyond those required for personal protection. The law encouraged private individuals to harass Roman Catholics by granting to anyone who discovered that a recusant had harbored a Roman Catholic priest, or that a Roman Catholic mass had been said on a recusant's premises, one-third of the fine paid or of the property forfeited by the recusant.[10] Other provisions deprived a recusant woman of two-thirds of her jointure and dower and deprived her of any part of her deceased husband's estate.[11] Such mean-spirited and vengeful laws were the product of the Gunpowder Plot and of the trials of the conspirators. Not surprisingly, the administration of these laws by the king and his officials was uneven, inconsistent, and frequently lax, circumstances which impelled Parliament to call regularly for their stricter enforcement.[12]

The Oath of Allegiance embedded within the first of the new penal laws became a bone of contention between the papacy and the English monarchy and, indeed, between Roman Catholic and Protestant spokesmen across Europe. But it seems actually to have been an attempt by James and his advisers to conciliate moderate Roman Catholics in England. As the king explained in a proclamation in 1610, the oath "was onely devised as an Acte of great favour and clemencie towards so many of Our Subjects, who though blinded with the superstition of Poperie, yet caried a dutifull heart towards our Obedience."[13] Thereby, James said, he and his officials could distinguish between Roman Catholics who were loyal subjects and those who accepted the doctrines and practices which had led to the "Powder-

---

[9] Ibid., "Act to Prevent and Avoid Dangers which May Grow by Popish Recusants," p. 95.
[10] Tanner, *Constitutional Documents of the Reign of James I*, p. 94.   [11] Ibid., p. 98.
[12] On the enforcement of the laws, see James J. La Rocca, "James I and His Catholic Subjects, 1606–1612: Some Financial Implications," *Recusant History*, 18, 3 (May 1987), 251–262. See also Thomas Malcolm Coakley, "The Political Position and Domestic Policy of Robert Cecil, First Earl of Salisbury, 1603–1612," Ph.D. thesis, University of Minnesota, 1959, pp. 257–272; Martin J. Havran, *The Catholics in Caroline England* (Stanford: Stanford University Press, 1962), pp. 12–17; Elliot Rose, *Cases of Conscience: Alternatives Open to Recusants and Puritans Under Elizabeth I and James I* (Cambridge: Cambridge University Press, 1975), pp. 55–57, 231–232; John Bossy, *The English Catholic Community, 1570–1850* (London: Darton, Longman, and Todd, 1975), pp. 121–125, 280; and J. C. H. Aveling, *The Handle and the Axe: The Catholic Recusants in England from Reformation to Emancipation* (London: Blond and Briggs, 1976), pp. 145–146, 156–159. For examples of the suffering caused by the laws, see Philip Caraman, ed., *The Years of Siege: Catholic Life from James I to Cromwell* (London: Longman, 1966), pp. 51–57, 60–63, 66–68, 72–73.
[13] James F. Larkin and Paul L. Hughes, eds., *Stuart Royal Proclamations*, 2 vols. (Oxford: Clarendon Press, 1973–1983), vol. I, p. 249.

Treason."[14] The king's intention seems to have been that once the latter group, the perceived enemies of his regime, had been confined under the penalties of *praemunire*, he could again practice a limited, if unofficial, toleration.

The oath was based in part on forms of submission drafted by secular priests – Roman Catholic clergy who were not members of religious orders – in the period 1602 to 1604 as part of their attempt to secure toleration in exchange for a profession of civil loyalty. In negotiations with Richard Bancroft, then bishop of London, members of this group tried to distinguish themselves sharply from the Jesuits, whom they accused of political subversion, and thereby win for themselves the freedom to pursue their pastoral activities.[15] "An oath of Allegeance thowght upon by some Catholickes" in about 1602, for example, acknowledged Elizabeth as lawful queen and affirmed that all her subjects were bound to obey her, "notwithstandinge any forayne or domesticall power, preheminence or authoritye, or any doctrine, opinion or writinge, that eyther hath allready or that shall hereafter affirme, comaund or teach the contrarye."[16] Bancroft, who became archbishop of Canterbury in 1604, negotiated covertly with the secular priests, partly as a way of splitting the clerical leadership of the Roman Catholic community.[17] Bancroft himself was responsible for a draft of the oath which eventually became a part of parliamentary legislation in 1606. He may have been assisted by Sir Christopher Perkins, a former Jesuit who was then a member of the House of Commons. In any case, the oath was the object of much consultation and was frequently revised during Parliament's sessions. James himself undoubtedly had a hand in the oath's composition.

The Oath of Allegiance required a subscriber to make seven affirmations. First, that King James "is lawful and rightful king of this Realm." Second, that the pope had no "power or authority to depose the King, or to dispose any of his Majesty's kingdoms or dominions, or to authorise any foreign prince to invade or annoy him or his countries, or to discharge any of his subjects of their allegiance and obedience to his Majesty."[18] Third, that

[14] Ibid., p. 249.

[15] Roland G. Usher, *The Reconstruction of the English Church*, 2 vols. (New York: Appleton, 1910), vol. I, pp. 160–188; vol. II, pp. 101–109, 310–320.

[16] Ibid., vol. II, p. 312.

[17] The divisions between secular priests and Jesuits in the period 1595–1604 resulted in two appeals to Rome by seculars unhappy over the leadership of the Archpriest George Blackwell, thought to be under the domination of the Jesuits. See John Bossy, "Henri IV, the Appellants, and the Jesuits," *Recusant History*, 8 (1965), 80–122, and *The English Catholic Community, 1570–1850*, pp. 34–48; and Arnold Pritchard, *Catholic Loyalism in Elizabethan England* (Chapel Hill: University of North Carolina Press, 1979), pp. 78–101, 120–174, 204–207.

[18] Notestein, *The House of Commons, 1604–1610*, pp. 153, 521 note.

regardless of any "declaration or sentence of excommunication or depriva-
tion . . . by the pope or his successors . . . or any absolution of the said
subjects from their obedience," the taker would bear true allegiance to the
king and defend him against all conspiracies. Fourth, that the taker would
disclose to the king "all treasons and traitorous conspiracies which I shall
know or hear of." Fifth, that "I do from my heart abhor, detest, and abjure,
as impious and heretical, this damnable doctrine and position, that princes
which be excommunicated or deprived by the Pope may be deposed or
murdered by their subjects or any other whosoever." Sixth, that "neither
the Pope nor any person whatsoever hath power to absolve me of this
oath." And, seventh, that the oath was "lawfully ministered unto me."[19]
The oath concluded with an assurance that the taker understood these
words in their plain and common meaning and had taken the oath "without
any equivocation or mental evasion or secret reservation whatsoever"[20] – a
reference to the doctrine of equivocation devised by Roman Catholic priests
to enable them to avoid answering directly the questions put to them when
they were in official custody.

Most of these affirmations were aimed at proponents of the activist
political ideology that flourished in England as well as in France and Spain
during the latter part of Queen Elizabeth's reign. Pope Pius V and Cardinal
William Allen had declared the queen an unlawful usurper, had declared
her deposed, and had called upon her subjects to withhold their obedience
from her. James and his advisers believed that this ideology had strongly
influenced the conspirators who planned to blow up the Parliament House
in November 1605. Yet times had changed with James's accession and,
especially, as a result of the peace made between England and Spain in
1604. Roman Catholics in England had been admonished by the pope not
to engage in violent acts against the English government. James hoped – in
vain, as it turned out – that Pope Paul V would publicly condemn the
Gunpowder Plot and those who were convicted of participating in it.[21] He
may well have expected that the pope would endorse the Oath of Allegiance
as a way of assuring the political authorities in England that Roman
Catholics were not a threat to the peace and stability of the realm. The oath
did not deny directly the spiritual authority which Roman Catholics

---

[19] Tanner, *Constitutional Documents of the Reign of James I*, p. 90 – for the first two
provisions of the oath.
[20] Ibid., p. 91 – for the remaining five provisions.
[21] Condemnation did come in the form of letters to the papal nuncio in Brussels: "letters are
come hether from the Pope, to his Nuntio, which doe declare his great detestacõn of the late
abominable treason, with acknowledgment how much the deallers therein deserue punishment, and insisting for some intervention to be used, that for respect greater severyties may
not be inforced against the reste of the Catholiques in England." London, Flanders, SP 77/8,
fol. 16 verso (Sir Thomas Edmondes to Salisbury, January 23, 1606).

believed the pope exercised by divine right. It did not deny that the pope could excommunicate an English king. But it sought to neutralize the political effect of such beliefs by affirming that subjects still owed allegiance to their lawful ruler. This deliberate separation of the issues of the pope's spiritual and temporal authority was insisted upon by James in order to make the oath more palatable to his Roman Catholic subjects. Nevertheless, there were features of the oath that were bound to be disquieting to Roman Catholics, whether lay or clerical, secular priests or Jesuits. To say that the pope had no power or authority to depose a ruler was to deny the papacy a right it had long claimed and had recently sought to put into practice; the deposing power had, moreover, been upheld by many distinguished theologians. Moreover, as the Jesuit Joseph Creswell observed in 1611, to say that the pope could not take steps to bring down a government seemed to ignore such possible cases as a king who forced his Christian subjects to become "Mohometans, Iewes, Pagans, or Infidels."[22] Even more disturbing was the assertion that the papal deposing power, which enjoyed wide support among Roman Catholic theologians, was "impious and heretical" and a "damnable doctrine."[23] Not only did a taker of the oath have to disavow a theological doctrine in good standing in the Roman Catholic world, but the taker would in effect recognize that the English Parliament and king could define doctrine in an authoritative way. "How came the English Parliament by authoritie to censure doctrine?" asked Creswell; "who deliuered them this Power? who made them assurāce of Gods infallible spirit?"[24] To say, moreover, that the pope had no power to absolve anyone of the obligations undertaken under the oath could trouble the conscience of anyone who recognized the pope as the supreme authority on earth in moral and spiritual matters.

Pope Paul V soon responded. In a letter or brief dated September 22, 1606, the pope forbade Roman Catholics in England to "come unto the churches of the Heretikes, or heare their Sermons, or communicate with them in their Rites," or to "binde your selves by the Oath," which he quoted in full.[25] To the pope it seemed self-evident that the oath was dangerous: "it must evidently appeare unto you by the words themselues,

[22] Joseph Creswell, *A Proclamation Pvblished vnder the Name of Iames, King of Great Britanny; With a Briefe & Moderate Answere Thereunto; Whereto Are Added the Penall Statutes Made in the Same Kingdome against Catholikes* ([St. Omer: English College Press,] 1611), p. 81.
[23] Tanner, ed., *Constitutional Documents of the Reign of James I*, p. 91.
[24] Creswell, *A Proclamation Pvblished vnder the Name of Iames*, p. 82.
[25] James I, *Triplici nodo, triplex cuneus: or, An Apologie for the Oath of Allegiance, against the Two Breues of Pope Pavlvs Qvintus, and the Late Letter of Cardinal Bellarmine to G. Blackwell the Arch-priest* (London: Robert Barker, 1607), p. 10. The pope's letter is dated "the tenth of the Calends of October, 1606" (p. 16).

that such an Oath cannot be taken without hurting of the Catholique Faith, and the Saluation of your Soules, seeing it conteines many things, which are flat contrary to Faith and Saluation."[26] Just what those "many things" were, he did not specify. The letter expressed the pope's compassion for Roman Catholics in England for "the tribulations and calamities, which ye haue continually susteined for the keeping of the Catholike Faith."[27]

The pope's letter was not, however, distributed by the Archpriest George Blackwell, who had served as the head of the Roman Catholic community in England since his appointment by Pope Clement VIII in 1598. Blackwell had been horrified by the Gunpowder Plot, about which he had written to Roman Catholic priests in England on November 7, shortly after the plot was discovered. He saw the plot as "an intolerable, uncharitable, scandalous, and desperate" act, contrary to a decree of the Council of Constance and the judgement of the "best catholic writers of our age."[28] He called upon his fellow priests to instruct the faithful that "private violent attempts cannot be thought of, much less may be aided and maintained by catholics."[29] Apprehended on the night of June 24, 1607, he was questioned by Archbishop Bancroft and others the next day. He had, he said, approved of the Oath of Allegiance when it had become law in the previous summer and had "divulged his iudgement and direction for the lawfulnesse of the taking of that oath," though only in conversation with priests and not in writing.[30] When he received the pope's letter, he decided not to publish it. Now, in captivity in the Gatehouse Prison, he sent a letter to his fellow priests dated July 7, 1607 in which he declared that in his opinion it would not be lawful or just for the pope to excommunicate King James, but if that were to happen, the king's subjects "would still be bound in the same way as now to maintain their loyalty" to the crown.[31] He urged his brethren to take the oath as he himself had done. "So shall we shake off the false and grievous imputation of Treason."[32] Blackwell's view of the oath as expressed in this letter was not given freely and spontaneously. But his view does not seem to

---

[26] Ibid., p. 13.

[27] Ibid., p. 9.

[28] [Hugh Tootell,] *Dodd's Church History of England from the Commencement of the Sixteenth Century to the Revolution in 1688*, ed. M. A. Tierney, 5 vols. (London: C. Dolman, 1839–1843), vol. IV, pp. cxi–cxii. See also *Calendar of State Papers, Domestic Series, of the Reigns of Edward VI, Mary, Elizabeth, and James I*, 12 vols. (London: HMSO, 1856–1872), vol. VIII, p. 243.

[29] [Tootell,] *Dodd's Church History*, vol. IV, p. cxii. See also *Calendar of State Papers, Domestic*, vol. VIII, p. 243.

[30] George Blackwell, *His Answeres vpon Sundry His Examinations; Together with His Approbation and Taking of the Oath of Allegeance; And His Letter Written to His Assistants and Brethren, Moouing Them Not Onely to Take the Said Oath but to Aduise All Romish Catholikes So to Doe* (London: Robert Barker, 1607), p. 9; see also p. 14.

[31] Ibid., pp. 23–24.   [32] Ibid., p. 39.

have been contrary to his conscience. He was evidently fed up with the theory and practice of political militancy and eager to shed the opprobrium brought on himself and his co-religionists by the Gunpowder Plot and the trials of the conspirators. On the other hand, the sort of accommodation to the king which Blackwell's example represented was bound to concern the pope, presaging, as it seemed to do, the eventual absorption of Roman Catholics in England into the political and religious establishment.

In a second letter to Roman Catholics in England, dated August 23, 1607, Paul V noted that some of his flock were reported to doubt the authenticity of his first letter. He affirmed that that letter had been written "not onely upon our proper motion, and of our certaine knowledge, but also after long and weightie deliberation."[33] English Roman Catholics were, he reiterated, forbidden to take the oath, whatever interpretations were put on it to persuade them to the contrary. Cardinal Robert Bellarmine, one of the leading Roman Catholic theologians, also wrote to George Blackwell on September 28, 1607, taking sharp issue with what he called Blackwell's "slip and fall" from constancy in not refusing an unlawful oath.[34] It made little difference, wrote Bellarmine, whether the language of the oath was moderate or not. The basic issue for him, as it was to be for many other Roman Catholics in the controversy which soon followed, was that the oath "tends to this end, that the authoritie of the head of the Church in England, may bee transferred from the successour of S. Peter, to the successour of K. Henry the eight."[35] The oath had been contrived in such a way that to profess civil allegiance to the king, the taker was forced to "denie the Primacie of the Apostolike Sea."[36] Blackwell answered Bellarmine in a letter on November 13, 1607 in which he claimed the support of "the writings of Catholics" for his action in taking the oath.[37] Those divines, he claimed, had never subscribed to the view that "the most holy successor of S. Peter" had "an Imperiall and Ciuill power" to depose a king.[38] In a letter to Roman Catholics in England written from the Clink prison on January 20, 1608, Blackwell called attention to the pope's two letters and to Bellarmine's letter to him. He held the view that the pope was "head of the Catholicke Church" and that all rulers were "subiect in some cases vnto his

---

[33] James I, *Triplici nodo, triplex cuneus: or, An Apologie for the Oath of Allegiance*, p. 33. The pope's second letter is dated "the x. of the Calends of September, 1607" (p. 33).

[34] Ibid., p. 37. The date of the letter is given in George Blackwell, *A Large Examination Taken at Lambeth According to His Maiesties Direction, Point by Point, of M. George Blakwell, Made Archpriest of England by Pope Clement 8, vpon Occasion of a Certaine Answere of His, without the Priuitie of the State, to a Letter Lately Sent unto Him from Cardinall Bellarmine Blaming Him for Taking the Oath of Allegeance* (London: Robert Barker, 1607), sig. (c₄).

[35] James I, *Triplici nodo, triplex cuneus: or, An Apologie for the Oath of Allegiance*, p. 38.

[36] Ibid., p. 39.

[37] Blackwell, *A Large Examination Taken at Lambeth*, sig. (e₂) verso.   [38] Ibid.

spirituall censures"; but that for the pope "to eradicate them, or to depose them" by any claim to temporal power *jure divino*, either directly or indirectly derived from his spiritual power, was unacceptable.[39] The allegiance which English subjects owed to their king was, he claimed, the same which the ancient Christians had owed to the emperor.[40] Whatever other theological and historical issues were involved, one theme in Pope Paul's and Cardinal Bellarmine's letters was clear. Not to obey the pope's orders on the oath was to ignore the pope's authority. Not surprisingly, Blackwell was deprived of his position of archpriest, on January 22, 1608, and replaced by George Birkhead (or Birket), whom the pope admonished to dissuade Roman Catholics in England from taking the oath and from attending Protestant services.[41] Despite this step and the pope's and the cardinal's letters, the oath was taken by many of the Roman Catholic laity, beginning with its general administration in the summer of 1607.

The controversy over the oath, though it involved major European figures, was as yet little known beyond the circles of those directly involved. But James was deeply moved by a conviction that his government's motives had been misunderstood in Rome and that his sovereign powers were being undermined by the pope's directives to Roman Catholics in England. According to James Montague, who edited the king's collected writings in 1616, James, having decided to have Thomas Bilson, bishop of Winchester, prepare an answer to Bellarmine, called "for penne and incke" and devoted himself to making notes for Bilson's use.[42] In six days, the king had prepared a manuscript which Archbishop Bancroft and Bishop Lancelot Andrewes pronounced a sufficient answer "both to the Pope and Cardinall."[43] The result was the *Triplici nodo, triplex cuneus: or, An Apologie for the Oath of Allegiance*, dated 1607, which appeared anonymously about the middle of February 1608. Latin and French translations were published soon afterwards. If, as seems likely, James received a good deal of scholarly assistance from Montague, as well as, perhaps, Bancroft and Andrewes, there is no reason to doubt that the book was essentially his.[44]

---

[39] Ibid., p. 158.   [40] Ibid., p. 166.

[41] *Calendar of State Papers, Domestic*, vol. VIII, p. 397.

[42] James I, *The Workes of the Most High and Mightie Prince Iames, by the Grace of God King of Great Britaine, France and Ireland, Defender of the Faith*, ed. James Montague (London: Robert Barker and John Bill, 1616), sigs. d₂–d₂ verso. Montague, the first master of Sidney Sussex College, Cambridge, from 1595, was dean of the Chapel Royal; in 1608 he became bishop of Bath and Wells. From there he was translated to Winchester in 1616. Bilson, a learned and prolific controversialist in the latter part of Elizabeth's reign, contributed only indirectly to the Oath of Allegiance controversy by a Latin translation in 1611 of his *The Perpetual Government of Christes Church* (1593), a defense of episcopal – not papal or presbyterian – government in the Church.

[43] James I, *Workes*, ed. Montague, sig. d₂ verso.

[44] James I, *Triplici nodo, triplex cuneus: sive Apologia pro iuramento fidelitatis, adversus duo*

The *Apologie* is not a scintillating work. James endeavored to deal straightforwardly with the arguments advanced by Pope Paul V and Cardinal Bellarmine and to set forth a persuasive rationale for the oath. Despite James's occasional bursts of indignation and some intemperate language, he argued his case with considerable discretion and restraint. His professed intention, once he had raised questions about the pope's and the cardinal's letters and had stated the issues as he saw them, was to leave it up to his readers "wisely and vnpartially" to judge whose arguments were the more convincing.[45] James described the oath as a means of separating loyal from disloyal subjects. He distinguished between "so many of his Maiesties Subiects, who although they were otherwise Popishly affected, yet retained in their hearts the print of their naturall duetie to their Soueraigne" and those who would use their religion as "a safe pretext for all kinde of Treasons, and rebellions against their Soueraigne."[46] The king expressed surprise that the pope would interfere in the affairs of England without first stating his objections to the oath. If he had done so, some alterations could, perhaps, have been made. James had tried, since the beginning of his reign, to be conciliatory to Roman Catholics in his realm.[47] Neither of the pope's two letters, the king pointed out, cited anything specific in the oath that was contrary to Christian faith and practice. Obedience to temporal authorities had never been considered "against Faith and saluation of soules," as the pope's first letter seemed to allege.[48] As for the cardinal's letter, its author made a fundamental mistake, said the king, in asserting that the oath dealt with the pope's supremacy in spiritual matters. Unlike the Oath of Supremacy of Elizabeth's reign, which Bellarmine had apparently confused with the Oath of Allegiance, the present oath did not dispute the pope's spiritual authority. He denied that in "any part of this Oath the primacie of Saint Peter is any way meddled with."[49] James marshalled an array of historical

brevia P. Pauli Quinti & epistolam Cardinalis Bellarmini ad G. Blackvellum Archipresby-terum nuper scriptam (London: R. Barker, 1607); Triplici nodo, triplex cuneus: ou Apologie pour le serment de fidelite, que de Roy de la Grand Bretagne veut estre faict par tous ses sujets, contre les deux brefs du Pape Paul cinquième & l'epistre, ou lettre, nagueres envoyee par le Cardinal Bellarmin à G. Blackwel Archiprestre (Leyden, 1608). For the authorship of the book, see David Harris Willson, "James I and His Literary Assistants," Huntington Library Quarterly, 8 (1944–1945), pp. 38–42, and King James VI and I (New York: Henry Holt, 1956), pp. 229–233. Willson argues plausibly that Montague's description is a simplified and dramatic account of a longer process. On the basis of the reports of the French and Venetian ambassadors, he contends that James spent much of December 1607 closeted with Montague, who supplied him with data, including critiques of Bellarmine's earlier writings. Nevertheless, the actual writing of the book, which he credits largely to James, could, he says, have taken place in the period of time described by Montague. See Willson, King James VI and I, p. 232.

[45] James I, *Triplici nodo, triplex cuneus: or, An Apologie for the Oath of Allegiance*, p. 112.
[46] Ibid., pp. 3–4.   [47] Ibid., pp. 6–7, 19.   [48] Ibid., p. 27.
[49] Ibid., p. 62.

evidence to subvert what he called Bellarmine's "strongest argument": viz. that no pope had ever "either commanded to be killed, or allowed the slaughter of any Prince whatsoever, whether he were an Heretike, an Ethnike, or Persecutor."[50] The king noted that Bellarmine had singled out murdering, while omitting "deposing, degrading, stirring vp of Armes, or Rebelling against them."[51] But, in any case, for "the Popes allowing of killing of Kings," the evidence was extensive and hardly to be denied.[52] "How many Emperors did the Pope raise warre against?"[53] In more recent times, how many attempts were made by papal agents on Queen Elizabeth's life? What about the panegyric made by Pope Sixtus V in "praise and approbation" of the murderer of King Henry III of France?[54] The deposing power, James argued, was but slenderly supported by any evidence that could be found in the scriptures and in the writings of the ancient fathers of the Church. But this was certainly not the case with the king's temporal supremacy in his own realm, for which he cited scriptural, theological, and historical support.[55] This oath dealt solely with "the Ciuill Obedience of Subiects to their Soueraigne," as earlier oaths approved by ancient councils had done.[56]

With the publication of the *Apologie*, which included the texts of the pope's and the cardinal's letters as well as the Oath of Allegiance itself, the controversy over the oath entered a more public phase. Latin and French translations of the *Apologie* were published in 1607 and 1608. James's authorship was soon suspected. Paul V asked Cardinal Bellarmine, whose views had been sharply challenged by the king, to reply to the *Apologie*. Bellarmine published his *Responsio* pseudonymously under the name of his chaplain, Matteo Torti. In addition to stressing the authority of the pope, as the vicar of Christ and head of the Church, to "direct and correct all Christians, even if they should be kings and princes,"[57] Bellarmine dropped a bombshell about James's correspondence with Pope Clement VIII in the 1590s, while the king was in Scotland. James, Bellarmine pointed out, was born of Roman Catholic parents and baptized with the traditional rites of the Roman Catholic Church.[58] At the time of Queen Elizabeth's death, his accession to the English throne was facilitated by Clement VIII in response to the king's promising better treatment of his Roman Catholic subjects. As king of Scots, James, along with his ministers, had created in Rome the impression that he did not "abhor the Catholic faith."[59] The king had

[50] Ibid., p. 64.   [51] Ibid., p. 65.   [52] Ibid.
[53] Ibid.; see also pp. 72–74.   [54] Ibid., p. 67.   [55] Ibid., pp. 105–109.
[56] Ibid., p. 47; see also pp. 53–55.
[57] Robert Bellarmine, *Matthaei Torti, presbyteri & theologi papiensis, responsio ad librvm inscriptvm, Triplici nodo, triplex cuneus, sive apologia pro iuramento fidelitatis* ([St. Omer: English College Press,] 1608), p. 60.
[58] Ibid., pp. 91–92, 96–98.   [59] Ibid., p. 47.

written letters full of goodwill to the pope himself, as well as to Cardinal Aldobrandini, in which "he asked that someone from the Scottish people be created a cardinal" so that he would have an official through whom he could conduct business with the pope.[60] Bellarmine contended that James had bitterly disappointed those with whom he had dealt in Rome. It was not surprising, therefore, that the current pope was frustrated in his dealings with the king.[61]

James pursued vigorously the charge that he had misled the papacy about his intentions in a letter to the pope before his accession in England. In October 1608, James challenged James Elphinstone, now Lord Balmerino, his secretary of state in Scotland, to reveal what he knew about the alleged letter. Balmerino, who had been the king's secretary in the years immediately before James's accession in England, acknowledged that he had obtained the king's signature for a letter which James had not read.[62] He repeated his confession before the English Privy Council, which had been charged by James to investigate the matter. In 1609, in Scotland, Balmerino was condemned to death for his crime, but he was sentenced to remain confined to his house for the rest of his life. The effect of these actions was largely to clear the king's name. James did not feel it necessary to mention the letter or Balmerino in his subsequent answer to Bellarmine. In any case, the full story is more complicated than Balmerino's confession suggested. A letter was sent from James to Clement VIII, dated September 24, 1599, in which the king asked the pope to name as cardinal the Scot William Chisholm, then bishop of Vaison, near Avignon, where he had succeeded his uncle by special license of Pope Gregory XIII. The bishop would thereby be better able to conduct business between the Scottish king and the papacy.[63] Elphinstone may indeed have obtained James's signature without the king's being aware of what he was signing. But the initiative of establishing contact with Rome was not the secretary's. James was engaged in a complex and delicate diplomatic effort to prepare the way for his peaceful accession to the English throne.[64] The letter may have been an

---

[60] Ibid.   [61] Ibid.

[62] Samuel R. Gardiner, *History of England from the Accession of James I to the Outbreak of the Civil War, 1603–1642*, 10 vols. (London: Longmans, Green, 1883), vol. II, pp. 31–34; Willson, *King James VI and I*, pp. 234–235; Maurice Lee, Jr., *Government by Pen: Scotland under James VI and I* (Urbana: University of Illinois Press, 1980), p. 93.

[63] Arnold Oskar Meyer, "Clemens VIII. und Jakob I. von England," *Quellen und Forschungen aus italienischen Archiven und Bibliotheken*, 7, 2 (1904), pp. 271, 274, 277.

[64] See, in addition to Meyer, "Clemens VIII. und Jakob I. von England," 286–306: Thomas Graves Law, ed., "Documents Illustrating Catholic Policy in the Reign of James VI," *Miscellany of the Scottish History Society*, vol. I (Edinburgh: Scottish History Society, 1893), pp. 1–70; G. F. Warner, "James VI and Rome," *English Historical Review*, 20 (1905), 124–127; A. W. Ward, "James VI. and the Papacy," *Scottish Historical Review*, 2 (1905) 249–252; J. D. Mackie, "A Secret Agent of James VI," *Scottish Historical Review*, 9

attempt by Elphinstone, a Roman Catholic, to push James further in the direction of closer relations with the pope than the king had intended to go. In any case, the letter did not say anything about James's being ready for conversion or about his plans for the treatment of Roman Catholics in England.

Meanwhile James's *Apologie* had been answered by Robert Parsons, the head of the English College in Rome, who professed not to know that the king was the author. Roman Catholics, said Parsons, were prepared to obey their king in all situations except "when the cause of Christ commeth in hand, who is Lord of our Consciences, or any matter concerneth the same."[65] This was the kind of obedience the ancient Christians rendered to the emperors in St. Cyprian's time, when they refused "to yield to their Temporall Princes Commandements against God and their Religion: no not for any torments that might be layd vpon them."[66] Parsons's book was subsequently answered in 1609 by William Barlow, bishop of Lincoln and one of the king's chaplains, who pressed Parsons and other supporters of the papacy to show specifically where the oath contained any matter "contrary to the will of God, either reuealed in his word, or by speciall message and commission deliuered."[67] James asked Lancelot Andrewes to answer Bellarmine's *Responsio*, which he did in his *Tortvra Torti*, a stout Latin volume published in 1609. It contained, among other things, an account of the Balmerino incident and the text of Balmerino's "Declaration and Confession" concerning the letter sent from James's court to Clement VIII.[68]

Having already stated his views on the oath and the arguments of the pope and the cardinal, James could have remained discreetly in the background, allowing his formidable array of theological advisers to answer any

(1912), 376–386, "The Secret Diplomacy of King James VI. in Italy Prior to His Accession to the English Throne," *Scottish Historical Review*, 21 (1924), 267–282, and *Negotiations between King James VI. and I. and Ferdinand I., Grand Duke of Tuscany* (London: Oxford University Press for St. Andrews University, 1927), pp. iii–xxiii, 7–11, and *passim*; Helen Georgia Stafford, *James VI of Scotland and the Throne of England* (New York: Appleton-Century, 1940), pp. 225–249.

[65] Robert Parsons, *The Ivdgment of a Catholicke English-man, Living in Banishment for His Religion, Written to His Priuate Friend in England, Concerning a Late Booke Set Forth, and Entituled, Triplici nodo, triplex cuneus, or An Apologie for the Oath of Allegiance* ([St. Omer: English College Press,] 1608), p. 53.

[66] Parsons, *The Ivdgment of a Catholicke English-man*, p. 64.

[67] William Barlow, *An Answer to a Catholike English-Man (So by Him-selfe Entitvled) Who, without a Name, Passed His Censure vpon the Apology, Made by the Right High and Mightie Prince Iames by the Grace of God King of Great Brittaine, France, and Ireland, &c. for the Oath of Allegeance* (London: Mathew Law, 1609), p. 163.

[68] Lancelot Andrewes, *Tortvra Torti: sive, ad Matthaei Torti librvm Responsio, qui nuper editus contra Apologiam serenissimi potentissimiqve principis, Iacobi, Dei gratia, Magna Britanniae, Franciae, & Hiberniae Regis, pro ivramento fidelitatis* (London: Robert Barker, 1609), pp. 181–199 (Balmerino's "Declaration and Confession," pp. 191–194).

further attacks on the *Apologie*. Instead he chose to make his authorship of the *Apologie* public and to join to a reissue of the work a longer treatise, which was the most ambitious literary undertaking of his career. Why? Montague provided a plausible explanation. The king, he said, was resolved,

that if the Pope and Cardinall would not rest in his answere, and sit downe by it; take the Oath as it was intended for a point of Allegiance and Ciuill Obedience; Hee would publish the *Apologie* in his owne name with a Preface to all the Princes in Christendome; wherein hee would publish such a Confession of his Faith, perswade the Princes so to vindicate their owne Power, discouer so much of the Mysterie of Iniquitie unto them; as the Popes Bulles should pull in their hornes, and himselfe wish he had neuer medled with this matter.[69]

James had decided to appeal the broader political issues to the temporal rulers of Christendom, who might, in their turn, bring about such changes in the Church as would eliminate once and for all a major threat to their peace and security.

James's preface was the *Premonition* or warning addressed to the Holy Roman Emperor Rudolph II, and "to All Other Right High and Mightie Kings; and Right Excellent Free Princes and States of Christendome: Our louing Brethren, Cosins, Allies, Confederates and Friends."[70] His claim to their friendship was not ill-founded. James had strenuously pursued a policy of peace with all nations both before and after his accession in England and he believed, with some justification, that he was without an enemy among the rulers of Europe.[71] In the 1590s he had sent emissaries to France, Spain, Venice, the United Provinces, and elsewhere to seek their friendship and, if possible, their support for his claim to the English throne. His marriage to Anne of Denmark brought him into close contact not only with her native

---

[69] James I, *Workes*, ed. Montague, sigs. d₂ verso–d₃.

[70] James I, *An Apologie for the Oath of Allegiance: First Set Forth without a Name, and Now Acknowledged by the Author, the Right High and Mightie Prince, Iames by the Grace of God, King of Great Britaine, France and Ireland, Defender of the Faith, &c.; Together with a Premonition of His Maiesties to All Most Mightie Monarches, Kings, Free Princes and States of Christendome* (London: Robert Barker, 1609) [hereafter cited as *Premonition*], sigs. a₂–a₂ verso, p. 1. For Rudolph, an eccentric Roman Catholic who had become increasingly antagonistic to the papacy for political reasons, see R. J. W. Evans, *Rudolf II and His World: A Study in Intellectual History, 1576–1612* (Oxford: Clarendon Press, 1973), esp. pp. 84–115.

[71] The major study of James's peace policy is Maurice Lee, Jr., *James I and Henri IV: An Essay in English Foreign Policy, 1603–1610* (Urbana: University of Illinois Press, 1970), pp. 3–16, 168–185, and *passim*, where, however, James is presented as more passive in pursuit of his aims than the evidence suggests. See also Simon Adams, "Spain or the Netherlands?: The Dilemmas of Early Stuart Foreign Policy," in Howard Tomlinson, ed., *Before the English Civil War: Essays on Early Stuart Politics and Government* (London: Macmillan, 1983), pp. 79–101; G. M. D. Howat, *Stuart and Cromwellian Foreign Policy* (London: Adam and Charles Black, 1974), pp. 1–24; and Charles H. Carter, *The Secret Diplomacy of the Habsburgs, 1598–1625* (New York: Columbia University Press, 1964), pp. 11–22, 109–119.

land but with northern German states whose princes were related or connected to Anne and her brother, Christian IV of Denmark.[72] James had discussed a marriage between Prince Henry and one of the daughters of the Grand Duke Ferdinand of Tuscany and his wife the Grand Duchess Christina, who was James's cousin through his grandmother, Mary of Guise.[73] He kept in touch with his Guise cousins, especially the duke of Lorraine. While still in Scotland James had cultivated cordial relations with Flanders, which was nominally sovereign – though still closely attached to Spain – under its rulers, the Archduke Albert of Austria and the Archduchess Isabella of Spain. These relationships were reinforced after James's accession in England. A treaty of friendship and alliance was signed with France in 1603 and, the next year, a peace treaty with Spain and Flanders. There were difficulties in relations with Flanders over that country's refusal in 1606 to extradite Hugh Owen and Father William Baldwin, suspected of complicity in the Gunpowder Plot, but relations between Britain and Spain continued normally.[74] The same was the case with disputes between the English and French over English cloth exports to France and the repayment of debts owed by France for English aid given to Henry IV during his struggle to secure the French throne.[75] Anne of Denmark's three sisters were married to the duke of Holstein, the landgrave of Hesse, and the duke of Brunswick, respectively, all three of whom were on close terms with James's

[72] Stafford, *James VI of Scotland and the Throne of England*, pp. 124–156.

[73] Mackie, "The Secret Diplomacy of King James VI. in Italy Prior to His Accession to the English Throne," pp. 278–282, and *Negotiations between King James VI. and I. and Ferdinand I*, pp. xiii–xx, 66–67, 71–73.

[74] PRO SP 77/7, fol. 273 (Salisbury to Edmondes, November 14, 1605); 77/7, fols. 285–286 (Edmondes to Salisbury, November 19, 1605); 77/7, fol. 295 verso (Edmondes to Salisbury, November 25, 1605); 77/7, fols. 312–315 (Edmondes to Salisbury, December 20, 1605); 77/8, fol. 15 (Edmondes to Salisbury, January 23, 1606); 77/8, fol. 40 (Edmondes to Salisbury, February 19, 1606). Edmondes had complained of Owen, an associate of Sir William Stanley, the former commander of the English regiment, and Baldwin, a Jesuit who was vice-prefect of the English mission, even before the discovery of the plot; he called them the "Patriarches" of the radical Roman Catholics in Flanders. SP 77/7, fol. 251 (October 9, 1605). The archduke took Owen and Baldwin into custody but declined to extradite them to England on the grounds that Owen was the servant of Spain and Baldwin was a priest and thus free from the normal civil procedures; he also pointed out that no explicit evidence had been disclosed to link them to the plot.

[75] The issue of the ill-treatment of English cloth merchants in France, about which James remonstrated with Henry (SP 78/49, fols. 111–111 verso, James I to Henry IV, December 24, 1604; SP 78/49, fols. 112–113, James I to Henry IV, February 15, 1605; SP 78/49, fols. 113–113 verso, James I to Henry IV, April 13, 1605), was largely settled in late 1605. The debt, which Sir Thomas Parry identified in 1604 as an issue hindering closer relations between the two countries (SP 78/51, fols. 4 verso–6, Parry to Cecil, January 5, 1604), was frequently brought up with French officials by Parry's successor, Sir George Carew (SP 78/54, fol. 125, Carew to Salisbury, July 6, 1608; SP 78/54, fols. 160–161, Carew to Salisbury, September 15, 1608; SP 78/54, fols. 221–222, Carew to Salisbury, December 7, 1608). A firm French commitment to begin repayments did not come until 1610.

family and court.[76] Marriage negotiations were discussed with Spain, though without much urgency on either side.

James's relations with foreign countries in his first seven years in England were aimed not only at winning friends for Great Britain but at establishing lasting stability in Europe. He supported Venice in its dispute with the papacy in 1606 to 1607, but worked for a peaceful solution to a conflict that threatened to involve Spain and to turn northern Italy once again into an international battleground.[77] His French allies, on good terms with both Venice and the papacy, negotiated a settlement. England and France had committed themselves in 1603 to settling the continuing war between the United Provinces on the one side and Spain and Flanders on the other. After several years of difficult negotiations, that war was halted temporarily by the Truce of Antwerp in March 1609, which established a period of twelve years free from hostilities.[78] It might have seemed in James's interests to allow the war to continue. The Dutch constrained the powerful Spaniards with the help of a subsidy from France. But James wanted a Europe entirely at peace. Unfortunately, shortly after the war in the Netherlands ended, a disputed succession in Cleves–Jülich in northwestern Germany threatened to bring several Protestant states as well as the Holy Roman emperor into conflict; but James believed that crisis, like others, could be resolved peacefully.[79]

[76] Roy Strong, *Henry, Prince of Wales, and England's Lost Renaissance* (London: Thames and Hudson, 1986), pp. 77–78.

[77] Sir Henry Wotton saw the dispute – for which, see below – as an attempt by Pope Paul V to encroach on the civil jurisdiction and thus the sovereignty of Venice (Wotton to James I, May 26, May 16, English style, 1606, PRO State Papers, Venice, SP 99/3, fols. 82 verso–83). James's view was that the Venetians were to be highly commended for "their wisdom and courage, in defending their honor against that usurped authoritie at Rome," thus providing a salutary example for other "Christian Princes, and States that have subiected themselves under that yoake." Yet he believed that some "meanes wrought by mediation" would be found. (PRO SP 99/3, fols. 111–111 verso, Salisbury to Wotton, June 16, 1606.)

[78] When preparations were being made in October 1607 for negotiations to end the Spanish–Dutch war, James laid down in his instructions to Sir Richard Spencer and Sir Ralph Winwood the principles of peace: the independence of the United Provinces and the continued maintenance of the Protestant religion there (PRO State Papers, Miscellaneous, France and Holland, SP 104, p. 163). He wished to avoid too strong a commitment to the defense of the United Provinces in association with France as inconsistent with his treaty with Spain and as a possible incitement to war (PRO SP 104, pp. 174, 176, Council to Commissioners, November 9, 1607, December 15, 1607). Spain and Flanders finally accepted the principles of independence and the continuation of Protestantism, though only on a temporary basis. The results, however, were highly beneficial to the Dutch. See Pieter Geyl, *The Revolt of the Netherlands, 1555–1609*, second edition (London: Ernest Benn, 1962), pp. 250–259; and Geoffrey Parker, *Spain and the Netherlands, 1559–1659: Ten Studies* (London: Fontana, 1979), pp. 73–74.

[79] Henry IV told Carew in early April 1609 that so long as the king of Spain or the Holy Roman emperor did not secure Cleves, he did not care which of the two contending Protestant princes got it, but he would not allow the Habsburgs to advance to his very

James's *Premonition* was thus directed to political leaders whose friendship he believed he could count on. The official, revised edition of the book
bore the date April 8, and was published in 1609. Latin and French editions
were published in London; a Latin edition was published in Amsterdam and
a Dutch edition in Leyden. Lancelot Andrewes may have assisted the king in
writing the book.[80] James's diplomatic agents were to ensure that copies of
the work reached the European heads of state.

In this book James recalled that the Oath of Allegiance was part of the
parliamentary legislation enacted after the discovery of the Gunpowder
Plot, a treason which had been "plotted onely by Papists, and they onely led
thereto by a preposterous zeale, for the aduancement of their Religion."[81]
Parliament had wanted to discover "whether any more of that minde, were
yet left in the Countrey."[82] During the oath's formulation, James had
insisted on a change which had the effect of separating the issues of the
pope's spiritual and temporal authority. When the House of Commons
wanted to include a provision that the pope had no power to excommunicate the king, James insisted that this be altered to specify that no papal
excommunication "can warrant my Subiects to practise against my person
or State."[83] Takers of the oath were, in other words, not required to
disavow the pope's power to excommunicate anyone but rather his power
to depose kings. Concerning the severer laws enacted against Roman
Catholic recusants in England following the discovery of the plot, James
asserted that not even the heated atmosphere of those months had led him
to abandon a policy of moderation. "And yet so farre hath both my heart
and gouernment bene from any bitternes, as almost neuer one of those
sharpe additions to the former Lawes, haue euer yet bene put in execution."[84] As for the letters of Pope Paul V forbidding Roman Catholics to

doorstep. PRO SP 78/55, fol. 65 (Carew to Salisbury, April 5, 1609). By November 1609,
James had sent Sir Ralph Winwood to Düsseldorf to show his support for the Union of
Evangelical Princes whose representatives were gathered there and to seek a solution to the
crisis in association with France and the United Provinces. PRO SP 78/55, fol. 232 verso
(Salisbury to William Becher, November 19, 1609).

[80] James I, *Apologia pro iuramento fidelitatis: primum quidem ἀνώνυμος, nunc vero ab ipso
auctore, serenissimo ac potentiss. principe, Iacobo, Dei gratia, Magnae Britanniae, Franciae
& Hiberniae Rege, fidei defensore, denuo edita; cui praemissa est praefatio monitoria
sacratiss. Caesari Rodolpho II., semper augusto, caeterisque Christiani orbis sereniss. ac
potentiss. monarchis ac regibus, celsissimisque liberis principibus, rebus publicis atque
ordinibus incripta* (London: J. Norton, 1609). For other editions and translations, see
Charles H. McIlwain, ed., *The Political Works of James I* (Cambridge, Mass.: Harvard
University Press, 1918), p. civ. For the authorship of the *Premonition*, see Willson, "James I
and His Literary Assistants," p. 46; Paul A. Welsby, *Lancelot Andrewes, 1555–1626*
(London: SPCK, 1958), pp. 144–145.

[81] James I, *Premonition*, p. 6.   [82] Ibid., p. 8.   [83] Ibid., p. 9.

[84] Ibid., p. 8. The king's statement gives the impression that religious persecution under the
penal laws was rare, which was certainly not the case. Government officials, including local
priest-hunters known as pursuivants, made life miserable for many Roman Catholics;

take the oath and the letter and subsequent treatise of Cardinal Bellarmine attacking it, these, said James, had neglected the major issues in the debate, issues which were of general, not just local, concern. What was at stake was nothing less than the authority of kings and of "all supereminent Temporall powers."[85] Bellarmine, by asserting the papal claim to be able to depose kings as well as excommunicate them, had attempted to justify a usurpation of power contrary to "the rule of all Scriptures, ancient Councels, and Fathers."[86] Furthermore the claim conveyed a threat to European peace and stability. This threat was to the security of all heads of state but was even greater to those who were Roman Catholics than to those who were not. Since the pope claimed, on the basis of several familiar New Testament texts describing St. Peter's commission, "so ample a power over Kings, to throne or dethrone them at his pleasure (and yet onely subiecting Christian Kings to that slauery)," it was evident that "so many of you as professe the Romish religion" were especially vulnerable.[87] Bellarmine had, James observed, dealt in other works with political allegiance in such a way as to be equally unsettling. "Speaking *de Clericis*," for example, Bellarmine had asserted "that Church-men are exempted from the power of earthly Kings; and that they ought [owe] them no subiection euen in temporall matters, but onely *vi rationis*, and in their owne discretion, for the preseruation of peace and good order."[88] James reminded his fellow sovereigns that some of the greatest among them had almost a third of their subjects in the clerical estate, and asked them to "consider and weigh, what a feather he pulls out of your wings, when he denudeth you of so many subjects."[89]

James showed that he was aware that the issue of the pope's temporal authority was nothing new in European political affairs. To the examples of aggressive papal actions against kings and emperors cited in his *Apologie*,

---

prisons where priests were confined were wretched places in which to live; fines on the laity were sometimes levied and frequently threatened. Yet by one index religious persecution was far less severe than in Elizabeth I's reign. Not counting the Gunpowder Plot conspirators, some seventeen Roman Catholic priests were executed for their faith during James's reign. Under Elizabeth, the number was 124. See Havran, *The Catholics in Caroline England*, p. 17; Kenyon, *The Stuart Constitution, 1603–1688*, second edition, p. 167. The level of fines, even at the height of imposition in the years 1606–1612, was lower than could have been expected. See La Rocca, "James I and His Catholic Subjects, 1606–1612: Some Financial Implications," pp. 253–259. Puritans sometimes complained that the king accorded Roman Catholics better treatment than they received. See "King James and the English Puritans: An Unpublished Document," *Blackwoods Magazine*, 188 (September 1910), 402–413, which discusses *An Humble Supplication for Toleration* (1609) from Puritan ministers and James's comments on it.

[85] James I, *Premonition*, p. 1.   [86] Ibid., p. 17.

[87] Ibid., p. 18. The scriptural passages cited in favor of the pope's temporal power over princes which were discussed by James were Matthew 16: 19 ("I will give you the keys of the kingdom of heaven") and John 21: 17 ("Feed my sheep").

[88] James I, *Premonition*, p. 20.   [89] Ibid., p. 22.

he added the resolutions of French and English kings to resist the political encroachments of ambitious popes.[90] James's point was that Bellarmine was trying to make as "one of the chiefe Articles of the Catholicke faith" a papal temporal authority which Christian kings and emperors had opposed for hundreds of years.[91] The kings of France, James reminded his fellow rulers, had "euer stoken to their Gallican immunitie, in denying the Pope any temporall power ouer them, and in resisting the Popes as oft as euer they prest to meddle with their temporall power, euen in the donation of Benefices."[92] James clearly had a good deal of history – from the Investiture Controversy to the conflict between Pope Boniface VIII and King Philip IV of France – on his side.

James was offended by Bellarmine's having called him an apostate from the Catholic faith. If he were to be formally accused of heresy by the pope in a conclave of cardinals, his accusers "would haue hard prouing me an Heretike, if he iudged me by their owne Ancient orders."[93] James said that he had always professed the faith in which he had been brought up. That faith, though it differed in important respects from that of his mother, he did not hesitate to call Catholic: "I am such a Catholicke Christian, as beleeueth the three Creeds; that of the Apostles, that of the Councell of Nice, and that of Athanasius . . . and I beleeue them in that sense, as the ancient Fathers and Councels that made them, did understand them."[94] Similarly, he held "the foure first generall Councels, as Catholike and Orthodoxe," as declared by acts of Parliament and accepted by the Church of England.[95] He revered the writings of the ancient fathers in the same way St. Augustine had, as worthy of belief where they agreed with the scriptures. James proceeded to describe the ways in which the Church of England honored and remembered the saints, and the esteem in which the Blessed Virgin Mary was held as "the mother of Christ, whom of our Sauiour tooke his flesh, and so the mother of God."[96] The beliefs and practices associated with private masses, communion in one kind, transubstantiation, adoration of the host, works of supererogation, and veneration of images were all "new Articles of faith, neuer heard of in the first 500. yeeres after Christ," and James therefore rejected them.[97]

As for the primacy of the Apostolic See, which Bellarmine had said was an essential part of the Catholic faith, James put the issue in the context, again, of the system of belief to which he had long adhered. He had ever maintained, against considerable opposition in Scotland, that "Bishops ought to be in the Church" and were apostolic in origin and so ordained by God.[98] He also acknowledged "Rancks and degrees amongst Bishops."[99]

[90] Ibid., pp. 25–32.   [91] Ibid., p. 22.   [92] Ibid., p. 26.   [93] Ibid., p. 33.
[94] Ibid., p. 35.   [95] Ibid.   [96] Ibid., p. 37.   [97] Ibid., pp. 38–39.
[98] Ibid., pp. 43–44.   [99] Ibid., p. 45.

He knew that patriarchs had been a part of the Church's structure since ancient times and that there had been contention among them for the first place. "If that were yet the question," he said, "I would with all my heart giue my consent, that the bishop of Rome should have the first Seate; I being a westerne King, would goe with the Patriarch of the West. And for his temporall Principality ouer the Signory of Rome, I doe not quarrell it neither; let him in God his name be *Primus Episcopus inter omnes Episcopos*, and *Princeps Episcoporum*; so it be no otherwise but as Peter was *Princeps Apostolorum*."[100] These titles, "first bishop among all bishops," and "prince of bishops" as St. Peter was "prince of the apostles," would seem to take the king a long way towards recognizing the Petrine Supremacy claimed by Rome. But James qualified his affirmations by denying that the Church had any earthly monarch "whose word must be a Law, and who cannot erre in his Sentence by an infallibility of Spirit."[101] All of this substantiated James's claim in his address to his first Parliament in England that he wished to be neither "an hereticke in Faith" nor a "schismatick in matters of Pollicie."[102] James's *Premonition* was, among other things, his attempt to stake out a broad middle ground of faith and practice on which, he hoped, Christians could agree.

Nevertheless much in the treatise had an anti-papal character, making it certain to anger many of James's intended readers. To the king's profession of faith was appended a long section – almost half the length of the book – devoted to the doctrine of the Antichrist. The king made it clear, albeit in undogmatic fashion, that he believed it likely that the modern papacy was the Antichrist described in the Book of Revelation. He was led towards this conclusion by the popes' claim to universal temporal dominion and their stirring up of political strife. The offense given to Roman Catholics by this section of the book was probably the result of the images employed as much as the message itself. The papacy was associated with all those marks of degradation described in scriptural prophecies: murder, sorcery, fornication, and theft.[103] James explained the seeming contradiction between the view of

---

[100] Ibid., p. 46. [101] Ibid.
[102] McIlwain, *The Political Works of James I*, p. 276.
[103] James I, *Premonition*, pp. 51–106. James said that he did not presume to bind anyone to his view, "if his owne reason lead him not thereunto" (p. 72). The view that the pope was the Antichrist was widely held as an article of faith among Protestants. For discussions of its importance in England, see Christopher Hill, *Antichrist in Seventeenth-Century England* (London: Oxford University Press, 1971), *passim*; Richard Bauckham, *Tudor Apocalypse* (Abingdon: Sutton Courtenay Press, 1978), pp. 91–112, 173, 236; Paul Christianson, *Reformers and Babylon: English Apocalyptic Visions from the Reformation to the Eve of the Civil War* (Toronto: University of Toronto Press, 1978), pp. 9–10, 15–17, 23, 38, 47–48, 111–112, 244–246; and Peter Lake, "The Significance of the Elizabethan Identification of the Pope as Antichrist," *Journal of Ecclesiastical History*, 31, 2 (April 1980), 161–178.

the papacy given here and that expressed elsewhere in the book in a
conversation with the French ambassador which was subsequently reported
to Rome. On July 1, 1609, Antoine le Fevre de la Boderie wrote to Brûlart
de Puysieulx, secretary of state at the French court, that James "does not
wish to say that the pope is the Antichrist except in so far as he [the pope]
maintains that he has the power to depose princes; that if he [the pope]
wishes to give up this pretension, he [the king] is willing to accept him as the
first among bishops."[104]

James believed that the means existed for reconstructing the Church and
freeing the temporal rulers from the threat of deposition and religiously
inspired subversion. The legitimate institution for effecting such a change, a
general council, had largely been eclipsed by the College of Cardinals, those
electors and advisers of popes who had come to be "so strangely exalted
aboue their first originall institution" as priests and deacons of the parishes
of the city of Rome.[105] Yet the monarchs, acting in concert, might still
achieve what was needed: the reform and reunion of Christendom.
Certainly, "if euer there were a possibilitie to bee expected of reducing all
Christians to an uniformity of Religion," wrote James,

> it must come by meanes of a generall Councell; the place of their meeting being
> chosen so indifferent, as all Christian Princes, either in their own Persons, or their
> Deputie Commissioners; and all Churchmen of Christian profession, that beleeue
> and professe all the ancient grounds of the true, ancient, Catholike, and Apostolike
> Faith, might have *tutum accessum* thereunto; All the incendiaries, and Nouelist fire-
> brands on either side being debarred from the same, as well Iesuites as Puritaines.[106]

James's *Premonition* thus sounded publicly that appeal for an ecumenical
council to deal with the disorders of Christendom which he had communicated prior to the Gunpowder Plot to several Roman Catholic rulers and
to Pope Clement VIII – and to which he had briefly alluded in his first
speech to Parliament.[107] This time the appeal was directed to the Christian
rulers and states rather than to the papacy. James's dislike of Jesuits and
Puritans had grown as a result of his experience with them. He considered
that they were the sects on the two sides that were least likely to compromise
and were also least respectful of the rights of Christian monarchs.

In his concluding exhortation to Christian princes and states, James called
upon all of them to oversee the "planting and spreading" of the worship of
God according to God's revelation.[108] James declared that he assumed that

---

[104] Antoine le Fevre de la Boderie, *Ambassades de Monsieur de la Boderie en Angleterre, sous
le regne d'Henri IV. & la minorité de Louis XIII. depuis les années 1606. jusqu'en 1611*, 5
vols. ([Paris,] 1750), vol. IV, p. 387. See also Ludwig von Pastor, *The History of the Popes
from the Close of the Middle Ages*, 40 vols. (St. Louis: B. Herder, 1936–1953), vol. XXVI,
p. 177.
[105] James I, *Premonition*, p. 109.   [106] Ibid., pp. 110–111.
[107] See chapter 2, above.   [108] James I, *Premonition*, p. 129.

those who had "gone out of Babylon" or were, in other words, part of that Protestant community that the king reckoned as "almost the halfe of all Christian people" would be in agreement with what he had written.[109] He nevertheless urged Protestants to "keepe fast the unity of Faith amongst your selues," avoiding idle controversies as well as misplaced zeal for "indifferent things."[110] He urged his Roman Catholic "Brethren and Cosins" to follow St. Paul's injunction to "search the Scriptures, and ground your Faith upon your owne certaine knowledge, and not vpon the report of others, since euery Man must be safe by his owne faith."[111] Calling the attention of Roman Catholics to the recent example of "the Popes ambitious aspiring ouer your temporall power," presumably in Venice, he urged them to maintain the "lawfull liberties" of their crowns and commonwealths.[112] The argument and tone of this conclusion – and, indeed, of much of the treatise – suggested that though the *Premonition* was addressed to all the princes and states of Christendom, it was principally aimed at Roman Catholic rulers. Only if they were won to James's point of view were the changes he envisioned likely to take place. If this was his intention, however, the section on the Antichrist was surely a tactical mistake.

II

In referring to the reception given to King James's literary works by his theological opponents, James Montague observed: "they looke upon his Maiesties Bookes, as men looke upon Blasing-Starres, with amazement, fearing they portend some strange thing, and bring with them a certain Influence to worke great change and alteration in the world."[113] This quality of intense apprehension seemed to characterize the reaction of the curia in Rome to James's *Premonition*. A substantial part of the diplomatic correspondence in the Vatican Archives for the months following the publication of the *Premonition* is devoted to "il libro del Re d'Inghilterra."[114] Almost every papal concern in Europe – Gallicanism in France, heterodoxy at the emperor's court, the anti-papal stance of Venice, the growth of Calvinism in the Rhineland, and the loyalty of Roman Catholics

---

[109] Ibid., p. 130.   [110] Ibid., pp. 130–131.
[111] Ibid., p. 131. The words at the end are from Habakkuk 2: 4.
[112] Ibid., p. 132.   [113] James I, *Workes*, ed. Montague, sig. C$_4$ verso.
[114] For a survey of some of the materials in the Vatican Archives for James's reign, see Dominic Conway, "Guide to Documents of Irish and British Interest in Fondo Borghese, Series I," *Archivium Hibernicum: Irish Historical Records*, 23 (1960), 1–147, and the sequel, dealing with Series II–IV, in the same journal, 24 (1961), 31–102. For the Roman Catholic reaction to James, see Robert Peters, "Some Catholic Opinions of King James VI and I," *Recusant History*, 10 (1969–1970), 293–303.

in Britain – seemed likely to be affected in some way by the British king's manifesto.[115]

Papal officials exhorted the intended recipients of the king's book to refuse to accept it, even if it were brought by an official envoy. Cardinal Scipione Borghese, the papal secretary of state, writing to Guido Bentivoglio in Flanders on July 18, 1609, urged the nuncio to see that the Archduchess Isabella remained deaf to the pleas of the English ambassador; if she refused to accept the king's book she would clearly demonstrate her piety.[116] With considerable satisfaction the cardinal wrote again to Bentivoglio on August 1, praising the Archduke Albert and the archduchess for declaring their unwillingness to receive the book.[117] On August 15, the cardinal commented favorably on the refusal of "the pernicious book of the king of England" by the ambassador of Spain at London.[118] On the same day a letter was sent from the papal secretary Confaloniero to Attilio Amalteo, nuncio in Cologne, warning him that the book of the king of England had penetrated into Italy; certain princes there had ignored the censure of the book by the Congregation of the Holy Office, which had prohibited the volume. The nuncio was to inform the princes and prelates of his province of the importance of this matter.[119] Cardinal Borghese wrote to the same effect on the same day to Ladislao d'Aquino, nuncio in Switzerland, urging him to see that government officials there not only refused to accept the book but took steps to repress it.[120] On the previous day he had sent a warning to Valerianus Muti, nuncio in Naples, that the king had sent emissaries to Italy bearing copies of the book, and asking the nuncio to make special representations to the viceroys to prevent the introduction or distribution of the book there. A list of heresies contained in the book was also sent to the viceroys by the pope's direction.[121] A list of heresies was also sent to Berlingerio Gessi, the nuncio in Venice, in mid-July, and a similar list was given to the secretary of the Venetian ambassador at Rome. On September 26 Cardinal Borghese rejoiced at the news that, in spite of an appeal by the English ambassador to the Venetian Senate, that body had refused to allow the book to be published or sold in the republic.[122] The government received its official copy but apparently deposited it, unread, in the Venetian State Archives.[123]

[115] The religious instability of Europe in this period is skilfully described in Marvin R. O'Connell, *The Counter Reformation, 1559–1610* (New York: Harper & Row, 1974), pp. 307–336.

[116] Rome, Vat. Arch., Fondo Nunziatura Fiandra 136 A, fols. 238 verso–239.

[117] Vat. Arch., Fondo Borghese, Ser. I, 914, fol. 5.   [118] Ibid., fol. 12 verso.

[119] Ibid., 898, fol. 15.   [120] Ibid., 901, fol. 7 verso.   [121] Ibid., fols. 170 verso–171.

[122] Ibid., 897, fols. 111–111 verso, 135, 139 verso.

[123] Logan Pearsall Smith, *The Life and Letters of Sir Henry Wotton*, 2 vols. (Oxford: Clarendon Press, 1907), vol. I, p. 104; Willson, *King James VI and I*, p. 238.

Despite papal efforts to prevent the reception of the king's book in Roman Catholic countries, the book was accepted and given a thoughtful reading by members of the court of Henry IV in France. James wrote to Henry on May 15, 1609 commending the book to the French king's attention and thanking him for the efforts made by the French ambassador at Rome to ease the controversy which had flared up between the English government and the papacy. The book which he was sending, said James, concerned "the state and liberty of all the Christian princes" and was especially appropriate for Henry who, like his predecessors, had maintained "the liberty of the Gallican Church to the immortal honor of your Crown."[124] Sir George Carew presented the book to the French king in early June with a short speech in which he asserted that the pope had acted "very hastely and peremptorily" in forbidding the taking of the oath, contrary to the advice of the French ambassador at the Vatican, and that the two replies from Rome in answer to James's *Apologie* had been not only largely "impertinent" but "very voyde of all modesty."[125] James's new preface admonished "other Christian Princes, how neerly this example touched them."[126] Henry accepted the king's book and letter, and on Carew's departure he turned them over to Nicolas de Neufville, seigneur de Villeroy, his secretary of state. On July 13 Henry told Carew that he had found "many good things" in the book.[127] Carew also reported that the king had delivered the book to Cardinal Jacques Davy du Perron, who had held a consultation about it in order to determine whether something profitable might not be drawn from it "for setling of controuersies in Religion."[128]

In a long despatch of July 2, 1609, Roberto Ubaldini, the nuncio in France, wrote to Cardinal Borghese to report on his recent interview with the French king about James's book. After accepting the book, Henry had turned it over to four of the leading theologians in France to examine. They had reported that though the book contained errors, it also affirmed many things "which today all heretics deny."[129] The king himself had declared to Ubaldini that the book offered grounds of hope. Henry believed that when James had been assured of the security of his life and realm he would become much more tractable. Even if he were not won over to Roman Catholicism he might be persuaded to treat his Roman Catholic subjects more gently.[130] On the same day the nuncio met with the king's theological advisers, for whom Cardinal du Perron was the spokesman. Du Perron said

---

[124] Paris, BN, MS. Français, Ancien Fonds, vol. 15984, fol. 341 verso.
[125] PRO SP 78/55, fols. 105–105 verso (Carew to Salisbury, June 15, 1609).
[126] Ibid., fol. 105 verso.
[127] Ibid., fol. 132 verso (Carew to Salisbury, July 21, 1609).   [128] Ibid., fol. 132 verso.
[129] Vat. Arch., Fondo Borghese, Ser. I, 915, fol. 227 verso. The other theologians were Cardinal François de la Rochefoucauld, Pierre Coton, and Fronton du Duc.
[130] Ibid.

that in view of the approval James had expressed of the ancient councils, the teachings of the fathers, and the place of the see of Rome in the early Church, and of his declared intention not to exact any except civil obedience from his Roman Catholic subjects, there seemed to be a promising opportunity to achieve positive results with the king.[131] But du Perron urged that quite a different course be taken with James from that which had so far been followed. Stinging literary attacks would only arouse the king's fears and suspicions of Roman Catholics, intensifying his anxiety, which stemmed from the recent plot against him.[132]

Stinging literary attacks from both sides became, however, the order of the day. Papal attempts to suppress the king's book were accompanied by attempts to find scholars able and willing to answer it,[133] and the flood of published works that came from European presses was sufficient to make James's ideas familiar to any educated person with the slightest interest in ascertaining what they were. Montague wrote that

as soone as his Maiestie dealt against the Pope, tooke the Cardinall in hand, made the world see the usurped power of the one, and Sophistry of the other; Good Lord, what a stirre we had; what roaring of the wilde Bulls of Basan, what a commotion in euery countrey; Insomuch, that I thinke, there is scarce a People, Language or Nation in Christendome, out of which his Maiestie hath not receiued some answere or other; either by way of refuting, or at least by rayling.[134]

A modern writer has called it "such a battle of books as the world had never seen before."[135] One reason both Catholic and Protestant authors were

---

[131] Ibid., 915, fols. 228–228 verso.   [132] Ibid., fol. 228 verso.

[133] Vat. Arch., Nunziatura Fiandra 136 A, fol. 236 verso (Borghese to Bentivoglio, July 11, 1609); Fondo Borghese, Ser. I, 915, fols. 237–237 verso (Ubaldini to Borghese, July 21, 1609); Fondo Borghese, Ser. I, 915, fols. 255–256 (Ubaldini to Borghese, August 2, 1609); Fondo Borghese, Ser. I, 907, fol. 8 (Borghese to Ubaldini, *c.* September 1, 1609).

[134] James I, *Workes*, ed. Montague, sig. d$_2$.

[135] James Brodrick, *Robert Bellarmine, 1542–1621*, 2 vols. (London: Longmans, Green, 1950), vol. II, p. 224. For overall treatments of the Oath of Allegiance controversy, see McIlwain, ed., *The Political Works of James I*, pp. xlix–lxxx; Brodrick, *Robert Bellarmine, 1542–1621*, vol. II, pp. 169–260; D. Harris Willson, *King James VI and I* (New York: Henry Holt, 1956), pp. 228–242; J. H. M. Salmon, *The French Religious Wars in English Political Thought* (Oxford: Oxford University Press, 1959), pp. 70–79; Clancy, *Papist Pamphleteers*, pp. 90–106; Manfred Ebert, *Jakob I. von England (1603–1625) als Kirchenpolitiker und Theologe* (Hildesheim: Gerstenberg, 1972), pp. 112–139; Johann Peter Sommerville, "Jacobean Political Thought and the Controversy over the Oath of Allegiance," Ph.D. thesis, Cambridge University, 1981; Kenneth L. Campbell, *The Intellectual Struggle of the English Papists in the Seventeenth Century: The Catholic Dilemma* (Lewiston, N.Y.: Edwin Mellen Press, 1986), pp. 39–75; and Donna B. Hamilton, *Shakespeare and the Politics of Protestant England* (London: Harvester Wheatsheaf, 1992), pp. 128–162. See also, for comments on the issues raised in the controversy, J. P. Sommerville, *Politics and Ideology in England* (London: Longman, 1986), pp. 9–56, 203–211, and Glenn Burgess, *The Politics of the Ancient Constitution: An Introduction to English Political Thought, 1603–1642* (University Park: Pennsylvania State University Press, 1993), pp. 115–119, 129–138, 188. For other

eager to express their views on the issues raised in James's book was that these issues seemed, in the spring of 1610, to have considerable urgency. On May 14 in that year King Henry IV of France was assassinated by a one-time lay monk believed to have been influenced by Roman Catholic theologians who justified tyrannicide.[136] In England the Oath of Allegiance was extended by Act of Parliament to all persons over eighteen years of age, and was made a requirement for entering the learned professions.[137] Subscription by Roman Catholics in England was widespread, though certainly not universal.[138] Abroad, the issues raised by the controversy seemed relevant to every nation's political circumstances.

In the literary warfare that followed the publication of the king's book in 1609, Cardinal Bellarmine was ably supported by two well-regarded Jesuit theologians in Germany, Martin Becanus[139] and Jacobus Gretser,[140] and by

treatments of James's part in the controversy, see the books and articles on his political thought cited in chapter 1, above.

[136] Roland Mousnier, *The Assassination of Henry IV: The Tyrannicide Problem and the Consolidation of the French Absolute Monarchy in the Early Seventeenth Century*, trans. Joan Spencer (London: Faber and Faber, 1973), pp. 36–60, 97–105.

[137] Tanner, *Constitutional Documents of the Reign of James I*, pp. 105–109. James also responded to a petition from Parliament for the restraint of recusants and Roman Catholic priests by issuing a proclamation on June 2, 1610 for the strict enforcement of the penal laws, including the imposition of the Oath of Allegiance as required by law. See Larkin and Hughes, *Stuart Royal Proclamations*, vol. I, pp. 245–250.

[138] For subscriptions by Roman Catholics, see Usher, *The Reconstruction of the English Church*, vol. II, pp. 253–254. For indictments in London of persons who refused to take the oath, see Hugh Bowler, ed., *London Session Records, 1605–1685* (London: Catholic Record Society, 1934), Publications of the Catholic Record Society, vol. XXXIV, pp. 51–53, 56, 65, 71, 73, 81–82, 86, 383–385. For examples of both submission and refusal – and of the suffering caused by the imposition of the oath – see Clarence J. Ryan, "The Jacobean Oath of Allegiance and the English Lay Catholics," *Catholic Historical Review*, 28, 2 (July 1942), 159–183.

[139] Martin Becanus, *Serenissimi Iacobi Angliae Regis Apologiae & Monitoriae praefationis ad imperatorem, reges & principes refvtatio* (Mainz: Ioannes Albinus, 1610); *Refvtatio Torturae Torti seu contra sacellanum Regis Angliae, quod causam sui regis negligenter egerit* (Mainz: Ioannes Albinus, 1610); *Dvellvm Martini Becani, Societatis Iesv theologi cum Gulielmo Tooker* (Mainz: Ioannes Albinus, 1612); *Dissidivm anglicanvm de primatv regis, cum brevi praefatione ad Catholicos in Anglia degentes* (Mainz: Ioannes Albinus, 1612); *Controversia anglicana de potestate regis et pontificis, contra Lancelottvm, sacellanum Regis Angliae, qui se Episcopum Eliensem vocat, pro defensione illustrissimi Cardinalis Bellarmini* (Mainz: Ioannes Albinus, 1612); *Examen concordiae anglicanae de primatu ecclesiae regio* (Mainz: Ioannes Albinus, 1613). Two of Becanus's books were translated into English: *The Confutation of Tortura Torti: or, Against the king of Englandes Chaplaine, for That He Hath Negligently Defended His Kinges Cause* ([St. Omer: English College Press,] 1610) and *The English Iarre: or, Disagreement amongst the Ministers of Great Brittaine Concerning the Kinges Supremacy* ([St. Omer: English College Press,] 1612).

[140] Jacobus Gretser, βασιλικον Δωρον, *sive commentarivs exegeticvs in serenissimi Magnae Britanniae Regis Jacobi Praefationem monitoriam et in Apologiam pro iuramento fidelitatis* (Ingolstadt: Adam Sartor, 1610); *Antitortor Bellarminianus Joannes Gordonius Scotus pseudodecanus et capellanus Calvinisticus* (Ingolstadt, 1611).

the redoubtable Spanish Jesuit Francisco Suarez. Suarez's reply to James in 1613, the *Defensio fidei Catholicae*, was a fundamental work in political theory.[141] Becanus published six books in three years, beginning in 1610. There were two formidable opponents in France, the Dominican Nicolas Coeffeteau, who attempted to follow Henry IV's advice to use moderation in dealing with the ideas of the English king, and the Jesuit Andreas Eudaemon-Joannes, a vigorous controversialist who defended Bellarmine against attacks by English writers.[142] Bellarmine himself was ordered by the pope to answer James's *Premonition* and promptly brought out his *Apologia*, an expanded version of his *Responsio*, in 1610.[143] Writers on the side of the cardinal and the pope also included the Flemish Jesuit Leonard Lessius, the Dutch theologian Adolf Schulcken, the English Jesuits Thomas Fitzherbert and Anthony Hoskins, Humphrey Leech, a recent English convert to Rome, and Matthew Kellison, head of the English College at Douai.[144] Robert Parsons left his reply to Barlow unfinished on his death in 1610, but the work was completed and published by Fitzherbert, with a preface attacking Barlow written by the English Jesuit Edward Coffin.[145]

[141] Francisco de Suarez, *Defensio fidei Catholicae et apostolicae aduersus anglicanae sectae errores, cum responsione ad Apologiam pro iuramento fidelitatis & Praefationem monitoriam serenissimi Iacobi Angliae Regis; ad serenissimos totius Christiani orbis Catholicos reges ac principes* (Coimbra: Gomez de Loureyro, 1613).

[142] Nicolas Coeffeteau, *Responce a l'Advertissement adressé par le serenissime Roy de la Grande Bretagne Iacque I. à tous les princes & potentats de la Chrestienté* (Paris: François Hvby, 1610). Andreas Eudaemon-Joannes, *Ad actionem proditoriam Edouardi Coqui, apologia pro R. P. Henrico Garneto anglo* (Cologne: Joannes Kinckium, 1610) – a defense of Garnet against Sir Edward Coke, but the book deals with issues discussed in the controversy over the oath; *Parallelvs Torti ac tortoris eivs L. Cicestrensis: sive responsio ad Torturam Torti pro illvstr^mo Card. Bellarmino* (Cologne: Joannes Kinckius, 1611).

[143] Robert Bellarmine, *Apologia Roberti S. R. E. Cardinalis Bellarmini pro responsione sua ad librum Iacobi Magnae Britanniae Regis cuius titulus est Triplici nodo triplex cuneus: in qua apologia refellitur Praefatio monitoria regis eiusdem; accessit eadem ipsa responsio iam tertio recusa qua sub nomine Matthaei Torti anno superiore prodierat* (Rome: Bartholomew Zannetti, 1609).

[144] Leonard Lessius, *De Antichristo et eius praecursoribus disputatio apologetica gemina, qua refutatur Praefatio monitoria falso vt creditur adscripta Magnae Britanniae Regi* (Antwerp: Plantin, 1611). Adolph Schulcken, *Apologia Adolphi Schulckenii Geldriensis, S.S. theologiae apud Ubios doctoris et professoris atque ad D. Martini pastoris pro illustrissimo domino D. Roberto Bellarmino S.R.E. Card. de potestate Romani Pont. temporali* (Cologne, 1613). Thomas Fitzherbert, *A Supplement to the Discussion of M. D. Barlowes Answere to the Iudgment of a Catholike Englishman &c. Interrupted by the Death of the Author F. Robert Persons of the Society of Jesus* ([St. Omer: English College Press,] 1613). Anthony Hoskins, *A Briefe and Cleare Declaration of Sundry Pointes Absolutely Dislyked in the Lately Enacted Oath of Allegiance Proposed to the Catholikes of England* ([St. Omer: English College Press,] 1611). Humphrey Leech, *Dutifull and Respective Considerations upon Foure Severall Heads of Proofe and Triall in Matters of Religion* ([St. Omer: English College Press,] 1609). Matthew Kellison, *The Right and Iurisdiction of the Prelate and the Prince: or, A Treatise of Ecclesiasticall and Regall Authoritie* (Douai: P. Auroi, 1617).

[145] Robert Parsons and Thomas Fitzherbert, *A Discvssion of the Answere of M. William*

James had an array of allies, including several Roman Catholics. The Roman Catholic William Barclay, a Scot who taught in Lorraine, had already written against those whom he called "monarchomachs" – Calvinists such as George Buchanan, as well as radical Roman Catholics such as Jean Boucher and G. Rossaeus.[146] A manuscript by Barclay dealing with the powers of popes and kings was published just after his death in 1608 by his son John, after some editing and revision by Archbishop Bancroft. Though Barclay did not justify the oath, he took the Gallican approach on the powers of the papacy by limiting those powers to spiritual matters.[147] The English Roman Catholics George Blackwell and Thomas Preston had the misfortune of writing from prison, though they were apparently well treated there. Preston, a Benedictine priest who wrote under the name of Roger Widdrington, was the most prolific contributor to the entire controversy.[148] Richard Sheldon, another Roman Catholic priest, embraced the Church of England the year after his book appeared. William Warmington, a Roman Catholic priest of the Congregation of St. Ambrose, won release from prison by the publication of his book.[149] A Roman Catholic layman, William Barrett, was influenced to take the king's side by the arguments of

Barlow, *D. of Divinity, to the Booke Intituled The Iudgment of a Catholicke Englishman Living in Banishment for His Religion &c. Concerning the Apology of the New Oath of Allegiance* ([St. Omer: English College Press,] 1612).

[146] William Barclay, *De regno et regali potestate, adversus Buchananum, Brutum, Boucherium, & reliquos monarchomachos* (Paris: G. Chavdière, 1600). Barclay seems to have coined the term "monarchomachs" or king-fighters to describe the writers who justified armed resistance to kings in the late sixteenth century.

[147] William Barclay, *De potestate papae: an & quatenus in reges & principes seculares ius & imperium habeat*, ed. John Barclay ([London: Eliot's Court Press,] 1609). Barclay's book was translated into English as *Of the Avthoritie of the Pope: Whether and How Farre Forth He Hath Power and Authoritie over Temporall Kings and Princes* (London: William Aspley, 1611). At the time of his death in 1608, Barclay was professor of civil law at Angers in France. For the Gallican tradition on the respective powers of king and pope, and the similarities between Gallican views and those of James and his supporters, see J. H. M. Salmon, "Gallicanism and Anglicanism in the Age of the Counter-Reformation," in his *Renaissance and Revolt: Essays in the Intellectual and Social History of Early Modern France* (Cambridge: Cambridge University Press, 1987), pp. 155–188.

[148] George Blackwell, *In Georgivm Blacvellum Angliae archipresbyterum a Clemente Papa Octavo designatum quaestito bipartita: cuius actio prior archipresbyteri iusiurandum de fidelitate praestitum; altera eiusdem iuramenti assertionem contra Cardinalis Bellarmini literas continet* (London: J. Norton, 1609) – a translation into Latin of *A Large Examination Taken at Lambeth* (1607).

[149] Roger Widdrington [Thomas Preston], *Apologia Cardinalis Bellarmini pro ivre principvm: aduersus suas ipsius rationes pro auctoritate papali principes seculares in ordine ad bonum spirituale deponendi* ([London: Richard Field,] 1611); *A Cleare, Sincere, and Modest Confutation of the Unsound, Fraudulent, and Intemperate Reply of T. F. Who Is Known To Be Mr. Thomas Fitzherbert, Now an English Iesuite* ([London: Edward Griffin,] 1616). Preston published fourteen other books, including three translations. See Peter Milward, *Religious Controversies of the Jacobean Age: A Survey of Printed Sources* (London: Scolar Press, 1978), pp. 99–113.

Blackwell and Barclay.[150] Among the king's most effective supporters were foreign Protestants, including Isaac Casaubon, the foremost classical scholar of his day, who came to England from France after Henry IV's death,[151] and Pierre du Moulin, the Calvinist pastor in Charenton, near Paris, who made two trips to England.[152] Marco Antonio De Dominis, the Roman Catholic archbishop of Spalato, defected – temporarily – to England, where he published his massive *De republica ecclesiastica*.[153] The king could also count upon the support of his own learned clergy in the Church of England, including Lancelot Andrewes, one of Bellarmine's major opponents,[154] the poet John Donne, whose contributions to the controversy were so well received that the king apparently urged him to enter the ministry,[155] and a host of bishops, cathedral deans, university scholars, and parish clergy.

The many Roman Catholic attacks on James made serious demands on the clergy of the English Church. William Tooker, dean of Lichfield Cathedral, answered Becanus, as did Robert Burhill, rector of parishes in Norfolk and Cambridgeshire, Richard Harris, rector of a parish in Essex, and Richard Thomson, rector of a parish in Cambridgeshire.[156] John

---

[150] William Barret, *Ius regis, sive de absoluto & independenti secularium principum dominio & obsequio eis debito* ([London: N. Okes,] 1612).

[151] Isaac Casaubon, *Ad Frontonem Dvcaevm S. J. theologum epistola, in qua de apologia disseritur communi Iesuitarum nomine ante aliquot menses Lutetiae Parisorum edita* (London: Ioannes Norton, 1611); *De rebus sacris et ecclesiasticis exercitationes XVI. ad Cardinalis Baronii prolegomena in Annales & primam eorum partem* (London: Norton, 1614) – includes a *Digressio adversus Andream Eudaemono-Iohannem*, pp. 37–46.

[152] Pierre du Moulin, *Defense de la foy Catholique contenue au livre de trespuissant & serenissime Roy Iaques I Roy de la Grand' Bretagne & d'Irlande: contre la Response de F. N. Coeffeteau, docteur en theologie & vicaire general des Freres Prescheurs* ([Paris ?] 1610).

[153] Marco Antonio De Dominis, *De repvblica ecclesiastica pars secunda continens libros qvintrum et Sex^{tvm}* (London: John Bill, 1620). This second volume of a work which includes three volumes (1617–1622) contains a *Responsio ad magnam partem Defensionis fidei P. Francisci Suarez*, pp. 877–1009.

[154] Lancelot Andrewes, *Responsio ad Apologiam Cardinalis Bellarmini quam nuper edidit contra Praefationem monitoriam serenissimi ac potentissimi principis Iacobi, Dei gratia Magnae Britanniae, Franciae, & Hiberniae Regis, fidei defensoris, omnibus Christianis monarchis, principibus, atque ordinibus inscriptam* (London: Robert Barker, 1610).

[155] John Donne, *Pseudo-Martyr: Wherein out of Certaine Propositions and Gradations This Conclusion Is Evicted, That Those Which Are of the Romane Religion in This Kingdome May and Ought To Take the Oath of Allegeance* (London: W. Burre, 1610); *Conclaue Ignati: siue, eivs in nvperis inferni comitiis inthronisatio* ([London: William Hall, 1611]) – translated into English as *Ignatius His Conclaue: or, His Inthronisation in a Late Election in Hell* (London: Richard More, 1611). For Donne's vocation to the ordained ministry, see R. C. Bald, *John Donne: A Life*, corrected impression (Oxford: Clarendon Press, 1986), p. 227; the idea that the king urged Donne to enter the ministry goes back to Isaak Walton.

[156] William Tooker, *Dvellum siue singvlare certamen cum Martino Becano Iesuita, futiliter refutante Apologiam et Monitoriam praefatione* (London: N. Butter and R. Mab, 1611); Robert Burhill, *Pro Tortura Torti contra Martinum Becanum Iesuitam, Responsio* (London: R. Barker, 1611); *Contra Martini Becani Iesuitae Moguntini Controversiam anglicanam auctam & recognitam: assertio pro iure regio proque reu^{di} Episcopi Eliensis*

Gordon, the Scottish dean of Salisbury, wrote three books against Bellarmine.[157] Samuel Collins, chaplain to Archbishop Bancroft's successor, George Abbot, replied to Eudaemon-Joannes and to Thomas Fitzherbert.[158] George Carleton, formerly vicar of a parish in Sussex, John Buckeridge, bishop of Rochester, and Thomas Morton, bishop of Coventry and Lichfield, all answered books by Bellarmine.[159] Responding to both the Gunpowder Plot and the assassination of the French king, David Owen, a recent B.D. from Cambridge, and George Hakewill, a recent D.D. from Oxford, wrote books condemning the deposing and murdering of kings, citing the scriptures, the ancient fathers of the Church, and a long succession of theologians.[160] Robert Abbot, Regius professor of divinity at Oxford, published lectures opposing the teachings of both Bellarmine and

Responsione ad Apologiam Bellarmini (London: N. Butter, 1613); *De potestate regia et vsurpatione papali pro Tortvra Torti, contra Parallelum Andreae Evdaemonioannis Cydonii Iesuitae responsio* (Oxford: Joseph Barnes, 1613); Richard Harris, *Concordia anglicana de primatu ecclesiae regio: adversus Becanum de Dissidio anglicano* (London: G. Hall, 1612) – translated into English as *The English Concord: In Answer to Becane's English Iarre, Together with a Reply to Becan's Examen of the English Concord* (London: M. Lownes, 1614). Richard Thomson, *Elenchus refutationis Torturae Torti: pro reverendissimo in Christo patre domino Episcopo Eliense adversus Martinum Becanum Iesuitam* (London: R. Barker, 1611).

[157] John Gordon, *Antitortobellarminvs, siue refutatio calumniarum, mendaciorum et imposturarum laico-Cardinalis Bellarmini contra iura omnium regum et sinceram, illibatamque famam serenissimi, potentissimi piissimique principis Iacobi, Dei Gratia, Magnae Britanniae, Franciae et Hiberniae Regis, fidei Catholicae antiquae defensoris et propugnatoris* (London, 1610); *Orthodoxo-Iacobus et papapostaticus: sive theses confirmatae testimoniis Graecorum et Latinorum patrum qui vixerunt usque ad millesimum a Christo annum; quibus probatur serenissimum Regem Maximae Britanniae &c. esse Catholicae fidei verum defensorem & propugnatorem* (London: F. Kyngston, 1611); *Anti-Bellarmino-tortor, sive Tortus retortus & Iuliano-papismus* (London: R. Field, 1612).

[158] Samuel Collins, *Increpatio Andreae Eudaemono-Iohannis Iesuitae de infami Parallelo et renovata assertio Torturae Torti, pro clarissimo domino atque Antistite Eliensi* (Cambridge: C. Legge, 1612); *Epphata to F. T. or, The Defence of the Right Reverend Father in God, the Lord bishop of Elie, Lord High-Almoner and Privie Counsellour to the Kings Most Excellent Maiestie, Concerning His Answer to Cardinall Bellarmines Apologie* (Cambridge: C. Legge, 1617).

[159] George Carleton, *Iurisdiction Regall, Episcopall, Papall, Wherein Is Declared How the Pope Hath Intruded upon the Iurisdiction of Temporall Princes and of the Church: The Intrusion Is Discovered and the Peculiar and Distinct Iurisdiction to Each Properly Belonging, Recovered* (London: I. Norton, 1610). John Buckeridge, *De potestate papae in rebus temporalibus sive in regibus deponendis usurpata: adversus Robertum Cardinalem Bellarminum, libri duo* (London: Norton, 1614). Thomas Morton, *Causa regia, sive de authoritate et dignitate principum Christianorum dissertatio: adversus Rob. Cardinalis Bellarmini tractatum De officio principis Christiani inscriptum, edita* (London: John Bill, 1620).

[160] David Owen, *Herod and Pilate Reconciled: or, The Concord of Papist and Pvritan (against Scripture, Fathers, Councels, and Other Orthodoxall Writers) for the Coercion, Deposition, and Killing of Kings* (Cambridge: Cantrell Legge, 1610). George Hakewill, *Scvtum regivm: id est, adversvs omnes regicidas et regicidarvm patronos ab initio mundi vsque ad interitum Phocae Imp. circa annum ab incarnatione domini 610, ecclesiae Catholicae consensus orthodoxus* (London: John Budge, 1612).

Suarez.[161] James even tried to establish a college where learned divines could "be imployed to write, as occasion shall require, for maintaining the Religion professed in Our Kingdomes, and confuting the Impugners thereof."[162] An Act of Parliament provided for the college's support from the income from a water system supplying London; an endowment was raised, largely on the basis of the benefaction of Matthew Sutcliffe, the first provost; and seventeen divines together with two historians were appointed to the college in May 1610. But Chelsea College, which survived until the 1650s, never flourished, perhaps because of the jealousy of Oxford and Cambridge. One of its purposes was to give a group of English theologians the freedom from academic and pastoral duties which, it was believed, Roman Catholic theologians abroad often enjoyed.[163]

Bellarmine's political theory had been taught to students in Louvain and Rome for more than thirty years and was well known through his scholarly publications. As James Brodrick has shown, Bellarmine's was basically a view which had developed in the middle ages:

> In that grandest of all historical conceptions, Church and State, the twin spiritual and temporal powers, were to share amicably and according to recognized principles all the sovereign authority of the West. The Church in her own spiritual sphere was to have complete control, and the State, as by nature the lesser power, must listen to and be guided by her advice, even in such matters as had only an indirect bearing on the salvation of souls . . . At his coronation the king became the Lord's anointed – *Dei gratia rex* – and at the same time, he swore an oath that he would be the loyal protector of the Church . . . Should he, then, fail in his duty to the Church, the Pope might revoke his benediction and declare his crown forfeit.[164]

In his *Responsio* to James, expressed in the name of his chaplain, Bellarmine explained that the pope was the Vicar of Christ, as had been acknowledged in a multitude of general councils, "from which it manifestly follows, that he is able to direct and correct all Christians, even if they should be kings or princes."[165] In his *Apologia*, written to answer James's *Premonition*, he explained further that the popes were the successors of the Apostle Peter to

---

[161] Robert Abbot, *De suprema potestate regia exercitationes habitae in academia Oxoniensi contra Rob. Bellarminum & Francisc. Suarez* (London: Norton, 1616).

[162] Fuller, *The Church-History of Britain*, Bk. X, p. 52 – the quotation is from King James's letter to the archbishop of Canterbury in 1616 asking him to solicit support for the college from the bishops and other clergy in his province. The original fellows, appointed in 1610, included Thomas Morton and Robert Abbot, both of whom contributed books to the controversy which stemmed from the oath, and Richard Field, who developed the Church of England's conciliar theology, partly in response to the controversy. One of the two historians appointed to the college was John Hayward, who wrote in favor of the Royal Supremacy in matters of religion in 1606 (see below).

[163] Fuller, *The Church-History of Britain*, Bk. X, pp. 51–54.

[164] Brodrick, *Robert Bellarmine, 1542–1621*, vol. I, pp. 219–220.

[165] Bellarmine, *Matthaei Torti . . . responsio ad librvm inscriptvm triplici nodo, triplex cuneus*, p. 60.

whom Christ had entrusted the Church as a flock to a shepherd.[166] The spiritual authority of the popes thus derived immediately from God. The political or temporal authority of kings also came from God but was mediated through the people whom they governed. The two spheres, spiritual and temporal, were thus distinct, but there could be no doubt which was superior. Although the pope was not the temporal head of the Christian world, he did have an indirect temporal power which he could exercise in the event the spiritual well-being of the Church was threatened. He could, for example, depose a prince who was bent on subverting the Christian faith of his subjects.[167] Concerning James's exhortation to the Protestant princes to maintain their unity in the faith while avoiding needless controversies, Bellarmine asked pointedly how Protestants could avoid contentions when they admitted no judge except the scriptures, "which each one twists in favor of his own judgment and his own opinions?"[168] As for the king's urging Roman Catholic rulers to read the scriptures and to find there the standard of belief and the foundation of a personal faith, this was to open the door to all heresies. What James was arguing, said Bellarmine, was similar to the argument of the English theologian William Whitaker a few years earlier: namely that each person ought to be judge in matters of faith, "and to submit to his own judgement rather than that of the Church, or Councils, or Pope."[169]

Suarez, an equally formidable opponent of the king, was, like Bellarmine, deeply indebted to the thought of St. Thomas Aquinas. His political thought developed out of a tradition of Spanish scholasticism which had significantly influenced Roman Catholic theology in Europe for almost a century.[170] For Suarez, who was finishing a massive work on jurisprudence when he was asked to answer James's book, monarchy was of human origin and was the result of arrangements originally entered into by popular consent. But this did not mean that the power exercised by kings was not of divine origin – it was. Kings, moreover, were sovereign, though

---

[166] Bellarmine, *Apologia . . . pro responsione sva ad librvm Iacobi Magnae Britanniae Regis*, second edition (Rome: Bartholomew Zannetti [actually St. Omer: English College Press], 1610), p. 183.

[167] Brodrick, *Robert Bellarmine, 1542–1621*, vol. I, pp. 238, 261, 264, 266; vol. II, pp. 165–166, 169–224.

[168] Bellarmine, *Apologia . . . pro responsione sva ad librvm Iacobi Magnae Britanniae Regis*, second edition, p. 184.

[169] Ibid., p. 186. William Whitaker, Regius professor of divinity at Cambridge, had frequently taken issue with Bellarmine in his lectures. One volume of lectures directed against Bellarmine was published in 1588; others were published posthumously in 1599, 1600, 1608, and 1611.

[170] Bernice Hamilton, *Political Thought in Sixteenth-Century Spain: A Study of the Political Ideas of Vitoria, De Soto, Suárez, and Molina* (Oxford: Clarendon Press, 1963), *passim*. See also Francisco de Vitoria, *Political Writings*, ed. Anthony Pagden and Jeremy Lawrance (Cambridge: Cambridge University Press, 1991), pp. xiii–xxiii.

only in their proper, temporal sphere. The Church, which had its origin in divine positive law, had a mission superior to that of the civil authority – to prepare its members for eternal life. In carrying out that mission, the Church counseled, influenced, and directed its members as was appropriate for their spiritual destiny. But the Church, as a "perfect" or complete society and one therefore fully equipped to fulfill its purpose, might find it necessary to act more forcefully on occasion in order to carry out its mission. In an extreme case, if a king were a notorious tyrant or a heretic who persecuted the faithful, the Church could go so far as to depose him for his spiritual crimes and for the danger he represented to his own people.[171] Though Suarez did not call for such action in the case of England, he argued that the English king and the Church of England were heretical[172] and that the Oath of Allegiance imposed on English Roman Catholics was unjust and spiritually injurious. As for the papacy's being the Antichrist, he contended that the Antichrist could not be an institution or a succession of individuals but must be a single figure. Turning the tables on James, he asserted that whoever attacked the Chair of St. Peter and sought to undermine the authority of the apostle's legitimate successors, was himself a precursor of the Antichrist.[173]

On the other hand, the Roman Catholic writer William Barclay, whose posthumous book was dedicated to Pope Clement VIII, attacked the papal assertion of temporal authority over kings and princes as destabilizing and frequently counterproductive. In his *Of the Avthoritie of the Pope*, Barclay cited Boniface VIII's confrontation with Philip IV of France and the harm done to the Church by the succeeding era of the Avignon papacy and the Great Schism. More recent examples of the harm done by popes in attempting to exercise temporal power included Julius II's military efforts and diplomacy against Louis XII of France, and Pius V's attempt to depose Elizabeth.[174] Such policies forced rulers to seek the support of opponents of the papacy. The papacy had never had any legitimate right to depose princes and had never interfered in the temporal affairs of princes before Pope Gregory VII's time. Bellarmine's theory of the indirect temporal power of the papacy was a theory of absolute power in disguise. How could kings be superior in temporalities if "an other may by law take their temporalities from them and give them to another"? This was to make the pope superior in temporal things.[175] Barclay had no doubt of the spiritual supremacy of

---

[171] Pierre Mesnard, *L'essor de la philosophie politique au XVIe siècle*, third edition (Paris: J. Vrin, 1969), pp. 620–634, 648–652. Suarez's *De legibus* was published in 1612.

[172] Suarez, *Defensio fidei Catholicae et apostolicae aduersus anglicanae sectae errores*, pp. 65–71.

[173] Mesnard, *L'essor de la philosophie politique au XVIe siècle*, p. 642.

[174] Barclay, *Of the Avthoritie of the Pope*, sig. 2, pp. 163–164.   [175] Ibid., pp. 62–63.

the pope or of his power to excommunicate erring members of the Church, even kings. But he denied that the pope had any temporal authority over princes and that the purported power to depose them was contrary to the Church's interests. The way for Roman Catholics to win kings from policies of repression to moderation and from error to truth was by political obedience and persuasion.[176]

Roman Catholics who wrote on the ecclesiastical supremacy of the pope were of three schools, as David Owen pointed out in 1610. There were canon lawyers like Alexander Carerius who granted the pope "absolute power over all the World, both in Ecclesiasticall, and Politicall Things"; a middle group, including Bellarmine, which denied the pope temporal power over kings directly, but gave him virtually unlimited temporal power "by an indirect prerogatiue"; and those who, like William Barclay and George Blackwell, allowed the pope "spirituall power to excommunicate Kings" but no temporal power, directly or indirectly, "to afflict the persons of Kings, to transpose their kingdomes, to perswade forrainers to make warres, or subiects to rebell against them."[177] Owen showed also the parallels between Roman Catholic theories which justified resistance to rulers and the theories of Protestants from Calvin to Buchanan to Hotman justifying such resistance. Roman Catholic and Protestant extremists were thus largely in agreement, like the Jewish ruler Herod and the Roman procurator Pilate in their condemnation of Christ. In contrast, the scriptures, fathers, and ancient councils required loyalty and obedience to temporal rulers. Their teachings still remained valid: all persons in a ruler's dominions "stand bound in lawe, allegiance, and conscience" to obey their temporal king.[178] Andrewes confronted Bellarmine and other Roman Catholics directly on the doctrine of the pope's temporal power. The doctrine had frequently been challenged on historical as well as theological grounds. It was not *de fide*, only a matter of opinion. Roman Catholic writers themselves had objected to the deposing and the dispensing powers. As a practical matter such powers produced instability in international relations. What treaty could be secure if the pope could release one or more signatories from the obligation to keep it?[179] Preston also opposed Bellarmine on the issue of the deposing power. Using the theory of "probabilism" which many Jesuits – Bellarmine's own order – employed, Preston argued that it was only probable at best that the pope had such temporal power

---

[176] Ibid., p. 163. See also Salmon, *The French Religious Wars in English Political Thought*, pp. 34–35, 72–74.

[177] Owen, *Herod and Pilate Reconciled*, sigs. ¶²–¶² verso.

[178] Ibid., sigs. ¶² verso–¶⁴; pp. 41–42, 46–51, 75.

[179] Andrewes, *Tortvra Torti*, pp. 16–31, 58–61. See also Paul A. Welsby, *Lancelot Andrewes, 1555–1626* (London: SPCK, 1958), p. 147.

and authority and that he could depose princes. In the light of the objections raised to the doctrine, it could hardly be considered binding on the faithful. In the case of the Oath of Allegiance, which condemned the deposing power, a Roman Catholic could subscribe to the oath even if it were more probable that the pope had such a power.[180] John Donne asserted that he was from a family which had suffered much for its Roman Catholicism, but that not every pretense of the pope was worth defending by martyrdom.[181] Supporters of the pope's temporal power had never adequately explained the origin of this power or what, if anything, its limitations were. The exercise of temporal power by the papacy had been opposed by many Catholic leaders and spokesmen: "how can that be so [much a] matter of faith, which is vnder disputation and perplexitie with them"?[182] To call the doctrine of the deposing power "heretical," as the Oath of Allegiance did, was not to call into question the pope's spiritual power. It was to point out that the deposing power was "inducing of Heresy" by impugning the civil obedience which was a part of every Christian's faith and duty.[183]

One of the conspicuous features of the controversy was the attention given to the history, nature, and purpose of general councils. This is hardly surprising, considering the importance of conciliar decrees in the development of Christian doctrine and the reliance by writers on both sides of the controversy on evidence provided by councils since antiquity. But James's discussion, in his *Premonition*, of the general council as a means of bringing Roman Catholics and non-Roman Catholics back together made the subject one of particular interest and concern. After the publication of the *Premonition*, Bellarmine responded to James's charge that the College of Cardinals had largely usurped the place of general councils in the governance of the Church by pointing out how many councils had been held with the help and support of the cardinals.[184] In responding to the king's statement that "if euer there were a possibilitie to bee expected of reducing all Christians to an uniformity of Religion, it must come by meanes of a generall Councell," he defended the Council of Trent as the Church's effort to do just that. The council, Bellarmine observed, had been attended by representatives of the emperor and many kings, as James wished such a council to be. Its location

[180] Widdrington [Preston], *A Cleare, Sincere, and Modest Confutation*, "Epistle to English Catholikes," sigs. B₂–D₃ verso; p. 33. See also Maurus Lunn, "English Benedictines and the Oath of Allegiance, 1606–1647," *Recusant History*, 10 (1969–1970), 146–163, and "The Anglo-Gallicanism of Dom Thomas Preston, 1567–1647," in Derek Baker, ed., *Schism, Heresy and Religious Protest* (Cambridge: Cambridge University Press, 1972), Studies in Church History, IX, pp. 239–246.

[181] Donne, *Pseudo-Martyr*, sigs. ¶₁, C₃.

[182] Ibid., p. 204; see also pp. 15–17, 69–77, 182.

[183] Ibid., p. 385. See also Bald, *John Donne: A Life*, pp. 200–227.

[184] Bellarmine, *Apologia . . . pro responsione sva ad librvm Iacobi Magnae Britanniae Regis*, p. 28.

had been convenient to both Germany and Italy. Protestants had been invited, and safe-conducts offered to them.[185] Bellarmine seemed to be saying that if Protestants had not been won back by the Council of Trent, there was no reason to think that another council would have a different result. On this subject, Humfrey Leech, with the help of Robert Parsons, developed further the idea of the implacability of the Protestants and the impracticality of attempting to arrive at an agreement with them in a council. If general councils were the key to unity, why "haue the Protestants in our dayes (hauing now almost had a full age, since their defection from Catholicke Roman Religion) neuer as yet called a generall Councell amōgst themselves, to repaire their owne breaches, reconcile their owne enmities, determine and decide their owne controuersies"?[186] The reason, he said, was their insistence upon the scriptures as the norm and rule for decisions, a principle the Lutherans specified as a condition of their attendance at Trent. Since Protestants did not all understand key scriptural passages in the same way, they had not been able to achieve agreements among themselves in "Conferences, Colloquies, Disputations, Synods or Councells."[187] As for James's acceptance – and the English Parliament's acceptance – of the first four general councils, why did he not accept the Church that assembled there: visible, magnificent, and endued with sanctity? If James accepted the first four councils, why not the "fourteene other no lesse Generall, from that of Chalcedon to the last of Trent"?[188] Becanus took Andrewes's discussion of what should characterize a general council seriously enough to suggest that Protestants should not start from the position that the pope is Antichrist any more than Roman Catholics should start from the position that Lutherans and Calvinists are heretics.[189] If factitious churchmen were to be excluded, what country had more of them than England?[190] Suarez took issue with James's assertion that popes were subject to general councils, as demonstrated by the Council of Constance, where three popes were deposed or induced to abdicate and a fourth was elected. Suarez asserted that none of the three was legitimate. Once the true pope was elected, "in him was the fulness of papal power, superior to that same council, because he did not have his power from the council but from Christ."[191]

The treatment of the subject of general councils by James's supporters drew on the history of the earliest councils, whose validity these writers

---

[185] Ibid., pp. 28–29.
[186] Leech, *Dvtifvll and Respective Considerations*, p. 170. For the contribution of Parsons to the book, see Thompson Cooper's article on Leech in *The Dictionary of National Biography*, 22 vols. (London: Oxford University Press, 1959–1960), vol. XI, p. 827.
[187] Leech, *Dvtifvll and Respective Considerations*, p. 175.   [188] Ibid., pp. 160, 169.
[189] Becanus, *Controversia Anglicana*, p. 169.   [190] Ibid., p. 171.
[191] Suarez, *Defensio fidei Catholicae*, p. 311.

accepted. They were also influenced by late medieval conciliar theory, which placed the authority of the general council above that of the pope, and by the example of the fifteenth-century councils of Constance and Basel. Andrewes, writing in defense of James against Bellarmine, cited documents from antiquity to show that the first four general councils – Nicaea, Constantinople, Ephesus, and Chalcedon – were all convened by the Christian emperors of the fourth and fifth centuries to safeguard the purity of the faith. Furthermore, despite the honor paid to bishops of Rome by the councils and the emperors themselves, it was the emperors who confirmed these councils' decrees.[192] If, as Bellarmine claimed, only the pope had the legitimate power to call a council, why, asked Andrewes, were there no general councils called to meet in Rome in the ancient period?[193] The emperor's sole right to call councils was reflected in imperial law, which forbade any assembly to be convened for the sake of religion unless the emperor had given his prior consent.[194] Burhill showed from the decrees of the first four general councils that the sees of Antioch, Alexandria, and Constantinople shared the prestige accorded to Rome.[195] Preston used late medieval conciliar theory to show that some questions in theology had not been settled. Though Cardinal Thomas de Vio Caietan asserted in the early sixteenth century that the pope was superior to a general council, this view was challenged by his contemporaries the Roman Catholic theologians John Major and Jacques Almain, and it had earlier been opposed as erroneous and heretical by Jean Gerson.[196]

In further support of James's urging of a general council, Carleton cited the decree *Haec sancta* from the Council of Constance to show that the general council was the appropriate body to settle theological disputes, heal schisms, and undertake reforms in the Church. After discussing the councils of Constance and Basel Carleton commented that "we are the children of them that held these councils."[197] If the Council of Trent had followed the examples of Constance and Basel and had met several other criteria – including free access to all nations and the acceptance of the scriptures as "the onely iudge of controuersies" – then "would wee admit that Councell to bee free and generall."[198] Carleton's treatment of councils and their place in the governance of the Church drew on the writings of Gerson, Nicholas of Cusa, and Aeneas Sylvius Piccolomini before he became Pope Pius II.[199] The conciliar theology expressed by supporters of the king had been developed in the Church of England quite apart from the controversy over

[192] Andrewes, *Tortura Torti*, pp. 165–166.   [193] Ibid., p. 168.   [194] Ibid., p. 350.
[195] Burhill, *De potestate regia*, pp. 98–100, 126.
[196] Widdrington [Preston], *A Cleare, Sincere, and Modest Confutation*, pp. 33–34.
[197] Carleton, *Iurisdiction: Regall, Episcopall, Papall*, pp. 274, 280.   [198] Ibid., p. 280.
[199] Ibid., pp. 283–301.

the oath. The canons of the Church which were drawn up by Convocation in 1606, though they never received the royal assent, defined the "one Catholick Church of Christ" as visible on earth "by the several, and particular Churches in it, and sometimes by general and free Councils lawfully assembled."[200] In the same year the historian John Hayward wrote a book about "supreme power in affairs of religion" in which he wrote that whenever "any great schisme or disturbance was maintained in the church" in the ancient period, the emperors would "assemble their Bishops in common Councell" to resolve them.[201] He cited Nicholas of Cusa to show that "the Emperours and their Iudges, with the Senate, had the primacie and office of presidence in the [first] eight generall Councels."[202] This was also the year in which the first volume of Richard Field's *Of the Church* was published. Field, a friend and disciple of Richard Hooker, described the general council as the highest level of jurisdiction in the Church, where disputes about the interpretation of scripture could be definitively settled: "they haue supreme power, that is the Bishoppes assembled in a generall Councell, may interpret the scripture, and by their authoritie suppresse all them that shall disobey such determinations as they consent vppon, to excommunication and censures of like nature."[203]

Discussion of general councils also turned up in some unexpected places. In late May 1606, James ordered eight Scottish ministers to come to his court in England to deliberate with him about "matteres concerneing the peice of our Kirk of Scotland."[204] The immediate issue was a bitter controversy in Scotland over whether a General Assembly of the Kirk could be held without first obtaining the king's permission. James had ordered the postponement of the summer meeting of the General Assembly in 1605, but a meeting had nevertheless been held at Aberdeen in early July. This

---

[200] John Overall, *Bishop Overall's Convocation-Book, MDCVI., Concerning the Government of God's Catholick Church and the Kingdoms of the Whole World* (London: Walter Kettilby, 1690), p. 273. For James's reasons for rejecting the canons, see Edward Cardwell, ed., *Synodalia: A Collection of Articles of Religion, Canons, and Proceedings of Convocations in the Province of Canterbury, from the Year 1547 to the Year 1717*, 2 vols. (Oxford: Oxford University Press, 1842), vol. I, pp. 330–334.

[201] John Hayward, *A Reporte of a Discovrse Concerning Svpreme Power in Affaires of Religion: Manifesting That This Power Is a Right of Regalitie, Inseparably Annexed to the Soueraigntie of Euery State* (London: Iohn Hardie, 1606), p. 30.

[202] Ibid., pp. 31–32.

[203] Richard Field, *Of the Church, Five Bookes* (London: Simon Waterson, 1606), p. 228. For Field's relationship with Hooker, see Richard Hooper on Field in the *Dictionary of National Biography*, vol. VI, p. 1276; and Nathaniel Field, *Some Short Memorials Concerning the Life of That Reverend Divine, Doctor Richard Field, Prebendarie of Windsor and Dean of Glocester*, ed. John Le Neve (London: Henry Clements, 1717), p. 19.

[204] James Melville, *The Autobiography and Diary*, ed. Robert Pitcairn (Edinburgh: Wodrow Society, 1842), p. 636. See also James Kerr Cameron, ed., *Letters of John Johnston, c. 1565–1611, and Robert Howie, c. 1565–c. 1645* (Edinburgh: Oliver & Boyd for the University of St. Andrews, 1963), pp. lxix–lxxi.

subsequently led to the imprisonment of a substantial number of ministers on charges of treason, some of whom were found guilty in early 1606.[205] The eight ministers summoned to the king's presence included Andrew Melville, the most influential leader of the Kirk and his nephew James Melville. The continuing controversy over the holding of assemblies in the summer of 1606 coincided with action in the Scottish Parliament in 1606 providing endowments for the recently revived episcopal sees. This was a critical moment in the history of the Kirk. James's long-range policy of seeking greater control over the Kirk in the interest of achieving peace and stability in Scotland and of bringing the Scottish and English churches into greater conformity with one another seemed to be taking effect.

The visiting ministers were treated to four sermons between September 21 and 30, 1606 by leading preachers in the Church of England, all of whom sought to inculcate their northern brethren with the point of view of the English Church. William Barlow, bishop of Rochester, preached on church government by bishops; John Buckeridge, president of St. John's College, Oxford, preached on the royal supremacy; Lancelot Andrewes preached on "the right and power of calling assemblies"; and John King, dean of Christ Church, Oxford, preached on ecclesiastical discipline.[206] All but King's sermon discussed general councils, which were hardly at issue in Scotland, though the subject was, of course, related to both bishops and the convening of ecclesiastical assemblies. Barlow sought to ground the "conuenting of Bishoppes and the inferior Clergie" in councils – provincial, national, and ecumenical – on the fifteenth and twentieth chapters of the Book of Acts.[207] Buckeridge cited the examples of the calling of the first four general councils by Christian emperors as instances of the exercise of the ecclesiastical supremacy by temporal rulers: "Since Emperours became (like Constantine) fathers of the Church, the causes of the Church haue depended vpon their will: And therefore the greatest Councels haue bene, and yet are called by their Authoritie."[208] Andrewes's treatment of the subject accorded councils immense significance in the life of the Church. Heresies, he noted, "haue

[205] Melville, *The Autobiography and Diary*, pp. 560–625; Lee, *Government by Pen*, pp. 47–56.
[206] William Barlow, *One of the Foure Sermons Preached before the Kings Maiestie, at Hampton Court in September Last: This Concerning the Antiquitie and Superioritie of Bishops, Sept. 21, 1606* (London: Matthew Law, 1606); John Buckeridge, *A Sermon Preached at Hampton Court before the Kings Maiestie on Tuesday the 23. of September, Anno 1606* (London: Robert Barker, 1606); Lancelot Andrewes, *A Sermon Preached before the Kings Maiestie at Hampton Court Concerning the Right and Power of Calling Assemblies, on Sunday the 28. of September, Anno 1606* (London: Robert Barker, 1606); John King, *The Fovrth Sermon Preached at Hampton Covrt on Tuesday the Last of Sept. 1606* (Oxford: Joseph Barnes, 1606).
[207] Barlow, *One of the Foure Sermons*, sig. B₁.
[208] Buckeridge, *A Sermon Preached at Hampton Court*, p. 34; see also 30–33.

euer bin best put to flight by the Churchs Assemblies, (that is) Councels, as it were by the Armies of Gods Angels (as Eusebius calleth them)."[209] Likewise abuses had been redressed by canons made by the Church in councils "and not elsewhere."[210] Once the temporal rulers became Christians, provincial, national, and general councils were held under their authority, and all seven ancient general councils – the only general councils, since only they included bishops from both East and West – were convened by emperors. Subsequent general councils were of the western church only, with the exception of the abortive council of Ferrara – Florence, called to help the East in its losing struggle against the Ottomans.[211] The convening of western councils by popes was a usurpation on their part of the function which properly belonged to kings and emperors. The right to call assemblies of both the congregation and the camp – that is, the Church and the body politic – had been given by God to Moses, Andrewes asserted, at the same time that he had been given the divine law.[212]

Despite elaborate efforts to persuade the eight ministers of the rightness of the points urged by the king's four preachers – efforts which involved the Scottish Council as well as Scottish and English bishops – James seemed to make little headway with them. Finally, Andrew Melville overstepped himself by writing scurrilous verses about the English liturgy and by insulting Archbishop Bancroft in the king's presence.[213] In April 1607 he was sent to the Tower, while his nephew was shortly afterwards sent to Newcastle in the north of England, where he was forced to remain. The other six ministers were allowed to return to Scotland. Meanwhile six ministers convicted of treason in Scotland were exiled abroad. Andrew Melville followed them when he was appointed in 1611 to a chair in theology at the Reformed Academy in Sedan in France. With the king's opposition in the Kirk thus crippled, a functioning system of episcopacy, operating in conjunction with the General Assembly, was instituted in Scotland in 1610.[214]

A proposal for a general council was also a part of James's diplomacy during the crisis in relations between the papacy and Venice between 1605 and 1607. At issue was the whole framework of laws and customs by which the Republic of Venice sought to control and direct the Church within its borders. Pope Paul V found particularly objectionable two recent decrees

---

[209] Andrewes, *A Sermon Preached before the Kings Maiestie*, p. 1.   [210] Ibid., p. 11.
[211] Ibid., p. 33. Andrewes said of his treatment of the seven general councils that it was based on "the very actes of the Councels themselves." (p. 33) At the end of the sermon he acknowledged his source: "The Edition of the Councels here alledged, is that of Venice, by Dominicus Nicolinus in fiue Tomes" (p. 55).
[212] Ibid., pp. 1–3, 45.
[213] Melville, *The Autobiography and Diary*, pp. 653–683.
[214] Ibid., pp. 683–710, 792–804.

that provided that no ecclesiastical building could be erected and no real property could be conveyed to the Church without the permission of the state. In addition, the pope was concerned about the cases of two clerics who had been accused before civil rather than ecclesiastical courts.[215] In April 1606 Pope Paul announced that he intended to excommunicate the Senate and place the territory under interdict – prohibiting the administration of the sacraments – if the two decrees were not repealed and the imprisoned clerics handed over to him. The crisis involved not just Venice and the papacy but much of Italy as well as France and Spain. Venice forbade the publication of the interdict, while the monk Paolo Sarpi, who became the official theologian and canon lawyer of Venice, argued in print that the pope had misused his powers and must be resisted.[216] The possibility of opposing alliances began to take shape. In May 1606 Sir Henry Wotton, the English ambassador, offered Venice his country's support and proposed a league including France, some of the Swiss cantons, and possibly a German principality for the defense of the republic.[217] Philip III of Spain backed the papacy. In the autumn of 1606 fear was almost palpable in northern Italy that Spain, which controlled Milan, would use this crisis as a pretext to invade Venice.

James had quite a different proposal for resolving the issues in dispute. In discussing his ideas on this subject with Zorzi Giustinian, the Venetian ambassador in England, on June 14, 1606 he first made clear his support of Venice in the matter of the republic's laws concerning ecclesiastical property and the treatment of clerics accused of civil crimes: "They are pious, most just, most necessary laws. Not only do I approve, I commend and sustain them. The world would indeed be fortunate if every Prince would open his eyes and behave as the Republic does."[218]

---

215 Roberto Cessi, *Storia della Repubblica di Venezia*, 2 vols. (Milan: Giuseppe Principato, 1944–46), vol. II, pp. 146–147; William J. Bouwsma, *Venice and the Defense of Republican Liberty: Renaissance Values in the Age of the Counter Reformation* (Berkeley: University of California Press, 1968), pp. 339–350. See also Pastor, *The History of the Popes*, vol. XXV, pp. 114–126.

216 Bouwsma, *Venice and the Defense of Republican Liberty*, pp. 358–370; David Wootton, *Paolo Sarpi: Between Renaissance and Enlightenment* (Cambridge: Cambridge University Press, 1983), pp. 1–11, 45–76, 131–135.

217 *Calendar of State Papers and Manuscripts, Relating to English Affairs Existing in the Archives and Collections of Venice, and in Other Libraries of Northern Italy*, 40 vols. (London: HMSO, 1864–1947), vol. X, pp. 348–349; Logan Pearsall Smith, ed., *The Life and Letters of Sir Henry Wotton*, 2 vols. (Oxford: Clarendon Press, 1907), vol. I, p. 349 note. Discussions of a military alliance for the defense of Venice took place in London and Venice in September and October, 1606. See PRO SP 99/3, fols. 168–168 verso (Wotton to Salisbury, September 12, 1606), fols. 187–190 (Salisbury to Wotton, October 2, 1606), fols. 200–201 (Wotton to Salisbury, October 24, 1606); *Calendar of State Papers, Venetian*, vol. X, pp. 409–411 (Zorzi Giustinian to the Doge and Senate, October 11, 1606).

218 *Calendar of State Papers*, Venetian, vol. X, pp. 359–360; Enrico Cornet, ed., *Paolo V. e la*

He continued by holding out the prospect of treating the Venetian crisis in a forum in which the larger problems of Christendom could be resolved:

I have no greater desire than to see the Church of God reformed of those abuses introduced by the Church of Rome. There is nothing I am more desirous of than the convocation of a legitimate Council. I have informed the king of France, with whom I am on good terms, and who knows but that through these present troubles of the Republic God may open the way for the effectuation of my pious purpose.[219]

The idea of appealing Venice's case to a general council was in fact being talked about in Venice and was not without supporters. It was, however, eventually discarded by the republic's statesmen as being too unpredictable.[220]

The mobilization of troops by Spain and France helped to bring Venice and the papacy to the realization that another war of the kind which had devastated Italy in the previous century ought to be avoided if at all possible. By the end of 1606 negotiations were making real progress, especially after Henry IV sent his kinsman, Cardinal François de Joyeuse, to help make peace.[221] The final settlement was expertly framed to protect the sensibilities of both parties, while restoring as much as possible the situation which had existed earlier. The two imprisoned clerics were handed over to Cardinal Joyeuse, who turned them over to representatives of the papacy. The laws which had offended the papacy were not withdrawn, though the republic pledged to the kings of Spain and France that they would be used moderately. The interdict, which the republic had not allowed to be effective, was withdrawn. By June 1607 the crisis was over.[222] At the same time an opportunity passed for a broader settlement of issues between the papacy and the temporal states of Europe. James saw Venice as the victim of papal encroachments in the political sphere at a time when his own throne had been threatened by Roman Catholics. The pamphlet warfare during the Venetian crisis turned out to be a rehearsal for the more extensive controversy over the Oath of Allegiance.

The fullest exposition of English conciliar theory was published in 1610

Repubblica Veneta: Giornale dal 22. Ottobre 1605 – 9. Giugno 1607 (Vienna: Tendler, 1859), p. 109.

[219] *Calendar of State Papers*, Venetian, vol. X, p. 360; Cornet, ed., *Paolo V. e la Repubblica Veneta*, p. 109.

[220] Cessi, *Storia della Repubblica*, vol. II, p. 147; Bouwsma, *Venice and the Defense of Republican Liberty*, p. 370. Sarpi had begun his career as official spokesman for Venice by issuing a tract by the conciliarist Jean Gerson. See Wotton, *Paolo Sarpi*, p. 48.

[221] PRO SP 99/3, fol. 248 (Wotton to Salisbury, December 1606); Pastor, *The History of the Popes*, vol. XXV, pp. 167–183; Bouwsma, *Venice and the Defense of Republican Liberty*, pp. 412–416.

[222] For an outline of the terms of the settlement, see Wotton's letter to Sir Thomas Edmondes, English ambassador at Brussels, May 18, 1607, in Smith, *The Life and Letters of Sir Henry Wotton*, vol. I, p. 389.

in the fifth book of Richard Field's *Of the Church*, a treatise evidently intended to be a semiofficial treatment of ecclesiology and a companion work to Hooker's *Laws of Ecclesiastical Polity*.[223] In addition to dealing more comprehensively with the conciliar issues treated by Andrewes, Barlow, Buckeridge, and James himself, Field spoke of the general council in a way which suggested that it was still a live possibility. This is not surprising since the king's own proposal, set forth in his *Premonition*, was already on the table. Field's concept of the membership of the Church was inclusive: all whom God had called in Christ to salvation and eternal life.[224] The Catholic or universal Church therefore included the churches of Greece, Armenia, Ethiopia, and Russia, though they had been condemned as heretical or schismatic by Rome. The Latin Church, despite its abuses and superstitions, was undoubtedly a member. So too were the various Protestant churches.[225] The way to settle disputes within the Catholic Church had long since been provided for in various councils, including those at the diocesan, metropolitan, and patriarchal level. At the highest level was the general council, where the bishop of Rome was entitled to the chief place: "And in such cases as could not be so ended, or that concerned the faith, and the state of the whole Vniuersall Church, there remained the iudgement, and resolution of a generall Councell; wherein the bishop of the first Sea was to sit as President, and moderatour; and the other Bishops of the Christian world, as his fellow Iudges, and in the same commission with him."[226]

Field stressed the important place of the papacy both in a general council and in the life of the Church. He made it clear that the bishop of Rome, though he had no temporal authority nor an "infallible iudgement in discerning" was the appropriate presiding officer in a general council.[227] "The greatest thing that eyther hee can challenge or wee yeeld vnto him, is to bee the prime Bishop in order and honour."[228] In association with others, especially "in the companies, assemblies, and synodes of Bishops and Pastors" he was to manage the affairs of the Church.[229] The "highest and most excellent exercise of the supreme Ecclesiasticall iurisdiction, is in Generall Councels"; they "are the best meanes of preseruing of vnity of doctrine, seuerity of discipline, and preuenting of Schismes."[230] As presiding

---

[223] Richard Field, *The Fifth Booke, Of the Chvrch, Together with an Appendix, Containing a Defense of Such Partes and Passages of the Former Bookes as Have Bene Either Excepted against or Wrested to the Maintenance of Romish Errours* (London: Simon Waterson, 1610).

[224] Ibid., sig. A₃. Compare Field, *Of the Church, Five Bookes*, p. 15.

[225] Field, *The Fifth Booke, Of the Chvrch*, pp. 371, 175. Compare Field, *Of the Church, Five Bookes*, pp. 71–72.

[226] Field, *The Fifth Booke, Of the Chvrch*, sig. B₁.   [227] Ibid., p. 367.   [228] Ibid.

[229] Ibid., pp. 367–368.   [230] Ibid., p. 371.

officer, the bishop of Rome would be entitled "to propose things to bee debated, to direct the actions, and to giue definitiue sentence, according to the voyces and iudgement of the Councell."[231] To be effective, the council must permit freedom of speech; those attending would be expected to seek "the common good, that priuate respects, purposes and designes bee not set forward vnder pretence of religion."[232] The calling of general councils, however, was the responsibility of the prince. In the ancient period, general councils were invariably called by emperors. Now that the political control exercised by the emperor extended over a smaller area, the right of calling such general councils lay "in the concurrence of Christian Princes, without which no lawfull Generall Councell can euer bee had."[233]

Two further books aimed at readers on the continent took up the appeal for a general council, though neither seems to have generated much enthusiasm. An anonymous French tract, now attributed to George Marcelline, appeared in 1609 and in an English translation as *The Triumphs of King Iames*, the year after.[234] It called upon the kings, the protectors of the churches, to "make of vs one heritage, that this seame-lesse Garment of our Lord may no more be torn in peeces."[235] To achieve this end, "it is necessary, that a good, free, and lawfull Counsell should bee called and assembled, by you Princes and Soueraigne Estates"[236] The time was right for such a step, since there was a willingness by many to submit themselves to such a council's decisions. The author described James in flattering terms and asserted that he was capable of presiding over such a council as Constantine had done at Nicaea.[237] He hoped that James would deliver the nations from the tyranny of Antichrist and "vnder the name and family of Steuart" bring Christendom together under his absolute rule.[238] In Paris, the moderate Roman Catholic Pierre de l'Estoile, found the book to resemble cicadas: "for it is thin and cries very loud."[239]

The other book, a *Svpplicatio* to the emperor, kings, and princes of Europe, published in 1613, originated in Italy and was probably the work of Giacomo Antonio Marta, a Paduan professor of law. William Crashaw translated the book into English in 1622 as *The New Man*, the name by which it is generally known.[240] The Church of Rome, the author asserted,

---

[231] Ibid., pp. 384–385.   [232] Ibid., pp. 377–378.   [233] Ibid., p. 414.

[234] [George Marcelline,] *Les trophees dv Roi Iacques I. de la Grande Bretaigne, France, et Irelande* ([London ?] A. Elevtheres, 1609); *The Triumphs of King Iames the First of Great Brittaine, France, and Ireland, King* ([London:] Iohn Budge, 1610).

[235] [Marcelline,] *The Triumphs of King Iames the First*, pp. 24–25 (incorrectly numbered as 14–19).

[236] Ibid., p. 26.   [237] Ibid., p. 27.   [238] Ibid., pp. 63, 69.

[239] Pierre de l'Estoile, *Journal pour le règne de Henri IV*, ed. Louis-Raymond Lefèvre and André Martin, 3 vols. (Paris: Gallimard, 1948–1960), vol. III, p. 29.

[240] [Giacomo Antonio Marta,] *Svpplicatio ad imperatorem, reges, principes, svper cavsis generalis concilij convocandi contra Pavlvm Qvintvm* (London: Bonham Norton, 1613);

was "destitute of a Pastor, and all the world rings of the Intrusion, Symony and sluggishness now raigning in Rome."[241] He appealed to James to enlist the aid of the emperor, kings, and princes of Europe for a "vniuersall reformation."[242] Unlike King James, the author considered that Pope Paul V had not been energetic enough in defending the jurisdiction of his see in the altercation with Venice, where the pope had made an ignominious surrender. Venice's example, the author complained, would now be taken up by other Italian states.[243] A French version published in Leyden was a free translation and expansion by Nicolas de Marbais, who had apparently left Roman Catholicism for Protestantism.[244] De Marbais elaborated on the crimes and vices of the pope and the cardinals, as described in the *Svpplicatio*, and excoriated the temporal pretensions of the papacy which had caused such difficulties for Henry IV of France and had ultimately cost the king his life.[245]

III

As much as anything else the controversy over the Oath of Allegiance showed the highly wrought intellectual and emotional state of Europe during the interval between two devastating wars in which religion played a major role. The peace which European statesmen had achieved at the beginning of the century seemed destined to be short-lived, if the intensity of feeling which these writings communicated was any indication. James, of course, had hoped to recover something of the lost unity of Christendom by

---

The New Man: or, A Svpplication from an Vnknowne Person, a Roman Catholike vnto Iames, the Monarch of Great Brittaine, and from Him to the Emperour, Kings, and Princes of the Christian World, Touching the Causes and Reasons That Will Argue a Necessity of a Generall Councell To Be Forthwith Assembled against Him That Now Vsurps the Papall Chaire vnder the Name of Paul the Fifth, trans. William Crashaw (London: George Norton, 1622). Crashaw's dedication to the marquis of Buckingham names "that famous Doctor Marta" as the likely author (sig. b₁ verso). Marta was, beginning in 1612, an informant in the service of England. See *Calendar of State Papers, Domestic*, vol. IX, pp. 174, 244; Smith, ed., *The Life and Letters of Sir Henry Wotton*, vol. II, pp. 98–99, 104, 141, 472; Norman Egbert McClure, ed., *The Letters of John Chamberlain*, 2 vols. (Philadelphia: American Philosophical Society, 1939), vol. I, pp. 333, 340. Marco Antonio De Dominis has been suggested as a possible candidate, but it seems unlikely that he was the author. See Noel Malcolm, *De Dominis (1560–1624); Venetian, Anglican, Ecumenist and Relapsed Heretic* (London: Strickland and Scott, 1984), pp. 41, 114.

241 [Marta,] *The New Man*, sig. A₁.   242 Ibid., sig. A₁ verso.
243 Ibid., pp. 35–36.
244 [Marta,] *Svpplication et reqvette à l'emperevr, aux roys, princes, estats, republiques & magistrats Chrestiens, sur les causes d'assembler un concile general contre Paul Cin-quiesme*, trans. Nicolas de Marbais (Leyden: Elzevier, 1613). For the translator's apparent change of faith, see the dedication, sigs. * xii–* xii. De Marbais comments that he has expanded the original Latin text (sig. ** ii).
245 [Marta,] *Svpplication et reqvette à l'emperevr, aux roys, princes, estats, republiques*, pp. 28, 30–32, 41–44, 70–75, 86, 141, 173–174.

bringing Protestants and Roman Catholics together in a general council to affirm their common heritage in the Catholic faith of antiquity and to settle or at least reach an accommodation over their theological differences. But this was the part of his message which few members of his international audience – with, as events were to show, some notable exceptions – seemed to hear. By far the most common response to James's *Premonition*, by Roman Catholics and Protestants alike, was to comment on his statement of his religious faith in such a way as to build an impregnable defense of one religious position or another. Soon the religious differences so tenaciously held to were being used to justify a conflict far more violent than this battle of the books.

If James failed in one of his endeavors, he may, nevertheless, have succeeded in another. Montague, writing in 1616, commented "that upon the comming foorth of that Booke, there were no States, that disauowed the Doctrine of it in that point of the Kings power."[246] He added that the Venetians had maintained James's doctrine of the state's temporal authority in theory and put it into practice, while the Sorbonne in Paris had steadfastly defended it.[247] James had, all along, claimed to be defending the right of every nation to be governed by its own laws and its own officials without interference from the ecclesiastical institution which claimed to be able to depose rulers on religious and moral grounds. On the level of abstract argument Bellarmine and Suarez made an effective case for the deposing power, but on the level of practical politics that power was, or was about to become, a dead letter.[248] James had spoken up for the sovereignty and autonomy of the national state at a time when the political theories of the Counter-Reformation were still at the height of their influence. How seriously his ideas were taken can be seen in the attention given to political theory in the books which poured from European presses following the publication of the *Premonition*. As a result, the discussion of fundamental political issues reached every corner of Europe. The king may fairly be said to have been one of the prophets of the new age of sovereign, independent states.[249]

[246] James I, *Workes*, ed. Montague, sig. d₃.   [247] Ibid.
[248] For a thoughtful essay on Robert Bellarmine's defense of the temporal authority of the papacy, see John Courtney Murray, "St. Robert Bellarmine on the Indirect Power," *Theological Studies*, 9 (1948), 491–535. Murray argues that the relation between the spiritual and temporal realms needs to be thought out anew in each age in the light of political circumstances (p. 492). Bellarmine, who stated his view "with magnificent vigor and sureness" (p. 492), stood too close to the medieval tradition to see that the so-called right of deposition, which had served a useful purpose in earlier times, was a limited, contingent, and relative one; it was unnecessary or inappropriate in the political circumstances of the seventeenth century (pp. 531–532). See also Thomas Clancy, "English Catholics and the Papal Deposing Power, 1570–1640," *Recusant History*, 6 (1961–1962), 205–227, and 7 (1963–1964), 2–10.
[249] See McIlwain, ed., *The Political Works of James I*, pp. xv, xxii–xxvii, xlix–lvi; Lorenzo

Another of James's conspicuous achievements was to bring English Protestants together in a common front which, for the moment at least, obscured the theological and ecclesiological differences among them. More than any other event in his reign, the Oath of Allegiance controversy forged a religious consensus among the English people that had been slow in coming to a country in which the Reformation had begun three-quarters of a century earlier.[250] That consensus was broadly Protestant and explicitly anti-Roman Catholic. To James's credit, he managed to mitigate the effects of this anti-Roman Catholicism by requiring, as he contended, only an expression of civil obedience in the Oath of Allegiance, and by treating peaceable Roman Catholics more leniently than the harsh penal laws specified. The years of the controversy over the oath may be said to mark the coming of age of the Church of England. The English Church had, the essayist and theologian Joseph Hall asserted in 1611, "such bishops, as may justly challenge the whole consistory of Rome; so many learned doctors and divines, as no nation under heaven more."[251] In addition, in its conciliar theology, the English Church developed a distinctive set of doctrines which recognized the authenticity of many expressions of Christianity within the one Church and which held out the prospect of a visible manifestation of that unity if and when the churches and nations of the Christian world were ready to take the appropriate steps to achieve it.[252]

The Oath of Allegiance, James's defense of it, and the resulting international controversy present a set of paradoxes which are difficult to resolve. The central paradox is the king's attitude towards the papacy. In the *Premonition* he argued that the pope was Antichrist while, in the same treatise, he recognized the important role of the popes as patriarchs of the

d'Avack, *La ragione dei re: il pensiero politico di Giacomo I* (Milan: A. Giuffrè, 1974), pp. 6–12, 35–37, 91, 194.

[250] For the religious consensus – never, of course, complete or without serious tensions – see Patrick Collinson, *The Religion of Protestants: The Church in English Society, 1559–1625* (Oxford: Clarendon Press, 1982). For the effect of the Oath of Allegiance in forging a broad Protestant unity in England, see Hamilton, *Shakespeare and the Politics of Protestant England*, pp. 128–137, 153–162. For the slow progress of Protestantism in gaining general acceptance in England, see Christopher Haigh, ed., *The English Reformation Revised* (Cambridge: Cambridge University Press, 1987), pp. 1–33, 176–215, and *English Reformations: Religion, Politics, and Society under the Tudors* (Oxford: Clarendon Press, 1993); additional evidence from a variety of sources is provided in Eamon Duffy, *The Stripping of the Altars: Traditional Religion in England, c. 1400–1580* (New Haven: Yale University Press, 1992), pp. 377–593.

[251] Joseph Hall, letter to James Montague, bishop of Bath and Wells, in *Epistles*, vol. III (1611), in *The Works of the Right Reverend Joseph Hall, D.D., Bishop of Exeter and Afterwards of Norwich*, ed. Philip Wynter, revised edition, 10 vols. (Oxford: Oxford University Press, 1863), vol. VI, p. 250.

[252] See Charles John Fenner, "The Concept and Theological Significance of Ecumenical Councils in the Anglican Tradition," Ph.D. thesis, Catholic University of America, 1974, pp. 77–259.

West. The contest with Pope Paul V and his supporters over the deposing power helped to forge a Protestant and anti-papal consensus in England, but also provided a spur to the development of a conciliar theology which, as expressed in Field's *Of the Church*, reserved a significant place for the pope in the reforming and reuniting of the universal Church. James believed deeply in the English conception of the crown as supreme in all spiritual as well as temporal affairs within the realm, but was apparently willing, as Field was, to accord the pope a certain preeminence among bishops. As James interpreted the Oath of Allegiance, those of his subjects who believed in the spiritual supremacy of the pope were allowed freedom of conscience on this point, as long as they acknowledged the king and the civil obedience due to him. The most likely explanation for these paradoxes is that James was torn between viewing the papacy as a threat to his own life and crown, as well as to the stability of the English Church and nation, and viewing it – in conjunction with a general council – as a focus of unity for western Christians.

Despite the lack of an immediate response from the temporal rulers to his appeal for a general council, James continued in the years which followed the publication of his *Premonition* to work for a broad religious settlement. Following his own advice to his fellow Protestant rulers, he actively encouraged greater unity among the Protestant churches in Europe, while awaiting a suitable opportunity for a general religious rapprochement that would include Rome.

4

Foreign visitors

One of the results of the Oath of Allegiance controversy was to make King James I of England a celebrated figure in Protestant circles in Europe. The Oath of Allegiance, required by law in England in 1606, was intended to separate Roman Catholics who adhered to the doctrine that a pope could depose a temporal ruler from Roman Catholics who did not hold this view and could therefore be considered loyal subjects. The king not only defended the oath in print, but in doing so opposed Pope Paul V, who condemned the oath, and Cardinal Robert Bellarmine, who defended the papal deposing power. In his writings James stated his own religious faith clearly and succinctly and denounced the temporal claims of the papacy. As the translators of the authorized or King James version of the Bible wrote in 1611, when the translation appeared: "the zeale of your Maiestie towards the house of God," already shown in support for preaching God's word at home, "doth not slacke or goe backward, but is more and more kindled, manifesting it selfe abroad in the furthest parts of Christendome, by writing in defence of the Trueth."[1] The king of Scotland, Ireland, and England, the most important Protestant ruler in Europe, thereby became one of the most widely admired figures in the Protestant community. Expressions of this admiration came from some unexpected quarters. In 1609, in Rakow, in Poland, then the center of unitarianism in that country, Jerome Moscorovius translated the Racovian Catechism, first published in Polish in 1605, into Latin for a European audience. It was dedicated to James I. The religious group at Rakow, founded in the late sixteenth century by the radical reformer Faustus Socinus, was large and prosperous by the early seventeenth century and had established both a college and a printing press.[2] According to the dedication, these unitarians wanted to set

[1] *The Holy Bible, Conteyning the Old Testament and the New: Newly Translated out of the Originall Tongues and with the Former Translations Diligently Compared and Reuised, by His Maiesties Speciall Cōmandement* (London: Robert Barker, 1611), sig. A₂ verso.

[2] Thomas Rees, ed., *The Racovian Catechism, with Notes and Illustrations, Translated from the Latin: To Which Is Prefixed a Sketch of the History of Unitarianism in Poland and the*

124

forth a theology consistent with the scriptures. James was one whose renown had "spread through the Christian world."[3] The dedication stated that James "recognizes that divine truth itself is contained in Divine Letters, and therefore considers that controversies in the Christian religion should be decided in accordance with the decrees of Sacred Letters, not the opinions of men."[4] Another dedication came with a translation of John Calvin's *Institutes of the Christian Religion* into the Czech language by Georgius Streizius, published in the Upper Palatinate in 1615. The dedication of the book, described on the title page as "for the common use of all peoples of the most widely spread Slavonic language," was signed by the theologian Johannes Opsimathes at Amberg in April 1616.[5] This volume was evidently prepared for presentation to James during Opsimathes's visit to England in July 1616, a journey encouraged by the Elector of the Palatinate, who was married to James's daughter Elizabeth. The dedication referred to James's reputation for wisdom and faith as extending throughout the Christian world, even to the arctic region, and called him the "patron of a re-cleansed Christian Religion."[6] Opsimathes's dedication was accompanied by verses addressed to James by scholars at Bremen, Prague, and Nuremberg.[7]

The controversy over the Oath of Allegiance had just begun when James attracted the attention of Johannes Kepler, the Imperial Mathematician in Prague, who sent a copy of his book, *De stella in pede serpentarii*, to the king in 1607 by way of the English ambassador. Kepler, originally a Lutheran but later considered too much a Calvinist to be appointed to the faculty of Tübingen University in his native Württemberg, found the eclectic

---

Adjacent Countries (London: Longman, Hurst, Rees, Orme, and Brown, 1818), pp. xxix–xxxi, lxxviii–lxxix.

[3] *Catechesis ecclesiarum quae in Regno Poloniae & Magno Ducatu Lithuaniae & aliis ad istud regnum pertinentibus provinciis affirmant neminem alium praeter Patrem Domini Nostri Jesu Christi esse illum Unum Deum Israelis, hominem autem illum Jesum Nazarenum, qui ex Virgine natus est, nec alium praeter aut ante ipsum Dei Filium Unigenitum & agnoscunt & confitentur* (Rakow, 1609), sig. a₄, a₆.

[4] *Catechesis ecclesiarum*, sig. a₄ verso.

[5] John Calvin, *Institutio Christianae religionis, in quatuor libros digesta, Johanne Calvino auctore, in Bohemicam vero Lingvam a Georgio Streyzio versa, et in communem usum omnium latissimae Slavonicae linguae populorum a Johanne Opsimathe edita* (Amberg in the Upper Palatinate: Léta Páně, 1615), p. 9. The volume in the library of Sidney Sussex College, Cambridge, has the unique copy of a twelve-page dedication to King James I. The book's location there may have some connection with the fact that James Montague, master of the College from 1595 to 1608, was the editor of James's *Workes* in 1616, or that Samuel Ward, master from 1610 to 1643, was one of the representatives sent by the king to the Synod of Dort in 1618–1619. The volume is described in E. P. Tyrrell and J. S. G. Simmons, "Slavonic Books before 1700 in Cambridge Libraries," *Transactions of the Cambridge Bibliographical Society*, vol. 3, part V (1963), 382–400.

[6] Calvin, *Institutio Christianae religionis . . . in Bohemicam vero Lingvam . . . versa*, pp. 3, 5.

[7] Ibid., pp. 10–12.

culture of the court of the Emperor Rudolph II very congenial.[8] Kepler's admiration for James was based as much on the king's learning as his religious faith. Kepler's letter, accompanying the book, asked God to "ordain that your Majesty rule so happily over Britain that you never feel compelled to abandon philosophy because of excessive business."[9] It also asked that God would grant the king power to effect "the pacification and improvement of the church reborn under most difficult circumstances to the well-being of Christendom and the safety of the realms entrusted to him."[10] Kepler followed up this letter with a dedication prepared several years later. In 1619, he dedicated to James his important *Harmonices mundi*, one of the sources for the third Keplerian law, recalling "what attention the prince of Christendom gives to divine studies."[11] He noted that James "as a youth considered the astronomy of Tycho Brahe, upon which my work rests, worthy of his intellect."[12] James "successfully bore the hereditary enmity of the bitterly hostile nations" of Scotland and England.[13] Kepler hoped that this book, which dealt with the harmony of the heavenly bodies, would appeal to one who sought "harmony and unity in the ecclesiastical and political spheres."[14] This tribute to James's efforts on behalf of religious and political reconciliation, from one of the most significant scientists of the early seventeenth century, must have given the king immense satisfaction. It

[8] Carola Baumgardt, *Johannes Kepler: Life and Letters* (New York: Philosophical Library, 1951), pp. 23–25, 59–69, 76–77, 100–101; R. J. W. Evans, *Rudolf II and His World: A Study in Intellectual History, 1576–1612* (Oxford: Clarendon Press, 1973), pp. 136, 152–153, 187, 190, 245–247, 272, 279–280, 291. *De stella nova in pede Serpentarii* was published in Prague in 1606.

[9] Johannes Kepler, *Gesammelte Werke*, ed. Walther von Dyck and Max Caspar, 20 vols. (Munich: C. H. Beck, 1937–), vol. XVI, p. 104; Max Caspar and Walther von Dyck, eds., *Johannes Kepler in Seinen Briefen*, 2 vols. (Munich: R. Oldenbourg, 1930), vol. I, p. 298.

[10] Kepler, *Gesammelte Werke*, ed. von Dyck and Caspar, vol. XVI, p. 104; Caspar and von Dyck, *Johannes Kepler in Seinen Briefen*, vol. I, p. 298.

[11] Kepler, *Gesammelte Werke*, ed. von Dyck and Caspar, vol. VI, p. 9; Caspar and von Dyck, *Johannes Kepler in Seinen Briefen*, vol. II, p. 118.

[12] Kepler, *Gesammelte Werke*, ed. von Dyck and Caspar, vol. VI, p. 9; Caspar and von Dyck, *Johannes Kepler in Seinen Briefen*, vol. II, p. 118.

[13] Kepler, *Gesammelte Werke*, ed. von Dyck and Caspar, vol. VI, p. 10; Caspar and von Dyck, *Johannes Kepler in Seinen Briefen*, vol. II, p. 120.

[14] Kepler, *Gesammelte Werke*, ed. von Dyck and Caspar, vol. VI, p. 11; Caspar and von Dyck, *Johannes Kepler in Seinen Briefen*, vol. II, p. 120. For Kepler's achievement in this book, see J. V. Field, *Kepler's Geometrical Cosmology* (Chicago: University of Chicago Press, 1988), pp. 96–166. The third law deals with what Kepler called "the proportion between the periods of any two planets" (p. 143). In August 1620, Sir Henry Wotton, then in Linz, urged Kepler to come to England, where he was assured of a warm reception by James I. Wotton was on his way to Vienna to try to negotiate an end to the war which had broken out over the accession of Frederick, James's son-in-law, as king of Bohemia. In a letter to a friend in the same month, Kepler wrote: "I do not think I ought to leave this second home of mine." Baumgardt, *Johannes Kepler: Life and Letters*, pp. 147–148. See also Logan Pearsall Smith, *The Life and Letters of Sir Henry Wotton*, 2 vols. (Oxford: Clarendon Press, 1907), vol. I, pp. 169–173.

was published just as James's emissaries were seeking peace in central Europe between the forces of the Bohemian Protestants and those of the Austrian Habsburgs.

One reason for James's celebrity among Protestants of very different kinds was that he had written in his *Premonition* in 1609, the preface to a reissue of his *Apologie for the Oath of Allegiance* of 1607, that the most feasible way to achieve a religious reconciliation was by means of a general council supported by the Christian princes. At such a council all those who adhered to "the ancient grounds" of the Christian faith would have access to a forum in which the disagreements threatening to wrack the continent could be discussed and resolved.[15] The proposal struck a responsive chord in those thinkers and leaders who could see the stark possibilities facing Europe if the religious tensions then current were not somehow lessened. For a decade after James's *Premonition* appeared, the English court became one of the European centers for the discussion and dissemination of ideas aimed at restoring peace to a Christendom torn by religious dissension and scarred by persecution. Among those who came to England in these years were three scholars who cherished the idea of a religious peace and sought throughout their careers to find effective ways to implement that idea.

The first to arrive was Isaac Casaubon, a Genevan-born French Huguenot who had gone to Paris in 1600 on the invitation of King Henry IV. There, as a protégé of Jacques-Auguste de Thou, the irenic Roman Catholic historian and councillor of state, Casaubon became the keeper of the king's library.[16] His scholarly activities, focused on the editing of classical texts and writing illuminating and discursive commentaries, made him known throughout the scholarly world. After his friend Joseph Juste Scaliger died in 1609, Casaubon was the leading humanistic scholar in Europe.[17] He clung resolutely to his Protestant faith in the midst of immense pressures

---

[15] James I, *An Apologie for the Oath of Allegiance: First Set Forth without a Name, and Now Acknowledged by the Author, the Right High and Mightie Prince, Iames by the Grace of God, King of Great Britaine, France and Ireland, Defender of the Faith, &c.; Together with a Premonition of His Maiesties to All Most Mightie Monarches, Kings, Free Princes and States of Christendome* (London: Robert Barker, 1609), pp. 110–111.

[16] Mark Pattison, *Isaac Casaubon, 1559–1614*, second edition (Oxford: Clarendon Press, 1892), pp. 121–122, 134–135, 177–179; Marcel Simon, "Isaac Casaubon, Fra Paolo Sarpi et l'Eglise d'Angleterre," in Marcel Simon, ed., *Aspects de l'Anglicanisme: Colloque de Strasbourg (14–16 juin 1972)* (Paris: Presses universitaires de France, 1974), pp. 39–40; Gaetano Cozzi, "Paolo Sarpi tra il cattolico Philippe Canaye de Fresnes e il calvinista Isaac Casaubon," in *Paolo Sarpi tra Venezia e l'Europa* (Turin: Einaudi, 1979), pp. 12–15. For de Thou, see Hugh Trevor-Roper, *Queen Elizabeth's First Historian: William Camden and the Beginnings of English 'Civil History'* (London: Jonathan Cape, 1971), pp. 11–21.

[17] Pattison, *Isaac Casaubon, 1559–1614*, second edition, pp. 125, 238–239, 256, 287, 448–466. For a favorable estimate of his scholarship, see Anthony Grafton, "Protestant versus Prophet: Isaac Casaubon on Hermes Trismegistus," *Journal of the Warburg and Courtauld Institutes*, 46 (1983), 78–92.

from members of the Roman Catholic hierarchy and from Henry IV himself to conform to the dominant religion in France.[18] As Casaubon confided to Sir George Carew, the English ambassador at Paris, in February 1609, "the Card. of Eureux [Jacques Davy Du Perron, bishop of Evreux, cardinal, then archbishop of Sens] is perpetually in hande wth him, to get him to theyr syde; Pere Coton [Pierre Coton, Jesuit confessor to Henry IV] plieth his wife to the same end."[19] Carew mentioned a proposal made by Sir Henry Savile, warden of Merton College, Oxford, some six months before, to bring Casaubon to England. Carew promised that he would "deale for him, wth his M^{tie}." on his return to England.[20] Casaubon's religious views did not endear him to some of his French Protestant associates. While it seemed clear to him, as it did to most other Protestants, that the Roman Catholic Church had made innovations in the ancient faith and tolerated corruptions, it also seemed clear to him that the Reformed churches had distorted elements of that ancient faith and had failed to preserve much that was of value in traditional liturgy and polity.[21] Casaubon's hopes for a renewed Church had much in common with those of other members of de Thou's circle – the Huguenot Jean Hotman de Villiers and the Roman Catholics Pierre de l'Estoile, Philippe Canaye de Fresnes, Pierre Dupuy, and François Pithou.[22] Casaubon and other friends of de Thou were evidently members of the group described by Ambassador Carew as a "third party." This party, Carew wrote in 1609, sought a reconciliation between the reformed party and the party of Rome, believing that the former had taken too extreme a course in the Reformation while the latter still needed to be reformed "both in doctrine and government in the papacy."[23] The emerging third party, wrote Carew, "acknowledgeth the reformation of the church of

[18] Pattison, *Isaac Casaubon, 1559–1614*, second edition, pp. 123–127, 136–145, 175–178, 187–191, 207–217; Pierre de l'Estoile, *Journal de l'Estoile pour le règne de Henri IV*, ed. Louis-Raymond Lefèvre and Andre Martin, 3 vols. (Paris: Gallimard, 1948–1960), vol. II, pp. 25, 574.

[19] London, PRO, State Papers, France, SP 78/55, fol. 46 verso (Sir George Carew to the earl of Salisbury, February 20, 1609).

[20] Ibid.

[21] Pattison, *Isaac Casaubon, 1559–1614*, second edition, pp. 219–226; Simon, "Isaac Casaubon, Fra Paolo Sarpi et l'Église d'Angleterre," pp. 40–52; Cozzi, "Paolo Sarpi tra il cattolico Philippe Canaye de Fresnes e il calvinista Isaac Casaubon," pp. 47–48.

[22] Pattison, *Isaac Casaubon, 1559–1614*, second edition, pp. 115–121; Corrado Vivanti, *Lotto politica e pace religiosa in Francia fra Cinque e Seicento* (Turin: Einaudi, 1963), pp. 53–56, 189, 293, 323, 347, 373, 385–390, 408; Cozzi, "Paolo Sarpi tra il cattolico Philippe Canaye de Fresnes e il calvinista Isaac Casaubon," pp. 17, 20–43.

[23] George Carew, "A Relation of the State of France, with the Characters of Henry IV. and the Principal Persons of that Court, drawn up by Sir George Carew, upon his Return from his Embassy there in 1609, and addressed to King James I," in Thomas Birch, *An Historical View of the Negotiations between the Courts of England, France, and Brussels, from the Year 1592 to 1617* (London: A. Millar, 1749), p. 445. "The president [of the Parlement] De Thou, and many of their learned lawyers, are held to be of this opinion" (p. 445).

England to approach nearest unto the form of the primitive church, of any that hath hitherto been made."[24]

The immediate cause of Casaubon's departure from France was the assassination of King Henry IV by François Ravaillac, a Roman Catholic who claimed to have acted out of concern for the Church and his co-religionists. The assassination was profoundly disturbing to French Protestants. They also worried about the direction which the government of Marie de Medici, the queen mother and regent, might take in its religious policy.[25] For several years Casaubon had feared a return of religious repression in France, despite the guarantees of the Edict of Nantes; and he had considered both Venice and England as places of refuge. As early as March 1610, proposals for his settlement in England had been made by Carew, now back in his native country. On April 1, 1610 Casaubon confided in his diary that he had decided to go to England.[26] An official invitation came from Richard Bancroft, the archbishop of Canterbury, in July. In October Casaubon reached England in the company of the English ambassador extraordinary, Lord Wotton of Marley, the brother of the poet and diplomatist Sir Henry Wotton, whom Casaubon had met earlier in Geneva.[27] Though the invitation to Casaubon had come from Archbishop Bancroft, it seems certain to have been encouraged by King James. The king had read Casaubon's *De libertate ecclesiastica* in 1608, a book begun during the crisis over religious and political authority in Venice, and for several days he could apparently talk of little else.[28] In Casaubon he saw an eminently useful ally in the battle of the books which had been provoked by the Oath of Allegiance. But he also saw in Casaubon an influential spokesman for the plans for religious reconciliation he had been pursuing since the beginning of his reign in England. If Casaubon saw England as a place where he could pursue his scholarship uninterrupted by other tasks, he was destined to be disappointed. Some years later, Hugo Grotius recalled that Casaubon had told him that when he came to England he set aside his work on the classical historians who had written on military events, since

---

[24] Carew, "A Relation of the State of France," p. 446.

[25] Roland Mousnier, *The Assassination of Henry IV: The Tyrannicide Problem and the Consolidation of the French Absolute Monarchy in the Early Seventeenth Century* (London: Faber and Faber, 1973), pp. 21–38, 232–239; Victor-L. Tapié, *France in the Age of Louis XIII and Richelieu* (Cambridge: Cambridge University Press, 1984), pp. 48–50, 62–68.

[26] Isaac Casaubon, *Ephemerides, cum praefatione et notis*, ed. John Russell, 2 vols. (Oxford: Oxford University Press, 1850), vol. II, pp. 730–731; Pattison, *Isaac Casaubon, 1559–1614*, second edition, pp. 246–256, 262–273; Cozzi, "Paolo Sarpi tra il cattolico Philippe Canaye de Fresnes e il calvinista Isaac Casaubon," pp. 113–114.

[27] Pattison, *Isaac Casaubon, 1559–1614*, second edition, pp. 40–42, 273. Lord Wotton was returning from a mission to congratulate Louis XIII on his accession.

[28] Ibid., p. 272. For the Venetian crisis of 1606 to 1607, see chapter 3, above.

James, in contrast to Henry IV, considered martial affairs less important than peace and religion.[29]

The welcome given Casaubon was cordial, and his hosts provided for his entertainment and expenses. Though a layman, Casaubon was made a prebendary of Canterbury Cathedral, a position carrying a stipend, and he was given a pension from the exchequer. The king frequently invited Casaubon to attend him at meals, where they conversed freely on scholarly subjects. Casaubon reported to de Thou that James was well informed about theological controversies and very familiar with sacred literature.[30] Among the members of the clergy, John Overall, dean of St. Paul's Cathedral, was particularly hospitable, taking Casaubon and his family into the deanery for a year. Casaubon spent many hours with Lancelot Andrewes, bishop of Ely, who was a frequent preacher at court; with the bishop Casaubon visited Cambridge University, where he was warmly received.[31] When a son was born in 1612 to Isaac and Florence Casaubon, he was baptized by James Montague, bishop of Bath and Wells, and John Buckeridge, bishop of Rochester, acting for George Abbot, Bancroft's successor as archbishop of Canterbury.[32] But Casaubon's stay in England was not regarded in France as a permanent arrangement. De Thou, with great tact, managed to have Casaubon's appointment as librarian continued with its emoluments ready to be reclaimed. This was on the strength of de Thou's assurances to the queen regent and her advisers that Casaubon intended to return and had only undertaken a journey to England for the sake of his studies.[33] As Casaubon became involved in literary controversies

[29] Hugo Grotius, *Briefwisseling*, ed. P. C. Molhuysen and B. L. Meulenbroek, 13 vols. (The Hague: Martinus Nijhoff, 1928–), vol. III, p. 352. The letter is from Grotius to Joachim Camerarius, July 27, 1628. For relations between Grotius and Casaubon and their significance for the Jacobean Church of England, see Hugh Trevor-Roper, *Catholics and Puritans: Seventeenth Century Essays* (London: Secker and Warburg, 1987), pp. 42–59, 195–198; and *From Counter-Reformation to Glorious Revolution* (London: Secker and Warburg, 1992), pp. 47–82. See also his lecture, *Edward Hyde, Earl of Clarendon* (Oxford: Clarendon Press, 1975).

[30] For Casaubon's reception in England, see John Chamberlain, *The Letters of John Chamberlain*, ed. Norman Egbert McClure, 2 vols. (Philadelphia: American Philosophical Society, 1939), vol. I, pp. 316–317, 332, and 385. Casaubon was described by Chamberlain in his letter to Sir Dudley Carleton on November 20, 1611 to be "scant contented with his entertainment of 300^{li} a yeare," especially compared to compensation received by Théodore Turquet de Mayerne, the king's Huguenot physician (pp. 316–317). For Casaubon's conversations with the king and his report to de Thou, see Lucien Rimbault, *Pierre du Moulin, 1568–1658: un pasteur classique à l'âge classique* (Paris: Librairie Philosophique J. Vrin, 1966), pp. 76–79.

[31] Pattison, *Isaac Casaubon, 1559–1614*, second edition, pp. 278, 292–294, 347–348. Later in his stay Casaubon visited Oxford with Sir Henry Savile, the warden of Merton College (pp. 354–372). Casaubon's wife Florence came to England to join him in February 1611 (p. 410).

[32] McClure, *The Letters of John Chamberlain*, vol. I, p. 385.

[33] Jacques-Auguste de Thou, *Choix de lettres françoises inédites* (Paris: Société des Bibliophiles, 1877), pp. 56–57, 80–81, 95.

with French ecclesiastics, there were rumblings from the French court about an imminent recall of the royal librarian.[34] Casaubon endeavored to stay on good terms with the queen regent's government, and in the last months of his life he promised the French ambassador in London that he would return to France if adequate provisions were made for his family and himself.[35] As events turned out, he was still in England when he died on July 1, 1614. Among the most frequent subjects of conversation between James and Casaubon was the controversy over the Oath of Allegiance. The number of writers who had published treatises on both sides of the controversy was prodigious, and James was determined not to be overwhelmed by the attacks coming from the citadels of Roman Catholicism abroad. Casaubon had not heretofore participated in the debate, but the assassination of King Henry IV by a man who claimed to be acting from religious motives gave concerns about the papal claim to the deposing power a new relevance and urgency. James was thus able to enlist the influential *littérateur* in his defense.

Just before Casaubon left France, a friend of his, Fronton du Duc (or Fronto Ducaeus), a Jesuit priest, gave Casaubon a short *apologia* for the Jesuits to be taken to James. This *Response apologetique* had been written in answer to an attack on Pierre Coton, the late King Henry's confessor, whose political views had come under attack following the king's murder. Fronton du Duc apparently hoped that the British king would be induced by the book to look more favorably upon the Society of Jesus. On the contrary James exploded with indignation after reading it and declared to Casaubon that it contained the same heinous ideas about the temporal power of the papacy which Cardinal Bellarmine had defended.[36] Casaubon was accordingly asked by James to prepare a response defending the king's position. Casaubon's epistle *Ad Frontonem Ducaeum* is a courteous and even-tempered work. He referred throughout the book to his fellow classicist and editor as "most erudite."[37] But he made clear that he could not accept the

---

[34] London, PRO, State Papers, France, 78/57, fols. 164 verso–166 (May 10, 1611), 176 verso (May 22, 1611); 78/58, fol. 22 verso (June 25, 1611).

[35] PRO 31/3/42 (French ambassador's reports, June 24, 1611–June 12, 1614).

[36] James Brodrick, *Robert Bellarmine, 1542–1621*, 2 vols. (London: Longmans, Green, 1950), vol. II, p. 227. The anonymous *Response apologetique a l'Anticoton* (1610), written by a priest, perhaps Coton himself, was an answer to the anonymous *Anticoton ou refutation de la lettre declaratoire du Pere Coton* (1610), which accused the Jesuits of being the authors of the "execrable parricide" of Henry IV. See Peter Milward, *Religious Controversies of the Jacobean Age: A Survey of Printed Sources* (London: Scolar Press, 1978), pp. 123–124.

[37] Isaac Casaubon, *Isaaci Casavboni ad Frontonem Dvcaevm S. J. theologum epistola, in qua de apologia disseritur communi Iesuitarum nomine ante aliquot menses Lutetiae Parisiorum edita* (London: John Norton, 1611). Casaubon and du Duc had been collaborators in a project supported by Henry IV to publish works of the church fathers from manuscripts in the royal library.

theory that the pope had the right to intervene in a nation's temporal affairs, nor could he accept the idealized picture of Henry Garnet as a martyr innocent of any complicity in the Gunpowder Plot.[38] Casaubon explained his book to Nicolas de Neufville, sieur de Villeroi, the secretary of state to the queen regent in France, by saying that James had expressed his concern over the "books which are written every day by those for whom it is a meritorious work to kill a king."[39] "It was," Casaubon wrote, "by the express commandment of the king that I have done this little book."[40] The author of the *Response apologetique*, "who had refuted the Anticoton," said Casaubon, "had openly taught this detestable doctrine while defending all those who had written of it."[41]

Casaubon also became a close collaborator with the king on plans for achieving a religious peace. Casaubon brought to his discussions with the king an outlook shaped by years of study as well as the experience of having lived much of his life in a country torn by a long civil war over religion. In 1607 Casaubon published a letter of Gregory of Nyssa, one of the Cappadocian fathers of the fourth century, which dealt with the contested issue of the two natures of Christ and with the concord of the Church.[42] The publication of Gregory's letter, heretofore not available in Greek or Latin, enabled Casaubon to express his views on the current state of the Church. He did so in the dedication of the work to Benjamin of Buwinck-hausen, the duke of Württemberg's ambassador to Henry IV. Where was now that "constructive charity spoken of by Paul the Apostle"? asked Casaubon. Where was the spirit of gentleness?[43] Instead the Church in Europe was marked by strife and hatred. While the clash of arms had ceased as a result of the sensible actions of the princes, especially Henry IV, Christians now fought with pens. They ignored the counsel of the ancient fathers of the Church that "love is the way."[44] Casaubon cited an image of Basil the Great to describe the Church in the early seventeenth century: a ship tossing on the waves, heading for imminent danger, while the pilots and sailors, oblivious to their common peril, fought furiously hand to hand.[45] Such a spectacle, said Casaubon, had thrown him back to find out from the early Christian writers, "what was the early faith, what was the

---

[38] Casaubon, *Ad Frontonem Dvcaevm*, pp. 32–44, 100–108.
[39] Paris, Bibliothèque Nationale, MS. Français Ancien Fond 15985, fol. 311. The letter was written from London, December 26, 1611, French (i.e., new) style.
[40] Ibid., fol. 311 verso.
[41] Ibid., fol. 311 verso. In letters to de Thou, Casaubon made clear his opposition to this "satanic doctrine" which he believed had taken the life of the French king. BN Collection Dupuy 16, fol. 35 verso (May 1611) and fol. 39 (August 1612).
[42] Isaac Casaubon, ed., *B. Gregorii Nysseni ad Evstathiam, Ambrosiam & Basilissam epistola* (Hanau: Wechel, 1607), pp. 11–13.
[43] Ibid., pp. 8–9.   [44] Ibid., pp. 9–10   [45] Ibid., p. 9.

form of ecclesiastical discipline, what were indeed the ancient rites."[46] He never doubted, he said, that what was most ancient was best and what was held everywhere and always was truest.[47] A writer like Gregory of Nyssa, Casaubon believed, could help to point the way towards concord.

An even clearer expression of Casaubon's views on the religious dissensions in Europe was his response to a book by Cardinal Jacques Davy du Perron. Du Perron, the son of a Huguenot pastor and formerly a Protestant, was one of those who had given instruction to Henry IV before the king's abjuration of Protestantism and his reception into the Roman Catholic Church. Cardinal du Perron tried diligently to convert Casaubon to Roman Catholicism.[48] Before Casaubon left Paris, du Perron sent him a letter in which he said of King James that except for "the Title of Catholike, there was nothing wanting in his Royall Person, to express the liuely patterne of a Prince, completely endued with all Princely vertues."[49] Casaubon showed the letter to the king, who was pleased by its general tenor, but insisted that he *was* a Catholic, since "he believed all those things, which the ancient Fathers with vniforme consent esteemed necessary to saluation."[50] Du Perron heard of the king's reaction and thereupon wrote a short treatise on what it meant to be a Catholic. Apparently without du Perron's permission, the work was published in Paris in 1612 and then translated into English by the Jesuit Thomas Owen.[51] Du Perron sought to demonstrate that on several key doctrines – the meaning of the eucharist, for example – James and the English Church were opposed to the teachings of the ancient fathers. His more important point was that the term *Catholic* denoted not simply belief but communion with the Catholic Church.[52] This communion, he argued, was what the king obviously lacked. But he hoped that James would become a Catholic in the generally accepted sense, since this could lead the way to unity among Christians: "he would become a Mediatour for the reconciliatō of the Church, which would be vnto him a more triumphant Glory, then that of all Alexanders, and Cesars."[53] It was du Perron's treatise – in the form of a letter – which Casaubon set out to answer.

In his own treatise, published in English and Dutch, as well as Latin,

---

[46] Ibid., p. 11. [47] Ibid.

[48] Pattison, *Isaac Casaubon, 1559–1614*, second edition, pp. 189–191, 212–216, 268–270.

[49] Jacques Davy du Perron, *A Letter Written from Paris by the Lord Cardinall of Peron to Mons' Casavbon in England* ([St. Omer: English College Press,] 1612), p. 3.

[50] Du Perron, *A Letter Written from Paris*, p. 3.

[51] Jacques Davy du Perron, *Lettre de Monseignevr le cardinal dv Perron envoyée au sieur Casaubon en Angleterre* (Paris: Iean Laqvehay and Iean Bovillette, 1612). Owen's translation appeared as du Perron, *A Letter Written from Paris*, already cited. See Milward, *Religious Controversies of the Jacobean Age*, pp. 128–129.

[52] Du Perron, *A Letter Written from Paris*, pp. 5–8, 39–40. [53] Ibid., p. 50.

Casaubon dealt directly with the issues du Perron had raised of what constituted catholicity and how the king could best serve the cause of Christian unity.[54] Casaubon asserted that the passage in his treatise refuting du Perron's argument about the term Catholic came from James himself.[55] The king had evidently seized on du Perron's argument that to be a Catholic was to be in communion with the Catholic Church. This argument, said James, simply called attention to a central problem, namely, that the various members of the Catholic Church were out of communion with each other. "The Church of Rome," he said, "the Greek Church, the Church of Antioch, and of Aegypt, the Abyssine, the Moschouite and many others, are members much excelling each other in sinceritie of doctrine, and faith: yet all members of the Catholike Church, whose ioynture, in regard of the outward forme was long since broken."[56] The Church of England, James maintained, was a member of the Catholic Church like the others. It had continuity of doctrine with the ancient Catholic Church. It also had continuity of persons in its succession of bishops: "behold the names of our Bishops, and their continuance from the first without any interruption."[57] James declared that he was willing to put the question of the catholicity of the teaching of the Church of England to the test. "Let vs have a free Councell which may not depend vpon the will of one," he proposed.

The Church of England is readie to render an account of her faith, and by demonstration to euince, that the authors of the reformation here, had no purpose to erect any new Church, (as the ignorant and malicious doe cauill) but to repaire the ruines of the old, according to the best forme: and in their iudgement that is best which was deliuered by the Apostles to the Primitive Church, and hath continued in the ages next ensuing.[58]

According to Casaubon, the king had also pursued at length the cardinal's argument that the English Church's concept of the eucharist was erroneous, and the king had turned his defense of the Church of England on this point into a plea for unity. James argued that the English Church had not rejected the ideas of the presence of Christ and of sacrifice in the eucharist, as du

---

[54] Isaac Casaubon, *The Answere of Master Isaac Casavbon to the Epistle of the Most Illustriovs and Most Reuerend Cardinall Peron, Translated out of Latin into English, May 18. 1612* (London: William Aspley, 1612); *Isaaci Casavboni ad Epistolam Illvstr. et Reuerendiss. Cardinalis Peronii responsio* (London: John Norton, 1612); *Antwoort Isaaci, Casavboni op den Brief vanden seer Door-luchtighe ende Eerwaerdighen Cardinael Perronius, Gheschreven wt den name ende van weghen den Alder-door-luchtichsten Koninck Iacobus, Koninck van groot-Britanien etc.* (n. p., 1612).
[55] Casaubon, *The Answere . . . to the Epistle of . . . Cardinall Peron*, p. 5. For a discussion of the theology of this treatise in its historical context, see Frederick Shriver, "Liberal Catholicism: James I, Isaac Casaubon, Bishop Whittingham of Maryland, and Mark Pattison," *Anglican and Episcopal History*, 66, 3 (September 1987), 303–317.
[56] Casaubon, *The Answere . . . to the Epistle of . . . Cardinall Peron*, p. 11.
[57] Ibid., p. 13.   [58] Ibid.

Perron claimed, but held them in the sense that the ancients had. Thus the Church of England believed Christ's words "This is my body" to refer to the bread in the eucharist, but was "not inquisitive" about the manner of Christ's presence in the element of bread, holding this to be a sacred mystery.[59] As for sacrifice, the service was itself a commemoration of Christ's sacrifice on the cross.[60] James urged, as a way to unity and peace, that Christians agree to worship together and allow the theologians to pursue the knotty problems of doctrine in an appropriate academic setting: "For the communion of the faithful consisteth much in the publike exercises of pietie: and this is the chiefe bond of vnion so much desired by good men. Wherefore if Christians could but agree about this, why might not all Europe communicate together? only, granting a libertie to schoole–Diuines with moderation to debate other opinions."[61] James's commitment to the cause of reconciliation among Christians was, according to Casaubon, one of the overriding themes of his life and career:

As for his most excellent Maiestie of Great Britaine, in whose Court I have now lived a whole yeere and more, I dare promise you, and with all manner of asseueration confirme, that he is so affected, and that the course of his whole life hath bin so ordered, that all men may easily vnderstand there is nothing dearer to him than the carefull endeuour for religion. Neither private businesse, nor the publike cares of his kingdome do vsually so affect his Maiestie, as a kinde of vnmeasurable desire by all meanes to promote religion, and (which consideration most beseemes so great a King) an exceeding affection by all right and honest meanes to procure peace amongst the dissenting members of the Church.[62]

Just how James's objectives of Christian unity and peace might be achieved was suggested in Casaubon's dedication of the treatise to Sir Thomas Edmondes, the English ambassador in France. Like good and intelligent Christians on both sides, said Casaubon, the king favored "publike agreement amongst Christian people."[63] But peace and concord must be coupled with truth. Peace could only be attained by agreement based on the teachings of Christ, the apostles, and the primitive Church.[64] How could the leaders of the churches arrive at such an agreement? The way which had the authority of antiquity behind it was by the convocation of a general council:

Now, to come vnto so great a benefit, there lieth but one kings streete, as it were, which from the entrance of the Church hath been beaten by our ancestors, namely the free celebration of a Generall Councell: wherein the complaints of all nations may be heard, wherein controversies may be determined, and peace for the time ensuing, by Gods mercie bee established. For the rooting of bad opinions out of mens mindes, and for the reconciliation of nations diuided by dissention, the Church

---

[59] Ibid., p. 30.   [60] Ibid., pp. 32–33.   [61] Ibid., p. 37.   [62] Ibid., p. 2.
[63] Ibid., sig. A₂ verso. The dedication is dated April 10, 1612.
[64] Ibid., sigs. A₂ verso–A₃.

in all ages knew no other course but this, nor vsed other but this; they vsed not violence nor armes.[65]

Casaubon's elaboration of the idea that the general council was the "kings streete" to unity carried conviction, especially as it was supported by his own detailed knowledge of the role of such councils in antiquity. Du Perron's final response to Casaubon was some time in coming and was apparently never finished – though it ran to over a thousand pages in the French edition of 1620.[66] What evidently happened was that du Perron decided to make his response a kind of *summa* of post-Tridentine theology. He discussed at length the history and theory of general councils, but touched only briefly on James's proposal for such a council to deal with the problems of dissension in his own time. He rejected any idea of a "free councell" if this meant a council free from the authority and direction of the papacy.[67] A council could not "perfectly represent the vniversal Church, if the visible head of the Church, be neither there personallie, representatively, or confirmatively."[68] On one matter, however, he left the door slightly ajar. He was ready to join in either a formal council or a verbal conference to discuss the claims of the English Church to be in conformity with the ancient Church.[69] Since the work was published posthumously, there was no occasion to take up this offer.

After the publication of his replies to Fronton and du Perron, Casaubon devoted himself to a task requiring greater scholarly attention but likely to be even more controversial. The task was to refute the work of the foremost Roman Catholic historian of the day. At the time of his death in 1607, Cardinal Cesare Baronio or Baronius had completed the twelfth volume of a massive history of the Church, intended to be the answer to the Magdeburg *Centuries*, a similarly ambitious work in thirteen volumes, published by a team of Protestant scholars between 1559 and 1574.[70] Casaubon undertook to expose what he saw as the faulty scholarship, the superstition, and the credulity characterizing Baronius's volumes. He intended thereby to display that "genuine antiquity" that was the only adequate foundation for

---

[65] Ibid., sig. A₃.

[66] Jacques Davy du Perron, *Réplique à la response dv serenissime Roy de la Grand Bretagne par l'illvstrissime et reverendissime cardinal du Perron, archeuesque de Sens, primat des Gaules & de Germanie & Grand Aumosnier de France* (Paris: Antoine Estiene, 1620). An English translation appeared a decade later: Jacques Davy du Perron, *The Reply of the Most Illustriovs Cardinall of Perron to the Answeare of the Most Excellent King of Great Britain* (Douai: M. Bogart, 1630). The Admonition to the Reader states that du Perron left the book unfinished at his death (sig. E₁).

[67] Du Perron, *The Reply . . . to the Answeare of the . . . king of Great Britain*, p. 436.

[68] Ibid., pp. 436–437.   [69] Ibid., p. 437.

[70] For Baronius's *Annales ecclesiastici*, 12 vols. (1588–1607), see Cyriac K. Pullapilly, *Caesar Baronius: Counter-Reformation Historian* (Notre Dame: University of Notre Dame Press, 1975), pp . 33–66, 144–177.

Christian faith and practice.[71] In October 1612 Jacques-Auguste de Thou assured Nicolas Brûlart, sieur de Sillery, the French chancellor, that Casaubon touched "only on what concerns antiquity and the question of legitimate jurisdiction, without entering on a discussion of dogmas and questions of doctrine."[72] But this was a distinction difficult if not impossible to maintain. During these years de Thou was relying upon Casaubon to supply him with historical materials from England relating to Scottish as well as English affairs for his own history of recent events. James wished to see the record put straight from his own point of view and had enlisted the efforts of the historian William Camden as well as the scholar and book collector Sir Robert Cotton in preparing manuscripts for Casaubon to send to de Thou.[73] Where Baronius had sought, with considerable success, to bury the Magdeburg centuriators' work in an avalanche of information and documentary evidence, all testifying, he believed, to the authenticity and sanctity of the Church of Rome, Casaubon sought to puncture Baronius's illusions with the tools of humanistic scholarship. He had little difficulty in showing that Baronius accepted documents at their face value, without subjecting them to philological and historical analysis. Casaubon thus helped to undermine Baronius's claim that the Church of Rome had preserved the Christian faith without significant alteration.[74] But Casaubon was drawn into discussing a wide range of issues beyond those which de Thou advised him to deal with. Despite its nearly 800 pages, Casaubon's *Exercitationes*, which dealt with only half of Baronius's first volume, failed to provide an adequate basis for Casaubon's alternative view of antiquity. That view, which stressed the value of the beliefs and practices of Christian antiquity as a means of revitalizing and reuniting the fragmented Church of his own time, was, however, to have a decisive influence on a German visitor who arrived while Casaubon was writing his refutation of Baronius.

In the spring of 1612 Georg Calixtus, a young German Lutheran theologian who shared many of Casaubon's interests, came to England to consult the French scholar. Calixtus's theological point of view, which had been shaped by his upbringing as the son of a Lutheran pastor and his

---

[71] Pattison, *Isaac Casaubon, 1559–1614*, second edition, p. 416. For discussion of Casaubon's *De rebus sacris et ecclesiasticis exercitationes XVI. ad Cardinalis Baronii prolegomena in Annales & primam eorum partem* (London: Norton, 1614), see pp. 322–341, 373–376, 415–416, 421–423.

[72] De Thou, *Choix de lettres françoises inédites*, p. 80.

[73] Trevor-Roper, *Queen Elizabeth's First Historian: William Camden and the Beginnings of English 'Civil History'*, pp. 16–17; de Thou, *Choix de lettres françoises inédites*, pp. 57, 61–64, 82–83, 86; Kevin Sharpe, *Sir Robert Cotton, 1586–1631: History and Politics in Early Modern England* (Oxford: Oxford University Press, 1979), pp. 87–95.

[74] Pattison, *Isaac Casaubon, 1559–1614*, second edition, pp. 332–340. See also Pullapilly, *Caesar Baronius: Counter-Reformation Historian*, pp. 163–171, for instances of Baronius's shortcomings in determining the authenticity of documents incorporated in his volumes.

education at the University of Helmstedt, was closer to Philip Melanchthon's unpolemical and conciliatory Protestantism than to that of most of the Lutheran theologians of Calixtus's day. Three years earlier Calixtus had taken an exploratory journey to visit the centers of Lutheran, Reformed, and Roman Catholic theology in Germany. He then became acquainted with the irenic Calvinist theologian David Pareus in Heidelberg. Now he was on a similar journey that had already taken him to the Netherlands and would soon take him to France to visit de Thou.[75] Calixtus deeply admired Casaubon for his scholarship and seems to have looked upon him as a model for his own career.[76] Details of Calixtus's visit to England are scant, though it is known that he visited several bishops as well as the universities of Oxford and Cambridge.[77] But the effects of the visit on Calixtus seem clear. He eventually became an exponent of what some of his critics called "syncretism," a theological method according to which a union of Lutherans, Calvinists, and Roman Catholics was supposed possible on the basis of the first five centuries of the Church's life. Like Casaubon and like the Flemish Roman Catholic scholar Georg Cassander in the mid-sixteenth century, Calixtus saw the ancient period as normative for Christian thought and practice. In his career as a professor at Helmstedt and as a representative at conferences involving several competing Christian denominations, Calixtus urged his contemporaries to look to the patristic writers and the theological formularies of antiquity as a way of evaluating and getting behind the conflicting confessions of their own time.[78]

According to Johann Balthasar Schupp, a contemporary of Calixtus, "it was not so much his teachers in Germany who led Calixtus to the reading of the fathers and church history, as the bishops in England, who possess most splendid libraries."[79] Another contemporary, Christoph Schrader, a col-

---

[75] Hermann Schüssler, *Georg Calixt: Theologie und Kirchenpolitik, eine Studie zur Ökumenizität des Luthertums* (Wiesbaden: Franz Steiner, 1961), pp. 1–4; W. C. Dowding, *German Theology during the Thirty Years' War: The Life and Correspondence of George Calixtus, Lutheran Abbot of Königslutter, and Professor Primarius in the University of Helmstadt* (Oxford: John Henry and James Parker, 1863), pp. 45–61.

[76] Ernst Ludwig Theodor Henke, *Georg Calixtus und Seine Zeit*, 2 vols. (Halle: Waisenhause, 1853), vol. I, p. 141.

[77] Ibid., vol. I, p. 149.

[78] For Cassander and Calixtus and the relation between them, see Friedrich Wilhelm Kantzenbach, *Das Ringen um die Einheit der Kirche im Jahrhundert der Reformation: Vertreter, Quellen und Motive des "ökumenischen" Gedankens von Erasmus von Rotterdam bis Georg Calixt* (Stuttgart: Evangelisches Verlagswerk, 1957), pp. 203–249, and Schüssler, *Georg Calixt: Theologie und Kirchenpolitik*, pp. 40–81. On Calixtus's thought, see also John T. McNeill, *Unitive Protestantism: The Ecumenical Spirit and Its Persistent Expression*, revised edition (London: Epworth Press, 1964), pp. 269–273, and, for a more critical interpretation, Hans Leube, *Kalvinismus und Luthertum im Zeitalter der Orthodoxie* (Aalen: Scientia Verlag, 1966 – originally published, 1928), pp. 257–305.

[79] Henke, *Georg Calixtus und Seine Zeit*, vol. I, p. 149; Dowding, *German Theology during the Thirty Years' War*, p. 58.

league at Helmstedt, said in the course of his funeral oration for Calixtus in 1656 that his friend had "a joyful memory through the whole of his life, that in London he had called on Isaac Casaubon, the greatest man of his age, whose conversations he related to us on literature, our holy religion, its corruptions and reformation, and the concord which ought to exist among Christians."[80] Calixtus himself wrote of his deep regret that Casaubon had not lived to complete the *Exercitationes* on Baronius, in which Casaubon could have expressed his ideas more fully, but he testified that Casaubon was "most desirous of bringing back concord" to the Church of Christ and was "very far removed" from the factional disputes among theologians of his time.[81] Though Schupp did not mention by name the English ecclesiastics whom Calixtus visited, they probably included John Overall, dean of St. Paul's Cathedral, who became bishop of Coventry and Lichfield two years later, and Lancelot Andrewes, bishop of Ely and a frequent preacher at court. Both were especially hospitable and encouraging to Casaubon.[82] Overall and Andrewes shared Casaubon's view of the importance of the ancient writers of the Church as well as the scriptures for the understanding of the Christian faith.[83] Andrewes, in fact, formulated this principle in a memorable way in 1613. Speaking in a sermon of the sources which determined the boundaries of the faith as the English Church understood it, he listed them as: "One canon put into written form for us by God, two testaments, three creeds, the first four councils, five centuries, and the series of fathers in that period."[84]

In the meantime one of the most extraordinary younger scholars of his generation had begun corresponding with Casaubon about the same subjects that Casaubon discussed with Calixtus. Hugo van Groot, or Grotius, classicist, historian, and jurist, had been Advocaat Fiscaal, or attorney general, of the Province of Holland since 1607.[85] As his earliest

---

[80] Henke, *Georg Calixtus und Seine Zeit*, vol. I, p. 148; Dowding, *German Theology during the Thirty Years' War*, pp. 59–60.

[81] Henke, *Georg Calixtus und Seine Zeit*, vol. I, pp. 147–148.

[82] Pattison, *Isaac Casaubon, 1559–1614*, second edition, pp. 277–278, 291–295, 300–301, 347–353, 417.

[83] For Andrewes, see Paul A. Welsby, *Lancelot Andrewes, 1555–1626* (London: SPCK, 1958), pp. 155–156 and *passim*. Welsby comments that for Andrewes, the "standard or norm of faith for the Church . . . was exhibited in its purest form in the New Testament and in the first five centuries of Church history" (p. 156).

[84] Lancelot Andrewes, *Concio Latine habita, coram regia maiestate, XIII° Aprilis, A.D. MDC XIII* (1629), in Andrewes, *Opuscula quaedam posthuma* (Oxford: J. H. Parker, 1852), Library of Anglo-Catholic Theology, vol. X, p. 91.

[85] R. W. Lee, *Hugo Grotius* [British Academy Lecture] (London: Humphrey Milford, 1930), pp. 6–11; William S. M. Knight, *The Life and Works of Hugo Grotius* (London: Sweet and Maxwell, 1925), pp. 122–127; Dieter Wolf, *Die Irenik des Hugo Grotius nach ihren Prinzipien und biographisch-geistesgeschichtlichen Perspektiven* (Marburg: N. G. Elwert Verlag, 1969), pp. 15–17. For Grotius's work as a historian, which bore early fruit in his

theological work, *Meletius*, clearly shows, Grotius was deeply concerned about the religious divisions of Christendom, partly because of the effects of such divisions upon his own country.[86] Written in 1611, though not rediscovered and published until 1988, *Meletius* expressed what were purportedly the views of Meletius Pegas, patriarch of Alexandria until his death in 1601, who had been deputized to serve as patriarch of Constantinople in 1597 and 1598. Grotius presumably knew of Meletius from a friend, Johannes Boreel, who had travelled in the Near East and had become acquainted with the patriarch.[87] Meletius was deeply concerned about the efforts of Roman Catholic missionaries in the East who sought to proselytize Greek Orthodox Christians, thus spawning bitter rivalries and theological disputes on issues which separated the eastern and western churches. The plea which the book made for agreement among believers on major doctrines and for an end to dissension was quite plausible as an expression of Meletius's views. But the argumentation was distinctly Grotius's and the approach was one he took in dealing with religious disputes throughout his life. Already in 1601, Grotius had written to the classical scholar Justus Lipsius that, whenever he wrote on religious issues, he would strive to be " 'catholic and ecumenical,' as the ancient Fathers would say."[88] Grotius's approach to the problem of rival theological and ecclesiastical traditions was as conciliatory as Casaubon's but far broader in its philosophical orientation and potential applicability. Grotius began with the nature of religion itself, which he found to be based on the belief that God exists. He asserted that this was an idea that enjoyed nearly universal support and was partly derived from the order and harmony of the physical world. In a few sentences, filled with references to ancient philosophers, he sought to establish that God was an intelligent being with a will that is free, that God attended to the created world, including human beings, and that God was good.[89] Human beings were also intelligent beings with free-will, but were under the "superior free agent," that is, God, whose activity

De antiquitate reipublicae Batavicae (1610), see E. O. G. Haitsma Mulier, "Grotius, Hooft and the Writing of History in the Dutch Republic," in A. C. Duke and C. A. Tamse, eds., *Clio's Mirror: Historiography in Britain and the Netherlands* (Zutphen: De Walburg Pers, 1985), pp. 55–72.

[86] G. H. M. Posthumus Meyjes, "Hugo de Groot's 'Meletius' (1611), His Earliest Theological Work, Rediscovered," *Lias*, 11 (1984), 147–150. For the Latin text, published for the first time, together with an English translation and a critical introduction, see Hugo Grotius, *Meletius sive de iis quae inter Christianos conveniunt epistola*, ed. Guillaume H. M. Posthumus Meyjes (Leiden: E. J. Brill, 1988). Grotius's work as a theologian is assessed in Henk J. M. Nellen and Edwin Rabbie, eds., *Hugo Grotius, Theologian: Essays in Honour of G. H. M. Posthumus Meyjes* (Leiden: E. J. Brill, 1994).

[87] Grotius, *Meletius*, ed. Posthumus Meyjes, pp. 20, 22, 103–104.

[88] Grotius, *Briefwisseling*, ed. Molhuysen, vol. I, p. 20.

[89] Grotius, *Meletius*, ed. Posthumus Meyjes, pp. 105–106.

towards human beings was expressed by law or authority.[90] Human beings who kept the law should be rewarded and those who broke it should be punished. These, wrote Grotius, "are the principles which the Christian religion has in common with all religions," including natural religion and the Mosaic religion.[91] Grotius considered religion to be "the most important thing in the world," the source of right thinking and acting.[92] But Grotius was not mainly concerned with particular theological doctrines: his basic concern was with law, community, and political order.[93]

Grotius's argument in this treatise was not, like Casaubon's, that the key to religious reconciliation was to restore the Church to its ancient state; instead it was that Christians could find unity on the basis of first principles. Nevertheless, he and Casaubon shared a great deal of common ground. Like the early Christian apologists, whose writings he had recently read, and like the Christian humanists of the sixteenth century, Grotius argued that classical philosophers and poets had anticipated and helped to prepare the way for Christian revelation, and that the ideas and values of these writers were epitomized in the Christian religion. In *Meletius*, he defined the supreme good, a philosophical principle, as the enjoyment of God forever.[94] Such enjoyment was an intellectual pleasure but one which would be accompanied at the Last Day by the restoration or resurrection of the body. There were, Grotius argued, both theoretical and practical elements of Christianity, as there were of all religions. The theoretical elements, or dogmas, included the oneness of God, which was not inconsistent with the trinitarian idea of several *hypostases*. In the case of the sun, by analogy, "we know the celestial body as such, its light and its fiery power," yet we know it as one, nevertheless.[95] Similarly one could speak of God as three, yet one. On another such matter, he argued that human beings, created free and the "most worthy of all visible things," were not what they ought to be; they had fallen into depravity, causing relations among them to be "fraught with hatred and dissension."[96] Grotius tried to steer a middle course between the contending parties in the Netherlands on the issues of free-will and grace. He argued that it was God who made possible "the remission of sins as well as a restoration of fallen man," through the death of a mediator who was both God and man.[97] But God's grace was offered "on condition of

[90] Ibid., p. 106.   [91] Ibid., p. 107.   [92] Ibid.
[93] Ibid., pp. 31–40. Compare G. H. M. Posthumus Meyjes, "Hugo Grotius as an Irenicist," in *The World of Hugo Grotius (1583–1645): Proceedings of the International Colloquium Organized by the Grotius Committee of the Royal Netherlands Academy of Arts and Sciences, Rotterdam, 6–9 April 1983* (Amsterdam and Maarssen: APA–Holland University Press, 1984), pp. 46, 50–54.
[94] Grotius, *Meletius*, ed. Posthumus Meyjes, pp. 107–109.
[95] Ibid., p. 110.   [96] Ibid., pp. 113–114.   [97] Ibid., pp. 116–117.

penitence and belief."[98] Through revelation, the example of Christ, and the power of the Holy Spirit, human beings could be restored. This would be done, however, only if human beings urgently wanted to be restored. Like the strict Calvinists, he thus stressed the power and indispensability of God's grace in human salvation, but like the Arminians, he also stressed the important part human belief and action played in that process.

The practical elements of Christianity, or ethical precepts, were described by Grotius in a way which not only showed their kinship with ancient moral philosophy but recognized certain distinctive Christian truths. These included the importance of duties towards God and the virtue of humility. According to Grotius, the Christian religion taught that human beings were to be loving, forgiving, and merciful to one another just as they expected God to be to them.[99] Faithfulness between husbands and wives within "the indissoluble bonds of matrimony" was an essential part of the Christian life.[100] So was obedience to those in authority, as long as they "do not run counter to God's commands."[101] Honest labor for oneself and one's family as well as the use of one's resources to help those in need were enjoined by the Christian religion. Indeed, "if Christian life would answer to its name all over the world," Grotius asserted, "we would live in a truly Golden Age, without wars, without quarrels, without poverty, in the greatest peace and harmony, an age of plenty for every single one of us."[102] Grotius quoted Meletius as saying that "it was amazing that people who agreed on so many points yet seemed so diverse and out of harmony."[103] Meletius is represented by Grotius as concluding that human beings preferred to argue about dogmas rather than to live in accordance with ethical precepts. The remedy for religious dissensions was to limit the number of necessary articles of faith and to leave the others to be discussed "with charity and under the guidance of the Holy Scriptures."[104] Grotius thus approached Christianity with the resources of his reason and on the basis of his wide reading in classical literature. Furthermore, he had a profound appreciation for the potential practical value of the Christian faith in creating a peaceful community on the national and the international levels. Evidently just beginning his study of the ancient Christian writers, Grotius was attracted to Casaubon as the acknowledged authority on that subject.

Grotius had written to Casaubon in April 1610, while the latter was still in France, acknowledging the Genevan's ascendance in the community of scholars, now that Scaliger, that great "leader of the Muses," had been

---

[98] Ibid., p. 118. For discussion of the theological controversies over grace in the United Provinces from 1610 to 1619, see chapter 8, below.
[99] Grotius, *Meletius*, ed. Posthumus Meyjes, pp. 126–127.
[100] Ibid., p. 128.   [101] Ibid., pp. 128–129.   [102] Ibid., p. 132.   [103] Ibid.
[104] Ibid., pp. 133–134.

taken away.[105] Casaubon wrote from London, towards the end of 1611, enclosing a copy of his reply to Fronton. In a long letter of January 7, 1612, Grotius acknowledged the treatise in approving terms and outlined a plan for ending the factionalism and violence afflicting the European world. Like Casaubon he yearned for "the retention and restoration of the peace of the Church."[106] The most effective way to begin, he asserted, was for those churches not acknowledging the "overlordship" of the bishop of Rome to bear witness to their common faith in a public confession.[107] This confession of the churches of the Reformation ought to appeal to moderate Roman Catholics, who could see thereby that good works had not been dismissed, or traditional rites abolished, or the theological views of antiquity condemned.[108] To draw up such a confession, a council or assembly would be required. Grotius recommended Britain as the place for this assembly and "the Most Wise King, the prince of princes of all those of this persuasion" as moderator and president.[109] Other princes and the States-General of the Netherlands would be invited to send representatives. Whether the Greek and other eastern churches should be invited he left up to the king and his advisers to decide.[110] Grotius's plan for a council, aimed at drawing up a document expressing theological agreement that would then be promoted by the Protestant princes under King James's leadership, was essentially the same as plans being discussed by Pareus and his circle in the Palatinate and by Philippe Duplessis-Mornay and other Huguenots in France.[111] A proposal for a common confession had in fact been advanced as far back as 1581 by the French and Belgic Reformed Churches in the preface to *Harmonia confessionvm fidei*, a collection of confessions published in Geneva.[112] The times, Grotius's letter suggested, gave this proposal a peculiar urgency.

Casaubon wrote to Grotius on February 6, 1612 that he had discussed this plan with the king, who approved of it highly.[113] Concerning the winning over of moderate Roman Catholics, James had observed that there were Catholics groaning under the tyranny of the pope who were willing to follow their own consciences. Casaubon reported that some of the English bishops were wrestling "night and day" with ideas similar to Grotius's.[114] Casaubon was convinced that, once a suitable opportunity arose, "the Most Serene King and the whole English Church" would

[105] Grotius, *Briefwisseling*, ed. Molhuysen, vol. I, p. 165.   [106] Ibid., p. 192.
[107] Ibid.   [108] Ibid.   [109] Ibid.   [110] Ibid., p. 193.
[111] Wolf, *Die Irenik des Hugo Grotius*, pp. 15–17.
[112] [Jean François Salvard, ed.,] *Harmonia confessionvm fidei, orthodoxarum, & reformatarum ecclesiarum, quae in praecipuis quibusque Europae regnis, nationibus, & prouinciis, sacram euangelij doctrinam pure profitentur* (Geneva: Petrus Santandrea, 1581), sigs. *ij–*** i verso.
[113] Grotius, *Briefwisseling*, ed. Molhuysen, vol. I, p. 196.   [114] Ibid.

further the plan.[115] On February 22 Casaubon wrote further that "a Synod of the Reformed Churches was something the king had prayed for over the course of many years," though James was unsure that he had the right to convene such a council on his own initiative. If the States-General of the Netherlands was willing to advance this proposal, the king was ready to further the project as far as he was able.[116] Grotius, his enthusiasm undiminished, responded on April 4 that the right to convene such a synod was that of kings and princes. Who, therefore, had a better right than the one who ruled over "the greatest and noblest part of the Reformed Church"?[117] Grotius believed, as he wrote on June 6, that some of the German princes would ask James to carry out this task – a not unreasonable assumption in light of James's treaty of alliance with the German Evangelical Union in March.[118] On August 11, Casaubon wrote to Grotius that the court was awaiting the arrival of Frederick, the young elector of the Palatinate, the intended husband of James's daughter Elizabeth; Casaubon would "leave no stone unturned" in his efforts to further the project for a council during the forthcoming visit.[119]

Grotius visited England for two months in the spring of 1613 as a member of a negotiating team sent to deal with the problem of English shipping in areas of the East Indies that the Dutch had recently wrested from Portuguese control. Formerly the upholders of freedom of navigation, Grotius and his colleagues now wanted restrictions on English merchantmen in the Far East.[120] During this visit Grotius hoped to win the king to the views of Johann van Oldenbarnevelt, Grand Pensionary or executive head of the Province of Holland, on the religious disputes in the Netherlands.

---

[115] Ibid.   [116] Ibid., p. 198.   [117] Ibid., pp. 205–206.

[118] Ibid., pp. 210–211.

[119] Ibid., p. 217. The close relations between England and the Evangelical Union did provide an opportunity for religious as well as political cooperation. James's son, Prince Henry, who died in November 1612, after the young elector of the Palatinate, the head of the Evangelical Union, arrived for the wedding festivities, had been viewed as one who would help to lead an international coalition against the Habsburg and Roman Catholic powers of Europe. Nevertheless, the wedding of Elizabeth and Frederick V in February 1613 marked a new stage in English relations with the Palatinate and the other Protestant states of Germany. The political, religious, and cultural overtones of the wedding are provocatively described in Frances A. Yates, *The Rosicrucian Enlightenment* (London: Routledge and Kegan Paul, 1972), pp. 1–14, and *Shakespeare's Last Plays: A New Approach* (London: Routledge and Kegan Paul, 1975), pp. 17–37, 57–59, and 97–104; and David Norbrook, "'The Masque of Truth': Court Entertainments and International Protestant Politics in the Early Stuart Period," *The Seventeenth Century*, 1, 2 (July 1986), 81–110. See also, for Prince Henry and the contemporary hopes which revolved about his future role: Roy Strong, *Henry, Prince of Wales and England's Lost Renaissance* (London: Thames and Hudson, 1986), pp. 7–85, 220–225.

[120] Lee , *Hugo Grotius*, pp. 15–23; G. N. Clark and W. J. M. Van Eysinga, eds., *The Colonial Conferences between England and the Netherlands in 1613 and 1615*, 2 vols. (Leiden: E. J. Brill, 1940–1951), vol. I, pp. 1–2, 27–81.

During the course of his stay, Grotius became a fast friend of Overall and Andrewes, and met, but incurred the dislike of, George Abbot, Bancroft's successor as archbishop of Canterbury. The archbishop found Grotius tediously prolix, with theological views too close to those of the late Jacobus Arminius. Arminius was the liberal Dutch theologian who had died in 1609 but whose views had inspired a controversial *Remonstrance* by his followers the year after. Abbot considered Grotius "practically a heretic," Grotius commented to the king.[121] As for James, he was apparently delighted with Grotius, despite differences with the Dutch over the maritime issues in dispute. In a letter of April 13, 1613 to Daniel Heinsius, the Dutch philologist and poet, Casaubon declared: "It is impossible to proclaim sufficiently my good fortune in having the company of that most excellent man, Hugo Grotius . . . Nor should you think that only I have been seized by admiration for that man, all learned and pious men whom he has met have been similarly affected. The king especially so."[122] On the theological and political issues then dividing the Netherlands, however, Grotius and the king proved to be on opposing sides. Grotius was a supporter of the Remonstrants, who followed in Arminius's footsteps, and of Oldenbarnevelt, while James subsequently became a supporter of the Counter-Remonstrants, the more strictly Calvinist party, and of Maurice, the prince of Orange. This explains, no doubt, why Grotius and the king did not become more closely associated in the years ahead in the cause of religious reunion, to which both were deeply committed.

When Isaac Casaubon died on July 1, 1614, his refutation and correction of Cardinal Baronius's *Annales* was far from complete, though the first installment of his *Exercitationes* had been published earlier in the year.[123] On his deathbed he received the eucharist from Bishop Andrewes; at his burial in Westminster Abbey his funeral sermon was preached by John Overall, recently consecrated as bishop of Coventry and Lichfield.[124] Casaubon was buried, as Thomas Fuller said, on the west or historical side of the south aisle of the abbey, where William Camden was subsequently buried, rather than on the east or poetical side, with Chaucer and Spenser.[125] Casaubon's tomb, said Fuller, was "erected at the cost of

---

[121] Ralph Winwood, *Memorials of Affairs of State in the Reigns of Q. Elizabeth and K. James I*, 3 vols. (London: T. Ward, 1725), vol. III, pp. 459–460; Grotius, *Briefwisseling*, ed. Molhuysen, vol. I, pp. 230–231, 233, 239–240; Lee, *Hugo Grotius*, p. 20.

[122] Isaac Casaubon, *Epistolae, insertis ad easdem responsionibus, quotquot hactenus reperiri potuerunt*, ed. Theodore Janson, third edition (Rotterdam: Caspar Fritsch and Michael Böhm, 1709), p. 529.

[123] Casaubon and Grotius exchanged comments about the book in letters early in May 1614. Grotius, *Briefwisseling*, ed. Molhuysen, vol. I, pp. 309–311.

[124] Pattison, *Isaac Casaubon, 1559–1614*, second edition, pp. 417–418.

[125] Thomas Fuller, *The Church-History of Britain; From the Birth of Jesus Christ untill the Year M. DC. XLVIII* (London: John Williams, 1655), Bk. X, p. 69.

Thomas Moreton [Morton], bishop of Durham, that great lover of Learned men, dead or alive."[126] The physician who attended him, Raphael Thorius, reported that Casaubon died regretting that his work on ecclesiastical history, dedicated "to the glory of God and Christian concord," was left unfinished.[127] Casaubon was thus given a burial appropriate to an especially distinguished scholar. The friendship of Bishops Andrewes, Overall, and Morton demonstrated his acceptance by the English Church.

Earlier in the year, reports of some of King James's conversations at court on the subject of a religious accord reached Rome. On January 28, 1614, Cardinal Roberto Ubaldini, the papal nuncio at Paris, wrote to Cardinal Scipione Borghese, nephew of Pope Paul V, about a proposal for a general council. The nuncio had received an account from an informant in London that, for some days, "the king has spoken very freely and in the presence of many, that he would greatly wish that His Holiness should wish to convene a General Council to which he would be able to send some of his bishops or ministers with a sure safeconduct in order to dispute with the prelates of the Council, and to appeal with all humility to what should be resolved there."[128] Concerning the Oath of Allegiance, the king had said that he had no other intention in requiring the oath than "to secure himself against evil designs."[129] It would be reassuring, the king had added, if the pope would "declare himself inimical to the Gunpowder Treason," and state just how much authority he claimed over princes.[130] In Ubaldini's opinion the king had broached the possibility of a council "more for the purposes of discussion than because he has a sincere and serious intention of searching for opportune means of uniting himself to the Holy Catholic Apostolic Church," and he reported from other sources that conditions had recently been made more difficult for Roman Catholics in England.[131] The reply to Ubaldini from Pope Paul V, dated February 27, 1614, concurred with the nuncio's skepticism: "Our Master, His Holiness, has read the information sent to Your Lordship by your friend in England, about the king's apparent desire for a General Council to be called to the end indicated, but His Holiness believes that it is all guile and that little can be hoped for from him, especially as you say he is persecuting the poor Catholics more than ever before."[132] The pope advised Ubaldini to work through the French ambas-

---

[126] Ibid., p. 70. Fuller refers to Morton as bishop of Durham, the see to which he was translated in 1632 from Coventry and Lichfield. In 1614 he was dean of Winchester.

[127] BN Collection Dupuy 16, fol. 114 verso.

[128] Hugo Laemmer, ed., *Meletematum Romanorum mantissa* (Ratisbon: G. J. Manz, 1875), pp. 325–326.

[129] Ibid.   [130] Ibid., p. 326.   [131] Ibid., pp. 325–326.

[132] Ludwig Pastor, *The History of the Popes from the Close of the Middle Ages*, 40 vols. (St. Louis: B. Herder, 1891–1954), vol. XXVI, p. 184. The generally hostile papal policies towards the religious and political authorities of Protestant England are analyzed by D. M.

sador in London to try to mitigate the rigors which Roman Catholics in England had to endure.[133]

Grotius's commitment to the cause of religious reconciliation survived the bitter conflict in the Netherlands in the years following his visit to England. This conflict culminated in 1619 in the suppression of the Arminian party, the execution of Oldenbarnevelt, and the sentencing of Grotius to imprisonment for life.[134] By a daring ruse, Grotius escaped from the island fortress of Louvestein in which he was confined, became an exile in Paris, and there published in 1625 his *De jure belli ac pacis*, one of the fundamental treatments of international law.[135] Two years later, in 1627, he outlined those beliefs which Christians, regardless of sect, had in common – an elaboration of the argument of *Meletius* – in a book entitled *De veritate religionis Christianae*. Translated into many languages, it became by far the most widely circulated of his writings.[136] Meanwhile, in 1614, Grotius had begun to correspond with the French diplomatist Jean Hotman de Villiers, a Huguenot member of de Thou's circle and one of the most assiduous advocates of religious reconciliation in France. Hotman, the son of the distinguished jurist and political thinker François Hotman, whose *Franco-Gallia* advanced a theory of limited constitutional monarchy, would become a close friend of Grotius and a literary collaborator with him on historical and religious projects.[137] Grotius's letter to Jean Hotman on

Loades, "Relations between the Anglican and Roman Catholic Churches in the 16th and 17th Centuries," in J. C. H. Aveling, D. M. Loades, and H. R. McAdoo, *Rome and the Anglicans: Historical and Doctrinal Aspects of Anglican–Roman Catholic Relations*, ed. Wolfgang Haase (Berlin: Walter de Gruyter, 1982), pp. 1–53, and Gerhard Müller, "Papal Policy and Schismatic Movements in the Sixteenth and Seventeenth Centuries," in David Loades, ed., *The End of Strife* (Edinburgh: T. and T. Clark, 1984), pp. 94–113.

[133] Pastor, *The History of the Popes*, vol. XXVI, p. 184.

[134] Wolf, *Die Irenik des Hugo Grotius*, pp. 17–37.

[135] For a recent assessment of Grotius's importance for the understanding of international relations, including international law, see Hedley Bull, Benedict Kingsbury, and Adam Roberts, *Hugo Grotius and International Relations* (Oxford: Clarendon Press, 1990), esp. pp. 65–93, 267–312.

[136] Hugo Grotius, *Sensvs librorvm sex qvos pro veritate religionis Christianae* (Leyden: Johannes Maire, 1627); Grotius, *Meletius*, ed. Posthumus Meyjes, p. 25. Subsequent editions had the title of the second edition: *De veritate religionis Christianae* (Leyden: Johannes Maire, 1628). For the influence of this book on Grotius's English contemporary William Chillingworth, see Robert R. Orr, *Reason and Authority: The Thought of William Chillingworth* (Oxford: Clarendon Press, 1967), pp. 32–33, 106, 118, 123. For its reception and influence, see Jan Paul Heering, "Hugo Grotius' *De Veritate Religionis Christianae*," in Nellen and Rabbie, *Hugo Grotius, Theologian*, pp. 41–52.

[137] For Hotman's career, see F. Schickler, "Hotman de Villiers et son temps," *Bulletin de la Societé de l'histoire du Protestantisme Français*, 17 (1868), 97–111, 145–161, 401–413, 464–476, 513–533; David Baird Smith, "Jean de Villiers Hotman," *Scottish Historical Review*, 14 (1917), 147–166; Vivanti, *Lotta politica e pace religiosa*, pp. 189–245; and G. H. M. Posthumus Meyjes, "Jean Hotman and Hugo Grotius," *Grotiana*, new series, 2 (1981), 3–29.

August 26, 1614 expressed his thanks for a gift of books written on behalf of "the most despaired of peace of Christendom, so terribly torn apart."[138] The gift evidently included writings by Melanchthon and Cassander, since Grotius commented: "if Luther had had the mind of Melanchthon, and the Patriarch of the West [the pope], the sympathies of Cassander," the affairs of Europe would have been much improved.[139] Grotius believed that Hotman had read his own book on the religious affairs of Holland, published two years before. Grotius's *Ordinum* presented a reasoned case for the exercise of authority in the ecclesiastical sphere by the government of Holland, and attempted to show that the authors of the *Remonstrance*, the controversial statement by followers of Arminius, were not heretics.[140] The book was intended to influence King James as well as to calm the contending religious factions in the Netherlands. Grotius asked, in the same letter of August 26, that Hotman remember his promise to provide him with historical materials for the earl of Leicester's expedition to the Netherlands in 1586 to 1587, when Hotman served as the earl's secretary.[141]

Hotman had had many years of experience in England, having served as guardian of the two sons of Sir Amyas Paulet, English ambassador in France, when they were undergraduates at Oxford, and having become a friend of several prominent figures at Queen Elizabeth's court. He had also served as an emissary of Henry of Navarre to King James VI in Scotland, after the Huguenot leader's accession to the French throne. In a letter to Hotman on 25 December 1593, William Fowler, a poet and secretary to Anne of Denmark, James's wife, had written from Edinburgh that the king was very pleased with a gift of books from Hotman. The king had already read parts of Hotman's father's collected works, which Hotman had edited on his return to Basel.[142] Hotman subsequently translated James's *Basilikon Doron* into French.[143] Hotman's contacts with James in Scotland help to explain how it was that the king was ready to propose a general council to advance the cause of a broad religious pacification soon after his accession

[138] J. W. van Meel, ed., *Francisci et Joannis Hotomanorum patris ac filii et clarorum virorum ad eos epistolae* (Amsterdam: G. Gallet, 1700), p. 397; Grotius, *Briefwisseling*, ed. Molhuysen, vol. I, p. 347.
[139] Meel, *Francisci et Joannis Hotomanorum . . . epistolae*, pp. 397; Grotius, *Briefwisseling*, ed. Molhuysen, p. 347.
[140] Hugo Grotius, *Ordinum Hollandiae ac Westfrisiae pietas ab improbissimis multorum calumnijs, praesertim vero a nupera Sibrandi Lvbberti epistola* (Leyden: J. Patius, 1612).
[141] Meel, ed., *Francisci et Joannis Hotomanorum . . . epistolae*, pp. 397–398; Grotius, *Briefwisseling*, ed. Molhuysen, p. 348.
[142] Meel, ed., *Francisci et Joannis Hotomanorum . . . epistolae*, pp. 379. The letter is addressed to "N. N.," but from its contents Jean Hotman appears to be the intended recipient.
[143] Meel, ed., *Francisci et Joannis Hotomanorum . . . epistolae*, pp. 368–369. This letter, undated, was addressed to "a certain Englishman," presumably Fowler, since it seems to be a belated answer to the letter on p. 379. Hotman complains here that he has not been rewarded for his translation of the king's book.

in England in 1603. Through Hotman, who was collecting irenic texts by Martin Bucer as early as 1593,[144] James must have known of the proposals of King Henry IV and his advisers in the late 1580s and the 1590s. These proposals called for either a national council of the Roman Catholic Church in France or a general council of the whole Church to resolve the religious issues at stake in the civil wars then being fought in France.[145] James's own proposal, as has been shown above, was rooted in the conciliar traditions of Scotland and England. But it no doubt owed a good deal as well to the conciliar tradition of France, where Henry IV and his advisers and publicists had advocated a council as a solution to the problems confronting France and other countries in Europe. Conciliarism came as naturally to Henry IV and his circle in France as it did to James VI and I and those who shared his concern about a divided Christendom.[146] Hotman apparently never lost his admiration for King James or for the Church of England. Carew, while English ambassador at Paris, wrote to Salisbury in November 1607 that Hotman was "a great admirer and magnifier of our Ecclesiasticall gouverment in England; insomuch as he hath spread the same opinion, into the mindes of many of worthe and learning here."[147]

Hotman had been collecting books and manuscripts on the theme of religious concord since the 1590s but he evidently found it impossible to publish a bibliography of such works in France. Grotius, however, was finally able to get Hotman's *Syllabus* published in Strasbourg in 1628 with a preface addressed "to the reader zealous for Christian peace and concord" by the German historian and philosopher Matthias Bernegger.[148] Bernegger

---

[144] Meel, ed., *Francisci et Joannis Hotomanorum . . . epistolae*, pp. 376–377. This letter, written by Hotman from Basel in 1593 to an unnamed correspondent, presumably in France, asked for help in obtaining three texts of Martin Bucer. Bucer's writings, which Hotman placed on the same level as those of Melanchthon, were, he noted, used by Edward VI in the restoration of the English Church.

[145] W. B. Patterson, "Henry IV and the Huguenot Appeal for a Return to Poissy," in Derek Baker, ed., *Schism, Heresy and Religious Protest* (Cambridge: Cambridge University Press, 1972), Studies in Church History, IX, pp. 247–257, and "Jean de Serres and the Politics of Religious Pacification, 1594–96," in Derek Baker, ed., *Church, Society and Politics* (Oxford: Basil Blackwell, 1975), Studies in Church History, XII, pp. 223–244; Vivanti, *Lotta politica e pace religiosa*, pp. 132–291.

[146] J. H. M. Salmon, "Gallicanism and Anglicanism in the Age of the Counter-Reformation," in his *Renaissance and Revolt: Essays in the Intellectual and Social History of Early Modern France* (Cambridge: Cambridge University Press, 1987), pp. 155–188. See also William J. Bouwsma, "Gallicanism and the Nature of Christendom," in Anthony Molho and John A. Tedeschi, eds., *Renaissance Studies in Honor of Hans Baron* (De Kalb: Northern Illinois University Press, 1971), pp. 809–830.

[147] PRO SP 78/53, fol. 362 (Carew to Salisbury, 28 November 1607).

[148] [Jean Hotman], *Syllabus aliquot synodorum et colloquiorum, quae auctoritate et mandato caesarum et regum, super negotio religionis ad controversias conciliandas, indicta sunt; doctorum item aliquot ac piorum virorum utriusque religionis, tam Catholicae Romanae, quam Protestantium, libri & epistolae, vel ex iis excerpta* (Orléans [actually Strasbourg], 1628), sigs.)(2–)(2 verso. For the publishing of this book and authorship of the preface,

claimed that these works showed how to achieve "the reconciliation of
controversies in religion and, indeed, peace, in a Europe torn apart by those
disagreements."[149] If the way they described had not been effectively
applied before, this might, Bernegger suggested, have been because the
disease had not yet reached the critical point at which a remedy could best
be applied. Now, however, public calamities had reached the level of a
debilitating fever. The "heads of the Christian world," that is, the temporal
rulers, could, however, apply a permanent cure through conciliation.[150]
Hotman's *Syllabus* suggested by its very length and diversity that conciliation was possible. Included were almost equal numbers of books and
manuscripts by Protestant and Roman Catholic authors, over 150 titles in
all. In France the authors included both Protestants and Catholics in Henry
IV's circle: Philippe Duplessis-Mornay, Jean de Serres, and Isaac Casaubon
on the one hand; Jacques-Auguste de Thou, Henry Constable, and Pierre
Coton on the other. In the Netherlands they included the Protestants
François Junius, Grotius's mentor in his student days, and Grotius himself,
and the Catholics Erasmus of Rotterdam and Georg Cassander.[151] The list
also included works by Italian, German, and English authors. The French
Jesuit Pierre Coton was represented by his *Institvtion catholiqve* of 1610
which, in a long preface to Protestant readers, identifies Catholic themes in
the writings of Luther, Calvin, Bucer, and in the Thirty-Nine Articles of the
Church of England.[152] Citing Calvin's admonition to unity in Book IV of
his *Institutes of the Christian Religion*, Coton held out the prospect of
reconciliation.[153] According to Hotman's annotation in the *Syllabus*, Henry

see G. H. M. Posthumus Meyjes, "Jean Hotman's Syllabus of Eirenical Literature," in
Derek Baker, ed., *Reform and Reformation: England and the Continent, c. 1500–c. 1750*
(Oxford: Basil Blackwell, 1979), Studies in Church History, Subsidia 2, pp. 175–193, and
"Jean Hotman and Hugo Grotius," pp. 8–10, 25–27.

[149] Hotman, *Syllabus*, sig.)(2.   [150] Hotman, *Syllabus*, sigs.)(2–)(2 verso.
[151] Hotman, *Syllabus*, sigs. A₁ – [E]₁. For the widespread interest in recapturing a genuine
catholicity in the early seventeenth century, see Martin Schmidt, "Ecumenical Activity on
the Continent of Europe in the Seventeenth and Eighteenth Centuries," in Ruth Rouse and
Stephen Charles Neill, eds., *A History of the Ecumenical Movement, 1517–1948*, second
edition (London: SPCK, 1967), pp. 73–120. See also Friedrich Heer, *Die Dritte Kraft: Der
europäische Humanismus zwischen den Fronten des konfessionellen Zeitalters* (Frankfurt-
on-Main: S. Fischer, 1959), for the view that a "third way," identified with humanism,
existed alongside Rome and the Protestant Reformation and included both Roman Catholics and Protestants.
[152] Pierre Coton, *Institvtion catholiqve, ou est declarée & confirmée la verite de la foy, contre
les heresies et svperstitions de ce temps; diuisee en quatre liures, qui seruent d'antidote aux
quatre de l'Institution de Jean Caluin* (Paris: Claude Chappelet, 1610), sigs. i ij–i iiii.
Coton's preface is only partly conciliatory; he also challenges Protestants to cite any
scriptural support for some thirty distinctively Protestant doctrines (sigs. c iiii–c iiii verso).
[153] Coton, *Institvtion catholiqve*, sigs. i iiii verso–k ij. See also his preface to the French king,
where Coton celebrates Henry IV's achievement in bringing peace to France and to
Christendom (sigs. a iij–a iiii), and his preface to the queen mother and regent – the book
having appeared after Henry IV's death – in which he says that her late husband was a

IV had approved of Coton's approach and had communicated his support to Pope Paul V.[154] As G. H. M. Posthumus Meyjes has shown, Hotman's list omits notoriously heterodox or heretical authors; instead, the authors represent "the established churches of Europe," backed by the various temporal governments.[155] The civil rulers could, Hotman and Grotius believed, achieve a reconciliation by the responsible use of their sovereign powers. Grotius later published an abbreviated version of this list along with seven short texts, including four of his own, in a book entitled *Via ad pacem ecclesiasticam* in 1642.[156] The key text here was Cassander's *Consultatio*, commissioned by the Emperor Ferdinand I and published in 1577.[157] Cassander had sought to reconcile two opposing doctrinal points of view represented by formularies included in Grotius's book: Melanchthon's Augsburg Confession and the Tridentine Creed authorized by Pope Pius IV. Cassander's model, like Casaubon's and Calixtus's, was the early Church, recourse to which could help to overcome the confessional divisions of the Reformation era.

Grotius himself continued to see a latter-day model of a reunited Church in the Church of England. After becoming Sweden's ambassador to France, Grotius proposed in 1637 a union between the Swedish Lutheran Church, in which episcopacy had been preserved, as in England, with the Church of England. Such a step, he believed, could bring Lutheran churches and perhaps even some Reformed churches into a larger union. It might even attract French Roman Catholics.[158] There was little positive response from Archbishop William Laud in England, a country now beset with religious divisions of its own. Grotius retained an admiration for the English liturgy and episcopal system of government to the end of his life. Before his death

principal shaper of the book which follows (sigs. a ij–a ij verso). The passage in Calvin's *Institutes* is cited as IV, 1, xviii, concluding words (sig. i iiii verso).

[154] Hotman, *Syllabus*, sigs. B₄–B₄ verso. The approach taken by Coton of emphasizing points of agreement between Protestants and Roman Catholics was consistent with that of Henry's Huguenot adviser Jean de Serres in the late 1590s. See Patterson, "Jean de Serres and the Politics of Religious Pacification, 1594–98," pp. 223–244.

[155] Posthumus Meyjes, "Jean Hotman's *Syllabus* of Eirenical Literature," p. 191.

[156] Hugo Grotius, *Via ad pacem ecclesiasticam* (Amsterdam: I. Blaev, 1642). For the origin of the list in an earlier work of Hotman's, see Posthumus Meyjes, "Jean Hotman and Hugo Grotius," pp. 22–28.

[157] Georg Cassander, *De articvlis religionis inter Catholicos et Protestantes controversiis consvltatio* (Cologne: Henricus Aquensis, 1577). For Cassander's thought, see Maria E. Nolte, *Georgius Cassander en zijn oecumenisch Streven* (Nijmegen: Centrale Drukkerij, 1951), pp. 248–254, and André Stegmann, "Georges Cassander: victime des orthodoxies," in *Aspects du libertinisme au XVIᵉ siècle: actes du colloque international de Sommières* (Paris: J. Vrin, 1974), pp. 199–214.

[158] W. J. Tighe, "William Laud and the Reunion of the Churches: Some Evidence from 1637 and 1638," *Historical Journal*, 30, 3 (1987), 717–727. The three letters reproduced here, which discuss Grotius's proposal, were written by Viscount Scudamore, Charles I's ambassador at Paris, to Archbishop Laud.

in 1645, when the English Church was being altered at home almost beyond recognition, Grotius commended to his wife and friends the services of the Church of England being held in the house of the English ambassador at Paris.[159] In his last years Grotius concluded that no effort to unite the Protestant churches was likely to succeed unless it was part of a fresh approach to Rome, which could serve as the center of a general reunion.[160] In 1642, in a booklet entitled *Votum pro pace ecclesiastica*, he delineated three ways to achieve an ecclesiastical union: by the authority of the pope, by a truly ecumenical council, or by a colloquy convened by the princes.[161] With the Thirty Years' War still raging, the problems of religious dissension were even more pressing than when he had discussed them with Casaubon and King James many years before.

Casaubon's sojourn in Jacobean England from 1610 to 1614 and the shorter visits of Calixtus and Grotius during this period helped to make England a center of irenic activity. The letters and books of the three scholars kept the idea of a religious concord before a European audience. Casaubon and Grotius maintained an extensive correspondence in Latin with scholars, diplomatists, jurists, and political leaders across national borders. This literary network constituted a Republic of Letters whose members were committed to peaceful means of resolving the increasingly inflammatory religious and political conflicts of the day.[162] By giving shelter to Casaubon and entertaining Grotius, James could, in effect, use these two influential intellectuals as publicists for his own conciliatory proposals. They, in turn, saw him as someone who might actually be able to effect an international religious settlement. In the Church of England, both men saw qualities which might provide a basis for a reunited Church. This was possible despite abuses and corruption in the English Church that marred its ecclesiastical life, as Puritan spokesmen pointed out, and despite the persecution in England of Protestant nonconformists and Roman Catholic recusants. As Roman Catholic controversialists asserted, Protestants had far more freedom in France than Roman Catholics had in England. Casaubon could nevertheless write to his wife, six months after his arrival in England: "You know how much I admire the Church of

---

[159] Hugo Grotius, *The Truth of the Christian Religion*, ed. John Le Clerc, thirteenth edition (London: F. C. and J. Rivington, 1809), "Testimonies Concerning Hugo Grotius's Affection for the Church of England," pp. 341–352. For Grotius's influence in England, see Johannes van den Berg, "Grotius' Views on Antichrist and Apocalyptic Thought in England," in Nellen and Rabbie, *Hugo Grotius, Theologian*, pp. 169–183.

[160] Posthumus Meyjes, "Hugo Grotius as an Irenicist," p. 61.

[161] Hugo Grotius, *Votum pro pace ecclesiastica, contra examen Andrae Riveti & alios irreconciliabiles* (n. p., 1642), pp. 11–17.

[162] G. H. M. Posthumus Meyjes, "Protestant Irenicism in the Sixteenth and Seventeenth Centuries," in Loades, *The End of Strife*, pp. 77–93; Sharpe, *Sir Robert Cotton, 1586–1631*, pp. 95–110.

England, where abuses have been removed which past ages had introduced into the Roman Church, and where the form of the ancient Church has been preserved."[163]

Hugh Trevor-Roper, Lord Dacre of Glanton, who has illuminated the subject treated here in several of his essays, has argued that "in the reign of James I, the Church of England had pretensions to be an ecumenical church, a third force, competing with the international Church of Rome and international Calvinism."[164] He finds the origins of this ecumenism in the "original Erasmian impulse which had been the intellectual inspiration of the English Reformation."[165] This Erasmian impulse, he believes, was reasserted in the early seventeenth century by scholars like Casaubon and Grotius, who were encouraged by a king who shared many of their interests. The ecumenical phase in England did not last, he contends, because of theological controversies at home and abroad. In the next reign, he points out, the Church of England became increasingly insular, absorbed in its own concerns.[166] The Church of England did have such an ecumenical phase in the early seventeenth century. The Elizabethan Church had tended to identify itself with Protestant, especially Calvinist, Europe. The Caroline Church of James's son, under the ecclesiastical leadership of Archbishop Laud, became very much aware of those special characteristics that distinguished it from both continental Protestantism and Roman Catholicism. It was the Jacobean Church that sought closer ties with Protestant Churches abroad, established contact with the Orthodox to the East, and developed a conciliar theology which prepared the way for a possible rapprochement with the Church of Rome. Casaubon and Grotius – as well as Calixtus – played significant roles in this process. Both Casaubon and Grotius were Christian humanists in the Erasmian mold, and Grotius had the added distinction of having one of the finest legal minds of his day.[167] But Trevor-Roper's interpretation needs to be modified to do justice to the critically important role played by King James. It was the king's conception of the mission of the Church of England that largely defined its place in Europe in the early seventeenth century. James, a political theorist and theologian as well as a statesman, does not really fit the Erasmian pattern. He was a Calvinist in theology, though more tolerant of theological differences than many Calvinists of his day. A European in outlook, as befitted a Scottish

---

[163] London, British Library, MS. Burney 367, fols. 92–92 verso.
[164] Trevor-Roper, *Catholics, Anglicans and Puritans*, p. ix.   [165] Ibid., p. 42.
[166] Ibid., pp. 52–59, 68, 90, 98, 195–198; Trevor-Roper, *From Counter-Reformation to Glorious Revolution*, pp. 47–58; Trevor-Roper, *Edward Hyde, Earl of Clarendon*, p. 7. See also, for Erasmus and Richard Hooker, H. R. Trevor-Roper, *Renaissance Essays* (London: Secker and Warburg, 1985), pp. 59–75, 103–120.
[167] Posthumus Meyjes, "Hugo Grotius as an Irenicist," pp. 50–53.

ruler of the late sixteenth century,[168] he sought to resolve international disputes, both religious and political; and he was a persistent proponent of a general council to promote a lasting religious settlement in Europe. He did not see the Church of England as a competitor to international Calvinism or an implacable foe to Roman Catholicism. Instead, like Hotman and de Thou, he wanted to include international Calvinism as well as the Church of Rome in a larger union. It was he who was chiefly responsible for fostering an intellectual and religious climate in England which was congenial to Casaubon, Calixtus, and Grotius. In this task he was ably assisted by English scholars and bishops, especially Overall and Andrewes.

James earned the admiration of individuals abroad as diverse as the translator of the Racovian Catechism, the scholars who associated themselves with the edition in the Czech language of Calvin's major work, and Johannes Kepler, the scientist and philosopher who formulated several fundamental laws for the understanding of the physical universe. He stated his faith publicly in a way which he hoped would cut across religious and national divisions. Protestant scholars from near and far saw the British king as an ally. To the extent that the Jacobean Church of England had an ecumenical outlook, it was James who was largely responsible for it. It is not surprising that some of the best spokesmen for the point of view James advanced were foreign visitors.

---

[168] Jenny Wormald, *Court, Kirk, and Community: Scotland, 1470–1625* (London: Edward Arnold, 1981), pp. 5, 149–150, 194.

5

The Synod of Tonneins

Beginning in late 1609, King James became more closely associated with Protestantism on the European continent. His action was consistent with the position he had taken as a defender of the Protestant faith against the papacy in the Oath of Allegiance controversy. It also resulted from the adroit diplomacy of Henry IV of France, who sought to form a coalition of states strong enough to counter the power of the Habsburgs in Spain and Austria and to resolve a succession crisis in Cleves–Jülich. Henry hoped that such a coalition would, as the English agent William Becher wrote from Paris in early 1610, "assure the succession and tranquility of the Dolphin [dauphin or prince, later Louis XIII], agaynst the practises or violence of the Spaniarde."[1] James followed these developments closely. In 1609, he joined a coalition including France, the United Provinces of the Netherlands, and the recently formed Union of Evangelical States in Germany, an alliance formed by Henry IV to assure that Rudolph II, the Holy Roman emperor, would not deny the rights of three claimants, all Protestants, to Cleves–Jülich, formerly ruled by a Catholic. The disputed territory lay strategically on both sides of the Rhine near the border of the divided Netherlands. When the assassination of Henry IV in May 1610 forestalled an allied invasion of the disputed territory, James's ambassador in France, Sir Thomas Edmondes, urged the new French ruler, the Queen Regent Marie de Medici, to carry out her late husband's plan to liberate the town of Jülich from Imperial control by the Archduke Leopold.[2] James had the satisfaction of seeing a combined French, English, German, and Dutch force do exactly

---

[1] London, PRO, State Papers, France, 78/56, fol. 7 verso (Becher to Salisbury, January 20, 1610). For the politics of the Cleves–Jülich dispute, see Maurice Lee, Jr., *James I and Henri IV: An Essay in English Foreign Policy, 1603–1610* (Urbana: University of Illinois Press, 1970), pp. 146–173; Simon Adams, "Spain or the Netherlands? The Dilemmas of Early Stuart Foreign Policy," in Howard Tomlinson, ed., *Before the English Civil War: Essays on Early Stuart Politics and Government* (London: Macmillan, 1983), pp. 86–95; and J. Michael Hayden, *France and the Estates General of 1614* (Cambridge: Cambridge University Press, 1974), pp. 10, 40–53, 98–99.
[2] PRO SP 78/56, fol. 146 (Edmondes to Salisbury, June 2, 1610).

that in August 1610. He subsequently supported negotiations, lasting until 1614, which resolved the succession dispute by dividing the territory between two of the claimants. In an effort to further peaceful negotiations James sent Sir Stephen Lesieur to the Imperial court at Vienna in 1612 to restrain the new emperor, Matthias, from "taking any violent resolutions," as Edmondes explained to Nicolas de Neufville, seigneur de Villeroy, the French secretary of state.[3]

After Henry IV died, James moved closer to the Evangelical Union, allying his country officially with the Union in 1612. One consequence of this policy was the English marriage treaty with the Palatinate of the Rhine, a Calvinist stronghold whose ruler Frederick V, an elector of the Holy Roman Empire, headed the Union. In February 1613, Frederick V and Princess Elizabeth were married in England in a ceremony which seemed to link James to one side in an increasingly serious religious and political division in Germany.[4] Sir Ralph Winwood, James's ambassador to the United Provinces, successfully urged that country to ally itself with the Union. Edmondes tried but failed to persuade the regency government in France to take the same step.[5] James was concerned that Marie de Medici and her ministers would not respect the rights of the French Protestant minority in the way Henry IV had done. Accordingly he made himself in effect the protector of the French Protestants and kept in close touch with several of their leaders, including the influential noblemen Philippe Duplessis-Mornay, governor of Saumur, and Henri de La Tour d'Auvergne, duke of Bouillon, governor of Sedan.[6] These steps might suggest that James

---

[3] PRO SP 78/61, fol. 95 verso (Edmondes to James I, March 16, 1613). For Lesieur's embassy, which began in September 1612, see PRO State Papers, Holy Roman Empire, 80/2, fols. 211–213 verso (instructions for Lesieur September 9, 1612), 225–233 (Lesieur to James I, January 6, 1613).

[4] G. M. D. Howat, *Stuart and Cromwellian Foreign Policy* (London: Adam and Charles Black, 1974), pp. 17–18; Claus-Peter Clasen, *The Palatinate in European History, 1555–1618*, revised edition (Oxford: Blackwell, 1966); Frances A. Yates, *The Rosicrucian Enlightenment* (London: Routledge and Kegan Paul, 1972), pp. 1–14, and *Shakespeare's Last Plays: A New Approach* (London: Routledge and Kegan Paul, 1975), pp. 31–35; David Norbrook, "'The Masque of Truth': Court Entertainments and International Protestant Politics in the Early Stuart Period," *The Seventeenth Century*, 1, 2 (July 1986), 81–110.

[5] PRO SP 78/60, fols. 74–74 verso (Edmondes to James I, September 6, 1612), 78/61, fol. 51 verso (Edmondes to James I, February 8, 1613), 78/61, fol. 76 verso (Edmondes to James I, February 20, 1613); Charles Maffit McAllister, "'The Boisterous Secretaire': The Political Career of Sir Ralph Winwood (1563?–1617)," Ph.D. thesis, University of Virginia, 1983, pp. 106–108. For the origins of the Union and its formation in 1608, see L. Anquez, *Henri IV et l'Allemagne, d'après les mémoires et la correspondance de Jacques Bongars* (Paris: Hachette, 1887), pp. 121–132.

[6] James's instructions to Edmondes at the beginning of his embassy to France, about May 14, 1610, stated that concerning "those, that profess the trew Religion in that kingdome . . . you may declare our selfes soe well affected, as we will never fayle to doe them all good offices, towards the king their souverayne, for contynewing those Priveledges and Indulgences, wch they inioyed under the king his father." PRO SP 78/56, fol. 106. Similarly, his instructions to

was playing a partisan role in the confessional politics which was turning Europe once again into two armed camps. On the contrary, James hoped to maintain the position, rapidly becoming more difficult, of a leading Protestant ruler able to remain on close, even cordial, terms with Catholic countries. He negotiated with Spain, France, Savoy, and Tuscany for a marriage treaty for his elder son Henry and, after Henry's death in 1612, pursued such negotiations on behalf of his younger son Charles with both Spain and France.[7] James's principal aims in foreign policy remained what they had been from the beginning of his reign in England: to maintain friendly relations with all nations and to seek to preserve the peace and stability of Europe.[8] James characteristically urged the French to pursue gentler means of persuasion in June 1613, when French troops stood poised to march into Savoy to counter the duke of Savoy's siege of Casale and his capture of several towns in the marquisate of Montferrat in northern Italy. As it happened, Spain, which ruled Milan, exerted sufficient diplomatic pressure on the duke of Savoy to force him to withdraw from Casale, thus averting a dangerous confrontation.[9]

Along with international peace, James sought the complementary goal of religious reconciliation. From the beginning of his reign in England, James had striven to alleviate the problem of religious disunity through an

Edward, Lord Wotton, ambassador extraordinary to France, August 24, 1610, directed him to express to his Protestant friends "that wee are resolved to imploy our best meanes to support these causes wch concern the body of religion in that authority libertie and safety wch they may iustly claime by virtue of their Edicts." PRO SP 78/56, fols. 242–242 verso. Exchanges with Duplessis-Mornay and the duke of Bouillon are numerous in the diplomatic correspondence between England and France. See PRO SP 78/56–61 (1610–13). For political relations between James and the French Protestants, see Simon L. Adams, "The Road to La Rochelle: English Foreign Policy and the Huguenots, 1610 to 1629," *Proceedings of the Huguenot Society of London*, 22, 5 (1975), 414–429, esp. pp. 416–420.

[7] Roy Strong, *Henry, Prince of Wales, and England's Lost Renaissance* (London: Thames and Hudson, 1986), pp. 80–84, and "England and Italy: The Marriage of Henry Prince of Wales," in Richard Ollard and Pamela Tudor-Craig, eds., *For Veronica Wedgwood These Studies in Seventeenth-Century History* (London: Collins, 1986), pp. 59–87; J. D. Mackie, "The Secret Diplomacy of King James VI in Italy Prior to His Accession to the English Throne," *Scottish Historical Review*, 21 (1924), 280–282, and *Negotiations between King James VI. and I. and Ferdinand I., Grand Duke of Tuscany* (London: Oxford University Press for St. Andrew's University, 1927), pp. 66–67, 71–74. For the start of negotiations for a marriage between Prince Charles and the French Princess Christine, following the death of Prince Henry, see PRO SP 78/61, fols. 5–7 verso (Edmondes to James I, January 9, 1613), SP 78/61, fol. 151 (Edmondes to James I, May 6, 1613), SP 78/61, fols. 196–197 verso (Edmondes to James I, July 29, 1613).

[8] Expressions of James's peace policy may be found in PRO SP 78/56, fol. 105 verso (instructions for Edmondes, about May 14, 1610), SP 80/2, fol. 211 verso (instructions for Lesieur, September 9, 1612), SP 80/2, fol. 288 (James I to Lesieur, May 14, 1613).

[9] Edmondes, surprised to receive these directions, nevertheless communicated James's advice promptly to Villeroy and the queen regent, as he reported back to James on June 19. SP 78/61, fols. 179–181. The duke of Nevers of the French branch of the House of Gonzaga had already gone to the aid of Casale.

international assembly of divines, if possible with the support of the papacy. During the years 1610 to 1614, he employed the celebrated French classical scholar Isaac Casaubon, then in England, in stimulating support for his ideas, especially in learned circles on the continent. Casaubon's death in July 1614 deprived James of a zealous ally in the cause of Christian reunion, but it did not end the campaign to which they had committed themselves. By this time James was involved in the most ambitious reunion plan of his career, the result of his collaboration with Pierre du Moulin, pastor of the Reformed Church in Paris and one of the leading theologians and polemicists in France.

I

James and du Moulin had corresponded for a good many years. According to Pierre du Moulin's son Peter, "King James of blessed and glorious memory before his coming to the Crown of England, sent expressions of Royal favour to the Consistory of Paris, who chose du Moulin to address their humble thanks by Letters to his Majesty."[10] The friendly relations thus established were renewed when James became involved in the theological controversy which followed in the wake of the Oath of Allegiance.[11] When James issued his *Premonition* in 1609, he apparently sent a personal copy to du Moulin – and du Moulin subsequently undertook to defend the king's book against the attack of the French Dominican, Nicolas Coeffeteau.[12] Du Moulin's *Defence of the Catholicke Faith Contained in the Booke of the Most Mightie and Most Gracious King Iames the First*, published in 1610,[13] was followed in 1614 by a treatise which sought to expose the usurpations of temporal power by the papacy and to refute the views of James's adversary Cardinal Bellarmine.[14] Du Moulin had a formidable reputation as a controversialist. In numerous publications, he attacked both Roman

[10] Peter du Moulin, "The Authors Life," prefixed to Pierre du Moulin's *The Novelty of Popery, Opposed to the Antiquity of True Christianity* (London: Francis Tyton, 1662), sig. ***4.

[11] For this controversy, see chapter 3, above.

[12] James's *Premonition . . . to All Most Mightie Monarches, Kings, Free Princes, and States of Christendome*, was issued to accompany a second edition of his *An Apologie for the Oath of Allegiance: First Set Forth without a Name, and Now Acknowledged by the Author, the Right High and Mightie Price, Iames by the Grace of God, King of Great Britaine, France and Ireland, Defender of the Faith &c.*; see chapter 3 above. The evidence for du Moulin's having received a copy of the *Premonition* from the king is in Pierre de l'Estoile, *Journal pour le règne de Henri IV*, ed. André Martin, 3 vols. (Paris: Gallimard, 1948–1960), vol. II, p. 471 (July 10, 1609).

[13] London: Nathaniel Butter and Martin Clerke, 1610. There were French editions in 1610 and 1612.

[14] Pierre du Moulin, *De monarchia temporali Pontificis Romani* (London: Norton, 1614), dedicated to King James (sigs. A_2–A_6).

Catholic and Protestant theologians with whom he disagreed. The story is reported by du Moulin's son that a guest at the table of Cardinal Jacques Davy du Perron once remarked "that Du Moulin was an Ass." At this the Cardinal replied, "You do him wrong Sir; He is such an Ass, that no man ever rubbed against him, but returned with a kick."[15] In spite of his activities as a polemicist, however, du Moulin became deeply interested in the cause of unity among Christians – at least among those who had broken with the papacy.[16]

In early 1612 a theological controversy erupted in the Reformed Churches of France which threatened to divide the French Protestants into warring factions. The controversy was between du Moulin and Daniel Tilenus, a professor at the Reformed Academy at Sedan, and concerned Christology, justification, and several related theological issues. By distinguishing sharply between the two natures in Christ, the human and the divine, Tilenus tended, according to du Moulin, to exclude the human nature of Christ from the person of the divine mediator. Tilenus thus called into question, argued du Moulin, the imputation of Christ's saving merits to humanity. This undermined the Protestant doctrine of justification. Du Moulin's dispute with Tilenus was not easily resolved. Du Moulin and Tilenus were enjoined to live in peace by synods of the Reformed Churches of France, by the Company of Pastors in Geneva, and by Philippe Duplessis-Mornay, the Huguenot soldier, statesman, and pamphleteer, who was one of the most influential Protestants in France.[17] King James made strenuous

[15] Peter du Moulin, "The Authors Life," sig. ***₂. For du Moulin's career, see also the "Autobiographie de Pierre du Moulin, d'après le manuscrit autographe, 1564–1658," *Bulletin de la Société de l'Histoire du Protestantisme Français*, 71 (1858), pp. 170–182, 333–344, 465–477; Lucien Rimbault, *Pierre du Moulin, 1568–1658: un pasteur classique à âge classique* (Paris: J. Vrin, 1966); J. van der Meij, "Pierre Du Moulin in Leiden, 1592–1598," *Lias*, 14, 1 (1987), 15–40; and Brian G. Armstrong, "The Changing Face of French Protestantism: The Influence of Pierre Du Moulin," in Robert V. Schnucker, ed., *Calviniana: Ideas and Influence of Jean Calvin* (Kirksville, Mo.: Sixteenth Century Journal Publishers, 1988), pp. 131–149.

[16] For du Moulin's irenic activities during these years, see W. B. Patterson, "Pierre Du Moulin's Quest for Protestant Unity, 1613–18," in Robert Swanson, ed., *Unity and Diversity in the Church* (Oxford: Basil Blackwell, 1996), Studies in Church History, XXXII, pp. 235–250; and Brian G. Armstrong, "Pierre Du Moulin and James I: The Anglo-French Programme," in Michelle Magdelaine, Maria Cristinà Pitassi, Ruth Whelan, and Antony McKenna, eds., *De l'humanisme aux lumières, Bayle et le protestantisme: mélanges en l'honneur d'Elisabeth Labrousse* (Oxford: Voltaire Foundation, 1996), pp. 17–29.

[17] For Mornay's role in the dispute between du Moulin and Tilenus, see below. Mornay's career is described in rich detail in Raoul Patry, *Philippe du Plessis-Mornay: un huguenot homme d'état (1549–1623)* (Paris: Fischbacher, 1933). The basic documentary sources are in *Mémoires et correspondance de Duplessis-Mornay* (Paris: Treuttel and Würtz, 1824–25), 12 vols. For the attempted mediation by the Company of Pastors, see Geneva, Bibliothèque Publique et Universitaire, MS. fr. 421, fol. 10 (duke of Bouillon to the Company of Pastors, April 22, 1612); 421, fol. 11 (du Moulin to Simon Goulart, April 26, 1612); 421, fol. 13 (du Moulin to the Company of Pastors, May 10, 1612); 421, fols. 14–15 verso (Company of

efforts over a period of two and a half years to persuade the two theologians to cease accusing one another of heretical teachings. He did this by directing Edmondes to calm du Moulin, as well as by writing to du Moulin himself and by seeking the aid of the duke of Bouillon, the patron of the academy in which Tilenus taught.[18] James was not uncritical about du Moulin's interpretations of the scriptures himself. He took issue with du Moulin, who had defended James's book against Coeffeteau, for having in various places given "a cleane contrary interpretaōn to the text of Scripture, then that wch we give in o^r booke."[19] Du Moulin defended himself at length for his conduct in the controversy with Tilenus in a letter to James on March 1, 1613. His adversary, he argued, had continued to publish views which threatened to undermine the faith of the French Reformed Churches and to bring them into disrepute abroad. Du Moulin was anxious to answer Tilenus, since the issue at stake was the central doctrine of justification.[20] At the end of the letter, however, he asserted that he wanted to work constructively to achieve peace and harmony in the French Church in the way the king had urged him to do. "In order to obey you," he wrote, "I have projected some means of accord and union among all the Churches which have thrown off the yoke of the Pope, which I submit to the judgement of your Majesty, who is someone that it seems that God has raised up for a work so excellent."[21] Enclosed with du Moulin's letter was a three-page document entitled "Overtures for striving for the union of the

Pastors to Bouillon, June 13, 1612); 421, fols. 18–18 verso (Bouillon to the Company of Pastors, August 11, 1612); 421, fols. 26–27 verso (Bouillon to the Company of Pastors, October 15, 1612); 421, fols. 32–35 verso (Company of Pastors to du Moulin, October ?, 1612); 421, fols. 36–37 (du Moulin to the Company of Pastors, November 16, 1612). The issues in dispute between du Moulin and Tilenus are dealt with in Edinburgh, National Library of Scotland, Wodrow MS. Quarto XXII, fols. 139 verso–141 verso (the Provincial Synod, Ile de France, to the National Synod of Tonneins March 17, 1614), fols. 154–154 verso (Bouillon to the Reformed Church of Paris), fols. 150 verso–153 verso (Tilenus to the Reformed Church in Paris, March 25, 1614), and fols. 144–148 (du Moulin to the National Synod of Tonneins, April 1614).
18 James's, Edmondes's, and Bouillon's efforts to resolve the dispute between du Moulin and Tilenus can be traced in PRO SP 78/59, fol. 131 (James I to Bouillon, May 1, 1612), SP 78/60, fol. 145 (Edmondes to James I, October 15, 1612), SP 78/61, fols. 44–44 verso (Bouillon to James I, February 6/16, 1613), SP 78/61, fols. 91–91 verso (James I to Edmondes, March 9, 1613), and SP 78/61, fol. 123 (du Moulin to James I, April 6/16, 1613).
19 PRO SP 78/58, fol. 272 verso (James I to Edmondes, December 19, 1611). James disagreed with several interpretations in du Moulin's book *De l'accomplissement des propheties*, as he indicated plainly in a letter to du Moulin shortly after its publication. See Paris: Bibliothèque Nationale, Collection Dupuy 571, fols. 60–63 verso (December 16, 1611). The king cited instances in which du Moulin was too harsh in his criticisms of fathers of the Church and of Pope Gregory I. See also SP 78/58, fol. 270 (Salisbury to Edmondes, December 19, 1611) and SP 78/58, fol. 274 (Notes concerning du Moulin's book).
20 PRO SP 78/61, fols. 66–66 verso (du Moulin to James I, February 19/March 1, 1613).
21 Ibid., fol. 67.

Churches of Christendom and pacifying the differences which have already arisen or which might arise in the future."[22]

Du Moulin's plan, with twenty articles, sought to find a basis for bringing together the Reformed churches, including the Church of England, and, subsequently, for bringing together these churches and the Lutheran churches. This would be done in two stages by means of an international assembly held with the support of the civil rulers of the Protestant states, especially the king of Great Britain, who is described in the first article as "the greatest and most powerful" of the sovereign princes of countries not under the subjection of the pope.[23] The international assembly described in the plan would be a meeting of two theologians sent by the British king, two by the churches of France, two by those in the Netherlands, two by the Swiss cantons, and "one or two from each prince of Germany of our confession."[24] In addition, King James and the Elector Palatine might seek the support of some of the Lutheran princes, especially the king of Denmark and the dukes of Saxony, Württemberg, and Brunswick, in sending representatives there. The deputies at the assembly would put on the table the Reformed confessions of the various churches, including those of England and Scotland, and draw up a common confession. Some matters "not necessary to salvation" might be passed over, including the opinions of Arminius on predestination.[25] Once this doctrinal accord had been drawn up, the delegates would formally declare that their churches did not condemn each other because of differences in ceremonies and ecclesiastical polity. The deputies would then seek to meet with deputies of the Lutheran churches in order to enlarge this association. On the perennially contentious issues of the necessity of baptism, the manner of Christ's presence in the Lord's Supper, and the reception of the body of Christ in the Supper, agreement would be sought with the Lutherans on broad theological principles.[26] But where complete agreement could not be reached, differing views would be tolerated among the churches. At the conclusion of the assembly a celebration of the Lord's Supper would be held at which the Lutheran pastors and the others would communicate together. During the holding of the assembly, King James would be kept informed of its proceedings. His advice would be sought by the assembly at its conclusion when the whole body would journey to England to meet with him. After their return home, the deputies would submit their work for the approval of their respective churches, while the princes would seek to abolish the names of Lutheran, Calvinist, and Zwinglian in favor of the name Christian Reformed Churches. Once all of this had been accomplished, "then would

---

[22] Ibid., fols. 68–69.   [23] Ibid., fol. 68.   [24] Ibid.
[25] Ibid.   [26] Ibid., fol. 68 verso.

be the time to seek the accord of the Roman Church."[27] Even if such an accord was not feasible, "we will be much more considerable and will speak with more authority when we will be in agreement."[28] James's initial response to du Moulin's plan was favorable, though guarded. In a letter to du Moulin on March 7, 1613 he wrote: "We have received your . . . letter with the project that you had conceived to unite the reformed churches, which we have not yet had the leisure to consider so seriously as well as we desire, but we will keep it near us in order to think more about how to further it, and we will serve it the best that it will be possible for us to the good of the Church of God."[29]

One of the people with whom du Moulin discussed this cause was Duplessis-Mornay, who, as president of the Huguenot political assembly at Saumur in 1611 and in subsequent years, had sought to guide his co-religionists peacefully through the uncertainties of the period following Henry IV's death.[30] Mornay's interest in bringing the French Protestants into closer association with Protestants abroad had arisen during the dark days of the religious wars, when the Huguenots desperately needed foreign allies. But his hopes for a Protestant union, or reunion, were still very much alive in the years of peace which followed the Edict of Nantes in 1598.[31] The accession of James VI of Scotland as James I of England seemed to him to mark the advent of an era in which this union could be effected. As Mornay wrote, on March 26, 1604, in a letter to Robert Le Maçon, sieur de La Fontaine, the pastor of the church for French Protestant refugees in London, James seemed "born and brought up to unite or assuage the differences in matters of religion among all the Protestant Churches of Europe."[32]

As early as March 1605 Mornay had tried to involve James in a broad scheme for Protestant union that originated in Germany among Protestant princes who were concerned over the tensions between Lutheran and Calvinist states. Mornay prepared a memorandum on a proposed national synod in Germany, where the problem was to be discussed, urging that James be informed of the result of the negotiations and asked to make England a party to the agreement which Mornay hoped would be forth-

[27] Ibid., fol. 69.   [28] Ibid.

[29] Ibid., fol. 88 (James I to du Moulin, March 7, 1613).

[30] Arthur L. Herman, "The Saumur Assembly of 1611: Huguenot Political Belief and Action in the Age of Marie de Medici," Ph.D. thesis, Johns Hopkins University, 1984, esp. pp. 66–131, 299–441; Jack Alden Clarke, *Huguenot Warrior: The Life and Times of Henri de Rohan, 1579–1638* (The Hague: Martinus Nijhoff, 1966), pp. 25–47.

[31] Patry, *Philippe du Plessis-Mornay*, pp. 375–462. For Duplessis-Mornay's activities on behalf of Protestant unity, beginning in 1580, see Robert D. Linder, "The French Calvinist Response to the Formula of Concord," *Journal of Ecumenical Studies*, 19, 1 (Winter 1982), 18–37, esp. pp. 22–29.

[32] Mornay, *Mémoires et correspondance*, vol. IX, p. 538.

coming.[33] Later Mornay was disappointed not only that this proposal foundered, but that James did not seem to take a more active part in leading the Protestant churches towards closer and more fraternal relations. In 1608 Mornay instructed his envoy to Venice – who went there to work circumspectly to further the Protestant cause and to bring Venice into closer association with the Protestant states – to communicate this disappointment to the English ambassador.[34] Again, in a letter of January 2, 1612 to Jacques Bongars, the representative of the French crown to the Protestant princes of Germany, Mornay expressed the wish that James would undertake "the healing of our diseases and divisions" as he had so often been exhorted to do. For reasons which must have been as much political as religious, Mornay declared his commitment to the "pursuit of so good a work."[35] By October 4, 1613 Mornay had reason to feel that his long-cherished hope was a good deal closer to realization. Writing on this date to Jacques de Jaucourt, sieur de Rouvray, deputy general of the French Reformed Churches at the royal court, Mornay mentioned having discussed with du Moulin a plan for the reunion of the Protestant churches:

> We have discussed together, M. Dumoulin and I, the proposal for the reunion of all the Protestant Churches, towards which I have worked for a long time and I have praised God that it is set in motion. I strongly approve the means that he has set forth; only I shall wish that the execution of it be effected by stages and degrees, as I explained, because I should be afraid that in pushing the whole thing at once one would succeed in injuring it.[36]

He disclosed also that he was writing to the English ambassador on this subject.[37]

Mornay wrote to the ambassador, Sir Thomas Edmondes, on the same day. He reminded Edmondes that he had himself been in touch with James and his ambassadors in France since the beginning of the king's reign, urging that steps be taken to bring about an accord among the Protestant churches:

---

33 Ibid., vol. X, pp. 75–78. In a letter to André Rivet, Pastor of Thouars, on May 22, 1605, Mornay commented that he had "written amply and seriously concerning this matter to persons of importance who can be useful in it." *Mémoires et correspondance*, vol. X, p. 92.

34 See the *Instructions* prepared for David de Licques, August 1, 1608, in Mornay's *Mémoires et correspondance*, vol. X, p. 239. Sir Henry Wotton, to whom de Licques was to communicate Mornay's message, had been engaged for some time in the task of furthering Protestantism in Venice. See Logan Pearsall Smith, *The Life and Letters of Sir Henry Wotton*, 2 vols. (Oxford: Clarendon Press, 1907), vol. I, pp. 75–107.

35 Mornay, *Mémoires et correspondance*, vol. XI, p. 376.

36 Ibid., vol. XII, p. 420. Jacques de Jaucourt, sieur de Rouvray, Ménétreux, and Saint-Andeux, had been chosen one of two deputies general by the queen regent in 1611. He was the brother of Jean de Jaucourt, seigneur de Villarnoul, who was Mornay's son-in-law. Patry, *Philippe du Plessis-Mornay*, 431, 491 note.

37 Mornay, *Mémoires et correspondance*, vol. XII, p. 420.

Monsieur, a little after it had pleased God to call the king your sovereign to this great estate, I proposed that there was no work more worthy of his piety, wisdom, and greatness, than the concord of all the Protestant Churches of Christendom, and for the sake of this I conferred several times, both by writing and in person with Messieurs his ambassadors in this kingdom, [and] even made to them some proposals about means which I believed very expedient in order to succeed, and I think you may have heard them talked about.[38]

Mornay commented that he had been disappointed not to see such a project advanced, though it had apparently always met with the king's approval.

Now, however, the Huguenot leader had been greatly encouraged to learn from du Moulin that James wished to undertake the work of bringing about an accord among the Protestant churches. He commended du Moulin and warmly endorsed the latter's plan, though with certain qualifications:

I therefore greatly praised God, Monsieur, when M. Dumoulin, having come to see us in these quarters, told me that this great king, your sovereign, wished to embrace this necessary work, if there ever was one in Christendom, and communicated to me a certain project, which he had drawn up, of steps to be taken to a successful end, which proceeded from so holy a zeal and so excellent a spirit that I could only greatly praise and approve it; only in the execution of them, as I advised him, it seemed to be necessary to proceed by degrees and stages, for reasons which he will know more easily how to declare to you.[39]

Mornay became almost lyrical in describing the contribution which this project could make to the pacification of Europe. Referring to the impending visit of du Moulin to the ambassador, he said:

I beseech you therefore, Monsieur, according to the desire which I know you have for the advancement of the glory of God, to wish to hear everything from his mouth, in order that by your holy initiatives this salutary design can be achieved under the authority of your sovereign; a design, in truth, requiring a long wind, and which, moreover, requires a continual care with patience; but certainly at the end of which will be seen prepared a crown of incomparable glory for the king your sovereign, who will by this means make the whole of Europe sing the song of the angels, and to so many honest people who long for this accord give reason to close their lives with the song of Simeon.[40]

Mornay promised to spend his remaining days supporting this project.[41]

On the same date Mornay wrote a memorandum entitled "Advice on the reunion of the confessions of all the Protestant Churches of Christendom," in which can be seen some of the qualifications which he evidently suggested to du Moulin. He advised that the "princes, estates, and Churches of the Confession of Augsburg," the Lutherans, not be brought into the discussions until after "the Churches of our confession" had reached general

---

[38] Ibid., p. 421.   [39] Ibid., pp. 421–22.   [40] Ibid., p. 422.   [41] Ibid.

agreement.[42] In order to reach this point there should be a "pro-synod" of the type proposed by du Moulin, namely, a meeting of the Reformed or Calvinist churches only.[43] Mornay felt that in order to have the French Protestants represented at such a meeting it would be necessary to submit the proposal to a national synod, and to refer it to the local churches afterwards. He urged that since the national synod met only every two years, it would accelerate matters to submit the plan to the very next national synod.[44] He observed further that some would be suspicious of the plan as an attempt by the king of Great Britain to change the form of discipline and polity of other Reformed churches – an apparent reference to James's strong predilection for episcopacy. For this reason it would be good to declare that, for the sake of peace and concord, the churches would "support fraternally the polity and discipline of one another."[45]

Lucien Rimbault has argued convincingly that the plan of union accepted by the Twenty-First National Synod of the Reformed Churches of France, meeting at Tonneins, May 2–June 3, 1614, was mainly du Moulin's work, even though du Moulin was not present at the synod.[46] Rimbault believed that a plan of du Moulin's was revised in accordance with Mornay's suggestions. He also, correctly, surmised that a form of the plan published at The Hague in 1617, apparently by du Moulin's theological opponents, was an earlier version which du Moulin revised after meeting with Mornay.[47] But Rimbault evidently did not know about du Moulin's letter of March 1, 1613 to King James, in which du Moulin enclosed an even earlier version of his plan. The "Overtures" that du Moulin sent to James were the heart of the plan of union accepted at Tonneins. The relation between the plan sent to James by du Moulin early in 1613 and the plan included in the acts of the synod in 1614 can be briefly described.[48]

[42] Ibid., p. 423.   [43] Ibid.   [44] Ibid.   [45] Ibid.

[46] Rimbault, *Pierre du Moulin*, pp. 71–75. For the presbyterian/synodal polity of the Reformed Churches of France, including the central role played by the National Synod, see Elisabeth Labrousse, "Calvinism in France, 1598–1685," in Menna Prestwich, ed., *International Calvinism, 1541–1715* (Oxford: Clarendon Press, 1985), pp. 285–315, esp. pp. 285–293.

[47] Rimbault, *Pierre du Moulin*, pp. 74–75, 235–238. Rimbault identifies the editor of du Moulin's plan in 1617 as an Arminian opposed to du Moulin's strict Calvinism. See Pierre du Moulin, *Copie de la suite ou seconde partie de la lettre de Monsieur du Moulin, Ministre en l'Eglise Reformée à Paris, omise de propos delibere, & par tromperie, en l'edition de Schiedam; ensemble des Ouvertures dudit sieur pour travailler à l'union des églises de la Chrestienté, & à appaiser les differens, &c.* (The Hague: Hillebrant Iacobssz, 1617), pp. 12–18. For the issues which separated Arminians from strict Calvinists, see chapter 8, below.

[48] Du Moulin's earlier plan is enclosed in his letter to James, PRO SP 78/61, fols. 68–69 (February 19/March 1, 1613); the text of the later plan of union is contained in the acts of the Synod of Tonneins (May 2–June 3, 1614), Montpellier, Faculté de Théologie Protestante, MS. 16400: Recueil des actes des Synodes Nationaux des Eglises Reformées du royaume de France, 1559–1620, no pagination or foliation. The text of the plan in SP 78/61

Changes, mostly additions, were made in seven of du Moulin's earlier articles. One important change was to delete any reference to Lutheran deputies at the initial assembly. The word *reformed* was added to describe the churches expected to participate in the initial assembly in order to show that the first assembly would be made up of deputies of the Reformed or Calvinist churches, including the Church of England.[49] The crucial difference between the two plans is that there were two distinct assemblies in the plan submitted to the Synod of Tonneins. This later plan specified that the first assembly would begin with a fast, by the deputies and the host church, and would end with a celebration of the "Holy Supper," during which the pastors of England and France would communicate together.[50] It further specified that, after the first assembly, the king of Great Britain and the authorities of the various Reformed churches would ask the Lutheran princes and churches to send deputies to a second assembly to work for an accord.[51] The effect of these changes was to distinguish clearly the two stages in the project of bringing the Protestant churches together and to stress the key role to be played by King James. The king would be expected to help to bring about the union of the Reformed churches with the Church of England, and he would then be expected to encourage the Lutheran princes and churches to send deputies to a second assembly, which would, it was hoped, unite the major Protestant churches.

The plan found in the acts of the synod seems to have been brought to Tonneins by David Home, a Scot, who held – or had held – an appointment as pastor in a French Reformed congregation. His appearance at the synod is described in the proceedings as follows:

Having been informed that M. David Home, formerly Pastor of the Church of Duras, in lower Guienne, was in this place, newly returned from his country of Scotland, and that having passed through England, the Most Serene King of Great Britain had entrusted him with a letter for this Company, which concerns the differences which have arisen concerning a point of the doctrine of the churches of this realm.[52]

---

is different in several ways from that in du Moulin, *Copie de la suite*. There are several slight changes in phrasing and in the numbering of the articles. There are also some additions to the earlier plan sent to James which are incorporated in the plan in the acts of the synod. But the plan in *Copie de la suite* is not identical to the text incorporated in the acts of the synod. All of this suggests that the version in Moulin's *Copie de la suite* is a revision of the plan that du Moulin sent to King James in early 1613.

[49] PRO SP 78/61, fol. 68; Montpellier MS. 16400, [fol. 1 verso].
[50] Montpellier MS. 16400, [fol. 1 verso].   [51] Ibid., [fol. 2].
[52] Jean Aymon, ed., *Tous les Synodes Nationaux des Eglises Réformées de France*, 2 vols. (The Hague: Charles Delo, 1710), vol. II, p. 5. See also John Quick, ed., *Synodicon in Gallia Reformata: or, The Acts, Decisions, Decrees, and Canons of Those Famous National Councils of the Reformed Churches in France*, 2 vols. (London: T. Parkhurst and J. Robinson, 1692), vol. I, p. 395. Aymon, *Tous les Synodes*, vol. II, p. 5; Quick, *Synodicon*, vol. I, p. 395.

The synod's brief narrative of Home's journey neglects the drama of what actually happened. Early in 1614 France was in the midst of an incipient rebellion led by discontented nobles, including Bouillon and the prince of Condé, a "prince of the [royal] blood."[53] Letters, partly in cipher, from the French ambassador in London, Samuel Spifame, sieur de Buisseaux, to Villeroy and Pierre Brûlart, vicomte de Puysieulx, secretaries of state at the French court, reveal that Home was arrested.[54] In April he had been stopped near Orléans, evidently on his way to Tonneins, and found to be carrying suspicious papers. Buisseaux, in response to a query from the French court, identified Home as minister at Duras, learned, and very zealous in his religion, who had recently spent five or six months in England.[55] Home carried letters from King James, the elector of the Palatinate, and the duke of Bouillon. He had, it seemed, come from Bouillon's base at Sedan. Since Bouillon had already been involved in 1612 in an attempt to stir up opposition to the regency government by leading members of the nobility, and had then acted with English support, the French authorities had every reason to be vigilant.[56] Buisseaux discussed the matter with James in early May, after the king himself asked if there was any news about the Scottish minister arrested in France. James said that he had sent Home to Sedan to seek an accommodation between the theologians Tilenus and du Moulin, from whence Home was to go to the Synod of Tonneins, bearing a letter from himself to the synod on the same subject. The king denied sending any other memoranda to the synod.[57] By May 21, Buisseaux had a more complete picture. The "true and only" reason that Home had been sent to the synod by the king was, he wrote, to carry there "an overture which has been drawn up by the minister du Moulin to try to

---

[53] Hayden, *France and the Estates General of 1614*, pp. 54–60.

[54] PRO PRO 31/3/47 contains transcripts of the letters of Buisseaux in England to Villeroy and Puysieulx in France in 1614. For the key to the cipher used by Buisseaux, I am indebted to H. R. Trevor-Roper, Lord Dacre of Glanton.

[55] Ibid. (April 22, 1614).

[56] That James knew about and encouraged plans for an uprising by Bouillon and other nobles disaffected by the regency government in the late summer of 1612 is clear from Edmondes's despatches from Paris. Bouillon as well as James feared that a marriage agreement recently concluded between France and Spain would draw the French government towards aggressively Catholic policies at home and abroad. See PRO SP 78/60, fols. 93–93 verso (Edmondes to James I, September 14, 1612), SP 78/60, fols. 156–156 verso (Edmondes to Rochester, October 7, 1612), SP 78/60, fols. 166–166 verso (Edmondes to James I, October 10, 1612), SP 78/60, fols. 178–178 verso (Edmondes to James I, October 22, 1612). The death of Charles de Bourbon, comte de Soissons, uncle of Henri de Bourbon, the prince of Condé, in October 1612, brought this intended "reformation" of the government to an end. See also Adams, "The Road to La Rochelle: English Foreign Policy and the Huguenots, 1610 to 1629," pp. 416–419. Early in 1614, as Adams shows, the French government faced another attempt by Bouillon; this time James sought to play the role of mediator.

[57] PRO PRO 31/3/47 (May 11, 1614).

unite all the churches which pretend to be reformed."[58] According to Buisseaux, the British king had shown this proposal to some of his bishops, who had not initially found it a very likely plan. But Bouillon and Duplessis-Mornay, said Buisseaux, considered it to be "very necessary and feasible" and urged that it be carried to the synod.[59] Bouillon and Duplessis-Mornay, he reported, were also engaged in the same attempt as the king to pacify Tilenus and du Moulin. Buisseaux concluded that there was no political danger in Home's mission, which is apparently what the French authorities in Paris had themselves concluded after reading the papers which Home was carrying. Home had been permitted to continue his journey to Tonneins for the meeting of the synod.

The synod ordered that before the letter from James was officially received, a copy should be given to Rouvray, deputy general of the Reformed Churches of France at court, so that he could be ready to demonstrate, if need be, that the deputies were not communicating with a foreign prince on matters of state.[60] Home was allowed to give an oral summary of the message to the delegates:

The said Monsieur Home, having been shown in, gave a verbal representation to the effect that the king of Great Britain had charged him to exhort this Company, on his behalf, to procure and achieve a happy Conformity of doctrine among the pastors, professors, and all the leaders of the churches of this realm, without giving offence to those who teach theology in the Churches of Germany, and others who have not the same sentiments.[61]

James's concern, as the letter showed, was with the theological controversy between du Moulin and Tilenus, over the two natures of Christ.[62] The king had been attempting to appease this disagreement since the preceding national synod, held at Privas, in 1612.[63] James was not the only political leader who had shown concern over this controversy. The proceedings state:

The letters of the king of Great Britain, received at the opening of the Assembly, and those of the Church of Geneva, having been read again, likewise those which have been given following, on behalf of my lord the Elector Palatine and Monsieur the Marechal de Bouillon, written to this Company, concerning the differences between du Moulin and Tilenus: the Company deputed some pastors to see the Inventory sent by the said M. Tilenus, and the Confession of the said M. du Moulin, concerning the effects of the hypostatic union [of the two natures].[64]

[58] Ibid. (May 21, 1614).   [59] Ibid. (May 21, 1614).
[60] Aymon, *Tous les Synodes*, vol. II, pp. 5–6; Quick, *Synodicon*, vol. I, p. 395.
[61] Aymon, *Tous les Synodes*, vol. II, p. 6; Quick, *Synodicon*, vol. I, p. 395.
[62] Aymon, *Tous les Synodes*, vol. II, p. 6; Quick, *Synodicon*, vol. I, p. 395.
[63] Rimbault, *Pierre du Moulin*, pp. 57–59, 71.
[64] Aymon, *Tous les Synodes*, vol. II, p. 37; Quick, *Synodicon*, vol. I, p. 418.

Apparently the Elector Palatine and the duke of Bouillon were as concerned as James that there not be a split in the ranks of the Reformed churches. The synod found that, though harsh words had been attributed to du Moulin in defending his views against attacks from Tilenus, du Moulin's theology was orthodox. It therefore ordered that du Moulin and Tilenus go to Saumur, on the Loire, where Mornay was governor and an important academy was located, and there, under the influence of the governor, the professors, and the pastors of the place, become reconciled. This procedure was to be reported to James and the other correspondents who had urged that the dispute be settled.[65]

So far there had been no mention of a larger plan of union. It seems to be alluded to, however, in James's letter, where the king said:

That honor in which God has clothed us, in elevating us to the first and most eminent place in the church, for the defence of the truth, and in order to serve with all our strength in our royal dignity, and the very ardent desire that we have to see a good Peace and Union flourish among those who sincerely profess the Christian faith, and the care that we take concerning your preservation, as being the first to have thrown off the yoke of idolatry, leads us to speak freely with you.[66]

James took seriously what he considered to be his responsibility as the head of an important Protestant state to foster "Peace and Union" among his coreligionists. He credited the French Protestants with a priority which could hardly be demonstrated when he said they had been the first to throw off "the yoke of idolatry."[67] But his use of this phrase connects his letter to the plan of union, as will be seen.

The letter sent to James by the synod expressed in elaborate terms the gratitude of the French Protestants for the king's interest in them:

Sire, The zeal with which it has pleased God to inflame your Royal Spirit, and the great care which your Most Serene Majesty deigns to take in the Christian Churches, obliges all the good servants of God to address prayers and continual votive offerings to the Lord of Glory, that it may please him to prolong the days of Your Majesty, and make your reign prosper. The Churches of France, in the name of which we are here assembled, have the most profound feelings of obligation, because they have received very often, and to their great advantage the consoling influences of this brilliant star in the sky of the Church of God, for which they render glory to God, and to Your Majesty our very humble thanks.[68]

---

[65] Aymon, *Tous les Synodes*, vol. II, p. 38; Quick, *Synodicon*, vol. I, p. 418.

[66] Aymon, *Tous les Synodes*, vol. II, p. 63; Quick, *Synodicon*, vol. I, p. 438.

[67] For the early history of the Calvinist Reformation in France, see Menna Prestwich, "Calvinism in France, 1555–1629," in Prestwich, *International Calvinism, 1541–1715*, pp. 71–107, which stresses French conditions; and Robert M. Kingdon, *Geneva and the Coming of the Wars of Religion in France, 1555–1563* (Geneva: Droz, 1956), which stresses the role played by Calvin's Geneva. For the earliest French Protestants, see Mark Greengrass, *The French Reformation* (Oxford: Basil Blackwell, 1987), pp. 1–20.

[68] Aymon, *Tous les Synodes*, vol. II, pp. 63–64; Quick, *Synodicon*, vol. I, p. 438.

After reporting their actions aimed at healing the breach between Tilenus and du Moulin, the delegates then mentioned in their letter a certain "Heroic Design" of James's which they had received from David Home:

> In regard to the Heroic Design of Your Majesty . . . to reunite the Churches of several Nations in one and the same Confession and Doctrine, we regard it as an enterprise worthy of such a great king, and one which answers to the holy zeal with which the Celestial Majesty has embraced your royal soul, and from our side we will contribute to it of our offerings, and make our contributions in the proper time and place. We pray also with all our heart and all the faculties of our soul: that this holy work might advance for the greatest Glory of God, to the confusion of the enemies of the Truth, whose detestable doctrine of regicide we condemn, which violates the Sacred Majesty of Kings, and their proposition by which they maintain that the Pope is able to put under interdict a whole realm.[69]

Who was David Home, the man entrusted with this delicate mission by King James? He was the second son of Sir David Home, or Hume, seventh baron of Wedderburn in Berwickshire. After attending St. Andrews University, where he matriculated in 1578, he visited France and Switzerland in his early twenties. Later he became a semi-permanent resident of France, probably spending the greater part of his life there, though he seems also to have resided at intervals on his estate at Godscroft in Berwickshire. A pamphleteer on many subjects, religious and political, he seems also to have been a gifted Latin poet.[70] Home and King James were allied in the pamphlet war over the rights of kings, which had been precipitated by the Oath of Allegiance. Home published a work in 1612 entitled *Le contr'assassin*, in which he attacked the political views of the Jesuits, especially Cardinal Bellarmine.[71] In dedicating the work to James, he declared his intention to demonstrate that "the doctrine that Your Majesty has learned from his youth," particularly on the relation between church and state, was "altogether pure and conformable to the Holy Scriptures."[72] This work, said Home, was one to which he was impelled by "nature and your benefactions to those to whom I have the honor to belong"[73] – by which he presumably meant the Reformed Churches of France. In a letter to James

---

[69] Aymon, *Tous les Synodes*, vol. II, pp. 64–65; Quick, *Synodicon*, vol. I, p. 439.

[70] On Home's life, see Thomas Bayne on David Hume (1560?–1630?), *Dictionary of National Biography*, 22 vols. (London: Oxford University Press, 1959–1960), vol. X, pp. 213–214; and Eugène and Emile Haag, *La France protestante*, 9 vols. (Paris: Joël Cherbuliez, 1847–1859), vol. V, p. 518.

[71] D. H. [David Home], *Le contr'assassin, ou response à l'apologie des Jesuites, faite par un pere de la Compagnie de Jesus de Loyola* (n. p., 1612). The Jesuit apologist whose work Home was answering was Pierre Coton, who defended the political teachings of his order after the assassination of Henry IV in 1610. See Roland Mousnier, *The Assassination of Henry IV: The Tyrannicide Problem and the Consolidation of the French Absolute Monarchy in the Early Seventeenth Century*, trans. Joan Spencer (London: Faber and Faber, 1973), pp. 63–105, 213–228.

[72] Home, *Le contr'assassin*, sig. *iiii.   [73] Ibid., sig. *iii.

which accompanied a copy of his book, Home asked the king to accept a letter from one he did not know.[74] James responded by way of Edmondes that Home's book had shown him to be a man of "discrecōn and iudgement."[75] Home had been, as the proceedings of the Synod at Tonneins indicate, the pastor of the Reformed church at Duras, located in Guienne, some twenty miles northwest of Tonneins. He had apparently been pastor there since 1604.[76] On his return from Scotland with messages from King James he must have been shocked to find his church under another's charge. The synod "declared him free to exercise the functions of his ministry in the same Province where he was, or in other Churches of this realm, where God will call him by the ordinary means of a legitimate vocation."[77]

To recapitulate briefly, the plan in the proceedings of the Synod of Tonneins seems to have originated with Pierre du Moulin, who modified it on the basis of suggestions from Philippe Duplessis-Mornay. Du Moulin sent the plan on to James, probably through the English ambassador in Paris. James entrusted the plan to David Home to present to the National Synod of the Reformed Churches of France. It must be assumed, since James's name is associated with the plan in the synod's proceedings and since it was he who gave it to Home, that he approved of the contents of the proposal. Indeed, the responsibility for the plan's final form must lie with the king. This is not to say that anything in the plan was necessarily written by James or his advisers in England – only that the final opportunity for editing or altering the proposal before it was sent to an official ecclesiastical body belonged to the king.

In the synod's proceedings, the plan is entitled "Overtures for striving for the union of the Christian Churches which have shaken off the yoke of the Papacy, and pacifying the differences which have already arisen or which might arise in the future."[78] There are twenty-one articles, of which the first eleven concern the union of the Reformed churches among themselves, and the next nine, the union of the Reformed with the Lutheran churches. The twenty-first article concerns a possible rapprochement with Rome. The plan is marked throughout by boldness of conception and an irenic spirit on the subject of theological differences. It tries, in articles eleven to twenty, to go

[74] PRO SP 78/60, fols. 32–33 (Home to James I, August 15/25, 1612).
[75] PRO SP 78/60, fol. 151 (October 6, 1612).
[76] Haag and Haag, *La France protestante*, vol. V, p. 518.
[77] Aymon, *Tous les Synodes*, vol. II, p. 38; Quick, *Synodicon*, vol. I, p. 419.
[78] Montpellier MS. 16400, [fol. 1]. Compare Aymon, *Tous les Synodes*, vol. II, p. 57; Quick, *Synodicon*, vol. I, p. 434. My analysis is based on the text of the Montpellier manuscript of the acts of the synod, which I have compared to the two published editions. As Brian G. Armstrong has shown, there are many extant manuscript copies of the acts of the various national synods. See his "*Semper Reformanda*: The Case of the French Reformed Church, 1559–1620," in W. Fred Graham, ed., *Later Calvinism: International Perspectives* (Kirksville, Mo.: Sixteenth Century Journal Publishers, 1994), 119–140.

at least half-way to meet the Lutherans; the theological ideas endorsed in this section have, nevertheless, a decidedly Calvinistic tone. The articles stress the necessity of having the backing of the temporal princes whose states would be involved in the plan. The first article of all declares that "no accord can be reached without the aid, assistance, and leadership of the sovereign princes whose lands have been withdrawn from the subjection of the Pope."[79] This article also makes clear that the king of Great Britain was considered the chief of these rulers and was expected to be the key mover of the plan. The essence of the plan was that there should be two assemblies, the first composed of deputies of the Reformed churches and the Church of England, the second of these together with deputies of the Lutheran churches.

The plan got down to practical matters almost at once. Article two deals with the number of deputies to be invited to the first assembly: "two theologians sent by His Majesty [of Great Britain], two by the Churches of France, two by those of the Low Countries, two by the Cantons of Switzerland, [and] one or two by each Prince of Germany of our confession."[80] The place of the meeting, dealt with in articles two and three, was evidently considered a matter of some importance. It should be readily accessible to the countries involved and secure from possible interference. Zeeland, the province at the southwestern extreme of the United Provinces of the Netherlands, seemed most nearly ideal: it was convenient to the ports of England and within easy reach of other countries.[81] At this first assembly the deputies would not begin by debating theological issues. Such discussion would probably lead only to wrangles, with the result that the deputies would never give in but return thinking of victory.[82] Instead, according to article four, they were to lay on the table "the Confessions of the Churches of France, England, and Scotland, the Low Countries, Switzerland, [and] the Palatinate."[83] This collection would presumably include the Thirty-Nine Articles of the Church of England, the Scots Confession, the Gallican Confession, the Belgic Confession, the Helvetic Confession, and the Heidelberg Catechism. On the basis of these already existing confessions a new one would be drawn up which would serve all the churches concerned. In

---

[79] Montpellier MS. 16400, [fol. 1]. Compare Aymon, *Tous les Synodes*, vol. II, p. 57; Quick, *Synodicon*, vol. I, p. 434.

[80] Montpellier MS. 16400, [fol. 1]. Compare Aymon, *Tous les Synodes*, vol. II, p. 57; Quick, *Synodicon*, vol. I, p. 434.

[81] Montpellier MS. 16400, [fol. 1]. Compare Aymon, *Tous les Synodes*, vol. II, p. 57; Quick, *Synodicon*, vol. I, p. 434.

[82] Montpellier MS. 16400, [fol. 1]. Compare Aymon, *Tous les Synodes*, vol. II, p. 57; Quick, *Synodicon*, vol. I, p. 434.

[83] Montpellier MS. 16400, [fol. 1]. Compare Aymon, *Tous les Synodes*, vol. II, p. 57; Quick, *Synodicon*, vol. I, p. 434.

this common confession, some debatable matters could be omitted: "One would take no notice of many things, without the knowledge of which one can be saved, as is the question of Piscator, and many subtle opinions proposed by Arminius about free will, the perseverance of the saints, [and] predestination."[84] This is a startling statement, coming as it does only four years before the Synod of Dort! Furthermore these were matters which concerned salvation in the most fundamental way. It was further observed in this article that the two sources of real errors in religion were curiosity and avarice. If it was the latter which had ruined the Church of Rome, it was the former which threatened the Reformed churches. How much better it would be, then, to be content to know only what concerned salvation.[85] Once this common confession had been drawn up, it would be subscribed to – not only by the deputies present but by the rulers of the countries whose churches were involved in the deliberations, and by the National Synod of the French Reformed Churches.[86] Article five further specified that what was intended was a permanent association of churches which could act to help resolve doctrinal disputes: "it would be necessary. . . that a rule be established that henceforth, if in England or France or Germany or the Low Countries or Switzerland some controversy should come up, nothing can be concluded or decided, even less innovated, without the consent of all the provinces which have entered into this accord."[87]

Such a plan threatened, of course, to run afoul of the various customs and aspirations of the churches involved. Nevertheless, article six expressed optimism about the prospects for such an agreement. After all, it was claimed, the Reformed churches were already largely in accord on the fundamental articles of the faith and differed "only in certain ceremonies and in ecclesiastical polity" or on particular matters of theology about which no official ordinances had yet been passed.[88] On the subject of these differences, article seven had a reassuring word to say to those who felt that their liturgical practices and polity would be endangered by the proposed accord:

On which ceremonies and polity a mutual declaration must be made and added to

---

[84] Montpellier MS. 16400, [fol. 1]. Compare Aymon, *Tous les Synodes*, vol. II, p. 57; Quick, *Synodicon*, vol. I, p. 434. Johann Piscator, a strict Calvinist, taught at Herborn University in Nassau, in the Rhineland. For Arminius, see chapter 8, below.

[85] Montpellier MS. 16400, [fol. 1]. Compare Aymon, *Tous les Synodes*, vol. II, pp. 57–58; Quick, *Synodicon*, vol. I, p. 434.

[86] Montpellier MS. 16400, [fol. 1]. Compare Aymon, *Tous les Synodes*, vol. II, p. 58; Quick, *Synodicon*, vol. I, p. 434.

[87] Montpellier MS. 16400, [fols. 1–1 verso]. Compare Aymon, *Tous les Synodes*, vol. II, p. 58; Quick, *Synodicon*, vol. I, p. 434.

[88] Montpellier MS. 16400, [fol. 1 verso]. Compare Aymon, *Tous les Synodes*, vol. II, p. 58; Quick, *Synodicon*, vol. I, p. 435.

the said Confession by which the said deputies, in the name of those who sent them, will declare that the churches do not at all condemn each other for this difference, which would by no means prevent our agreeing on the faith and true doctrine and our embracing each other as truly faithful and members of the same body.[89]

This assurance must have been important to Huguenots, who were aware of the liturgical and ecclesiological differences between their own church and the Church of England.[90] As if to demonstrate that the liturgical differences within this group were no bar to communion and fellowship in the Body of Christ, article eight specified that after this first assembly the Lord's Supper would be celebrated, during which the pastors of England and France would communicate together. The assembly would have begun with a fast not only by the deputies but by the church of the place in which the assembly was meeting, in order to "beseech the assistance of God for so holy and important a plan."[91]

The articles stressed the necessity of proceeding with the backing of the temporal authorities. In article nine it was stated that the deputies should "come furnished with power and letters amply authorizing them" to act.[92] These letters should convey the commitment of those who issued them to receive the conclusions of the assembly and work to put them into effect.[93] Special efforts should be made to see that King James was a party to all that would be decided. "During the holding of this assembly," according to article ten, "there might be persons going from and coming to the king of Great Britain so that nothing takes place without his advice and authority."[94] Moreover, after the assembly had done its work, the deputies were to cross over to England, "in order to render their respects to His Majesty, to thank him and to receive his wise counsel concerning the means of putting into practice" their agreement.[95]

Plans for the second assembly were to be made before the first was finally dissolved. To be held the next year, this second assembly was intended to deal with any problems which had been encountered in the realization of the matters agreed to at the first. As it was pointed out in article eleven,

---

[89] Montpellier MS. 16400, [fol. 1 verso]. Compare Aymon, *Tous les Synodes*, vol. II, p. 58; Quick, *Synodicon*, vol. I, p. 435.

[90] Compare Rimbault, *Pierre du Moulin*, p. 72.

[91] Montpellier MS. 16400, [fol. 1 verso]. Compare Aymon, *Tous les Synodes*, vol. II, p. 58; Quick, *Synodicon*, vol. I, p. 435.

[92] Montpellier MS. 16400, [fol. 1 verso]. Compare Aymon, *Tous les Synodes*, vol. II, p. 58; Quick, *Synodicon*, vol. I, p. 435.

[93] Montpellier MS. 16400, [fol. 1 verso]. Compare Aymon, *Tous les Synodes*, vol. II, p. 59; Quick, *Synodicon*, vol. I, p. 435.

[94] Montpellier MS. 16400, [fol. 1 verso]. Compare Aymon, *Tous les Synodes*, vol. II, p. 59; Quick, *Synodicon*, vol. I, p. 435.

[95] Montpellier MS. 16400, [fol. 1 verso]. Compare Aymon, *Tous les Synodes*, vol. II, p. 59; Quick, *Synodicon*, vol. I, p. 435.

"there may be some provinces which will disapprove of some part of what will be agreed to, or which will provide some better expedient."[96] But it was made clear in article twelve that it was at this juncture that the Lutherans would be asked to participate. The invitation was to come from the highest levels: "The time that shall elapse between these two assemblies or synods will be used by His Majesty of England and by the provinces of our confession to accomplish it so that in the second assembly there will be Lutheran pastors and doctors sent by their princes and Lutheran churches to work towards an accord between them and us."[97]

It was remarked in article thirteen that the differences between the Reformed and the Lutheran churches were of two kinds. In the first place, there were differences which could readily be resolved. These included matters of ceremonial, or liturgical practice. The differences which existed here could "very easily be borne with and tolerated," since they were a matter of decorum rather than necessity.[98] The article also included predestination in this category. The plan suggested that this doctrine could be dealt with in the common confession of the Reformed churches in so circumspect a way that agreement with the Lutherans could be reached without difficulty. It recommended that the example of the Augsburg Confession might be followed, where mention is made of this question with a great deal of caution.[99] The same article suggested that the different emphases laid on the importance of baptism by the two groups of churches could be easily dealt with. The necessity of baptism might be affirmed in effect by saying that it was necessary to celebrate baptism in the Christian Church and necessary for each individual not to disregard it, "without pushing further the question of necessity."[100]

Differences which would not be so easy to reconcile were dealt with in the following three articles. There were, it seemed, two main issues in dispute, both concerning the interpretation of the Lord's Supper. Calvinists of the early seventeenth century were unable to accept what they understood as the Lutheran doctrine of "the ubiquity of the Body of Christ,"[101] according

---

[96] Montpellier MS. 16400, [fol. 2]. Compare Aymon, *Tous les Synodes*, vol. II, p. 59; Quick, *Synodicon*, vol. I, p. 435.

[97] Montpellier MS. 16400, [fol. 2]. Compare Aymon, *Tous les Synodes*, vol. II, p. 59; Quick, *Synodicon*, vol. I, p. 435.

[98] Montpellier MS. 16400, [fol. 2]. Compare Aymon, *Tous les Synodes*, vol. II, p. 59; Quick, *Synodicon*, vol. I, p. 435.

[99] Montpellier MS. 16400, [fol. 2]. Compare Aymon, *Tous les Synodes*, vol. II, p. 59; Quick, *Synodicon*, vol. I, p. 436.

[100] Montpellier MS. 16400, [fol. 2]. Compare Aymon, *Tous les Synodes*, vol. II, p. 60; Quick, *Synodicon*, vol. I, p. 436.

[101] Montpellier MS. 16400, [fol. 2]. Compare Aymon, *Tous les Synodes*, vol. II, p. 60; Quick, *Synodicon*, vol. I, p. 436. On this dispute, and its origins in the teachings of Luther, Melanchthon, Zwingli, and Calvin, see Pontien Polman, *L'élément historique dans la*

to which it was possible for Christ's body to be present simultaneously in heaven, at the right hand of the Father, and on earth, in the bread used in the celebration of the Lord's Supper. Differences between the Lutheran view of the real presence of Christ in the elements of the eucharist and the symbolist/memorialist view of the Swiss reformers had divided the two traditions ever since the Marburg Colloquy of 1529. In an effort to get around this difficulty, the plan proposed that the Calvinist side put forward a number of propositions about Christ's Incarnation· with which the Lutherans could be expected to agree. These included the statements that Jesus Christ, born of the Virgin Mary, had a true human body; that, throughout his life on earth and even after his burial, his body was always in one place at one time; that since his Ascension he is seated on God's right hand; that his present glorification has not destroyed the reality of his human nature; and that he will return in the same flesh which he received in the womb of the Virgin Mary when he comes to judge the living and the dead.[102] The implication of these propositions would seem to be that Christ could not be present in his human body in two places at once. But in reference to the divine nature of Christ, one of the propositions stated: "That the eternal Son of God is present everywhere."[103] The plan recognized that this would probably not be enough to satisfy the Lutherans, since it urged a mutual toleration if there were still differences of opinion. It would be especially important "not to write any more books on the subject, or employ any further invective or preaching until God has given more clarity to those who err."[104]

The other – and related – problem concerned the manner in which the faithful received or participated in the Body of Christ in the Lord's Supper. At issue was whether Christ was truly present in the bread and wine used in the service, as the Lutherans asserted, or whether in the act of recalling the saving acts of Christ and sharing in the sacred meal instituted by him the faithful fed on Christ's body in a spiritual sense, as the Calvinists asserted. The plan proposed a way of avoiding a direct confrontation on this issue by .

controverse religieuse du XVIe siècle (Gembloux: J. Duculot, 1932), pp. 35–36, 55–62, 129; Reinhold Seeberg, *Lehrbuch der Dogmengeschichte*, fourth edition, IV, Part I (Leipzig: Werner Scholl, 1933), pp. 457–479; Otto Ritsch, *Dogmengeschichte des Protestantismus*, vol. IV (Göttingen: Vandenhoeck & Ruprecht, 1927), pp. 1–32, 70–106; and Erwin Iserloh, Joseph Glazik, and Hubert Jedin, *Reformation and Counter Reformation* (New York: Crossroad, 1990), pp. 356–361, 385–390.

[102] Montpellier MS. 16400, [fol. 2–2 verso]. Compare Aymon, *Tous les Synodes*, vol. II, p. 60; Quick, *Synodicon*, vol. I, p. 436.

[103] Montpellier MS. 16400, [fol. 2 verso]. Compare Aymon, *Tous les Synodes*, vol. II, p. 60; Quick, *Synodicon*, vol. I, p. 436.

[104] Montpellier MS. 16400, [fol. 2 verso]. Compare Aymon, *Tous les Synodes*, vol. II, p. 60; Quick, *Synodicon*, vol. I, p. 436.

setting out four principles on which both sides, presumably, could agree. These were that the elements of bread and wine in the Lord's Supper were "not naked signs and simple figures, destitute of truth"; "that in the Supper, we participate really in the Body of Christ"; that the bread does not cease to be bread when it is consecrated – that is, is not transubstantiated; and that since it does not cease to be bread, it should not be adored.[105] There followed a genuinely Calvinistic note, and one which also recalled the *sursum corda* of the English Prayer Book, that rather than adoring the sacrament, "we should lift up our hearts on high."[106] The plan proposed that rather than inquiring more deeply into the manner of participation in the Body of Christ in the sacrament, the two sides content themselves with the teaching of Ephesians 3:17 that "Jesus Christ dwells in our hearts through faith" – "from which it follows that he does not inhabit the hearts of those who have no faith."[107] If there were disagreements over the manner of participation, however, the holders of differing views ought to be tolerated rather than persecuted. In those things on which agreement had been reached, "let us march together."[108]

Mutual toleration was therefore the final step in a process which seemed unlikely to result in complete agreement. That the Lutheran and the Reformed churches did not differ widely in their external acts and observances was looked upon in article seventeen as an immense advantage. Members of each group would presumably not hesitate to attend in joint services of worship, even though they might differ on important matters like Christology, predestination, and free-will.[109] In contrast, the differences which existed between the modes of worshipping in Protestant churches and in the Roman Catholic Church were a major obstacle to their joint participation in the Holy Communion: "But if I come to receive communion with someone who adores the bread or pretends to sacrifice Jesus Christ, this action would scandalize me and make me flee that place, out of fear of

---

[105] Montpellier MS. 16400, [fol. 2 verso]. Compare Aymon, *Tous les Synodes*, vol. II, p. 60; Quick, *Synodicon*, vol. I, p. 436.

[106] Montpellier MS. 16400, [fol. 2 verso]. Compare Aymon, *Tous les Synodes*, vol. II, p. 60; Quick, *Synodicon*, vol. I, p. 436. For a close parallel, see John Calvin, *Institutes of the Christian Religion*, ed. John T. McNeill, 2 vols. (Philadelphia: Westminster Press, 1961), vol. II, pp. 1380–1381. In the Prayer Book service of Holy Communion of 1552 the *sursum corda* introduced the canon or fixed part of the service with the words "Lyfte up your heartes," to which the congregation responded, "We lyfte them up unto the Lorde." See *The First and Second Prayer Books of Edward VI* (London: Dent, 1910), p. 387.

[107] Montpellier MS. 16400, [fol. 2 verso]. Compare Aymon, *Tous les Synodes*, vol. II, p. 60; Quick, *Synodicon*, vol. I, p. 436.

[108] Montpellier MS. 16400, [fol. 2 verso]. Compare Aymon, *Tous les Synodes*, vol. II, p. 61; Quick, *Synodicon*, vol. I, p. 436.

[109] Montpellier MS. 16400, [fol. 2 verso–3]. Compare Aymon, *Tous les Synodes*, vol. II, p. 61; Quick, *Synodicon*, vol. I, p. 436.

participating in idolatry or in a false sacrifice."[110] If a model for such an accord between groups of churches were needed, there was one available. Article eighteen suggested that the "Concordat of the Polish Churches, drawn up at Sendomir, in the year 1570, and since reaffirmed at the Synod of Vladislaw in 1583," deserved to be imitated.[111] This was an agreement among three Protestant churches in Poland – the Lutheran, the Reformed, and the Bohemian Brethren – according to which the three were pledged to work together in peace and charity for the good of the whole Church.[112] This document was to be made available to the deputies for their guidance.

The second assembly was, according to article nineteen, to have several features in common with the first. Among these features was the provision for a fast at the beginning, and a celebration of the Lord's Supper at the conclusion. At this celebration, "the Lutheran pastors and ours would communicate together."[113] It was also to be the case at the second assembly that there would be "the same respect shown to His Majesty of England" as at the first.[114]

Article twenty looked forward to the day of fulfillment, when this union of the major Protestant churches would become a reality. It declared that it would be "absolutely necessary that the princes promise to employ their authority so that these names of Lutherans, Calvinists, and Sacramentarians be abolished."[115] In this unified body of Christians all churches would henceforward be known as Christian Reformed Churches. The use of invectives against other Christians would be strictly forbidden, whether in sermons or tracts, under the threat of heavy penalties. As a result, "the Catalogue of the Frankfurt [Book] Fair would no longer be filled with injurious titles, as it ordinarily is."[116] The same article paid special attention to the situation in Germany, where deep divisions existed between Lutheran and Calvinist states. After the union had been completed, the Protestant princes of Germany, on a day which they had agreed upon, would see that their pastors exchanged churches with those of a neighboring state. On this

110 Montpellier MS. 16400, [fol. 3]. Compare Aymon, *Tous les Synodes*, vol. II, p. 61; Quick, *Synodicon*, vol. I, p. 437.
111 Montpellier MS. 16400, [fol. 3]. Compare Aymon, *Tous les Synodes*, vol. II, p. 61; Quick, *Synodicon*, vol. I, p. 437.
112 See Ruth Rouse and Stephen C. Neill, eds., *A History of the Ecumenical Movement, 1517–1948*, second edition (London: SPCK, 1967), pp. 62–63.
113 Montpellier MS. 16400, [fol. 3]. Compare Aymon, *Tous les Synodes*, vol. II, p. 61; Quick, *Synodicon*, vol. I, p. 437.
114 Montpellier MS. 16400, [fol. 3]. Compare Aymon, *Tous les Synodes*, vol. II, p. 61; Quick, *Synodicon*, vol. I, p. 437.
115 Montpellier MS. 16400, [fol. 3]. Compare Aymon, *Tous les Synodes*, vol. II, pp. 61–62; Quick, *Synodicon*, vol. I, p. 437.
116 Montpellier MS. 16400, [fol. 3]. Compare Aymon, *Tous les Synodes*, vol. II, p. 62; Quick, *Synodicon*, vol. I, p. 437.

day, designated as a solemn occasion, there would be a celebration of the Lord's Supper at which the princes and their peoples would receive the sacrament at the hands of the visiting divines.[117] This service would therefore become a tangible expression of the unity existing among Christians. It was obviously hoped that the unhappy divisions existing in Germany among Protestants would gradually be healed by this means.

The last article expressed wistfully and without much expectation of its realization the hope that a reconciliation could then be achieved between these Christian Reformed Churches and Rome: "If it should please God to bless so holy and praiseworthy a project, which would secure an immortal crown for His Majesty of Great Britain, and for the princes who should act together with him, then it would be time to seek an accord with the Church of Rome."[118] This would be the time for a truly ecumenical council, but the article did not express optimism about the prospects of such a meeting being convened. The reason given was that "the Pope does not allow any council or conference unless he presides over it."[119] In any case, once the union of Protestant churches had been completed, they would be a much more formidable body than any one of the churches had been before, and their ministers would be able to speak with much more authority.[120] However qualified the hope expressed in article twenty-one, it did look forward to an eventual reunion which would include Rome. The effect is breathtaking in its boldness and its apparent disregard of a century of bitterness and conflict that had followed Luther's Ninety-Five Theses of 1517.

It appears from the proceedings of the Synod of Tonneins that the Reformed Churches of France were receptive to the eventual reunion of Christendom. Dour, practical, and zealous about orthodoxy these Calvinists may have been – as their co-religionists elsewhere are reputed to have been – but they were yet willing to endorse the plan, offer their prayers for its success, and promise more concrete support when the time was ripe. How surprising is this? Actually, not surprising at all, as these churches had been actively pursuing a similar goal for over three decades.

Their first significant steps had been taken in 1578, at the Ninth National Synod, meeting at Sainte-Foy, where it was decided to respond favorably to an invitation from Germany to attend a meeting of representatives from the

---

[117] Montpellier MS. 16400, [fol. 3]. Compare Aymon, *Tous les Synodes*, vol. II, p. 62; Quick, *Synodicon*, vol. I, p. 437.

[118] Montpellier MS. 16400, [fol. 3 verso]. Compare Aymon, *Tous les Synodes*, vol. II, p. 62; Quick, *Synodicon*, vol. I, p. 437.

[119] Montpellier MS. 16400, [fol. 3 verso]. Compare Aymon, *Tous les Synodes*, vol. II, p. 62; Quick, *Synodicon*, vol. I, p. 437.

[120] Montpellier MS. 16400, [fol. 3 verso]. Compare Aymon, *Tous les Synodes*, vol. II, p. 62; Quick, *Synodicon*, vol. I, p. 437.

Lutheran and Reformed churches in order to draw up a uniform confession of faith for all Protestants.[121] When nothing came of this proposal, the French tried, at the Twelfth National Synod, meeting at Vitré in 1583, to revive the plan by sending a theologian to talk with leaders of the German churches.[122] Plans were made at the same synod to strengthen ties with the Reformed Church in the Netherlands by allowing deputies from that church to attend the meetings of the national synods in France. Similar arrangements were approved at later synods.[123] In 1603, at the meeting of the National Synod at Gap, the idea of a union with the Lutheran churches of Germany was reopened, and the synod sent letters to universities in Germany, England, Scotland, Switzerland, and the Netherlands to ask for their help in establishing such a union.[124] The response, as reported at the National Synod at La Rochelle, in 1607, was encouraging – and was evidently the basis on which the deputies at Tonneins hoped to proceed. At La Rochelle it was stated that favorable responses had been received from the Elector Palatine, the Ecclesiastical Senate of the Palatinate, the University of Heidelberg, and the provincial synods of Holland, Zeeland, and Hanau, as well as from classes in Berne and Geneva, all of whom approved the French Confession of Faith. Those gathered at La Rochelle called for prayers for this union.[125] The plan of union of 1614, coming as it did from England, represented support from an important new quarter.

The plan presented to the National Synod of Tonneins was thus not only a logical outgrowth of James's interest in finding means of working towards Christian reunion, but it was the climax to a protracted campaign pursued by the French Reformed community for the achievement of a similar objective.[126] The most significant difference which distinguished James from the French Protestants on this subject was his more pacific attitude towards Rome. The artfully phrased article twenty-one looks very much like a compromise designed by du Moulin to be acceptable to both the British king and his co-religionists in France.

---

[121] Aymon, *Tous les Synodes*, vol. I, pp. 131–133; Quick, *Synodicon*, vol. I, pp. 120–22.
[122] Aymon, *Tous les Synodes*, vol. I, p. 170; Quick, *Synodicon*, vol. I, p. 153. Though a common confession was not drawn up, a collection of confessions was edited by the Palatine pastor Jean François Salvard entitled *Harmonia confessionvm fidei* (Geneva: Petrus Santandrea, 1581), which showed the similarities among the Reformed confessions.
[123] Aymon, *Tous les Synodes*, vol. I, pp. 157, 201, 227; Quick, *Synodicon*, vol. I, pp. 143–144, 180, 200. See also G. De Félice, *Histoire des Synodes Nationaux des Eglises Réformées de France* (Paris: Grassart, 1864), p. 107, and Linder, "The French Calvinist Response to the Formula of Concord," pp. 31–32.
[124] Aymon, *Tous les Synodes*, vol. I, p. 274; Quick, *Synodicon*, vol. I, p. 239.
[125] Aymon, *Tous les Synodes*, vol. I, p. 300; Quick, *Synodicon*, vol. I, pp. 263–64.
[126] Cf. De Félice, *Histoire des Synodes Nationaux*, pp. 160–163.

II

The plan formed by King James and by key spokesmen for the Protestants of France, which was launched so hopefully at the Synod of Tonneins in 1614, was rather quickly – and unhappily – outrun by events. At first, however, the sponsors of the proposal had reason to feel that they were making progress. Du Moulin's reconciliation with Tilenus, which James had urged, was effected in October 1614 according to a process prescribed at the Synod of Tonneins. Home wrote to James on June 9, 1614 that the synod had named Philippe Duplessis-Mornay to serve as arbiter of the dispute at his seat at Saumur, along with some neighboring pastors.[127] Home also reported that he had "made the overture to the synod of means of reaching an accord between our churches and the Lutherans . . . following the project of M^r. du Moulin," and that the synod had "lent its ear to this and given charge to the deputies of the provinces to think about it carefully for the next national synod."[128] On October 16, 1614 Home wrote to Ambassador Edmondes that, as James had charged him, he had seen to the reconciliation of du Moulin and Tilenus. Writing from Saumur, he said that the two men had reached an accord "by the good conduct of Monsieur du Plessis and of the pastors attached to this place."[129] Both men had been absolved of the charges they had brought against each other and of the blame they had brought upon themselves. After this they "embraced and promised solemnly to hold to the decisions of the ancient councils."[130] In du Moulin's own account, written to James from Paris, he thanked the king for having appeased the discord between Tilenus and himself, and added that he hoped that James would embrace with enthusiasm the plan for a general union of the churches.[131] After speaking to the ambassadors from the United Provinces and the princes of Germany, du Moulin had found that they were very favorably inclined to the plan. He added that it was not surprising "that all the Princes and Republics seeing Your Majesty employing yourself with it" were ready to follow his example and work towards such a worthy goal under James's leadership.[132]

In February 1615 James sent word to du Moulin, by way of the royal

---

127 BL Stowe MS. 174, fol. 347 (Home to James I by way of Edmondes, June 9, 1614).
128 Ibid.
129 BL Stowe MS. 175, fol. 76 (Home to Edmondes, October 16, 1614).
130 Ibid.
131 PRO SP 78/58, fols. 230–230 verso. This undated letter from du Moulin to James is filed as November 22, 1611 by the PRO, but from its contents it seems certain to have been written after the reconciliation prescribed by the Synod of Tonneins. The letter describes the same procedure at Saumur described by Home in his letter of October 16. Du Moulin's letter should probably be dated as late October or early November 1614.
132 Ibid., fol. 230 verso.

physician Théodore de Mayerne, then on a visit to France, that he wished the Parisian pastor to come to England. Mayerne was a French Calvinist who had migrated to England in 1611, anxious for his safety and concerned about his professional prospects following the assassination of Henry IV. After obtaining permission from his consistory for a temporary absence, du Moulin left for England in early March.[133] Before going, however, he wrote to Mornay of his plans for advancing the project of union while he was there. He would, he said, be able to speak with the king "about the Union in Religion of which I have shown you the project, and to urge him to exert himself for it. Concerning these matters I implore you to write me confidentially, or to instruct M. de Rouvray well concerning your intentions, who will do me the honor of communicating them to me."[134] In his letter du Moulin reported an initially favorable response from the Netherlands and Protestant princes in Germany. In this receptive climate du Moulin was especially anxious that the provincial synods in France go forward with their discussions of the proposal. Here, he felt, Mornay could be of considerable assistance. He asked that

since at the Synod of Tonneins the provinces were charged to make preparations for the project of Union which had been sent to the said Synod by the king of Great Britain with the exhortation to think about it and prepare for it, it would please you to exhort them so that at the provincial synods which will be held this spring this business may be brought forward, for I learn that the Estates of the Low Countries and the Princes of Germany are disposed to it. Whatever impediment there may be on the side of England I will try to remove when I am there; and it would be a shame if, when all the foreign churches were inclining to this accord, we only should remain behind. You are the one who can accomplish the most and whom our Churches, with good reason, respect more than any other, which obliges us to pray God for your prosperity and preservation.[135]

During du Moulin's stay of approximately three months in England, he felt compelled to concern himself with a matter which King James probably felt was more pressing than the plan of union. In the preceding January, Cardinal du Perron had given a speech in the French Estates-General intended to quash a proposed law dealing with political allegiance in France. The cardinal found the proposed law to bear an uncomfortably close resemblance to the Oath of Allegiance in England. James, anxious to defend himself, sought du Moulin's assistance in composing a French reply

---

[133] "Autobiographie de Pierre du Moulin, d'après le manuscrit autographe, 1564–1658," p. 342. For Théodore de Mayerne, also known as Théodore Turquet, see Hugh Trevor-Roper, "Medicine at the Early English Court," in his *From Counter-Reformation to Glorious Revolution* (London: Secker and Warburg, 1992), pp. 27–46.

[134] Du Moulin to Du Plessis-Mornay, 5 March 1615, in *Bulletin de la Société de l'Histoire du Protestantisme Français*, 33 (1884), p. 402.

[135] Ibid., p. 403.

to du Perron's oration at the meeting of the Estates-General. One of the demands of the prince of Condé and the other nobles who had been pacified after their threatened rebellion early in 1614 had been for a meeting of the Estates-General, presumably to correct the shortcomings of the queen regent's government. But Marie de Medici was herself quite willing to assemble the three estates in the autumn of 1614, when the young king would have just attained his majority (aged thirteen) and could publicly endorse and extend the regency government's authority to direct the nation's affairs.[136] All three estates – the clergy, the nobility, and the bourgeoisie – were eager to reform aspects of government policy and practice. Members were concerned about the sale of ecclesiastical and political offices, the egregious amount of the pensions being granted to prominent figures at court, and the toll of the taxes which fell, principally, on the Third Estate. The clergy also wanted to see the decrees of the Council of Trent, which had been concluded in 1563, finally accepted in France. A pent-up demand for the redress of grievances was understandable. The three most recent meetings of the Estates-General had been in 1560, 1576, and 1588, during the era of the religious wars. Not one meeting had been held in the reign of Henry IV. Hopes were thus high for the meeting which began in Paris on 14 October.[137]

One item which appeared in the *cahier* or notebook of the *gouvernement* of Paris and the Ile de France, having been placed there in June 1614, dealt with the allegiance due to the king. The framers, concerned in part with the recent assassination of Henry IV by a former friar who cited religious reasons for his act, wanted to condemn the theory that the pope could declare a king of France deposed. The proposal in the *cahier* was introduced in the chamber of the Third Estate on December 15. It requested that the king declare in the assembly of the Estates-General, "as a Fundamental Law of the Kingdom": "that since he is known to be sovereign in his state, holding his crown from God alone, that there is no power on earth whatever, spirituall or temporal, which has any authority over his kingdom, to take away the sacred nature of our kings, to dispense [or absolve] their subjects of the fidelity and obedience which they owe them for any cause or pretext whatsoever."[138]

This proposal, which became known as the First Article of the Third Estate, also specified that all French subjects were to hold this law "as

---

[136] Hayden, *France and the Estates General of 1614*, pp. 54–66. The peace treaty with the prince of Condé and most of the other nobles was signed on May 15, 1614.

[137] Hayden, *France and the Estates General of 1614*, pp. 97, 108, 112, 121, 126; Victor-L. Tapié, *France in the Age of Louis XIII and Richelieu*, trans. D. McN. Lockie (Cambridge: Cambridge University Press, 1974), pp. 72–75.

[138] Text in Hayden, *France and the Estates General of 1614*, p. 131.

conforming to the word of God." Holders of governmental and ecclesiastical offices, teachers, and preachers were to swear to and sign a statement
to this effect. All books which affirmed "the contrary opinion," namely,
"that it is lawful to kill and depose our kings, to rise up and rebel against
them, to shake off their [the subjects'] yoke of obedience" would be held to
be seditious and damnable. Foreigners who held this contrary view would
be considered "enemies of the crown"; French subjects holding the view
would be "guilty of treason in the first degree."[139] The supporters of the
original proposal clearly shared much of the viewpoint of the Parlement of
Paris, the kingdom's leading law court, which had condemned books of
political theory by Juan de Mariana and Robert Bellarmine as well as the
recent answer of Francisco Suarez to King James's defense of the Oath of
Allegiance. Mariana's, Bellarmine's, and Suarez's books had been found to
contain views dangerous to the French king in sections dealing with regicide
and the papal deposing power.[140] The overwhelming support for the article
in the Third Estate probably owed a great deal to the fact that a majority of
its members were royal office-holders concerned to preserve the health and
security of the bureaucratic state. The article also drew on the *politique*
theories of the late sixteenth century, which sought to find a middle ground
between the opposed political theories of the Huguenots and the Catholic
ligueurs by stressing the claims of the kingdom over those of religious
authorities. The article had links, also, to a recently revived Gallicanism and
conciliarism in learned circles in France. This body of thought stressed that
the French king was sovereign within his kingdom and that decrees of popes
or councils could only be admitted with the king's consent.[141]

But the article generated formidable opposition. It was threatening to the
bishops of the First Estate for jurisdictional as well as theological and
political reasons. The theory which the article sought to condemn was held
not only by respectable theologians, past and present, but, apparently, by
Pope Paul V himself. Furthermore the article, by its references to the word
of God and its use of the term *damnable*, seemed to encroach on the clergy's
area of responsibility. The article was also embarrassing to the government
of the queen regent and the royal council, which was trying to foster

---

[139] Ibid.
[140] Pierre Blet, "L'article du Tiers aux Etats Généraux de 1614," *Revue d'histoire moderne et
    contemporaine*, 2 (1955), 81–106. Blet also sees in the article an effort to weaken the
    Jesuits and, if possible, secure their expulsion from France.
[141] Edmond Richer, *De ecclesiastica et politica potestate* (Caen, 1612), translated into English
    as *A Treatise of Ecclesiasticall and Politike Power* (London: Iohn Budge, 1612), sigs.
    E₃–H₄; discussion in J. H. M. Salmon, "Gallicanism and Anglicanism in the Age of the
    Counter-Reformation," in his *Renaissance and Revolt: Essays in the Intellectual and Social
    History of Early Modern France* (Cambridge: Cambridge University Press, 1987),
    pp. 155–188, esp. pp. 181–188.

political harmony in the kingdom and saw this as a potentially divisive issue both at home and abroad. Even before receiving an official copy of the article from the Third Estate, leaders of the clergy went to the nobility for assistance; by compromising on several other key issues concerning political and financial matters, the First Estate won the Second Estate's support. Cardinal du Perron spoke effectively to the nobles against the article at the end of December. On January 2, 1615 he also spoke to the Third Estate in an address lasting two and a half hours, which was subsequently published. So successful were these efforts that on January 15, the king ordered the article removed from the *cahiers*.[142] The Third Estate subsequently reminded him of it, however, in the revised version of its First Article.[143] In his address of January 2, du Perron defended the papal deposing power on narrow grounds. He claimed that there was one case on which all writers on the subject agree that the subjects' oath of fidelity to the crown could be dissolved: if a king, sworn to uphold Catholicism, became a heretic or an apostate and attempted to subvert the religion of the nation. In such a case a pope or a general council could pronounce such a dissolution of the subjects' oath of fidelity. To force persons to assert that this could not be done would be to "intangle their consciences."[144] He asserted fervently that if the laity was allowed to make binding theological canons like that contained in the article, all order and authority in the Church would be overthrown.[145] If the article were to be adopted, moreover, the result would be a schism separating France from the rest of the Catholic Church and also separating Catholics from one another within France. The result would be, he said, that France would go the way of England, where faithful Catholics were persecuted and the bulk of the population was isolated from Catholic Christendom. The article was, he argued, an import from England: it had a fish's tail from swimming the narrow seas.[146] The king of France, du Perron asserted, did not need this kind of security. His greatest security was to be in union with the Catholic Church and the Apostolic See. Recent history – the religious wars – showed how destructive religious divisions in France could be.[147]

Edmondes, James's ambassador in Paris, complained at once about du

[142] Hayden, *France and the States General of 1614*, p. 144; Blet, "L'article du Tiers aux Etats Généraux de 1614," p. 103.
[143] Hayden, *France and the Estates General of 1614*, p. 146.
[144] Jacques Davy du Perron, *Harangve faicte de la part de la Chambre ecclesiastiqve en celle du Tiers estat, sur l'article du serment* (Paris: Antoine Estiene, 1615), translated into English as *An Oration Made on the Part of the Lordes Spirituall, in the Chamber of the Third Estate (or Communalty) of France, vpon the Oath (Pretended of Allegiance) Exhibited in the Late Generall Assembly of the Three Estates of That Kingdome* ([St. Omer: English College Press,] 1616), pp. 13–16.
[145] Du Perron, *An Oration Made on the Part of the Lordes Spirituall*, pp. 16, 67–72.
[146] Ibid., pp. 17, 97–100, 115–117.   [147] Ibid., pp. 117, 125–128.

Perron's speech to Villeroy and soon afterwards to the queen regent. He denied the cardinal's assertion that English agents were responsible for the article.[148] In June, Edmondes made a formal protest in the name of James to the young king and his mother which was published as part of his *Remonstrances*.[149] Meantime, soon after du Moulin's arrival in London in March, James enlisted the French pastor's help in formulating a considered and scholarly reply to du Perron, comparable in length to the published oration. In the French *Declaration*, published in London in 1615, du Moulin added an *Advertissement*:

The Reader will be advised that during my sojourn at the Court of the Most Serene king of Great Britain, his majesty received a copy of the harangue of Monsieur the Cardinal du Perron, in which having found several things which outrage the honor of God and the common cause of Kings, touching in particular the honor of his person and the dignity of his crown, he resolved to make a response, which, having written with his own hand, he was pleased to communicate to me, and commanded me to give it some polishing in the French language, not trusting himself in it, although our language is very familiar to him.[150]

Du Moulin asserted that he had a copy in the king's own hand, which made clear that the "matter and a part of the French style" was the king's.[151] In his autobiography, however, du Moulin claimed more credit. "His Majesty asked me to make a response" to du Perron's printed oration, he wrote, "which I did." Du Moulin added: "I presented my response to him, which was printed under his name."[152]

James's – and du Moulin's – *Declaration*, published in an English translation in the following year as *Remonstrance . . . for the Right of Kings and the Independance of Their Crownes against an Oration of the . . . Card. of Perron*, followed du Perron's argument closely. It began,

[148] PRO SP 78/63, fols. 8 verso–9, 11–11 verso (Edmondes to Winwood, January 9, 1615).

[149] Thomas Edmondes, *Remonstrances Made by the Kings Maiesties Ambassadovr vnto the French King and the Queene His Mother, Iune Last Past, 1615, Concerning the Marriages with Spaine, as also Certayne Diabolicall Opinions Maintayned by Cardinall Perron about the Deposing and Murthering of Kings* (London: Nathaniel Butter, 1615). For Edmondes's "Declaration . . . vnto the French King, and the Queene his Mother, Concerning an Oration Made by the Cardinall of Perron," see sigs. C₁–C₃ verso. The document entitled "Remonstrance made by the Ambassador of Great Britain to the King and the Queen his mother," undated, SP 78/63, fols. 16–17, filed as if it were enclosed in Edmondes's letter of January 9, is evidently the French version of the speech Edmondes made in June.

[150] James I, *Declaration dv serenissime Roy Iaqves I. Roy de la Grand' Bretaigne, France et Irelande, Defenseur de la Foy, povr le droit des rois & independance de leurs couronnes, contre la harangve de l'illvstrissime Cardinal du Perron prononcée en la Chambre du Tiers Estat le XV. de Ianuier 1615* (London: John Bill, Printer to the King, 1615), sig. Q₄. James and du Moulin must have been misinformed about the date of du Perron's oration, which was on January 2, according to the French (new style) calendar.

[151] Ibid.

[152] "Autobiographie de Pierre du Moulin d'après le manuscrit autographe, 1564–1658," p. 343.

however, by defending James's literary intervention in the affairs of another country. The reason James gave was his sorrow over the murder of Henry IV and his deep concern about the attempt of the Gunpowder plotters on his own life – both of which he saw as the result of the application of the theory of the papal deposing power.[153] He cited what he believed were serious inconsistencies in du Perron's argument, including the fact that the examples du Perron gave of papal depositions did not, for the most part, concern heresy or schism – the grounds on which du Perron sought to defend the deposing power.[154] Moreover du Perron had by his own account served Henry IV faithfully at a time when the pope had declared the French king deposed as a relapsed heretic.[155] James also noted that du Perron had asserted that a person who opposed a king on religious grounds might kill him in a pitched battle but not in private, a distinction which James treated with scorn.[156] Du Perron's claim that the deposing power had the support of the Church's teaching for 1,100 years contained, the king asserted, a significant concession. Du Perron had omitted the first 500 years, the period of the New Testament and the ancient Church, when nothing had been said of the doctrine.[157] Furthermore, the tradition of support for the deposing power was certainly not unbroken, especially in France. French theologians, the Parlement of Paris, the University of Paris, and the French crown had traditionally and regularly opposed the exercise of temporal power by the papacy within France.[158] Du Perron's historical arguments, which James discussed in detail, were, the king asserted, based on papal actions, not on right – and were all taken from the period in which the papacy had tried to bring the civil rulers of Europe under its control.[159] Pope Gregory VII, whose example was celebrated by du Perron, provoked widespread wars in Christendom by his sentence of excommunication against the Emperor Henry IV. Was this an example to be followed?[160] The question at issue, according to the king, was "whether such a Prince can be vnthroned by the Pope, by whom he was not placed in the Throne; and whether the Pope can

---

[153] James I, *Declaration*, p. 1; *Remonstrance of the Most Gratiovs King Iames I. King of Great Brittaine, France, and Ireland, Defender of the Faith, &c. for the Right of Kings and the Independance of Their Crownes against an Oration of the Most Illustrious Card. of Perron, Pronounced in the Chamber of the Third Estate. Ian. 15. 1615* (Cambridge: Cantrell Legge, Printer to the University of Cambridge, 1616), sig. A₁. The book was translated into English by Richard Betts. There was also a Latin translation in 1616, published in London by John Bill.

[154] James I, *Declaration*, p.10; *Remonstrance*, sig. B₄.

[155] James I, *Declaration*, pp. 6, 37; *Remonstrance*, sigs. B₁, pp. 73–75.

[156] James I, *Declaration*, pp. 9, 102; *Remonstrance*, sig. B₃–B₃ verso, p. 219.

[157] James I, *Declaration*, pp. 10, 55–67; *Remonstrance*, pp. 19, 111–137.

[158] James I, *Declaration*, pp. 26–43; *Remonstrance*, pp. 51–88.

[159] James I, *Declaration*, p. 51; *Remonstrance*, p. 100.

[160] James I, *Declaration*, pp. 22–24; *Remonstrance*, pp. 45–47.

despoile such a Prince, of that Royaltie which was neuer giuen him by the Pope?"[161] Framed in this way, the question seemed answerable only in the negative.

James made a surprising concession of his own by granting that "if a King shall commaund any thing directly contrary to Gods word, and tending to the subuerting of the Church; that clerics in this case ought not onely to dispense with subiects for their obedience, but also expressly to forbid their obedience: For it is always better to obey God then man."[162] The reason, presumably, was that this principle – that where there was a divine command, one ought to obey God rather than man – was scriptural (Acts 5: 29), and was stated explicitly in Calvin's *Institutes*. It was, furthermore, the bedrock of the Huguenot resistance theory which had seen du Moulin's spiritual forebears through several decades of civil war in France.[163] But to James this principle did not necessarily justify armed resistance. He argued, in fact, that it was better to suffer under a heretical king than to raise a rebellion against him. Two wrongs, in effect, did not make a right.[164] Du Moulin was, presumably, ready to take this more passive approach. By the early seventeenth century, French Protestant thinkers generally stressed obedience to political authority and loyalty to the crown, though some Protestant members of the nobility used religion as a pretext for radical political activity. Moreover the French Reformed community, through its political assemblies, pressed the government regularly to adhere strictly to the provisions of the Edict of Nantes.[165]

The concession that a subject could refuse to obey if the king commanded something contrary to God's law was not mentioned in James's *God and the King*, a dialogue also published in 1615 but intended for a domestic audience. James had learned to despise the idea of resistance to constituted authority while he was in Scotland. In the dialogue the interlocutor Theodidactus defended the penal laws against Roman Catholics, upheld the Oath of Allegiance, and denied that the pope had any authority to dispense

[161] James I, *Remonstrance*, p. 155; compare *Declaration*, p. 74.
[162] James I, *Remonstrance*, pp. 110–111; compare *Declaration*, p. 55.
[163] See Calvin, *Institutes of the Christian Religion*, ed. McNeill, vol. II, pp. 1519–1521; Julian H. Franklin, ed., *Constitutionalism and Resistance in the Sixteenth Century: Three Treatises by Hotman, Beza, and Mornay* (New York: Pegasus, 1969), pp. 101–108, 133–135, 142–158.
[164] James I, *Declaration*, pp. 55–62; *Remonstrance*, pp. 111–125.
[165] See W. J. Stankiewicz, *Politics and Religion in Seventeenth-Century France: A Study of Political Ideas from the Monarchomachs to Bayle, as Reflected in the Toleration Controversy* (Berkeley: University of California Press, 1960), pp. 64–90; and Hartmut Kretzer, *Calvinismus und französische Monarchie im 17. Jahrhundert: Die politische Lehre der Akademien Sedan und Saumur, mit besonderer Berücksichtigung von Pierre Du Moulin, Moyse Amyraut und Pierre Jurieu* (Berlin: Duncker und Humblot, 1975), esp. pp. 131–193, for a treatment of du Moulin's political thought.

with the law of nature or the law of the scriptures. He cited both natural law and the scriptures in support of obedience to political authority.[166] When Philalethes, the partner in the dialogue, raised the point of whether a prince who sought to oppose the whole Church, or to extinguish Christianity, should be repudiated, Theodidactus said no. The Church, he argued, would survive. In sternly Augustinian terms, James argued that the only recourse for the subjects of such a king was repentance for their sins, which had brought on this punishment.[167]

In any case, in the *Remonstrance*, James defended the French Protestants, who had fought a long series of military campaigns to win recognition and toleration. In the early stages of the civil wars, James argued, the French Protestants had fought to defend themselves against attack. In the latter stages, they had come to the rescue of Kings Henry III and Henry IV and had stood by them to the end.[168] As for du Perron's charge that Protestants across Europe had continually spread sedition, James argued that the work of the Protestant reformers in England and the Netherlands had been immensely beneficial to both countries.[169] He also defended the French Protestants against the charge of heresy. Their faith and his had never been declared heretical in a fair and legitimate general council: "it was neuer yet hissed out of the Schooles, nor cast out of any Council . . . where both sides haue been heard with like indifferencie."[170] The only council which had ever been offered to Protestants was one in which the pope, a party in the case, was "Iudge of Assize," and where safe access to the place of meeting and protection while there were not assured.[171] The *Remonstrance* thus wound up by being a defense of French and European Protestantism as well as kingship and the British king's handling of the issue of political allegiance.

Du Moulin had lived in England previously, from 1588 to 1592, when he was tutor to the young Roger Manners, earl of Rutland, and was himself a student at Cambridge University. There he had attended the lectures of the Calvinist theologian William Whitaker before going to teach, first at the Latin school in Leyden and then at the University of Leyden, in the United Provinces. Among his students at Leyden University was Hugo Grotius. King James welcomed du Moulin back to England enthusiastically and

---

[166] James I, *God and the King: or, A Dialogue Shewing that Our Soueraigne Lord King Iames, Being Immediate vnder God within His Dominions, Doth Rightfully Claime Whatsoeuer Is Required by the Oath of Allegiance* (London: By the King's Command, 1615), pp. 15–81. The book has been attributed to Richard Mocket.
[167] Ibid., pp. 88–89.
[168] James I, *Declaration*, pp. 120–121; *Remonstrance*, pp. 266–268.
[169] James I, *Declaration*, pp. 123–124; *Remonstrance*, pp. 274–275.
[170] James I, *Remonstrance*, p. 171; compare *Declaration*, p. 82.
[171] James I, *Remonstrance*, pp. 171–172; compare *Declaration*, p. 82.

invited the French pastor to stand behind his chair at meals, as was customary for visitors, and discuss matters of religion with him. During du Moulin's stay, from late March to late June 1615, he accompanied the king to Cambridge, received the degree of Doctor of Divinity there, and was made a prebendary of Canterbury Cathedral with a handsome annual stipend. He took the customary oath before the canons of the cathedral chapter in Canterbury on the understanding that it did not compromise his allegiance to his own king or his commitment to the polity of the Reformed church in France.[172] In June du Moulin preached in French at the Chapel Royal at Greenwich on the king's invitation, where he stressed the power of preaching the gospel as a work of reconciliation; he also spoke of the faith that bound him and the congregation together, and the contributions of King James to the welfare of the Christian Church.[173] Du Moulin's ties to England were long-lasting. He visited James in March 1625, shortly before the king's death, and was absentee rector of a parish in Wales for another decade. Two of his sons settled in England, but took different sides in the conflicts of the following decades: Peter became a divine and a royal chaplain; Lewis became a historian and a religious nonconformist.[174] Like Casaubon – and Grotius in later years – du Moulin found the episcopal system of polity as practised in England appealing. In 1624 he even asked James to consider him for the vacant bishopric of Gloucester.[175] Du Moulin was faithful to his word in using this visit to further the plan of union. He sent copies of the plan from London to "the Churches of France & the Low Countries," where they found their way to interested persons.[176] In May the

---

[172] "Autobiographie de Pierre du Moulin d'après le manuscrit autographe, 1564–1658," pp. 177–182, 342–343; Rimbault, *Pierre du Moulin*, pp. 20–23, 75–79; Norman Egbert McClure, ed., *The Letters of John Chamberlain*, 2 vols. (Philadelphia: American Philosophical Society, 1939), vol. I, pp. 591, 602.

[173] Pierre du Moulin, *A Sermon Preached before the Kings Maiesty at Greenwich the 15. of Iune. 1615.* (Oxford: Henry Cripps, 1620), pp. 1, 19–21, 35. The sermon was translated by John Verneuil.

[174] "Autobiographie de Pierre du Moulin d'après le manuscrit autographe, 1564–1658," p. 474; Rimbault, *Pierre du Moulin*, pp. 108–114; John Venn and J. A. Venn, eds., *Alumni Cantabrigiensis*, Part I (to 1751), 4 vols. (Cambridge: Cambridge University Press, 1922–27), vol. III, p. 197; John Goldworth Alger on Lewis, Peter, and Pierre du Moulin in *Dictionary of National Biography*, vol. XIII, pp. 1097–1099.

[175] See Armstrong, "The Changing Face of French Protestantism: The Influence of Pierre Du Moulin," pp. 139–144. Also Bernard Cottret, *The Huguenots in England: Immigration and Settlement, c. 1550–1700*, trans. Peregrine and Adriana Stevenson (Cambridge: Cambridge University Press and Paris: La Maison des Sciences de l'Homme, 1991), pp. 81–96; and Elisabeth Labrousse, "Great Britain as Envisaged by the Huguenots of the Seventeenth Century," in Irene Scouloudi, ed., *Huguenots in Britain and Their French Background, 1550–1800* (Totowa, N.J.: Barnes and Noble, 1987), pp. 143–157.

[176] David Blondel, *Actes avthentiqves des Eglises Reformées de France, Germanie, Grande Bretaigne, Pologne, Hongrie, Païs Bas, &c., touchant la paix & charité fraternelle* (Amsterdam: Jean Blaev, 1655), pp. 10–11, 72.

Provincial Synod of the Ile de France wrote to thank him for its copy. The plan was subsequently published by David Blondel, in a collection of irenic religious documents in 1655, and by Gerard Brandt, in his history of the theological controversies in the Netherlands which appeared in Dutch in 1671 and in an English translation in 1721.[177] Both Blondel and Brandt assumed that the plan was drawn up during du Moulin's visit to England in 1615, probably because the copies which reached them originally came from du Moulin during or shortly after his stay in England.

In the Palatinate of the Rhine, one of the leading Calvinist theologians in Europe saw in the activities of King James and others an opportunity to try to bridge the theological and ecclesiological gulf between Calvinists and Lutherans in Germany. German Lutherans had been rent by divisions in the mid-sixteenth century over issues concerning the sacraments, salvation, Christology, and predestination. These divisions had been definitively settled for Lutherans by the Formula of Concord and the Book of Concord, in 1577 and 1580 respectively. But the concord which had been reached excluded "crypto-Calvinists" as well as most professing Calvinists.[178] In his *Irenicum* of 1615, subtitled, "the union and synod of the evangelicals," David Pareus discussed what could be accomplished to bring Lutherans and Calvinists together by an ecumenical council, or at least an evangelical synod, and what specifically might be expected of King James VI and I.[179] Pareus struck a cautionary note in his *Irenicum* by pointing out that the Roman Catholics, by excluding the Protestants from the Council of Trent, had exacerbated the schism resulting from the Reformation, and that the Lutherans had deepened the divisions within the ranks of the Protestants by excluding the Calvinists from their deliberations in Saxony which produced the Formula of Concord. Away, then, with such limited synods![180] What was needed was a truly ecumenical council, which would bring all Christians together and help them to resolve their differences. He argued that it should be composed of both ecclesiastical and civil leaders who would seek

---

[177] Blondel, *Actes avthentiqves*, pp. 72–76; Gerard Brandt, *The History of the Reformation and Other Ecclesiastical Transactions in and about the Low-Countries, from the Beginning of the Eighth Century down to the Famous Synod of Dort*, 4 vols. in 2 (London: John Childe, 1720–1723), vol. II, pp. 153–157. Brandt's work was first published in Dutch in 1671. Du Moulin's plan is reproduced in an abridged form in Jaques Courvoisier, "Forerunners of the World Council: Pierre du Moulin," *Ecumenical Review*, 1, 1 (Autumn 1948), 76–82.

[178] Linder, "The French Calvinist Response to the Formula of Concord," pp. 21–22, 29–31; W. Brown Patterson, "The Anglican Reaction," W. Robert Godfrey, "The Dutch Reformed Response," and Jill Raitt, "The French Reformed Theological Response," in Lewis W. Spitz and Wenzel Lohff, eds., *Discord, Dialogue, and Concord: Studies in the Lutheran Reformation's Formula of Concord* (Philadelphia: Fortress Press, 1977), pp. 150–190.

[179] David Pareus, *Irenicum, sive de unione et synodo evangelicorum concilianda liber votivus paci ecclesiae & desideriis pacificorum dicatus* (Heidelberg: Jonas Rose, 1615).

[180] Ibid., pp. 22–23.

the guidance of the Word of God about issues in contention. The appropriate convener would be, not the pope, but the Holy Roman emperor, and one of the first essential actions of such a council would be to annul the decrees of the Council of Trent.[181] If such a council proved not to be feasible, however, then a synod of evangelicals should be undertaken. The leadership of the highest political authorities would again be needed. Among the Lutherans, whose adherents dominated Saxony, Thuringia, Silesia, Prussia, and the kingdoms of Denmark and Sweden, Christian IV of Denmark would be an appropriate convener. Among the Reformed, who were most numerous in the Palatinate, Hesse, the United Provinces, Great Britain, and parts of Switzerland, as well as parts of France, Bohemia, and Hungary, James VI and I, Christian IV's brother-in-law, would be an appropriate convener. The two monarchs, Christian and James, seemed destined to bring their respective communities of co-religionists together.[182] Pareus's proposal, which was a logical application of du Moulin's plan, came, appropriately, from the state in which James's daughter Elizabeth was now settled with her husband, the Elector Frederick V, and where English cultural influences were now strong. In 1616, at a degree ceremony at Heidelberg University attended by the elector, Pareus defended his book against a Jesuit opponent in Mainz and a Lutheran opponent in Tübingen.[183] This apparently important support from Heidelberg was not, however, welcomed at James's court. James disliked Pareus's political theories, which restated the Reformed view that political resistance was sometimes justified, and he did not welcome Pareus as an ally.[184]

At the Twenty-Second National Synod of the French Reformed Churches, meeting at Vitré in May and June 1617, the provinces all reported that they had done as much as they could to help realize the project proposed at Tonneins. The synod felt it was necessary now "to wait for those who made

---

[181] Ibid., pp. 24–30.   [182] Ibid., pp. 30–32.

[183] David Pareus, *De pace & unione ecclesiarum evangel. oratio inauguralis habita in solenni Universitatis Heidelbergensis* (Heidelberg: Jonas Rose, 1616), pp. 5–22. According to Pareus's son Philipp, a great many attacks were made on the *Irenicum*, especially from Swabia and Saxony. See Philipp Pareus, "Narratio historica de curriculo vitae & obitu scriptisque reuerendissimi patris D. Davidis Parei," in David Pareus, *Opervm theologicorum partes quatuor*, ed. Philipp Pareus, 3 vols. (Frankfurt: Jonas Rose, 1647), vol. I, sig. C5.

[184] Pareus earned King James's enmity for his political theory in a commentary on Romans (1613), in which he argued that where the magistrates are tyrannical, subjects may, under the direction of the lesser magistrates, defend themselves, the commonwealth, and the true religion (*Opervm theologicorum*, vol. II, pp. 246–263). The commentary was condemned by Cambridge University in 1619, and answered by David Owen in 1622. See Pierre Bayle, *Dictionnaire historique et critique*, third edition, 4 vols. (Rotterdam: Michel Bohm, 1720), vol. III, pp. 2176–2179, and Thompson Cooper on David Owen in the *Dictionary of National Biography*, vol. XIV, pp. 1295–1296.

such Overtures to press this Affair further."[185] In the meantime a committee of four ministers was appointed, made up of André Rivet, pastor of Thouars, Jean Chauve, pastor of Sommières, Daniel Chamier, pastor and professor at Montauban, and Pierre du Moulin, to confer with Duplessis-Mornay at Saumur to work out further and more detailed plans as opportunities presented themselves. Their proposals were to be submitted to the provinces and then acted upon at the following national synod.[186] In the following year, however, the committee found itself facing new responsibilities. A theological dispute in the Netherlands had been following a tortuous course for some years and had now reached the point where it threatened the peace not only of the Reformed church there but of the state as well. The States-General of the United Provinces therefore called for a national synod, with representatives from foreign Reformed churches, to settle the issues involved.[187] This synod, to be held in the city of Dordrecht, or Dort, in November 1618, must have seemed to the committee appointed at Vitré an appropriate setting in which to work for the project of union. The members' attendance at Dort would also serve to give the French Protestants representation there. Encouraged by the church at Paris and by the deputies general at court, the members of the committee therefore made plans to attend – only to be forbidden to leave the country by order of King Louis XIII, who was evidently afraid such an assembly would draw his Protestant subjects into overt political action at home or abroad.

Jean Chauve reported to the Twenty-Third National Synod, meeting at Alès, from October to December 1620, the experience which he and Daniel Chamier had had:

He had set out to go to Holland and attend the synod of Dordrecht, following the Advice given to the Province of the Sevenes, by the said Lord Deputies General at Court, and by the Church of Paris, and how he had been diverted from this Journey in order to come into Languedoc, on the Advice which M. Chamier and himself received at Geneva, from the Prohibition which His majesty had issued concerning them, from attending this Assembly.[188]

Like their colleagues, Rivet and du Moulin were prevented from attending.[189] The Synod of Alès, presided over by du Moulin, nevertheless

185 Aymon, *Tous les Synodes*, vol. II, p. 108; Quick, *Synodicon*, vol. I, p. 499.
186 Aymon, *Tous les Synodes*, vol. II, pp. 108–109; Quick, *Synodicon*, vol. I, p. 499. For steps taken in France in support of the plan, see Rimbault, *Pierre du Moulin*, pp. 87–92, and Patry, *Philippe du Plessis-Mornay*, pp. 546–48.
187 See chapter 8, below.
188 Aymon, *Tous les Synodes*, vol. II, p. 156; Quick, *Synodicon*, vol. II, p. 3.
189 "Autobiographie de Pierre du Moulin, d'après le manuscrit autographe, 1564–1658," p. 470; Daniel Chamier, *Journal de son voyage à la cour de Henri IV en 1607 et sa biographie*, ed. Charles Read (Paris: La Société de l'Histoire du Protestantisme Français, 1858), pp. 346–349.

approved the canons of the Synod of Dort in 1620 in order to strengthen what it called "our Union with all the Reformed Churches."[190] It also commended the work of Dort as "a powerful Remedy to rid the Church of Corruption, and to root out Heresies contrary to the Dogma of Predestination, and to other Articles which depend upon it."[191] Perhaps it was – but Dort fell short of the reconciliation of the churches across confessional lines that du Moulin, Duplessis-Mornay, and King James had proposed.

James's policy towards France after the assassination of Henry IV was aimed at preventing France from becoming an ultramontanist Roman Catholic state in alliance with Spain and therefore a threat to the United Provinces and England, as well as to that country's own Protestant minority. Despite the order by the French crown in early 1615 that the First Article of the Third Estate be revoked and despite the exchange of princesses which was scheduled for later in the same year – Elizabeth of France to marry the future Philip IV of Spain, Anne of Spain to marry Louis XIII of France – James's objectives were largely met during Marie de Medici's regency. Her government, largely because it was dominated by experienced ministers from Henry IV's reign, continued to work for peace as the late king had sought to do, balancing commitments and alliances without giving any serious advantages to Spain. The First Article had been championed by both the Third Estate and the Parlement of Paris, though it had been successfully opposed by the First Estate and was finally withdrawn on orders from the crown. The decrees of the Council of Trent were *not* officially accepted by the Estates-General, though they were accepted by the clergy, acting independently, soon afterwards.[192] The French Protestants seemed reasonably secure in their enjoyment of the special status granted them by Henry in the Edict of Nantes. James's interest in the French Protestants did not escape the notice of the French government and this probably helped to preserve their liberties. James's policy towards France was at least a partial success.

The broader objective of James's foreign policy was to achieve some degree of religious reconciliation among the major Protestant churches, and, ultimately, between Protestants and Roman Catholics, as the basis of a lasting European peace. To accomplish this, he committed himself to a plan drawn up by du Moulin, revised after consultations with Duplessis-Mornay, and presented to the Synod of Tonneins by David Home, his own emissary. The plan was imaginative but naive. Differences between Lutherans and Calvinists were bitter and deep and could not be so easily papered over as the drafters seemed to believe. James no doubt recognized

---

[190] Aymon, *Tous les Synodes*, vol. II, p. 182; Quick, *Synodicon*, vol. II, p. 37.
[191] Aymon, *Tous les Synodes*, vol. II, p. 183; Quick, *Synodicon*, vol. II, p. 37.
[192] Hayden, *France and the Estates General of 1614*, pp. 140–141, 156, and 156 note.

this. On the other hand, a plan which promised to lessen the mutual suspicions among Protestant states now joined with England in a political alliance was only to be encouraged. It might at least get negotiations about religious unity under way. The Evangelical Union in Germany, made up of Lutheran as well as Calvinist states, needed the kind of ideological strengthening the plan envisioned, if the Union was not to disintegrate when put to the test. The French Protestants, whom James had promised to protect following the death of Henry IV, needed the help and support of neighboring Protestant countries in the new and threatening political environment in France. The plan presented at the Synod of Tonneins did not contain a perfect solution – no plan could have provided that – but it did provide a means of negotiating differences and of achieving a mutual toleration between Lutherans and Calvinists. It even held out a slender hope for a rapprochement between the churches of the Reformation and the see of Rome. With all its shortcomings, the plan aimed at the kind of reconciliation the king had long advocated, and it had been drawn up by and approved by the French Protestants, whom he considered his allies.

The plan presented at Tonneins was not the only avenue the king found open. While the plan was being considered by Protestants abroad, James took further steps to foster Christian unity by befriending leading figures in the Greek Orthodox Church as well as a Roman Catholic archbishop.

➻ 6 ➻

Relations with the Greek Orthodox Church

The Greek Orthodox Church, rich in history and tradition and linked through the centuries to the Hellenistic world in which Christianity first spread beyond Palestine, maintained a precarious existence in the early seventeenth century. The Ottoman Turks, who overran the remnants of the Byzantine Empire in the fourteenth and fifteenth centuries and captured Constantinople in 1453, allowed Christians to practice their religion. The Ottoman rulers, Muslims themselves, accorded Christians the status of a nation within the Ottoman Empire, entitled to worship according to Christian laws. In its profession of religious toleration, the Ottoman Empire was in advance of any state in western Europe. Yet, in practice, Ottoman rule was almost disastrous for the Greek Church.[1] Most of the prominent church buildings in Greece and Asia Minor were destroyed in war, allowed to fall into ruin, or converted into mosques. New church buildings could only be erected with special permission, which the Turkish authorities were often reluctant to give. Christians, like other subject peoples, were heavily taxed and forced to provide labor for the conquerors. Boys were regularly taken from Christian families to be brought up as Muslims and trained as bureaucrats or soldiers in the corps of Janissaries. Local officials harassed and exploited Christians through legal or extra-legal means to the point that many were impoverished or forced into exile.[2] Even more damaging for a

---

[1] Apostolos E. Vacalopoulos, *The Greek Nation, 1453–1669: The Cultural and Economic Background of Modern Greek Society*, trans. Ian and Phania Moles (New Brunswick: Rutgers University Press, 1976), pp. 101–148; Steven Runciman, *The Great Church in Captivity: A Study of the Patriarchate of Constantinople from the Eve of the Turkish Conquest to the Greek War of Independence* (Cambridge: Cambridge University Press, 1968), pp. 165–185; Timothy Ware, *The Orthodox Church* (New York: Penguin, 1969), pp. 96–100; G. Georgiades Arnakis, "The Greek Church of Constantinople and the Ottoman Empire," *Journal of Modern History*, 24, 3 (September 1952), 235–250.

[2] For Ottoman policies towards Christians within the empire, see Stanford J. Shaw, *History of the Ottoman Empire and Modern Turkey*, 2 vols. (Cambridge: Cambridge University Press, 1976–77), vol. I, pp. 58–59, 151–153. See Halil Inalcik, *The Ottoman Empire: The Classical Age, 1300–1600*, trans. Norman Itzhowitz and Colin Imber (London: Weidenfeld and Nicolson, 1973), pp. 77–118, for an assessment of the Turkish use of slaves from subject

church which had produced outstanding theologians and had preserved many of the texts of ancient Greek philosophy and literature, the Turks made it virtually impossible for most Greeks in the Empire, outside Istanbul itself, to receive more than the rudiments of an education. As a result Greek youths who could afford it had to go abroad for advanced study – to Padua, Florence, Pisa, Paris, or to the College of Saint Athanasius in Rome, where the papacy hoped they would imbibe the appropriate religious faith.[3] It was to help meet the Greek need for better-educated priests and bishops that King James and George Abbot, the archbishop of Canterbury, proposed scholarships for Greek Orthodox students to study in England.

Direct contact between English commercial and political officials and the Turkish and Greek authorities in Istanbul began early in the sixteenth century. English trade with the eastern Mediterranean in the middle ages had been in the hands of Italians, principally Florentines, Genoese, and Venetians. During the Italian wars of the early sixteenth century, when Venice was struggling to survive against invaders, including neighboring Italian states, English ships visited several Greek islands under Venetian control.[4] But it was the French who gained the ascendancy in the Levantine trade in the early sixteenth century, partly as a result of political alliances made with the sultans against the Habsburgs. English shipping to the area then declined until the visit to Istanbul of William Harborne in 1578, when he began negotiations for a formal agreement between Queen Elizabeth I and the Sultan Murad III. According to the charter of privileges for English traders, issued in 1580, Englishmen would enjoy equal rights with Venetians and Frenchmen – a considerable diplomatic and commercial achievement.[5] The representative of the Turkey Company and then, in succession, the Levant Company served both as the company's principal

peoples. Also Runciman, *The Great Church in Captivity*, pp. 186–207, for the effects of Turkish policies on the Greeks.
[3] Deno J. Geanakoplos, *Greek Scholars in Venice: Studies in the Dissemination of Greek Learning from Byzantium to Western Europe* (Cambridge, Mass.: Harvard University Press, 1962), pp. 41–70; Vacalopoulos, *The Greek Nation, 1453–1669*, pp. 151–186; Runciman, *The Great Church in Captivity*, pp. 208–225; Timothy Ware, *Eustratios Argenti: A Study of the Greek Church under Turkish Rule* (Oxford: Clarendon Press, 1964), pp. 5–11. Vacalopoulos takes a more favorable view of the available educational opportunities than most other commentators.
[4] C. G. A. Clay, *Economic Expansion and Social Change: England, 1500–1700*, 2 vols. (Cambridge: Cambridge University Press, 1984), vol. II, pp. 106–107, 129–130; D. M. Palliser, *The Age of Elizabeth: England under the Later Tudors, 1547–1603*, second edition (London: Longman, 1992), pp. 336–337; Albert C. Wood, *A History of the Levant Company* (London: Oxford University Press, 1935), pp. 1–5; Mortimer Epstein, *The Early History of the Levant Company* (London: Routledge, 1908), pp. 1–9.
[5] Arthur Leon Horniker, "William Harborne and the Beginning of Anglo-Turkish Diplomatic and Commercial Relations," *Journal of Modern History*, 14, 3 (September 1942), 289–316. The English traded lead, tin, and, especially, woolen cloth, for spices, medicines, wines, olive oil, currants, carpets, and raw silk.

agent and as the English ambassador to the Sublime Porte, as the Turkish government was frequently called. The company paid his salary. The English ambassador sought to protect English trading interests against the Venetians and the French, who had come earlier on the scene, and the Dutch, who followed the English there in the early seventeenth century. The ambassadors were in frequent contact with the Greek community in Istanbul and elsewhere, since Greeks made up much of the mercantile class in the Ottoman Empire.[6] They also reported on the affairs of the Greek Church and saw a good deal of the patriarch of Constantinople, the leading official in the Greek nation. Patriarchates were frequently of short tenure. Not only were elections and depositions of patriarchs much influenced by rivalries and cliques in the electing body – the Holy Synod, made up of leading metropolitans and ecclesiastical officials – but among the Greek merchant families, and even within the seraglio or sultan's household. The election of a patriarch had to be approved by the sultan and a significant fee paid to the government for that approval. Sometimes the office went to the highest bidder. Furthermore, the western ambassadors themselves sought to determine who held the office of patriarch and what his policies were. The Venetian and French ambassadors sought to push him in a pro-Roman direction, while the English and Dutch ambassadors sought to push him in an anti-Roman direction. So volatile was the situation that there were sixty-one changes of patriarch in the century from 1595 to 1695. Inasmuch as depositions were often followed by reinstatements, the changes involved only thirty-one individual patriarchs.[7] In the early seventeenth century, when England had become a major trading partner of the Ottomans and a diplomatic force in Istanbul, close relations were developed between the Church of England and the Greek Orthodox Church. King James, some-times directly but more often through his officials, worked to effect greater understanding and a deeper respect between the two churches. His efforts were to have a lasting effect.

I

One of the earliest official communications from a prelate of the Greek Church to the Church of England was sent to Archbishop Abbot in 1616. On January 21, Gabriel Severus, a prolific scholar and controversialist who

[6] Arthur Leon Horniker, "Anglo–French Rivalry in the Levant from 1583 to 1612," *Journal of Modern History*, 18, 4 (December 1946), 289–305; Inalcik, *The Ottoman Empire*, pp. 133–139; Vacalopoulos, *The Greek Nation, 1453–1669*, pp. 206–290. The Turkish government was called the "Sublime Porte" because of the high portal of the palace of the grand vizier or leading minister under the sultan.
[7] Runciman, *The Great Church in Captivity*, pp. 195–207; Ware, *The Orthodox Church*, pp. 98–99.

held the title of metropolitan of Philadelphia in Asia Minor, though he resided permanently in Venice, sent fraternal greetings to the English archbishop.[8] Educated at the University of Padua, Severus had had pastoral responsibility for the Greek Christians in Venice, under the authority of the patriarch of Constantinople, since 1577.[9] If he had the wings of a dove, Severus wrote to Abbot, he would "with great effort but still greater pleasure" fly to meet the archbishop, in order to converse, not about "vain and pretentious philosophy," but about "that sincere and blameless doctrine of faith which Jesus Christ handed down to us once and for all."[10] Since he was cut off by the expanse of the sea and by mountain ranges, he offered, instead, a "token and pledge of mutual love and affection," presumably one of his books.[11] He added his endorsement of the efforts made by Abbot in the cause of ecclesiastical harmony and peace: "I beg you to continue to entreat God for the longed-for harmony of the Christian World and of the true sons of the Church, and also for the cooperation and unity of its members in sound health."[12] Severus, who was familiar with western theological writings, both Roman Catholic and Protestant, could well have been responding to the professions British theologians had made about the nature of the Church, especially in the Oath of Allegiance controversy. He evidently wanted to assist in the project of restoring the Church's unity, but he died the next year. By that time, another prelate, even more prominent in the life of the Greek Church, was corresponding with the archbishop.

In about 1615, Cyril Lukaris, the Orthodox patriarch of Alexandria, then on official business in Constantinople, wrote a long letter in Greek to Archbishop Abbot.[13] The letter was in reply to one from Abbot, sent with the encouragement of King James I, whose interest in the Greek Church Lukaris found deeply encouraging. Lukaris had evidently initiated the

---

[8] Oxford, Bodleian Library: MS. Smith 36, fol. 44, Gabriel Severus, archbishop of Philadelphia, to George Abbot, archbishop of Canterbury, in Greek; ibid., fol. 33, Latin copy, dated January 21, 1616.

[9] Deno J. Geanakoplos, *Byzantine East and Latin West: Two Worlds of Christendom in Middle Ages and Renaissance* (Oxford: Blackwell, 1966), pp. 121, 132, 170, 172; Runciman, *The Great Church in Captivity*, pp. 214–217, 257, 279. Severus defended the Orthodox view of the *filioque* against a fellow Greek, Maximus Margounios, and of the sacraments against both Lutherans and Roman Catholics.

[10] Bodl. MS. Smith 36, fol. 44.   [11] Ibid.   [12] Ibid.

[13] Ibid., fols. 39, 41. The letter is undated. For Lukaris's turbulent career, see George A. Hadjiantoniou, *Protestant Patriarch: The Life of Cyril Lucaris (1572–1638), Patriarch of Constantinople* (Richmond: John Knox Press, 1961); Keetze Rozemond, ed., *Cyrille Lucar: Sermons, 1598–1602* (Leiden: E. J. Brill, 1974), pp. 1–17; Gunnar Hering, *Ökumenisches Patriarchat und Europäische Politik, 1620–1638* (Wiesbaden: Franz Steiner, 1968); Emile Legrand, ed., *Bibliographie Hellénique, ou description raisonnée des ouvrages publiés par des Grecs au dix-septième siècle*, 5 vols. (Paris: Alphonse Picard, 1894–1903), vol. IV, pp. ix–xi, 161–175. See also Colin Davey, *Pioneer for Unity: Metrophanes Kritopoulos (1589–1639) and Relations between the Orthodox, Roman Catholic and Reformed Churches* (London: British Council of Churches, 1987), pp. 67–68.

correspondence by asking if the English Church could assist in educating members of the Greek clergy. Lukaris began his letter to Abbot by excusing himself for not answering sooner. He had been called away to give aid to the Orthodox peoples of the Balkans and Poland who were threatened with an "anti-Christian tyranny" as a result of the "art and cunning of the Jesuits" – a reference to the vigorous effort being made in those areas to bring the Orthodox within the jurisdiction of the papacy.[14] Under the agency of the Jesuits this same effort was being made in the city of Constantinople itself. Lukaris noted that the two religions existed in single households and that conflict and argument were endemic among eastern Christians. Under the circumstances Lukaris found the communication from England, containing an offer of help, to be heartening, and he expatiated upon the qualities of that monarch whose loving concern had been so expressed. King James's classical wisdom and charitable heart had made him unique among the then reigning monarchs – "a philosopher-king in every respect."[15] James's Christian qualities were no less evident than his generosity, and these attributes had carried his reputation to the East and across the world. Finally Lukaris turned to the invitation which had elicited such an outpouring of gratitude. Soon, he said, he would depart for Alexandria, and "from there I will gladly send to your piety men whom I select and judge to be pleasing to Christ as skilled in the service of the Gospel."[16]

Having reached Egypt, Lukaris wrote again, on March 1, 1617, confirming his earlier letter and commenting in more detail on the proposal Abbot had made to him. The king and the archbishop, he said, had been the authors of a plan "by which we should send someone from among us who would do careful work in sacred theology."[17] Accordingly the patriarch had selected a young presbyter, Metrophanes Kritopoulos, who had already shown promise in scholarship, and who was "very ready to absorb more profound learning."[18] He therefore commended Kritopoulos to the care of the archbishop and the Most Serene King. Archbishop Abbot, in turn, wrote to the patriarch, on November 17, 1617, to say that Kritopoulos had been entered at "the illustrious University of Oxford" and that he would be provided with whatever help was required. The king, the archbishop noted, had given instructions that Kritopoulos be received with "humanity and friendship."[19] Abbot asked for the patriarch's prayers for the British Church and offered his own for the Greek Church, "that she

---

[14] Bodl. MS. Smith 36, fols. 39, 41.   [15] Ibid., fols. 39, 41 verso.
[16] Ibid., fols. 39, 41 verso–42.
[17] Paulus Colomesius, ed., *S. Clementis epistolae duae ad Corinthios* (London: James Adamson, 1694), p. 329.
[18] Ibid., p. 329.   [19] Ibid., pp. 334–335.

together with the whole Catholic stronghold . . . may be strengthened in truth and peace."[20] Thus was inaugurated a scheme, now little known, for educating Greek students in England, a step which marked the beginning of official relations between the Church of England and the Greek Orthodox Church.[21] The scheme, though it involved a journey for the Greeks to the other side of Europe, was well conceived as a contribution to the needs of the Orthodox. Greek churchmen were able to maintain very few institutions for the academic education of their clergy, apart from the Patriarchal Academy in Constantinople. Moreover they were increasingly subjected to the proselytizing efforts of Jesuits and of Greeks educated in Rome. An education abroad offered aspiring young theologians the opportunity of learning at first-hand the methods and achievements of the scholars of western Europe. At the same time the scheme would enable British Christians to gain a greater understanding of eastern traditions in theology and piety.

Lukaris was interested in forging ties with England partly because he had studied Calvinist theology and was increasingly influenced by it. A native of Crete, which had long been under Venetian control, he was educated partly in Venice and partly at a monastery in Candia, and then at the University of Padua, where he read philosophy. After being ordained by his cousin Meletius Pegas, patriarch of Alexandria, he served in Poland for five years as the patriarch's representative, to help to shore up the Orthodox against the Jesuits and the Uniat Eastern Church which was under the supervision of Rome. In 1601 he succeeded his kinsman as patriarch of Alexandria. Soon afterwards, Lukaris met Cornelius van Haga, the Dutch ambassador to the Sublime Porte, and through him received books on theology and other subjects from the Netherlands.[22] By 1612–1613, he was corresponding with Johann Uytenbogaert, a prominent minister and member of

[20] Ibid., p. 335.
[21] Compare Steven Runciman, "The Church of England and the Orthodox Churches in the Seventeenth and Eighteenth Centuries," in E. G. W. Bill, ed., *Anglican Initiatives in Christian Unity* (London: SPCK, 1967), pp. 5–7; Methodius Fouyas, *Orthodoxy, Roman Catholicism, and Anglicanism* (London: Oxford University Press, 1972), pp. 35–36; and, the fullest treatment of the significance of relations between the two churches in this era, H. R. Trevor-Roper, "The Church of England and the Greek Church in the Time of Charles I," in Derek Baker, ed., *Religious Motivation: Biographical and Sociological Problems for the Church Historian* (Oxford: Blackwell, 1978), Studies in Church History, XV, pp. 213–240.
[22] Hadjiantoniou, *Protestant Patriarch*, pp. 9–40; Lucar, *Sermons, 1598–1602*, ed. Rozemond, pp. 4–16; Runciman, *The Great Church in Captivity*, pp. 259–269; Germanos [Strenopoulos], Metropolitan of Thyateira, *Kyrillos Loukaris, 1572–1638: A Struggle for Preponderance between Catholic and Protestant Powers in the Orthodox East* (London: SPCK, 1951), pp. 9–19; R. Belmont, "Le patriarche Cyrille Lukaris et l'union des églises," *Irénikon*, 15, 4 (July–August 1938), 342–362; 15, 6 (November–December 1938), 535–553.

the Arminian party at The Hague.[23] Were he and Uytenbogaert, Lukaris asked in 1612, not pastors under one Supreme Pastor, by whom they were constituted pastors?[24] A declaration of his emerging views was made in a letter of September 6, 1618 to Marco Antonio De Dominis, the archbishop of Spalato, near Venice, who had migrated to England in 1616. Lukaris wrote to thank De Dominis for the first volume of the latter's *De republica ecclesiastica*, a study of the nature and constitution of the Church, which had been published in 1617.[25] Lukaris noted that De Dominis had been "reformed" from his previous Roman Catholic views, and the patriarch commented that he was reforming his own faith.[26] He had once been deluded into thinking that Roman Catholic dogmas were sound, except for the papal supremacy in the Church and several fairly minor matters about which the Latins and Greeks disagreed. But this was before he discovered "the pure and clear word of God."[27] He now recognized that reformed theology was the closest to "the doctrine of Christ."[28] He saw original sin as remaining after baptism, free-will to be dead except in those reborn by grace, and the partaking of the body and blood of Christ in the eucharist to be sacramental and spiritual rather than physical, in accordance with the sacrament's institution.[29] Furthermore, he declared that the use of images in the East had degenerated in some quarters into idolatry and that the invocation of the saints frequently obscured the place and work of Christ as Savior.[30] Lukaris was alarmed that "the satellites of the Antichrist have as it were occupied the whole East," where they worked unceasingly to corrupt "the souls of the simple" beneath "the false shell of Catholicism."[31] For this reason he welcomed the opportunity of sending someone like Metrophanes Kritopoulos to the most flourishing Church of England to prepare himself to nourish his people with the "pure food of the gospels" and to defend and restore the apostolic faith.[32] Lukaris said that his own faith had been nourished by Cornelius van Haga, who represented the States-General of the Netherlands in the Turkish capital. Despite the obstacles represented by the tyranny under which he lived, Lukaris looked for eventual success with the aid of the English Church.[33]

---

[23] Christian Hartsoeker, ed., *Praestantium ac eruditorum virorum epistolae ecclesiasticae et theologicae*, third edition (Amsterdam: Franciscus Halma, 1704), pp. 314–315, 357–365.

[24] Cyril Lukaris to Johann Uytenbogaert, May 30, 1612, in Hartsoeker, *Praestantium ac eruditorum virorum epistolae*, p. 315.

[25] Cyril Lukaris to Marco Antonio De Dominis, September 6, 1618, in Legrand, *Bibliographie Hellénique*, vol. IV, pp. 329–340. On De Dominis, see below, chapter 7.

[26] Legrand, *Bibliographie Hellénique*, vol. IV, p. 330.   [27] Ibid., p. 333.

[28] Ibid., p. 334.   [29] Ibid., pp. 334–336.   [30] Ibid., p. 336.   [31] Ibid., p. 338.

[32] Ibid., p. 339.   [33] Ibid., p. 340.

II

A good many Greeks had, in fact, already found their way to England, where they had achieved a mixed reputation. It was not uncommon in the early seventeenth century for Greeks who had been ruined by the actions of local Turkish officials, or who had a child or other relative in a Turkish prison as security for a fine, to come to England to try to ameliorate their unhappy condition. In 1609, for example, Patrick Young, the keeper of the king's library, whose philhellenic actions earned for him the jocular title of "the patriarch of the Greeks," sent letters to several friends in England on behalf of Anastasios Joseph, a native of Cappadocia. The latter was described as an honest Christian, who had been a wealthy trader – a fact demonstrated by testimonials. Now deprived by the Turks of all his financial resources and with his only son in captivity, he had come seeking Christian alms, "that he himself may be delivered from poverty and his son from this tyranny and confinement."[34] When Joseph had met with some success in England he went on to Scotland, carrying with him a letter from Patrick Young to Sir George Young of Wilkinton, a royal councillor there. James's librarian asked the councillor to provide Anastasios with an official letter "for soliciting charitable contributions in Scotland," in order that he might be rescued "from the waves of miseries in which he is tossing."[35] A common practice was for Greeks in such a situation to procure a letter of commendation from the British king, entitling them to proceed under royal protection to collect such funds as they were able. Letters of this kind were provided by King James for Chariton, metropolitan of Dyrrachios, who had been driven from his see and stripped of his fortune,[36] and for Pankratios Grammatikos, a merchant of Wallachia, who had been robbed of his business and forced to leave his son in captivity until a ransom could be raised.[37] Later King Charles I provided such a letter for Gregorios Argyropoulos, a monk and landowner of Thessalonica, who had lost his land after a Turkish soldier had been slain there. Charles's letter, written in response to a request by Cyril Lukaris, admonished "pastors, vicars, and sacristans" to urge their flocks and local officials to show zeal for this benevolent work.[38] That other Greeks sought and received aid in England –

---

[34] Johannes Kemke, *Patricius Junius (Patrick Young), Bibliothekar der Könige Jacob I. und Carl I. von England* (Leipzig: M. Spirgatis, 1898), pp. 118–121. See also Andreas Tillyrides, Ἀνέκδοτοσ Ἀλληλογραφία ἐκ τῶν ἐν Ἀγγλίᾳ Ἐπιδημησάντων Ἑλλήνων τινων τοῦ 17ου Αἰῶνος (reprinted from θεολογία (Athens, 1974), pp. 37–39.

[35] Kemke, *Patricius Junius*, p. 121.

[36] Ibid., p. 133; Tillyrides, Ἀνέκδοτοσ Ἀλληλογραφία, pp. 15–19.

[37] Kemke, *Patricius Junius*, p. 133.

[38] Ibid., pp. 134–135. For Cyril Lukaris's letter to Charles I in 1632, asking that the monk be given such royal assistance, see Bodl. MS. Smith 36, fols. 37–38.

for which they often expressed a deep gratitude – is clear from Patrick Young's correspondence.[39]

Inevitably, perhaps, the arrival of no small number of wandering Greeks, with tales of oppression in distant lands, led to a certain skepticism on the part of the English and Scots. Even Patrick Young was forced to recognize this mood. In a letter to John Williams, principal of Jesus College, Oxford, in the spring of 1612, Young said, in the course of commending Dionysios Koronaios, that he was not unaware that "the first love of the majority for the Greeks has now cooled." Nor was he ignorant, he went on to say, of the crookedness of their character and of their supreme love of lying – "the race seems indeed to have been born to invent fables."[40] Despite this, the letter asked Williams, "in the interest of the common Christian will," to urge his friends to contribute something to the Greek's necessity, "one much (as I may use the words of the patriarch of Constantinople), one little, each according to his own power and good resolution."[41] At least one of the Greeks who came to England in this period was a scholar, and his example must have helped to prepare the way for the admission of other Greeks into the English universities. Christophoros Angelos, a native of the Peloponnesus, was persecuted by the Turkish authorities in Athens and imprisoned, but was allowed to sail on an English ship to Yarmouth in 1608. In East Anglia he had the good fortune to be befriended by John Jegon, the bishop of Norwich, and other members of the clergy of that diocese, who contributed money to help support him and who sent him on to Cambridge. As he related his own story in 1617:

the doctors of Cambridge received me kindly and frankly, and I spent there almost one whole yeare . . . Then I fell sicke, that I could scarce breath, and the physitians and doctors counselled me to goe to Oxford, because (said they) the aire of Oxford is far better than that of Cambridge. And so I came to this famous universitie of Oxford: and now I live here studious these many yeares.[42]

Angelos became a member of Balliol College on migrating to Oxford, and there he gave instruction in the Greek language. He also published four books between 1617 and 1624, including an account, in Greek and Latin, of the liturgical rites of the Greek Church. King James declared, in a document prepared for Angelos's leave-taking, that the Greek scholar had spent seventeen years in the English universities, "in which without infraction or offence, he has lived soberly and piously, certainly with profit to

[39] Kemke, *Patricius Junius*, pp. 134–136; Tillyrides, Ἀνέκδοτοσ Ἀλληλογραφία, pp. 24–26, 40.

[40] Kemke, *Patricius Junius*, p. 122.   [41] Ibid., p. 123.

[42] Ibid. See also Tillyrides, Ἀνέκδοτοσ Ἀλληλογραφία, pp. 8, 22, and the anonymous article on Christopher Angelus in the *Dictionary of National Biography*, 22 vols. (London: Oxford University Press, 1959–1960), vol. I, pp. 415–416.

himself and not unprofitably to others."[43] As it turned out, however, Angelos remained in Oxford until his death in February 1639, "leaving behind him," said Anthony à Wood, "the character of a pure Grecian and an honest and harmless man."[44]

Cyril Lukaris's first scholar in England, Metrophanes Kritopoulos, was also placed at Balliol College, the undergraduate college of Archbishop Abbot. Kritopoulos evidently entered there not long after his arrival in England in the latter part of 1617. Though this young priest, of a good family in Macedonia, could not endure the beer served in his new surroundings, he found a great deal of congenial scholarly company in Oxford and in London.[45] In an album or autograph book kept by Kritopoulos are to be found complimentary messages about him by John Prideaux, the Oxford theologian and rector of Exeter College; Robert Burton, the author of the *Anatomy of Melancholy*; Richard Corbet, the poet and dean of Christ Church, Oxford; and John Bainbridge, the Savilian professor of Astronomy at Oxford. An entry by the mathematician Henry Briggs suggests that Kritopoulos had studied at least briefly at Gresham College, London, before going up to Oxford.[46] From other sources it is clear that Kritopoulos was a close friend of Andrew Downes, the Regius professor of Greek at Cambridge. Kritopoulos also seems to have been a friend of the king's physician, the Frenchman Raphael Thorius.[47] Finally Daniel Featley, the chaplain to Archbishop Abbot, paid tribute to Kritopoulos as "the choice flower of all the Greeks" who had come to England, "the marrow of pleasant Attica, of piety, modesty, [and] humanity."[48] That there was at least one other Greek studying at Oxford in the next few years and that there were still others who wished to study there is revealed by several Greek letters, though unfortunately information beyond what they contain is largely lacking. In

[43] Kemke, *Patricius Junius*, p. 124.
[44] Anthony à Wood, *Athenae Oxonienses: An Exact History of All the Writers and Bishops Who Have Had Their Education in the University of Oxford*, ed. Philip Bliss, 4 vols. (London: F. C. and J. Rivington, 1813–1820) [originally published, 1691], vol. II, col. 633.
[45] On Metrophanes Kritopoulos's career, see Colin Davey, *Pioneer for Unity*; Markos Rhenieres, Μητροφάνησ Κριτόπουλος καὶ οἱ ἐν Ἀγγλίᾳ καὶ Γερμανίᾳ φίλοι αὐτοῦ (1617–1628) (Athens: Perre, 1893); Trevor-Roper, "The Church of England and the Greek Church in the Time of Charles I," pp. 222–224, 240; Kemke, *Patricius Junius*, pp. 124–130; Legrand, *Bibliographie Hellénique*, vol. V, pp. 192–218; Tillyrides, Ἀνέκδοτοσ Ἀλληλογραφία, pp. 5–6, 35.
[46] F. H. Marshall, "An Eastern Patriarch's Education in England," *Journal of Hellenic Studies*, 40 (1926), pp. 187–189; Davey, *Pioneer for Unity*, pp. 102–111. For Greek excerpts from the album, see Rhenieres, Μητροφάνησ Κριτόπουλος, pp. 12–23. The album, which was first discovered by Rhenieres in Egypt, contains signatures and testimonials dated in the autumn of 1622, near the end of Kritopoulos's stay at Oxford.
[47] Tillyrides, Ἀνέκδοτοσ Ἀλληλογραφία, p. 10.
[48] Rhenieres, Μητροφάνησ Κριτόπουλος, pp. 14–15. See also Tillyrides, Ἀνέκδοτοσ Ἀλληλογραφία, pp. 10, 34–35. Featley no doubt used Attica to suggest the culture of ancient Greece, even though Kritopoulos was from Macedonia.

1633 Jacobos Vlastos wrote from Balliol College to Patrick Young to ask him for news of the departure of a mutual friend for Constantinople. Young is described as "one dearest to me" by Vlastos, who entreated the Englishman to write and maintain the friendship between them.[49] Two years before, two Greek archimandrites, both called Gregory, one with the surname Kantakouzenos, the other with the surname Makedonios, petitioned King Charles I, Archbishop Abbot, and William Laud, the bishop of London, to allow them to study at Oxford. Greece, they lamented to the king, had formerly been a divine workshop of wisdom; now it was destitute of learning.[50] To the archbishop they proclaimed that the ruin of Greece was worth a jeremiad on the order of that for Jerusalem; well should Rachel weep for her children. They wished to be liberated from their servile state by attending the "sacred academy of Oxford." "We wish to stay there and pursue your philosophy and holy theology, but we cannot accomplish this unless you supply us with the provisions for sustenance, and all the necessities of our living."[51]

The second well-attested student sent by Lukaris was Nathaniel Konopios, a native of Crete. By the time he was chosen, in the late 1630s, Lukaris had been patriarch of Constantinople intermittently since 1620, having gone there from Alexandria only to find himself repeatedly victimized by intricate and destructive intrigues. In the spring of 1623, some two and a half years after his election as patriarch of Constantinople in late 1620, a party of Greek clergy, with the support of the French ambassador, succeeded in deposing him. The rival party apparently favored giving effect to the union of the Latin and Greek Churches agreed to at the Council of Ferrara–Florence in 1438–1439, but never accepted in the East. They accused Lukaris to the sultan of being in treasonable correspondence with the czar of Russia, an Orthodox Christian who was a potent rival of the Ottomans in the north.[52] Lukaris's theological views were also a factor in these procedures. Sir Thomas Roe, the English ambassador, wrote in 1622 to Bishop John Williams, lord keeper of the Great Seal in England, that Lukaris was "a man of more learning and witt then hath possessed that place in many yeares, and in religion a direct Calvinist; yett he dares not

[49] Tillyrides, Ἀνέκδοτοσ Ἀλληλογραφία, pp. 8, 23.
[50] Ibid., pp. 9, 28; Kemke, *Patricius Junius*, p. 133.
[51] Tillyrides, Ἀνέκδοτοσ Ἀλληλογραφία, p. 30.
[52] Hadjiantoniou, *Protestant Patriarch*, pp. 57–61; Runciman, *The Great Church in Captivity*, pp. 269–271; Thomas Roe, *The Negotiations of Sir Thomas Roe in His Embassy to the Ottoman Porte, from the Year 1621 to 1628 Inclusive*, ed. Samuel Richardson (London: Society for the Encouragement of Learning, 1740), pp. 146–147 (Roe to Abbot, May 2, 1623) and 757–758 (Roe to Charles I, February 22, 1628, with a "Relation of the Practices of the Jesuits against Cyrillus, Patriarch of Constantinople"); Michael J. Brown, *Itinerant Ambassador: The Life of Sir Thomas Roe* (Lexington: University Press of Kentucky, 1970), p. 157.

shewe yt."[53] Lukaris's successor had an even briefer tenure of office, as did that prelate's successor. By October 1623 Lukaris was again on the patriarchal throne, which he retained until 1638 with interruptions caused by depositions in 1633, 1634, and 1635.[54]

Lukaris stirred up controversy by sponsoring a translation of the New Testament into vernacular Greek and, even more, by publishing his own *Eastern Confession of the Christian Faith*. The confession was first published in French and Latin in Sedan in 1629, then in Greek in Geneva in 1631. Its publication in Geneva was the result of Lukaris's friendship with Antoine Léger, a Swiss pastor who was chaplain to van Haga.[55] The patriarch's intent, as Jaroslav Pelikan has written, was evidently "to achieve a synthesis of Eastern Orthodox dogma and mildly Calvinist theology, in which the genius of each tradition would be articulated without doing violence to the other."[56] Lukaris's definitions of the Trinity, the Incarnation, and the nature of the Creation are rooted in Orthodox language and concepts. There are three persons or hypostases, but one God. Jesus Christ was conceived by the Holy Spirit in the womb of "the ever virgin Mary"; in the Incarnation, he "emptied Himself, that is, He assumed man's nature into his own substance."[57] In Creation, "the one God in Trinity, the Father, Son, and Holy Ghost . . . hath created all things good, and He cannot do any evil."[58] On the issue of the *filioque* ("and the Son"), long a source of dispute between the Latin West and the Greek East, Lukaris's confession offers a compromise: "the Holy Ghost proceeding from the Father by the Son," rather than simply "from the Father," as in the Greek – the original –

[53] Roe, *Negotiations*, p. 36 (Roe to Williams, April 29, 1622).
[54] Ibid., p. 185 (Roe to Sir Dudley Carleton, October 4, 1623); Hadjiantoniou, *Protestant Patriarch*, pp. 113–121; Runciman, *The Great Church in Captivity*, pp. 282–284.
[55] Runciman, *The Great Church in Captivity*, pp. 275–276; Davey, *Pioneer for Unity*, pp. 284–285. An English translation is included as an appendix in Hadjiantoniou, *Protestant patriarch*, pp. 141–145. The edition of 1629 was entitled the *Confessio Fidei* of Cyril, patriarch of Constantinople. The Greek edition of 1631 has the title used here. Lukaris acknowledged his authorship of the confession in conversation with the French ambassador in December 1631; see Bodl. MS. Tanner 461, p. 81 (letter of Cornelius van Haga, January 7, 1632).
[56] Jaroslav Pelikan, *The Christian Tradition: A History of the Development of Doctrine*, 5 vols. (Chicago: University of Chicago Press, 1971–1989), vol. II, *The Spirit of Eastern Christendom (600–1700)*, pp. 282–283; see also pp. 283–286, 293. For other commentaries on Lukaris's confession, see George P. Michaelides, "The Greek Orthodox Position on the Confession of Cyril Lucaris," *Church History*, 12 (1943), 118–129, which examines arguments for and against Lukaris's authorship, and J. Mihalcesco, "Les idées calvinistes du patriarche Cyrille Lucaris," *Revue d'histoire et de philosophie religieuses*, 11 (1931), 506–520, which argues that Lukaris was imbued with Calvinist ideas and wanted a union of the Orthodox and Protestant churches. Also Runciman, *The Great Church in Captivity*, pp. 272–282, and Hadjiantoniou, *Protestant Patriarch*, pp. 94–99.
[57] Hadjiantoniou, *Protestant Patriarch*, p. 142.   [58] Ibid.

Nicene Creed.[59] Many of the theological issues which were contested in the West in the sixteenth century had been little discussed in the East, and had not been definitively dealt with by the Greek Church. Lukaris stated the faith of the Orthodox in such a way as to distinguish it from that of Rome and to leave an opening to the Protestantism practiced and professed in the Netherlands and in England. As a result, many statements in the confession reflect the views of the Protestant Reformers, especially those in the Calvinist tradition. These statements include an affirmation of the primacy of the scriptures: "We believe the authority of the Holy Scripture to be above the authority of the Church."[60] Also an affirmation of justification by faith: "We believe that without faith no man can be saved;" and "We believe that man is justified by faith and not by works."[61] The "object of faith," Lukaris understood as "the righteousness of Christ, which . . . faith apprehends."[62] The confession affirmed, furthermore, that God "hath predestinated His elect unto glory before the beginning of the world, without any respect unto their works."[63] The corollary to this proposition was stated in Calvinist fashion: "He hath rejected whom He would" in accordance solely with his will, but he governs the world in his providence in accordance with the principles of mercy and justice.[64] Lukaris found that there were only two "Evangelical Sacraments," in the sense that they were instituted in the gospel, namely, baptism and the eucharist. Both of them conferred grace through faith.[65] Lukaris's approach to Protestantism left many of his co-religionists behind. Moreover it gave his enemies, many of them pro-Roman in theology and ecclesiastical politics, a list of propositions which could be the basis of attacks on him. Shortly after Lukaris's death in 1638, his confession was condemned at synods in Constantinople in 1638 and 1642 and in Jassy in Moldavia in 1642. From 1642 to 1672, the Orthodox faith was defined by the theologians Peter of Moghila and Dositheus of Jerusalem to show that Lukaris's confession was heretical.[66] Lukaris's death was violent. Accused by his enemies of encouraging the Russian cossacks to attack the Turks, he was executed in 1638 on the orders of Sultan Murad IV.[67]

After Lukaris's execution the young priest Konopios went to the English

---

[59] Ibid., p. 141. For the *filioque* controversy, see Pelikan, *The Christian Tradition*, vol. II, pp. 183–198, 275–278.
[60] Hadjiantoniou, *Protestant Patriarch*, p. 141.   [61] Ibid., pp. 142–143.
[62] Ibid., p. 143.   [63] Ibid., p. 141.   [64] Ibid., pp. 141–142.
[65] Ibid., pp. 143–144.
[66] Ware, *The Orthodox Church*, pp. 106–110, *Eustratios Argenti*, pp. 8–16.
[67] Lukaris's death is described by John Greaves, who had been sent by Archbishop Laud to Constantinople to procure manuscripts, in a letter of August 2, 1638: *Miscellaneous Works of Mr. John Greaves, Professor of Astronomy in the University of Oxford*, 2 vols. (London: J. Brindley, 1737), vol. II, pp. 434–435. See also Runciman, *The Great Church in Captivity*, pp. 285–286; Hadjiantoniou, *Protestant Patriarch*, pp. 127–133.

ambassador in Constantinople, Sir Peter Wyche, to seek his assistance. Wyche helped him to make the journey to England and provided him with a commendation to Abbot's successor, Archbishop William Laud.[68] As a result of Laud's intercession Konopios was admitted to Balliol College in 1639.[69] The next few years were, of course, extremely eventful for England and hardly conducive to study. Konopios seems, nevertheless, to have pursued his studies with genuine zeal at Oxford, where he had the distinction of being one of the first persons to drink coffee there. On January 31, 1643 he received the Bachelor of Divinity degree. Not until nearly the end of the Civil War, in 1645, did he leave Oxford for Leyden, the home of the Netherlands' most celebrated university.[70] He alluded to his experience in England in a petition for financial support which he prepared for the States-General in the Netherlands in about 1646. After serving as chaplain to Lukaris, the patriarch of Constantinople, Konopios related, he had come to England on his patriarch's suggestion in order to study, and he had been received there with kindness and courtesy. There he remained "for six whole years," while making considerable progress in theology and the Latin language. In order to pursue his studies further, he had crossed over to the Netherlands, where he had enjoyed the company of learned men. During this period of a year and a half he had secured "orthodox books to spread the Religion and Gospel of Christ" in his homeland, and it was to help bear the cost of transporting these books, as well as himself, that he sought assistance from the States-General.[71] But Konopios seems not to have made his journey at that time. He was soon afterwards appointed chaplain at Christ Church, Oxford, a position he held until ejected by the parliamentary commissioners in November 1648. By that time, however, he had been chosen as metropolitan of Smyrna, where he was to end his career.[72]

The final months of Kritopoulos's stay in England, more than twenty years earlier, were marred by a disagreement which threatened to discredit the scholarship scheme early in its development and which may explain the wide hiatus in time between the first of the official scholars and the second. Writing to the ambassador, Sir Thomas Roe, on August 13, 1623, Archbishop Abbot reported – erroneously, as it happened – that Metrophanes

[68] For Laud's attitude towards the Greek Church, see Trevor-Roper, "The Church of England and the Greek Church in the Time of Charles I," pp. 213–214, 228–230, 235, 239.
[69] Kemke, *Patricius Junius*, pp. 136–137; Tillyrides, Ἀνέκδοτοσ Ἀλληλογραφία, pp. 7, 20–21.
[70] Kemke, *Patricius Junius*, pp. 137–138; Wood, *Athenae Oxonienses*, vol. IV, col. 808.
[71] Kemke, *Patricius Junius*, p. 138; Gerardus Joannes Vossius, *Gerardi Joan. Vossii et clarorum virorum ad eum epistolae*, ed. Paulus Colomesius, 2 pts. (London: Samuel Smith, 1690), part II, p. 145.
[72] Kemke, *Patricius Junius*, p. 138; Tillyrides, Ἀνέκδοτοσ Ἀλληλογραφία, pp. 7–8.

Kritopoulos had left for the continent, bound for Constantinople.[73] Abbot had already written on November 20, 1622 that Kritopoulos, having spent five or six years at Oxford with good report, and having acquired considerable learning, including "some reasonable knowledge of the English tongue," was about to leave for the East.[74] The delay in Kritopoulos's departure evidently affected the archbishop's opinion of him adversely. "I bred him full five yeers in Oxford," wrote Abbot in his letter of 1623,

> with good allowance for diett, cloaths, bookes, chamber, and other necessaries; so that his expence, since his comeing into England doth amount almost to three hundred pounds. Whiles hee was in that university, hee carried himselfe well; and at Michaelmas last I sent for him to Lambeth, taking care that in a very good shippe hee might bee conveyed to that port [Constantinople], with accommodation of all thinges by the way.[75]

At this point, however, Kritopoulos had apparently gone to Newmarket to see King James before leaving the realm; and, at court, while enjoying the king's hospitality, he devised a plan for buying books to take home to Cyril Lukaris. His plan involved the king's selling two titles of honor and one benefice, which prompted Abbot to oppose the idea. But to fulfil the Greek's desire, the archbishop purchased out of his own pocket "many of the best Greeke authors, and among them Chrysostomes eight tomes."[76] He also supplied other books in Latin and English, making, as he saw it, a fitting present for the patriarch.

Kritopoulos, however, was in no hurry to leave the country. "Since Michaelmas last," continued Abbot,

> I lodged him in my owne house, I sett him at my owne table, I cloathed him, and provided all conveniences for him; and would once againe have sent him away in a good shippe, that hee might safely have returned: butt hee fell into the company of certaine Greeks, with whom wee have bene much troubled for collections, and otherwise; and although I knew them to bee counterfeits and vagabonds, (as sundry times you have written vnto mee) yet I could not keepe my man within dores, but hee must be abrode with them, to the expence of his time and mony. In breefe, writing a kind of epistle vnto mee, that he would rather loose his bookes, suffer imprisonment, and losse of his life, then go home in any shippe; but that he would see the parts of Christendome, and better his experience that way.[77]

Abbot's patience now being exhausted, he dismissed Kritopoulos with £10

---

[73] Roe, *Negotiations*, pp. 171–172. For Roe's career in Constantinople, where he was a staunch friend of Lukaris, see Brown, *Itinerant Ambassador*, pp. 119–169, and Michael Strachan, *Sir Thomas Roe, 1581–1644: A Life* (London: Michael Russell, 1989), pp. 134–183.

[74] Roe, *Negotiations*, p. 102.   [75] Ibid., p. 171.

[76] Ibid., p. 172. The edition of St. John Chrysostom's works referred to here was no doubt the Greek edition prepared by Sir Henry Savile at Eton College and published in eight folio volumes in 1610–1613.

[77] Roe, *Negotiations*, p. 172.

leaving him in the care of Sir Paul Pindar, former English ambassador to Constantinople. What confounded Abbot was that anyone with an English education could have behaved so abominably: "I had heard before of the basenes and slavishnes of that nation; but I could never haue beleeved, that any creature in humane shape, having learning, and such education as hee hath had heere, could, after so many yeeres, haue bene so farre from ingenuity, or any gratefull respect."[78] Thereafter Abbot found it impossible to say anything favorable about the patriarch's scholar. On June 23, 1624 the archbishop wrote to the ambassador that Kritopoulos was still in England and that despite the Greek's entreaties he had refused to provide any further assistance. Of "what hee intendeth," wrote Abbot, "I can yeeld no account."[79] By March 30, 1625 Abbot was able to say that Kritopoulos had left "with pretence to traveile throughe Germany by lande, in whiche course I cannot see how hee should carye the bookes alonge with him."[80] The archbishop added that he was afraid that Kritopoulos had "fared so well in these parts" that he would have difficulty conforming again to the monastic life of the Greek Church.[81] Kritopoulos's plan to return by land was, however, no mere whim on his part. It was probably the result of a commission from Lukaris that he make contact with Protestant churches on the continent. He subsequently assured the Genevans that his patriarch would welcome close relations between the Orthodox Church and the Reformed churches.

One activity which probably occupied Kritopoulos during his last months in England was assisting Nikodemos Metaxas, a Greek monk from Cephalonia, in making arrangements to transport a printing press from London to Constantinople.[82] Though there were Greek presses in Venice, which were used chiefly for printing classical and patristic texts and works of classical scholarship, there was not a single Greek press in the East which the Orthodox could use to print theological works, liturgical texts, and the scriptures, let alone polemical tracts to counter similar Roman Catholic materials.[83] Metaxas, who met Kritopoulos in late 1622 or early 1623, was a member of a distinguished family and evidently paid for the press and the voyage himself.[84] He reached Constantinople in June 1627 with the press

---

[78] Ibid.   [79] Ibid., p. 253.   [80] Ibid., p. 373.   [81] Ibid.

[82] Evro Layton, "Nikodemos Metaxas, the First Greek Printer in the Eastern World," *Harvard Library Bulletin*, 15 (1967), 140–168; R. J. Roberts, "The Greek Press at Constantinople in 1627 and Its Antecedents," *Library*, 22, 1 (1967), 13–43.

[83] For the development of publishing in the Greek language at Venice – in which Greek scholars played a conspicuous part – see Geanakoplos, *Greek Scholars in Venice*, pp. 57–60, 117–158, 171–176, 226–229, 263–278, 282–291. As Geanakoplos shows, Greeks were also active in the establishment of Greek presses in Florence, Rome, and Alcalá.

[84] Layton, "Nikodemos Metaxas, the First Greek Printer in the Eastern World," pp. 141, 144. Kritopoulos mentions Metaxas's arrival in England in an undated letter probably written in

and two Netherlanders skilled in using it. Metaxas subsequently installed the press in a house near the residence of Sir Thomas Roe, who had befriended him, and began printing books in Greek.[85] But the Turkish authorities became suspicious of this activity, and the French ambassador opposed the press as a threat to the Jesuit mission to win the Greeks to the Roman obedience. In January 1628, Janissaries broke into Metaxas's house, and carried away books and equipment.[86] In the end, the Venetian government asked Metaxas as a Venetian subject – since Cephalonia was controlled by Venice – to give up operating the press. In compensation, Lukaris named Metaxas the archbishop of Cephalonia, Zante, and Ithaca. Metaxas took his press to Cephalonia and apparently never operated it again.[87] Because of a complex set of religious and political circumstances, therefore, the first Greek press in the Levant – brought from England by a Greek who enjoyed the support of the English ambassador – survived in Constantinople for only a little more than a year. Abbot's view of Kritopoulos had become one of undisguised distaste, but King James thought well of him and was evidently pleased that he had helped to forge close links between the Greek Church and the Church of England. In the letter of safe conduct James provided to Kritopoulos in 1623, the king related that Kritopoulos, who had been sent by his patriarch to study in England, had been recalled to his own land to serve as priest and archimandrite of the Greek Church.[88] Kritopoulos had had the courtesy of coming to take his leave of the king "that he who entered these lands by our wishes, might return with our good favour and peace to his own people."[89] "We understand," continued James,

that the said Metrophanes in our University of Oxford, where he has spent this period of five years, has been assiduous in the reading of the Holy Fathers and Doctors of the Church and in all parts of sacred study, conversations with learned men of every kind not in the meantime having been neglected, for which (as he makes clear by testimonies from them) a great desire has remained with him in going out as in journeying here; a moderation of soul has been seen of that one throughout his stay and sanctity of character has been joined with distinguished learning.[90]

1622 or 1623. Metaxas had gone to London to visit a brother who was a merchant connected to the Levant Company.

[85] Roe, *Negotiations*, p. 663 (Roe to Thomas Goad, chaplain to Archbishop Abbot, July 7, 1627), pp. 760–761 (Roe to Charles I, February 22, 1628 – "Relation of the Practises of the Jesuits").

[86] Roe, *Negotiations*, p. 739 (Roe to Edward, Lord Conway, secretary of state, January 26, 1628), pp. 761–763 (Roe to Charles I, February 22, 1628).

[87] Layton, "Nikodemos Metaxas, the First Greek Printer in the Eastern World," pp. 147–151; Roberts, "The Greek Press at Constantinople in 1627 and Its Antecedents," pp. 28–37.

[88] Rhenieres, Μητροφάνησ Κριτόπουλος, p. 24.   [89] Ibid.

[90] Ibid. As this passage suggests, one of the pleasures of studying at Oxford for the Greeks was the opportunity of reading the Greek fathers of the Church. This safe conduct was found in Hamburg, the first stop on the route Kritopoulos followed home.

James's letter is a wholehearted endorsement, not only of Kritopoulos's record at Oxford, but of the arrangements which had brought him to England.

III

Kritopoulos used his extended journey home as an opportunity to find out more about Protestantism on the continent and to share with his hosts his own detailed knowledge of the theology and liturgy of the East. His route took him through Germany, where he managed to elude the marauding armies of both sides in the Thirty Years' War. Scholars, universities, and civic authorities extended hospitality to a visitor whom they found scholarly, engaging, and eager to learn. Kritopoulos spent eight months at Helmstedt in Germany as a guest in the home of Georg Calixtus, the irenic Lutheran theologian.[91] He also visited Wittenberg and spent almost a year at Nuremberg and the nearby University of Altdorf. At the University of Tübingen, where he spent a winter, he met Lucius Osiander, the son of a prominent member of a group of Lutheran theologians who had corresponded with the Patriarch Jeremias II about a union between the Lutherans and the Orthodox half a century earlier.[92] At Berne and Geneva, he declared his hope to further the prospects of a union between the Reformed and Orthodox churches.[93] After a stay of almost three years in Venice, where he taught and preached in the Greek community, Kritopoulos returned to Alexandria in late 1630 or early 1631.[94] Despite the blemishes Abbot saw in Kritopoulos's character, the Oxford-educated Greek priest found himself in a few years discharging an office with major responsibilities. He himself became patriarch of Alexandria in 1636, where he served until his death in 1639.[95] Unfortunately the divisions in the Greek Church which brought down his patron threatened his own career. In 1638, after Lukaris's downfall, Kritopoulos was compelled by the new patriarch of Constantinople, Cyril Contaris, to sign a repudiation of Cyril Lukaris's confession.

Kritopoulos himself had written a confession, actually a lengthy theological treatise, on Orthodox beliefs and practices in 1625, while a guest of Georg Calixtus. It was not published until 1661. Kritopoulos's discussion of theology was not only more extensive than Lukaris's, it was more an attempt to present Orthodoxy in terms likely to make it intelligible to

[91] Legrand, *Bibliographie Hellénique*, vol. V, p. 201; Davey, *Pioneer for Unity*, pp. 147–158.
[92] Davey, *Pioneer for Unity*, pp. 188–252. For Lucius Osiander and the Lutheran approach to the Greeks at the time of the patriarchate of Jeremias II, see Runciman, *The Great Church in Captivity*, pp. 226–258, esp. 254–256.
[93] Legrand, *Bibliographie Hellénique*, pp. 202–208; Davey, *Pioneer for Unity*, pp. 253–263.
[94] Davey, *Pioneer for Unity*, pp. 263–288.
[95] Legrand, *Bibliographie Hellénique*, vol. V, p. 209.

westerners than to integrate Orthodox and Calvinist theology. Like Lukaris's confession it dealt with some of the issues then being discussed in the West. On predestination, the subject of intense and bitter debate at the Synod of Dort in 1618 to 1619, he affirmed with Acts 13:48 that "there believed in him [Christ] as many as were ordained to eternal life."[96] But he described God's relationship with human beings as one in which God justifies sinners by the blood of the Son, calls them by the Holy Spirit, and predestines to salvation those whom he foresees as worthy of grace. His treatment was explicitly Pauline, stressing Romans 8:29–30, but it did not state an extreme doctrine of predestination.[97] Kritopoulos identified three sacraments, namely baptism, the eucharist, and penance, as necessary for salvation, and four others as appropriate channels of grace under certain circumstances. These four were chrism (the counterpart to confirmation, administered by a priest immediately after the sacrament of baptism), ordination, marriage, and holy unction. He defended the view that the consecrated bread and wine in the eucharist were the body and blood of Christ, but without reference to transubstantiation, consubstantiation, or any particular theory of divine presence in the elements as an explanation for this mystery. Kritopoulos criticized Roman Catholics for having reduced unction, the rite of healing, to extreme unction, a rite for the dying.[98] He presented an elaborate defense of the use of leavened rather than unleavened bread in the eucharist, and a rationale with scriptural and patristic citations for traditions such as venerating icons and relics, praying for the dead, and taking monastic vows.[99] In one of his most distinctive formulations, he described the Church as a body marked by internal harmony, a deep respect for tradition, an unwillingness to persecute, and reliance on the scriptures.[100] Unlike the situation with regard to Lukaris's confession, Kritopoulos's confession was never condemned in the East, and is regarded by the Orthodox as a valuable, though unofficial, statement of the faith.[101]

James's and Abbot's scholarship scheme for Greek Orthodox students did not survive the English Civil War, but it had considerable influence. An attempt to found a Greek college at Oxford in the late seventeenth century was one legacy of the scheme. At that time, some ten to fifteen Greek students were selected by the Orthodox ecclesiastical authorities in the East, brought to England by the Levant Company, and entered at Gloucester

---

[96] Davey, *Pioneer for Unity*, pp. 163–164. For Kritopoulos's confession, see also Pelikan, *The Christian Tradition*, vol. II, pp. 286–293.

[97] Davey, *Pioneer for Unity*, pp. 164–166.   [98] Ibid., pp. 166–169, 173–174, 176–180.

[99] Ibid., pp. 175–176, 180–185.   [100] Ibid., pp. 171–172.

[101] Ware, *The Orthodox Church*, pp. 109, 211; Pelikan, *The Christian Tradition*, vol. II, pp. 286–287.

Hall, the predecessor of Worcester College.[102] The scheme, which began with the arrival of five students in 1699, had foundered by 1705, chiefly because of financial difficulties, the dissatisfaction of some students with the arrangements in Oxford, the withdrawal of support by the Levant Company, and, most important, the refusal of the Greek Church to send any more students. "The irregular life of some priests and laymen of the Greek Church living in London has greatly disturbed the Church," explained the registrar of the Greek Church in Constantinople.[103] Later conversations of a variety of kinds between Anglican and Orthodox churchmen on theological issues with the objective of achieving a better understanding between the churches were surely another legacy. From the beginning of English–Orthodox relations, the easterners apparently felt comfortable with their counterparts in the Church of England, sensing no desire by the English to proselytize them.[104] When Christophoros Angelos fled from the Turks in Athens, he asked many merchants "where I might find wise men, with whom I might keepe my religion and not loose my learning. They told me: In England you may have both, for the English men love the Grecians and their learning, and it is a monarchie where are found many very honest, wise and liberall men"; and so, he said, "I came in a streight course to England."[105] One of the most tangible results was the gift by Cyril Lukaris to King James of the early fifth-century Greek manuscript of the Bible which is now known as the Codex Alexandrinus. The gift was in recognition of James's contributions to the Greek Church and his support of Lukaris in his struggles to retain control of the patriarchate in Constantinople. Under the direction of James and Abbot, Roe had consistently and effectively assisted Lukaris against his enemies. The volume arrived in England in 1627. Believed by Lukaris to be "written by the hand of Tecla, the protomartyr of the Greeks," it was regarded by the patriarch as "the greatest relique of the Greeke church."[106] The

---

[102] E. D. Tappe, "The Greek College at Oxford, 1699–1705," *Oxoniensia*, 19 (1954), 92–111.

[103] Ibid., p. 102.

[104] Compare Fouyas, *Orthodoxy, Roman Catholicism, and Anglicanism*, pp. 35, 64–65; V. T. Istavridis, *Orthodoxy & Anglicanism*, trans. Colin Davey (London: SPCK, 1966), pp. 149–151. See also Kallistos Ware and Colin Davey, eds., *Anglican–Orthodox Dialogue: The Moscow Statement Agreed by the Anglican–Orthodox Joint Doctrinal Commission, 1976* (London: SPCK, 1977); *Anglican–Orthodox Dialogue: The Dublin Agreed Statement, 1984* (Crestwood, New York: St. Vladimir's Seminary Press, 1985); and Colin Davey, *Anglicans and Eastern Christendom* [paper given at a conference on "The Anglican Church" in Milan in 1984] (London: privately printed, 1984).

[105] Kemke, *Patricius Junius*, p. 123.

[106] Roe, *Negotiations*, p. 344 (Roe to the duke of Buckingham, January 24, 1625). The sending of this Bible, "formerly presented to his late majestie," now dedicated to Charles I, is noted in Roe, *Negotiations*, p. 618 (Roe to Archbishop Abbot, February 17, 1627). Tecla or Thecla, a virgin martyr and teacher, appears in several of the apocryphal Acts of

codex has proved to be one of the foundations of modern biblical scholarship.

The Jacobean establishment of scholarships for Greek students in England clearly had as one of its main purposes the bringing together of the Church of England and the Greek Orthodox Church in some form of closer association. This was made clear in a letter of 1619 to a Greek prelate, presumably Cyril Lukaris, by De Dominis, archbishop of Spalato, who was then close to King James and the leading bishops in England. De Dominis referred to the Eastern Church as "the first mother of all Churches of Christ."[107] This historic body was, he commented, doubly unfortunate in having to contend for its life against a hostile, unbelieving temporal ruler and an aggressive Roman Catholic mission in the East, aimed at bringing Greek Orthodox Christians into the papal fold. For the preservation of the liberty and purity of the Greek Church, he recommended a close union with the *Anglicana Ecclesia*, which did not seek to subjugate the Greeks as the pope sought to do.[108] Such a union would be founded on the basis of the unity of a common faith, grounded in the canonical scriptures of the Old and New Testaments and in the ancient creeds – the Apostles', the Nicene, and the Athanasian. The problem of the *filioque* clause – the phrase declaring that the Holy Spirit proceeded from the Father "and the Son," which was a part of the Nicene Creed in the West but not in the East – should be discussed seriously and amicably. If agreement could not be reached, each church should then follow its own tradition, without being subjected to censures from the other. The union would also recognize as authoritative the ancient ecumenical councils – the first five, with certain provisions of the sixth and seventh. Ecclesiastical polity and sacramental worship would be in accordance with the canons of the early Church. It would not be necessary to designate a specific number of mysteries or sacraments, but to affirm the centrality of baptism and the eucharist in the life of the Church. The manner of Christ's presence in the elements of the eucharist would be understood as spiritual and ineffable. There would be equality among bishops, though the jurisdiction exercised by metropolitans

---

Paul the Apostle. The Codex Alexandrinus contains not only most of the Greek Bible but the First and Second Letters of the patristic writer Clement. See *The Interpreter's Dictionary of the Bible*, 5 vols. (New York: Abingdon, 1962–1976), vol. I, p. 81, vol. III, pp. 678–679. On Thecla, see also Elisabeth Schüssler Fiorenza, *In Memory of Her: A Feminist Theological Reconstruction of Christian Origins* (New York: Crossroad, 1989), pp. 173–175.

[107] Marco Antonio De Dominis to Cyril Lukaris (?), London 1619, in J. H. Hessels, ed., *Ecclesiae Londino–Batavae archivum*, 3 vols. in 4 (Cambridge: Cambridge University Press, 1887–1897), vol. II, p. 949. There had been an exchange of letters between De Dominis and Lukaris in 1618, occasioned by De Dominis's sending the patriarch a copy of the first volume of his *De republica ecclesiastica*. See above in this chapter.

[108] Hessels, ed., *Ecclesiae Londino–Batavae archivum*, vol. II, p. 950.

and patriarchs would be affirmed. After such a union between the Greek and English churches had taken place, eastern Christians could expect to receive further support from England, especially from the king of Great Britain, the Defender of the Faith.[109] De Dominis invited his correspondent to send four patriarchs, two bishops, and a learned presbyter to confer with the leaders of the Church of England, especially King James, about this plan of union. De Dominis would see that their expenses were paid for their trip to England and return. By this means, he hoped, God would enable the participants to begin to reintegrate the divided Church.[110]

A union of the English and Greek churches in the early seventeenth century would seem to have been highly unlikely, even with a patriarch of Constantinople like Cyril Lukaris, who shared important theological convictions with Reformed thinkers in the West. The Church of England had been shaped and reshaped in the course of the English Reformation. The Greek Orthodox Church, largely isolated from the West during the sixteenth century, had been little affected by either the Protestant movement or the Roman Catholic Council of Trent. But this very fact meant that there was a theological openness in the East in the early seventeenth century which made the initiatives from England for closer relations timely and promising. Western churches, including the Church of Rome, were reaching out to the East, trying to establish closer theological and ecclesiological relations. From the point of view of the Greeks, an alliance with the English, increasingly a potent force in the Levantine trade, made sense. England could provide moral and material support for the Orthodox struggle to survive against both the Turks and the agents of Roman Catholicism. At the same time the English Church could gain important support from the Greeks in its ideological struggle against Rome and in its continuing search for religious self-understanding and identity. English theologians – including Thomas Cranmer, John Jewel, and Richard Hooker – had long contended that the Church of England was the continuation of the ancient Catholic Church in the island. Union, or at least closer association, with the Greeks would make that claim more credible. The Greek Orthodox Church had a continuity with the ancient Church which Rome could not deny. Indeed, in its links with the ancient sees of the eastern Mediterranean, with the culture and language of the New Testament, and with the ancient ecumenical councils, all of which were held in the East, it had a claim to apostolicity and catholicity equal or even superior to that of Rome.

However well disposed Lukaris was to closer relations with the English Church, no such conference as De Dominis proposed ever occurred. Formidable obstacles stood against its taking place: the subsequent preoccu-

---

[109] Ibid., pp. 950–953.   [110] Ibid., p. 953.

pation by Lukaris with maintaining his hold on the patriarchate in Constantinople and the preoccupation of King James with peace-making at the outset of a major European war. Furthermore, neither the Greek nor the English Church was yet ready to move with much alacrity to engage in detailed negotiations. Yet there was probably a good deal of support for such a union at James's court. The ideas expressed in De Dominis's letter were surely not his alone. De Dominis was, in 1619, at the height of his influence in England, and he no doubt discussed relations with the Greek Orthodox Church with English bishops and with the king himself. De Dominis's letter outlines a plan of union as ambitious as that enunciated in Isaac Casaubon's letters to Cardinal du Perron or that outlined in the document drawn up by Pierre du Moulin and sent to the French Reformed Synod of Tonneins. It shows James working through his allies and advisers to seek a "broader Christian union."[111] Such a union was intended eventually to include not only the Protestant churches and the Roman Catholic Church, but the Orthodox Church in the East. Just how much James, his bishops, or scholars in England knew about the Greek Church is open to question. They certainly knew, or knew about, the writings of the ancient Greek fathers of the Church: St. Athanasius, St. John Chrysostom, the Cappadocian Fathers – St. Basil, St. Gregory of Nazianzus, and St. Gregory of Nyssa – and St. Cyril of Alexandria. References to Greek patristic writers were frequent in English theology. The eastern liturgies had been studied ever since Cranmer's time and were increasingly well known.[112] Classical Greek was taught in English schools and universities, with the result that some English bishops and scholars could correspond with the Greeks in that language. But it is doubtful that many English bishops and scholars were familiar with later Greek theologians – St. Maximus the Confessor and St. John of Damascus in the seventh and eighth centuries, St. Simeon the "New Theologian" in the eleventh century, or St. Gregory Palamas in the fourteenth century.[113] It is even less likely that they would have been familiar with Russian theologians such as St. Sergius of

---

[111] See above, chapters 2, 4, 5.

[112] G. J. Cuming, "Eastern Liturgies and Anglican Divines, 1510–1662," in Derek Baker, ed., *The Orthodox Churches and the West* (Oxford: Blackwell, 1976), Studies in Church History, XIII, pp. 231–238. For knowledge of the Greek Church in England, see Davey, *Pioneer for Unity,* pp. 78–82, 129–136. For some of the theological reasons English writers were interested in the Greek Church, see Anthony Milton, *Catholic and Reformed: The Roman and Protestant Churches in English Protestant Thought, 1600–1640* (Cambridge: Cambridge University Press, 1995), pp. 272, 309, 378–381.

[113] For the rich texture of theology and mysticism in the last two centuries of the Byzantine Empire, see Donald M. Nicol, *Church and Society in the Last Centuries of Byzantium* (Cambridge: Cambridge University Press, 1979), esp. pp. 31–97. For the writers named, see also Pelikan, *The Christian Tradition,* vol. II, and J. M. Hussey, *The Orthodox Church in the Byzantine Empire* (Oxford: Clarendon Press, 1986).

Radonezh or St. Nilus Sorsky. English theologians had devoted relatively
little attention to such issues as the *filioque* clause in the western version of
the Nicene Creed, the use of leavened or unleavened bread in the eucharist,
or the proper use of icons in worship – all subjects of great interest in the
East.[114] Few Englishmen, except for those who knew Greeks in England or
had come into contact with Greeks in the Levant, had much idea of
contemporary Greek religious practices and piety. Some English writers,
indeed, described Greek Christians as degenerate and backward.[115]

Yet there were features of the Greek Church that were extremely
attractive to the English. Like Hugo Grotius in his account of the Greek
faith in *Meletius*, some Englishmen saw Greek theology as a purer form of
Christian belief than the conflicting western versions.[116] The Greek Church,
like the English, was episcopal in polity. Liturgy was centrally important to
both churches – more so than verbal orthodoxy. Music figured prominently
in both traditions. Both churches stressed the importance of the scriptures,
the writings of the Greek fathers, the ancient conciliar formulations of the
faith, and the historic creeds. Equally important, the two churches shared a
view of ecclesiastical authority: that it was not centered in one official or
episcopal see but was shared by the great sees and expressed in ecumenical
councils. Richard Field's conciliar theology had much in common with the
Greek view of the centrality of the "pentarchy" of ancient sees – Rome,
Constantinople, Antioch, Alexandria, and Jerusalem – and the need for
their full participation in any decision-making which was truly ecumenical.[117] In any future conversations concerning the reunion of Christendom, the Greek Church and the Church of England would be likely to
have much in common. Despite difficulties experienced on both sides,
George Abbot, Patrick Young, Thomas Roe, Gabriel Severus, Cyril Lukaris,
and Metrophanes Kritopoulos, with King James's encouragement, laid a
foundation on which future generations could build.

[114] William Laud knew the issues and defended the Greeks, claiming Peter Lombard in his
support. He also criticized the Roman Church for adding the *filioque* to the Nicene Creed
and then anathematizing the Greeks for not having it: "it is hard to add and anathematize
too." See William Laud, *Works*, 9 vols. (Oxford: J. H. Parker, 1847–1860), vol. II, p. 29.
[115] Samuel C. Chew, *The Crescent and the Rose: Islam and England during the Renaissance*
(New York: Oxford University Press, 1937), pp. 133–138.
[116] See above, chapter 4.
[117] Hussey, *The Orthodox Church in the Byzantine Empire*, pp. 297–299; Davey, *Pioneer for
Unity*, pp. 83–84. For Field's conciliar thought, see above, chapter 3.

---- **7** ----

Marco Antonio De Dominis

The fullest and most systematic treatment of the ideas on church unity advocated by King James was written by an Italian, Marco Antonio De Dominis, formerly the Roman Catholic archbishop of Spalato. De Dominis's *De republica ecclesiastica*, published in Latin between 1617 and 1622 in three stout folio volumes, reached a European-wide audience. Its impact was blunted, however, because De Dominis's "shiftings in religion" caused him, by the time of his death in 1624, to be regarded as an apostate by both Roman Catholics and Protestants.[1] De Dominis arrived in England on December 6, 1616 from Venice, after two and a half months of travel across northern Italy, Switzerland, the Rhineland, and the Netherlands. He had left Italy disguised as a Ragusan merchant, and had been joined on his journey by Robert Barnes and David Murray, two of King James's subjects.[2] According to the historian Arthur Wilson, De Dominis was "old and corpulent, unfit for Travel, being almost at his journies end by Nature"; yet he began to speak out vigorously against the faith and practices of the Church of Rome

---

[1] For De Dominis's life and career, see S. Ljubić, "O Markantunu Dominisu Rabljaninu, historičko-kritičko iztraživanje navlastito po izvorih mletačkoga arkiva i knjižnice arsenala parizkoga," *Rad Jugoslavenske Akademije Znanosti i Umjetnosti*, 10 (Zagreb, 1870), 1–159; Delio Cantimori, "Su M. A. De Dominis," *Archiv für Reformationsgeschichte*, 49, 1–2 (1958), 245–258, "L'utopia ecclesiologica di M. A. De Dominis," in *Problemi di vita religiosa in Italia nel cinquecento: atti del Convegno di Storia della Chiesa in Italia (1958)* (Padua: Antenore, 1960), pp. 103–122; Antonio Russo, *Marc'Antonio De Dominis, Arcivescovo di Spalato e Apostata (1560–1624)* (Naples: Istituto della Stampa, 1965); David L. Clark, "Marco Antonio de Dominis and James I: The Influence of a Venetian Reformer on the Church of England," *Papers of the Michigan Academy of Science, Arts, and Letters*, 53 (1968), pp. 219–230; Dušan Nedeljković, *Marko Dominis u nauci i utopiji na delu* (Belgrade: Serbian Academy of Sciences and Arts, 1975); and Noel Malcolm, *De Dominis (1560–1624): Venetian, Anglican, Ecumenist and Relapsed Heretic* (London: Strickland and Scott, 1984). For documents relating to De Dominis, see S. Ljubić, "Prilozi za životopis Markantuna de Dominisa Rabljanina, spljetskoga nadbiskupa," *Starine*, 2 (1870), 1–260, and Veselin Kostić, *Kulturne veze iz medju jugoslavenskih zemalja i engleske do 1700 godine* (Belgrade: Serbian Academy of Sciences and Arts, 1972), pp. 442–491.

[2] Malcolm, *De Dominis (1560–1624)*, pp. 42–44; Ljubić, "Prilozi za životopis Markantuna de Dominisa," pp. 146–161.

soon after his arrival in England.³ Warmly welcomed by George Abbot, the archbishop of Canterbury, and by the king, De Dominis was given several appointments in the Church of England – including that of dean of the Chapel Royal at Windsor and master of the Savoy in London – and became a prominent anti-Roman Catholic controversialist, as well as a spokesman for a reorganized and more inclusive universal Church. Then, after five and a half years in England, De Dominis, like a wandering star in the Ptolemaic system, went "Retrograde, placing himself again in the Roman Calendar."⁴ What moved De Dominis to undertake so arduous a physical and spiritual journey as that which led him to England in the first place? And why, having found an honored place among ideological allies, did he leave it for the very citadel of the ecclesiastical power he had attacked?

I

The island of Rab, where De Dominis was born, is just off the eastern Adriatic coast, some 120 miles across the sea from Venice. De Dominis was a member of a prominent Roman Catholic family long settled in the area. After receiving his early education in Loreto, on the eastern Italian coast, at a school directed by the Jesuits, De Dominis himself entered the Society of Jesus in 1579. Following further education in Verona and Padua, he became well known as a professor of mathematics at the University of Padua and of rhetoric and philosophy at the University of Brescia. As a philosopher of nature, De Dominis made significant contributions to the science of optics. After resigning from the Society of Jesus, he was elected bishop of Segna, on the eastern Adriatic coast, in 1597, succeeding an uncle who had been killed by Turkish raiders. This was a part of the Mediterranean world where political and religious jurisdictions overlapped, often with destructive consequences. Rab was controlled by Venice, but nearby Segna, on the mainland, where De Dominis served as bishop until 1602, was in Habsburg-controlled Croatia, and was near the frontier of the Ottoman Empire.⁵ In

³ Arthur Wilson, *The History of Great Britain: Being the Life and Reign of King James the First, Relating to What Passed from His First Access to the Crown, Till His Death* (London: Richard Lownds, 1653), p. 102. De Dominis was fifty-six when he entered England.
⁴ Ibid.
⁵ For De Dominis's career as a Jesuit, see Pietro Pirri, "Marc'Antonio De Dominis fino all'episcopfrom the Gato," *Archivum historicum Societatis Iesu*, 27 (1959), 265–288. His book on optics, *De radiis visus et lucis in vitris perspectivis et iride*, written c. 1590, was published in Venice in 1611. The political situation along the Dalmatian coast is described in L. S. Stravrianos, *The Balkans Since 1453* (New York: Holt, Rinehart and Winston, 1958), pp. 74–80, 137; and Vladimir Dedijer, Ivan Božić, Sima Cirković, and Milorad Edmečić *History of Yugoslavia*, trans. Kordija Kveder (New York: McGraw-Hill, 1974), pp. 125–126, 142–153, 172–188.

Segna refugees known as the Uskoks, from Ottoman-controlled lands, were supported by the Austrian Habsburgs to harass the Turks. But the Uskoks also conducted a vicious campaign of piracy against Venetian shipping, ostensibly because some of the goods the ships carried were the property of Muslims and Jews. As bishop of Segna, De Dominis made strenuous efforts to end hostilities between the Venetians and the Uskoks and to negotiate an agreement with the Emperor Rudolph II by which the Uskoks would be withdrawn to the Croatian interior.[6]

De Dominis's archiepiscopal see of Spalato, to which he was translated in 1602, was at the center of a long stretch of Dalmatian coast governed by Venice, but much of his archdiocese lay in Ottoman territory, where episcopal supervision was difficult or impossible to exercise. Ecclesiastically he stood at the edge of the western Church. Serbian Orthodox parishes were situated virtually alongside his own, and there were Greek Orthodox parishes on the Venetian-controlled islands of Corfu, Cephalonia, and Zante, as well as on the Greek mainland to the south. De Dominis may have been partly of South Slavic descent, though his family had used a name Italian in form since the fourteenth century.[7] It is not surprising that De Dominis was concerned about religious reconciliation and peace and was almost preoccupied with questions of ecclesiastical jurisdiction.

It was to Venice that De Dominis owed his appointment at Spalato, and it was to *la Serenissima* that De Dominis looked for guidance throughout his career as archbishop. Venice was fiercely independent. A hundred years earlier it had withstood the forces of the League of Cambrai – the papacy, France, the Holy Roman Empire, and Spain – which had sought to subjugate the republic and dismember its Italian possessions along with its maritime empire.[8] In the crisis of 1606–1607, Venice again defied the papacy and successfully stood up against Spain, which ruled neighboring Milan. The dispute tested Venetian resolve to subject "criminous clerks" to its laws and to regulate the church's acquisition of real estate.[9] An

---

[6] Malcolm, *De Dominis (1560–1624)*, pp. 15–19. For the Venetian struggle against the Uskoks, see Alberto Tenenti, *Piracy and the Decline of Venice, 1580–1615*, trans. Janet and Brian Pullan (Berkeley: University of California Press, 1967), pp. 3–15, 56–57, 89–90, and M. E. Mallett and J. R. Hale, *The Military Organization of a Renaissance State: Venice, c. 1400 to 1617* (Cambridge: Cambridge University Press, 1984), pp. 242–247, 327–330, 482–493.

[7] Compare Nedeljkovič, *Marko Dominis*, p. 173.

[8] See, for the strain of the war and its political effects on Venice, Felix Gilbert, "Venice in the Crisis of the League of Cambrai," in J. R. Hale, ed., *Renaissance Venice* (London: Faber and Faber, 1973), pp. 274–292.

[9] William J. Bouwsma, *Venice and the Defense of Republican Liberty: Renaissance Values in the Age of the Counter Reformation* (Berkeley: University of California Press, 1968), pp. 293–338, 417–482. For the course of the conflict in 1606–1607, see above, chapter 3. A. D. Wright has argued that Venice was trying to achieve the same control over the church within its borders already achieved by France, Spain, Florence, and Spanish-controlled

ideological campaign waged by Venetian spokesmen, especially the friar Paolo Sarpi, stressed the order, stability, and moderation of Venice's constitution and the republic's determination to preserve its freedom from foreign interference by Pope Paul V and his political allies. In effect the contest was between the papacy, acting as a universal ecclesiastical monarchy, and a state seeking to manage its own affairs, including the church within its borders. In Sarpi's own history of the crisis, he stressed the diplomatic support England had given Venice throughout its struggle.[10] King James was the only European ruler who had sided with Venice during the dispute, though his support was more moral than material. His ambassador, Sir Henry Wotton, along with the embassy chaplain William Bedell, saw strained relations between Rome and Venice as an opportunity to promote Protestantism in Italy.[11] Bedell, a considerable scholar and linguist, became a close friend of Sarpi as well as of De Dominis during his service in Venice from 1607 to 1610. De Dominis, who supported Venice in its struggle with the papacy, evidently saw the conduct of relations between the temporal and ecclesiastical authorities in the republic as one of the keys to a reformed and reunified international Church.

De Dominis was not reticent about his intentions in coming to England. In a little book entitled *Consilium profectionis*, first published in Heidelberg in the course of his journey northwards and published in London as *A Manifestation of the Motives* soon after his arrival there, the archbishop undertook to explain the motives for his departure. His decision, he said,

Naples: "The Venetian View of Church and State: Catholic Erastianism?" *Studi Secenteschi*, 19 (1978), 75–106. For church–state relations in northern Italy as well as Venice, see Wright, "Why the Venetian Interdict?" *English Historical Review.* 89 (July 1974), 534–550.

10 Paolo Sarpi, *The History of the Quarrels of Pope Paul V. with the State of Venice* (London: John Bill, 1626), pp. 117–118, 175–176, 183–186, 237–240. See also Enrico Cornet, ed., *Paolo V e la Repubblica Veneta: giornale dal 22. Octobre 1605–9. Giugno 1607* (Vienna: Tendler, 1859), pp. 108–109, 152–153; Logan Pearsall Smith, *The Life and Letters of Sir Henry Wotton*, 2 vols. (Oxford: Clarendon Press, 1907), vol. I, pp. 75, 86, 89–95, 349, 352–361; *Calendar of State Papers and Manuscripts, Relating to English Affairs, Existing in the Archives and Collections of Venice, and in Other Libraries of Northern Italy*, 40 vols. (London: HMSO, 1864–1947), vol. X, pp. 21–22, 359–360. For the text of the papal interdict against Venice in 1606, see David Chambers and Brian Pullan, eds., *Venice: A Documentary History, 1450–1630* (Oxford: Blackwell, 1992), pp. 225–227.

11 For the activities of William Bedell in Venice as chaplain to Wotton, see Thomas Wharton Jones, ed., *A True Relation of the Life and Death of the Right Reverend Father in God William Bedell, Lord Bishop of Kilmore in Ireland* (Westminster: Camden Society, 1872) [an account written by Bedell's son William], pp. 10–12, 101–104, 135–139; E. S. Shuckburgh, ed., *Two Biographies of William Bedell, Bishop of Kilmore, with a Selection of His Letters and an Unpublished Treatise* (Cambridge: Cambridge University Press, 1902), [the first is that by Bedell's son, the second is by Alexander Clogie, who was Bedell's chaplain in Ireland], pp. 83–89, 239–251; and Gilbert Burnet, *The Life of William Bedell, D.D., Bishop of Kilmore in Ireland* (London: John Southby, 1685), pp. 5–18, 22, 30.

was "the ful-ripe fruite of ten yeeres deliberation at the least."[12] He described
his upbringing, education, and early career to explain that decision adequately. He had been educated by the Jesuits, whose society he had joined,
and he had been a lecturer in humanities at Verona before being ordained as
a priest. Later, he had taught mathematics at Padua, and rhetoric, logic, and
philosophy at Brescia. Only after becoming bishop of Segna, however, did he
undertake a serious study of the fathers of the Church, in order to prepare
himself for preaching. "From these lampes," he said,

> a new and strange light darted forth vpon me, the beames whereof, though vnwilling,
> and shutting mine eyes, I could not but perceiue. As for dogmaticall points in
> Diuinity, I found in the Fathers many passages diuers wayes repugnant to the
> common Tenets of the Schoolemen, in whom I was formerly lessoned . . . As for
> Church-discipline, I saw, and wondered to see the spirituall gouernement of these
> times so far wide and different from the ancient.[13]

De Dominis related that he had continued these studies after being made
archbishop of Spalato and primate of Dalmatia and Croatia. But a practical
problem interrupted his theological reflections. He was struck by "the vast
omnipotencie of the Court of Rome daily encroaching, and eating vpon my
Metropoliticall rights."[14] Furthermore he was disgusted by the "Roman-
izing pamphlets" that appeared during the papal interdict against Venice,
pamphlets that vilified the bishops, such as himself, within the Venetian
territories.[15] All of this had led him to dream of a Church constituted, as the
ancient Church had been, of more or less independent bishoprics all sharing
a common faith. He had described the way that ancient form could be
recovered in his forthcoming book on the ecclesiastical commonwealth. In
leaving Italy he had no intention of leaving what he considered to be the
Catholic Church: "I hye me vp into some safe place, where the true
Catholique Religion holdeth vp her head, and taketh free breath."[16] In such
a place "I meane, as my dutie bindes, and as my strength affoards, to

[12] Marco Antonio De Dominis, *A Manifestation of the Motives, Whereupon the Most Reuerend Father, Marcvs Antonivs De Dominis, Archbishop of Spalato, (in the Territorie of Venice) Vndertooke His Departure Thence: Englished out of His Latine Copy* (London: John Bill, 1616), p. 1. De Dominis's book, entitled *Consilium profectionis*, originally appeared in Heidelberg in Latin and Italian in the autumn of 1616; the text was dated at Venice, September 20, 1616.
[13] De Dominis, *A Manifestation of the Motives*, pp. 16–17. De Dominis had received permission from the general of the Society of Jesus, Claudio Acquaviva, to leave the Jesuits. At the time, De Dominis was a candidate for the see of Segna. Russo, *Marc'Antonio De Dominis*, p. 31.
[14] De Dominis, *A Manifestation of the Motives*, p. 18.
[15] Ibid., p. 19. The Republic of Venice largely succeeded in its efforts to compel clerics to continue carrying out their sacerdotal duties during the papal interdict, thus making them accomplices in the resistance to Rome. The Jesuits, who were bound to the papacy by a special vow of obedience, refused to obey the orders of the republic and were expelled.
[16] Ibid., p. 39.

display and publish that trueth which I haue learned, and to lay forth the
wayes for remoueall of Schismes, and reducing of the Church to vnity." [17]

Roman Catholic answers to De Dominis's *Consilium* paint a different
picture, emphasizing his pride, inconstancy, and greed. John Floyd, an
English Jesuit, accused De Dominis of wanting to extend his "Metropolitan
Priuiledges" over his suffragans and abridge the rights of the pope.[18] He
poured scorn on De Dominis's plan to bring together the various churches
that professed faith in Christ according to the ancient creeds. He described
such churches as "so many and so repugnant, the one against the other,
Grecians, Lutherans, Calvinistes, Libertines, Anabaptists," their doctrines
disagreeing "allmost infinitely the one from the other."[19] John Sweet,
another English Jesuit, argued that De Dominis had come to England
because he needed a stipend, having resigned his archbishopric to his
nephew.[20] He also denied De Dominis's assertion that Catholics and
Protestants were united on the fundamental doctrines of the faith. He drew
upon the writings of the Fathers to show that Protestants were heretical on
the doctrines of original sin in relation to baptism and on free-will.[21] The
divisions among Protestants showed, moreover, that some were heretical
even by the Protestants' own standards.[22] De Dominis's migration to
England was one of the sensational events of 1616, giving comfort to
Protestants and causing embarrassment to the archbishop's former co-
religionists. In addition to Latin and Italian editions of the *Consilium*
published in Heidelberg, there were soon Latin and English editions
published in London. A French edition was published by the Huguenots at
Saumur and a Dutch edition at The Hague.[23]

---

[17] Ibid., pp. 39–40.
[18] John Floyd, *A Svrvey of the Apostasy of Marcvs Antonivs de Dominis, Sometyme Arch-bishop of Spalato* (n.p., 1617), p. 47.
[19] Floyd, *A Svrvey of the Apostasy*, p. 84.
[20] John Sweet, *Monsigʳ. fate voi, or a Discovery of the Dalmatian Apostata, M. Antonivs De Dominis, and His Bookes* ([St. Omer,] 1617), p. 29. De Dominis had asked on November 23, 1613 for the election of a bishop coadjutor with the right to succeed him, but the papacy demurred. Finally, in May 1616, the papacy ruled that De Dominis could renounce his episcopal charge in favor of his nephew, Sforza Ponzone, who entered Spalato in December. See Russo, *Marc'Antonio De Dominis*, p. 39, and Malcolm, *De Dominis (1560–1624)*, pp. 42–43. This information was evidently not available to Floyd, or was ignored by him, since he charged De Dominis with inventing a new doctrine: "That a Bishop for feare of persecution may forsake his flock, and leaue it wholy destitute." Floyd, *A Svrvey of the Apostasy*, p. 123.
[21] Sweet, *Monsigʳ. fate voi*, pp. 130–145. [22] Ibid., pp. 145–151.
[23] De Dominis, *Svae profectionis consilivm exponit* (London: John Bill, 1616); *Declaration de Marc Antoine de Dominis, archevesque de Spalato, metropolitain des deux royaumes de Croatie & Dalmatie; sur les raisons qui l'ont meu à se departir de l'Eglise Romaine* (Saumur: T. Portau, 1616); *Verclaringhe van de Motiven ende Oorsaecken daer door de E. heere Marcvs Antonivs de Dominis, Aerts-bischop van Spalaten* (The Hague: Hillebrant Jacobsz, 1616).

De Dominis clearly felt that he had suffered from unjust ecclesiastical procedures almost from the time he was elected archbishop in 1602. That election, made in a papal consistory, on the recommendation of the doge of Venice, carried with it an agreement that Marzio Andreucci, dean of Udine, was to receive a pension from the new archbishop's income. When Andreucci was himself elected bishop of Traù in 1604, De Dominis refused, on the grounds of his own poverty, to pay Andreucci the required pension. The papacy insisted upon the rights of the bishop of Traù, a decision which led to a protracted dispute.[24] By 1609 another issue had arisen. De Dominis protested to Berlingerio Gessi, papal nuncio in Venice, that the nuncio had taken away from the Dalmatian bishops the responsibility for revising and publishing vernacular liturgical books for their dioceses.[25] In other conflicts involving relations with his cathedral chapter and his episcopal jurisdiction, De Dominis found the papacy opposing him.[26]

Such experiences with the intrusive papal administration, coupled with his own close association with Venice, had inclined De Dominis to the Venetian side in the celebrated crisis of 1606–1607, when Pope Paul V and the Republic of Venice contested the extent of papal authority within the dominions of the city-state. During the crisis De Dominis wrote, anonymously, two books which long remained in manuscript. In his *Admonitio* of 1606 addressed to Cardinal Cesare Baronius, who had written a *Paraenesis* to urge Venice to obey the papal demands, De Dominis defended the republic in uncompromising terms. No ancient or modern theologian, De Dominis argued, had ever affirmed that "the jurisdiction of the Pope extends to temporal affairs and that he is able to limit the natural power of a Prince where there is no question of the faith and religion being involved."[27] Venice, in other words, should be allowed to exercise its governmental responsibilities without interference by the papacy, particularly since there was no doubt about the republic's adherence to the Catholic faith. De Dominis went on to call attention to abuses

[24] Russo, *Marc'Antonio De Dominis*, pp. 32–38; Malcolm, *De Dominis (1560–1624)*, pp. 21–23. The registers of letters in the Vatican Archives for 1612–1613 show that Scipione Caffarelli, Cardinal Borghese, the papal secretary, urged the nuncio, Berlingerio Gessi, bishop of Rimini, to reach an amicable settlement between De Dominis and Andreucci if at all possible. Vat. Arch., Fondo Borghese, Series I, vol. 905, fol. 15 verso (January 28, 1612), fols. 71–71 verso (April 22, 1612), fols. 83 verso–84 (May 5, 1612), fol. 91 verso (May 19, 1616).

[25] Oliver Logan, "The Ideal of the Bishop and the Venetian Patriciate: *c.* 1430–*c.* 1630," *Journal of Ecclesiastical History*, 29, 4 (October 1978), p. 447 and note; Malcolm, *De Dominis (1560–1624)*, p. 23.

[26] Russo, *Marc'Antonio De Dominis*, pp. 33–37; Malcolm, *De Dominis (1560–1624)*, pp. 22–23.

[27] De Dominis, *Reipublicae Venetae admonitio ad Caesarem Baronium S.R.E. Cardinalem contra ipsius paraenesim*, in De Dominis, *Scritti giurisdizionalistici inediti*, ed. Antonio Russo (Naples: Luigi Loffredo, 1965), p. 27. For commentary, see pp. 5–22.

by the Roman curia – the sale of offices and dispensations, the suppression of criticism, the condemnation of even the best writers to prison or to violent death – and repeated the fifteenth-century conciliar call for a reform of the Church "in head and members."[28] In his other contribution to the controversy De Dominis discussed in detail the issues at stake as of May 1606, the date given at the end of the text. *Martellino* is a "Dialogue Concerning the Dissensions between the Supreme Pontiff, Pope Paul V, and the Most Serene Republic of Venice," as the subtitle states.[29] Addressed to the members of the Senate in Venice, it may have been transcribed and distributed to them by the Delle Rose family to whom De Dominis entrusted the manuscript.[30] The interlocutors – a learned and assertive Paduan, Martellino, and a more cautious country priest, Timorelli – eventually reach a consensus. Without compromising the principle of the temporal authority of the state, Martellino proposes that the laws be stated in general terms to cover all citizens and that both sides seek a way out of the current confrontation.[31]

The issues that concerned De Dominis in 1606 continued to be central to his research and writing. By 1612 the papal nuncio in Venice reported to Rome that the archbishop of Spalato was composing a work against the authority of the pope and of the Holy See; the nuncio was urged to use all peaceful means to dissuade the archbishop from the project.[32] By the end of October 1613, the papal secretary spoke of De Dominis's book as nearly complete: "if it arrives here it will be looked at and diligently considered."[33] The book which had so alarmed the authorities is apparently lost, but its contents seem clear from De Dominis's own description of it in a letter to the doge of Venice on October 8, 1616, written from Coire, Switzerland: "a defence of the most serene republic . . . [and] of the legitimate authority and power of temporal princes to make laws and to govern the state, against the vain pretensions of the Roman Curia."[34] In his letter to the doge De

---

[28] De Dominis, *Scritti giurisdizionalistici inediti*, ed. Russo, pp. 62–63.
[29] De Dominis, *Martellino: Dialogo sopra li dispareri tra il Sommo Pontefice Paulo Papa V. et la Serenissima Republica di Venetia*, in De Dominis, *Scritti giurisdizionalistici inediti*, ed. Russo, pp. 67–87. See also S. Ljubić, "Prilog k razpravi o Markantunu Dominisu Rabljaninu," *Starine*, 14 (1872), 1–18.
[30] De Dominis, *Scritti giurisdizionalistici inediti*, ed. Russo, p. 15.
[31] Ibid., p. 87.
[32] Rome, Vat. Arch., Fondo Borghese, series I, vol. 905, fol. 63 verso (April 14, 1612), fol. 70 verso (April 21, 1612), fols. 337 verso–338 (July 27, 1613). In the letter of July 27, Cardinal Borghese expresses satisfaction that the nuncio has apparently dissuaded De Dominis from his project through the influence of one of the archbishop's relatives.
[33] Vat. Arch., Fondo Borghese, series I, vol. 905, fol. 378 (October 26, 1613).
[34] Ljubić, "Prilozi za životopics Markantuna de Dominisa," p. 148. Compare De Dominis, *Scritti giurisdizionalistici inediti*, ed. Russo, p. 16. See also the report of two Venetian diplomats who encountered De Dominis on October 9 at Coire, Switzerland, and who carried back the archbishop's letter to the doge. They reported that De Dominis had written

Dominis confided that he felt his life had been in danger from plots of the Roman curia.[35]

De Dominis had been encouraged to seek asylum in England by its official representatives in Venice, as a series of letters exchanged in 1614–1615 shows. Contacts between De Dominis and the English embassy began as much as a decade earlier. Bedell, the chaplain to Ambassador Wotton, was said by a contemporary biographer to have given De Dominis valuable assistance in the writing of his major theological work.[36] But it was Sir Dudley Carleton, Wotton's successor beginning in late 1610, who made the initial arrangements for De Dominis's departure for England.

Early in Carleton's stay he encouraged two other Italians to go to England, but with disappointing results. On March 16, 1614 Archbishop Abbot wrote to Carleton that two friars whom Carleton had sent to England had been entertained by himself and by Tobias Matthew, the archbishop of York, and had visited Oxford and Cambridge. Now, however, they had returned to their former faith, having been "tampered with," that is, persuaded of the need to remain loyal Roman Catholics, by the chaplain to the Venetian ambassador and by the Spanish ambassador. Though briefly apprehended, they had escaped and fled from the country. He was glad that De Dominis remained firm.[37] The two friars, Giulio Cesare Vanini and Battista Maria Genochi, were described by the historian Thomas Fuller as "onely racking, no thorough-paced Protestants," who "watched their opportunity to run away."[38]

De Dominis, no doubt aware of the cases of Vanini and Genochi, seemed determined to provide Carleton and Abbot the assurance they needed about the depth of his commitment to a new religious outlook. De Dominis wrote to Carleton on May 15, 1614 that he was in a labyrinth, his writings known to all, through the "little faithfulness" of his scribes, and considered unacceptable in Rome.[39] He sought refuge in a land where "Christian freedom has lifted its head," under the protection of the "no less learned

---

a book *de potestate principum*, which he believed he would not be able to publish "in any place subject in spiritual matters to the Roman Church." Ljubić, "Prilozi," as above, p. 147.

[35] Ljubić, "Prilozi za životopis Markantuna de Dominisa," pp. 148–149; Russo, *Marc'Antonio De Dominis*, pp. 39–40.

[36] Jones, ed., *A True Relation of the Life and Death*, pp. 135–139.

[37] *Calendar of State Papers, Domestic Series, of the Reigns of Edward VI, Mary, Elizabeth, and James I, 1547–1625*, 12 vols. (London: HMSO, 1856–1872), vol. IX, p. 227. For the two friars, see the illuminating article by Calvin F. Senning, "Vanini and the Diplomats, 1612–1614: Religion, Politics, and Defection in the Counter-Reformation Era," *Historical Magazine of the Protestant Episcopal Church*, 54, 3 (September 1985), 219–239.

[38] Thomas Fuller, *The Church-History of Britain, from the Birth of Jesus Christ untill the Year M. DC. XLVIII* (London: John Williams, 1655), Bk. X, p. 100.

[39] PRO, SP, Venice: SP 99/16, fol. 2.

than religious" king of Great Britain.[40] De Dominis said that he had already written in support of the king's *Apologie* and *Premonition* and against Cardinal Bellarmine.[41] On September 7, 1614 De Dominis wrote to Carleton again about his need for "a refuge in a safe house" under the benevolent King James.[42] He was delighted that this opportunity had apparently been assured through the commendations of the king and the archbishop of Canterbury. On October 15, 1614 De Dominis wrote Archbishop Abbot a letter rich in metaphors about the Church. He had once thought of the various Christian churches as proceeding in straight lines from the center of a circle, gradually moving further and further apart. But unity was to be found at the center of the circle and that center was Christ.[43] On the other hand the Church was a tree with many branches, some flourishing, some not, but nourished by one holy root. Unity was to be found by returning to the center and to the root. He found it an act of benevolence and clemency for Archbishop Abbot to provide "a small corner on your pleasant soil" for him.[44] He hoped that the private meeting of the two of them would be the beginning of a public joining of all the churches of Christ. On December 15, 1614 Abbot wrote to Carleton to review the arrangements made to date for De Dominis's relocation: De Dominis was to travel to England by way of Holland and was not to expect more from his hosts than a quiet life in a university with a moderate annual income.[45]

Early in 1615, on January 30, De Dominis wrote again to Abbot and also to King James. He commended the king for his efforts to purge and restore the Church to its ancient splendor. James's concern for the whole Church made him unique among monarchs.[46] He thanked Archbishop Abbot for offering him a shelter in a fortified city. Then, in a passage about King James which he evidently wanted the king to read, he called attention to the felicity of those "who stand always in your presence, and hear your wisdom."[47] God had set James on his throne to make "one undivided whole out of partition," a phrase with ecclesiological as well as political implications.[48]

In his letter to Carleton on September 7, 1614, De Dominis noted that the ambassador had asked that he should "freely and clearly" set forward his petition and desire.[49] The letter was his attempt "to set forth my case clearly to your Excellency."[50] He had, ever since he was a boy, found his intellectual and spiritual nourishment in sacred studies. For many years he had accepted scholastic teachings and the determinations of the Roman Catholic Church, even repressing doubts lest he should fall away from the

---

[40] Ibid., fol. 2 verso.   [41] Ibid.   [42] PRO SP 99/17, fol. 72.   [43] Ibid., fol. 190.
[44] Ibid., fol. 191.   [45] *Calendar of State Papers, Domestic*, vol. IX, p. 262.
[46] PRO SP 99/18, fol. 249.   [47] Ibid., fol. 250.   [48] Ibid.
[49] PRO SP 99/17, fol. 72.   [50] Ibid.

common faith. But as he pursued his studies through various academic levels he found himself in a state of anxiety rather than peace.[51] It bothered him that his masters and professors took extreme pains "lest books contrary to Roman doctrine" be available to anyone.[52] He found that when his teachers publicly opposed the opinions of others, they forbade their auditors, "under penalty of severest excommunication, to read the very writings of [those] adversaries."[53] Even as a bishop he had found it difficult to secure such books, so effectively were they suppressed and destroyed. He had yearned for greater intellectual freedom. Ever since the time of his ordination to the priesthood, he had, moreover, "nourished the desire . . . of seeing the union of all the churches of Christ": "The separation of the West from the East, and of the South from the North, I could never bear with a calm mind, and I anxiously desired to recognize the cause of so numerous and so great schisms and to find whether it was possible to think of some way to bring together the wandering churches of Christ to a sure and ancient union."[54] This ardent desire – fed by his awareness of "so many disagreements among the professors of the Christian faith and the bitterest hatreds" among the churches – had consumed him more and more.[55]

After being made a bishop, De Dominis had, he related, concentrated his studies on canon law and the writings of the fathers, being chiefly concerned with practical problems. He found that the "rule and practice of ecclesiastical discipline and spiritual governance" in his time were very different from what they had been in the ancient period.[56] The issues of discipline and polity became more acute when he became an archbishop and found himself troubled by relations with his own metropolitans. Then, in the midst of the controversy between Rome and Venice he was deeply offended by the Roman pamphlets which did not cease to disparage the bishops in the Venetian territories as "rustic, ignorant, and men of no conscience" – presumably for their obedience to the Venetian Republic during its campaign to nullify the effects of the papal interdict.[57] De Dominis now saw that "the Roman ecclesiastical monarchy" was a usurpation of human contrivance, not an institution of Christ.[58] He saw that as a result of the growth of papal power, the later general councils differed greatly from the earlier ones "in form, authority, doctrine, and decrees."[59] Many articles of faith had been intruded upon Christians without adequate basis, and many teachings of the so-called heretical churches were in fact more Catholic than those of the Roman Catholic Church. There were

---

[51] Ibid., fol. 72 verso.   [52] Ibid.   [53] Ibid., fol. 73.
[54] Ibid.   [55] Ibid.   [56] Ibid., fol. 73 verso.
[57] Ibid., fol. 74. Compare Bouwsma, *Venice and the Defense of Republican Liberty*, pp. 374–390.
[58] PRO SP 99/17, fol. 74.   [59] Ibid.

matters still in dispute among the churches that he wanted to investigate
further. What he craved was the opportunity to do so without threats,
repression, persecution, and plots against him. He longed for "a quiet and
private life" among learned and studious persons, without temporal cares
or responsibilities.[60] He wanted, in particular, to consider plans for "an
ecclesiastical unity, especially of the Eastern churches with the reformed."[61]

In addition to these theological and personal considerations, there was
another consideration that influenced De Dominis profoundly. Soon after
the archbishop's arrival in England, the first volume of his *De republica
ecclesiastica* began to be printed there. It was very nearly De Dominis's
lifework, an achievement by which he could reasonably hope to be
remembered. Eventually published in three volumes, the work contained
more than 2,200 folio pages in Latin, and touched upon most of the
theological disputes then raging in Europe. De Dominis sought to place
these disputes in the perspective of the Church's faith and practice since
antiquity and to find as much theological common ground as possible
between the rival churches of his own day. The restoration of unity, he
argued, could be achieved by returning to the ancient pattern of a communion of regional or national churches, episcopally governed, and bound
together by the scriptures and historic creeds. The role of the papacy would
be to encourage this unity while respecting the autonomy of the various
churches. De Dominis's difficulties with the papacy and the argument of the
book meant he would have found it virtually impossible to get the work
published in any Roman Catholic country. In November 1616, before the
De republica ecclesiastica had been published, a decree of the congregation
in Rome charged with compiling the Index of Prohibited Books forbade De
Dominis's book in all languages, "whether already printed or hereafter to
be printed."[62] By the end of May 1617 Cardinal Borghese had written to
the papal nuncio in Paris that De Dominis had had his impious book
published and that the Holy Roman emperor had forbidden its circulation
in Germany. He urged the nuncio to persuade the king of France to do
likewise.[63] In December 1617 a committee of divines at the Sorbonne
presented a list of propositions from the first volume of the work which its
members considered heretical, scandalous, and injurious to the Roman
Catholic Church and the Holy See. The Faculty of Theology condemned
forty-seven propositions in the book later in the same month.[64] Not to be

---

[60] Ibid., fols. 75–75 verso.   [61] Ibid., fol. 75 verso.
[62] De Dominis, *A Manifestation of the Motives*, sigs. I₁–I₃ – *Decretvm*, dated at Rome,
November 12, 1616.
[63] Vat. Arch., Fondo Borghese, series I, vol. 902, fol. 218 verso (Cardinal Borghese to Guido
Bentivoglio, May 27, 1617).
[64] BN, Nouvelles acquisitions latines, vol. 2456, fols. 99 verso–100; *Censvra Sacrae Facvltatis
Theologiae Parisiensis, in qvatvor priores libros De republica ecclesiastica, auctore Marco*

outdone, the Faculty of Theology at Cologne condemned some 376 propositions from the *De republica ecclesiastica* at the end of March 1618.[65]
England, on the other hand, seemed to welcome the work.

II

De Dominis's departure for England, planned by Carleton, did not occur
until Sir Henry Wotton arrived in Venice in 1616 for his second assignment
there as ambassador. Wotton wrote to King James from Venice on July 30,
1616 that De Dominis would set out within a week or so.[66] His journey,
which did not begin until September 20, brought him to London on
December 13, where he became a guest of Archbishop Abbot at Lambeth
Palace.[67] Early in January 1617 John Chamberlain, a friend of Carleton,
who was now ambassador in Holland, wrote him that De Dominis was
"well esteemed and respected everywhere specially at court."[68] In the
middle of January Chamberlain wrote to Carleton that De Dominis had
attended services at St. Paul's Cathedral and had been at the bishop of
London's palace, at Westminster, and "all about where any thing is to be
seen."[69]

   Rather than being settled in a university, as Abbot had suggested would
be the case, De Dominis was appointed to various ecclesiastical offices
which provided for his support. As early as January 4, 1617, he was
reported by Chamberlain to have been chosen to be dean of Windsor, the
collegiate church or chapel, dedicated to St. George, which was under the
king's patronage.[70] Fuller called it "one of the gentilest and entirest
Dignities of the Land."[71] But the appointment was delayed. Before the end
of the year, De Dominis had been promised the mastership of the Savoy, the
medieval palace which had been turned into a hospital, with chapel

   Antonio de Dominis quondam archiepiscopo Spalatensi (Cologne, n. d.) – the decree is
   dated December 15, 1617.

[65] *Censvra Sacrae Facvltatis Theologicae Coloniensis, in qvatvor priores libros De repvbl.
ecclesiastica M. Antonij de Dominis, quondam archiepiscopi Spalatensis* (Cologne, 1618).
The *De republica ecclesiastica* was attacked before its publication by John Sweet (1617),
and afterwards by Johannes Roberti (1619), Andreas Eudaemon-Joannis (1619), John Floyd
(1620, 1623), and Nicolas Coeffeteau (1623).

[66] Smith, ed., *The Life and Letters of Sir Henry Wotton*, vol. II, p. 100.

[67] Norman Egbert McClure, ed., *The Letters of John Chamberlain*, 2 vols. (Philadelphia:
American Philosophical Society, 1939), vol. II, pp. 43–44 (Chamberlain to Carleton,
December 21, 1616).

[68] Ibid., p. 48 (Chamberlain to Carleton, January 18, 1617).

[69] Ibid., p. 50 (Chamberlain to Carleton, January 18, 1617).

[70] Ibid., pp. 47–48; F. L. Cross and E. A. Livingstone, eds., *The Oxford Dictionary of the
Christian Church*, second edition (London: Oxford University Press, 1974),
pp. 1491–1492.

[71] Fuller, *The Church-History of Britain*, Bk. X, p. 94.

attached.[72] In the meantime, in February 1617, some bishops had undertaken to provide a living for him until something further had been done by the king. There was difficulty about the appointment at the Savoy, since Walter Balcanquhall, the son of a distinguished Scottish minister, was first given the position.[73] Finally, by March 1618, De Dominis had been made dean of Windsor and master of the Savoy, as well as a prebendary of Canterbury Cathedral.[74] In communicating with his assisting clergy at Windsor and the Savoy, he probably used Latin, at least in the early years; they no doubt carried out most of the pastoral duties associated with the two places. But De Dominis used Italian effectively in preaching at the Chapel of the Mercers' Company, the church for Italians living in London. Carleton noted two occasions in 1617–1618 when De Dominis delivered a sermon there. On November 30, 1617 De Dominis preached earnestly, according to a correspondent of Chamberlain, and with general approbation.[75] On November 14, 1618, when there was a fast at the Italian Church for the success of the Synod of Dort in the Netherlands, "the archbishop of Spalato preached there they say very well."[76] De Dominis assisted Archbishop Abbot at the consecration of Nicholas Felton as bishop of Bristol and George Montaigne as bishop of Lincoln, both in December 1617.[77] In the summer of 1617 he visited both Cambridge and Oxford and received a doctor's degree at each university.[78]

King James received De Dominis soon after his arrival in London and again, later in the year, at Windsor Castle.[79] On July 3, 1617 the king wrote

[72] *Calendar of State Papers, Domestic*, vol. IX, p. 500 (Chamberlain to Carleton, November 29, 1617).

[73] *Calendar of State Papers, Domestic*, vol. IX, pp. 432 (Chamberlain to Carleton, February 8, 1617); 504 (Chamberlain to Carleton, December 20, 1617); 510 (De Dominis to Carleton, January 2, 1618); 514 (Chamberlain to Carleton, January 17, 1618); 521 (William Lovelace to Carleton, February 10, 1618); 526 (Nathaniel Brent to Carleton, March 7, 1618). Balcanquhall was appointed as master in December 1617 but resigned the position to De Dominis and was given a reversionary grant. De Dominis became master in March 1618. See Robert Somerville, *The Savoy: Manor, Hospital, Chapel* (London: Duchy of Lancaster, 1960), pp. 68, 239–240.

[74] *Calendar of State Papers, Domestic*, vol. IX, p. 527 (De Dominis to Carleton, March 15, 1618).

[75] Ibid., pp. 500 (Chamberlain to Carleton, November 29, 1617), 501 (Gerard Herbert to Carleton, December 6, 1617).

[76] McClure, *The Letters of John Chamberlain*, vol. II, p. 183 (Chamberlain to Dudley, November 14, 1618).

[77] *Calendar of State Papers, Domestic*, vol. IX, p. 504 (Chamberlain to Carleton, December 20, 1617). Both of the new bishops apparently continued to reside in London. See Kenneth Fincham, *Prelate as Pastor: The Episcopate of James I* (Oxford: Clarendon Press, 1990), pp. 31, 306, 311 (Felton); 312, 321 (Montaigne).

[78] *Calendar of State Papers, Domestic*, vol. IX, pp. 475 (Edwin Sherburn to Carleton, July 5, 1617), 477 (De Dominis to Paul de la Ravoire, July 20, 1617), 482 (William Goodwin to Carleton, August 18, 1617).

[79] *Calendar of State Papers, Domestic*, vol. IX, pp. 417 (De Dominis to Carleton, December

to De Dominis from Stirling Castle in Scotland to thank him for a copy of the dedication to him of the first volume of *De republica ecclesiastica*, the printing of which was by then nearly complete.[80] James, in the midst of the only visit to Scotland he made during his reign in England, had just met a group of ministers and others protesting a bill before the Scottish Parliament. The bill would have declared the king able to make decisions affecting the "external policy of the kirk."[81] To many Scots his religious policy threatened the liberty and authority of the General Assembly of the Kirk and was part of an attempt to make the Kirk conform to English liturgical usage. In the face of widespread opposition, the king withdrew the bill from the agenda submitted to Parliament.[82] James's opening comment to De Dominis, after thanking him for his letter and the dedication, rings true: "we are oppressed and nearly overwhelmed by the number and weight of affairs."[83] James did want to bring the liturgical practices of the Scottish and English churches closer together by instituting a series of measures in Scotland which became known as the Five Articles of Perth. These measures included celebrating Christmas, Good Friday, Easter, Ascension Day, and Pentecost with appropriate services; requiring communicants to receive the elements of the eucharist while kneeling; presenting youths for confirmation by a bishop; permitting the administration of baptism in private homes; and permitting the celebration of the eucharist in private homes. To James such measures would encourage the churches of the two kingdoms to move closer together and would give the Kirk greater claim to being, as it claimed to be, part of the one universal Church through the ages. To many Scots, the measures were radically inconsistent with Reformation principles, as expressed in the official Scottish formularies of faith, worship, and discipline. After James left Scotland in August, a general assembly called for St. Andrews in November refused to approve the articles in the form the king requested. Although the articles were approved at the General Assembly at Perth in August 1618, and were subsequently ratified by the Scottish Parliament in 1621, they were not consistently enforced – some of them, indeed, were virtually ignored. And the provision for kneeling when receiving the elements of the eucharist was a divisive issue in the Kirk for the next two decades. While examining

31, 1616), 423 (Horace Vere to Carleton, January 8, 1617), 480 (Thomas Lake to Ralph Winwood, August 11, 1617), 488 (De Dominis to Carleton, October 16, 1617).

[80] Christiaan Hartsoeker, ed., *Praestantium ac eruditorum virorum epistolae ecclesiasticae et theologicae*, third edition (Amsterdam: Franciscus Halma, 1704), p. 482; *Calendar of State Papers, Domestic*, vol. IX, p. 470 (De Dominis to Carleton, May 28, 1617).

[81] Maurice Lee, Jr., *Government by Pen: Scotland under James VI and I* (Urbana: University of Illinois Press, 1980), p. 167.

[82] Ibid., p. 168; also pp. 160, 167, 174–189. See also Walter Roland Foster, *The Church before the Covenants: The Church of Scotland, 1596–1638* (Edinburgh: Scottish Academic Press, 1975), pp. 124, 182–192.

[83] Hartsoeker, *Praestantium ac eruditorum virorum epistolae*, p. 482.

De Dominis's book on the problems of a divided Christendom, James confronted a major obstacle in achieving greater consistency and harmony between the national churches of his own kingdoms.[84]

In his letter to De Dominis on July 3, 1617, the king declared his admiration for his visitor's recent actions in wholehearted terms: "He who left behind his native land, friends, and all things accustomed to be dear to his flesh for the sake of Christ the Lord, is he not rightly to be held most worthy?"[85] The more strenuously De Dominis was opposed by those who had persecuted him in his previous career, the more cordially he would be treated by James. The king was glad to be the patron of De Dominis's book. "When [your] adversaries have seen on what foundations that work rests, [and] by what a cloud of witnesses it is supported, they will not say that your departure from their band was done rashly."[86] The king was glad to be ready to begin, finally, "our return to you"; and in keeping with the archbishop's prayers for his speedy return, he offered his own prayers for De Dominis's delayed return "from the chariot-course of life," so that the archbishop might bring his "vast and distinguished" work to completion.[87]

De Dominis's Italian sermon at the Mercers' Chapel on November 30, 1617, the First Sunday in Advent, is a revealing statement of his own theological convictions and the reasons that he admired the Church of England. Though preached in Italian to a congregation made up mostly of Italian visitors and exiles, the sermon was soon translated and published in English. As required by the canons of the Church of England, De Dominis bade the congregation to pray with him before the sermon. The petitions followed the prescribed order, but were clearly phrased as the preacher wanted.[88] In this prayer De Dominis stated a coherent view of the nature of

---

[84] See Ian B. Cowan, "The Five Articles of Perth," in Duncan Shaw, ed., *Reformation and Revolution: Essays Presented to the Very Reverend Principal Emeritus Hugh Watt, D.D., D.Litt., on the Sixtieth Anniversary of His Ordination* (Edinburgh: Saint Andrew Press, 1967), pp. 160–177; Foster, *The Church before the Covenants*, pp. 63–64, 124–125, 181–192, 200–203; Lee, *Government by Pen*, pp. 160, 167, 175–189, 195, 205–206; and John D. Ford, "The Lawful Bonds of Scottish Society: The Five Articles of Perth, the Negative Confession and the National Covenant," *Historical Journal*, 37, 1 (1994), 45–64.

[85] Hartsoeker, *Praestantium ac eruditorum virorum epistolae*, pp. 482–483.

[86] Ibid., p. 483.   [87] Ibid.

[88] See Canon 55, "The Form of a Prayer to be used by all Preachers before their Sermons" (1604) in *The Constitutions and Canons Ecclesiastical and the Thirty-Nine Articles of the Church of England* (London: J. G. and F. Rivington, 1833), pp. 34–35. This form had its origins in the medieval "Bidding of the Bedes [prayers]," one of the oldest forms of intercessory prayer in the Christian liturgical tradition. See Massey H. Shepherd, Jr., *The Oxford American Prayer Book Commentary* (New York: Oxford University Press, 1950), pp. 47–48. For the Italian congregation in London, which first met for services in 1550, see Luigi Firpo, "La Chiesa italiana di Londra nel cinquecento e i suoi rapporti con Ginevra," in Delio Cantimori, Luigi Firpo, Giorgio Spini, *et al.*, eds., *Ginevra e l'Italia* (Florence: Sansoni, 1959), pp. 307–412. The congregation had been given the use of the chapel of Mercers' Hall in 1609 (p. 411).

the Church and suggested the importance of contemporary events in the unfolding of God's purposes. He prayed for God's blessing upon "his vniuersall holy Church, and that it would please him by his spirit to vnite all Christian Churches in the onely, true, pure, and holy faith, to combine them in perfect charity, to extinguish all disunions, to make vp all rents and schismes, to mollifie all hardned hearts, that they may cast off their obstinacie, and lay aside all humane respects, and deseignes; that so all obstacles, hindering this so important vnion, may be remooued."[89] De Dominis prayed that "all Christian Princes" would be inspired "to procure the generall reformation of the Church, and to set forward this holy vnion."[90] He prayed especially for King James, the "Defender of the true ancient, pure, & holy, Catholique, and Apostolique faith."[91] In addition, he prayed for the royal family, including the Elector Palatine and the Lady Elizabeth. He prayed also for the Venetians, "that God would deliuer them from their enemies, and preserue them in their full liberty."[92] He remembered before God "all Prelates, Priests, and Ministers of the holy Vniuersall Church: In speciall for those that manage the spirituall affaires in these kingdomes."[93] Thus, this "bidding prayer" linked together the various parts or branches of the universal Church, envisioned a special responsibility for the temporal rulers in reforming and reuniting the Church, recognized an important religious vocation for the British king, and even managed to suggest a connection between British national and religious interests and those of the Palatinate and Venice.

In the sermon proper De Dominis quoted Romans 1:29–31, St. Paul's catalogue of the sins of the Gentiles, especially in pagan Rome, and asserted that Rome "as now is" had the same characteristics.[94] But he went on to assert that the Church of Rome and the reformed churches – though their current adherents seemed to hate each other – actually shared a common faith. "The Religion of both," De Dominis said, "is in the maine essentials and fundamentals the very same," in that both had the same Saviour, apostles, gospel, and baptism.[95] The chief difference was that the ship of Rome, unlike that of the reformed churches, had thrown out its map and compass, namely "the infallible Card [chart] of the holy Scriptures, and the true compasse quartered out into the foure first generall councels, and seconded with the under-windes of the holy Fathers."[96] De Dominis himself was thankful for having emerged out of the night of papal errors – including

[89] De Dominis, *A Sermon Preached in Italian, by the Most Reuerend Father, Marc'Antony De Dominis, Archb. of Spalato, the First Sunday in Aduent, anno 1617; in the Mercers Chappel in London, to the Italians in That City, and Many Other Honorable Auditors Then Assembled* (London: John Bill, 1617), p. 4.
[90] Ibid.   [91] Ibid.   [92] Ibid., p. 5.   [93] Ibid., p. 6.
[94] Ibid., p. 23.   [95] Ibid., p. 31.   [96] Ibid., pp. 33, 36.

implicit (rather than justifying) faith, transubstantiation, and the corrupt practices associated with penance – into the light.[97] This was in accordance with Romans 13:12, his principal text: "The night is passed, the day is at hand: Let vs therefore cast off the workes of darknesse, and let us put on the armour of light."[98] Here in the British Isles, "the light of the trueth is freely, and openly let in."[99] The scriptures were studied carefully; there were many eminent scholars; the bishops were "learned, religious, and vigilant ouer their flocks"; the priests were "skilfull in the cure of soules"; the people were zealous in their spiritual duties.[100] Above all King James was "a matchlesse paterne to all the Kings and Princes of Christendome, of great zeale in purging, aduancing, and mainteining Christs holy Religion."[101] The sermon was published in its original Italian in London in 1617 and in an English translation in the same year. A Latin translation was published at Leeuwarden in the Netherlands in 1618, a German translation at Frankfurt in 1618, and a French translation at Charenton in 1619.[102] De Dominis had become the object of European-wide attention.

Two other books published by De Dominis in 1617–1618 sought to expose the shortcomings of the papacy. *Papatvs Romanvs* (1617) is largely a collection of Latin passages from the scriptures, the Fathers – especially St. Augustine, St. Ambrose, St. Jerome, and St. Cyprian – the decrees of the general councils, and canon law on the subject of the papacy, with spare interpretive comments.[103] The dedication to King James claimed that the king's efforts to recover and preserve the liberty of the Church against the see of Rome were supported by all the learned writers of antiquity as well as by many modern scholars.[104] De Dominis's *The Rockes of Christian Shipwracke*, published in English, Italian, French, and German in 1618,

[97] Ibid., pp. 38–48, 60. [98] Ibid., title page. [99] Ibid., p. 61.
[100] Ibid., pp. 61–62. [101] Ibid., p. 61.
[102] De Dominis, *Predica fatta da Mons'. Marc'Antonio De Dominis, Archiv°. di Spalato, la prima domenica dell'Auuento quest'Anno 1617. in Londra, nella Capella detta delli Merciari (ch'e la chiesa degl'italiani) ad essa natione italiana* (London: John Bill, 1617); De Dominis, *Concio habita italice a reverendo patre Marco Antonio De Dominis, archiepiscopo Spalatensi primo die dominico Adventus Anno 1617; Londini in Mercatorum Capella, coram italis ibi commorantibus, & aliis honorificis in illa synaxi & conventu* (Leeuwarden: Ioann Starter, 1618); De Dominis, *Erste Evangelische Predigt von Herrn Marco Antonio De Dominis, Erzbischoffen zu Spalato; nach dem er durch Gottes sonderbare schickung vom Bapstumb abgetretten; zu Londen in Engelland, am ersten sontag dess Advents, im Jahr 1617, gehalten; in der Capellen, genennt delli Merciari, welches der italianer Kirchedaselbst ist* ([Frankfurt?] 1618); De Dominis, *Sermon de M'e Marc Anthoine de Dominis . . . faict le premier dimanche de l'Advent de l'année 1617, à Londres, en la chappelle des Merciers, qui est l'église des italiens, a eux adressée [sic]* (Charenton: Mondière, 1619).
[103] De Dominis, *Papatvs Romanvs: liber de origine, progressu, atque extinctione ipsius* (London: John Bill, 1617).
[104] Ibid., sig. A₂.

took the argument against papal claims back to the apostles' time.[105] The book purported to offer advice by the Church of Christ to her children so that they might avoid the rocks – all of them beliefs and practices associated with the Church of Rome – which could lead to shipwreck and disaster. St. Peter himself, De Dominis argued, never pretended to be "an vniuersall Pope, or only Vicar generall of Christ."[106] The first bishops succeeded the apostles *in solidum*, that is, "euery particular Bishop, whatsoeuer hee bee, holdeth the place, and office of the Apostles," and has the same charge Christ gave to them.[107]

De Dominis's literary activity in England also included writing to the States-General of the United Provinces of the Netherlands concerning the controversy over Arminianism. De Dominis had taken a keen interest in the dispute almost from the time of his arrival, as a letter of John Overall, bishop of Coventry and Lichfield, to Hugo Grotius shows. While Overall was in King James's presence during Christmas, as he related in his letter of June 20, 1617, the king had asked Overall if he had discussed any theological matters with De Dominis.[108] The bishop replied that he had and that he very much agreed with one of De Dominis's observations. This was that controversies over predestination "did not seem to him to be of the Catholic faith, but matters of theological disputation."[109] It would be better to deal with them in private conversations on the basis of the scriptures and the testimony of antiquity than to allow agitators to attack one another publicly in hostile speeches. This opinion, Overall said, was approved by the king, who found highly presumptuous the claims of those who spoke as if they knew the secret counsels of God. The bishops who were present had all agreed.[110] De Dominis repeated much the same opinion in a letter of July 20, 1617 to Paul de la Ravoire, a friend who had gone to the Netherlands to seek employment with Carleton.[111]

De Dominis's own relations with the States-General were cordial. He sent that assembly a copy of the first volume of the *De republica ecclesiastica* on August 17, 1617, along with a letter expressing concern over the "dreadful

[105] De Dominis, *The Rockes of Christian Shipwracke, Discoured by the Holy Church of Christ to Her Beloued Children, That They May Keepe Aloofe from Them* (London: John Bill, 1618); De Dominis, *Scogli del christiano naufragio, quali va scoprendo la santa Chiesa di Christo* ([London]: 1618); De Dominis, *Les écueils du naufrage chrestien découverts par la sainte Eglise de Christ à ses bien aymez enfans affin qu'ils s'en puissent esloigner* (La Rochelle: J. Hebert, 1618); De Dominis, *Steinklippe dess christichen Schiffbruchs, welche die heilige Kirche Christ ihren vielgeliebten Sohnen entdeckt* (Frankfurt: Rosen, 1618).
[106] De Dominis, *The Rockes of Christian Shipwracke*, p. 5.
[107] Ibid., p. 17.
[108] Hartsoeker, *Praestantium ac eruditorum virorum epistolae*, p. 484.
[109] Ibid.   [110] Ibid.
[111] *Calendar of State Papers, Domestic*, vol. IX, p. 477 (De Dominis to Paul de la Ravoire, July 20, 1617); Malcolm, *De Dominis (1560–1624)*, p. 58.

quarrels" in the United Provinces which threatened a major schism within the church.[112] The States-General, in turn, sent De Dominis a letter of thanks and a gift, which the archbishop described in a letter to Carleton on January 2, 1618.[113] By this time De Dominis had also received a letter from Hugo Grotius, whom he had met in Rotterdam on his way to England. Grotius described with some asperity the theological views of those of his countrymen whose doctrine of divine grace in the process of salvation threatened to extinguish human free-will.[114] He sought De Dominis's support in these disputes as well as King James's. Grotius, an adherent of the Remonstrant or Arminian party, spoke uneasily of the strong opposition to the Remonstrants, expressed at a recent session of the States-General by De Dominis's friend Carleton.[115] De Dominis's own letter to the States-General on January 1, 1618 was timely. He thanked the assembly for its kind letter to him and for its splendid gift of silver goblets.[116] He then expressed his ardent longing for an end to ecclesiastical dissensions in the Netherlands and a strengthening of the republic. "Would that the disagreeing parties, overlooking all purely human counsels, might allow themselves to be guided and instructed by that charity which the Holy Spirit pours into our hearts!"[117] He wished that the two parties would quietly compose their differences between themselves, without interference by outsiders. The objective, De Dominis stressed, must be to find a way to live in peace, not for one party to suppress the other.[118] De Dominis believed, like Grotius, that it was one of the functions of temporal governments to prevent religious disputes from distracting and dividing the body politic.

Parallel to De Dominis's effort to perserve the unity of the Reformed Church of the Netherlands was his effort in 1619, already discussed, to bring about unity between the Church of England and the Greek Orthodox Church. De Dominis's proposal in his letter to the Patriarch Cyril Lukaris was that such a union be on the basis of the Christian faith as expressed in the canonical scriptures, the three historic creeds, and the decrees of the ecumenical councils of antiquity.[119] These documents, he felt, contained the fundamental beliefs – the common faith – of Christendom. De Dominis proposed to the Greeks that polity and worship should be on the ancient model and that the primitive equality among bishops should be respected. If the reunion of the South and North – to use De Dominis's terms in his letter

---

[112] Hartsoeker, *Praestantium ac eruditorum virorum epistolae*, p. 485.
[113] *Calendar of State Papers, Domestic*, vol. IX, p. 510 (De Dominis to Carleton, January 2, 1618).
[114] Hartsoeker, *Praestantium ac eruditorum virorum epistolae*, p. 488.
[115] Ibid.   [116] Ibid., p. 490.   [117] Ibid.   [118] Ibid.
[119] J. H. Hessels, ed., *Ecclesiae Londino–Batavae Archivum*, 3 vols. in 4 (Cambridge: Cambridge University Press, 1887–1897), vol. II, pp. 946–954. For discussion, see above, chapter 6.

to Carleton of September 7, 1614 – seemed a long way off, a significant part of the West could at least, he hoped, be joined to the East by the means he suggested.[120] De Dominis's initiative, including his invitation to Lukaris to send representatives to England to discuss a union, was the most concrete proposal he made in the way of furthering the cause of a reunited Church. Meanwhile De Dominis was absorbed in preparing for publication the literary work by which he sought to provide a theoretical basis for reunion and to combat ideas which he believed were a formidable obstacle to that reunion and to the political peace of Christendom.[121]

III

De Dominis's *De republica ecclesiastica* is a kind of Utopia, as Dušan Nedeljković has pointed out.[122] But like many other works in that genre it is firmly rooted in an analysis of history, and is directed towards solving what seemed to be pressing contemporary problems. From one point of view those problems were ecclesiological. De Dominis's work, like Richard Hooker's, dealt with "the laws of ecclesiastical polity," and attempted to show how the Church should be governed if it was to fulfill its divine mission and enjoy unity and concord.[123] From another point of view those problems were political. Wars were being fought on the pretext of religion, and some ecclesiastical leaders, including the pope, used the actions of the temporal authorities to gain their objectives. De Dominis's work treated not only the question of the right form of the Church but that of the right relation between church and state. Like King James he hoped to see the universal Church restored and purified according to the apostolic pattern and Christendom enjoying a new era of peace and stability.

120 PRO SP 99/17, fol. 73 (De Dominis to Carleton, September 7, 1614).
121 De Dominis's manuscript of Books I, II, and VI, with corrections, revisions, and insertions, is found in Oxford: Bodl., Tanner MSS. 462, 463, and 283, fol. 122. A note by William Sancroft states that he bought the manuscript at a bookshop by the gate of the Savoy, where De Dominis had once lived. Tanner MS. 462, fol. 16.
122 Nedeljković, *Marko Dominis u nauci i utopiji na delu*, pp. 7–8, 74–76, 98–99. Cantimori's "L'utopia ecclesiologica di M. A. De Dominis" had used the term earlier. Nedeljković's interpretation presents De Dominis as a social reformer who aimed at the democratization of the Church on the model of primitive Christian communities.
123 Compare Richard Hooker, *Of the Laws of Ecclesiastical Polity*, in W. Speed Hill, ed., *The Folger Library Edition of the Works of Richard Hooker*, 6 vols. in 7 (Cambridge, Mass.: Harvard University Press, 1977–1990, and Binghamton, N.Y.: Medieval and Renaissance Texts and Studies, 1993), vols. I–III. Hooker and De Dominis both defended episcopacy, the former against the English Puritans, the latter against the supporters of Counter-Reformation Rome; they both stressed the importance of general councils in the life of the Church; and they both had an irenic vision. Their treatments of polity complement each other in that Hooker's treatment is philosophical and theological, while De Dominis's is scriptural, patristic, and historical. De Dominis does not appear to have been directly influenced by Hooker.

De Dominis considered the Church constitutionally to be an association of bishops who carried out the work the apostles had been commissioned by Christ to perform. They proclaimed the gospel preserved in the scriptures, administered the sacraments by which the Church was sustained, and administered such temporal goods as the ongoing life of the Church required. Other orders of the ministry depended upon the bishops, as the ordination of priests and deacons by the bishops suggested. Among the bishops themselves there was an administrative hierarchy. Archbishops, metropolitans, primates, and patriarchs exercised a limited jurisdiction over other bishops. But all bishops were equally the descendants of the apostles. When disputes about doctrine or discipline arose, it was appropriate for the bishops to meet in regional, national, or general councils to resolve them.[124]

If this was the essential form of the Church, what had happened to alter it almost beyond recognition? The alteration had come, De Dominis felt, because of the rise of the papacy. He vigorously disputed Cardinal Bellarmine's interpretation of the Petrine texts of scripture, purportedly giving the bishops of Rome authority over the whole Church, and Cardinal Baronius's account of the historical basis of papal authority.[125] Such an authority was, to De Dominis, an encroachment upon the liberties of the Church. De Dominis did not deny that the Apostle Peter had enjoyed a certain primacy among the apostles and that he, along with the Apostle Paul, had been associated with the foundation of the see of Rome. These circumstances, along with the fact that Rome had been the mother of many other churches, gave Rome a special place of honor and respect in the Christian community. But they did not mean that the pope was justified in attempting to exercise a monarchical authority within the Universal Church. The Church in every country in Christendom, De Dominis argued, was threatened by papal claims to universal jurisdiction. The archbishop made a special appeal to his fellow bishops throughout the world to unite against papal intrusions upon their episcopal rights and to work together to bring about a genuine reconciliation of Christendom.[126] The popes, he argued further, had also attempted to exercise temporal jurisdiction over Christian princes. This, De Dominis contended in a long section of volume II directed against the Jesuit theologian Francisco Suarez, undermined the authority of the princes, led to internal rebellions, and played a conspicuous

---

[124] De Dominis, *De repvblica ecclesiastica libri X* (London: John Bill, 1617), pp. 1–2, 10–11, 25–26, 166, 194, 231–232, 472, 511–516. This volume was also published in Heidelberg (Johannis La Cellotti, 1618). In spite of the title, the volume contained only Books I–IV. The second volume contained Books V–VI; the third, Books VII and IX. Books VIII and X never appeared.

[125] De Dominis, *De repvblica ecclesiastica libri X*, pp. 32–34, 525–527, 676–682, 725–726.

[126] Ibid., "To the Whole Order of Divine Bishops of the Holy Catholic Church," sigs. A_1–B_3 verso.

part in causing international wars.[127] In strongly appealing to the princes of
Europe, De Dominis urged them to wield the authority entrusted to them by
God to reestablish order and to bring a disastrous era of religious dissension
to an end.[128]

De Dominis noted that he and Suarez had apparently decided to write on
the nature of the Church and its relation to the civil powers about the same
time, but they came to very different conclusions. Suarez justified the
obedience which he believed the Church owed the pope, while De Dominis
freed the Church from the bondage imposed on it by the papacy.[129] In his
detailed "Demonstration of the errors which Fr. Francisco Suarez, of the
Society of Jesus, has attempted to defend in his book which he entitled
Defensio fidei Catholicae," De Dominis was especially concerned to refute
Suarez's charges against King James's faith, the royal supremacy, and the
Oath of Allegiance.[130] Since Suarez had argued that the Church of England,
despite James's claims, had defected from the Catholic faith, De Dominis
drew upon his own experience in England to demonstrate that the English
Church was soundly Catholic. Having rid itself of many errors and
corruptions during its Reformation, the Church of England remained the
same church as in earlier centuries, professing the same faith. Suarez had
argued that since Henry VIII's time, vast changes had taken place in the
English Church: sacrifice abolished, altars destroyed, priests detested, parish
churches no longer named in honor of the saints. De Dominis countered
that Suarez had been misinformed: Christ's sacrifice was recalled at every
celebration of the eucharist; altars or holy tables for the eucharist were set
up in every church; the ancient orders of ministry were continued; and
parish churches bore the names of apostles, saints, martyrs, and the Blessed
Virgin Mary.[131] Furthermore daily public prayers were said each morning
and evening in the churches and sung in the principal ones; saints' days and
festivals were faithfully observed; and liturgical life was characterized by
great reverence and solemnity. De Dominis found the contemporary Church
of England and the ancient Catholic Church to be remarkably alike.[132]

On the subject of the royal supremacy, De Dominis denied that the
English kings had usurped a spiritual power. The governorship over the
English Church exercised by King James applied only to its external affairs
and was paralleled by the role of monarchs in the major Roman Catholic
countries.[133] The king did not exercise the cure of souls which could only be

---

[127] De Dominis, *De repvblica ecclesiastica, pars secvnda, continens libros qvintum et sextvm*
(London: John Bill, 1620), pp. 877–1009. This second volume was also published in
Frankfurt (Rulandius, 1620).
[128] De Dominis, *De repvblica ecclesiastica, pars secvnda*, pp. 637–639; also pp. 578–581.
[129] Ibid., p. 877.   [130] Ibid., pp. 877, 879–906, 925–948, 950–963.
[131] Ibid., pp. 880–882.   [132] Ibid., p. 882.   [133] Ibid., pp. 880, 891.

performed by those in holy orders: preaching, conducting services, pronoun-cing absolution, administering the sacraments. But whatever pertained to the external regulation of the Church the king considered an important part of his responsibilities: convening councils of the clergy, insisting upon the observance of the canons, providing for an effective ministry of the word and sacraments, supporting and even prescribing divine worship.[134] This did not mean that the king rejected any spiritual authority outside his kingdoms. In his *Premonition* James had affirmed that he accepted willingly the first four general councils as Catholic and orthodox, and that he was ready to support a general council, legitimately convened, in which all churches participated. He was even willing to acknowledge the bishop of Rome as patriarch of the West.[135] The contentious issue of the Oath of Allegiance turned, as De Dominis understood it, on the question of whether the king could require takers of the oath to renounce as heretical a power to depose monarchs which was claimed by the popes and defended by their spokesmen. De Dominis argued as James had that the oath required a civil allegiance only, such as that described in the scriptures, especially in Romans, chapter 13. He went on to draw the logical conclusion that if anyone, the pope included, claimed a power contrary to the clear teaching of the scriptures, that claim had already been sufficiently condemned, not by the king but by the scriptures themselves.[136] James had found De Dominis an effective defender, even against a theologian with the towering reputation of Suarez. De Dominis, like King James, recognized and affirmed the growing power of the state in religious affairs; Suarez's treatment of the relation between church and state was a spirited attempt to restore to the papacy a temporal power it had largely lost, despite the flood-tide of the Counter-Reformation.

This much of De Dominis's argument is contained in the first two volumes of his work, published in England by the king's printer in 1617 and 1620. But there was difficulty in publishing the third volume, which contained De Dominis's solution to the problems he recognized in the Europe of his day. His own explanation was that Archbishop Abbot, a man "most devoted" to Calvinist doctrine, was unsympathetic to De Dominis's plan for the reunion of the separated churches. Nor did Abbot and several other English bishops approve of the section of the work dealing with the Church's use of temporal possessions, since it suggested that in some ways the English Church, supported in part by tithes in the hands of lay impropriators and subject to the payment of annates formerly levied by the papacy but now by the crown, was still insufficiently reformed.[137] The

---

[134] Ibid., pp. 925–928. [135] Ibid., p. 928. [136] Ibid., pp. 952–953, 963.
[137] De Dominis, *De pace religionis: epistola ad venerabilem virum Iosephum Hallum, archipresbyterum Vigorniensem* (Besançon, 1666), pp. 10–11. Lay impropriators were the

bishops evidently prevailed. The third volume had to be published in Germany in 1622, by which time De Dominis was preparing to leave England.[138]

In the third volume De Dominis argued that the way for the schisms in the Church to be healed was through a general council of bishops and the leaders of non-episcopal churches. Such a council should recognize as Catholic Christians all those who professed the faith of the scriptures and the historic creeds, and who wished to enter into union with their brethren. The Council of Trent had not been truly ecumenical since its members had not included the eastern churches, most of the German churches, and the Church of England; and the council had paid scant heed to the representatives of the Gallican Church of France. Moreover it had been prevented from discussing and acting upon the problem of papal authority. To reunite the separated churches a general council would have to admit the Protestants to membership and be free from papal domination. Since the papacy was almost certain to oppose such a council, it was incumbent upon the princes of Europe to act in concert to assemble the bishops and other ecclesiastical leaders in a convenient place.[139]

The basis for settling disputes over the theological doctrines dividing Christians must be the scriptures. They constituted the "rule of faith," when properly understood.[140] It was not that they contained directions for every aspect of the Church's life, but they contained what was necessary for Christians to know for their salvation. They were "the treasury of all dogmas" and must be considered superior to all other sources.[141] General councils themselves were not infallible, however legitimate their convocation and proceedings. Their work, however, in times of contention and division, was indispensable: namely, to search out the truth, under the guidance of the Holy Spirit, and to set it forth clearly.[142] In the process of searching out the truth, the writings of the fathers of the Church and of other theologians were valuable as witnesses to the divine revelation of the

owners of former monastic properties who collected tithes and used some of this income to provide support for parish clergy.

[138] De Dominis, *De repvblica ecclesiastica, pars tertia, continens libros VII, VIII, IX, X* (Hanau: L. Hulsius, 1622). In the preface to the reader, the printer in Hanau notes that De Dominis had not yet completed Books VIII and X; he hopes that they can be added later. Book IX, which deals with tithes, appointments, benefices, collations, and simony is paginated separately (pp. 1–153). The citations which follow are from a later edition of volume three, published in Frankfurt (Joannes Rosa, 1658).

[139] De Dominis, *De repvblica ecclesiastica, pars tertia,* pp. 5–68, 105–116, 126–132, 146–155, 319–322.

[140] Ibid., pp. 1–2, 5–21, 126–132. For a detailed analysis of Book VII, which deals with the prospect of reunion within the context of a doctrine of the rule of faith, see Russo, *Marc'Antonio De Dominis,* pp. 97–131.

[141] De Dominis, *De repvblica ecclesiastica, pars tertia,* pp. 21–24.

[142] Ibid., pp. 39–44.

scriptures. But there could be no independent tradition equal in authority to the scriptures, whether that tradition was written or unwritten. The Roman pope was neither a universal nor an infallible judge of controversies of the faith.[143] To resolve the issues then in dispute, only a council representing the whole Church was likely to be adequate and effective. To convene such a council the combined efforts of Christian princes on all sides would be required.[144] The process of healing the rifts between East and West, North and South, however, was likely to be a long one. If the issues were not all resolved in a general council, as was likely to be the case, the particular churches, the living members of the one Catholic Church, could resolve to tolerate differences where they were not contrary to the rule of faith and to work for a more perfect union.[145]

In De Dominis's opinion, the time for such a council as King James of England had called for had arrived. In his dedication of volume II to the king in 1620, De Dominis had expressed the hope that James would proceed with all his strength towards a realization of "the union of the Christian Church."[146] By 1622, of course, the time had passed, if one of the purposes of such a council was to bring Protestants – still divided among themselves – and Roman Catholics together and to prevent the outbreak of war. But De Dominis's conciliar solution was one which he saw as having been used from the apostles' own time and one whose usefulness was not likely to be superseded. De Dominis's vision of a reunited Christendom and of the means by which it could be achieved was essentially the same as James's. From the time De Dominis had heard of King James's writings and observed his diplomatic activity on behalf of religious and political reconciliation – probably in the period of the Venetian crisis – the archbishop had seen in the king a kindred spirit. His dedications of the first two volumes to the king strongly suggest that he viewed the king as a mentor as well as a patron. De Dominis worked out his ideas in much more detail, of course, than James could ever have done, considering the demands of the king's position, but there is a remarkable consistency between the *De republica ecclesiastica* and James's writings about the Church, especially the *Apologie* and the *Premonition*.[147] In crossing Europe from the Adriatic Sea to the North Atlantic, partly at least to be able to publish his immense theological treatise, De Dominis became, in effect, a spokesman and publicist for James's own views. His work, in the Latin understood by all the learned in western Europe, was the fullest and most scholarly exposition of the

---

[143] Ibid., pp. 24–39, 65, 78–97.   [144] Ibid., p. 48.   [145] Ibid., p. 197.
[146] De Dominis, *De repvblica ecclesiastica, pars secvnda*, Dedication, p. 3.
[147] For a useful discussion of James's views on the Church, see Robert Peters, "The Notion of *the Church* in the Writings Attributed to King James VI & I," *Studies in Church History*, 3 (1966), 223–231.

theological ideas he and King James shared, particularly on the rule of faith, the nature of the Church, the relation between the temporal and spiritual authorities, and the means of achieving the reunion of the Church.[148]

When De Dominis was preparing the first two volumes of his *De republica ecclesiastica* for the press, he was also doing the same thing for Paolo Sarpi's *History of the Council of Trent*. Sarpi, eight years older than De Dominis, had been interested in the Council of Trent and in conciliar ideas since his student days in Mantua and Bologna.[149] He was also familiar with French discussions in the late sixteenth and early seventeenth centuries of the possibility of a national or general council to resolve the religious problems of France.[150] Through Sir Henry Wotton, William Bedell, and Giovanni Francesco Biondi, a former secretary to the Venetian ambassadors in Madrid and Paris who had settled in England, Sarpi had been brought into close contact with English writers and statesmen. King James, in fact, offered him hospitality in England during the period that Sarpi's friend Casaubon was there.[151] It was known by 1612 that Sarpi was writing a *History of the Council of Trent*, together with other historical works dealing with the recent conflict between the papacy and the Republic of Venice. For Sarpi the Council of Trent was a momentous event in the history of the Church and of Europe, inasmuch as it had helped to create the disturbing religious and political divisions of his own time.[152]

There was considerable mystery, at the time of its publication in London in 1619, about how the Italian text of the *History of the Council of Trent* got to England – and who its author was. Readers soon guessed who had written the book, but it has only been in the past sixty years that the fact of

---

[148] On the subject of De Dominis's scholarship, particularly in his treatment of the position of the bishop of Rome in the early centuries, Joseph Turmel has written, in his *Histoire de la théologie positive du Concile de Trente au Concile du Vatican* (Paris: G. Beauchesne, 1906): "Dominis does not just reproduce the ideas already set out by Calvin and the Centuriators. But he bases them on a list of testimonies [Gratian, the ancient church historians, the fathers] which had not to that time been drawn up. His dissertation was to be nearly the last word on a theory dear to the Protestants and, in general, to all enemies of the papacy" (p. 390).

[149] Paolo Sarpi, *Opere*, ed. Gaetano and Luisa Cozzi (Milan–Naples: Ricciardi, 1969), pp. 3–4.

[150] Ibid., pp. 9–10, 23–24. See also Paolo Sarpi, *Lettere ai gallicani*, ed. Boris Ulianich (Wiesbaden: Franz Steiner, 1961), pp. xiii–xvi, xxii–xxiv.

[151] Sarpi, *Opere*, ed. Cozzi, pp. 636–642; Sarpi, *Lettere ai gallicani*, ed. Ulianich, pp. cxlii, 51, 64–66. For Sarpi and Casaubon, see Gaetano Cozzi, "Paolo Sarpi tra il cattolico Philippe Canaye de Fresnes e il calvinista Isaac Casaubon," in his *Paolo Sarpi tra Venezia e l'Europa* (Turin: Einaudi, 1979), pp. 3–133. For Sarpi and King James, see also John L. Lievsay, "Paolo Sarpi's Appraisal of James I," in Heinz Bluhm, ed., *Essays in History and Literature Presented by Fellows of the Newberry Library to Stanley Pargellis* (Chicago: Newberry Library, 1965), pp. 109–117.

[152] Bouwsma, *Venice and the Defense of Republican Liberty*, pp. 570–572.

its publication in London has been satisfactorily explained.[153] Sarpi, who had begun his research as early as 1608, apparently finished his book in 1616. He was encouraged in his work by Ambassador Carleton. No doubt Sarpi recognized – as De Dominis did about his own major work – that it would be impossible to get a book highly critical of the papacy into print in Italy, even in the Republic of Venice. King James, who had offered his protection and favor to Sarpi in 1607 and 1612, saw advantages to the book's being published in England. Accordingly Archbishop Abbot sent the lawyer and scholar Nathaniel Brent to Venice to persuade Sarpi to allow his manuscript to be sent to England for publication. Brent succeeded in his mission. In 1618 Brent sent packets weekly to Abbot, who acknowledged them in his letters as *canzoni* in order to avoid suspicion if his letters were intercepted.[154] While the manuscript was being assembled in London, De Dominis, referred to as the "Old Man" in Abbot's letters to Brent, helped to prepare it for the press and added a dedication and a subtitle to the work. In 1620, a year after Sarpi's history had been published in Italian in London, an English translation by Brent was published there. A Latin translation was also published in London in 1620.[155] The author's name was given on the title-page as Pietro Soave Polano, which readers soon recognized as an anagram (with one "o" too many) of Paolo Sarpi Veneto. The book quickly found its way to Paris, Venice, Rome, and other major cities. There were four Latin editions by 1622. Additional translations in French and German were soon published.[156] Eventually a rival history of the Council of Trent by Cardinal Sforza Pallavicino was published in 1656–1657. Both accounts were widely read during the next three centuries. Sarpi's book, carefully

---

[153] See Luigi Salvatorelli, "La prima edizione autentica della 'Istoria del Concilio Tridentino' di Paolo Sarpi," *Pan*, 6 (1935), 351–360; Frances A. Yates, "Paolo Sarpi's 'History of the Council of Trent,'" *Journal of the Warburg and Courtauld Institutes*, 7 (1944), 123–143, reprinted in Frances A. Yates, *Renaissance and Reform: The Italian Contribution: Collected Essays*, 3 vols. (London: Routledge and Kegan Paul, 1983), vol. II, pp. 189–217, with a note on "A New Edition of Paolo Sarpi" (1975), pp. 218–222; Gaetano Cozzi, "Fra Paolo Sarpi, l'anglicanesimo e la 'Historia del Concilio Tridentino,'" *Rivista Storica Italiana*, 68 (1956), 559–619. Also John L. Lievsay, *Venetian Phoenix: Paolo Sarpi and Some of His English Friends (1606–1700)* (Lawrence, Kansas: University Press of Kansas, 1973), pp. 22–73.

[154] Lewis Atterbury, *Some Letters Relating to the History of the Council of Trent* (London: W. Hawes, 1705), pp. 2, 6–11; Lambert B. Larking, "Notes of Sir Roger Twysden on the History of the Council of Trent", *Notes and Queries*, second series, 4 (July–December 1857), pp. 122–123; Eugenia Levi, "King James I. and Fra Paolo Sarpi in the Year 1612," *The Athenaeum*, no. 3689 (July 9, 1898), 66–67, and "King James I. and Fra Paolo Sarpi in 1607," *The Athenaeum*, no. 4062 (September 2, 1905), 304–305.

[155] Paolo Sarpi, *Historia del Concilio Tridentino: nella quale si scoprano tutti gl'artificii della corte di Roma, per impedire che né la veritá di dogmi si palesasse né la riforma del papato & della chiesa si trattasse, di Pietro Soave Polano* (London: John Bill, 1619).

[156] Bouwsma, *Venice and the Defense of Republican Liberty*, p. 623; Cozzi, "Sarpi, l'anglicanesimo e la 'Historia del Concilio Tridentino,'" pp. 561, 584.

researched and written with the grace characteristic of humanist scholar-ship, has "some claim to be considered the last major literary achievement of the Italian Renaissance," according to William J. Bouwsma.[157]

The polemical subtitle added to Sarpi's *History* by De Dominis was: "in which are revealed all the artifices of the Roman Curia to prevent either the truth of dogmas from being made known or the reform of the papacy and the church from being discussed." De Dominis's dedication to King James was in the same vein. It gave the misleading impression that the archbishop had brought a copy of the work with him, along with other works by Italian writers, when he came to England.[158] Concerning the subject of the book, De Dominis wrote that in recent centuries the popes had been afraid of being discovered for what they were and "reformed, & reduced to what they ought to be" by the sacred councils of the Church.[159] Accordingly the popes had corrupted and oppressed those councils by fraud and even violence. This process "has been seen clearly in the late Council of Trent," although the council had been represented by Roman Catholic spokesmen as pure and holy.[160] The author of the book, said De Dominis, was one who was determined to reveal the truth about the Council of Trent, and was himself a "person born & educated under the obedience of the Roman Pontiff."[161] De Dominis, who signed the work from "the House of Savoy, 1 January 1619," expressed the hope that King James would thereby under-stand "why the Roman Curia has never wished to allow human eyes to see the Acts of this Council."[162] De Dominis's dedication did not please at least one discriminating reader. Writing to William Camden on July 15, 1619, Nicolas-Claude Fabri de Peiresc, a French Roman Catholic and a widely known man of letters, complained that the preface, with De Dominis's name attached, threatened to discredit a great work in the eyes of those "who are not of his opinion."[163] This preface, he feared, would prevent the history from making its way into the hands of Roman Catholics and even, as might otherwise have been possible, into Italy. [164]

Sarpi's *History of the Council of Trent* told a story of strict papal control over the council. This control was exercised by papal legates who presided over its sessions, controlled its agenda, limited its debates, and kept in close

[157] Bouwsma, *Venice and the Defense of Republican Liberty*, p. 623.
[158] Sarpi, *Historia del Concilio Tridentino*, sigs. A$_2$, A$_3$.
[159] Ibid., sig. A$_2$ verso.   [160] Ibid.
[161] Ibid. For the friendly relations between Sarpi and De Dominis in 1615, see C. Castellani, ed., *Lettere inedite di Fra Paolo Sarpi a Simone Contarini, ambasciatore Veneto in Roma, 1615* (Venice: Visentini, 1892), pp. 161–163.
[162] Sarpi, *Historia del Concilio Tridentino*, sig. A$_3$ verso.
[163] William Camden, *Gulielmi Camdeni et illustrium virorum ad G. Camdenum epistolae* (London: Richard Chiswell, 1691), p. 282.
[164] Ibid.

touch with a succession of popes in order to determine what actions would be acceptable to Rome and what actions would not be.[165] But the *History* told another story as well. Sarpi showed that the early years of the Reformation were marked by appeals for a general council by Lutherans in Germany and by the Holy Roman emperor.[166] When the council was finally convened in 1545, it did not satisfy the demand in Germany for a free council in German lands.[167] Some German Protestants attended in 1551–1552, but they were not allowed to introduce items of chief importance to them.[168] The appearance of the German Protestants and the hostile reception they received was the climactic moment in the *History*. But the last part was the most intensely interesting part of the work. The Holy Roman emperors continued to press for the inclusion of Protestants in a resumption of the council or in a new council.[169] Beginning in 1559, the French crown pressed for a national synod in France to include Protestants in order to help to resolve religious dissensions there.[170] The cardinal of Lorraine, who was known to want to institute reforms that might lead French Protestants back into the Roman fold, was an influential member of the council in 1562–1563.[171] But the cardinal of Lorraine's reform program was not approved; no Protestants attended the final sessions; the doctrinal decrees against Protestants enacted in earlier sessions were reaffirmed; and some issues were left unresolved – notably, the authority of bishops compared to that of the pope. The rift in the Church which was threatening in the 1520s had seemingly become permanent by the 1560s.[172] The subtitle of Sarpi's *History* might well have been: "how the opportunity was lost of reuniting the Church by means of a general council."

Sarpi's work had a melancholy tone and included passages of biting sarcasm, particularly when he described papal machinations.[173] It re-

---

[165] Paolo Sarpi, *The Historie of the Covncel of Trent: Containing Eight Bookes, in Which (Besides the Ordinarie Actes of the Councell) Are Declared Many Notable Occurences Which Happened in Christendome during the Space of Fourtie Yeeres and More, and, Particularly, the Practises of the Court of Rome, to Hinder the Reformation of Their Errors, and to Maintain Their Greatnesse*, trans. Nathanael Brent (London: Robert Barker and John Bill, 1620), pp. 73, 130, 134–135, 307, 350, 469, 497, 581, 625, 674.

[166] Ibid., pp. 11, 33, 36, 41, 47, 49–50, 54, 57, 60, 65, 77.

[167] Ibid., pp. 58, 61–62, 66, 76, 77, 81, 106.

[168] Ibid., pp. 328–376.   [169] Ibid., pp. 477, 530, 616, 677.

[170] Ibid., pp. 422–433.   [171] Ibid., pp. 602–603, 624, 629–632.

[172] Note Sarpi's own assessment: "For this Councell desired and procured by godly men, to reunite the Church which began to bee diuided, hath so established the Schisme, and made the parties so obstinate, that the discords are become irreconciliable; and being managed by Princes for reformation of Ecclesiasticall discipline, hath caused the greatest deformation that euer was since Christianity did begin: and hoped for by the Bishops to regaine the Episcopall authority, vsurped for the most part by the Pope, hath made them loose it altogether, bringing them into greater seruitude." Ibid., p. 2.

[173] Ibid., pp. 34, 58, 73.

sembled in this way the *History of Italy* by Francesco Guicciardini written three quarters of a century earlier, which described the disasters brought on Italy by foreign invaders and by the stratagems of Italian states, including Rome.[174] But Sarpi implied that there was a better solution to the issues which the Council of Trent had dealt with. In reading the book, Protestants could see that their spiritual ancestors had wanted a general council in order to reform and reunite the Church. Roman Catholic readers could see that the principal issues raised by the Protestant reformers had not been dealt with on the basis of a free and full discussion and that some important proposed reforms had been ignored. The kings of France and the Holy Roman emperors could see that their predecessors had not been satisfied with the final results, and that the council had left religious dissensions in their own territories unresolved. One conclusion might be that if a general council were now convened which would deal with the issues of doctrine and needed reforms in a way which the Council of Trent had not done, there was a real possibility of restoring the unity of Christendom and achieving a lasting peace. This was, of course, King James's vision.

Sarpi could well have intended the *History* to be used by James to help to further his plans for a council. He made an intriguing but obscure comment about the prospects for his book:

I assure my selfe, that this worke will be read by few, and is of a short life: not so much for want of forme, as for the nature of the subiect. And I am so perswaded, by that which I see happen in the like things. But not regarding perpetuity, or continuance of time, it shall suffice me that it will please some one, to whome I will shew it, because I know hee will make vse of it; and I am assured that, for hereafter, that will happen to it which the coniunctures shall comport.[175]

The "some one" who "will make vse of it" could, of course, be any one of the *literati* or statesmen of Sarpi's acquaintance; but it could also be King James, the prince who had undertaken to publish the book as part of an effort to convene a truly ecumenical council which would profit from the

---

[174] See Mark Phillips, *Francesco Guicciardini: The Historian's Craft* (Toronto: University of Toronto Press, 1977), pp. 107–156.

[175] Sarpi, *The Historie of the Covncel of Trent*, p. 269. For interpretations of Sarpi's *History*, see, in addition to the works already cited: Corrado Vivanti, "In margine a studi recenti sul Sarpi," *Rivista Storica Italiana*, 79 (1967), 1075–1095; William Bouwsma, "Venice, Spain, and the Papacy: Paolo Sarpi and the Renaissance Tradition," in Eric Cochrane, ed., *The Late Italian Renaissance, 1525–1630* (New York: Harper & Row, 1970), pp. 353–376; Enrico De Mas, *Sovranità politica e unità Cristiana nel seicento Anglo-Veneto* (Ravenna: Longo, 1975), pp. 110–121, 216–221; and David Wootton, *Paolo Sarpi: Between Renaissance and Enlightenment* (Cambridge: Cambridge University Press, 1983), pp. 1–7, 104–116, 132. On Sarpi's conciliarism, see Francis Oakley, "Constance, Basel and the Two Pisas: The Conciliarist Legacy in Sixteenth- and Seventeenth–Century England," *Annuarium Historiae Conciliorum*, 26 (1994), 85–118, esp. pp. 103–112, and "Complexities of Context: Gerson, Bellarmine, Sarpi, Richer, and the Venetian Interdict of 1606–1607," *Catholic Historical Review*, 82 (July 1996), 369–396.

mistakes of Trent. It is surprising – perhaps a remaining part of the mystery connected with the work – that De Dominis, who did so much to advance the conciliar plans of King James in volume III of the *De republica ecclesiastica*, did not choose to bring out the conciliar message of Sarpi's *History* in his dedication of the book to the king.

IV

The reputation De Dominis had earned as an outspoken opponent of the Roman Catholic Church makes his decision, in 1622, to return, not to Venice but to the city of Rome, seem foolhardy or even suicidal. What could possibly have moved him to such a course of action? From what both De Dominis and his English critics wrote, the basic reasons seemed to be that he found many of the leaders of the English Church less committed to the cause of reunion than King James and that he hoped to find a greater receptivity to that cause in Rome with the accession of Gregory XV than had been the case there in a great many years. Once again, De Dominis wrote his own explanation, called in an English translation his *Second Manifesto*. Here he complained of the very thing it might have been concluded from the *De republica ecclesiastica* he would have admired: the comprehensiveness of the Church of England. In this work, dated at Rome November 24, 1622, he said that the "milder Protestants" in England, "although they endeauour by all meanes to free themselves . . . from heresie, for that they seeme neither wholly to follow Luther nor Caluine: but the pure Doctrine of the English Church which they call reformed; yet can they not be free from the heresie both of the Puritanes, and Anabaptists; for that they communicate with them without scruple; for if any Puritane or Anabaptist come to their Ecclesiasticall assemblies, they neither auoyde, nor exclude him."[176] Indeed, De Dominis added, "Puritan Ministers . . . doe administer the very Sacraments of this false English Church." When he had discovered that the English Church was so deeply infected with heterodoxy, he decided that he "could not stay any longer in it."[177] He not only repudiated his error in seeking a spiritual home in England but he flatly

---

[176] De Dominis, *The Second Manifesto of Marcvs Antonivs De Dominis, Archbishop of Spalatro: Wherein for His Better Satisfaction, and the Satisfaction of Others, He Publikely Repenteth, and Recanteth His Former Errors, and Setteth downe the Cause of His Leauing England, and All Protestant Countries, to Returne vnto the Catholicke Romane Church*, trans. M. G. K. (Liège: G. Houius, 1623), sig. C₂. This is a translation of De Dominis, *Sui reditus ex Anglia consilium exponit* (Rome: Apostolic Camera, 1623). The book was also translated into English by E. Coffin as *M. Antonius De Dominis, Archbishop of Spalato, Declares the Cause of His Returne out of England* ([St. Omer: English College Press,] 1623).

[177] De Dominis, *The Second Manifesto*, sig. C₃; see also sig. A₂ verso.

declared that the works he had written after he had forsaken the Roman Church were full of heresies. These mistaken beliefs he listed and explicitly rejected.[178]

The *Second Manifesto* seems to have been written as a kind of spiritual purgation by one determined to show that he was free from heresy. More revealing is a long letter written while De Dominis was still in England in response to a letter from the theologian Joseph Hall, who had written to try to dissuade the archbishop from his plan to return to Rome.

Hall, then dean of Worcester, pointed to the dangers which would confront De Dominis in the city of seven hills which the archbishop's thunderbolts had so often struck.[179] Assuming that De Dominis was still committed to Christian unity, Hall argued that Rome had shown no signs of weakening in its opposition to those outside its ranks, nor was Rome likely to yield to entreaties to give up its claims to spiritual and temporal authority or its own distinctive doctrines.[180] The dean seemed frankly puzzled that one whom the English Church had welcomed and the king himself had bountifully entertained would now leave his newly made friends. Did the archbishop find the religion of the English, which he had once extolled, to be lacking in divine truth?[181] Hall reminded De Dominis of the inquisitorial prison in which certain English visitors in Rome had spent some seventeen years. The English theologian predicted that if De Dominis did not change his mind and remain in his adopted country, he would wish either that he had never seen Britain or else that he had never left it.[182]

According to De Dominis's answer, which remained unpublished until 1666, he had come to England with several objectives: to discover the causes of dissensions and schisms in the Church, to find a place where he could write freely, to work for Christian unity and concord, and to serve King James.[183] His experience in England had, De Dominis affirmed, taught

---

[178] Ibid., sigs. A_2 verso–C_1. Among the errors he acknowledged were denying that the pope was head of the visible Church, the mass was a true sacrifice, that transubstantiation occurred in the mass, and that auricular confession followed by absolution was a sacrament.

[179] Joseph Hall, "Reverendissimo viro, d°. Marco Antonio De Dominis, archiepiscopo Spalatensi, epistola discessus sui ad Romam dissuasoria," in *The Works of the Right Reverend Joseph Hall, D.D., Bishop of Exeter and Afterwards of Norwich*, ed. Philip Wynter, 10 vols. (Oxford: Clarendon Press, 1863), vol. X, pp. 208–209. This letter, which is not dated, was received by De Dominis in London on February 20, 1622. See De Dominis, *De pace religionis*, pp. 49–55.

[180] Hall, "Reverendissimo viro epistola," pp. 210–211.

[181] Ibid., p. 213.   [182] Ibid., pp. 212, 214.

[183] De Dominis, *De pace religionis*, p. 2. According to the printer, the manuscript of De Dominis's reply was obtained from an erudite Englishman who had passed through Besançon from Geneva (page opposite the title-page). De Dominis's letter is dated March 1, 1622 at the Savoy (p. 62).

him a great deal about the causes of schism in the Church. Schisms had occurred from the time of the Reformation because some groups of professed Christians insisted upon considering others heretics and refused to maintain fellowship with them. Both Roman Catholics and Protestants were guilty of this. De Dominis maintained that, in spite of the polemical writing produced by several generations of theologians, no one had shown that Roman Catholics were not sound in all the fundamental doctrines of the faith.[184] Since the English confession of faith, the Thirty-Nine Articles, was one of the most moderate in Christendom and seemed to be aimed at including a wide variety of Christians, he had expected to find a willingness among English churchmen to acknowledge the common ground shared by the Church of England and the Roman Catholic Church. He had found such a willingness in King James and many other ecclesiastical leaders. The king was well aware that Roman Catholics did not err in essential matters of the faith and he wished to tolerate those who were not a threat to the commonwealth. Unfortunately, said De Dominis, the Church of England was increasingly dominated by Puritans, even in the episcopal ranks, who refused to have any dealings with Roman Catholics, whom they condemned as heretics.[185] De Dominis argued that the recent participation of English churchmen, including Hall, in the Synod of Dort showed how closely the Church of England was associated with extreme Calvinist theology. This synod promised to make the schism between Rome and England far more difficult to heal. Largely because of this theological state of affairs, De Dominis had not found the intellectual freedom in England he had expected. The way had been blocked, in fact, to the publication of the third volume of his major theological work. As for serving King James, whose wisdom and learning so attracted De Dominis, he had been able to accomplish relatively little. De Dominis had therefore decided to accept the invitations he had received to return home to Italy.[186]

Further reasons were advanced by De Dominis in letters and statements while he was still in England. In a letter to Diego Sarmiento de Acuña, count of Gondomar, the Spanish ambassador in England, dated February 9, 1622, an extract of which was included in De Dominis's reply to Hall, the archbishop spoke of the assurances he had received from the ambassador over a period of some eight months relative to going to Italy. He was reassured by a letter from Cardinal Giangarzia Mellini in Rome concerning his reception on the continent.[187] De Dominis acknowledged that there were dangers in his planned journey back to Italy. But the Roman Catholic Church, he argued with what seems remarkable naïveté, dealt gently with

---

[184] Ibid., pp. 3–6.
[185] Ibid., pp. 13–15.   [186] Ibid., pp. 7–8, 10, 15.   [187] Ibid., pp. 16–17.

those who, though they disagreed with the authorities on some matters, were willing to be corrected. He was willing to submit his work to his fellow clerics for their judgement, and would revise it where necessary. De Dominis was confident that his faith was orthodox, and had been equally so while he had been among Roman Catholics and among Protestants. Though he was glad to be leaving Britain, he would never cease, so long as he lived, to work for religious union and concord.[188]

Some of the ways in which De Dominis planned to work for concord are suggested by the answers he gave to questions propounded to him by ecclesiastical officials in England in the early part of 1622, on orders from the king.[189] In a written statement in February, De Dominis asserted that he could help each side in the divided Christian community to understand the other and could, perhaps, adjudicate their differences. Much, of course, depended upon the attitude of the pope:

> if the Pope would vse some moderation (as I haue formerly saide) about his supremacy, and leaue vnto Princes their intire right of regiment; that then Protestants might tolerate some abuses, (since euen themselues want not their abuses) . . . that so Schisme might be remooued, and there might insue vnion in fundamentall Faith and Charitie . . . and then afterwards there might be more regular disceptation made of dogmaticall points of controversie.[190]

If he were able to advise the pope, De Dominis said, he would recommend not only that he give up the power he claimed over princes but that "he would approue the English Liturgie; that hee would grant them the vse of the cuppe; that hee would suffer the controuerted points of Faith to be handled by way of Councels, after the ancient vse of the Church; that in those points of the Councell of Trent, wherein the Protestants haue made good applications of their opinions, he would release his Anathematisme of them."[191]

De Dominis believed, furthermore, that many Roman Catholic practices strenuously protested against and used as a justification of schism by the Protestants could be satisfactorily explained to them by reviewing the use of such practices in the ancient Church. These included "reuerencing of Reliques, vse of the Crosse, and of Images, and of Chrisme, and of annointing the sicke, Intercession and inuocation of Saints, and priuate Masses." They might then be found "either good and holy, or laudable, or at least tolerable . . . And thus might Schisme be taken away, and vnion

---

[188] Ibid., pp. 56–57, 62.

[189] Richard Neile, *M. Ant. De Dñis, Arch-bishop of Spalato, His Shiftings in Religion: A Man for Many Masters* (London: John Bill, 1624), sig. A₂. De Dominis was interrogated at intervals between January 21 and March 30, 1622, when he was commanded to leave the realm within twenty days. A record of these proceedings is preserved in PRO SP 14/128/103. See also *Calendar of State Papers, Domestic*, vol. X, pp. 366–370.

[190] Neile, *M. Ant. De Dñis*, pp. 44–45.   [191] Ibid., p. 47.

reestablished."[192] De Dominis seemed confident that since the accession of Pope Gregory XV as Paul V's successor, the prospects for such a course of action had been much enhanced. He had, in fact, known Gregory earlier in his career in Italy, and he looked to the new pope for leadership in the cause of religious reconciliation.[193]

Quite a different account of De Dominis's motives was given by Archbishop Abbot, a man who had been in a position to know De Dominis well. Writing to Ambassador Roe in Constantinople, on November 20, 1622, Abbot described De Dominis as a *bestaccio* who had accepted the honors and emoluments granted to him without a word of thanks, "neither to the king, nor to mee, nor to any other person in England."[194] In spite of having "the mastership of the Savoy, the deanry of Windsor, one benefice, and another donative, besides plate given him every yeere from the kinge, to the value of 200 marks" and an additional annual contribution from the clergy of £200, he was dissatisfied with his rank and with his income.[195] The Spanish ambassador, Gondomar, who was anxious to get De Dominis out of England, had worked upon his pride and avarice with the help of several Italians in Rome. As a result, De Dominis was promised "a pension of 12000 crownes a yeere, or the bishopricke of Salerna in the kingdome of Naples, besides acceptation from the bishop of Rome," if he would return to his former profession.[196] De Dominis then asked permission of the king to go to Rome "vnder color to seeke some reconcilement betweene the reformed and the Roman churches."[197] The king, in order to ascertain the archbishop's intentions more fully, had prescribed a series of questions to be put to him. De Dominis's answers, in Abbot's view, showed the Italian "to bee a meere worldly man, without conscience or religion."[198] Rather than being given permission to leave England, De Dominis, who now appeared "odious both to God and man," was "inioyned by such a day to depart the realme, and not to returne vpon his perill."[199]

This explanation, based on the view that De Dominis was venal and self-

[192] Ibid., p. 48.
[193] Ibid., p. 89. For Gregory XV and De Dominis, see Ludwig von Pastor, *The History of the Popes from the Close of the Middle Ages*, 40 vols. (St. Louis: B. Herder, 1891–1954), vol. XXVII, pp. 106–107.
[194] Thomas Roe, *The Negotiations of Sir Thomas Roe in His Embassy to the Ottoman Porte, from the Yeare 1621 to 1628 Inclusive*, ed. Samuel Richardson (London: Society for the Encouragement of Learning, 1740), pp. 102–103.
[195] Ibid., p. 102.
[196] Ibid. Gondomar's brief comments to his government about De Dominis concern the archbishop's literary activities. See Diego Sarmiento de Acuña, Conde de Gondomar, *Correspondencia Oficial*, ed. Antonio Ballesteros y Beretta, 4 vols. (Madrid: Press of the Archives, 1936–1945), vol. I, p. 118; vol. II, p. 277.
[197] Roe, *The Negotiations of Sir Thomas Roe*, p. 102.
[198] Ibid.   [199] Ibid.

seeking, was evidently widely accepted in England. It was the basis of Thomas Middleton's play "A Game of Chess," where "the Fat Bishop" was portrayed as worldly, proud, and gullible, and a fitting victim of the machinations of the Black Knight (Gondomar), which were aimed at returning the prelate to the Kingdom of Darkness.[200] Thomas Fuller related the saga of "that arrant Apostata" in England in much the same sarcastic terms as Archbishop Abbot. Later in the century John Hacket also wrote a disapproving account of De Dominis in his life of Archbishop John Williams.[201] The very title of Richard Neile's collection of official documents – M. Ant. De Dñis Arch-bishop of Spalato, His Shiftings in Religion: A Man for Many Masters – reflects a similar view.[202]

If De Dominis aroused suspicions in England, the same was certainly the case in Rome. After receiving absolution in Brussels at the hands of the papal nuncio, according to the instructions of Cardinal Mellini, for all that he had said or written contrary to the Roman Catholic faith, De Dominis made his way to the Eternal City.[203] There he renewed his abjuration and was given housing, provisions, servants, and a modest benefice. In January 1623, he requested a more adequate income and was accordingly raised to a standard of living that active bishops might have envied. The treatment of De Dominis by Gregory XV, a friend of his from earlier years, did not, however, suit all the members of the Roman curia, and when Pope Gregory died in the summer of 1623, the archbishop's position was rapidly undermined. By April 17, 1624 he was under suspicion of heresy by the Inquisition and had been conducted as a prisoner into the Castel Sant'Angelo. There he remained for several months.[204] His Second Manifesto called forth a bitter comment from Jean Hotman de Villiers, a French Protestant who had worked for many years for an amelioration of religious differences

---

[200] Thomas Middleton, Works, ed. A. H. Bullen, 8 vols. (New York: AMS Press, 1964 – reprint of 1885 edition), vol. VII, pp. 1–135. On August 12, 1624, the Spanish ambassador protested against "a scandalous comedy, in which his Majesty the king of Spain, Count Gondomar, and the Archb. of Spalato are personified," a description which fits Middleton's play. Calendar of State Papers, Domestic, vol. XI, p. 325.

[201] Fuller, The Church-History of Britain, Bk. X, pp. 71, 93–100; John Hacket, Scrinia reserata: A Memorial Offer'd to the Great Deservings of John Williams, D.D. (London: Samuel Lowndes, 1693), part I, pp. 98–103.

[202] This book, cited above, was translated into Latin as Alter Ecebolius, M. Ant. De Dominis, arch. Spalatensis, pluribus dominis inseruire doctus (London: John Bill, 1624). Ecebolus was a follower of Julian the Apostate who sought reconciliation with the Church after the emperor's death.

[203] Paris, Bibliothèque de l'Arsenal, MS. 4111, pp. 13–25. De Dominis's deposition at the house of the nuncio, Guido di Bagno, is dated May 17, 1622.

[204] De Dominis's journey to Rome and his reception there were reported in England by T. H., Newes from Rome, Spalato's Doome: or, An Epitome of the Life and Behaviour of M. Antonius de Dominis, First Bishop of Segnia, Afterwards Archbishop of Spalato (London: Richard Whitaker, 1624), pp. 24–34.

in Europe. Writing to a friend on May 21, 1623, Hotman referred to the "retraction of this monster Spalato, considered such by both sides."[205]

De Dominis died in prison, of a fever, on September 9, 1624. Since, however, the Inquisition's proceedings had not been completed, his body remained unburied in a Roman convent. The case was finally decided on December 21, 1624, when the Congregation of the Holy Office decreed that De Dominis had died as a relapsed heretic and ordered his body and his books to be burned.[206] The summary of the proceedings of the Inquisition preserved in the Arsenal in Paris indicates the grounds on which this verdict was based. The final decree cited De Dominis's communications with heretics before his flight from Italy, his refusal to obey a command to appear before Pope Paul V, the writings published while he was in northern Europe, and a number of propositions which he had expounded on scripture and tradition, the sacraments, the authority of the Holy See, and the nature and content of the Catholic Faith. But much, if not all of this, had been included among the errors which De Dominis had confessed and for which he had been absolved in Brussels.[207] There was, however, an additional item in the decree which received considerable attention there. The archbishop had evidently not given up his design for a union of the separated members of the Catholic Church, that is, "the Roman, the Anglican, and all the Protestant Churches."[208] In fact, he had written out a sketch for such a union, presumed to have been composed after his reconciliation with the Roman Catholic Church in Brussels, and in it he showed that he wished "in every way to defend the necessity of a union with the Protestants."[209] This recognition by De Dominis of Protestants as fellow Christians, with whom closer relations were not only possible but necessary for the well-being of the Church, aroused the suspicions of the interrogators, convincing them that De Dominis had returned to his previous errors.[210] Meanwhile Sarpi, who also hoped for a peaceful reunion of Christians separated by the Reformation, died in 1623 in Venice, where he had continued until his death to be the principal theological adviser to the republic.

---

[205] Paris, BN, MSS. nouvelles acquisitions françaises, vol. 5130, fol. 56. For Hotman's career and irenic efforts, see Corrado Vivanti, *Lotta politica e pace religiosa in Francia fra cinque e seicento* (Turin: Einaudi, 1963), pp. 189–245.

[206] Bibl. de l'Arsenal, MS. 4111, pp. 63–73. A detailed account of the sentencing and execution is contained in the anonymous *A Relation Sent from Rome, of the Processe, Sentence, and Execution, Done Upon the Body, Picture, and Bookes of Marcvs Antonius De Dominis, Archbishop of Spalato, after His Death* (London: John Bill, 1624).

[207] Bibl. de l'Arsenal, MS. 4111, pp. 77–78.

[208] Ibid., p. 78.   [209] Ibid., p. 83.

[210] *A Relation Sent from Rome* lists sixteen heresies, five of which concern his views on church unity, including: "That the Church of Rome, and the Church of England are one and the same Church, both the one, and the other, Catholike and Orthodoxe" (sig. B₂–B₂ verso).

An explanation of De Dominis's movements which redounds far more to his credit than his detractors have allowed is consistent with the evidence presented here. De Dominis was not without worldly ambition – indeed he seems to have had more than his share of a vice considered particularly unbecoming in a cleric – but it is difficult to explain his movements on this basis alone. Both in his journey to England and in his journey to Rome he took great risks, and in both cases gave up a reasonably secure position for one much less certain. Hacket, in the late seventeenth century, saw him not only as a place-seeker but as a man obsessed with an idea: "He lived and died with General Councils in his Pate, with Wind-Mills of Union to concord Rome and England, England and Rome, Germany with them both, and all other Sister-Churches with the rest, without asking leave of the Tridentine Council."[211] That judgement rings true. De Dominis would not have gone to England, in all probability, except that he saw this as his best opportunity to see his ecclesiological *summa* published. But having communicated his ideas about a religious reconciliation to the scholarly world he finally concluded that his plan of union could never be realized without the support of the papacy. The election of De Dominis's friend Gregory XV as pope seemed to present a favorable opportunity in Rome, and made the journey back to Italy a risk worth taking. De Dominis was not a martyr for Roman Catholicism nor for Anglicanism – neither tradition, indeed, has wished to claim him[212] – but died for an ecumenical ideal which is only now, perhaps, beginning to be understood and appreciated.

De Dominis was not a "thorough-paced" Protestant, to use Thomas Fuller's phrase, any more than the two friars, Vanini and Genochi, were. But neither was he an impostor or a dissimulator who came to England to seek his fortune and, because his worldly ambitions were not fully satisfied, returned to the Roman Catholic fold, as many of his English critics seemed to believe. De Dominis attempted, before going to England, to develop a theology which was Catholic but non-papal. His ecclesiology owed a great deal to the example of Venice, in that De Dominis envisioned a Church which was a congeries of particular churches enjoying a large degree of autonomy but linked together by faith and episcopal polity, while being subject to the temporal laws of individual states. De Dominis's ecclesiology also owed a great deal to the conciliar movement of the fourteenth and

[211] Hacket, *Scrinia reserata*, part I, pp. 104–105.
[212] Note, however, the favorable comments on De Dominis by John Cosin, *Works*, 5 vols. (Oxford: Parker, 1844–1855), vol. IV, pp. 160–162, and J. S. Brewer, in his edition of Thomas Fuller, *The Church-History of Britain*, 6 vols. (Oxford: Oxford University Press, 1845), vol. V, pp. 510–512, 529–530. Joseph Crehan, in "The Dalmatian Apostate," *Theological Studies*, 22, 1 (March 1961), 41–58, argues that De Dominis contributed significantly to the views of Cosin and Laud on scripture and tradition, the role of the papacy, and the place of the English Church in the universal or Catholic Church.

fifteenth centuries in that he saw the universal Church as governed on the highest level by general councils representing the whole body of the faithful. The passion in De Dominis's life was to reunite the Church. Where that desire came from it is difficult to say, though his associations with English representatives in Venice during the Venetian crisis with Rome must have had something to do with it. Through them he learned first-hand about the theology and practices of a national episcopal church separate from the Church of Rome. The writings and example of King James were probably important to his theological development long before he left for England. It was during the years between the Venetian crisis and De Dominis's departure for England, roughly a decade, that he apparently wrote most of his *De republica ecclesiastica*, a book which powerfully supported the British king's theological and political views and his call for the reunion of the Church by conciliar means.

Combined with De Dominis's passion for the reunion of the Church was a deep hostility to the papacy – again a result of his Venetian experience but also the result of clashes over financial and jurisdictional issues with papal officials. There was a tension in post-Tridentine Roman Catholicism between the ideal of a renewed episcopate, made up of responsible men who were dedicated to their pastoral and administrative duties, and the over-riding power and authority of the pope, who could and did treat bishops as his agents, dependent on his will and subject to his policies. De Dominis was deeply influenced by the ideal of a renewed episcopate, but he rebelled against the reality of papal power. The paradox in De Dominis's life and career is that a person of settled antipathy to the Counter-Reformation papacy went back, not just to Roman Catholicism but to the very city in which the papacy had its seat. Vanity played its part. De Dominis was not welcomed by some English Protestants, whose behavior he found insulting. Disappointment also played its part. He found that not all English bishops and theologians shared King James's vision of an inclusive, reunited Church. In the end, however, what led De Dominis to Rome was the hope that he cherished for a reunited Church under the leadership of a pope whom he would be able to influence. De Dominis's move was the desperate attempt of a lonely, egotistical, and gifted man to find personal and spiritual fulfillment and, at the same time, to help to restore unity and coherence to a Europe being torn apart by religious conflict and war.

8

The Synod of Dort

The Synod of Dort, which met in the United Provinces of the Netherlands from November 1618 to May 1619 to settle theological issues threatening to plunge that country into civil war, was convened with the encouragement of King James and attended by representatives of the Church of England. These representatives played an active part in the synod and helped to formulate its decrees. On their return home, they received approbation and tangible rewards from the king, who expressed considerable satisfaction with their work. As spokesmen for a theological tradition which had developed for over a half century at the two English universities and in the Church of England, they had reason to feel that theirs was the faith of a broad section of English Protestants.[1] Yet within a few years the synod had become the focus of a bitter controversy that threatened to split the English

---

[1] For treatments of the synod in relation to English history see Nicholas Tyacke, *Anti-Calvinists: The Rise of English Arminianism, c. 1590-1640* (Oxford: Clarendon Press, 1987), esp. pp. 87–180; Christopher Grayson, "James I and the Religious Crisis in the United Provinces, 1613–19," in Derek Baker, ed., *Reform and Reformation: England and the Continent, c. 1500 – c. 1750* (Oxford: Basil Blackwell, 1979), Studies in Church History, Subsidia 2, pp. 195–219, and John Platt, "Eirenical Anglicans at the Synod of Dort," in the same collection, pp. 221–243; John Platt, "Les anglais à Dordrecht," in M. Peronnet, ed., *La controverse interne au protestantisme (XVIe–XXe siècles)* (Montpellier: Universitaire Paul Valéry, 1983), pp. 109–128; Peter White, *Predestination, Policy and Polemic: Conflict and Consensus in the English Church from the Reformation to the Civil War* (Cambridge: Cambridge University Press, 1992), pp. 175–214, and *passim*; and Anthony Milton, *Catholic and Reformed: The Roman and Protestant Churches in English Protestant Thought, 1600–1640* (Cambridge: Cambridge University Press, 1995), pp. 418–435. The involvement of English diplomats and of King James in the controversies which led up to the synod is treated in Jan den Tex, *Oldenbarnevelt*, 2 vols. (Cambridge: Cambridge University Press, 1973), vol. II, pp. 519–654. Other studies of English participation in the synod include M. W. Dewar, "The British Delegation at the Synod of Dort, 1618–1619," *Evangelical Quarterly*, 46, 2 (June 1974), 103–116; W. Nijenhuis, "The Controversy between Presbyterianism and Episcopalianism surrounding and during the Synod of Dordrecht," in his *Ecclesia Reformata: Studies on the Reformation* (Leiden: E. J. Brill, 1972), pp. 207–220; Robert Peters, "John Hales and the Synod of Dort," in G. J. Cuming and Derek Baker, eds., *Councils and Assemblies* (Cambridge: Cambridge University Press, 1971), Studies in Church History, vol. VII, pp. 277–288; and G. P. Van Itterzon, "Engelse belangstelling voor de canones van Dordrecht," *Nederlands Archief voor Kerkgeschiedenis*, 48 (1968), 267–280. A. W.

Church while it coincided with a political and constitutional crisis of ominous proportions.[2] Despite the attention given in recent years to the synod and its consequences in England and the Netherlands, it is still not entirely clear why King James sent British representatives to Dort and what he hoped to achieve by doing so. Compelling evidence in contemporary documents suggests that these actions were a significant part of his larger plan for religious and political pacification.

I

In some ways James's support of the Synod of Dort was very much in keeping with policies he had been pursuing for many years. He was deeply concerned about the strength and unity of the Dutch Republic, since that nation had had a special relation with England and was England's natural ally. He feared that religious disputes there could easily disrupt England. He was also concerned that divisions within the United Provinces of the Netherlands could leave that country more vulnerable to Spain, which was eager to regain it as part of the Spanish Netherlands to the south.[3]

Harrison, *The Beginnings of Arminianism to the Synod of Dort* (London: University of London Press, 1926), is a valuable older study.

[2] For recent analyses of the discussions about the synod in England in the 1620s, see Sheila Lambert, "Richard Montagu, Arminianism and Censorship," *Past and Present*, 124 (August 1989), 36–68; Kenneth Fincham, "Prelacy and Politics: Archbishop Abbot's Defence of Protestant Orthodoxy," *Historical Research*, 41 (February 1988), 36–64; P. G. Lake, "Calvinism and the English Church, 1570–1635," *Past and Present*, no. 114 (February 1987), 32–76; Kenneth Fincham and Peter Lake, "The Ecclesiastical Policy of King James I," *Journal of British Studies*, 24, 2 (April 1985), 169–207; J. Sears McGee, "William Laud and the Outward Face of Religion," in Richard L. De Molen, ed., *Leaders of the Reformation* (Selingsgrove, Pa.: Susquehanna University Press, 1984), pp. 318–344; Peter White, "The Rise of Arminianism Reconsidered," *Past and Present*, 101 (November 1983), 34–54, and *Predestination, Policy and Polemic*, pp. 215–255; Dewey D. Wallace, Jr., *Puritans and Predestination: Grace in English Protestant Theology, 1525–1695* (Chapel Hill: University of North Carolina Press, 1982), pp. 79–104; and G. J. Hoenderdaal, "The Debate about Arminius outside the Netherlands," in T. H. Lunsingh Scheurleer and G. H. M. Posthumus Meyjes, eds., *Leiden University in the Seventeenth Century: An Exchange of Learning* (Leiden: Brill, 1975), pp. 137–159. Links between religion and politics in the decade are treated by Conrad Russell, *Parliaments and English Politics, 1621–1629* (Oxford: Clarendon Press, 1979), esp. pp. 147–165; Hillel Schwartz, "Arminianism and the English Parliament, 1624–1629," *Journal of British Studies*, 12, 2 (May 1973), 41–68; and Carl Bangs, "'All the Best Bishoprics and Deaneries': The Enigma of Arminian Politics," *Church History*, 40, 1 (March 1973), 5–16. See also A. W. Harrison, *Arminianism* (London: Duckworth, 1937), pp. 122–156; and Samuel R. Gardiner, *History of England from the Accession of James I to the Outbreak of the Civil War, 1603–1642*, 10 vols. (London: Longman, 1984), vol. VI, pp. 64–65, 122, 203–212, 329–330; and vol. VII, pp. 7–24, 35–76, 123–132.

[3] Grayson, "King James I and the Religious Crisis," pp. 198–209; Tex, *Oldenbarnevelt*, vol. II, pp. 528–533, 581, 611–630. For the struggle between the United Provinces and Spain, see Geoffrey Parker, *Spain and the Netherlands, 1559–1659: Ten Studies* (London: Fontana, 1979), *The Dutch Revolt* (London: Allen Lane, 1977), pp. 199–270, *The Army of Flanders and the Spanish Road, 1567–1659* (Cambridge: Cambridge University Press,

The synod which met at Dort in 1618 wrestled with religious disputes which had wracked the United Provinces for over a decade. The Remonstrant party, taking its name from a Remonstrance drawn up in 1610 by Protestants who wanted to provide for greater latitude in the official interpretation of predestination, generally followed the tenets of the liberal Calvinist, Jacobus Arminius. Arminius had been, until his death in 1609, a brilliant but controversial teacher at the University of Leyden in the province of Holland, the leading university in the United Provinces. The Counter-Remonstrant party opposed the Remonstrants and the distinctive tenets of Arminius in the name of a stricter and purer Calvinism. While the Remonstrants were numerous and influential in the populous province of Holland, with its flourishing commercial and industrial centers of Amsterdam, Rotterdam, and Leyden, the Counter-Remonstrants dominated the Reformed Church in the other six provinces of the country. By 1618, these doctrinal disputes had contributed to political and constitutional disputes which had led the country to the brink of civil war.[4] In the capital city of The Hague, a schism had developed between the followers of Prince Maurice of the house of Orange, the Stadholder or protector of most of the provinces, and the followers of Johan van Oldenbarnevelt, the advocate or chief executive of the province of Holland and the leading official in the States-General, the representative assembly of the country. Prince Maurice was as committed to the Counter-Remonstrants as Oldenbarnevelt was to the Remonstrants. Across the province of Holland in the summer of 1618 magistrates and citizen soldiers were unsure whom to obey as Prince Maurice moved to disband militia units which towns, with the encouragement of Oldenbarnevelt, had mobilized.

King James, just across the narrow seas, considered the United Provinces an indispensable ally in the alignments which were then taking shape on the continent. With the Twelve Years' Truce between the United Provinces and Spain due to expire in 1621 and with his daughter Elizabeth married to the elector of the Palatinate, a state closely linked to the Dutch Republic, King James needed a strong and united nation at the gateway to Europe and one on which he could rely. He had warned the States-General as early as 1610 about the danger posed by "seditious and hereticall preachers," and he had vigorously opposed the appointment of Conradus Vorstius as Arminius's successor as professor of theology at Leyden on the grounds of his

---

1972); Pieter Geyl, *The Revolt of the Netherlands, 1559–1609*, second edition (London: Ernest Benn, 1962), pp. 180–259; and R. A. Stradling, *The Armada of Flanders: Spanish Maritime Policy and European War, 1568–1668* (Cambridge: Cambridge University Press, 1992), pp. 1–36.
[4] Tex, *Oldenbarnevelt*, vol. II, pp. 609–644; Peter Geyl, *The Netherlands in the Seventeenth Century*, 2 vols. (London: Ernest Benn, 1961–1964), vol. I, pp. 51–61.

heterodoxy on fundamental doctrines.[5] In defending his intervention with the States-General over the issue of Vorstius's appointment, James stated that he feared a contagion, which "dispersing it selfe, might infect, not onely the bodie of their State, but all Christendome also; the danger whereof was so much greater to our Dominions then to many others, by how much the Provinces of the said States are neerer unto Vs in their situation."[6] Partly out of deference to the king's wishes Vorstius was removed to Gouda in the spring of 1612, where he lived for the next seven years. Theological disputes nevertheless continued at the University of Leyden and throughout the province of Holland over the teachings of Arminius. King James's support was sought by both parties. Finally, in March 1617, the king urged that a national synod of the Reformed Church in the Netherlands be held under the supervision of the States-General.[7] His acceptance of an invitation to send representatives to the synod thus had a clear political purpose. But his hopes for what the synod could achieve went well beyond settling the issues which had threatened the peace and security of the Netherlands.

The States-General, which approved the convening of a national synod in November 1617, was not content to have a purely national assembly. The contested matters which had divided the Church and nation were related to theological issues of deep importance for all the churches of the Reformation. If these issues were to be settled, the Reformed Church of the Netherlands needed the best advice and strongest support it could obtain. The States-General therefore invited representatives from a number of states and churches considered to share a common theological point of view. Invitations went to the elector Palatine, the landgrave of Hesse, the Protest-

---

[5] James I, *His Maiesties Declaration Concerning his Proceedings with the States Generall of the United Provinces of the Low Countreys, in the Cause of D. Conradus Vorstius* (London: Robert Barker, 1612), p. 4. For detailed discussions of the dispute about Vorstius, see Frederick Shriver, "Orthodoxy and Diplomacy: James I and the Vorstius Affair," *English Historical Review*, 85 (July 1970), 449–474; and W. Nijenhuis, "Saravia and James I's Moves against the Appointment of Vorstius," in his *Ecclesia Reformata: Studies on the Reformation* (Leiden: E. J. Brill, 1994), vol. II, pp. 206–224.

[6] James I, *His Maiesties Declaration*, p. 7.

[7] King James to the States-General of the Netherlands, March 20, 1616 [i.e., 1617], in Christiaan Hartsoeker, ed., *Praestantium ac eruditorum virorum epistolae ecclesiasticae et theologicae* (Amsterdam: Franciscus Halma, 1704), p. 482. See also Tex, *Oldenbarnevelt*, vol. II, pp. 580–581; and Harrison, *Beginnings of Arminianism*, p. 246. For the character and organization of the Reformed Church in the Netherlands, see Peter Y. De Jong, "The Rise of the Reformed Churches in the Netherlands," in De Jong, ed., *Crisis in the Reformed Churches: Essays in Commemoration of the Great Synod of Dort, 1618–1619* (Grand Rapids, Mich.: Reformed Fellowship, 1968), pp. 1–21; Alastair Duke, "The Ambivalent Face of Calvinism in the Netherlands, 1561–1618," in Menna Prestwich, ed., *International Calvinism, 1541–1715* (Oxford: Clarendon Press, 1985), pp. 109–134; and Derk Visser, "Establishing the Reformed Church: Clergy and Magistrates in the Low Countries, 1572–1620," in W. Fred Graham, ed., *Later Calvinism: International Perspectives* (Kirksville, Mo.: Sixteenth Century Journal Publishers, 1994), pp. 389–407.

ant cantons of Switzerland, the Reformed Churches of France, the Walloon churches, and the cities of Emden and Bremen, as well as to the king of Great Britain.[8] The result was that the synod had an international character. The foreign members were to enter a country where tensions were high. Only after the prince of Orange had arrested Oldenbarnevelt and his adviser Hugo Grotius in mid-August 1618 did the States of Holland, the provincial assembly of Holland, agree to the holding of a national synod in the city of Dordrecht, or Dort, which lay within the province.[9]

James had chosen the representatives from the Church of England carefully, to ensure that they could contribute to the discussions in an informed way and help to resolve difficult issues without rancor. Since he had always enjoyed the conversation of learned men, especially divines, he could be expected to know promising candidates.[10] Three of the representatives were Cambridge-educated and were all three, apparently, his own choice.[11] John Davenant was president of Queens' College, Cambridge, and Lady Margaret professor of divinity at Cambridge University; Joseph Hall was a well-known poet and prose writer as well as dean of Worcester; and Samuel Ward was the master of Sidney Sussex College, Cambridge. George Carleton, the bishop of Llandaff in Wales, an Oxford-educated theologian, was chosen by George Abbot, the archbishop of Canterbury.[12] The fact that Carleton was the only bishop in the delegation made him an appropriate choice as the leader of the group.

The king met with the English delegates at Newmarket before they departed, in order to give them their instructions. They were henceforth to use Latin among themselves so as to increase their facility in that language for the discussions at the synod. They were to confer among themselves about all issues being debated so that they could arrive at a common understanding. That understanding was to be "agreeable to the Scriptures, and the doctrine of the Church of England."[13] Their advice to the Netherlanders should be to avoid preaching abstruse points in the pulpits of their churches that would be more appropriate to the lecture halls of the universities. They were also to advise their Dutch colleagues not to introduce new doctrines but to uphold those which had been taught for the

---

[8] Geeraert Brandt, *The History of the Reformation and Other Ecclesiastical Transactions in and about the Low-Countries, from the Beginning of the Eighth Century, down to the Famous Synod of Dort*, 4 vols. in 2 (London: Timothy Childe, 1720–1723), vol. II, p. 388.

[9] Tex, *Oldenbarnevelt*, vol. II, pp. 644–654.

[10] D. Harris Willson, *King James VI and I* (New York: Henry Holt, 1956), pp. 197–199.

[11] Platt, "Eirenical Anglicans," p. 234. Davenant and Ward were royal chaplains; Hall had accompanied James to Scotland in 1617.

[12] PRO SP 14/109, fol. 157.

[13] Thomas Fuller, *The Church–History of Britain* (London: John Williams, 1655), Bk. X, p. 78.

past twenty or thirty years in their country and which were consistent with their own published confession – an evident reference to the Belgic Confession of 1566. In dealing with issues raised at the synod, the delegates were to try to make sure that the "positions be moderately laid down, which may tend to the mitigation of heat on both sides."[14] The delegates were to consult the English ambassador, Sir Dudley Carleton, who was well acquainted with the issues in dispute, and to be ready, from time to time, to "receive Our Princely directions, as occasion shall require."[15] James was concerned that agreements reached at Dort not cause a rift in the larger Protestant community. He directed the representatives to advise the Netherlanders not only to adhere to their own confession but to "conforme themselves to the publick Confessions of the neighbour-reformed Churches, with whom to hold good correspondency, shall be no dishonour to them."[16] Later the king talked for some two hours to Davenant and Ward at Royston, near Cambridge, shortly before the delegates left for the synod in mid-October.[17] The notes made by Davenant and Ward during their stay at Dort show the care they took to analyze the issues in dispute with reference to the principles expressed by Reformed theologians abroad and the formularies of the Church of England.[18]

Two of the English representatives elaborated publicly on the king's instructions at the beginning of their sojourn in the Netherlands. Bishop Carleton addressed the prince of Orange and the States-General upon his arrival in the Netherlands in early November 1618 in an oration on the theme of peace. The king of Great Britain, he said, was committed to the project of settling "Peace and concord amongst Christian Princes throughout the world; but especially . . . of procuring the good and tranquillity of this your state, to which he acknowledges his kingdom to bee linkt by the Tye of an ancienter and straiter League."[19] What was to be sought, he urged, was agreement within the Dutch Church and among fellow churches: "Your consent in Doctrine with other Churches, shall bee a sacrifice of sweet sauor vnto God . . . and it shall bee welcome newes vnto

---

[14] Ibid.   [15] Ibid.   [16] Ibid.   [17] Ibid.

[18] For Ward's detailed delineation of the issues, see the notes he made at the synod: Cambridge, Sidney Sussex College, MS. L, 1–14. They are described by Margo Todd, "The Samuel Ward Papers at Sidney Sussex College, Cambridge," *Transactions of the Cambridge Bibliographical Society*, 8, 5 (1985), 582–592. For Davenant's papers during his stay at the synod, including notes on the Five Articles discussed there, see Oxford, Exeter College, MS. 48, fols. 1–91 verso. One of the documents in Davenant's papers is John Overall's judgement on the Five Articles. For Overall's analysis of the articles in relation to the teachings of the English Church, see Cambridge University Library, MS. Gg 1, 29: Speeches and Letters of John Overall, fols. 6–14.

[19] George Carleton, *An Oration Made at the Hage before the Prince of Orenge and the Assembly of the High and Mighty Lords, the States Generall of the Vnited Prouinces* (London: Ralph Rounthwait, 1619), p. 2.

the Churches, and Honourable vnto your Lordships, when they shall vnderstand, that you hold Brotherly fellowship one with another in Christ."[20] Joseph Hall, in a Latin sermon delivered at the end of November at the synod, referred to the instructions of King James, in which the monarch had stressed that all present at Dort should adhere to the common faith expressed in the confessions of the Netherlands and other churches.[21] What, then, Hall asked, of those infamous names – Remonstrants, Counter-Remonstrants, Calvinists, and Arminians? "We are Christians, let us also be 'of like spirit.' We are one body, let us be also of one mind."[22]

The delegation from across the Channel was soon British rather than simply English. This was effected by the king's sending Walter Balcanquhall, a native of Scotland, to the synod in December to represent the Scottish nation.[23] Balcanquhall was the son of a Scottish pastor but was ordained in the Church of England. He was, at the time of his appointment, a fellow of Pembroke College, Cambridge. One of the original positions had to be refilled when Joseph Hall became ill in late December and was replaced by Thomas Goad, a former fellow of King's College, Cambridge, who served as chaplain to Archbishop Abbot.[24] Closely associated with the delegation was John Hales, formerly a lecturer in Greek at Oxford and a fellow of Eton College, who served as chaplain to Ambassador Carleton at The Hague. Hales's letters to Carleton, beginning in mid-November, were one of the means by which the English government was kept informed of the activities of the delegates.[25] After Hales's departure, at the beginning of February, Balcanquhall continued the task of sending regular reports to the ambassador, who, in turn, kept Secretary of State Sir Robert Naunton and King James supplied with news.

The issues in dispute between Remonstrants and Counter-Remonstrants were complex and had not been definitively settled by any conference or ecclesiastical body. Arminius's followers had consistently argued that his theological views were in keeping with the confession adhered to in the Reformed Church in the Netherlands. Arminius himself had asked in 1606 that the issues in dispute be referred to a national synod.[26] These issues may

[20] Ibid., pp. 8–9.

[21] Joseph Hall, *The Works of the Right Reverend Joseph Hall, D.D., Bishop of Exeter and Afterwards of Norwich*, ed. Philip Wynter, revised edition, 10 vols. (Oxford: Clarendon Press, 1863), vol. X, p. 261.

[22] Ibid.

[23] PRO SP 84/87, fol. 139; John Hales, *Golden Remains of the Ever Memorable Mr. Iohn Hales of Eton College* (London: Tim. Garthwait, 1659), part II, p. 44.

[24] Hales, *Golden Remains*, part II, pp. 43, 55, 66.

[25] Peters, "John Hales and the Synod of Dort," pp. 279–281. Hales became, in effect, a member of the delegation in mid-January. See Hales, *Golden Remains*, part II, pp. 58–60. Balcanquhall's letters were published with Hales's in this collection.

[26] Carl Bangs, *Arminius: A Study in the Dutch Reformation* (Nashville: Abingdon Press,

be briefly summarized from the statement Arminius's followers drew up soon after his death. The Remonstrants, in the Five Articles of 1610, contended that what should be taught about predestination was that God "by an eternal and unchangeable purpose in Jesus Christ his Son" determined to save those who, through the grace of the Holy Spirit, believed and persevered to the end; the unbelieving, he left "in sin and under wrath."[27] On the atonement, they believed that Christ "died for all men and for every man," but that "no one actually enjoys this forgiveness of sins except the believer."[28] On grace and free-will, they argued that "man has not saving grace of himself, nor of the energy of his own free will" to effect his own salvation, "but that it is needful that he be born again of God, in Christ, through his Holy Spirit, and [be] renewed."[29] Concerning grace, they asserted that it was "the beginning, the continuance and accomplishment of all good," but that it was not irresistible.[30] On the subject of perseverance they contended that "those who are incorporated into Christ by a true faith" are given the power, with the help of the grace of the Holy Spirit, to "win the victory," but that whether or not they could "through negligence" forsake their life in Christ "must be more particularly determined out of the Holy Scripture."[31] To the Counter-Remonstrants these propositions fatally undermined the absolute decrees of predestination and reprobation, implied that salvation was the fruit of human cooperation with divine grace, and severely weakened the strength of that grace by making its effectiveness depend on human efforts. The result, as they saw it, was to exalt human nature and to compromise the sovereignty and omnipotence of God.

The synod was made up of just over a hundred members, twenty from the States-General, five from Dutch academies and universities, fifty-six from provincial synods in the Netherlands, and twenty-three from foreign countries.[32] The Dutch representatives were overwhelmingly members of the Counter-Remonstrant party. Of the delegates elected by the provincial synods, which in most cases sent four ministers and two elders, only the

1971), pp. 275–280. On Arminius's theology, see also Richard A. Muller, "God, Predestination, and the Integrity of the Created Order," in Graham, ed., *Later Calvinism: International Perspectives*, pp. 431–446, and *God, Creation and Providence in the Thought of Jacob Arminius: Sources and Directions of Scholastic Protestantism in the Era of Early Orthodoxy* (Grand Rapids, Mich.: Baker Book House, 1991).

[27] Philip Schaff, ed., *The Creeds of Christendom*, 3 vols. (New York: Harper & Brothers, 1877), vol. III, p. 545.
[28] Ibid., p. 546.   [29] Ibid., pp. 546–547.   [30] Ibid., p. 547.
[31] Ibid., pp. 548–549.
[32] *A Catalogue of the Deputies of the High and Mightie States Generall of the Vnited Prouinces and of the Reuerend and Learned Divines Who Now Are Met in the Nationall Synode Celebrated in the Citie of Dordrecht in Holland, with a Short Narration of the Occasions and Introduction of the Said Synodicall Assembly* (London: Nich. Bourne and Nath. Newberie, 1618), pp. 1–10.

delegation from Utrecht had any Remonstrant members. Utrecht's delegation was divided exactly in half; two ministers and an elder from each party. Some prominent Remonstrant ministers had already fled the country by the time the synod opened, apparently fearing arrest after the seizure of Old-enbarnevelt and Grotius.[33] Thirteen Remonstrants, led by Simon Episco-pius, professor at the University of Leyden, were summoned to the synod, where they arrived in early December. During December 1618 they commented on and defended the Five Articles of 1610 and presented their objections to the official formularies, as ordered by the synod. But a protracted dispute over procedure ensued, marked by the Remonstrants' attempt to provoke a consideration of broader issues, especially the doctrine of reprobation. The Remonstrants in the country at large were justifiably alarmed by what seemed to be an assembly packed with their opponents. To most of the members of the synod, the behavior of the Remonstrants who appeared before them was obstinate and obstructionist. Silenced on December 29, the Remonstrant delegation made its last appearance on January 14, 1619.[34] In early February Hales, who was displeased with the synod's leadership, left Dort and was replaced as Ambassador Carleton's correspondent by Balcanquhall.[35] After the Remonstrants were dismissed, the synod devoted itself to discussing and drawing up decrees on each of the five theological doctrines dealt with in the Remonstrance. They endeavored to make up for the absence of Remonstrant spokesmen by referring to the writings of members of the party.

The early sessions of the synod saw a resolute attempt by one of King James's allies in the cause of church unity to get the subject of union on the synod's agenda. On December 8, 1618 Pierre du Moulin wrote a letter from Paris to Ambassador Carleton which the latter soon relayed to the king. Du Moulin had been elected as a delegate to the synod by the French Reformed Church, but had been forbidden by King Louis XIII to attend.[36] The king did not wish to see the members of the minority church in France in prolonged

---

[33] Harrison, *The Beginnings of Arminianism*, pp. 274, 285–288, 292–294.
[34] John Hales, *Golden Remains of the Ever Memorable M' Iohn Hales of Eton College* (London: Tim. Garthwait, 1659), part II, pp. 24, 31, 34–35, 42, 45, 60–61, 64–65, 70. Hales gives dates for sessions of the synod in *stylo novo*, used in the Netherlands.
[35] According to Hales, "I have a desire to returne to the Hague; first because the Synod proceeding as it doth, I do not see that is *opere pretium* for me here to abide; and then because I have sundry private occasions that call me to return." Letter of February 1, 1619, *stylo novo*. Hales, *Golden Remains*, part II, p. 77. The often quoted statement that Hales bade Calvin "good night" at Dort is based on Anthony Farindon's letter to the publisher of this volume: "when he was employed at that Synod, and at the well pressing 3. S. John 16. by Episcopius, – there, I bid John Calvin good night, as he has often told me." Hales, *Golden Remains*, sig. A₄.
[36] Lucien Rimbault, *Pierre du Moulin, 1568–1658: un pasteur classique à l'âge classique* (Paris: J. Vrin, 1966), pp. 88–89. The royal ordinance which prevented the delegates of the French Church from attending the synod was dated October 15, 1618.

contact with their co-religionists abroad. The memory of the religious wars in France apparently was still too strong. If he had been present, du Moulin wrote, he would have proposed "that so notable an assembly ought not to content itself with appeasing the troubles of the Church of the Netherlands but act also to prevent future evils" of a like kind.[37] This could be done in the present synod by drawing up a confession of faith based upon the confession of all the churches represented there, which all the delegates could then affirm. Once accepted by the respective churches this confession would become "the cement of our union." If any new controversy arose, "nothing should be concluded or innovated without the consent of all the Provinces and Churches which have entered into this accord."[38] But it was no less important, du Moulin continued, that the synod should undertake "a project of accord and reconciliation between ourselves and the Lutheran churches."[39] To this end the synod should write to Lutheran princes, academies, and churches to ask that representatives from their side meet with the representatives of the churches assembled at Dort to discuss an accord and mutual toleration. For this initiative to succeed, the active support of the king of Great Britain was essential. Du Moulin asked that the ambassador forward to the king his letter on this subject.[40]

The plan sent to Dort was essentially the one which du Moulin had helped to prepare for the National Synod of the French Reformed Church at Tonneins in 1614. The French delegation which was to have attended the Synod of Dort consisted of the four pastors – André Rivet, Jean Chauve, Daniel Chamier, and du Moulin – who had been appointed by the French National Synod at Vitré in 1617 to pursue the project of union introduced at Tonneins.[41] Du Moulin saw the Synod of Dort as an assembly of the kind described in the first part of the plan of union presented at Tonneins. He was eager to see the way prepared at Dort for a second assembly, which would include Lutheran representatives.

Ambassador Carleton wrote to Secretary Naunton on December 16, 1618, enclosing the letter to the king. Du Moulin had sent similar advice to other members of the synod, the ambassador reported, and he himself had discussed the proposal with Prince Maurice and his cousin Count William, whose enthusiasm was distinctly muted. But the ambassador felt that neither part of the proposal, the common confession or the subsequent meeting with the Lutherans, was unrealizable.[42]

---

[37] PRO SP 84/87, fol. 111. This letter is printed in Dudley Carleton, *The Letters from and to Sir Dudley Carleton, Knt., during His Embassy in Holland, from January 1615/16 to December 1620* (London: 1780), pp. 325–326.
[38] PRO SP 84/87, fol. 111.   [39] Ibid., fol. 111 verso.   [40] Ibid.
[41] Rimbault, *Pierre du Moulin*, pp. 88–89. See above, chapter 5.
[42] PRO SP 84/87, fols. 152–152 verso. This letter is printed in Carleton, *Letters*, pp. 318–319.

The king himself responded in a conversation reported from Whitehall on December 22 by Secretary Naunton. James requested that the British theologians and "other of the most remarkable persons in that synod" consider du Moulin's proposal seriously.[43] If a common confession were to be drawn up, he would like to examine it. The king also sounded a cautionary note, which he evidently wished Ambassador Carleton to convey to the British delegates. James wanted the introduction of du Moulin's proposal to be done deliberately, with adequate support, lest the proposal be defeated and leave the churches represented at Dort in a weaker position:

He joins in [the] opinion that it will be a matter of great honor to the times and to that Synod, and of no lesse importance therein to the Church, if it shall succeede with such an issue as is propounded. But it must be handled with great care, and even temper; least the attempting of it without success should do more prejudice to our profession and give new occasion of infiltracion and triumph by the Common Enemie, who will be sure to traverse it all they can.[44]

He was ready, if the synod proposed it, to "interpose himselfe with and to the Lutheran princes."[45]

At Dort the British delegates agreed to "have trial made" of du Moulin's proposal, as Bishop Carleton reported on December 31.[46] The next day Hales wrote the ambassador that "a generall Confession of Faith, at least so farr as those Churches stretch who have Delegates here in the Synod," was very possible, "there being no point of Faith in which they Differ."[47] As for relations with the Lutherans, he viewed a "mutuall tolleration" as more feasible than a union, since there were seemingly irreconcilable differences between the Lutheran churches and those represented at Dort over such issues as "the ubiquity of Christs manhood, the Person of Christ, [and] the *communicatio idiomatum.*"[48] He wondered whether du Moulin was being realistic: "The French wits are naturally active and projecting; and withall carry evermore a favourable conceit to the possibility of their projects. Out of this French conceit I suppose proceeded this of M. Moulins."[49] Hales was seemingly unaware of King James's active involvement when du Moulin's plan had been formulated four and a half years earlier.

Hales pursued the matter with Johannes Bogerman, the pastor of Leeuwarden who was the synod's president, and after some delay he received the president's opinion. On January 22 Hales wrote that Bogerman had asked Bishop Carleton and Abraham Scultetus of the Palatinate to "conceive a forme of publick Confession," which, after it had been examined by those in authority at Dort, would be "sent to his Majesty, by

[43] PRO SP 84/87, fols. 174–174 verso.   [44] Ibid., fol. 174 verso.   [45] Ibid.
[46] Carleton, *Letters*, p. 330.   [47] Hales, *Golden Remains*, part II, p. 54.
[48] Ibid. *Communicatio idiomatum* refers to the interchangeable properties of the divine and human natures of Christ.
[49] Ibid., p. 55.

him to be revised and altered according to his pleasure, and so from him to be commended unto the Synod publickly."[50] As for an approach to the Lutherans, "he thinks it not fit that any word at all be made."[51] Meanwhile Bishop Carleton had written to the ambassador on January 14 that he intended to frame a confession on the basis of the Thirty-Nine Articles of the Church of England and to show it to the delegates from the Palatinate as well as others. "If there be a consent between our church and Palatines," he concluded, "all the rest will easily come over; for the Palatine confession is that, which carrieth most authority in these reformed churches."[52] After the middle of January, however, du Moulin's proposal, endorsed by the king, was not urged by the British delegates, presumably because it had little support. Echoes of it can, however, be heard in their later actions.

During the winter and spring of 1619 the British delegation significantly contributed to the deliberations of the synod on the key issue of Christ's atonement. The contribution was to insist that the decrees on the second article affirm that Christ died for all, not just for the elect. This affirmation was achieved despite seemingly overwhelming support in the synod for the view that the atonement was limited. The result was that the decrees of Dort were a more moderate statement – and one closer to the views of the Remonstrants – than would otherwise have been the case.

What was to end as a dramatic achievement began as a disagreement among the British representatives themselves. In the last of Hales's letters from Dort, on February 7, he reported that there had been "many private meetings" in Bishop Carleton's lodgings about points of considerable concern to Samuel Ward and Matthias Martinius of Bremen on the subject of grace.[53] As Balcanquhall explained in his report of February 9, there was disagreement in the synod and in the British delegation itself about the second article, dealing with Christ's death.[54] On the one hand Davenant, Ward, and Martinius believed that Christ died for all *particular* men; Carleton, Goad, and Balcanquhall himself believed that he died only for the elect, who consisted of all *sorts* of men. Meanwhile the British representatives, on the advice of the synod's president, had sought the advice of the archbishop of Canterbury on the disputed points.[55] Ward discussed the theology of Christ's sacrifice vigorously with President Bogerman in a series

---

[50] Ibid., p. 71. [51] Ibid.
[52] Carleton, *Letters*, p. 332. The authorized catechism in the Palatinate and the United Provinces was the Heidelberg Catechism of 1562.
[53] Hales, *Golden Remains*, part II, p. 80.
[54] Ibid., part III, p. 2. On the contribution of the British delegation to the discussions of the second article, see Platt, "Les anglais à Dordrecht," pp. 109–128. The subject is treated in detail in William Robert Godfrey, "Tensions within International Calvinism: The Debate on the Atonement at the Synod of Dort, 1618–1619," Ph.D. thesis, Stanford University, 1974.
[55] Hales, *Golden Remains*, second edition (London: Robert Pawlett, 1673), pp. 179–183. (The second edition of Hales's book contains many additional letters from Dort.)

of written responses to propositions the latter had advanced. In a manuscript preserved at Sidney Sussex College, the English theologian countered
the president's view that the merits of Christ's death were intended only for
those whom God had elected.[56] Ward asserted, on the contrary, that
Christ's offering of himself on the cross was the expression of God's love for
all human beings. In the New Testament, he asserted, Christ is called "the
Saviour of the World" and "the lamb of God who takes away the sins of the
world." In Christ, as St. Paul observed, "God reconciled the world to
himself."[57] Ward noted that in the Old Testament, salvation was promised
to all nations and peoples unto the ends of the earth.[58] In the New
Testament the promises of the Old Testament were fulfilled. These teachings, he said, could not be understood as restricting the merits of Christ's
death to the elect. God's expressed intention was that all human beings
might be redeemed. Through Christ, God had established a new covenant
by which those who were incorporated into Christ were made the sure
beneficiaries of grace. By this means the merits of Christ's death were
applied specifically and efficaciously to those who believed in Christ.[59]
Ward argued that all *possibility* of salvation was not thereby removed from
those who apparently did not respond to the gospel. He recalled to
Bogerman what he called "the greatest freedom of divine will in the
dispensation of supernatural gifts."[60] Even the wicked, he argued, could
hear the gospel preached and experience other spiritual gifts. Nevertheless,
he noted with reference to the parable in Matthew 22: "Many who have
been called do not come to the wedding feast," and "some come but
without wedding garments."[61] The merits of Christ, intended for all, thus
did not benefit all alike.

Davenant's viewpoint was similar to Ward's. Both Balcanquhall and
Bishop Carleton, in their letters to Ambassador Carleton, said that Davenant's ideas about "the universal grace of redemption" would not be
acceptable to the synod.[62] But Davenant, like Ward, was determined to
uphold his position, declaring that rather than withdraw his theses, "he
would rather to have his right hand cut off."[63] Moreover he seems to have
devoted himself to gathering evidence from the scriptures, an array of
theological writers, and the Reformed confessions of faith. By February 18,
before any advice had arrived from Archbishop Abbot, the British delegates

---

[56] Sidney Sussex MS. L, 4: "Concerning the Attaining [of Merits] Made through the Death of
Christ: Debate between D. W. [Doctor Ward] and the President of the Synod of Dort,"
pp. 1, 4, 8, 9.
[57] Ibid., pp. 15–16.   [58] Ibid., p. 15.   [59] Ibid., pp. 2, 16.
[60] Ibid., p. 6. For the argument about the possibility of those outside the covenant receiving the
benefits of Christ's sacrifice, see pp. 2–7.
[61] Ibid., p. 14.   [62] Hales, *Golden Remains*, part III, p. 4; second edition, p. 181.
[63] Ibid., second edition, pp. 181–182.

had reached agreement on the second article.[64] What they agreed to is contained in a letter from the whole British delegation to the archbishop, dated March 11, stating their "Reasons of enlarging Grace beyond Election."[65] They had evidently received advice to the contrary from Archbishop Abbot by this time and were eager to defend their decision. They had also heard from King James himself by way of John Young, dean of Winchester, one of the king's closest advisers. Young wrote to Ward on February 25 that James "lykes veri weal of your *media via*" on the issues under discussion, and especially approved of their objective of formulating a statement which would not alienate the Lutheran churches from the churches represented at Dort.[66] Young expressed the hope that the delegates' actions would "make way one day by Gods blessing in his good tyme for the making up of the rent in our reformatione."[67] On February 19, a few days before Young wrote to Ward, Secretary Naunton wrote to Ambassador Carleton on the same subject. The king, said Naunton, wished the conclusions concerning Christ's death to be worded so as to ensure "that the same may be as aggreeable to the Confessions of the Church of England and other reformed churches and with as little distaste or umbrage to the Lutheran churches as may be."[68]

The agreement among the British delegates, as explained in their joint statement of March 11, was based on a theological treatise by Davenant entitled "Doctor Davenant touching the Second Article . . . of the Extent of Redemption."[69] The key proposition affirmed by the British delegates was that "God sent his Son . . . who paid the price of redemption for the sins of the whole world."[70] This proposition, they commented, "is equipollent to the express Article of the Church of England . . . Art. XXXI, which also is delivered *totidem verbis* in the Consecratory Prayer before the Receiving of the Holy Eucharist in the Book of Common Prayer."[71] The texts referred to here – the Articles of Religion and the Book of Common Prayer – were the authoritative theological formularies in the

---

[64] Ibid., second edition, pp. 183–184.
[65] Ibid., second edition, pp. 184–186. A Latin version is found in Hartsoeker, *Praestantium ac eruditorum virorum epistolae*, pp. 561.
[66] Bodl., Tanner MS. 74, fol. 196.   [67] Ibid.   [68] PRO SP 84/88, fol. 217.
[69] Hales, *Golden Remains*, second edition, pp. 186–190; Hartsoeker, *Praestantium ac eruditorum virorum epistolae*, pp. 561–563.
[70] Hales, *Golden Remains*, second edition, p. 187.
[71] Ibid. Article XXXI, "Of the one Oblation of Christ finished upon the Cross," reads in part: "The offering of Christ once made is the perfect redemption, propitiation, and satisfaction, for all the sins of the whole world, both original and actual, and there is none other satisfaction for sin but that alone." This teaching was directed against the proposition that Roman Catholic priests at the celebration of the mass offered Christ as a sacrifice for the living and the dead. See E. J. Bicknell, *A Theological Introduction to the Thirty-Nine Articles of the Church of England*, third edition by H. J. Carpenter (London: Longman, 1955), pp. 410–419.

Church of England. The fact that they explicitly affirmed that Christ died for the sins of the whole world was no doubt decisive in bringing the British delegation to a single mind about the second article. The relevant phrase in the prayer of consecration in the Prayer Book referred to God the Father's having given his "Son Jesus Christ to suffer death upon the cross for our redemption; who made there (by his one oblation of himself once offered) a full, perfect, and sufficient sacrifice, oblation, and satisfaction for the sins of the whole world."[72] Each of the British delegates at Dort would have used these words whenever he celebrated the Holy Communion. The reasons the British delegates gave for affirming the view stated by Davenant included their belief that this doctrine "is the undoubted Doctrine of the holy Scriptures, and most consonant to Antiquity, Fathers, and Councils, to whom our Church will have all Preachers to have special respect in doctrinal points."[73] They asserted that "there is no confession of any Reformed Church, that doth restrain Christ's death only to the Elect," as many of the Counter-Remonstrants held.[74] They commented further: "We verily think that the strictness of the Contra-Remonstrants in this Second Article is one chief reason which keepeth the Lutheran Churches from joyning with us. And we think that if way were given in the Synod herein, they would be the more easily brought to hold the Doctrine of Predestination according to the Opinion of St. Augustine, and the Church of England."[75]

Having achieved an agreement based on the views of Davenant and Ward, who were originally a minority of two among their colleagues, the British delegation went on to contend for this doctrine in an assembly which probably had a majority holding the opposite view. But the British view prevailed, perhaps because of the persuasiveness of the British representatives and the deference of the synod to the delegation from the largest national church represented at Dort – or, more likely, because of the strength of the case the British delegates presented. In any event the British view decisively influenced the final version of the decrees. The *lex orandi* of the Book of Common Prayer, a more elaborate liturgy than most of the delegates at Dort were accustomed to, had helped to shape the *lex credendi* of the major international gathering of Reformed theologians in early modern times. If the doctrine steered clear of the rigid exclusiveness of the Counter-Remonstrants, it also avoided the view that all were restored to a

---

[72] *The Book of Common Prayer and Administration of the Sacraments and Other Rites and Ceremonies of the Church according to the Use of the Church of England* (Oxford: Oxford University Press, [*c.* 1969]), p. 313. This passage first became part of the prayer of consecration in 1549. See *The First and Second Prayer Books of Edward VI* (London: J. M. Dent, 1910), p. 222.

[73] Hales, *Golden Remains*, second edition, p. 188.   [74] Ibid., p. 189.

[75] Ibid., p. 190.

state of grace by the atonement, which was widely understood as being taught by the Remonstrants. The British representatives affirmed in a way which embraced the positions of both of the contending parties that it was God's intention to apply the fruits of Christ's sacrifice by "conferring Faith and other Gifts" on those to whom God showed love and mercy.[76]

The British representatives submitted a written *Suffrage* on each of the five contested articles on March 6, 1619. These statements, they said, "wee beleive to be agreeable to the word of God, and sutable to the Confessions of so many reformed Churches."[77] They advised their fellow ministers to touch "warilie in due time and place" the mysteries of predestination and reprobation.[78] Concerning the atonement, they counseled: "we are so to determine of the precious merit of Christs death, that we neither sleight the judgement of the Primitive Church, nor yet the Confessions of the Reformed Churches, nor (which is the most principall point of all the rest) weaken the promises of the Gospel, which are to be propounded universally in the Church."[79] The decrees of the Synod of Dort were drafted by groups made up of both foreign and Dutch theologians and were debated by the whole assembly. In at least one instance during the final drafting of the decrees the influence of King James's instructions and his message of December 22 can be seen at work. On April 24, 1619 the British delegates warned that the phrase used in the decrees "according to the judgement of all Reformed Churches" implied too broad an agreement. They maintained that, however the other churches represented at Dort used the term *Reformed*, in the Church of England the Lutherans were held to be reformed, since the Reformation had first been undertaken by those of the Lutheran persuasion. The word *our* was therefore directed to be substituted for *all* in the phrase *according to the judgement of all Reformed Churches*, signifying the agreement reached at Dort. The British delegates stressed that their directions were to avoid insofar as possible offending the Lutherans.[80]

The nearest the delegates came to agreeing to a common confession was their affirmation of the Belgic Confession near the close of the Synod of Dort. This action brought forth a spirited defense of episcopal polity by Bishop Carleton, who did not want it supposed that the British representatives agreed with the idea of a parity of ministers expressed in the Belgic Confession.[81] The synod did not, in the end, make a deliberate effort to

---

[76] Ibid., p. 185.

[77] *The Collegiat Svffrage of the Divines of Great Britaine, Concerning the Five Articles Controverted in the Low Countries* (London: Robert Milbourne, 1629), p. 171.

[78] Ibid., p. 176.   [79] Ibid., p. 177.

[80] Hales, *Golden Remains*, second edition, pp. 155–156 (from the *Acta synodi*); Brandt, *History of the Reformation*, vol. III, p. 282.

[81] George Carleton, John Davenant, Walter Balcanquhall, *et al.*, *A Ioynt Attestation, Avowing That the Discipline of the Church of England Was Not Impeached by the Synode of Dort*

prepare the way for closer relations between the churches represented there and the Lutheran churches, as both du Moulin and King James had urged. The distance remaining between the two groups of churches was soon to be shown in the strained and even hostile relations between Lutheran and Calvinist states in Germany in the early years of the Thirty Years' War.

In their final form, as approved by the unanimous vote of the delegates, the decrees were read aloud in Latin in the Great Church at Dort on May 6, 1619. In the same year, they were published in an English translation in London.[82] The decrees are discursive and are aimed more at edifying the faithful than at resolving intractable philosophical and theological difficulties. On the whole they deal skilfully and intelligibly with issues of perennial concern to Christian theologians. Though they repudiate many of the characteristic teachings of the Remonstrants, they do not endorse the extreme positions of the Counter-Remonstrants. On the key issues of predestination and the atonement, the decrees are definitely not a supralapsarian document – that is, they do not link creation and election in the way many Counter-Remonstrants did in an effort to safeguard the integrity of the "eternal decrees." The British delegation would have made this distinction explicit by citing extreme positions on both sides that had been rejected.[83] Instead, only the teachings of the Remonstrants which the synod found unacceptable were cited. In the context of the theology of the Reformed churches of the early seventeenth century, however, the decrees may be seen as a deliberate and judicious compromise. They were aimed at expressing the "received doctrine," in language closely interwoven with that of the scriptures.[84]

Since the decrees of Dort are frequently oversimplified and distorted, it is worthwhile to look at what they actually say on the key issues in dispute.

(London: R. Mylbourne, 1626); George Carleton, *Bp Carletons Testimonie Concerning the Presbyterian Discipline in the Low-Countries and Episcopall Government Here in England* (London: Nath. Butter, 1642); Nijenhuis, "The Controversy between Presbyterianism and Episcopalianism surrounding and during the Synod of Dordrecht," pp. 207–220.

[82] *The Ivdgement of the Synode Holden at Dort, Concerning the Five Articles, As Also Their Sentence Touching Conradvs Vorstivs* (London: John Bill, 1619). The Latin edition is the *Ivdicivm Synodi Nationalis, Reformatarvm Ecclesiarvm Belgicarvm, Habitae Dordrechti Anno 1618 & 1619* ([Dordrecht,] 1619).

[83] Hales, *Golden Remains*, part III, p. 18.

[84] Pierre du Moulin viewed the decrees of Dort as moderate compared to the views of such theologians as Beza, Piscator, Gomarus, and Tronchin. See PRO SP 78/68, fols. 264–264 verso (du Moulin to Carleton (?), December 23, 1619). For comments on the decrees as a judicious compromise, see Walter Rex, *Essays on Pierre Bayle and Religious Controversy* (The Hague: Martinus Nijhoff, 1965), pp. 80–86. On their "popular," rather than "scholastic," style, see Donald Sinnema, "Reformed Scholasticism and the Synod of Dort (1618–19)," in B. J. Van der Walt, ed., *John Calvin's Institutes: His Opus Magnum* (Potchefstroom: Potchefstroom University for Christian Higher Education, 1986), pp. 467–506.

On the subject of predestination itself, the decrees assert that "all men have sinned in Adam, and are become guiltie of the curse, & eternall death," but that God in his love has sent his "Sonne into the world, that whosoever believeth in him might not perish, but have life everlasting."[85] Belief or faith is described as a gift of God, enjoyed by some and not by others. This election was made before the foundation of the world in order that those chosen would become, by God's grace, faithful and holy.[86] Those human beings chosen to salvation are assured of their election by observing in themselves such spiritual fruits as faith in Christ, fear of God, grief for sins, and a thirst for righteousness.[87] Concerning persons who do not have this assurance, the decrees state that "these ought not be cast downe at the mention of Reprobation, nor reckon themselves amongst the reprobate, but must diligently go forward in the vse of those meanes [which God has provided], and ardently desire, and humbly and reverently expect the good howre of a more plentifull grace."[88] Christians who do not experience the assurance associated with the recognition of God's love for them are not, therefore, to assume that they have been rejected, but are to work, hope, and pray in expectation of a fuller revelation of God's will for them.

On the subject of Christ's death and the redemption which springs from it, the decrees affirm that the "death of the sonne of God is the onely, and most perfit sacrifice, and satisfaction for sinnes, of infinite price, and value, abundantly sufficient to expiate the sinnes of the whole world."[89] The promise of the gospel – that "whosoeuer beleeues in Christ crucified, should not perish, but haue life euerlasting," – is to be proclaimed to all people.[90] The bestowing of "iustifying faith" is not, however, universal, but proceeds from God's "eternall loue toward the elect," which has been and hereafter will be fulfilled.[91] The sacrifice of Christ on the cross is thus sufficient for all, but is efficacious only for the faithful – that is, those to whom God has extended his grace.

Man's corruption and conversion to God are treated together in such a way that the bondage of sin and the power of divine grace are closely linked and strongly emphasized. Human beings "neither will, nor can (without the grace of the holy Ghost regenerating them) set streight their owne crooked nature."[92] This is despite "some remands of the light of nature," by which they distinguish good and evil, and manifest "some care of vertue."[93] But these abilities do not suffice "to come to the sauing knowledge of God."[94] That which neither the light of nature nor the delivery of the decalogue to Moses could do, "God bringeth to passe by the power of the holy ghost, through his word" concerning the Messiah.[95] God's "regenerating spirit,"

---

[85] *Ivdgement of the Synode*, p. 1.   [86] Ibid., p. 6.   [87] Ibid., pp. 7–8.
[88] Ibid., p. 10.   [89] Ibid., p. 22.   [90] Ibid., pp. 22–23.   [91] Ibid., pp. 24–25.
[92] Ibid., p. 32.   [93] Ibid., p. 33.   [94] Ibid.   [95] Ibid., p. 34.

moreover, works a real change in the human being, making "of a dead heart liuely, of an evill good," enabling it "like a good tree, to bring forth the fruits of good workes."[96] But "as for those, who are not as yet called, we must pray for them to God."[97] The Christian community should, therefore, have a special concern for those who have not yet heard God's call. Meanwhile those who are being regenerated are nourished by the word and sacraments. By such means "is the good gift of God working in vs made more sensible vnto vs, and his worke it selfe best commeth to perfection."[98]

Finally, under the heading of the perseverance of the saints, the decrees state that, even though the regenerate may sin as a result of their infirmity, "God is faithfull, who mercifully confirms them in the grace, wherein he hath once accepted them, and mightily preserueth them in the same, euen vnto the end."[99] Perseverance is thus the result of God's faithfulness in his dealing with sinful human beings, rather than the rectitude of the faithful. The "faithfull themselves may be and are ascertained, according to the measure of their faith," although they sometimes experience doubts and do not experience "this full assurance of faith."[100] The faithful are not, as a result, either proud or careless of the means of salvation. Instead they have "a farre greater care to walke more circumspectly in the waies of the Lord, which are prepared to this end, that by walking therein they may hold fast the certaintie of their perseverance."[101]

The decrees of the synod are frequently represented as expressing a narrow, exclusive, and intolerant faith, representing the hardening of theological divisions in the post-Reformation period. To some extent the treatment accorded the Arminians in the Netherlands supports such a view. Once the decrees were approved, Dutch officials carried out a severe political and religious repression. The Arminian clergy in the United Provinces were suspended from their positions. The leading statesman of the province of Holland, Johan van Oldenbarnevelt, the defender of the Arminians, was executed, though more for political than religious reasons. His colleague Hugo Grotius was sentenced to life imprisonment, from which he escaped a few years later.[102] The United Provinces avoided a civil war, but at considerable human cost and in a way that jeopardized the reputation of the country as a tolerant and humane society.[103] Moreover the condemnation of the Remonstrants by the synod gave encouragement to

[96] Ibid., p. 38.   [97] Ibid., p. 41.   [98] Ibid., p. 44.   [99] Ibid., p. 54.
[100] Ibid., pp. 58–59.   [101] Ibid., p. 60.
[102] Harrison, *Beginnings of Arminianism*, pp. 388–399; Tex, *Oldenbarnevelt*, vol. II, pp. 672–675; François Laplanche, *Orthodoxie et prédication: l'oeuvre d'Amyraut et la querelle de la grâce universelle* (Paris: Presses universitaires de France, 1965), pp. 30–33.
[103] Compare J. H. Huizinga, *Dutch Civilization in the Seventeenth Century and Other Essays* (London: Fontana, 1968), pp. 53–61.

the strict Calvinists in the Netherlands and to what has been called a "further reformation" in the church and in society.[104]

The decrees themselves, however, are a moderate expression of a biblical theology which originated in the European-wide Reformation a century earlier, especially in Protestant Switzerland. At the same time they reflect the discussion and elaboration of theological doctrines in the countries represented at Dort. For England, this process included the theological reflection represented in the Thirty-Nine Articles of Religion and the Book of Homilies, as well as the Lambeth Articles of 1595, which strikingly anticipated some of the positions adopted at Dort.[105] The process also included the teaching, disputations, and scholarship associated with Cambridge University in the age of John Whitgift, William Whitaker, William Perkins, and Laurence Chaderton, and with Oxford University in the age of Lawrence Humphrey, Richard Cole, and John Reynolds. The clergy and laity of the Church of England who were the products of this tradition were not all or even predominantly Puritans, in the sense of wanting to alter the liturgical forms or the ecclesiastical polity of the established Church in any fundamental way. Certainly the British representatives at Dort were not Puritans in this sense.[106] The comprehensiveness of the English tradition may be illustrated by the fact that the decrees of Dort were endorsed by the British delegation, led by a bishop; by an English Puritan exile, William Ames, who served as a theological adviser to Johannes Bogerman, the president of the synod;[107] and by an English separatist, John Robinson, the pastor of the Pilgrim Fathers, who wrote the first defense in English of the

---

104 Joel R. Beeke, *Assurance of Faith: Calvin, English Puritanism, and the Dutch Second Reformation* (New York: Peter Lang, 1991), pp. xv–xvi, 381–413.

105 Charles Davis Cremeans, *The Reception of Calvinistic Thought in England* (Urbana: University of Illinois Press, 1949), pp. 24–41, 60–82; H. C. Porter, *Reformation and Reaction in Tudor Cambridge* (Cambridge: Cambridge University Press, 1958), pp. 207–240, 277–287, 317–390, 408–409.

106 C. M. Dent, *Protestant Reformers in Elizabethan Oxford* (Oxford: Oxford University Press, 1983), pp. 74–125, 221–237; Peter Lake, *Moderate Puritans and the Elizabethan Church* (Cambridge: Cambridge University Press, 1982), pp. 1–76, 201–261. Compare the comments on Calvinism at Cambridge in William T. Costello, *The Scholastic Curriculum at Early Seventeenth-Century Cambridge* (Cambridge, Mass.: Harvard University Press, 1958), pp. 108–128. For the definition of Puritanism, see Basil Hall, "Puritanism: The Problem of Definition," in G. J. Cuming, ed., Studies in Church History, II (London: Nelson, 1965), pp. 283–296, esp. p. 290. For the development of a moderate, conformist, Calvinist tradition within the Church of England, see Peter Lake, "Matthew Hutton – a Puritan Bishop?" *History*, 64 (June 1979), 182–204; Margo Todd, "'An Act of Discretion': Evangelical Conformity and the Puritan Dons," *Albion*, 18, 4 (Winter 1986), 581–599; Kenneth Fincham, "Prelacy and Politics: Archbishop Abbot's Defence of Protestant Orthodoxy," *Historical Research*, 61 (February 1988), 36–64; Susan Holland, "Archbishop Abbot and the Problem of 'Puritanism,'" *Historical Journal*, 37, 1 (March 1994), 23–43; and Milton, *Catholic and Reformed*, pp. 377–418.

107 Keith L. Sprunger, *The Learned Doctor William Ames: Dutch Backgrounds of English and American Puritanism* (Urbana: University of Illinois Press, 1972), pp. 52–70.

synod's work, published in Leyden in 1624.[108] It is also evident that the British representatives at Dort were moderate spokesmen for this tradition and in this way represented the views of their king.

The Church of England in the early seventeenth century was not a monolithic institution theologically. King James, who described himself as a "Catholic Christian," encouraged a certain diversity among theologians and ecclesiastical leaders to help him to steer a middle way between the Scylla and Charybdis of Presbyterianism and Roman Catholicism.[109] There was, as recent scholarship has made clear, an anti-Calvinistic group with some prominent adherents. The theological point of view of this anti-Calvinistic group had its origins in the two universities in the 1590s, where protests were made over the predestinarianism then dominant in the chapels and lecture rooms. In the reign of King James, despite the prevailing Calvinist orthodoxy, opposition to Calvinism continued to characterize the theology of some of the Church's clergy, though they were usually discreet about expressing this view publicly.[110] The reaction to the Synod of Dort in England, especially after the accession of James's son Charles in 1625, brought this incipient conflict into the open in a dramatic way.

II

That King James approved of the synod's work may be judged from several pieces of evidence. Bishop Carleton visited the king on his return to England and stood by him during the mid-day meal on May 24, when they talked about the work the British representatives had done. An onlooker commented that the bishop was "much comended for his carriage in the Synode."[111] A few days later the bishop reported to Ambassador Carleton

[108] John Robinson, *A Defence of the Doctrine Propovnded by the Synode at Dort* ([Leyden,] 1624), pp. 9, 59–64, and *passim*.

[109] See Lake, "Calvinism and the English Church," pp. 49–51, and Fincham and Lake, "The Ecclesiastical Policy of King James I", pp. 170–171; James I, *A Premonition to All Most Mightie Monarches, Kings, Free Princes, and States of Christendome*, in the *Political Works of James I*, ed. C. H. McIllwain (Cambridge, Mass.: Harvard University Press, 1918), p. 122.

[110] Tyacke, *Anti-Calvinists*, pp. 29–86, 106–124. Tyacke's interpretation has been vigorously challenged by White, *Predestination, Policy and Polemic*, pp. x–xii, 101–123, 203–214, and *passim*, where White argues that the alleged dichotomy between Calvinists and Anti-Calvinists is too sharp, and that there had not been, in any case, a Calvinist "consensus" in the late Elizabethan and early Stuart Church of England, as Tyacke claims. But Calvinism is, as White himself says, a complex tradition (p. xii), and there were degrees of Calvinist belief on predestination as on other issues. King James was, on the evidence presented here, a moderate Calvinist, as were many, perhaps most, of the leading bishops and theologians in the Church of England of his day. Tyacke's interpretation is supported by Kenneth Fincham, *Prelate as Pastor: The Episcopate of James I* (Oxford: Clarendon Press, 1990), esp. pp. 248–276.

[111] PRO SP 14/109, fol. 100.

that he was being translated to a new see, which turned out to be the better-endowed bishopric of Chichester.[112] As vacancies occurred, the other delegates all received attractive appointments: Davenant became bishop of Salisbury; Ward, Lady Margaret professor at Cambridge; Balcanquhall, master of the Savoy; Goad, prebendary of Winchester Cathedral. Hall, who tried to mediate between those of his countrymen who accepted the synod and those who opposed it, was offered the bishopric of Gloucester, which he modestly declined. He became bishop of Exeter early in the next reign.[113] More significantly, perhaps, James acquiesced in Bishop Carleton's view that the Remonstrants were Pelagians, analogous to the opponents of St. Augustine of Hippo. On July 20, 1619, the bishop wrote to Ambassador Carleton that the king "hathe taken diverse occasions to speak against the Remonstrants as men not tollerable."[114]

Nevertheless the king did not act to give the decrees of Dort official standing in England, nor did he ask the convocations of the Church of England to do so. He was preoccupied in the years immediately following Dort with diplomacy aimed at bringing about a negotiated settlement of the issues which had plunged parts of Europe into an increasingly destructive war. His approach involved seeking the support of Spain in bringing the war to an end while negotiating a possible Anglo-Spanish marriage treaty.[115] Prospects for a marriage between Prince Charles and the Spanish infanta would undoubtedly have been hurt by identifying England more closely with the Protestant churches of Spain's enemies, especially in the Palatinate and the United Provinces of the Netherlands. More important, the king felt that continued discussion of the issues raised at Dort, particularly from the pulpit, would introduce into England some of the contagion which had threatened the Netherlands with a terminal illness. In this connection he sent a letter to Archbishop Abbot in 1622 with attached "Directions concerning preachers," which ordered that preachers refrain from treating "the deep points of predestination, election, reprobation, or of irresistibility of God's grace; but leave those themes to be handled by

[112] Ibid., fols. 117, 255; Norman Egbert McClure, ed., *The Letters of John Chamberlain*, 2 vols. (Philadelphia: American Philosophical Society, 1939), vol. II, pp. 240–241.

[113] On the favorable reception given the returning delegates and the significance of the king's appointments, see Fuller, *The Church-History of Britain*, Bk. X, p. 84. For Hall, see his autobiography in *Works*, ed. Wynter, vol. I, pp. xli–xlv.

[114] PRO SP 14/109, fols. 117–117 verso, 255. Cf. Willson, *King James VI and I*, pp. 399–400.

[115] S. L. Adams, "Foreign Policy and the Parliaments of 1621 and 1624," in Kevin Sharpe, ed., *Faction and Parliament: Essays on Early Stuart History* (Oxford: Oxford University Press, 1978), pp. 149–164; Robert Zaller, "'Interest of State': James I and the Palatinate," *Albion*, 6, 2 (Summer 1974), 144–175. See below, chapter 9.

learned men, and that moderately and modestly."[116] This policy was consistent with his instructions to the British representatives at Dort. Despite James's attempt to limit public discussion, Dort was vigorously discussed soon afterwards in treatises by learned men who were not notably restrained in the way the king had prescribed.

This public discussion was begun in the year following James's Directions by Matthew Kellison, the *nom de plume* for the Catholic publisher John Heigham, who, though he did not mention Dort, took English Protestants to task for maintaining several doctrines upheld by strict Calvinists. These included, in Kellison's words, that "by the fall of Adam, we have all lost our free will"; that "faith once had, cannot be lost"; that "God by his will and inevitable decree, hath ordained from all eternitie, who shall be damned, and who saved"; and that "everyone ought infallibly to assure him selfe of his salvation, and to believe that he is of the number of the predestinat." These propositions, clearly based on the decrees of Dort, he denied on the basis of biblical texts from the King James version. Kellison gave his book the provocative title, *The Gagge of the Reformed Gospell*.[117]

Kellison's views did not long go unchallenged. In 1624, Richard Montagu, who served as rector of Stanford Rivers in Essex, as well as archdeacon of Hereford, canon of Windsor, and chaplain to King James, published an answer entitled *A Gagg for the New Gospell? No, a New Gagg for an Old Goose*. Montagu related that he had been bothered by the activities of certain "Catholique Limitors," who, like the friars of old, had been disrupting the life of his parish. These men had been urging Montagu's parishioners to embrace the Roman faith. One of the visitors had left a copy of Kellison's *Gagge*.[118] In answer to its arguments, Montagu asserted that most of the doctrines attacked in the *Gagge* were not, in fact, doctrines of the Church of England, but were merely private opinions held by certain members of the English Church. He charged that some of these opinions had been "raked together out of the lay-stals of deepest Puritanisme, as much opposing the Church of England, as the Church of Rome."[119] Opinions which he denied as having the status of doctrines of the Church

---

[116] Edward Cardwell, ed., *Documentary Annals of the Reformed Church of England*, 2 vols. (Oxford: Oxford University Press, 1844), vol. II, p. 202.

[117] Matthew Kellison [John Heigham], *The Gagge of the Reformed Gospell, Briefly Discovering the Errors of Our Time, with the Refutation by Express Textes of Their Owne Approoved English Bible*, second edition ([St. Omer: Charles Boscard, 1623]), pp. 65, 76, 77, 79.

[118] Richard Montagu, *A Gagg for the New Gospell? No, A New Gagg for an Old Goose, Who Would Needes Vndertake to Stop All Protestants Mouths for Ever, with 276 Places out of Their Owne English Bibles* (London: Matthew Lownes and William Barret, 1624), "To the Reader." For the controversy which Montagu provoked see Wallace, *Puritans and Predestination*, pp. 84–92.

[119] Montagu, *A New Gagg*, "To the reader."

included several of those cited by Kellison relating to faith, predestination, and assurance.[120]

Montagu subsequently complained that "some Informers" had accused him of being a Papist and an Arminian. The complaint had come, it seems, from two Ipswich ministers, John Yates and Samuel Ward (not the delegate to Dort), who took issue with Montagu's views in his answer to Kellison and with another book of the same year. Among other things Montagu seemed to condone praying to the saints. Their complaint, sent to the House of Commons, was referred to Archbishop Abbot.[121] Montagu's answer, entitled *Appello Caesarem: A Iust Appeale from Two Uniust Informers*, was written as an appeal to King James. By the time it was published in 1625, however, James had died; the book was therefore dedicated to the new king, Charles I.[122]

In his appeal Montagu asserted at once that the charges of being a Papist and an Arminian were groundless, since, "I flatly defied and opposed the One; and God in Heaven knoweth that I never so much as yet read word in the other."[123] He noted that his opponents were willing to be called Calvinists, but he asserted that he did not wish to be accounted "Arminian, Calvinist, or Lutheran . . . but a Christian."[124] He declined to take a stand on the matter of final perseverance, but he noted that according to Article XVI of the Thirty-Nine Articles, human beings could fall from grace. On predestination, he was committed to Article XVII, which did not touch on "Rejection, Reprobation, or Desertion."[125] On this matter he stated: "I must confess my dissent thorough and sincere from the faction of novel-lizing Puritans."[126] God's action in response to the fallen state of human beings was to have compassion on them and, through Christ, to draw those to him "that took hold of mercy, leaving them there that would none of him." "If this bee Arminianisme, *esto*," he said, "I must professe it."[127]

On the Synod of Dort, Montagu asserted: "I derogate nothing from that Synode, nor any particular man in that Synod." In fact, he said, the leader of the British delegation was a friend and acquaintance of long standing who had become "my Reverend and much reverenced Diocesan."[128] Nevertheless Montagu did not accept the synod's conclusions any further than

---

[120] Ibid., pp. 177–183.

[121] Conrad Russell, *Parliaments and English Politics, 1621–1629*, pp. 207, 231–233, 240–241; article on Montagu by W. H. Hutton in *Dictionary of National Biography*, 22 vols. (Oxford: Oxford University Press, 1959–1960), vol. XIII, pp. 713–717.

[122] Montagu, *Appello Caesarem: A Iust Appeale from Two Uniust Informers* (London: Matthew Lownes, 1625), sigs. A₁–A₄ verso.

[123] Ibid., sig. A₃.   [124] Ibid., p. 10.   [125] Ibid., p. 51.   [126] Ibid., p. 60.

[127] Ibid., pp. 64–65.

[128] Ibid., p. 69. Montagu was rector of Petworth, Sussex, as well as Stanford Rivers, Essex. In the former, his diocesan was George Carleton, bishop of Chichester.

they agreed with the Articles of Religion approved by the Church of England. There had long been an attempt to insinuate "Genevanisme into Church and State," which would, if not resisted, ultimately bring an alien discipline as well as doctrine into the Church.[129] On free will, he found no "material difference betweene the Pontificians, at least of better temper, and Our Church."[130] He approved, in fact, part of the decrees of the Council of Trent on this subject.[131] Returning to the Synod of Dort, he asked: "Who bound the Church of England, or Me, a Priest, and a Member of the Church of England, unto defense of all the Decrees or Determinations of that Synod? Hath Prince? or Parliament? or Convocation? Edict? Statute? or Canon? I knowe none."[132]

The new king would soon receive specific advice on this matter. In early August 1625, Bishops John Buckeridge of Rochester, John Howson of Oxford, and William Laud of St. Davids wrote to the duke of Buckingham about the issues Montagu had raised. They urged that clergy of the Church of England not be forced to subscribe to any doctrinal opinions except those approved "in a National Synod and Convocation" of the Church of England, and asked that the king consider the "dangerous consequences" which might follow from submitting "to any other Judge."[133] Concerning the Synod of Dort, the opinions approved there had been treated at Lambeth, under Queen Elizabeth, but the queen had "caused them [the Lambeth Articles] to be suppressed" as inconsistent with "the practice of piety and obedience."[134] The three bishops argued that Dort was "a Synod of that nation, and can be of no authority in any other national church till it be received there by public authority." They hoped that "the Church of England will be well advised, and more than once over, before she admit a foreign Synod, especially of such a church as condemneth her discipline and manner of government."[135] Some months later, after King Charles had asked Lancelot Andrewes, bishop of Winchester, to confer with George Montaigne, bishop of London, Richard Neile, bishop of Durham, and other bishops about Montagu's book, five bishops wrote to the duke of Buckingham that Montagu had not "affirmed anything to be the doctrine of the Church of England, but that which in our opinion is the doctrine of the Church of England, or agreeable thereunto."[136] They urged that in order to keep the peace, the king prohibit all parties in the Church "any further

---

[129] Montagu, *Appello Caesarem*, p. 72.   [130] Ibid., p. 95.   [131] Ibid., pp. 96–105.
[132] Ibid., p. 107.
[133] William Laud, *The Works of the Most Reverend Father in God, William Laud, D.D., Sometime Lord Archbishop of Canterbury*, 7 vols. (Oxford: John Henry Parker, 1857–1860), vol. VI, p. 245.
[134] Ibid., p. 246.   [135] Ibid.
[136] Ibid., p. 249. The five bishops who signed were Andrewes, Montaigne, Neile, Buckeridge, and Laud.

controverting of these questions by public preaching or writing, or any other way."[137] By the spring of 1626, following a conference at York House in February, called by the duke of Buckingham to discuss the issues in dispute, it was evident that the duke had become, as one contemporary observer put it, "the great protector of the Montagutians."[138]

By the time this advice was given, there were numerous books and pamphlets in the press or soon to be submitted for publication dealing with the issues raised by Montagu. The most considerable one was a defense of the synod's decrees by Bishop Carleton, who disagreed in a fundamental way with Montagu's interpretation of the Church's teachings. In his *Examination* of Montagu's "Late Appeale," Carleton contended that, however much the Puritans of Elizabeth's day had disturbed the Church on matters of discipline, "they never mooved any quarrell against the Doctrine of our Church."[139] Carleton argued that Montagu had invented a new term in speaking of "a Puritane doctrine." Though there had been and were differences of opinion in England over discipline, and though the forms of ecclesiastical organization varied in England, Scotland, Geneva, and elsewhere, "yet the Doctrine hath beene hitherto held the same."[140] Montagu's intention, he charged, seemed to be "to make divisions where there were none."[141] As for the disaffection Montagu had expressed toward the Synod of Dort and the efforts of the British representatives there, Carleton affirmed that "they who were imployed in that service, were authorized by his Majesties Commission, directed by his Instructions, and when they returned rendring to his Majesty an account of their imployment, were most graciously approved by his Majesty."[142]

Carleton also joined with his colleagues Balcanquhall, Davenant, Goad, and Ward in 1626 in a *Ioynt Attestation*, in which they avowed both that they had assented at Dort only to what was "conformable to the received Doctrine" of the Church of England, and that they had not compromised in any way the English Church's views on polity.[143] When they had given their approval to the Belgic Confession at the conclusion of the synod, they had

---

[137] Ibid.
[138] Dr. Meddus to Joseph Mead, London, May 22, 1626, in Thomas Birch, ed., *The Court and Times of Charles the First*, 2 vols. (London: Henry Colburn, 1848), vol. I, p. 105. On the York House conference see John Cosin, *Works*, 5 vols. (Oxford: John Henry Parker, 1843–1855), vol. II, pp. 17–81; Tyacke, *Anti-Calvinists*, pp. 164–180; and Roger Lockyer, *Buckingham: The Life and Political Career of George Villiers, First Duke of Buckingham, 1592–1628* (London: Longman, 1981), pp. 306–308.
[139] George Carleton, *An Examination of Those Things Wherein the Author of the Late Appeale Holdeth the Doctrines of the Pelagians and Arminians To Be the Doctrines of the Church of England*, second edition (London: William Turner, 1626), p. 8.
[140] Ibid., pp. 121–122.   [141] Ibid.
[142] Ibid., p. 46.
[143] Carleton, Davenant, Balcanquhall, *et al.*, *A Ioynt Attestation*, pp. 5–7, 25–26.

approved only the doctrinal points, as they had been asked to do. Bishop Carleton had defended episcopacy in the synod as being derived from the practice of the apostles and the primitive Church.[144]

In the same year the parliamentarian Francis Rous argued in his *Testis Veritatis* that the views of James I, the theological tradition of the Church of England, and the weight of opinion among the fathers of the Church Catholic were opposed to Arminianism. This last was grounded in human pride and likely to lead to a revival of popery.[145] John Yates, whose complaint had helped to provoke Montagu's appeal, took issue, in his *Ibis ad Caesarem*, with the charge in his opponent's book that many who conformed to the discipline of the Church of England were Puritans on doctrinal grounds. Yates argued that, on the contrary, it was the doctrine championed by Montagu that threatened to cause a schism in England, as it had done in the Netherlands.[146] Henry Burton, rector of St. Matthew's, Friday Street, London, who had served in the royal household as clerk to both Prince Henry and Prince Charles, complained to the king in his *Plea to an Appeal* that King James's memory had been profaned by Montagu in the latter's treatment of Dort. As for the issues discussed there, he asked: were the learned representatives of the Church who sought to be faithful to their Church's formularies to be accepted as "interpreters of our Church doctrines" or was "singular Maister Mountagu" to be so accepted?[147] Other books by Anthony Watson, Daniel Featley, and William Prynne also appeared in 1626 taking issue with Montagu's views.[148]

Charles I, following his father's example, strove to contain the discussion

---

[144] Ibid., pp. 10–12. See also Carleton, *Bp Carletons Testimonie.* The discussion at Dort and afterwards is analyzed in Nijenhuis, "The Controversy between Presbyterianism and Episcopalianism surrounding and during the Synod of Dordrecht," pp. 207–220.

[145] Francis Rous, *Testis Veritatis: The Doctrine of King Iames, Our Late Soueraigne of Famous Memory, of the Church of England, of the Catholicke Chvrch, Plainely Shewed To Bee One in the Points of Praedestination, Free-Will, Certaintie of Saluation, with a Discouery of the Grounds both Naturall and Politicke of Arminianisme* (London: W. I., 1626), pp. 2–6, 21–22, 39–55, 98.

[146] John Yates, *Ibis ad Caesarem: or, A Svbmissive Appearance before Caesar, in Answer to Mr. Mountagues Appeale, in the Points of Arminianisme and Popery, Maintained and Defended by Him, against the Doctrine of the Church of England* (London: R. Mylbourne, 1626), part III, pp. 37–46.

[147] Henry Burton, *A Plea to an Appeale: Trauersed Dialogue Wise* (London: W. I., 1626), sig. P 3, pp. 88–89, 92.

[148] Anthony Wotton, *A Dangerous Plot Discovered: By a Discourse Wherein Is Proved that Mr. Richard Mountagu in His Two Bookes, the One Called A New Gagg, the Other, A Iust Appeale, Laboureth to Bring in the Faith of Rome and Arminius under the Name and Pretence of the Doctrine and Faith of the Church of England* (London: Nicholas Bourne, 1626); Daniel Featley, *Pelagius Redivivus: or, Pelagius Raked Out of the Ashes of Arminius and His Schollers* (London: Robert Mylbourne, 1626); Daniel Featley, *A Second Parallel, Together with a Writ of Error Sued against the Appealer* (London: Robert Milbourne, 1626); William Prynne, *The Perpetuitie of a Regenerate Mans Estate* (London: William Jones, 1626).

in 1626 by issuing a proclamation charging that all his subjects, especially clergymen, refrain from publishing or maintaining any opinions in religion other than such as were "clearly grounded and warranted by the Doctrine and Discipline of the Church of England heretofore published and happily established by authoritie."[149] In 1628 he applied this principle in even more explicit language to the Articles of Religion. His Declaration on the Articles directed that "no man hereafter shall either print, or preach, to draw the Article aside any way, but shall submit to it in the plain and full meaning thereof: and shall not put his own sense or comment to be the meaning of the Article, but shall take it in the literal and grammatical sense."[150] Even in the universities, the discussion was to be severely limited. No one in the universities was to "affix any new sense to any Article" or maintain in disputations, lectures, sermons, or books anything "other than is already established in Convocation with our royal assent."[151]

Meanwhile, however, Arminianism had become a major concern of the House of Commons. In 1625 Montagu was examined in the house on his two books and was censured.[152] Complaints were also raised about him there in 1626 and 1628. Among the points found unsatisfactory in his *Appello Caesarem* was his slighting of the Synod of Dort, "so honored by the [late] King."[153] In June 1628 a remonstrance to King Charles on the subject of religion called attention to "a general fear conceived in your people of secret working and combination to introduce into this kingdom innovation and change"; the house named Richard Neile and William Laud as among those "near about the King that are suspected for Arminians."[154] The members were not placated by the king's about-face in suppressing Montagu's *Appello Caesarem* in January 1629.[155] According to the Resolutions on Religion drawn up by a subcommittee of the House of Commons

---

[149] "A Proclamation for the establishing of the Peace and Quiet of the Church of England," June 14,1626, in James F. Larkin and Paul L. Hughes, eds., *Stuart Royal Proclamations, vol. II: Royal Proclamations of King Charles I, 1625–1646* (Oxford: Clarendon Press, 1983), pp. 90–93. This did not prevent William Prynne from publishing surreptitiously two further books on Arminianism three years later: *The Church of Englands Old Antithesis to New Arminianisme* (London: n.p., 1629) and *God No Imposter nor Deluder: or, An Answer to a Popish and Arminian Cavill* (n.p., 1629).

[150] "The King's Declaration Prefixed to the Articles of Religion," November 1628, in Samuel R. Gardiner, ed., *The Constitutional Documents of the Puritan Revolution, 1625–1660*, third edition (Oxford: Clarendon Press, 1906), p. 76.

[151] Ibid.

[152] Maija Jansson and William B. Bidwell, eds., *Proceedings in Parliament, 1625* (New Haven: Yale University Press, 1987), p. 333.

[153] Ibid., p. 331.

[154] Robert C. Johnson, Mary Frear Keeler, Maija Jansson Cole, and William B. Bidwell, eds., *Proceedings in Parliament, 1628*, 6 vols. (New Haven: Yale University Press, 1977–1983), vol. IV, pp. 311–313.

[155] Larkin and Hughes, *Stuart Royal Proclamations*, vol. II, pp. 218–220.

in February 1629, among the imminent dangers facing the kingdom was: "the subtile and pernicious spreading of the Arminian faction, whereby they have kindled such a fire of division in the very bowel of the State, as if not speedily extinguished, it is sufficient to ruin our Religion, by dividing of us from the Reformed Churches abroad, and amongst ourselves at home; and by casting doubts upon the Religion professed and established, which if faulty or questionable in four or five articles, will be rendered suspicious to unstable minds in all the rest."[156]

These resolutions, expressing anxiety about the future of Protestantism at home and abroad, reflect the alarm felt by members of Parliament as they watched French government forces overcome the Huguenots, just as Austrian and Spanish Habsburg forces had overrun the Palatinate, and Austrian Habsburg forces had overrun Bohemia. The result of these and other military actions had been, the parliamentarians believed, that "the [Protestant] Churches of Germany, France, and other places are in great part already ruined, and the rest in the most weak and miserable condition."[157] The committee saw a close connection between Arminianism and popery in Montagu's books; in the devotional writings of John Cosin, canon of Durham; in the repositioning of the communion table to the east end of many churches; and in the introduction of ceremonies such as standing, bowing, and crossing oneself at certain points in the service. The committee also saw evidence of an ascendancy of Arminianism in the English Church by the elevation of Montagu to a bishopric in 1628 and the advancement of John Buckeridge, John Howson, Richard Neile, and William Laud to positions of greater prominence.[158]

So preoccupied was the Commons with these issues that in the famous

---

[156] Wallace Notestein and Frances Helen Relf, eds., *Commons Debates for 1629* (Minneapolis: University of Minnesota Press, 1921), p. 97. For the parliamentary attention to the issue of Arminianism, see Conrad Russell, "The Parliamentary Career of John Pym, 1621–9," in Peter Clark, Alan G. R. Smith, and Nicholas Tyacke., eds., *The English Commonwealth, 1547–1640: Essays in Politics and Society Presented to Joel Hurstfield* (Leicester: Leicester University Press, 1979), pp. 147–165, and *Parliaments and English Politics, 1621–1629*, pp. 167–168, 231–233, 298–299, 379–384, 404–415, 423–429.

[157] Notestein and Relf, *Commons Debates for 1629*, p. 96. The fear of popery, especially in the context of the Thirty Years' War, is effectively linked with hostility to the party of Montagu by White, "The Rise of Arminianism Reconsidered," pp. 45–54. See also Caroline M. Hibbard, *Charles I and the Popish Plot* (Chapel Hill: University of North Carolina Press, 1983), pp. 6–13, 236–238; and Robin Clifton, "Fear of Popery," in Conrad Russell, ed., *The Origins of the English Civil War* (London: Macmillan, 1973), pp. 144–167. As Alexandra Walsham points out, Arminianism was probably more appealing than strict Calvinism to "church papists," those Roman Catholics who conformed to the established Church. Awareness of this appeal would only have increased the committee's suspicions. See Walsham, *Church Papists: Catholicism, Conformity and Confessional Polemic in Early Modern England* (Woodbridge, Suffolk: Royal Historical Society and Boydell Press, 1993), pp. 97–98, 115.

[158] Notestein and Relf, *Commons Debates for 1629*, p. 100.

Protestation of March 2, 1629, passed after the Speaker of the House had been forcibly held in his chair to prevent him from ending the session, the first item read: "Whosoever shall bring in innovation of Religion, or by favour or countenance, seek to extend or introduce Popery or Arminianism or other opinion disagreeing from the true and orthodox Church, shall be reputed a capital enemy to this Kingdom and Commonwealth."[159] With the monarch and the lower house of Parliament at loggerheads over religion, the established Church bitterly divided, and a European war menacing England and threatening to destroy its allies abroad, the situation strikingly resembled that which had existed in the Netherlands a decade earlier. Charles's dissolution of parliament in 1629, and his personal rule in the 1630s, only temporarily deflected the gathering storm.

The evidence of this decade suggests that the controversy over the Synod of Dort represented a critical turning-point in the development of the early Stuart Church. The formulation of the synod's decrees may be seen as culminating a theological tradition which had become dominant in England over a period of half a century and had made the Church of England a member of a company of churches which was conscious of a common religious heritage. The decrees themselves, especially those concerning the second article, resulted from the close collaboration between representatives of the Church of England and those of the Reformed churches abroad. But the controversy over the synod in England marked the beginning of a period in which a high degree of religious consensus was replaced by greater dissension, leading ultimately to severe dislocations in church, state, and society by the middle of the century. The Synod of Dort was the focus of this growing dissension in the 1620s.

During the controversy over the synod, the term *Arminian*, formerly applied to a theological party in the Netherlands, came to be used in England as the name for a domestic party. Its accuracy as a name for the rising ecclesiastical party of the 1620s and 1630s is still being debated.[160] What is clear is that English Arminianism was a complex phenomenon, consisting of a range of points of view. It was not a theological system of

---

[159] Ibid., pp. 101–102.
[160] Thomas A. Mason, *Serving God and Mammon: William Juxon, 1582–1663, Bishop of London, Lord High Treasurer of England, and Archbishop of Canterbury* (Newark: University of Delaware Press, 1985), pp. 14–15, 51–52, 61–62; Charles Carlton, *Charles I: The Personal Monarch* (London: Routledge & Kegan Paul, 1983), pp. 63–64, 109; Patrick Collinson, *The Religion of Protestants: The Church in English Society, 1559–1625* (Oxford: Clarendon Press, 1982), pp. 18, 79–82, 85; White, "The Rise of Arminianism Reconsidered," pp. 45–53; Schwartz, "Arminianism and the English Parliament, 1624–1629," pp. 41–68; White, *Predestination, Policy and Polemic*, pp. 238–255. White's view that the defenders of Richard Montagu were middle-of-the-road members of the established Church in the 1620s is unconvincing in the light of the hostility generated in Parliament and elsewhere by their activities.

beliefs, as was the case with Arminianism in the Netherlands. English Arminianism had several foci, including the liturgical practices and views associated with John Cosin, the stress on episcopal authority associated with William Laud, and the elaboration of the theory of divine-right monarchy associated with Roger Manwaring.[161] But there was also, from the beginning, a theological element which derived from the work of Richard Montagu. Montagu was not an Arminian in the sense of being a follower of Jacobus Arminius, but he recognized an affinity with the Arminians whose distinctive teachings were condemned at Dort.[162] In a strict theological sense he was at least quasi-Arminian, and the ecclesiastical party of which Laud was the recognized leader in the late 1620s and the 1630s continued to be characterized by a detachment from Calvinism cogently expressed in Montagu's books of 1624 and 1625. Laud himself denied being an Arminian, though he shared with Montagu a deep-seated disaffection for the Calvinism which had long prevailed in the established Church.[163]

III

King James sent British representatives to the Synod of Dort to preserve the unity and stability of the Dutch Republic – a natural ally, though a commercial and maritime rival – and to advance the plans he had long favored for the reunion of the churches. The latter objective has been little noticed with regard to the synod. Its importance, however, can be inferred from his instructions to the representatives he sent to Dort, his messages to them while there, and the actions and statements of the British representatives themselves. The key phrase for understanding James's religious objective was conveyed in Young's letter of February 25, 1619, where Young spoke of the work of the delegates as preparing "for the making up of the rent in our reformatione." The "rent in our reformatione" meant not the threatened rupture among Calvinists but the actual rupture between Calvinists and Lutherans that had occurred during the Reformation of the

---

[161] J. P. Sommerville, *Politics and Ideology in England, 1603–1640* (London: Longman, 1986), pp. 127–131, 222–224; Margaret A. Judson, *The Crisis of the Constitution: An Essay in Constitutional and Political Thought in England, 1603–1645* (New York: Octagon, 1964), pp. 208, 214–217.

[162] Montagu, *Appello Caesarem*, pp. 64–65.

[163] For recent discussions of Archbishop Laud's theology and policies, see Kevin Sharpe, *The Personal Rule of Charles I* (New Haven: Yale University Press, 1992), pp. 275–402; Julian Davies, *The Caroline Captivity of the Church: Charles I and the Remoulding of Anglicanism, 1625–1641* (Oxford: Clarendon Press, 1992), pp. 46–125, and *passim*; Kenneth Fincham, ed., *The Early Stuart Church, 1603–1642* (Stanford: Stanford University Press, 1993); and Milton, *Catholic and Reformed*, esp. pp. 63–92, 310–321, 353–373, 418–447.

sixteenth century. Du Moulin's plan, which James had helped to shape and continued to support, aimed to bring together the Church of England and the Reformed churches on the basis of a common confession. The next step was for those churches to approach the Lutheran churches to seek unity or at least a mutual toleration. The final point in the plan called for the united churches of the Reformation to make a fresh approach to Rome. James saw the Synod of Dort as a way to take an essential step. His sending of representatives was a deliberate move to realize his long-term goal of religious reconciliation. It was the most concrete action he took to fulfill the goal of church unity during his reign in England. Not having du Moulin present at the synod was a serious disadvantage. Du Moulin was dynamic and persuasive and he represented a prestigious member church of the family of Reformed churches. Nevertheless the British representatives devoted themselves to making the decrees at Dort a moderate, not an extreme, statement, especially on the key doctrine of the atonement, and to keeping the door open for future conversations with the Lutherans.

The irony of the Synod of Dort for England was that the British representatives, having worked for moderation at the synod, found themselves charged as extremists by Richard Montagu and other English "Arminians" – a term which, as we have seen, had a less precise theological meaning than in the Netherlands. Montagu and other members of his party received patronage and support from the king. Not only did James see no problem in having a degree of theological diversity in the Church of England, but he found the English Arminians more congenial than the strict Calvinists in the period when he was seeking the support of Spain in his foreign policy and the hand of the Spanish infanta for his son. The Arminians were less zealous about conducting an aggressively Protestant policy on the continent than those with views like Archbishop Abbot and many of the members of Parliament. James must have been surprised to see the furore provoked by Montagu's writings and perhaps by the contents of the writings themselves. Almost certainly he would have worked more adroitly and effectively than Charles did in dealing with the controversy between the defenders and the opponents of Dort in the later 1620s.

James saw the Synod of Dort as an opportunity both to restore peace and stability to the United Provinces of the Netherlands and to advance his project of bringing the churches of Europe closer together. Unfortunately the controversy over the synod that erupted at the end of his reign helped to cause an ominous rift within the English Church and nation. The role played by the British delegates at Dort deserves more attention than it has received. The delegates ably represented the Church of England and the moderate Calvinist tradition in English life and culture which had developed since the mid-sixteenth century. The performance of the British delegates at the synod in shaping its decrees and their defense of the synod's work afterwards were that tradition's finest hour. The British delegates were concerned in their deliberations at Dort to stress theological continuity, consistency, and antiquity, in accordance with the teachings and practices of the Church of England. But they were also concerned to further cordial relations between the English Church and foreign Protestant churches, both Calvinist and Lutheran. Like King James, they wanted to find a basis for a religious peace, not only in the Netherlands but elsewhere in Europe. With the king's encouragement they made a major contribution to the synod by insisting that Christ's atoning sacrifice was sufficient for all of humanity.

9

Outbreak of the Thirty Years' War

Despite King James's efforts to prevent it, war broke out in Europe in 1618 and lasted with varying degrees of intensity until 1648. This was the most destructive war in early modern European history, devastating much of the Holy Roman Empire as well as causing considerable loss of life and property in the Netherlands, Italy, France, and Spain. The war also brought dramatic changes in the standing of many of the European states, hastening the decline of Spain and leading to the dominance of France.[1] James could not have foreseen the consequences of the war or its length and complexity, but he sensed the momentous character of the Bohemian revolution, especially when it came to involve his son-in-law, the elector of the Palatinate. Like his fellow princes James was well aware of the timetable

---

[1] The idea that the series of conflicts between 1618 and 1648 constituted a single "Thirty Years' War" goes back to the time of the Peace of Westphalia in 1648. The idea makes most sense when applied to Germany, where fighting was continuous. From the point of view of nations outside Germany, the generation of war inevitably looks more episodic. For Spain and France, the struggle lasted beyond 1648 to the Peace of the Pyrenees in 1659 and can be seen as the continuation of the wars between France and Spain of 1494–1559 and of the last phases of the French religious wars of 1562–1598. See S. H. Steinberg, *The 'Thirty Years War' and the Conflict for European Hegemony, 1600–1660* (London: Edward Arnold, 1966), pp. v–vi, 1–28; Geoffrey Parker, *The Thirty Years' War* (London: Routledge & Kegan Paul, 1984), pp. xiii–xvi, 215–226; Myron P. Gutmann, "The Origins of the Thirty Years' War," *Journal of Interdisciplinary History*, 18, 4 (Spring 1988), 749–770; N. M. Sutherland, "The Origins of the Thirty Years War and the Structure of European Politics," *English Historical Review*, 107 (July 1992), 587–625. Parker's *The Thirty Years' War*, written in collaboration with nine other historians, is the best overall study in English. But three older studies are still valuable: C. V. Wedgwood, *The Thirty Years War* (London: Jonathan Cape, 1938), especially for central Europe; Georges Pagès, *The Thirty Years War, 1618–1648* (New York: Harper & Row, 1970 – French original, 1939), for France; and J. V. Polišenský, *The Thirty Years War*, trans. Robert Evans (London: Batsford, 1971 – Czech original, 1970), for Bohemia and eastern Europe. For the crucially important role played by Spain, see J. H. Elliott, *The Count-Duke of Olivares: The Statesman in an Age of Decline* (New Haven: Yale University Press, 1986), and John Lynch, *The Hispanic World in Crisis and Change, 1598–1700* (Oxford: Blackwell, 1992), pp. 84–172, the third edition of his *Spain under the Habsburgs, vol. II: Spain and America, 1598–1700*, first published in 1969. Other more specialized works are noted below.

provided by the approaching end of the Twelve Years' Truce between Spain and the United Provinces of the Netherlands. He made concerted efforts to resolve the immediate issues early in the war – efforts which provoked vigorous opposition at home – hoping to forestall a longer and more complicated conflict, fueled by religious passions. In an age of religious partisanship, he sought, as a key part of his efforts at pacification, to bridge the religious chasm which divided Europe.[2]

As 1618 began James had reason to think that the prospects for peace in Europe were good, owing in part to the diplomatic efforts of his own government. The second decade of the seventeenth century, like the first, had been fruitful for Jacobean peacemaking. Following his successful peace negotiations with Spain in 1604, he had helped to persuade Spain and the United Provinces to accept a truce in their long war in 1609. When the contested succession in Cleves–Jülich threatened repeatedly to lead to a major war, he worked for a negotiated peace. The settlement of 1614, the Peace of Xanten, by which the territories were divided between the rulers of Brandenburg and Neuburg, did not immediately eliminate all sources of conflict. Both the Archduke Albert of Flanders and Maurice, the prince of Orange, continued to hold territories which they occupied during and after the negotiations.[3] Despite the efforts of James's envoys, the various parties whom they tried to reconcile were reluctant to compromise. James's ambassador, Sir Stephen Lesieur, sent to the Holy Roman emperor and to several German princes in 1612–1613, met difficulties almost everywhere he went. In Vienna, both the Emperor Matthias and his adviser, Bishop

[2] For the extent to which contemporaries viewed the series of conflicts as a religious war, see Robert Bireley, "The Thirty Years' War as Germany's Religious War," in Elizabeth Müller-Luckner, ed., *Krieg und Politik, 1618–1648: Europäische Probleme und Perspektive* (Munich: R. Oldenbourg, 1988), pp. 85–106, and his *Religion and Politics in the Age of the Counterreformation: Emperor Ferdinand II, William Lamormaini, S. J., and the Formation of Imperial Policy* (Chapel Hill: University of North Carolina Press, 1981); Claus-Peter Clasen, *The Palatinate in European History, 1555–1618*, revised edition (Oxford: Blackwell, 1966), pp. 21–32, and *passim*; Michael Roberts, *Gustavus Adolphus: A History of Sweden, 1611–1632*, 2 vols. (London: Longmans, Green, 1953–1958), esp. vol. I, pp. 182–245; and Marvin Arthur Breslow, *A Mirror of England: English Puritan Views of Foreign Nations, 1618–1640* (Cambridge, Mass.: Harvard University Press, 1970). Alexandra Walsham's article "'The Fatall Vesper': Providentialism and Anti-Popery in Late Jacobean London," *Past and Present*, 144 (August 1994), shows how the collapse in 1623 of a building in London in which English Catholics were worshipping was seen by many English Protestants as a dramatic vindication of their cause in the international struggle then under way. For a penetrating analysis of the religious and political developments of the later sixteenth century which divided Europe along ideological lines, see J. H. Elliott, *Europe Divided, 1559–1598* (New York: Harper & Row, 1968).

[3] As Sir Thomas Edmondes reported from Paris on January 9, 1615 each side had accused the other of breaking the treaty by occupying territories in violation of the agreement. A year later, on January 2, 1616, he reported that discussions were under way for the rendering of places in Cleves–Jülich held by the Dutch. PRO SP 78/63, fol. 6, 78/65, fols. 18–18 verso.

Melchior Klesl, resented Lesieur's admonitions on behalf of peace in Cleves–Jülich, while the elector of Saxony was equally reluctant to accept his suggestions about how to settle the conflicting claims of Saxony and Brandenburg in the disputed territories.[4] Nevertheless a German war was averted. In France a revolt by the prince of Condé and leading Huguenots against the regency of Marie de Medici in 1615–1616 led to five months of internal tension and sporadic warfare. Instructed by James and by Sir Ralph Winwood, the secretary of state in London, to help to negotiate a peace in France, the English ambassador, Sir Thomas Edmondes, found the queen mother at first cold to his pleas and the nobles not much more receptive.[5] By January 10, 1616, however, with a negotiated settlement in sight, Edmondes reported that Marie de Medici was "nowe as well satisfied of my proceedings as before she had ben possessed with contrarie opinions thereof."[6] Meanwhile James's envoys had worked successfully to end the War of Kalmar between Denmark and Sweden, rivals for the control of the Baltic Sea.[7] The Peace of Knäred in 1613 was generally favorable to Denmark under James's brother-in-law Christian IV, but it was also welcomed by Gustavus Adolphus, then beginning his reign in Sweden. What is clear from the diplomatic records of this decade is that James was

---

[4] PRO SP 80/2, fols. 263 (Lesieur to King James, March 8, 1613), 272–272 verso (Lake to Lesieur, March 30, 1613), 281 (Lesieur to King James, April 15, 1613), 284–286 verso (Lesieur to King James, May 3, 1613), 297 (Lesieur to King James, June 3, 1613). Concerning the attitude of the elector of Saxony, Lesieur wrote: "for Saxe partly of himself and by the perswasion of his Conseil doth not willingly see that your Majestie or anie other Prince but the Emperor take notice of matters of state in the Empire" (fol. 286 verso). One reason that the elector of Brandenburg was more receptive to James's initiatives than the elector of Saxony was that Brandenburg belonged to the Evangelical Union of States, to which James was allied, while Saxony did not. Klesl's and the Emperor Matthias's suspicions were partly based on their belief that Lesieur had been involved in a plot against Matthias in 1611 during the reign of the Emperor Rudolf II. For Lesieur's mission, see E. A. Beller, "The Negotiations of Sir Stephen Le Sieur, 1584–1613," *English Historical Review*, 40 (January 1925), 22–33.

[5] PRO SP 78/64, fols. 17–20 (Edmondes to Winwood, September 16, 1615), 86–87 verso (Edmondes to Winwood, October 28, 1615), 104–104 verso (Du Moulin to Winwood, November 11, 1615), 173–175 verso (Edmondes to Winwood, December 1, 1615), 181–183 (Edmondes to Winwood, December 10, 1615), 219–221 (Edmondes to Winwood, December 22, 1615); SP 78/65, fols. 1–3 (Edmondes to Winwood, January 1, 1616). The uprising began before the exchange of princesses between France and Spain (Elizabeth of France to be the wife of Philip, the heir to the Spanish throne, Anne of Spain to be the wife of Louis XIII of France) in late October 1615, and was partly aimed at disrupting this dynastic alliance. A truce was agreed to following the intervention of Edmondes, who had won the confidence of the rebellious nobles and the leaders of the Huguenot Assembly, in January 1616.

[6] PRO SP 78/65, fol. 52 verso (Edmondes to Winwood, January 23, 1616).

[7] Roberts, *Gustavus Adolphus: A History of Sweden, 1611–1632*, vol. I, pp. 60–72. The War of Kalmar between Denmark and Sweden, fought over Sound dues levied by the Danes on shipping entering the Baltic Sea and over Swedish expansion in the eastern Baltic, was resolved in 1613 by negotiations conducted by Robert Anstruther, James's representative at Copenhagen, and James Spens, his representative at Stockholm.

a respected figure abroad and that he was served by a remarkably able corps of diplomats.[8]

As a monarch James was the preeminent practitioner of ecumenical politics of his time, a ruler determined to foster close relations between his country and both Protestant and Catholic states abroad. He hoped that his example and his diplomatic initiatives would help to resolve the hostilities which threatened western Christendom with a self-inflicted catastrophe. The outbreak of a war which ultimately lasted thirty years was the greatest challenge in James's lifetime to his irenic and ecumenical policies, and that war proved to be the undoing of much that he had worked for. But at the outset of the major European crisis of the early seventeenth century James's efforts to resolve the issues in dispute came closer to succeeding than most observers have recognized. His peacemaking efforts focused first on the Emperor Ferdinand and Bohemia, then on the Archduchess Isabella and the Palatinate of the Rhine, and finally on King Philip IV and an Anglo-Spanish marriage.

I

In 1618, the year of the Bohemian revolt which was soon to lead to the intervention of outside powers, a panegyric to peace was published in England, celebrating King James's achievements as a conciliator. _The Peace-Maker_, dedicated by James "to all our true-louing and peace-embracing subiects," pointed out that peace, which had formerly been a stranger in England, "is now become a sister, a Deere and Naturall sister."[9] Changing the metaphor, the text likened peace to a dove sent out from the ark "to see if the whole world were not yet couered with the perpetuall deluge of Blood and Enmity." Finding an olive branch in Britain, "heere now it hath remained full Sixteene yeeres."[10] Enlarging upon this theme, the work observed that England and Scotland had been reconciled in "their louing Vnion." Ireland, "that rebellious Outlaw," had been brought to recite the text *Beati Pacifici*. Spain, "that great and long-lasting opposite, betwixt

---

[8] See Maurice Lee, Jr., "The Jacobean Diplomatic Service," *American Historical Review*, 72, 4 (July 1987), 1264–1282.

[9] James I, *The Peace-Maker: or, Great Brittaines Blessing, Fram'd for the Continuance of That Mightie Happiness Wherein This Kingdomme Excells Manie Empires* (London: Thomas Purfoot, 1619) [first published 1618], sig. A3 verso. According to D. Harris Willson, *King James VI and I* (New York: Henry Holt, 1956), the king "probably wrote small portions" of the book, "and Lancelot Andrewes the rest" (p. 271). It has also been attributed to Thomas Middleton, the playwright. My own view is that the book was an effort by James and his literary assistants to generate support for the king's peacemaking efforts, and that James wrote much of it.

[10] James I, *The Peace-Maker*, sig. A4.

whome and England, the Ocean ranne with blood not many yeares before," had shaken hands "in friendly amity." Between Spain and her "with-standing Prouinces" in the Netherlands, "leagues of friendship" had been established. Other disputes had also been happily resolved: Denmark and Sweden, Sweden and Poland, Cleves and Brandenburg.[11] In the light of James's experience, it is not surprising that his first reaction to war in central Europe was to attempt negotiation.[12]

The Bohemian revolt, which erupted in the spring of 1618 over the religious and political policies of the pre-elected king of Bohemia, Ferdinand of Styria, designated as the successor to his cousin Matthias, was a problem which James soon recognized as a major threat to the peace of Europe. The revolt had not only resulted in the defenestration of two leading Habsburg officials, but had ranged Protestant forces against those of the country's Catholic rulers. Since his government's relations with Spain had been close in recent years it was natural that James should discuss a problem involving the Austrians with their politically and militarily powerful Spanish kinsmen

---

[11] Ibid., sigs. B$_1$–B$_1$ verso. See Lee, *James I and Henri IV: An Essay in English Foreign Policy, 1603–1610* (Urbana: University of Illinois Press 1970), pp. 12–13, 17–18, 61–70, 118–142, 175–176.

[12] For James's foreign policy during the years 1618 to 1625, see Charles H. Carter, *The Secret Diplomacy of the Habsburgs, 1598–1625* (New York: Columbia University Press, 1964), esp. pp. 109–133; Robert Zaller, *The Parliament of 1621: A Study in Constitutional Conflict* (Berkeley: University of California Press, 1971), and "'Interest of State': James I and the Palatinate," *Albion*, 6 (1974), pp. 144–175; Robert E. Ruigh, *The Parliament of 1624: Politics and Foreign Policy* (Cambridge, Mass., 1971); Martin J. Havran, *Caroline Courtier: The Life of Lord Cottington* (London: Macmillan, 1973), pp. 51–86; J. V. Polišenský and Frederick Snider, *War and Society in Europe, 1618–1648* (Cambridge: Cambridge University Press, 1978), pp. 59–67, 88–94, 109–112, 163–167; Arthur Wilson White, Jr., "Suspension of Arms: Anglo–Spanish Mediation in the Thirty Years War, 1621–1625," Ph.D. thesis, Tulane University, 1978; Simon L. Adams, "The Road to La Rochelle: English Foreign Policy and the Huguenots, 1610 to 1629," *Proceedings of the Huguenot Society of London*, 22, 5 (1975), 414–429, "Spain or the Netherlands? The Dilemmas of Early Stuart Foreign Policy," in Howard Tomlinson, ed., *Before the English Civil War: Essays on Early Stuart Politics and Government* (London: Macmillan, 1983), pp. 79–101, and "Foreign Policy and the Parliaments of 1621 and 1624," in Kevin Sharpe, ed., *Faction and Parliament: Essays on Early Stuart History* (Oxford: Clarendon Press, 1978), pp. 139–171; Conrad Russell, *Parliaments and English Politics, 1621–1629* (Oxford: Clarendon Press, 1979), pp. 70–203; Roger Lockyer, *Buckingham: The Life and Political Career of George Villiers, First Duke of Buckingham, 1592–1628* (London: Longman, 1981), pp. 76–88, 125–219; Thomas Cogswell, "England and the Spanish Match," in Richard Cust and Ann Hughes, eds., *Conflict in Early Stuart England: Studies in Religion and Politics, 1603–1642* (London: Longman, 1989), pp. 107–133, and *The Blessed Revolution: English Politics and the Coming of War, 1621–1624* (Cambridge: Cambridge University Press, 1989); Maurice Lee, Jr., *Great Britain's Solomon: James VI and I in His Three Kingdoms* (Urbana: University of Illinois Press, 1990), pp. 262–298; and Robert Brenner, *Merchants and Revolution: Commercial Change, Political Conflict, and London's Overseas Traders, 1550–1653* (Princeton: Princeton University Press, 1993), pp. 247–258.

and allies.[13] On September 27, 1618 the English *chargé d'affaires* in Spain, Francis Cottington, wrote to Sir Robert Naunton, secretary of state, that he had recently visited King Philip III at the Escorial palace. There he had acquainted the Spanish king that James was concerned that "those people who had taken armes against the king of Bohemia" had done so for the ostensible purpose of preventing "the execution of a cruell massacre intended against them meerly for theire religion," which was "the same the King my master professeth."[14] James could not in honor and conscience "leave them to be consumed by the sword, if what they pretended and alleadged were true."[15] Yet, "such was his respect to the generall peace and quiet of Cristendom and to the perfect friendship and brotherly amitie" between Philip and himself, that "he was resolved to use his utmost endeavours and to interpose his best credit and autoritie for compounding the difference" between the two parties.[16] A suggestion that such a course would be welcome had already been made by the Spanish king. Letters from Cottington to Sir John Digby and to Sir Thomas Lake, dated August 9, 1618, had stated that Philip would be willing for James to "interpose himself for the accommodating of the busines of Bohemia."[17] This was the origin of the ambitious diplomatic initiative launched by James in the

[13]　Carter, *The Secret Diplomacy of the Habsburgs, 1598–1625*, pp. 47–49 and "Gondomar: Ambassador to James I," *Historical Journal*, 7 (1964), 189–208; Havran, *Caroline Courtier*, pp. 51–60; White, "Suspension of Arms," pp. 1–3, 37–49; Adams, "Spain or the Netherlands?," pp. 88–89, 95–96; Lee, *Great Britain's Solomon*, pp. 264–265. For the composition and activities of the so-called Spanish party, whose influence was in decline in 1618, see Kenneth Morgan Peoples, "The Spanish Faction and the Exercise of Political Power in Jacobean England, 1612–1618," Ph.D. thesis, University of Virginia, 1980. In Bohemia, the rule of the Habsburgs was based on their inheritance of the claims of King Louis Jagellon, who was killed while fighting against the Turks in 1526. But the Diet of Bohemia insisted on its traditional right to elect the king. In order to ensure continuity, the Habsburgs presented the heir to the throne to be elected while his predecessor was still living. Thus, Ferdinand was pre-elected in 1617, while King Matthias was king of Bohemia and Holy Roman emperor. This procedure also gave the pre-elected king a vote in the election of the Holy Roman emperor, since the king of Bohemia was one of the seven electors specified in the Golden Bull of 1356. See Victor S. Mamatey, *Rise of the Habsburg Empire, 1526–1815* (Malabar, Florida: Krieger, 1978), pp. 14, 28–31, 49–51.

[14]　Samuel Rawson Gardiner, ed., *Letters and Other Documents Illustrating the Relations between England and Germany at the Commencement of the Thirty Years' War* (Westminster: Camden Society, 1865), p. 10. A second volume of documents with the same title was published in 1868, also edited by Gardiner and in the same Camden Society series. The two volumes will be distinguished here as vol. I and vol. II. For the circumstances in Bohemia which led to the "defenestration of Prague" on May 23, 1618, when a force led by Heinrich Matthias, Count Thurn, Protector of the Protestants, hurled the two leading members of the regency government, Jaroslav Bořita of Martinic and Vilem Slavata, from an upper floor of the royal palace, see Victor-L. Tapié, *The Rise and Fall of the Habsburg Monarchy*, trans. Stephen Hardman (New York: Praeger, 1971), pp. 54–87; Polišenský, *The Thirty Years War*, pp. 86–99; and Parker, *The Thirty Years' War*, pp. 38–49.

[15]　Gardiner, *Letters and Other Documents*, vol. I, p. 10.
[16]　Ibid.　　[17] Ibid., p. 4.

following year. Recent research suggests that Spain was not simply trying to neutralize a potential supporter of the Bohemians by this suggestion. Within the Spanish Council of State opinion was divided as to whether it was in the interest of Spain to aid the Austrians in their dispute in faraway Bohemia. By September 1618 it had been decided that aid would be granted. But King Philip III also believed that Ferdinand would be wise to make peace by compromise with the Bohemians.[18]

The count of Gondomar, who had represented Spain in England since 1613, returned to Spain for reasons of health in the late summer of 1618, where he was in a position to interpret the actions of the English government to his superiors. On September 30, 1618, the marquis of Buckingham wrote to Gondomar, stating that King James was committed "to do all that he can and that lies in his power" to resolve the Bohemian problem peaceably.[19] On January 14, 1619 Gondomar wrote a *consulta* for his government on the plans which had been developed for this negotiation. "These good offices of the king of England," he wrote, "were owing to his [James's] inclination to peace, and to his expectation of the difficulties into which the Palatine and the Protestants of Germany would bring him," if they were to provoke a wider conflict.[20] It was this desire for peace, said the ambassador, "which has more to do with his good offices than your Majesty's friendship or than the representations made to him by the Count of Gondomar."[21] Gondomar's analysis was accurate. James was worried that the Bohemian conflict would become a general religious war, which might sweep his nation and others into a desperate struggle for survival. Buckingham wrote to Cottington in November 1618 that James was glad that winter was approaching, since this would impede further fighting. James was confident that Philip III would find him as impartial a negotiator as he had been in the Cleves–Jülich dispute.[22] Even before an embassy could be sent to Germany, James was pressured by the Evangelical Union of

---

[18] Peter Brightwell, "The Spanish Origins of the Thirty Years' War," *European Studies Review*, 19 (1979), pp. 409–431. This account corrects that in Bohdan Chudoba, *Spain and the Empire, 1519–1643* (Chicago: University of Chicago Press, 1952), pp. 216–221, which focuses on the militant policies of the Spanish ambassador to the Imperial court, Iñigo Vélez de Guevara, Count of Oñate, and his predecessor, Baltasar de Zúñiga, who had become a leading member of the council in Madrid. Cottington reported to Lake from Madrid on September 26, 1618 that Spain was to support Ferdinand with 500,000 ducats sent from Genoa – "yet on the other side they labour by all wayes possible to compound it [the quarrel in Bohemia] by all faire meanes, as that which eles is likely to cost them many millions." Gardiner, *Letters and Other Documents*, vol. I, p. 12. Spain had long had an interest in Bohemian affairs and had even insisted on Philip III's claim to the Bohemian throne in the five years before Ferdinand's election. See Magdalena S. Sánchez, "A House Divided: Spain, Austria, and the Bohemian and Hungarian Successions," *Sixteenth Century Journal*, 25, 4 (1994), 887–903.

[19] Gardiner, *Letters and Other Documents*, vol. I, p. 13.

[20] Ibid., p. 30.   [21] Ibid.   [22] Ibid., p. 25.

States to back the Bohemian rebels. In January 1619 Christoph von Dohna, a member of a politically prominent family in the Palatinate, negotiated a renewal of the defensive alliance between the Union and England which had first been agreed to in 1612.[23] Soon the representatives of several European states were in England seeking men and supplies. By late spring, the escalation of military activity in central Europe had brought in Silesia and Moravia on the side of Bohemia, as well as Spain on the side of Austria; intensive fighting had broken out around Vienna itself. Moravia, Silesia, and Upper and Lower Lusatia joined Bohemia in a *Confederatio bohemica* of states rebelling against the Austrian Habsburgs. Upper and Lower Austria were also in revolt. Meanwhile, Ferdinand officially succeeded the Emperor Matthias as king of Bohemia upon the emperor's death in March.[24]

With the chances for peace rapidly diminishing, a large embassy was organized and sent to the continent. Under the leadership of the privy councillor James Hay, Viscount Doncaster, the mission consisted of 150 persons and required two ships to cross the Channel.[25] As early as February 19, 1619, it was reported from London that Doncaster was "to goe Embassador to the princes of Germany, and soe to Bohemia."[26] Not until April 14 did Doncaster receive his instructions from James at Royston. Preparations for the journey had been time-consuming, but the main reasons for the delay resulted from Queen Anne's death on March 1; James's own illness, which provoked fears that his death was near; and the death of the Emperor Matthias, which necessitated a reassessment of the political situation in Germany. The king's directions to Doncaster were that he should seek a cessation of hostilities in Bohemia and an eventual settlement, based on a recognition by the Bohemians of Ferdinand's

---

[23] Samuel R. Gardiner, *History of England from the Accession of James I. to the Outbreak of the Civil War, 1603–1642*, 10 vols. (London: Longmans, Green, 1883–1884), vol. III, pp. 285–286; Gardiner, *Letters and Other Documents*, vol. I, pp. 41–42 (Dutch Commissioners to the States-General, February 2/12, 1619; Naunton to Carleton, February 4, 1619). See also, for Palatine foreign policy at this time, Clasen, *The Palatinate in European History, 1555–1618*, pp. 21–24, and Elmar Weiss, *Die Unterstützung Friedrichs V. von der Pfalz durch Jakob I. und Karl I. von England im Dreissigjährigen Krieg (1618–1632)* (Stuttgart: W. Kohlhammer, 1966), pp. 4–10.

[24] Tapié, *The Rise and Fall of the Habsburg Monarchy*, pp. 87–88; Parker, *The Thirty Years' War*, pp. 49–51. For the eastern frontier, see J. V. Polišenský, "Bohemia, the Turk and the Christian Commonwealth (1462–1620)," *Byzantinoslavica*, 14 (1953), 82–108.

[25] For Doncaster's embassy, see Edward McCabe, "England's Foreign Policy in 1619: Lord Doncaster's Embassy to the Princes of Germany," *Mitteilungen des Instituts für Österreichische Geschichtsforschung*, 58 (1950), 457–477; Roy E. Schreiber, *The First Carlisle: Sir James Hay, First Earl of Carlisle as Courtier, Diplomat and Entrepreneur, 1580–1636* (Philadelphia: American Philosophical Society, 1984), pp. 22–32; and Gardiner, *Letters and Other Documents*, vol. I, pp. 45–209, vol. II, pp. 1–109.

[26] Gardiner, *Letters and Other Documents*, vol. I, p. 45 (Sir Thomas Wynn to Sir Dudley Carleton, February 19, 1619).

authority as king, the exclusion of Jesuits from political affairs there, the restoration of the religious freedom formerly enjoyed by the Protestants, and the return to political office of those Protestants who had been expelled.[27] James must have felt confident that his advice would be heeded. Juan de Ciriza, secretary of the Council of State in Spain, had written to Cottington on January 22, 1619 that Philip III was pleased that James was willing to work for the public peace in Bohemia, and he pledged the assistance of the Spanish ambassador in Vienna, Iñigo Vélez de Guevara y Tassis, Count of Oñate, in accordance with the understanding and friendship between the kings of England and Spain.[28] James believed that his ambassador would therefore be well received by Ferdinand as well as by the Bohemians. He counted also on the support of his resident ambassadors in France, Flanders, the United Provinces, Spain, and Savoy, as well as on Sir Henry Wotton, who was returning from Venice.

Doncaster's itinerary after his landing at Calais in early May 1619 took him to many of the major centers of political power in areas threatened by war. In Brussels, the Archduke Albert, the brother of Ferdinand, welcomed Doncaster and gave him a letter to Ferdinand supporting the proposal for a cessation of arms.[29] In Heidelberg, the Elector Frederick, however, spoke more of war than of peace, especially of his intention to provide for the defense of the Upper Palatinate, a separate part of his state which bordered on Bohemia as well as Bavaria. He persuaded Doncaster to ask James to send aid to the Palatinate.[30] In early July, after Doncaster had written to the elector of Saxony and visited the duke of Bavaria to ask for their support, he finally intercepted Ferdinand at Salzburg, where the Habsburg ruler had stopped on his way to Frankfurt for the forthcoming meeting of the Imperial Diet. Doncaster was surprised to find Ferdinand cool towards James's message. After Doncaster had offered his master's "interposition" and his own service in mediating a peace between Ferdinand and his subjects in Bohemia, Ferdinand responded "that he thought his Ma[ty] of Great Brittayne was not well informed how the Bohemians his subjects had behaved themselves toward him."[31] Pressed by Doncaster about whether he accepted James's offer to mediate, Ferdinand replied that a counselor of his would respond for him. The counselor's message was not encouraging. He said that Ferdinand had tried negotiations and had found the Bohemians determined to draw the Austrians, Moravians, and others into rebellion

---

[27] Ibid., pp. 69–74. [28] Ibid., p. 37.
[29] Ibid., pp. 102–103 (Doncaster to Naunton, May 30, 1619), 128 (Doncaster to the count of Oñate, June 19, 1619).
[30] Ibid., pp. 118–127 (Doncaster to James, June 18, 1619, Doncaster to Buckingham, June 18, 1619, Frederick V to Doncaster, June 19, 1619).
[31] Ibid., p. 159 (Doncaster to Naunton, July 9, 1619). See also pp. 135–138 (Doncaster to Naunton, June 19, 1619), 144–148 (Doncaster to Naunton, July 2, 1619).

with them.[32] As for James's offer of help, he said that Ferdinand had received similar offers from other rulers and had decided to refer the matter to four German princes – the electors of Mainz, the Palatinate, and Saxony, and the duke of Bavaria – and that to withdraw it from them would only lead to confusion.[33] One circumstance which had changed, as Doncaster reported at the beginning of his letter, was that the Habsburg forces were no longer on the defensive. The forces of Ernst, the count of Mansfeld, fighting for the Bohemians, had been badly beaten by those of the Imperial commander, Charles Bonaventure, the count of Bucquoy, in June. Since then, Doncaster wrote, Bucquoy's troops had "burned above fifty townes and villages, putting the people, without regard of sexe or age, to the sword."[34]

When he finally met the Spanish ambassador, the count of Oñate, in Frankfurt, on July 26, Doncaster received an equally unsatisfactory response. Oñate made no excuse for Ferdinand's not taking up James's offer to mediate. Doncaster asked him bluntly "why my master's intervention had beene so earnestly intreated by his master, if it could not now be accepted?"[35] Oñate replied evasively that Ferdinand could not ignore the four German princes, three of them electors, but would turn to James in the end. Doncaster then pressed him for an assurance "of a present cessation of armes, upon usuall and reasonable conditions, and then of a treaty to ensue, with persons, time, and place appoynted for it."[36] Doncaster was eager to have such an assurance so that he could offer it to the Bohemians and then return before the Frankfurt Diet was over. On August 3 an answer came from Ferdinand in a letter conveying the same discouraging message that Doncaster had received at Salzburg. The next day Oñate provided his interpretation. The ambassador said that, now that Ferdinand had invested so much in an army and that the army had gained the upper hand, the only solution was for the Bohemians to sue for peace or face destruction by the sword.[37] About the same time Doncaster heard from William Norreys, whom he had sent to Bohemia to communicate with the Protestant leaders. They evidently resented Doncaster's not coming in person and declared that they were ready to sacrifice everything for "the liberty of their religion and country."[38] On August 28, 1619 Ferdinand was elected Holy Roman

---

[32] Ibid., p. 160.   [33] Ibid.

[34] Ibid., p. 157. Doncaster had reported Bucquoy's victory over Mansfeld at Budweis on June 29, 1619 (p. 141).

[35] Ibid., p. 189 (Doncaster to Naunton, August 7, 1619).

[36] Ibid., p. 191.

[37] Ibid., pp. 181–182, 192–194.

[38] Ibid., pp. 196–197; see also pp. 165–167. Also McCabe, "England's Foreign Policy in 1619: Lord Doncaster's Embassy to the Princes of Germany," pp. 473–476.

emperor, as Ferdinand II, in Frankfurt. Two days before, by a remarkable coincidence, Frederick of the Palatinate was elected king of Bohemia by the Diet in Prague, where the pre-elected Ferdinand was declared deposed. Frederick, believing that delay would only jeopardize the Bohemian cause, decided at the end of September to accept the crown.[39]

Frederick's election as king of Bohemia in August 1619 put James in a position which became steadily more difficult. In order to maintain credit with the Spanish court, where discussions were going on not only about ending the war but about linking Spain and England in a marriage treaty, the English government felt it necessary to show that Doncaster had had nothing to do with Frederick's election as king. This was demonstrated to Sir Walter Aston by Doncaster, Digby, and Naunton in mid-January 1620, before Aston left to become the resident ambassador at Madrid. Digby had already sent assurances to the English representative in Madrid to be conveyed to the Spanish government.[40] James had advised Frederick against accepting the crown when it was offered. Even when the new monarch, together with James's daughter Elizabeth, had taken up residence in Prague, James continued to ask for evidence that the monarchy of Bohemia was elective and that the Diet which had deposed Ferdinand and elected Frederick had acted legally and constitutionally. He reportedly told Frederick's emissary "that he did not hear without displeasure of the introduction by the people of the practice of dethroning kings and princes."[41] But the Rhenish Palatinate was another matter, and James was insistent that this territory, threatened by Spanish troops, should remain in Frederick's possession. On September 25, 1620, however, Elizabeth asserted in a letter to Buckingham from Prague that the Spanish general Spínola "hath taken three towns of the King's [Frederick's] in the Lower Palatinat: two of them are my jointur: he will, if he can, take all that countree." She urged Buckingham to "move his Majestie now to shew himself a loving father to us, and not suffer his children's inheritance to be taken away."[42] In a

[39] Gardiner, *Letters and Other Documents*, vol. II, p. 48 (Doncaster to Naunton, September 27, 1619, old style). Following new instructions issued in September 1619, Doncaster went to Vienna to congratulate Ferdinand on his accession as Holy Roman emperor and then returned to England by way of the United Provinces, where he gave an account of his mission before the States-General in December (pp. 57–58, 80–81, 108–109).

[40] Samuel R. Gardiner, ed., *The Fortescue Papers, Consisting Chiefly of Letters Relating to State Affairs, Collected by John Packer* (Westminster: Camden Society, 1871), p. 114 (Naunton to Buckingham, January 13, 1620); Gardiner, *Letters and Other Documents*, vol. II, p. 59 (Digby to Cottington, September [no day given] 1619), pp. 120–123 (instructions for Aston, January 5, 1620).

[41] Gardiner, *Letters and Other Documents*, vol. II, p. 148 (Girolamo Lando to the doge of Venice, January 30, 1620). For other conversations on this subject, see pp. 90, 141, 165, 174, 177.

[42] Gardiner, *The Fortescue Papers*, p. 138.

postscript, she added: "tell the King that the enemie will more regard his blowes then his wordes."[43]

Louis XIII of France, like James, wanted a peaceful settlement of the conflict in Germany, though for somewhat different reasons. The French king could hardly take Ferdinand's side in the conflict without strengthening the house of Austria, France's traditional adversary. On the other hand, as king of the largest Catholic country, Louis was reluctant to back Frederick and to risk seeing Protestantism triumph in Bohemia and much of south-eastern Germany. The way out of these dilemmas was to negotiate a peaceful settlement, a project which the French government resolved to undertake towards the end of 1619. On December 14 Sir Edward Herbert, the English ambassador at Paris, reported that the French government was short of money and feared "an universall warre."[44] Rather than yield to the entreaties of the count of Fürstenberg, the Imperial ambassador extraordinary, who was seeking aid for Ferdinand, Louis's government resolved to encourage negotiations.[45] There were also important domestic reasons to steer clear of military commitments in Germany. A squabble between Louis's government and a faction headed by the duke of Epernon and Marie de Medici had almost led to civil war in 1619. Louis's project of restoring Roman Catholicism to a dominant position in Béarn, part of Henry IV's ancestral kingdom of Navarre, had been announced in 1617 and was certain to encounter stiff resistance. Civil war in France, requiring whatever military resources Louis XIII had, was a possibility in either situation.[46]

France's subsequent mediation between the forces of the Catholic League and the Evangelical Union in the summer of 1620 had unexpected results. Towards the end of June, French envoys arrived in Ulm, on the River

---

[43] Ibid.

[44] Gardiner, *Letters and Other Documents*, vol. II, p. 105 (Herbert to Naunton, December 14, 1619). Herbert claimed credit for fostering close relations between his "pacific prince" and the French monarchy. This no doubt encouraged the French to seek peaceful ways of resolving the German conflict. See Sidney Lee, ed., *The Autobiography of Edward, Lord Herbert of Cherbury*, second edition (London: Routledge, 1906), pp. 106–107, 113.

[45] Gardiner, *Letters and Other Documents*, vol. II, pp. 112–114 (Herbert to King James, December 31, 1619), 114 (Herbert to Naunton, January 1, 1620), 175 (Herbert to Naunton, February 18, 1620). When a French embassy to Germany was formed, its mission was "to mediate a cessation of armes," to be followed by a Diet, at which the French would help to achieve a settlement. See pp. 180–181 (Herbert to Naunton, February 20, 1620). For a detailed treatment of this subject, see Victor-L. Tapié, *La politique étrangère de la France et le début de la Guerre de Trente Ans (1616–1621)* (Paris: Leroux, 1934), pp. 338–629.

[46] Victor–L. Tapié, *France in the Age of Louis XIII and Richelieu*, trans. D. M. Lockie (Cambridge: Cambridge University Press, 1984), pp. 69, 95, 106–108, 117. In December 1620, the Reformed Churches of France and Béarn appealed to James for diplomatic and military assistance in face of the violent persecution they were suffering. See London, Lambeth Palace Library, Gibson MS. 941/177, fols. 1–2.

Danube between Württemberg and Bavaria, just before the armies of the two alliances converged on the city. Charles of Valois, duke of Angoulême, prevented a battle by getting the two sides to retire in opposite directions – the Protestant forces to the Palatinate and the Catholic forces to Austria. From the French point of view Germany had been, at least temporarily, neutralized, with the two armies sent back to defensive positions.[47] But in fact the army of the Catholic League could now join the Imperial army for an attack on Bohemia, which was carried out early in November. At an elevation outside Prague called the White Mountain, Frederick's forces were routed on November 8, 1620, forcing him to flee the country.[48] Ferdinand was thus able not only to reestablish control over Bohemia but to begin a process which, in a few years, made the monarchy there securely hereditary in the Habsburg family, largely stamped out Protestantism, and substituted pro-Imperial and Roman Catholic landowners for many of the Protestant burgers and nobility.[49] As a result the Habsburgs, France's traditional enemies, were in a significantly stronger position. Louis's peacemaking, like James's, had had anything but the desired effect.

II

The autumn of 1620 had brought such disasters to Frederick and Elizabeth that James was forced to make preparations for a more militant policy. Not only had Spanish troops invaded the Rhenish Palatinate in force, but the army assembled by his son-in-law, the elector of the Palatinate, had been decisively defeated in Bohemia, sending the derisively styled "Winter King" and his queen into exile. Money raised in England by subscription was soon on its way to Heidelberg to assist the elector. James evidently felt that he could do nothing other than call a Parliament to advise him and to provide the means to defend the Palatinate of the Rhine against attack.[50] In his opening speech to Parliament on January 30, 1621, the king approached

[47] Tapié, *France in the Age of Louis XIII and Richelieu*, pp. 113–114; Pagés, *The Thirty Years War*, pp. 70–71. Angoulême went on to Vienna after negotiating the Treaty of Ulm on July 3, hoping to restore peace with the help of the emperor. But the duke found Ferdinand determined to subjugate the rebels in Bohemia.

[48] See Polišenský, *The Thirty Years War*, pp. 110–115, for a discussion of why the battle turned out as it did and of the immediate consequences. See also Polišenský and Snider, *War and Society in Europe, 1618–1648*, pp. 62–65. For the participation of English and Scottish volunteers in the forces committed to Frederick, see J. V. Polišenský, "'Gallants to Bohemia,'" *Slavonic and East European Review*, 25 (April 1947), 391–404.

[49] Tapié, *France in the Age of Louis XIII and Richelieu*, p. 114; Polišenský and Snider, *War and Society in Europe, 1618–1648*, pp. 202–216.

[50] Zaller, *The Parliament of 1621: A Study in Constitutional Conflict*, pp. 6–36. For events in central Europe, see Polišenský, *The Thirty Years War*, pp. 98–132. Sir Albert Morton, James's envoy, arrived in Heidelberg with funds in late 1620. Lambeth Palace Library, Gibson MS. 930/118, fols. 1–1 verso.

this subject with evident regret. In the eighteen years he had been in England, he said, the country had been at peace, and he considered it a privilege "that you should live quietly under yor vines and fig trees reapinge the frutes of yor owne labours."[51] Now, however, "the miserable and torne estate of Christendome, wch none that hath an honest heart can looke on wth out a weepinge eye" urgently required attention.[52] He had not been the cause of this state of affairs; instead, he had attempted to forestall it by Lord Doncaster's mission, which had cost him £30,000. Now that the Rhenish Palatinate itself was in danger of falling, despite James's efforts to preserve it, he needed a speedy grant of supply.

James did not, however, give up his search for peace by negotiation. The return of the count of Gondomar to England in March 1620 had provided an appropriate occasion for resuming talks aimed at a marriage between Prince Charles and the Infanta Maria, a matter which was being seriously discussed before the Spanish ambassador's departure in the summer of 1618.[53] Now, however, the match had an even larger political significance. If a firm Anglo-Spanish alliance were concluded by this means, then the two nations might be able to work out a just and lasting settlement in the Palatinate, where their interests overlapped. The marriage negotiations were watched carefully by Rome and by papal nuncios in Brussels and Madrid, in the hope that the results would ameliorate conditions for Roman Catholics in England. Rome's insistence that papal permission would be required for such a marriage meant that a speedy conclusion was not likely.[54] In the meantime James had developed another, more direct strategy for dealing with the crisis on the continent.

John, now baron, Digby was a man of long political experience at home and abroad, and he had played a major part in earlier negotiations for a Spanish marriage.[55] James evidently hoped that, with these discussions again under way with the Spanish government, Digby could bring the contenders in Germany at least to a truce, after which a permanent peace could be made with the help of the rulers of Austria and Spain. Once again, then, an English embassy was prepared for a tour of the European capitals. Digby went on a preliminary visit to Brussels, where, in early March 1621, he prevailed upon the Archduke Albert to recommend a truce in the

---

[51] Folger MS. Z. e. 1 (15): Historical Papers of the Time of James I, fol. 2. For a shorter version of this speech, see John Rushworth, *Historical Collections*, 7 vols. (London: George Thomason, 1659–1701), vol. I, pp. 21–23.

[52] Folger MS. Z. e. 1 (15), fol. 2 verso.

[53] Gardiner, *History of England*, vol. III, pp. 37–71, 338, 377.

[54] Rome, Vatican Secret Archives, Fondo Borghese, ser. II, vol. 103: Reports from the nuncio in Flanders (May 16, 1620), fols. 54–54 verso; Fondo Borghese, ser. I, vol. 827 bis: instructions to the nuncio in Spain (April 5, 1621), fols. 95–96.

[55] Zaller, "'Interest of State,'" p. 155; see below in the present chapter.

Palatinate to the Spanish government in Madrid and to General Spínola. With the Twelve Years' Truce between Spain and the United Provinces due to expire in April the archduke would be glad, it seems, to have the general nearer at hand for the defense of the Spanish Netherlands. No sooner had Digby's initial task been successfully accomplished, however, than Spain suddenly became a less predictable ally. Philip III died at the end of March, leaving as his successor a sixteen-year-old son, Philip IV, whose intentions were still little known.[56]

Other diplomatic missions were aimed at supporting Digby's project. Sir Edward Villiers was sent in January and again in September to persuade Frederick to accept James's strategy of seeking the security of the Palatinate in return for Frederick's submission to the emperor and his abandoning any further claim to Bohemia.[57] Sir George Chaworth, who was sent to express James's condolences to the Archduchess Isabella for the Archduke Albert's death in mid-July, used the occasion to urge her to support a cessation of hostilities in the Palatinate.[58]

Digby's embassy, a large company with appropriate trappings to signify the importance its sponsors accorded to it, crossed the English Channel at the end of May 1621.[59] The king's instructions spelled out an ambitious assignment. Digby was to persuade the emperor to restore the Palatinate to its rightful rulers, in return for which James would see that Frederick gave up any further pretensions to Bohemia and that he submitted to the authority of the emperor in a manner appropriate to his own birth and rank.[60] The ambassador was to add expressions of amity towards the house of Austria, with whom a closer bond would soon be forged when the proposed marriage was agreed upon. In the event the emperor turned a deaf ear, he was to be told that the dispossession of the king of England's children was a matter that could only lead to "an immortall and irreconcile-able quarrell" between that king and the emperor, and that other lawful means would have to be found to right this wrong.[61] The same message and the same resolution were to be used in dealing with Spain, if the mission to Austria was not a success.[62] Frederick himself, under the Ban of the Empire, deserted by the Evangelical Union, which by this time had been effectively dissolved, and forced to live on the charity of the Dutch at The Hague,

---

[56] Gardiner, *History of England*, vol. IV, pp. 186–190; J. H. Elliott, *Imperial Spain, 1469–1716* (London: Edward Arnold, 1963), pp. 318–319, and *The Count-Duke of Olivares*, pp. 3–6, 40–45.

[57] Zaller, "'Interest of State,'" p. 153; White, "Suspension of Arms," pp. 133, 149–159, 242–243, 285.

[58] White, "Suspension of Arms," pp. 221, 264–266.

[59] Zaller, "'Interest of State,'" p. 160.

[60] PRO SP 80/4, fols. 22–23 (instructions for Digby, May 23, 1621).

[61] Ibid., fol. 24.   [62] Ibid., fols. 24–24 verso.

played almost no part in these negotiations on his behalf. A bitter anecdote from one of his supporters in the next year stated that "while the king of Denmark would reinforce Frederick's non-existent army with a thousand pickled herrings, and the Hollanders would raise ten thousand butter-boxes, the English contingent would be a hundred thousand ambassadors."[63]

Though the final results hardly reflected the fact, Digby seems to have carried out his diplomatic responsibilities in a vigorous and skilful way. He obtained the truce he sought in the Palatinate from Archduke Albert and Spínola and met with members of Frederick's council to inform them of his mission and obtain their support. Having reached Vienna at the beginning of July 1621, he presented his proposals to the Emperor Ferdinand.[64] It was soon clear that the emperor and his councilors were seriously interested in them. Not only did war threaten to erupt on the northern, eastern, and western borders of Bohemia, giving the emperor every reason to look for a peaceful settlement, but Madrid and Brussels were in favor of a pacification, as was the Protestant but pro-Imperial state of Saxony. For the better part of two months Digby strove to work out with the emperor and other diplomatic envoys a plan whereby the temporary cessation of arms in the Rhenish or Lower Palatinate might be converted into a secure peace. The difficulties were formidable. Not only did the count of Mansfeld, the commander of an army committed to defending the Upper Palatinate, show no sign of wanting to give up his military operations; but his master Frederick, as aggressive as ever, exhibited a new interest in his former kingdom of Bohemia. On the other side Maximilian of Bavaria was ambitious to annex the Upper Palatinate to his own dominions and take Frederick's electoral title for himself. By the time Digby left Vienna, on September 5, 1621, a settlement still seemed possible, especially as the emperor had written to Brussels to urge that fighting be suspended as long as practicable.[65] Digby returned to England by way of Munich, Heidelberg, and Brussels, where he sought to give effect to the agreement tentatively reached in Vienna.[66] Before he arrived home, however, Maximilian of Bavaria had invaded the Upper Palatinate with Ferdinand's approval, and

[63] McCabe, "England's Foreign Policy," p. 473.

[64] PRO SP 84/4, fols. 37–38 (Digby to Carleton, May 28, 1621), 54 (Digby to Spínola, June 4, 1621), 63–63 verso (Digby to Calvert, June 14, 1621), 65–65 verso (Digby to Archduke Albert, June 18, 1621), 82–82 verso (Digby to Calvert, June 19, 1621), fols. 89–89 verso (Digby to Calvert, June 24, 1621), 97–97 verso (Digby to Calvert, July 2, 1621). See also Zaller, "'Interest of State,'" pp. 161–162; Gardiner, *History of England*, vol. IV, pp. 204–205.

[65] Gardiner, *History of England*, vol. IV pp. 206–216.

[66] James asked that word be sent to Spínola in September that Frederick had had no hand in Mansfeld's movements, a matter on which Digby would soon be able to give assurance; he asked Spínola to continue to work for a settlement. See Gardiner, *The Fortescue Papers*, pp. 160–161.

Mansfeld had fled to the Lower Palatinate, where Spanish troops controlled much of the country.

By the time Digby reached England at the end of October, the collapse of the Rhenish Palatinate seemed so imminent that James called Parliament back into session almost at once to vote supplies for its defense. On November 21, the second day of the session, Digby described the negotiations he had conducted. The emperor, he said, had been "very inclinable" to a peaceful settlement, though discussions had been slow to reach a conclusion.[67] Ferdinand had been expecting a meeting of the Diet and had had many consultations with the German princes. Maximilian, on the other hand, had been peremptory and rude, declaring that the only peace he sought had already been attained by his bribing Mansfeld to stay out of the way. The Archduchess Isabella at Brussels "seemed to understand by the Empo^r lres [letters] that he did rather prepare for warre than peace, & would geve noe direct answer untill she heard from the K. of Spayne."[68] The Spanish king, though he had so far maintained his neutrality, "hathe at this instant five Armyes in motion."[69] With an enlargement of the war likely, "it will not misbecome the wisdome of this state to feare the worst."[70] In the debates which followed in the House of Commons, speakers ranged widely over the subject of foreign policy, many of them returning to the threat posed by Spain and its alleged agents, the English Roman Catholics. On the subject of the match with Spain there was a widespread feeling that such a move was inappropriate on religious and political grounds, besides being remarkably untimely.[71] James, informed of the drift of the debate while he was staying at Newmarket, showed his anger in a letter delivered to the speaker of the House on December 3. The king accused "some fiery & turbulent spirites" with having meddled "wth matters farre above their capacityes wch tends to the infringing of o^r prerogative royall."[72] Accordingly the House was directed not to deal further with "o^r governm^t or misteryes of state namely o^r Sonnes mariage" nor disparage "the k. of Spayne, and other of o^r frends and allyes."[73]

---

[67] Folger MS. V. b. 303: *Speeches delivered in Parliament and Other Political Documents*, p. 233. The speech is given in a different form in Rushworth, *Historical Collections*, vol. I, p. 39.

[68] Folger MS. V. b. 303, p. 233.   [69] Ibid.   [70] Ibid.

[71] Zaller, *The Parliament of 1621*, pp. 145–156; Conrad Russell, "The Foreign Policy Debate in the House of Commons in 1621," *Historical Journal*, 20 (1977), 289–309; S. L. Adams, "Foreign Policy and the Parliaments of 1621 and 1624," in Kevin Sharpe, ed., *Faction and Parliament: Essays on Early Stuart History* (Oxford: Clarendon Press, 1978), pp. 149, 159–164; Conrad Russell, *Parliaments and English Politics, 1621–1629* (Oxford: Clarendon Press, 1979), pp. 124–126, 129–132.

[72] Folger MS. V. b. 303, p. 233.

[73] Ibid. The letter is to be found with some differences in Rushworth, *Historical Collections*, vol. I, p. 43.

The House of Commons, in failing to heed this advice, showed just how far its members were from the king on the fundamental principles to be followed in the international crisis. Where the king wanted money to defend the Palatinate of the Rhine, while pressing on with his diplomatic measures to secure a settlement, many in the Commons – to judge by its debates and the petition of December 3, to which the king took exception even before it was passed – wanted a war with Spain, a Protestant marriage for the prince, and stronger enforcement of the laws against Roman Catholic recusants.[74] Unfortunately for the effective implementation of any policy this session of Parliament ended in a vociferous struggle over parliamentary privilege, especially the exercise of free speech.[75] If there is still uncertainty about whether the House had overstepped its constitutional bounds in discussing foreign policy, as the king claimed, it is certainly clear why James reacted strongly to its policy recommendations.[76] By its proceedings the House of Commons threatened to undermine James's entire diplomatic program, followed since the beginning of the Bohemian revolt, which was aimed at reaching an understanding with the Habsburg powers, particularly Spain. This program was not, however, one to which most of James's subjects were likely to be sympathetic, nor was it one he took the trouble to explain in any detail to Parliament.

Meanwhile the truce in the Upper Palatinate had been broken by Mansfeld in July 1621 and by the Emperor Ferdinand and Maximilian of Bavaria in September and October. In the Palatinate of the Rhine, the English commander, Sir Howard Vere, sent to maintain garrisons of English soldiers in cities still loyal to Frederick, also violated the truce by moving troops into the nearby bishopric of Speyer in August. Mansfeld arrived in the Rhineland with his army from the Upper Palatinate in October where he was hotly pursued by Jean 't Serclases, Count of Tilly, and the army of the Catholic League.[77] The Twelve Years' Truce in the Netherlands, which had been temporarily extended, ended in August 1621. Paradoxically the resumption of fighting on these fronts made the prospects for negotiations more promising by the end of the year. Ferdinand was sharply criticized by the elector of Saxony, usually his ally, for not having committed himself to

---

[74] Gardiner, *History of England*, vol. IV, pp. 246–248. Compare Russell, *Parliaments and English Politics, 1621–1629*, pp. 132–138, where it is argued that there were misunderstandings on both sides, making the gap between the Commons and the king look wider than was actually the case.

[75] Zaller, *The Parliament of 1621*, pp. 156–187.

[76] Compare Russell, "The Foreign Policy Debate," pp. 292–299, 309, and Zaller, *The Parliament of 1621*, pp. 156–159. See also Russell, *Parliaments and English Politics, 1621–1629*, pp. 139–142.

[77] White, "Suspension of Arms," pp. 184, 215–219, 232, 249–260; Parker, *The Thirty Years' War*, pp. 63–65.

James's peace initiative. Moreover Ferdinand's unpredictable foe, Bethlen Gabor, had shown the weakness of the Imperial position in Hungary, and Ferdinand's perennial enemy, the Ottoman Turks, were threatening him from further east. Hoping to reduce tensions in both east and west, Ferdinand became much more receptive to James's conciliatory efforts. His change of heart opened the way for James's major effort at negotiating a settlement in the following year.[78]

The Brussels Conference, which convened in May and lasted until the end of September 1622, was the focus of European diplomacy and hopes for a lasting peace. Initially proposed by James in a letter of late November 1621 to the Archduchess Isabella, it had the official support of the emperor and the Spanish king. Its aim was to achieve a truce or suspension of arms which would be followed by a general peace agreement.[79] James was represented by Sir Richard Weston, who had already been sent along with Sir Edward Conway on a mission to negotiate peace in Brussels, in Heidelberg, and in Prague from July to November 1620.[80] The emperor was represented by Count George Louis von Schwarzenberg, an Austrian nobleman called away from his country estates, while the archduchess was represented by Peter Pecquius, chancellor of Brabant and a privy councillor, and Ferdinand de Boisschot, baron of Saventhem, a former envoy to France. The Spanish resident ambassador in Brussels, Alonso de la Cueva, marquis of Bedmar, was closely involved in the negotiations. After some delay, Frederick and Mansfeld sent representatives in early June. William Trumbull, James's resident agent in Brussels, assisted Weston. Digby was meanwhile on his way to Madrid in May to further the negotiations for an Anglo-Spanish marriage.[81]

Preparations for the Brussels Conference began in January 1622, when prospects for a cessation of the fighting and for peace negotiations looked favorable in Vienna, Madrid, and London, as well as Brussels. But the conference did not convene for many months because of preliminary diplomatic activities. By the time the conference actually started, there had already been more fighting in Germany than had occurred in the area since the end of 1620. Frederick, who had returned to the Lower Palatinate in the spring of 1622, suffered severe defeats in late April and early May at the hands of the army led by the count of Tilly. By the end of June the Imperialists controlled everything in the Palatinate of the Rhine except for

---

[78] White, "Suspension of Arms," pp. 283–288, 295–300; Polišenský, *The Thirty Years War*, pp. 148–152. Ferdinand and Bethlen Gabor signed a truce on January 6, 1622 at Nikolsburg.

[79] White, "Suspension of Arms," pp. 293–294; Parker, *The Thirty Years' War*, p. 65.

[80] White, "Suspension of Arms," pp. 116–130, 149.

[81] Ibid., pp. 309–311, 319, 336, 339, 340, 357, 359; Carter, *The Secret Diplomacy of the Habsburgs*, pp. 86, 217, 283, 285.

the cities of Mannheim, Frankenthal, and Heidelberg. The emperor now seemed inclined to accept the verdict of the battlefield, and he had a different plan to settle the remaining issues more quickly – namely at an Imperial Diet.[82]

In the early weeks of the conference, discussions turned inevitably but unprofitably to commissions – that is, to the questions of whether Isabella was fully authorized and empowered by the emperor to order a cessation of fighting by Imperial troops and whether Frederick was fully committed to abide by the pacific policies of James and his diplomatic representatives.[83] Despite their best efforts, neither James and his agents nor Isabella and hers could effect a lasting cessation of the fighting. As the events of the summer showed, Frederick and his allies did not hesitate to ignore James's orders and entreaties. Tilly acted largely independently of Isabella. Tilly's immediate commander was Maximilian of Bavaria, head of the Catholic League, who was determined to subjugate the Palatinate. Frederick's allies, Mansfeld and Christian of Brunswick, were basically entrepreneurs, using their armies for plunder and for securing military and political advantages for themselves. Even Córdoba, the Spanish commander, did not always heed Isabella. He had standing orders from Spain to coordinate his military actions with those of Tilly.[84] Mediation over the issue of the Palatinate began in earnest in early June when Arthur, baron Chichester of Belfast, whom James had sent as his envoy to Frederick, was named at the conference to try to persuade both sides to accept a three-week truce. Though Frederick and Mansfeld agreed, Tilly and Córdoba did not. After a renewed discussion of commissions and powers in Brussels, agreement was reached that places in the Palatinate held by one party or another would be retained for the present, no new fortifications would be built, and commerce in the area would be allowed to resume. Despite assurances given to Weston by Bedmar, Tilly moved to besiege Heidelberg, leading Weston to make the strongest protest to Isabella. James was similarly outraged.[85] A new proposal from Isabella's government in late July was that the three cities in the Palatinate which remained outside Imperial control be put under her protection – a solution Weston considered tantamount to surrendering them. Mansfeld and his troops subsequently fought their way through Isabella's territories to join the Dutch, leading her to denounce Weston for having done nothing to prevent this invasion.[86] In early September Weston pressed Isabella for a cessation of Tilly's siege of

---

[82] White, "Suspension of Arms," pp. 330–334, 337, 387–390.
[83] Ibid., pp. 340–348.
[84] Ibid., pp. 335, 353–355, 365–366, 391, 404, 419, 424, 449, 453–456; Wedgwood, *The Thirty Years War*, pp. 149–152; Parker, *The Thirty Years' War*, p. 65.
[85] White, "Suspension of Arms," pp. 404–408, 412.
[86] Ibid., pp. 419–420, 432–438, 445–448, 451; Wedgwood, *The Thirty Years War*, pp. 154–157.

Heidelberg, but she was powerless to stop it. Tilly stormed the city, completing his conquest on September 19. Shortly after receiving the news of the city's fall, Weston took leave of Isabella to return to London, and the Brussels Conference came to an end.[87]

James now employed a dramatic and unprecedented stratagem aimed at damping down the fires of conflict before they became a conflagration. In early July 1622, a congregation of cardinals, assembled by Pope Gregory XV, had delivered its judgement on the proposed articles of the Anglo-Spanish marriage treaty. George Gage, the English envoy in Rome, was told that, in order to be acceptable, these articles would have to provide for the free exercise of the Roman Catholic faith in England. The statement went on to suggest that James – whose conversion had long been desired – declare himself a Roman Catholic, since his studies must have convinced him that the Roman faith alone was that true and ancient one in which he could find salvation.[88]

James chose to answer this message with a letter of his own to Pope Gregory. Dated the last day of September 1622 at Hampton Court, the letter began with the traditional papal title, "Most Holy Father" – a usage most Protestants would have deplored.[89] After noting what must have seemed anomalous, "that one differing from you in point of Religion should now first salute you with o[r] Letter," James declared his deep concern over "these calamitous discords and bloodshedds w[ch] for these late yeares by-past have so miserably rent the Christian world."[90] It had been his "care and dayly solicitude to stoppe the course of these growing evils," especially since "wee all worshipp the same most blessed Trinity, nor hope for salvation by any other meanes then by the blood and meritts of one Lord and Saviour Christ Jesus."[91] Having stated his desire for peace and the ecumenical creed on which, at least in part, that desire was based, James sought to move the pope "to putt yo[r] hand to so pious a worke and so wourthy of a Christian Prince" – namely, ending the war.[92] He went on to express the hope that, once these storms had ceased, "the harts of those Princes, whom it any way concernes, may bee reunited in a firme and unchangeable friendshippe."[93] James did not doubt "but yo[r] Holinesse out of yo[r] singular piety, and for the creditt and authority that you have with the parties, both may and will further this worke in an extraordinary

---

[87] White, "Suspension of Arms," pp. 449–457, 463–472. Weston had been instructed by James to issue an ultimatum to Isabella that unless a cessation was ordered in the Palatinate, he would leave Brussels. Tilly ignored Isabella's pleas for an end to the siege.

[88] Gardiner, *History of England*, vol. IV, pp. 351–352.

[89] Oxford, Bodl., Tanner MS. 73, fol. 236. A Latin version is in the same collection: Tanner MS. 73, fol. 235. See also Gardiner, *History of England*, vol. IV, p. 372.

[90] Bodleian Tanner MS. 73, fol. 236.

[91] Ibid.   [92] Ibid.   [93] Ibid.

manner."[94] There was, he declared, no way in which one could act more deservingly of "the state of Christendome."[95] There is something profoundly moving about the spectacle of the leading Protestant prince, in a time of sectarian bitterness and turmoil, writing to the spiritual leader of the Roman Catholic Church to establish their common religious and political concerns and to ask the pope to use his influence to help stop the fighting. The letter, however, seems not to have had any immediate effect. The papacy was heavily committed, morally and materially, to the Catholic League and to Ferdinand II, who were seen as struggling to defend and strengthen Roman Catholicism in Germany.[96]

III

Despite these setbacks, James still had an important card to play in his continuing campaign to achieve peace in Europe: the Spanish match.[97]

[94] Ibid., fols. 236–236 verso.   [95] Ibid., fol. 236 verso.

[96] Parker, *The Thirty Years' War*, pp. 59, 92; Bireley, *Religion and Politics in the Age of the Counterreformation*, p. 43. The generous subsidies provided by Gregory XV to Ferdinand and Maximilian dried up under Urban VIII, who was elected pope in August 1623.

[97] The Spanish match has been neglected by historians since Gardiner's magisterial but hostile account in his *History of England*, vol. III, pp. 37–71, vol. IV, pp. 325–411, and vol. V, pp. 1–214, an interpretation followed closely by Willson, *King James VI and I*, pp. 362–372, 412–423, and *passim*. Several recent books and articles, however, throw additional light on the king's project. For the role played by Buckingham, see Lockyer, *Buckingham*, pp. 125–176. For that played by Olivares, see Elliott, *The Count-Duke of Olivares*, pp. 203–222. The popular and parliamentary opposition to the match is illustrated and analyzed by Thomas Cogswell, "Crown, Parliament and War, 1623–25," Ph.D. thesis, Washington University, 1983, pp. 1–105; *The Blessed Revolution*, pp. 6–53; and "England and the Spanish Match." For Cottington, who served as Prince Charles's Secretary, see Havran, *Caroline Courtier*, pp. 67–86 and *passim*. See also, for a detailed study of the diplomatic, political, and military context of the marriage negotiations, White, "Suspension of Arms." For broader issues in English foreign policy, see Adams, "Spain or the Netherlands? The Dilemmas of Early Stuart Foreign Policy" and "Foreign Policy and the Parliaments of 1621 and 1624." For the perspectives of English Catholics, see the account in [Hugh Tootell,] *Dodd's Church History of England*, ed. M. A. Tierney, 5 vols. (London: Dolman, 1839–1843), vol. V, pp. 115–149. Printed sources, on the other hand, abound. See Edward Hyde, Earl of Clarendon, *State Papers*, ed. R. Scrope and T. Monkhouse, 3 vols. (Oxford: Clarendon Press, 1767–1786), vol. I, pp. 3–14, appendix, pp. i–xxxi; Philip Yorke, earl of Hardwicke, ed., *Miscellaneous State Papers from 1501 to 1726*, 2 vols. (London: W. Strahan and T. Cadell, 1778), vol. I, pp. 399–522; [Tootell,] *Dodd's Church History of England*, ed. Tierney, vol. V, pp. cclxxxi–ccclxi; Gardiner, *Letters and Other Documents*, vol. II, pp. 120–131, *Narrative of the Spanish Marriage Treaty* [by Francisco de Jesus] (London: Camden Society, 1869), and "The Earl of Bristol's Defence of His Negotiations in Spain," in *The Camden Miscellany*, vol. VI (London: Camden Society, 1871), pp. i–xxxix, 1–56; Antonio Ballesteros y Beretta, ed., *Correspondencia oficial de Don Diego Sarmiento de Acuña, Conde de Gondomar*, 4 vols. (Madrid: Archives, 1936–1945), vol. I, pp. 131–147, 226–230, 277–286, 304–306, 316–357, and *passim*; and Albert J. Loomie, ed., *Spain and the Jacobean Catholics*, 2 vols. (London: Catholic Record Society, 1973–78), vol. II.

Negotiations for an Anglo-Spanish marriage went back to the Anglo-Spanish treaty in 1604. They began again in earnest soon after Diego Sarmiento de Acuña, later made count of Gondomar, arrived in England as resident ambassador in 1613. Sir John Digby, as he then was, had gone to Spain in 1611 on an unsuccessful mission to negotiate a marriage between Prince Henry and the Infanta Anna. After Henry's unexpected death, Digby went back to discuss a marriage between Prince Charles and the Infanta Maria. By 1614, Spain, England, and the papacy were all in consultation about such a marriage.[98] Sarmiento favored the match partly because he genuinely wanted closer relations between the two countries and partly because a marriage settlement could ease the stringent conditions under which his co-religionists, the English Roman Catholics, lived.[99] James found the prospect of a Spanish match attractive because it would provide a close link between his kingdom and the most powerful nation and dynasty in Europe. A substantial Spanish dowry would also help to solve his government's perennial financial problems. Equally important, the match would support his long-term project of achieving a stable peace and a significant measure of religious reconciliation in Europe. An Anglo-Spanish alliance could give him the kind of leverage with leading Roman Catholic states which he already had with Protestant states as head of the Evangelical Union, a long-time ally of the United Provinces of the Netherlands, the brother-in-law of the king of Denmark, and the *de facto* protector of the Huguenots in France. He would thus be in a strong position to move forward with his irenic diplomacy in a time of increasing political and religious tensions in Europe.

By February 1617, a *junta* or council of theologians had been appointed in Madrid to advise the Spanish Council of State about the proposed marriage, and in March of that year a committee of seven council members and advisers had been appointed by James to consider the state of the marriage negotiations.[100] According to Sarmiento, as reported to the Spanish Council of State, every member of James's committee "voted that there was nowhere in the world a marriage or alliance more suitable for the

[98] Loomie, *Spain and the Jacobean Catholics*, vol. II, pp. 42–43 (Council of State, Spain, to Philip III, August 30, 1614); Gardiner, *Narrative of the Spanish Marriage Treaty*, pp. 105–106, 110–121; [Tootell,] *Dodd's Church History of England*, ed. Tierney, vol. V, p. 115.

[99] The traditional view of Sarmiento/Gondomar as sly, unscrupulous, and conniving, and one who exercised undue influence over James, has been effectively challenged by Carter, "Gondomar: Ambassador to James I," 189–208, and *The Secret Diplomacy of the Habsburgs, 1598–1625*, pp. 120–133, 233–244; and Loomie, *Spain and the Jacobean Catholics*, vol. II, pp. xiv–xxii.

[100] Loomie, *Spain and the Jacobean Catholics*, vol. II, pp. 79–81 (Luis de Aliaga to Philip III, February 27, 1617), 83–84 (Council of State to Philip III, April 29, 1617); Gardiner, *Narrative of the Spanish Marriage Treaty*, pp. 298–305.

prince and accordingly it was proper and honorable to seek it publicly by sending a person for this purpose."[101] Accordingly Digby, who had returned from Spain in February 1616, having established that there was serious interest in the match in Spain, was sent back to Madrid as ambassador extraordinary in August 1617.[102] Digby was told in his instructions that the articles on religion given to him in a private conference on his visit to Spain in 1616, which James had examined and responded to, would be an appropriate basis for an agreement.[103] Digby found the Spanish court publicly receptive to the marriage proposal. As he wrote on October 8, 1617 from Burgos: "Whatsoever hath beene written by the duke of Lerma or spoken by the Spanish Ambassador in England unto yor Ma^{ty}, is by this king fully avowed, . . . this king professeth an extraordinary desire to make the Match, and is resolved of it, yf [the] poynt of Religion can be accommodated."[104] Sarmiento – now made count of Gondomar – also understood from sources in Spain that there was "a very strong approval of the marriage" there.[105] In January 1618 Digby reported that the Spanish king was prepared to work hard to obtain the necessary dispensation from the pope.[106] By March Digby could report that he had "now almost brought all my businesses to an issue."[107] He knew that Gondomar had been recalled to Spain, but he reported that the Spanish king had agreed that his ambassador could stay in London until Digby arrived back, so that "all thinges may be agreed on, before his Coming away."[108] Digby, back in London, reported in June that he had "performed al those particulars wch he [King James] gave me in charge to deliver unto the Spanish Ambassador."[109] By the time the revolt in Bohemia broke out, the marriage negotiations between England and Spain were well advanced, though obtaining a dispensation for the marriage from Rome promised to be a serious obstacle.

---

[101] Loomie, *Spain and the Jacobean Catholics*, vol. II, p. 84. The committee members appointed by James were Thomas Howard, earl of Suffolk; William Herbert, earl of Pembroke; Thomas Howard, earl of Arundel; George Villiers, earl of Buckingham; Thomas Erskine, viscount Fenton; Sir Thomas Lake; and Digby.

[102] PRO SP 94/22, fol. 16 (Cottington to Winwood, March 13, 1616). Digby's summary of his assigned task in Spain includes this item: "To propound the marriage of the Prince of Wales, with the Infanta of Spayne . . . but not to treate till there was an Assurance, that the proposition in generall, was very acceptable unto those of Spayne, and likewise, that they would undertake, the cleering of such difficulties, as on their side might arise, of the pcuring a dispensation, from the Pope, by reason of the difference in poynt of Religion" (fol. 102).

[103] PRO SP 94/22, fols. 120–120 verso (instructions for Digby, April 4, 1617).

[104] Ibid., fol. 196 (Digby to King James, October 8, 1617).

[105] Loomie, *Spain and the Jacobean Catholics*, vol. II, p. 99 (Gondomar to Philip III, December 30, 1617).

[106] PRO SP 94/23, fol. 4 (Digby to King James, January 15, 1618).

[107] Ibid., fol. 12 (Digby to Lake, March 7, 1618).

[108] Ibid., fol. 16 (Digby to Lake, March 10, 1618).

[109] Ibid., fol. 45 (Digby to Lake, June 16, 1618).

To show his good intentions towards his Roman Catholic subjects – a major concern to Gondomar, to many other Spaniards, and, of course, to the papacy – James took a series of steps to ease their civil disabilities. Before leaving England, Gondomar wrote to Cardinal Bellarmine on July 4 1618: "Because of my intervention this king has granted freedom to all priests who had been imprisoned and condemned to death [,] who number seventy-two."[110] This number included Father William Baldwin, accused of complicity in the Gunpowder Plot, who had been in prison for eight years. Lord Chancellor Bacon, baron Verulam, was instructed by the king to see that the activities of the pursuivants, who ruthlessly searched, ransacked, and frequently destroyed the property of Roman Catholics in their search for priests and incriminating evidence, were investigated and restrained "as soon as possible."[111] Julian Sanchez de Ulloa, the Spanish resident agent after Gondomar's departure, reported on July 30 that "this king has exerted considerable care that the pursuivants be suppressed."[112] On September 24 he wrote to Philip III: "At the moment one can now say that there is no persecution."[113] Gondomar's confessor, Diego de la Fuente, who remained in England, was asked by the Spanish king to report to King James regularly on the progress of the negotiations in Spain. Fuente wrote to Philip III on November 16, 1618 that James would do everything he could and more if, "at the arrival of the count of Gondomar at your Majesty's court, the good news that he longed for might come."[114]

The near-success which James had achieved in the marriage negotiations with Spain in 1618, before the outbreak of war on the continent, was a major reason why he did not give up the prospect of a marriage when war brought disasters for the Bohemian Protestants, the Evangelical Union, and his daughter and son-in-law in the Palatinate. By 1622, both the young Philip IV and James were strongly attracted to the marriage as a way of dealing with pressing international problems. Spain, now stretched to support the Emperor Ferdinand's military operations in central Europe as well as its own operations in northern Italy, the Rhineland, and the Netherlands, feared a war at sea with England. James, anxious to recover the Palatinate for Elizabeth and Frederick but aware that England lacked the military power on land to take it by force, saw the negotiations for a marriage as the best means of persuading Spain to relinquish territory which Spanish soldiers, under Imperial ensigns, had invaded and occupied.

Meanwhile the focus of attention in negotiations for the match shifted to Rome, where envoys from both Spain and England converged in 1621.

[110] Loomie, *Spain and the Jacobean Catholics*, vol. II, p. 109.
[111] Ibid., p. 111 (Verulam to Gondomar, July 22, 1618).
[112] Ibid., p. 113 (Sanchez de Ulloa to Philip III, July 30, 1618).
[113] Ibid., p. 115.   [114] Ibid., p. 119.

Diego de la Fuente, Gondomar's confessor, who had won the confidence of King James during his long stay in England, went to Rome in January 1621 to assist the Spanish ambassador, the duke of Alburquerque, in soliciting for the dispensation. After Paul V's death in late January 1621, Fuente's credentials were renewed for the new pope, Gregory XV, as soon as the result of the papal election was known. In March, Philip III died, but his son decided shortly after his accession to continue the negotiations.[115] In May James sent George Gage, an English Catholic, to speak on behalf of his fellow Catholics in England in favor of the dispensation. He was joined in November by John Bennett, an English Roman Catholic priest, who reported on the steps taken by James to relieve the Catholics' suffering.[116] The prospects for papal approval of the marriage were much enhanced by the advent of Gregory XV's pontificate.

The Spanish match reached its climactic stage in 1622–1623. Digby set out from London to travel to Madrid in May 1622, the same month in which Carlos Coloma, ambassador extraordinary representing Spain – though he had long lived in the Spanish Netherlands – journeyed to London. After Coloma and Gondomar had conferred, Gondomar returned to Madrid to assist in the negotiations; he retained the title of resident ambassador in England.[117] Digby, who had energetically pursued James's conciliatory policies in Germany in 1621, was, as Weston had been at the Brussels Conference, concerned that the remaining English enclaves in the Palatinate be preserved from the Imperialist army under Tilly. In Madrid Digby complained in September that the letters sent by Philip IV to Isabella urging her to order Tilly to raise the siege of Heidelberg had not been strong enough. The *junta* of the Spanish Council that considered Digby's protest agreed and urged Isabella to order Tilly to cease hostilities, lest the Brussels Conference be disrupted. By the time the message arrived in Brussels, Heidelberg had fallen, Weston had departed, and the conference was over.[118] Digby, who was made earl of Bristol in September 1622, evidently concluded, as King James had, that the best remaining hope for the restitution of the Palatinate and a general peace was to conclude the marriage negotiations in Madrid as quickly as possible.

Even as the negotiations for peace in Brussels were breaking down, prospects for a papal dispensation for an Anglo-Spanish marriage were improving. George Gage returned to England from Rome late in August

[115] Gardiner, *Narrative of the Spanish Marriage Treaty*, pp. 162–163; Loomie, *Spain and the English Catholics*, p. 144 (Gondomar to Philip III, February 18, 1621).

[116] Gardiner, *Narrative of the Spanish Marriage Treaty*, pp. 164, 169; [Tootell,] *Dodd's Church History of England*, vol. V, pp. 119–124, ccxciii–ccxcv.

[117] White, "Suspension of Arms," pp. 319, 361; Loomie, *Spain and the Jacobean Catholics*, vol. II, pp. xix–xx.

[118] White, "Suspension of Arms," pp. 481–482.

1622, carrying cordial messages from the cardinals who had considered James's negotiations with Spain. In September, after he had had three meetings with James and the prince, Gage informed the cardinals that the king seemed favorable to their requests.[119] Taking a circuitous route back to Rome, Gage journeyed to Paris and then to Madrid, where in November he declared that he was carrying assurances to the pope which would also be certain to give Philip IV satisfaction.[120] Meanwhile, in Rome, Marco Antonio De Dominis, formerly archbishop of Spalato and more recently dean of Windsor in England, had arrived to reaffirm his Roman Catholicism and to cultivate an earlier friendship with Gregory XV. De Dominis made a public declaration of penitence and an abjuration of his errors in leaving the see of Spalato to go to England. When Pope Gregory asked his opinion of the proposed Anglo-Spanish marriage and whether the Holy See should agree to it, De Dominis answered that the conditions should be such as to advance the cause of the Roman Church by securing liberty of conscience for Roman Catholics in England. Such liberty, he said, could certainly be granted by James since the king already allowed liberty "to every kind of [Protestant] sect, however contrary they might be to one another."[121] De Dominis considered it highly anomalous that such Protestant extremists enjoyed religious liberty in England while Roman Catholics, who professed the true and pure religion, were "subjected to discouragement, captivity, and oppression."[122]

In October 1622 the earl of Bristol began a concentrated effort in Madrid to bring the protracted negotiations to a conclusion. He pointed out in a memorandum to Philip IV that it had been five years since the articles concerning religion had been given him in Spain and that James had long ago agreed to them. In early 1621, Diego de la Fuente had been sent to Rome to secure a dispensation. Bristol was astonished that new and impossible things were now being asked of his king.[123] He renewed his diplomatic offensive in November by expressing his and King James's frustration that no progress had been made on the two matters he had been sent to negotiate: the marriage of the prince of Wales and the restitution of the Palatinate.[124] As a result of Bristol's entreaties, supported by the embassy of Endymion Porter, a member of the marquis of Buckingham's household who arrived from England in November, Philip IV wrote a

---

[119] Gardiner, *Narrative of the Spanish Marriage Treaty*, pp. 172–178.
[120] Ibid., pp. 182–184.
[121] Ibid., pp. 185–186 (the quotation is on p. 186).   [122] Ibid., p. 186.
[123] Ibid., p. 179; Gardiner, "The Earl of Bristol's Defence of His Negotiations in Spain," pp. 19–20.
[124] Gardiner, *Narrative of the Spanish Marriage Treaty*, p. 187. James had written to Bristol in October prescribing time limits to the negotiations. Gardiner, "The Earl of Bristol's Defence of His Negotiations in Spain," pp. 22–23.

conciliatory letter to James on December 12. Here he stated that he had sent a message to the pope saying that what James had agreed to concerning the religious articles was considered in Spain to be sufficient and asking that a dispensation for the marriage be granted. While they waited for the dispensation, Philip continued, the temporal articles could be settled. He added that immediately after the dispensation arrived, by March or April at the latest, arrangements could be completed for the infanta's departure for England later that spring.[125] Bristol wrote to James on December 26, 1622 urging that these terms be accepted.[126] Both Bristol and Francisco de Jesus, a Carmelite priest who served as preacher to Philip IV, stated in their accounts that the negotiations had been essentially completed by this date.[127] Bristol added that the remaining details were actually settled in the next few weeks: the dowry to be paid, the person who would accompany the infanta to England, and the date of the marriage ceremony *per verba de praesenti* or by proxy – namely, within twenty days after the arrival of the dispensation.[128]

The news from the Palatinate had been discouraging during the autumn of 1622, but even on this issue Bristol provoked or shamed the Spanish king and his advisers into trying to save the two remaining cities not under Tilly's control – as a preliminary step to a negotiated settlement. After the fall of Heidelberg, Bristol asked the count of Olivares, the rising statesman in the king's inner circle, to see that Tilly was ordered not to attack Mannheim and Frankenthal. Bristol also boldly requested that, if Tilly did not lift his sieges of the two cities, the Spanish general Córdoba be ordered to assist the English commander, Sir Horace Vere, in defending the cities.[129] The *junta* of state on English affairs replied that Philip had already written to Ferdinand, Maximilian of Bavaria, and Isabella to stop Tilly from further sieges. In response to Bristol's urging, the *junta* sent an order on October 29, to Isabella directing her to take the two cities under protection if Tilly did not comply with her order. It added that, if there was any difficulty, the Spanish army was to assist the *English* garrisons under Vere.[130] But the letter reached Brussels just too late to save Mannheim. Vere had surrendered the city to Tilly on November 4. Tilly then marched directly to Frankenthal. Isabella offered to sequester the cities – a solution that James was willing to

---

[125] Gardiner, "The Earl of Bristol's Defence of His Negotiations in Spain," pp. 25–26. Philip had submitted what Bristol had shown him of James's response to Rome to a *junta* of state. The *junta* had decided that James's response was satisfactory and had recommended that Philip seek the necessary dispensation from Rome. Gardiner, *Narrative of the Spanish Marriage Treaty*, pp. 196–197.

[126] Gardiner, "The Earl of Bristol's Defence of His Negotiations in Spain," pp. 26–27.

[127] Ibid., p. 27; Gardiner, *Narrative of the Spanish Marriage Treaty*, p. 197.

[128] Gardiner, "The Earl of Bristol's Defence of His Negotiations in Spain," p. 27.

[129] White, "Suspension of Arms," p. 495.   [130] Ibid., pp. 496–499.

accept – but the archduchess was horrified at the suggestion that she should order military action against the army of the Catholic League. Tilly, in any case, rejected her order to surrender the captured cities, though he reduced his operations before Frankenthal to a blockade.[131] Bristol, however, was reluctant to accept defeat. When he learned of the fall of Mannheim, he demanded that it and Heidelberg be returned to the English and their allies within seventy days. In December Philip wrote to Ferdinand saying that a cessation of fighting in the Palatinate of the Rhine must be agreed to.[132] Though Spain had not, by year's end, provided any concrete help to the beleaguered cities, Bristol had at least obtained an important commitment from Philip IV – namely, that Spain would use force if necessary to resolve the issue of the Palatinate in a way that recognized James's and ultimately Frederick's interests there.[133]

Bristol's courier, Walsingham Gresley, set out for London from Madrid in February 1623 with the results of the latest negotiations in Spain so that James could prepare for the infanta's arrival in England in the spring. As he entered France he encountered two familiar figures claiming, improbably, to be Tom and Jack Smith, merchants from England. They were, in fact, Prince Charles and the marquis of Buckingham, travelling in disguise and in great haste so as to arrive in Madrid unannounced. They opened Gresley's letters and thus apprised themselves of the current state of the negotiations.[134] The autumn visit of Endymion Porter, now on his way back to Spain, had been, in part, a reconnaissance mission to see if it were feasible for James's son along with his favorite to visit the Spanish court in person. Charles and Buckingham intended to complete the negotiations and return home with the infanta shortly. They arrived in Madrid at Bristol's house in the evening of March 7, apparently taking the ambassador completely by surprise. Their journey, which had begun only on February 17, soon after Porter's return to London, seems to have been Charles's idea.[135] When James, deeply upset over the planned journey at the time Buckingham first broached it, asked the opinion of Francis Cottington, who had long experience as the English agent in Madrid, the latter replied sensibly that once the prince was in Spain, Philip and his advisers might raise their

[131] Ibid., pp. 500–508, 511–516. By mid-November, James had accepted in principle the proposal that Isabella sequester for a limited time cities still in English hands (pp. 503, 518–520).
[132] White, "Suspension of Arms," pp. 509–510.
[133] Gardiner, "The Earl of Bristol's Defence of His Negotiations in Spain," pp. 38–39.
[134] Ibid., pp. 27–28; Havran, *Caroline Courtier*, p. 71.
[135] Gardiner, "The Earl of Bristol's Defence of His Negotiations in Spain," p. 28; Gardiner, *Narrative of the Spanish Marriage Treaty*, pp. 202–203; Havran, *Caroline Courtier*, pp. 70–72; Lockyer, *Buckingham*, pp. 135–140. Lockyer cites evidence that as early as May 1622, Charles had told Gondomar that he would, if Gondomar signaled that it would be acceptable, go to Madrid "incognito and only accompanied by two servants" (p. 135).

demands. Despite Buckingham's outrage over the envoy's honest but untactful reply, Cottington returned to Spain as the prince's secretary.[136] The arrival of the prince and the marquis in Madrid was seen by the Spanish government as convincing evidence of the British king's seriousness of purpose in the negotiations and, more important, of the prince's readiness to accept the faith of his intended spouse. There were great demonstrations of joy in Madrid and a new feeling of optimism in Rome in the weeks which followed.[137] The negotiations, which had already been substantially completed before the arrival of Charles and Buckingham, now entered a new phase, marked by rising expectations on the part of the prince's Spanish hosts.

James, who remained deeply concerned about the Palatinate, was determined that the match contribute to a resolution of issues which had long been in contention there. He was, as he wrote to Charles and Buckingham on March 15, 1623, disgusted by the duplicity of the Emperor Ferdinand, who had "thrice broken all his promises to me."[138] Ferdinand had taken steps to resolve the problem of the Palatinate in his own way and in accordance with promises he had made to Maximilian of Bavaria when the latter, with the army of the Catholic League at his command, had come to the emperor's aid in the war in Austria and Bohemia. In January Ferdinand had assembled at Regensburg a *Deputationstag* of princes of the Holy Roman Empire, a kind of mini-Diet, where he told the assembly that he had deprived Frederick of his office of elector and given it to Maximilian.[139] The Spanish and Flemish ambassadors in London, said James, had agreed to the "depositing of Frankendale in the king of Spain and the Archdutchess's hands."[140] If "this business [is to] be brought to a good end," wrote James, "it must now be done by the king of Spain's mediation betwixt the Emperor and me, whom he [the Emperor] hath so far wronged and neglected."[141] Frankenthal was handed over to officers of the Archduchess Isabella in March, pending a general peace conference.[142]

Charles and Buckingham found the Spanish officials "hankering upon a

---

[136] Havran, *Caroline Courtier*, p. 71.
[137] Gardiner, "The Earl of Bristol's Defence of His Negotiations in Spain," pp. 28–29; Gardiner, *Narrative of the Spanish Marriage Treaty*, pp. 206–207, 213; White, "Suspension of Arms," p. 533.
[138] Hardwicke, *Miscellaneous State Papers*, vol. I, p. 404.
[139] White, "Suspension of Arms," pp. 522–523, 536; Parker, *The Thirty Years' War*, p. 67. After considerable debate, the emperor concluded that Maximilian should be confirmed in his possession of the title for his lifetime, thus leaving the long-range future of the Palatinate still unsettled.
[140] Hardwicke, *Miscellaneous State Papers*, vol. I, p. 404.   [141] Ibid.
[142] Parker, *The Thirty Years' War*, pp. 65, 189; Wedgwood, *The Thirty Years War*, pp. 157, 507, 510. Spanish troops were to remain in Frankenthal until 1653.

conversion."[143] As the two of them wrote to James on March 17, their hosts held "that there can be no firm friendship without union in religion."[144] Olivares spoke to Charles of the constancy of the prince's grandmother, Mary Queen of Scots, in her Catholic faith. Philip IV assigned Olivares the responsibility of persuading Buckingham "that it was only right that the Prince should allow himself to listen to information in our Holy Catholic Faith," now that he had, "as it were, entered its gates."[145] To see what such a session would be like, Buckingham volunteered to meet with Olivares, Francisco de Jesus, and James Wadsworth, a Roman Catholic convert, who would serve as interpreter. Charles and Buckingham then met with a group of theologians on April 23. At this meeting the authority of the pope was discussed with reference to Luke 22:31–32, where Jesus said to Simon Peter at the Last Supper: "I have prayed for you that your faith may not fail; and when you have turned again, strengthen your brethren."[146] According to Francisco de Jesus, Charles commented that the text was being misinterpreted and he asked that it be read in French, which both he and Zacharias Boverio de Saluzo, the Capuchin priest who had raised the point, understood. The discussion so roused the ire of Buckingham that, in a show of temper, he withdrew, pulled off his hat and trampled it under foot.[147] There were no further conferences aimed at the prince's conversion.

James had a different strategy in mind: to show the Spaniards how much their Church and the Church of England had in common. On March 17 he wrote to Charles and Buckingham that he had sent two chaplains to Spain: Leonard Mawe, master of Peterhouse, Cambridge, and Matthew Wren, fellow of Pembroke Hall, Cambridge, "together with all stuff and ornaments fit for the service of God."[148] According to the king's directions for conducting services in Spain, issued at Newmarket on March 10, these items included surplices, copes, candlesticks, chalices, and patens. A room set aside for prayer was to be arranged "chappellwise with an altar, frontl, palls, lynnen coverings, [and] demy carppet."[149] The communion was to be celebrated "in due forme," and with oblations from every communicant.[150] In the sermons, there should be "no polemicall preaching to invaigh against them or to censure them but only to confirm the doctrine and tenets of the Church of England by all positive arguments either in fundamentall or

---

[143] Hardwicke, *Miscellaneous State Papers*, vol. I, p. 409.   [144] Ibid.

[145] Gardiner, *Narrative of the Spanish Marriage Treaty*, pp. 207–209 (the quotation is on p. 209).

[146] Ibid., p. 211. The translation I have used here is the Revised Standard Version.

[147] Gardiner, *Narrative of the Spanish Marriage Treaty*, p. 211. The meeting was held in Philip IV's own apartments, but the king declined to be present lest he hear something contrary to the Catholic faith.

[148] Hardwicke, *Miscellaneous State Papers*, vol. I, p. 406.

[149] Loomie, *Spain and the Jacobean Catholics*, vol. II, p. 186.   [150] Ibid.

moral points and especially to apply ourselves to morall lessons to preach CHRIST JESUS CRUCIFIED."[151] Thus, no disputes were to be raised, but if the resident ambassador, Sir Walter Aston, or the prince's secretary, Sir Francis Cottington, should be asked for further information about the English Church, the chaplains were to have suitable books available: the Articles of Religion, the Book of Common Prayer "in severall languages," and James's own religious works in English and Latin.[152] James's instructions, as he wrote to Charles and Buckingham, were that the services should "prove decent, and agreeable to the purity of the primitive church, and yet as near the Roman form as can lawfully be done, for it hath ever been my way to go with the church of Rome *usque ad aras*."[153] Mawe and Wren conducted services in Madrid at the residence of Ambassador Bristol.[154]

Charles and Buckingham came to Spain in the expectation that the arrangements for the marriage would be concluded quickly. They found the members of the Spanish court "by outward shows, as desirous of it [the marriage] as ourselves," as they wrote to James on March 17.[155] James had the same strong desire. He reported to the prince and marquis on April 10 that the fleet was nearly ready and could be sent to bring them home before May 1, if necessary.[156] Both sides were waiting for the papal dispensation. James assured Charles and Buckingham that it was on its way. He wrote to them on March 25 that he had agreed to the religious conditions specified by Spain and that a *consulto* in Rome had recommended that the pope grant the dispensation "for the weal of Christendom."[157]

James had already met the religious commitments demanded of him. In the preceding autumn Bristol had shown Philip IV the paper carried by Gage "containing his master's answer to the demand of His Holiness for a further explanation and extension to be made in some of the articles relating to religion; and also at the reply which he had given on the general point with regard to the common benefit of the Catholics."[158] Philip had submitted this answer to his *junta* of state, which had decided that the answer was satisfactory and recommended that Philip try to obtain the necessary dispensation by the following March or April.[159] In a letter in late

---

[151] Ibid.

[152] Ibid. Loomie notes that the Book of Common Prayer was translated into Spanish and copies sent to Prince Charles in Madrid so that the Spaniards would know what the English liturgy was like (p. 185). Cottington was made a baronet in February 1623.

[153] Hardwicke, *Miscellaneous State Papers*, vol. I, p. 406. *Usque ad aras*, "up to the altars," was to a point just short of the Roman Catholic celebration of the mass.

[154] Gardiner, *Narrative of the Spanish Marriage Treaty*, p. 212. Francisco de Jesus saw as the purpose of these arrangements to show "by these external forms how little, as they say, is the difference between themselves and us" (p. 212).

[155] Hardwicke, *Miscellaneous State Papers*, vol. I, p. 409.

[156] Ibid., p. 414.   [157] Ibid., p. 411.

[158] Gardiner, *Narrative of the Spanish Marriage Treaty*, p. 196.   [159] Ibid., p. 197.

December Philip sent the duke of Alburquerque, his ambassador in Rome, his own recommendation to this effect along with the paper Bristol had given him. James no doubt knew from Gage that this request had been received favorably by the pope and his advisers.[160]

The eagerly awaited dispensation arrived in Madrid on April 24, 1623. Accompanying it, however, was a list of conditions aimed at ensuring that James would fulfill the promises he had made. The papal nuncio at Madrid was given instructions about what he was to insist upon.[161] Charles and Buckingham knew that the dispensation had been granted when they wrote to James on April 22, and they also knew some of the further conditions which it contained: "two years more to the [infanta's supervision of the] education of the children; no other oath to be ministered to the Roman catholic subjects, than that which is given to the Infanta's servants, and that they [the English Roman Catholics] may all have free access to her church."[162] By April 27 they were able to report that the dispensation had arrived and to assure James that "we will not be long before we get forth of this labyrinth, wherein we have been entangled these many years; we beseech your Majesty to be secret in the conditions, and be assured we will yield to nothing, but what you may perform, both with your honour and conscience."[163] On May 11 James acted to hasten the conclusion of negotiations by sending the prince the necessary authorization to negotiate the final treaty.[164]

Charles soon received "a courteous letter" from Gregory XV, as he wrote to his father on June 6.[165] This letter of April 20 commended the prince's desire "to match with the house of Austria," and called upon him to remember the examples of his illustrious ancestors and to return to the ancient faith of the Roman Catholic Church.[166] Charles, in his reply to the pope on June 20, responded to this invitation by expressing eloquently his own and his father's intention of furthering the peace and unity of Christendom. Concerning the examples of his ancestors, Charles wrote that their zeal to make war on behalf of the Christian faith would be matched by his own zeal to make peace:

although it be true that they often adventured and put their estates and lives in danger, for no other reason than the propagation of the christian faith, yet their courage hath not been greater in setting upon the enemies of the cross of Christ with

---

[160] Ibid., pp. 197–201; White, "Suspension of Arms," p. 534. Philip's letter was sent on December 20/30, 1622.

[161] Gardiner, *Narrative of the Spanish Marriage Treaty*, p. 213.

[162] Hardwicke, *Miscellaneous State Papers*, vol. I, p. 414.

[163] Ibid., p. 416.   [164] Ibid., p. 419.   [165] Ibid.

[166] [Tootell,] *Dodd's Church History of England*, vol. V, p. 131.

open war, than shall be my care that peace and unity, which have been of long exiled from the christian commonwealth, may be reduced to a true concord.[167]

This intention, the prince said, had long been that of his father, King James, "for it grieveth him sore to consider the great and cruel misfortunes and slaughter, which have followed the discord of christian princes."[168] Charles accepted, as "most conformable to your holiness's charity and great wisdom," the pope's support of his desire to enter into a "treaty of alliance with the catholic king, by means of marriage with his sister." He added, concerning the infanta's religious faith, that "it is most certain, I would never so earnestly procure to tie myself with the strong bond of marriage unto a person whose religion I could not endure."[169] The prince was "far from plotting anything contrary to the Roman catholic religion."[170] He went on to affirm that Christians shared a common set of beliefs. "Even as we all acknowledge one God in Trinity and Unity, and one Christ crucified," he desired that "we may all profess one and the self-same faith."[171] Charles said that he would "refuse no labour" in order to advance the cause of unity.[172] The prince wrote this letter without consulting his father beforehand.[173] King James's ecumenical and irenic principles had never been expressed more aptly and forcefully.

Negotiations in Madrid were not easy, even though most matters of substance previously under discussion had already been resolved as a result of Bristol's diplomacy in late 1622. A chief reason for the difficult negotiations was that Gregory XV's instructions to his nuncio, Innocenzo De Massimi, were that once the dispensation was in the hands of Philip IV, there should be less difficulty "in obtaining the condition required for putting it into effect, that is to say, public liberty of conscience in England, together with the free and open exercise of the Roman Catholic religion, which should be first approved of by the Privy Council, and afterwards confirmed by the Parliament."[174] These matters were discussed in a series of meetings between Spanish commissioners appointed by the Council of State

---

[167] Ibid., p. 133. For the Latin text of the letter, see vol. V, pp. cccxiv–cccxv, and Hardwicke, *Miscellaneous State Papers*, vol. I, pp. 452–453.

[168] [Tootell,] *Dodd's Church History of England*, vol. V, p. 133.

[169] Ibid.   [170] Ibid.   [171] Ibid., pp. 133–134.   [172] Ibid., p. 134.

[173] Hardwicke, *Miscellaneous State Papers*, vol. I, p. 419. Compare Gordon Albion, *Charles I and the Court of Rome: A Study in 17th Century Diplomacy* (Louvain: Bibliothèque de l'Université, 1935), p. 41.

[174] Gardiner, *Narrative of the Spanish Marriage Treaty*, p. 214. These conditions, aimed at making the negotiations more difficult if not impossible, were added in Rome after Olivares had sent his emissary, Ruy Gomez, duke of Pastrana, in April to ask the pope not to grant the dispensation. The dispensation, however, had already been sent. The cardinal secretary, Luigi Ludovisi, then added new conditions, requiring complete liberty of conscience, including the public practice of Roman Catholicism confirmed by Parliament. See Albion, *Charles I and the Court of Rome*, pp. 28–31.

and the British delegation, which consisted of Buckingham – raised to the rank of duke in May – Bristol, Aston, and Cottington. Charles also attended the sessions.[175] Another reason for the difficult negotiations was that Olivares, despite his efforts to appear helpful to the prince and duke, had long had serious reservations about the whole project. As he explained to Philip IV, it was not to James's political advantage to make the concessions he was being called upon to make to the English Roman Catholics. Though James might not be opposed to the Roman Catholic religion, there was nothing in his career to suggest that he would take steps to enhance its position in England. The two countries were already on friendly terms. Olivares feared that further negotiations would be counterproductive.[176]

Olivares's doubts about the marriage actually ran much deeper. He knew that the Infanta Maria was herself unwilling to marry Prince Charles unless there were real prospects for improving the situation of the English Roman Catholics. She had sent Olivares a message in late 1622 that she would prefer to "enter a convent of barefooted nuns than be married with such defective conditions" as the treaty then contained.[177] Olivares also saw the fate of the Palatinate as a matter which only James and the Emperor Ferdinand could resolve in direct negotiations. If they could not agree, Spain would not be able to settle their differences. His own solution, which he had already set out in a memorandum to Philip IV, was a series of marriages: the infanta to Ferdinand's eldest son, Prince Charles to Ferdinand's eldest daughter, and the Elector Frederick's eldest son to Ferdinand's younger daughter.[178] The effect would be to link both Charles and Frederick to the Austrian Habsburgs and bring Frederick's son and heir under the influence of the Imperial court. Olivares worried about what would happen if the Anglo-Spanish marriage took place and England thereafter had no alternative to entering the European war in order to secure the return of the Palatinate. Spain would then be in the extremely awkward position of having to choose between England and the Austrian Habsburgs.[179]

The Spanish Council of State, apparently eager to conclude the treaty, decided in early May to proceed with negotiations without exacting such conditions as were being proposed by the nuncio. In contrast a *junta* of theologians which began meeting in late May reached a consensus that the marriage should only be approved if sufficient assurances were given that

[175] Gardiner, *Narrative of the Spanish Marriage Treaty*, pp. 215–216.
[176] Ibid., pp. 219–220. See also pp. 221–228. For Charles's and Buckingham's favorable comment on Olivares's role in the early stages of the negotiations, see Hardwicke, *Miscellaneous State Papers*, vol. I, p. 419.
[177] Gardiner, *Narrative of the Spanish Marriage Treaty*, p. 191.
[178] Ibid., p. 192.
[179] For the dilemmas facing Spain – of which Olivares was acutely aware – see Elliott, *The Count-Duke of Olivares*, pp. 203–222, esp. pp. 207–210.

the pope's conditions had been accepted in England. The theologians recommended that Philip agree to the marriage but delay sending the infanta to England for a year, by which time James would be expected to suspend the penal laws against Roman Catholics and grant them the right to "the free exercise of their religion in their own houses, and in those of their friends and neighbours."[180] When Cottington returned to England to inform the king of the latest developments in the negotiations, James was astonished and disconsolate. As he wrote to Charles and Buckingham on June 14, "Your letter by Cottington, hath strucken me dead."[181] He did not know what to say publicly or to the council. The fleet had already waited a fortnight for a favorable wind for sailing to Spain. He advised Charles and Buckingham that if the Spaniards "will not alter their decree," then to "come speedily away," breaking off the negotiations.[182]

Charles and Buckingham had meanwhile continued to encounter difficulties. On June 26, they commented in a letter to James on the long delay caused by "the foolery of the Condé of Olivares," who had given the treaty to a lawyer to put into finished form. The lawyer had "slipped in a multitude of new, unreasonable, undemanded, and ungranted conditions."[183] They were still confident, however, that they would be able to overcome all difficulties. When James's order to them to return arrived soon afterwards, they so informed Olivares, as they wrote to James on June 27. Olivares, however, told them that the process was moving forward and that the matter now rested with Philip IV. They told James, therefore, that they believed that they could return in a month's time, accompanied by the infanta.[184] Charles had been strongly opposed to the conditions insisted upon by the *junta* of theologians aimed at ensuring that religious liberty be granted to English Roman Catholics, and he asked that a simpler way be found to address the theologians' concerns.[185] The *junta*, however, declined to change its recommendation. According to Francisco de Jesus's account, a surprising development then took place. When the prince and duke, along with the two English ambassadors, went to Philip early in July, ostensibly to take their leave, Charles told him that he had decided "to accept the proposals made to him with respect to religion, and also to give the securities demanded for their due execution, and that this was the final determination of the King his father."[186]

James did agree to the final treaty by taking an oath in London on July 20

---

[180] Gardiner, *Narrative of the Spanish Marriage Treaty*, pp. 220, 232–236 (the quotation is on p. 236).
[181] Hardwicke, *Miscellaneous State Papers*, vol. I, p. 421. For Cottington's visit, see Havran, *Caroline Courtier*, pp. 74–75.
[182] Hardwicke, *Miscellaneous State Papers*, vol. I, p. 421.
[183] Ibid., p. 422.   [184] Ibid., pp. 423–424.
[185] Gardiner, *Narrative of the Spanish Marriage Treaty*, pp. 243–245.   [186] Ibid., p. 246.

in the presence of Coloma, the resident Spanish ambassador, and Juan de Mendoza, marquis de la Ynojosa, the ambassador extraordinary, along with his Privy Council.[187] Cottington was soon on his way back to Madrid from London with "a public instrument written on parchment" containing the king's and the Privy Council's oaths to fulfill the conditions for the marriage with respect to religion.[188] On July 25, 1623 Charles and Philip IV both signed the marriage treaty in Madrid. On August 5, in London, James wrote to Charles and Buckingham that he had "given order to put in execution, all that I have promised, and more."[189] This included discharging "all debts already owing to me by [Roman Catholic] recusants," amounting to £36,000 in England and Ireland.[190]

Exactly what had Charles and James agreed to? Much of the treaty dated back to 1617, though some changes had been made before Gondomar's return to Spain in 1620. Further revisions were made after Gage returned to England from Rome in August 1622 with the pope's notations and again after discussions between Bristol and the Spanish ministers in December 1622.[191] Like earlier versions, the treaty provided for the celebration of the marriage in Spain and for establishing the infanta's household in England, where she and her servants would "have the free use and public exercise of the Roman Catholic Religion."[192] The final version also provided for a public church near the infanta's residence where the sacraments would be celebrated according to the usage of the Roman Catholic Church and where there would also be a burial ground.[193] Twenty-four Roman Catholic priests and assistants would be named; they would serve under the supervision of a bishop in the infanta's household. A special oath of allegiance would be required of members of the infanta's household, including subjects of the British king, which would not compromise the consciences of Roman Catholics. Besides pledging fidelity to the king, the oath would require the taker to report immediately to the authorities any information about hostile actions being planned against the king, prince, infanta, or state. Children of

---

[187] Havran, *Caroline Courtier*, p. 75; Loomie, *Spain and the Jacobean Catholics*, vol. II, p. xx. Ynojosa came to England in May to announce that Prince Charles had arrived safely in Madrid; he stayed on to help to work out the details of the marriage treaty.

[188] Gardiner, *Narrative of the Spanish Marriage Treaty*, p. 247. See also Havran, *Caroline Courtier*, pp. 75–76.

[189] Hardwicke, *Miscellaneous State Papers*, vol. I, p. 445.

[190] Ibid., pp. 445–446.

[191] Gardiner, *Narrative of the Spanish Marriage Treaty*, p. 327. In this appendix to Francisco de Jesus's account, the Latin text of the treaty of 1617 is printed alongside that of 1623, with the pope's responses of 1622 (pp. 328–340). See also the Latin texts of the Articles for the Spanish Match as transmitted from Rome, July 28, 1622, and the Articles of the Spanish Match as adopted and sworn to by King James and his Council, July 20, 1623, in [Tootell,] *Dodd's Church History of England*, vol. V, pp. ccxcix–cccv and cccxxii–cccxxix.

[192] Gardiner, *Narrative of the Spanish Marriage Treaty*, p. 330.   [193] Ibid.

the marriage would be educated under the care of the infanta until the age of ten. Like other members of the infanta's household, the royal children would not be subject to laws against Roman Catholics, and they would enjoy the right of succession to the realms and dominions of Great Britain.[194]

In addition, the treaty contained secret articles sworn to by James on July 20, and by Charles and Philip IV on July 25, which were intended to satisfy the pope's insistence that there be religious toleration for the Roman Catholic subjects of the British king. The articles provided for the suspension of laws against Roman Catholics and "perpetual toleration of the exercise of the Roman Catholic Religion among private persons within the walls of houses," throughout England, Scotland, and Ireland.[195] James and Charles undertook, moreover, to see to it that Parliament would approve and ratify the treaty and would "abrogate and revoke all laws, particular as well as general, levied against Catholics and the Roman Religion."[196] Further, in secret articles sworn to by Charles and Philip IV alone on July 25, Charles promised to effect this abrogation of the laws against Roman Catholics within three years and to seek his father's approval for extending the years during which the infanta would supervise the education of the royal children from ten, as specified in the public treaty, to twelve.[197] The Spanish king undertook to see that the marriage was performed *verbis de praesenti*, once papal approval of these arrangements was received, and to see that the infanta was delivered to English representatives on March 1, 1624 in Madrid or on April 15 at a Spanish port.[198] These secret articles required actions by James and Charles which would be extremely difficult to fulfill, especially the abrogation of the penal laws by Parliament. James and Charles presumably understood the agreement as requiring that they make the best effort they could to carry out the articles under the existing circumstances.

Charles set August 30 as the date for his and Buckingham's departure, "offering to leave powers for the celebration of the marriage in his absence, if the expected permission did not arrive from Rome before his departure."[199] Delay in receiving approbation from Rome could be expected, since Gregory XV had died in early July. His successor, Urban VIII, was elected on August 6. Before leaving the Escorial, where the prince and duke were entertained on their way to the northern coast of Spain, Charles gave

---

[194] Ibid., pp. 332–339.

[195] Ibid., p. 341. James prepared a Patent with a form of Pardon and Dispensation to Catholics, September 8, 1623, but delayed its implementation until the results of the proceedings in Madrid were known. See [Tootell,] *Dodd's Church History of England*, vol. V, pp. 145, cccxxxviii–ccclxi.

[196] Gardiner, *Narrative of the Spanish Marriage Treaty*, pp. 341–342.

[197] Ibid., p. 343.   [198] Ibid., p. 344.   [199] Ibid., p. 251.

Bristol an authorization for the marriage to be celebrated soon after the approbation arrived from Rome. The authorization was to be valid until the coming Christmas. But, surprisingly, at Segovia he left another document with a servant, Edward Clerke, who was to take it to Bristol's house. Here Charles expressed his concern that the infanta might decide to become a member of a religious order after the proxy marriage had taken place and he asked that assurances be obtained that this would not happen; only then was the authorization he had left with Bristol to be used.[200] If Francisco de Jesus was right, that Clerke was to produce this letter only after the papal approbation had arrived, it suggests that Charles – or Buckingham – wanted to thwart the plans for a marriage made in the preceding weeks.[201] But Bristol, who was eager to complete the arrangements for the marriage after Charles and Buckingham left, quickly discovered the reason for Clerke's arrival at his residence and the contents of the prince's order. On September 24 Bristol requested James's permission to put the prince's authorization for the marriage into effect on the arrival of the papal approbation, providing that he had received appropriate assurances that the infanta would not enter a religious order after the marriage.[202] James gave him this permission on October 8, though he also asked Bristol to delay the marriage so that it could be celebrated during the Christmas season. The king thus put his ambassador in a new quandary, since the authorization from the prince was only valid until Christmas. In his letter to James on October 24, Bristol sought to clear up this apparent inconsistency.[203]

Meanwhile Bristol had reported to James on September 9 that at the Escorial he had found "the former distastes betwixt the Duke [of Buckingham] and the Condé of Olivares grown to a public professed hatred, and an irreconcilable enmity."[204] Buckingham's own letter to James on September 1 conveyed the bitterness he felt at not being able to bring the infanta along on his return journey: "I'll bring all things with me you have desired, except the Infanta, which hath almost broken my heart, because your's, your son's, and the nation's honour is touched by the miss of it; but since it is their fault here and not ours, we will bear it the better."[205] Bristol reported that Charles, in contrast to Buckingham, was generally well liked

---

[200] Ibid., pp. 257–258.   [201] Ibid., pp. 258–259.

[202] Hardwicke, *Miscellaneous State Papers*, vol. I, pp. 481–482.

[203] Ibid., pp. 483–484. James wrote to Bristol on November 13 that he had been unaware that his direction was inconsistent with the powers left by the prince. See Gardiner, "The Earl of Bristol's Defence of His Negotiations in Spain," p. 52. The liturgical Christmas season began with Christmas Day and continued until Epiphany on January 6.

[204] Hardwicke, *Miscellaneous State Papers*, vol. I, p. 479. Francisco de Jesus made several references to the enmity between the two men. See Gardiner, *Narrative of the Spanish Marriage Treaty*, pp. 208, 211, 254. See also Lockyer, *Buckingham*, pp. 148–151.

[205] Hardwicke, *Miscellaneous State Papers*, vol. I, p. 451.

in Spain, as Philip IV's letters to the prince showed. The ambassador told James that "all your great affairs will in the end have good success, if they be not, by the passions of the Ministers of the one side or the other, interrupted."[206]

After Charles's and Buckingham's departure, Bristol continued to press the Spanish king and his ministers to resolve the issue of the Palatinate. He reported several meetings on the subject as early as August 29, when he relayed the Spanish proposal that Frederick's eldest son be brought up in the emperor's court as a step towards full restitution of the Palatinate – a proposal Bristol knew to be unrealistic, since Frederick and Elizabeth were certain to oppose it.[207] On October 24 he wrote to James that he knew that the king "hath long been of opinion that the greatest assurance you could get, that the king of Spain would effectually labour the entire restitution of the Prince Palatine was, that he really proceeded to the effecting of the match."[208] He told James that he was seeking written assurance about the issue of the Palatinate from Philip IV. He believed that the Spaniards also wanted the issue settled before the infanta left for England, otherwise, as Olivares had said, "they might give a daughter, and have a war within three months after."[209] In any case, Bristol observed, the resolution of the problem of the Palatinate involved many other princes and could only be settled by a formal treaty, which would take time. He favored accepting the profession of the Spaniards "that they infinitely desire, and will, to the utmost of their powers, endeavour to procure your Majesty's satisfaction" in the matter of the Palatinate and then proceeding as quickly as possible to the marriage.[210]

The papal approbation arrived in Madrid on November 14, having been delayed by Urban VIII's untimely illness. Philip IV subsequently set November 29 as the date of the marriage.[211] Bristol so notified James. On November 26, however, he received a startling letter from James dated November 13 directing him to ask for written assurance on the issue of the Palatinate from the Spanish king before the marriage was celebrated. James said that he was astonished that a part of the Palatinate which provided much of Frederick's income had recently been seized by Spanish troops and that the Emperor Ferdinand had given its revenues to the archbishop of Mainz. He therefore directed Bristol to "procure from that King, by act or answer to you under his hand, or by letter to us, 'That he will help us to the restitution of the Palatinate and dignity, by mediation; or otherwise assist us, if mediation fail; and within what time the mediation shall determine,

---

[206] Ibid., p. 479.   [207] Ibid., p. 477.   [208] Ibid., pp. 484–485.
[209] Ibid., p. 485.   [210] Ibid., p. 487.
[211] Gardiner, *Narrative of the Spanish Marriage Treaty*, pp. 261–263.

and the assistance of arms begin.'"[212] James showed his good faith by
directing Prince Charles to defer the authorization for the marriage left with
Bristol the previous August and to renew it for a longer time, so that further
negotiations could take place.[213]

After Bristol sent a message to Philip IV that in order for the marriage to
be "firm and durable," the issue of the Palatinate would have to be
discussed further, the marriage was postponed. Gondomar, in a *consulta* to
the Spanish council, advised the Spanish king, who had been "ready to
conclude the alliance yesterday morning," to persevere in the negotiations.[214] But if James insisted on including the issue of the return of the
Palatinate, Gondomar said, Spain should include the issues of the conflicts
in Holland and the East Indies, where English help against the Dutch would
be extremely valuable.[215] Raising such issues as the war in the Netherlands
and the control of the East Indies would, of course, raise the stakes in
diplomacy dramatically and would no doubt be unacceptable to Britain. By
December 26, Bristol and Aston were able to report more fully on Philip
IV's response to the demand contained in James's letter of November 13.
The response was, as they had warned it would be in their letter of
December 6, "much worse and much more reserved than any we had
formerly received; it being rather indeed an expostulation than any direct
answer to any point by us propounded."[216] They pointed out that before
the king's recent declaration of policy, the Spanish council had, on
November 22, "resolved to procure your Majesty entire satisfaction; and
that the Condé de Olivares had wished us to signify so much to your
Majesty in this King's name . . . and that he had assured us we should
receive so much in writing before the *desposorios*."[217] Since receiving
James's message, however, the Spanish officials

plainly let us know, that this King, out of his love and desire of friendship with your
Majesty, was resolved to employ his utmost endeavours for the procuring your
Majesty entire satisfaction: but to have it extorted from him by way of menace, or
that it should now be added to the marriage by way of condition; and that his sister
must be rejected unless the King would undertake to give satisfaction, and that, by

[212] Clarendon, *State Papers*, vol. I, pp. 13–14 (James to Bristol, November 13, 1623). The
area concerned was "Berk Strott," i.e. Bergstrasse, called by White "the richest part of the
country." White, "Suspension of Arms," p. 569.
[213] Clarendon, *State Papers*, vol. I, p. 13.
[214] Loomie, *Spain and the Jacobean Catholics*, vol. II, p. 165.
[215] Ibid. Gondomar no doubt saw events in the Far East as creating an opportunity to effect
such a plan. In the East Indies, Spain was defending the formerly Portuguese colonies
against the Dutch, while the British East India Company was a rival of the Dutch. Fighting
between the English and Dutch traders had broken out in 1619. News of the execution of
ten English traders by Dutch officials on the island of Amboina in the Moluccas in February
1623 only reached England in May 1624.
[216] Hardwicke, *Miscellaneous State Papers*, vol. I, p. 490.   [217] Ibid.

declaring that he would make a war against the Emperor, if need were . . . he could neither with his honour, nor with the honour of his sister . . . make any other answer for the present, than what he had done.[218]

Under the officials' controlled, formal language, the message was that the Spanish king had been pushed beyond the limits of his patience.

The course of James's negotiations in the Spanish Netherlands in 1623 for a truce in the empire, to be followed by a peace conference, ran remarkably parallel to that for a marriage alliance in Spain. In April 1623 prospects for James's and the Archduchess Isabella's peacemaking looked very promising. Pleased by the reports he was receiving from Spain about Charles's reception there, James had reopened negotiations for a truce with the Spanish ambassadors in London. By April 22 a treaty was ready to be signed.[219] It called for a truce in the Holy Roman Empire to last for fifteen months. Isabella was to convene a peace conference at Cologne in three to four months. The truce would bind all military commanders, who would face suppression by the signatories if they violated it. James and Isabella hastened to ratify the treaty in early May. By May 23 the Emperor Ferdinand had also signed it. But Frederick held out, despite James's repeated assurances that this was the best way to get the Palatinate back.[220] Finally, on August 26, Frederick signed the treaty. Thus, the way was open for the peace conference at just the time when agreement had been reached in Spain for a proxy marriage between Prince Charles and the infanta. Isabella sent a message to the emperor in early September asking him to name a date for the conference and appoint his representatives. Despite Isabella's further entreaties, Ferdinand did not respond, but his actions spoke clearly. In the autumn of 1623 the emperor began to distribute Frederick's lands.[221] By early November the situation in the Rhineland looked a good deal less promising than it had looked two months before, as James's letter of November 13 showed. In order to secure the return of the Palatinate by diplomatic means, James needed more than ever a firm commitment of help from Spain.

December 1623 marked the effective end of the marriage negotiations, though desultory conversations in England and Spain continued into early 1624.[222] In February 1625 Gondomar was again named ambassador extra-

[218] Ibid., p. 491.   [219] White, "Suspension of Arms," pp. 547–549.
[220] Ibid., p. 556. On May 29, 1623, Isabella wrote to James that she had given formal approval for the conference to be held at Cologne, according to James's wish. Lambeth Palace Library, Fairhurst/Laud Papers 3473, fols. 82–82 verso.
[221] White, "Suspension of Arms," pp. 568–569.
[222] Gardiner, *Narrative of the Spanish Marriage Treaty*, pp. 268–282. Aston heard from James in April 1624 that Parliament had advised that negotiations with Spain over the marriage and the Palatinate be broken off (p. 280). On July 5 Philip ordered the negotiations ended (p. 282).

ordinary to England.[223] But by that time England was making preparations for a war with Spain, and Gondomar did not undertake another mission. James had tried to ensure that the Spanish match would not only bring him the political and diplomatic leverage he needed to secure a European peace – a cause for which he was willing to risk his own political fortunes at home – but that it would bring the Palatinate back to his daughter and son-in-law in the near future. In November 1623, with the solemnization of the Spanish marriage only a few days away, he had overplayed his hand. An alliance with England had clearly been attractive to Spain, but not at the risk of provoking an armed conflict with the Austrian Habsburgs.

However much James wanted to continue with plans for the marriage, the course of events in England after Charles's and Buckingham's return put him in an increasingly difficult position. The prince's arrival in London on October 6 was marked by popular celebrations featuring bonfires, the ringing of church bells, the firing of cannons, and the drinking of many healths. The celebrations had started in London with news of Charles's landing in England the day before, and they quickly spread with the news to Norwich, York, Chester, and other provincial cities.[224] People seemed overjoyed not only that the heir to the throne had returned safely from Spain but that he had not been converted to Roman Catholicism nor did he have the infanta as his bride. Charles and Buckingham, angered by their treatment at the Spanish court, used their newly found popularity to win political support for a change in foreign policy in the Privy Council and at court.[225] Buckingham wanted to cultivate the anti-Habsburg states of Europe around the support of the Dutch and the rightful claims of Elizabeth and Frederick to the Palatinate. He also worked to gain support for a Parliament which would supply resources for a war to effect the recovery of the Palatinate and the humbling of Spain at sea.[226] James had not lost control of foreign and domestic policy, but he faced an extremely serious challenge. The Spanish match had long been unpopular with much of the nation, though it enjoyed considerable support in the Privy Council. James's plan had been to conclude the marriage, then work with Spain to effect the return of the Palatinate. His letter of November 13 was not an attempt to scuttle the marriage – though Charles and Buckingham may have hoped it would have that effect. Instead, it was a bold and calculated attempt by James to hold onto the diplomatic initiative and keep his peace policy on track.

---

[223] Loomie, *Spain and the Jacobean Catholics*, vol. II, pp. xx–xxi.

[224] David Cressy, *Bonfires and Bells: National Memory and the Protestant Calendar in Elizabethan and Stuart England* (Berkeley: University of California Press, 1989), pp. 93–104.

[225] Cogswell, "Crown, Parliament and War, 1623–25," pp. 1–105, *The Blessed Revolution*, pp. 55–121, "The Spanish Match," pp. 107–133. See also chapter 10, below.

[226] Lockyer, *Buckingham*, pp. 168–178.

Bristol, who was recalled from Spain in January 1624, came home to face charges from Buckingham that he had played into the hands of the Spaniards over a long period of time and had failed to save the Palatinate.[227] In a series of written replies in 1624 and 1625, Bristol responded to questions from a special commission concerning his activities and judgements. He also provided a narrative of the negotiations with Spain from 1611 to 1624, citing despatches and events in convincing detail.[228] Bristol's overall judgement of the Spanish match is worth pondering. If, as he wrote in February 1625, Spain and England had proceeded with the match, the result would have been that King James

> should have speedily seene the marriage, which hee had so long sought, effected, that the Prince should have had a worthye ladie whom hee loved, that the portion [dowry] should have bene three tymes as much as was ever given in monye in Christendome, that the king of Spayne had engaged himselfe for the restitution of the Palatinate, for which the earl of Bristol conceaved a daughter of Spayne and 2 millions had bene no ill pawne.[229]

Concerning the alternative policy of waging war on the continent, Bristol "doubted [not] that the recovery of the Palatinate from the Emperor and the duke of Bavaria by force would prove of great difficultye, and that Christendome was like to fall into a generall combustion."[230] He had hoped that King James "might have had the honor and happinesse not only to have given peace, plenty, and increase to his owne subjects and crownes, but to have compounded the great differences that had bene these many yeares in Christendome, and by his pyete and wisdom to have prevented the shedding of so much Christian blood."[231]

On the basis of his long experience as an ambassador, Bristol probably knew more about foreign affairs than anyone else in England with the exception of the king himself, and he shared James's deep concern that the volatile political and religious issues of the day might lead to a protracted and general war. Bristol claimed that James's efforts to secure peace between 1618 and 1623 had come very near to succeeding. The ambassador said that he was "a most unfortunate man" to see "his Majesties affayres so neere the beeing setled to his Majesties content," only "to see the whole state of affayres turned upsyde downe without any the least fault of his."[232]

Historians of the Thirty Years' War have tended to ignore James's

---

[227] Gardiner, "The Earl of Bristol's Defence of His Negotiations in Spain," pp. i–viii.

[228] Ibid., pp. 1–56; Hardwicke, *Miscellaneous State Papers*, vol. I, pp. 494–522.

[229] Gardiner, "The Earl of Bristol's Defence of His Negotiations in Spain," p. 53. For the method by which Philip IV proposed to pay the dowry of two million crowns, see "His Catholick Majesty's Answer with regard to the Dowry and the Times of Payment," undated but probably 1623, in Clarendon, *State Papers*, vol. I, appendix, pp. xxx–xxxi.

[230] Gardiner, "The Earl of Bristol's Defence of His Negotiations in Spain," p. 53.

[231] Ibid.   [232] Ibid., pp. 53–54.

peacemaking efforts or to treat them as largely irrelevant to the major power struggles which began in 1618. But this is to misunderstand the conflict. There was nothing inevitable about the series of complications which prolonged the war from year to year and from decade to decade. To be sure, there were serious political problems which needed to be resolved. These problems included the disputes over politics and government within the Holy Roman Empire, the unresolved struggle in the Netherlands, the rivalry between France and the Habsburg powers of Spain and Austria, and the struggle for control of the Baltic Sea. Europe was also entering a period of severe economic difficulties which exacerbated political conflicts of all kinds. And there was the overarching issue of religion, which threatened to turn the whole of Europe into two warring camps. But it is entirely possible that each of the political problems could have been addressed with at least a limited prospect of success. Even the religious divisions of Europe could have been bridged in some measure. James believed, unlike many later commentators, that every conflict visible on the horizon in 1618 could be dealt with constructively by negotiation and that the religious issue could either be resolved or defused to the point at which it was no longer likely to spark what Bristol called a "generall conflagration."

With France, Spain, the Spanish Netherlands, and England all inclined to peace in Germany at one time or another between 1618 and 1623, why then was it not achieved? Aside from the inherent difficulties of coordinating different national policies, the answer seems to be that the belligerent parties – the Emperor Ferdinand, the Bohemian rebels, the Elector Frederick, and Duke Maximilian of Bavaria – were all determined to proceed with hostilities. The United Provinces was also ready to prosecute further its long war against Spain. The effect of these actions was to undermine James's efforts to resolve the Bohemian crisis by means of Doncaster's mission and then to stop the fighting in the Rhineland by the Brussels Conference and the mediation of Sir Richard Weston. Over the same period of time, negotiations in Spain were more successful. The Spanish match was, except for papal permission, ready to be concluded in 1618, about the time the Bohemian revolt occurred. By late 1622 revised terms had been agreed to, and early in 1623 the papal dispensation had actually been issued. By the time Charles and Buckingham arrived in Madrid, even the temporal articles had been settled. The visit of Charles and Buckingham in Madrid, however, prolonged the negotiations by allowing the Spaniards to raise their demands concerning the treatment of English Roman Catholics. Charles and his father agreed to terms which Parliament was not likely to approve and which he and his father would probably not have been able to implement fully. Yet the agreements, to whatever extent they could be realized, would have marked the dawn of a new day for Roman Catholics in James's dominions – the kind of resolution James had apparently favored before his coming to the English throne in 1603.

A negotiated settlement of the kind James urged was a far better solution than war, and the king advanced his plans at a time when the scale of the war was still limited and the issues were amenable to a diplomatic solution. James was zealous, energetic, and resourceful between 1618 and 1623 in pursuing a peace which he believed was in the best interests of his country and the whole of Europe. His peacemaking efforts came very close to succeeding in May 1622 with the convening of a broadly supported peace conference in Brussels, again in December 1622 with the settlement of terms for an Anglo-Spanish marriage, and yet again in September 1623 when arrangements were made for the proxy marriage of Charles and Maria in Madrid at the same time that the Archduchess Isabella called on the Emperor Ferdinand to set a date for a peace conference in Cologne. Had James's efforts succeeded, the war might well have ended before his death in 1625, and the Habsburg powers, whose friendship he aspired to, would have been well served. The same is true for England's traditional allies.

Last years and conclusion

On Christmas Eve 1618, when King James's hopes of being able to negotiate a peace in central Europe remained strong, he began to write *A Meditation vpon the Lords Prayer*, which he finished at the end of March 1619.[1] It was intended to guide, especially, the members of his own court, including the marquis of Buckingham, to whom the work was dedicated. James's little book is valuable in showing the importance he attached to personal religious devotion. "The service of God is the most due, necessary, and profitable action of a Christian man," he wrote, and prayer "is to be preferred to all other actions of a Christian man."[2] The book is also valuable in suggesting where he stood on contemporary issues of faith and practice at the time the Synod of Dort was in session. He considered St. Paul's admonition to "Pray continuallie," as especially needed in an age when the Puritans had turned it into "Preach continually."[3] James defended the use of the Lord's Prayer against those Puritans who objected to its being said more than once during particular services of the Church of England and those sectarians called Brownists who objected to any set prayers at all.[4] He commended private confession, especially as preparation for the sacrament of Holy Communion, citing Calvin in his support. But he objected to the mandatory use of confession in the Roman Catholic Church as inviting a priestly tyranny over Christians.[5] In commenting on the phrase "leade vs not into Temptation," he asserted that the Arminians "cannot but mislike the frame of this Petition; for I am sure, they would have it, and

---

[1] James I, *A Meditation vpon the Lords Prayer: Written by the Kings Maiestie, for the Benefit of All His Subiects, Especially of Such as Follow the Court* [first published in 1619], in James Montague, ed., *The Workes of the Most High and Mighty Prince, Iames, by the Grace of God Kinge of Great Britaine, France and Ireland, Defender of the Faith, &c.* (London: Robert Barker and John Bill, 1616–1620), pp. 572–573.

[2] James I, *A Meditation vpon the Lords Prayer*, p. 574.   [3] Ibid., p. 575.

[4] Ibid., pp. 575–576.

[5] Ibid., p. 584. The passage cited in Calvin is *Institutes*, III, 4, 12. There Calvin commends private confession to one's own pastor.

suffer us not to bee ledde into temptation."[6] Just as God alone draws sinful human beings out of their corruption, so God "is sayde to leade us into temptation, when by a strong hand hee preserues vs not from it."[7] James's stress in this volume on the loss of free-will by Adam's fall, the necessity for God's "effectuall grace," and his thankfulness for the light of the Gospel "in this Island" after "that more then Egyptian darknesse" of the past shows that he was, in his last years in England, as in his early years in Scotland, a moderate Calvinist for whom religion was of fundamental importance.[8]

James's *Meditation vpon the Lords Prayer* also reveals what he thought was the distinctive mark of his kingship:

I know not by what fortune, the dicton of PACIFICVS was added to my title at my comming in England; that of the Lyon, expressing true fortitude, hauing beene my dicton before; but I am not ashamed of this addition; for King Salomon was a figure of CHRIST in that, that he was a king of peace. The greatest gift that our Sauiour gave his Apostles, immediatly before his Ascension, was, that hee left his Peace, with them.[9]

Since his accession in England James had worked not only to maintain peace among his three kingdoms of England, Scotland, and Ireland and between his realms and the other European states, but to try to resolve conflicts abroad which threatened to disrupt Christendom. This task was bound up, as he saw it, with the need to reunite the Christian churches in a common body. The frontispiece of the *Meditation* showed a subdued but still determined James sitting on a throne, holding a scepter in his right hand and an orb in his left hand, under the slogan *Beati Pacifici*, "blessed are the peacemakers."

Just how difficult peacemaking was, especially in the months following the Elector Frederick's acceptance of the crown of Bohemia, was suggested by another book, whose dedication to Prince Charles was dated December 29, 1619. James's *A Meditation vpon the 27. 28. 29. Verses of the XXVII. Chapter of Saint Matthew: or, A Paterne for a Kings Inavgvration* concerned a passage at the end of St. Matthew's account of the passion of Christ, where "the Gouernors Souldiers mocked our Sauiour, with putting the ornaments of a King vpon him."[10] If James seemed close to sacrilege in associating himself in his book on the Lord's Prayer with Christ's granting peace to the apostles before ascending to heaven, he came even closer to it

---

[6] James I, *A Meditation vpon the Lords Prayer*, p. 594. For other critical comments on the Arminians, see pp. 578, 581.

[7] Ibid., p. 594.   [8] Ibid., pp. 594, 597.

[9] Ibid., p. 590. Dicton is probably a variant of diction, which meant a speech or verbal description in James's time.

[10] James I, *A Meditation vpon the 27. 28. 29. Verses of the XXVII. Chapter of Saint Matthew: or, A Paterne for a Kings Inavgvration* [first published in 1620], in Montague, *The Workes of the Most High and Mightie Prince, Iames*, p. 601. For comments on this book and on the *Meditation vpon the Lords Prayer*, see Kevin Sharpe, "The King's Writ: Royal Authors and Royal Authority in Early Modern England," in Kevin Sharpe and Peter Lake, eds., *Culture and Politics in Early Stuart England* (London: Macmillan, 1994), pp. 126–127.

in representing the mocking of Christ as a pattern of earthly kingship. James wrote to Prince Charles that as he had thought about the crown of thorns, he was reminded of a king's "thorny cares," something "I daily and nightly feele in mine owne person."[11] He recalled that the English King Henry IV had told his own son "that he was neuer a day without trouble since it [the crown] was first put upon his head."[12] James interpreted the three verses which describe the bringing of Jesus into a Common Hall among a throng of soldiers, his being adorned with a scarlet robe and a crown of thorns, and his being acclaimed as "king of the Ievves," as a model of a king's inauguration. However sardonically the soldiers had intended their actions, God had caused them to do that honor to his son which was appropriate.[13]

James formulated out of this brief passage in St. Matthew a political theology or Christian view of kingship. The crown, he observed, is given to the king by his people to remind him that he reigns by their love and consent. At the same time the king receives at his coronation a public acknowledgement of his people's "willing subiection to his person and authority."[14] It was nonetheless true that kings received their crowns, in the sense of their authority, from God alone. The plaited crown of thorns given to Christ was not only a reminder of the "stinging cares of Kings" but of "the anxious and intricate cares of Kings, who . . . must euen expect to meete with a number of crosse and intricate difficulties."[15] The reed put in Christ's right hand was a scepter, "thereby teaching Christian Kings that their scepters . . . should not be too much vsed or stretched, but where necessity requires it."[16] Just as hard blows would make a reed break, so too frequent use of a king's prerogative could weaken or destroy it.[17] The robe placed on a king's shoulders at his coronation signified his role as dispenser of justice and the color purple the ancient dye which "was of extreame long lasting, and could not be stayned."[18] The king's justice ought never to be stained by dishonor or corruption. James's view of divine-right monarchy thus stressed the responsibility of the king to his people as well as to God. The king must one day give account to God of "the good gouernment of his people, & their prosperous estate both in soules and bodies."[19] James intended his daringly Christological picture of kingship as a *vade mecum* for his son to prepare him for the day when he would assume the responsibilities of the monarchy. The book was a shorter and more somber version of the political theory of James's *Basilikon Doron* and *The Trew Law of*

---

[11] James I, *A Meditation vpon the 27. 28. 29. verses of the XXVII. Chapter of Saint Matthew*, pp. 601–602.
[12] Ibid., pp. 603–604.   [13] Ibid., p. 608.   [14] Ibid., pp. 611–612.
[15] Ibid., p. 613.   [16] Ibid., p. 614.   [17] Ibid.
[18] Ibid., p. 611; see also p. 621.   [19] Ibid., p. 621.

Free Monarchies, written several years before he left Scotland. As in *Basilikon Doron*, he described Christian kings as not simply "laikes" (laity) but as *mixtae personae*, mixed persons with religious as well as temporal responsibilities, "being bound to make a reckoning to GOD for their subjects soules as well as their bodies."[20] It was the king's responsibility, wrote James, "to ouersee and compell the *Church* to do her office," to purge the Church of abuses, and to see that the Church was reverenced and obeyed by his temporal subjects.[21]

James was both a Protestant in the Calvinist tradition and an advocate of closer relations among all the churches, including the Roman Catholic Church. His viewpoint was largely the result of his upbringing in Scotland during years of bitter sectarian conflict, but it also reflected his conviction that his was a religious faith based on scriptural revelation and consistent with the teachings of the ancient Church. Moreover, he believed that the liturgy, polity, and doctrinal standards of the Church of England were in the historic catholic tradition of Christianity. He therefore welcomed, even relished, religious discussions, and he worked towards the kind of organic unity which he believed the one, holy, catholic, and apostolic Church described in the Apostles' and Nicene creeds should exhibit. In the Europe of his day, moreover, he saw a resolution of differences between Protestants and Roman Catholics as imperative if a stable community of nations was to be created and sustained.

Some of these religious ideas and concerns were explored in a conference on May 24–26, 1622 at which James and two spokesmen of the Church of England exchanged views with John Percy, also known as John Fisher, a Jesuit. The conference, organized by the king and intended for the benefit of Mary, countess of Buckingham, mother of James's favorite, was occasioned by her announcement that she intended to become a Roman Catholic. Members of her family and members of the court were in attendance. On the first day the discussion was between Francis White, dean of Carlisle and royal chaplain, and Percy. On the second day it was largely between King James and Percy, though White also took part. On the third day the discussion was between William Laud, bishop of St. David's, and Percy. Much of the discussion was, inevitably, devoted to the claims of the Protestant churches and those of the Roman Catholic Church, and of relations among the churches.[22]

According to Percy's account of the second day's proceedings, which

---

[20] Ibid., p. 611.   [21] Ibid.

[22] For a description of the conference and Percy's account of the second day, see Timothy H. Wadkins, "King James I Meets John Percy, S. J. (May 25, 1622): An Unpublished Manuscript from the Religious Controversies Surrounding the Countess of Buckingham's Conversion," *Recusant History*, 19 (1988), 146–154.

remained unpublished until recently, James began by criticizing the Society of Jesus sharply for advancing doctrines and advocating practices which threatened the safety of princes. This was evident, he said, in the Gunpowder Plot, in which four Jesuit priests had been implicated. Percy replied that he detested the plot, but was unwilling to judge the persons whom James had named as instigators.[23] An exchange then followed concerning Cardinal Bellarmine's theory of the indirect power of the pope to depose princes for heresy or crimes. James contended that an indirect power was more threatening than a direct power, since it was insidious and difficult to oppose in a court of law or other open forum.[24] James then asked Percy what heresies the English Church could be accused of holding. Percy replied that one of them was "denying the Popes spirituall Supreme Power over the church."[25] James replied that the pope's claim to be universal bishop was advanced by popes only after Gregory the Great's death in the seventh century. Gregory had even called the title *universal bishop* antichristian.[26] After further exchanges about what Percy claimed was the care the popes had customarily taken for the whole Church, James said "he coulde be contente the Pope to bee cheife Patriarcke of the West."[27] On another issue of supposed heresy in the English Church, Percy charged that English Protestants denied "the reall presence of Christe in the Sacrament."[28] The king said that this was not so, since they only denied the manner of Christ's presence as professed by Roman Catholics, namely the doctrine of transubstantiation, which "he thought . . . to implie contradiction."[29] When asked by Percy if he himself believed that the substance of Christ inhered in the consecrated elements, James replied that he believed that it did.[30] When the discussion turned to Luther's revolt, James said that the revolt had been necessary, since there were "errours in the romaine church needinge reformation."[31] The discussion to which James contributed most thus showed that there was common ground between Protestants like himself and Roman Catholics, even on such contentious issues as the role of the papacy in the western Church and the theology of the eucharist, but that further refinement of doctrines on both sides would be needed if they were to reach agreement.

A discussion of the means of restoring Christian unity was left to the third day of the conference, when William Laud was the spokesman for the English Church. Laud acknowledged that the Roman Church was, as Richard Hooker too, had argued, a true church, since it received the scriptures as a rule of faith and the two sacraments of the gospel as "instrumentall Causes and Seales of Grace," even though Rome's under-

---

[23] Ibid., p. 148.   [24] Ibid., pp. 148–149.
[25] Ibid., p. 150.   [26] Ibid.   [27] Ibid., p. 151.   [28] Ibid.
[29] Ibid.   [30] Ibid., pp. 151–152.   [31] Ibid., p. 153.

standing of the rule and of the sacraments was defective.[32] He decried the "miserable Rent in the Church," as Calvin had done, but he argued that Protestants had been thrust away when they had called for the affirmation of theological truths and for the redress of abuses.[33] The way back to unity, however, was open, and the standard by which disputes could be settled was the Holy Scriptures. Where the meaning of the scriptures was in doubt, recourse must be had to the best interpreters – "the Exposition of the Primitiue Church" – or to a general council, "lawfully called, and fairely and freely held," where judgements would be based on the scriptures as the rule of faith.[34] The Council of Trent, he observed, was not a true general council, since it was controlled by the papacy, that part of the Church most needing to be reformed. Furthermore it lacked either the presence or the consent of the Eastern Orthodox Churches.[35]

Though these assertions were made by Laud rather than James, they undoubtedly were also the views of the king. James had advanced the same conciliar solution to the problem of the divided Church at the beginning of his reign in England and the same theme had been developed by his theological allies in the Oath of Allegiance controversy. Francis White, in his *Replie* in 1624 to the written answers to a set of questions propounded to Percy by James following the conference, linked the king directly to the issue of reunion.[36] With reference to Percy's argument that James should lead Christendom back towards unity by becoming reconciled with the see of Rome, White replied, first sarcastically, then in a deeply serious way:

> must his Maiestie haue the Office of a Proctor, and Factor, for the Court of Rome; nay, of a Lieutenant of the Papall Forces, to revnite all Protestants to the Church of Rome? Had you meant the procuring of a Free Generall Councell of all Christendome, or (at least) of all the Westerne Church, for the reducing eyther of the Deuiate parts home to the Truth, or the exasperated parts to a more charitable complying in things indifferent or tollerable (in which discussion, as well the Papacie it selfe, as other matters, might bee subiect to Tryall;) such a Worke might be fit for a Churchman to mooue, and for his Majestie to affect: than whom, no Prince (no, nor priuate Christian) is more forward in Zeale, and furnished in Wisedome, to purge the Distempers, and heale the Wounds of the Christian Church.[37]

In the last years of James's reign, White expressed the same hope James had

[32] William Laud, *An Answere to Mr Fishers Relation of a Third Conference betweene a Certaine B. (as He Stiles Him) and Himselfe*, ed. Richard Baily (London: Adam Islip, 1624), p. 38.

[33] Ibid., p. 39. The reference to Calvin is to the *Institutes*, IV, 1, 7.

[34] Laud, *An Answere to Mr Fishers Relation of a Third Conference*, p. 43.

[35] Ibid., pp. 43–44.

[36] Francis White, *A Replie to Iesuit Fishers Answere to Certain Questions Propoũded by His Most Gratious Matie King Iames* (London: Adam Islip, 1624), sigs., d$_1$–d$_4$.

[37] Ibid., sig. d$_4$. The institution of the general council is further discussed as a means to achieve unity on pp. 10–11, 152–157.

often expressed, and the king's supporters had expressed, that the Church's wounds might be healed by a general council of all the churches, where agreements could be reached on controversial issues or at least a "charitable complying in things indifferent or tollerable" arrived at. James himself never lost that hope, even in the bitterly contentious atmosphere created by the outbreak of a European war. Nor was anyone in his time "more forward in Zeale" to effect it.

As delighted as James was to have Prince Charles and the duke of Buckingham home on October 6, 1623, he experienced several difficult months after their return from Spain. Though officially the Spanish match was still one of the major objectives of English foreign policy and the long course of Anglo-Spanish negotiations seemed to have reached fruition, the prince and the favorite soon showed that they were opposed to the alliance.[38] They resented being delayed by Spanish promises that were not fulfilled. They were also acutely aware that the Spanish authorities and the papacy had used the opportunity to make the religious conditions for the marriage increasingly stringent. The prince and duke were upset that even after they had agreed to virtually every condition asked of them, the infanta was still not allowed to accompany them back to England. In addition Olivares and Buckingham had become bitter enemies. Buckingham was convinced that Olivares had dissimulated by pretending to encourage the match, when all along he had been implacably opposed to it. Within weeks of their return, Charles and Buckingham – whose relationship had become much closer during their sojourn abroad – were seeking the support of privy councillors and others at court for a radically revised foreign policy. If the negotiations with Spain on the match and on a truce in Germany were to be broken off, as Charles and Buckingham believed they should be, the only alternative seemed to them to be war.[39] James found this extremely difficult to accept, coming after his two decades of peacemaking. But his negotiations for peace and the return of the Palatinate had been undermined by the end of the year by the emperor's disposition of the Palatinate and the Spanish king's hostile reaction to James's request for firm assurance about the recovery of the Palatinate. A new approach was clearly needed. On December 28, James yielded to pressures at court by issuing his warrant for a Parliament.[40]

When Parliament met on February 19, 1624, James stressed in his

---

[38] Robert E. Ruigh, *The Parliament of 1624: Politics and Foreign Policy* (Cambridge, Mass.: Harvard University Press, 1971), pp. 22–34; Thomas Cogswell, *The Blessed Revolution: English Politics and the Coming of War, 1621–1624* (Cambridge: Cambridge University Press, 1989), pp. 57–69.

[39] Cogswell, *The Blessed Revolution*, pp. 77–105.

[40] Ruigh, *The Parliament of 1624*, p. 35.

opening speech that as a result of his government's policies, his subjects lived in peace, "when all the neighbour Countryes are in warr."[41] His concern for peace throughout Europe, as well as the peace of his own realms, had led him to conduct extensive negotiations, including those for a marriage between his son and the infanta of Spain. James said that as a result of Prince Charles's journey to Spain, "I awaked as a man out of a dreame," seeing that "the business is nothing advanced neither of the match nor of the palat[inate] for all the long treaties & great pmises . . ."[42] In order to inform Parliament fully of the course of events in Spain, "I will cause my Secretary to shew you my Letters & my sonne & Buck[ingham] shall declare all the pceedings."[43] When Parliament had considered all the evidence, "my desire is that you will give me yo[r] honest & sound advice."[44] The significance of this request could not have been lost on the members. In asking for advice on the Spanish treaties, which dealt with his son's marriage and with foreign policy, James had invited discussion of matters which in 1621 he had insisted were parts of the royal prerogative and thus exclusively his own responsibility.

By March 23 the outline of a new foreign policy, one which Parliament was willing to support with a significant levy of taxes, had begun to take shape. The stage had been set for a radical reappraisal of the issues involved by Buckingham's relation of events in Madrid, given on February 24. The duke laid the blame for the failure of negotiations squarely on Spain, with Digby as Spain's accomplice. Digby, he insisted, had known all along that the Spaniards had no intention of agreeing to the match or agreeing to the restitution of the Palatinate, yet he had kept King James's hopes alive.[45] When Charles and he arrived in Spain, said Buckingham, officials there made it clear that the match would not be acceptable unless the prince was converted to Roman Catholicism. Digby sought to persuade the prince "to be converted (at leste) in form."[46] After Charles and Buckingham returned and James demanded a "Resolute answer" of Philip IV on the issue of the Palatinate, the answer was returned "that Spayne will only treat wth the Empo[r] for Restitucōn of the Pallat. but will noe otherwise meddle therin."[47] After debates in both houses of Parliament and a conference between them, Archbishop Abbot presented their advice to James on March 8: "that ye treaties both for the Marriage and the Palatinate may not any long[r] be

---

[41] Washington: Folger Library MS. V. b. 303, p. 335. The text of this speech and of several others in the Folger collection differs significantly from that in John Rushworth, ed., *Historical Collections*, 7 vols. (London: George Thomason, 1659–1701), vol. I, pp. 115–146, and in *Journals of the House of Lords*, 19 vols. (London, 1767), vol. III, pp. 220–343.

[42] Folger MS. V. b. 303, p. 335.   [43] Ibid., p. 336.   [44] Ibid.

[45] Ibid., pp. 249–250; MS. V. a. 205, pp. 31–58.   [46] Folger MS. V. b. 303, p. 249.

[47] Ibid., p. 250.

contynued, wth the hono^r of yor Mat^{ie}, the safety of yor peace, and Welfare of yor Children and posterity, and also the assurance of yor ancyent allyes & confederates."[48] James thanked them for their advice, but stated reservations about it. As a "peaceable kinge" all the days of his life, he was not ready to undertake war unless there was a compelling reason. If there was no other way to recover the Palatinate, he would consider war, but only if he had sufficient funds to support it. Otherwise he would only be able "to showe my teeth, and doe noe more."[49]

James's answer on March 8 set off a new round of debates. Prince Charles urged Parliament to act expeditiously, and he assured the members that "You shall oblige mee who am now first enteringe into the worlde, when tyme shall serve hereafter you shall not think yor labo^{rs} ill bestowed."[50] By March 14 the two houses were ready with another address to the king. Archbishop Abbot stated on their behalf that both houses were ready "in a p[ar]liamentary manner wth our p[er]sons and abilities to assist yor Mat^{ie}."[51] James startled the archbishop by rejecting the suggestion in Abbot's introduction that the Spaniards had dealt insincerely in the negotiations, though this was certainly what Buckingham had said in his account. The king then amazed all the members of the parliamentary delegation by asking for a very large and explicit grant of funds for "this great Busines": five subsidies and ten-fifteenths for war and one subsidy and one-fifteenth for his own necessities and debts.[52] After an interruption by the prince, who said that his father would not ask anything for his own needs, James said that the sixth subsidy could also go to war, and he raised the total amount to six subsidies and twelve-fifteenths.[53] This was a huge amount, unprecedented even in Queen Elizabeth's reign, when England had fought Spain for a decade and a half. After extended debates, in which more than fifty members of the Commons spoke, the two houses offered on March 22 "the greatest aid which was ever granted in Parliament to be levied in so short a time: that is, three entire subsidies and three fifteenths."[54] These taxes were to be levied "upon your Majesty's public declaration of the utter dissolution and discharge of the two treaties of the marriage and Palatinate . . . towards the support of the war which is likely to ensue."[55] The two houses promised, moreover, that this grant was only the "firstfruits of our hearty oblation" and that "if you shall be engaged in a real war, we your loyal and

---

[48] Folger MS. V. a. 205, p. 76.   [49] Ibid., p. 82.   [50] Ibid.   [51] Ibid., p. 90.
[52] Ibid., pp. 90–93.   [53] Ruigh, *The Parliament of 1624*, pp. 209–212.
[54] J. R. Tanner, ed., *Constitutional Documents of the Reign of James I, A.D. 1603–1625, with an Historical Commentary* (Cambridge: Cambridge University Press, 1930), p. 300. For the debates, see Ruigh, *The Parliament of 1624*, pp. 212–228; Cogswell, *The Blessed Revolution*, pp. 197–215; and Conrad Russell, *Parliaments and English Politics, 1621–1629* (Oxford: Clarendon Press, 1979), pp. 186–189.
[55] Tanner, ed., *Constitutional Documents of the Reign of James I*, p. 300.

loving subjects will never fail to assist your Majesty in a Parliamentary way."[56]

In his speech to a parliamentary delegation on March 23 at Whitehall, James accepted their advice to break both of the treaties with Spain, and he described the main features of his new policy. His former forbearance had been "for the spareing the effusion of Christian bloud, and as the most easy and probable way to recover the Palat[inate]."[57] James made it clear that his purpose had been, as he had declared to Parliament in 1621, to secure the restitution of the Palatinate to his daughter and son-in-law. He had no doubt of the justice of this cause: "there was never any enemy of my sonne in law with whom I have talked of that busynes, or any other man that ever I spake with of that side, wch did not say and confesse that I had reason to have the Palat: one way or other."[58] He promised that the funds raised would be devoted solely to securing the Palatinate by military means. For the conduct of the war, he required "a faithfull and secret counsell of warr."[59] Subsidies would be controlled and used under the supervision of committees appointed by Parliament, as he had previously agreed. But James insisted that the ultimate responsibility for military operations and for foreign policy remained his: "whether I shall send 200, or 2000 men? whether by sea or land? whether East or West? whether by diversion or otherwise by invasion uppon the Bavarian or Emperor you must leave that to the kinge."[60] He acknowledged that he had "broken the Neck of 3. pliament^s one after the other" by dissolving them, but he hoped that this would be a happy Parliament.[61]

The Parliament of 1624 was in many ways a happy parliament for its members, not least because they discussed and influenced foreign policy and set controls on the use of subsidies. For James, on the other hand, it was frequently irksome and frustrating. Both houses petitioned him on April 10 that all laws against Jesuits, seminary priests, and others in holy orders "derived from the See of Rome," and against "all Popish recusants" be put in execution.[62] They asked, moreover, that in any negotiations for the marriage of the prince no commitment be made to ease the execution of these laws. James responded in a speech at Whitehall on April 24 that he regretted that he should be thought to need urging "to doe that wch my conscience and dutie binde me unto."[63] He reminded the members that he had clearly declared his own religion, for which he had been mocked and slandered – "never Kinge suffered more by ill tonges than I have done."[64] Yet he had never favored persecution, "for I ever thought, that noe waie

[56] Ibid.   [57] Folger MS. X. d. 150, fol. 1.   [58] Ibid., fol. 1 verso.   [59] Ibid.
[60] Ibid.   [61] Folger MS. V. a. 205, p. 207.
[62] Tanner, ed., *Constitutional Documents of the Reign of James I*, p. 301.
[63] Folger MS. Z. e. 1, fol. 1.   [64] Ibid.

ever more increases any Religion then Persecution, according to that sayinge *Sanguis martirum est semen ecclesiae,*" the blood of martyrs is the seed of the Church.[65] He agreed to issue a proclamation ordering Jesuits and priests to depart from the realm by a definite date and for judges to put all the laws against recusants into operation. But he insisted that in this matter "you must give me leave as a good horseman sometimes to use the reynes and not alwayes to use the spurre."[66]

A more agonizing problem emerged when accusations of profiteering, mismanagement, and favoritism were raised by members of both houses against Lionel Cranfield, earl of Middlesex, the lord treasurer. Cranfield had originally been a protégé of Buckingham, but he had irritated the duke and prince during their sojourn in Spain when he had raised questions about the costs of their mission. The treasurer was, moreover, known to have favored the Spanish match, partly for the sake of the dowry the infanta would bring, and he warned against the ruinous effects war would have on government finances and on trade. The House of Commons, acting as "Inquisitors-General" of the kingdom, voted on April 15 to impeach Cranfield and ask the Lords to try him.[67] On May 5 James defended Cranfield in a speech to the Lords at Whitehall in which he pointed out that Cranfield had been concerned about "abuses in the Exchequer, in the Navy, and a thousand other pticulers" before becoming treasurer.[68] His reforms had greatly benefited the crown, but also made him many enemies. James observed that there were "diverse things layd to his charge" which Cranfield had done with "my knowledge & approbation" and ought not to be held against him.[69] The king nevertheless asserted that "if here appeare false-hood, treacherie & deceipt under trust my Love [for him] is gone."[70] With Charles and Buckingham taking the side of the Commons in the Lords, Cranfield was found guilty of the charge of accepting bribes and of inadequately supplying the Ordnance Office. James, however, exercised his own discretion in evaluating the evidence and the sentence against Cran-field. The king found that the treasurer had mismanaged the accounts of the Royal Wardrobe, and agreed that Cranfield should lose his offices. Parlia-ment had sentenced him to imprisonment in the Tower at the king's pleasure and fined him £50,000. But Cranfield was soon released, and his fine reduced to £30,000 in July and then to £20,000 in November.[71]

On May 28, the day before Parliament adjourned, the Commons

---

[65] Ibid.   [66] Ibid., fol. 1 verso.
[67] J. P. Kenyon, ed., *The Stuart Constitution: Documents and Commentary*, second edition (Cambridge: Cambridge University Press, 1986), pp. 93–94.
[68] Folger MS. V. b. 303, p. 252.   [69] Ibid., p. 253.
[70] Ibid., p. 254.
[71] Menna Prestwich, *Cranfield: Politics and Profits under the Early Stuarts, the Career of Lionel Cranfield, Earl of Middlesex* (Oxford: Clarendon Press, 1966), pp. 439–474.

submitted a long list of grievances to the king for which the members sought redress. Many dealt with patents, that is grants by letters patent to individuals or groups giving them exclusive rights to engage in specific enterprises – fish the New England waters, or bring in coal to London by sea, or produce gold wire, for instance. It was to eliminate such grants that a Monopolies Bill had been passed in this Parliament. In his speech on the same day James promised to submit these grievances to his council and judges for review.[72] The speaker, Sir Thomas Crew, declared in his closing speech that with reference to "the great and waighty business" the two houses had been called to consider, "the true beleevers at home and our neighbors & confederats abroad may reioyce and sing a new song of ioy."[73] It is ironic that the only one of James's Parliaments to end on entirely good terms with him was one which was committed to a belligerent foreign policy of a kind which the king had opposed throughout his reign in England.

What does one make of this? One explanation that has been given is that this Parliament was managed by Charles and Buckingham to the exclusion of James, who was old, tired, isolated, and powerless.[74] It is true that Charles and Buckingham wanted a meeting of Parliament to break off negotiations with Spain and to grant support for an anti-Spanish war. They used their patronage and influence to secure the election of members of the Commons who were sympathetic to their views and they organized groups in both houses to further their political program. Furthermore they partici- pated actively in the sessions of the House of Lords and encouraged spokesmen with views similar to theirs to direct the debates and business of the Commons.[75] But the evidence of this Parliament's actions as presented by several recent historians shows that James was anything but a passive figure in the unfolding of events. It was James whom Parliament sought to satisfy during its month-long consideration of the Spanish treaties and of the support needed in case of war. James's objectives and tactics were not always the same as those of Charles and Buckingham. He specifically did not endorse Buckingham's view that Spain had been insincere in the marriage negotiations and he stated his financial needs in the event of war in such starkly honest terms as to surprise the delegation from Parliament. In his speech given at the time of Cranfield's impeachment by the Commons, James not only defended the lord treasurer to the Lords, but pointed out that it was Buckingham who had brought Cranfield into the royal service.

[72] Folger MS. V. a. 205, pp. 114–137; MS. V. b. 303, p. 255.

[73] Folger MS. V. a. 205, pp. 138, 144.

[74] Samuel R. Gardiner, *History of England, from the Accession of James I. to the Outbreak of the Civil War, 1603–1642*, 10 vols. (London: Longmans, Green, 1883), vol. V, pp. 159–160, 174; D. Harris Willson, *King James VI and I* (New York: Henry Holt, 1956), pp. 441–443; Ruigh, *The Parliament of 1624*, pp. 27–32.

[75] Ruigh, *The Parliament of 1624*, pp. 57–90.

In the Subsidy Bill James received a more generous grant than had been made to his predecessors without a declaration of war or even a commitment on his part as to exactly what kind of war he intended to wage. The Parliament of 1624 was as much the king's as it was the duke's or the prince's.

Another explanation that has been given is that James was forced by a combination of public opinion, the views of both houses of Parliament, and, especially, the convictions of his favorite and his son to abandon the search for peace in favor of confrontation and, eventually, war with Spain.[76] It is true that much of the political nation, including most of the members of Parliament, were anti-Spanish; and they saw England as the natural ally of the United Provinces and the German Protestant states. Opposition to the Austrian and Spanish Habsburgs had long been strong in England and had been intensified by the Bohemian revolt and the loss of the Palatinate.[77] But, on the evidence presented here, it can be seen that James was not forced to revise his foreign policy by domestic politics, including the activities of the two persons closest to him, so much as by events abroad. It was the actions of the Emperor Ferdinand, Duke Maximilian of Bavaria, the Elector Frederick, and Christian of Brunswick which undermined his negotiations for a truce and a peace conference in Germany. And it was Philip IV and Count Olivares of Spain who had shown themselves unwilling to risk a conflict with Austria over the status of the Palatinate. By the end of 1623, when James called for a meeting of Parliament, he saw no alternative to developing a new foreign policy. With the help of Charles and Buckingham, members of the Privy Council, and Parliament, whose advice he solicited in his opening address, James developed a new approach to foreign affairs, but it was not the same as that advocated by his son and favorite.

Charles and Buckingham wanted a war with Spain on both sea and land in cooperation with the anti-Habsburg states of Europe, Catholic as well as Protestant. James favored preparations for war, but his objectives were far more limited than theirs. What he wanted was the return of the Palatinate to his daughter and son-in-law. James told Parliament on March 23: "And for my part except by such meanes as God may putt into my hands I may recover the Palat: I could wish never to have bin borne; I am old but my onely sonne is younge, & I will promise for my selfe & him, that noe meanes shall be unused for the recovery of it, & this I dare say as old as I am, If I might doe good to the busynes I would goe in my owne person, & thinck my labour & travell well bestowed though I should end my dayes

[76] Cogswell, *The Blessed Revolution*, pp. 1, 310–315.
[77] Ibid., pp. 6–105, 137–226. See also S. L. Adams, "Foreign Policy and the Parliaments of 1621 and 1624," in Kevin Sharpe, ed., *Faction and Parliament: Essays on Early Stuart History* (Oxford: Clarendon Press, 1978), pp. 139–171.

there."[78] James resisted pressures for a "blue water" campaign against Spanish shipping or an all-out war on the European continent. To the extent England was to be actively engaged in military or naval conflict, he wanted such action to be restricted. The king's policy involved the threat of force and even the use of force, as in the financing of Mansfeld's ill-fated contingent of impressed Britons for use in the Palatinate. But he continued to seek diplomatic solutions for the return of the Palatinate as well as other issues in the war. In his conversations with the Spanish ambassadors he urged Philip IV to assist in the restoration of the Palatinate to Frederick and Elizabeth. Even when preparations for a war against Spain were being made during his last months, James never broke diplomatic relations with Spain. James's foreign policy during his last year of life was not bellicose.[79] His statement in his opening address to Parliament in February 1624 remained the theme of his reign: "I have bene treating these many yeares & yet still doe endeavour & have noe other Intencõn but onely to treate of the peace of Kingdomes in genãll & of this in more pticuler."[80]

If there was continuity in James's conduct of foreign policy in the last months of his life, the same is true of his approach to issues concerning differences between English Protestants and Roman Catholics. He responded to Parliament's request for more stringent measures against Catholic priests with a proclamation on May 6 ordering them to depart from the realm of England before June 14, 1624 or to suffer "the uttermost severity and punishment, which by the Lawes in that behalfe made, can bee inflicted upon them."[81] But he would clearly have preferred them to go into exile and thus avoid more severe punishment. Moreover his efforts to secure a French marriage for Charles showed just how far he was willing to go to relax the execution of laws against Roman Catholics in England.

James wanted a marriage alliance with France for some of the same reasons he had wanted one with Spain. To link the house of Stuart to the house of Bourbon would be to form a partnership with a predominantly Roman Catholic nation and with one of the most powerful monarchies in Europe. Negotiations for the hand of Princess Christine of France had been progressing for several years when they were superseded by those for the hand of the Infanta Maria in 1616. Christine had subsequently married Victor Amadeus of Savoy, but her younger sister Henrietta Maria was now of a marriageable age. An alliance with France might also give James a

---

[78] Folger MS. X. d. 150, fol. 1.
[79] Compare Ruigh, *The Parliament of 1624*, pp. 385–387; Russell, *Parliaments and English Politics, 1621–1629*, pp. 177, 185–186, 190, 201–208; Cogswell, *The Blessed Revolution*, pp. 314–315.
[80] Folger MS. V. b. 303, p. 335.
[81] James F. Larkin and Paul L. Hughes, eds., *Stuart Royal Proclamations*, 2 vols. (Oxford: Clarendon Press, 1973–83), vol. I, p. 592.

valuable supporter in his effort to secure the restoration of the Palatinate. To Buckingham, who began informal conversations on the subject of an Anglo-French marriage alliance with Tanneguy Leveneur, count of Tillières, the French ambassador, in December 1623, the stakes were even higher.[82] France, were it willing to play the part, could be the great power at the center of the anti-Habsburg coalition which Buckingham favored. As events showed, France, now under the influence of Armand-Jean du Plessis, Cardinal Richelieu, was not ready for so ambitious a policy, partly because of a rebellion under way in the French southwest, where Huguenots were numerous. But Louis XIII's government was quite willing to discuss a marriage which would, if it were successfully negotiated, keep England out of such an alliance with the Spanish Habsburgs.

Unofficial negotiations began in Paris in February 1624 when Henry Rich, Lord Kensington, arrived as ambassador extraordinary. By the time negotiations were officially under way in June, Kensington had been joined by the earl of Carlisle. The French government was represented in England by Antoine de Ruze, marquis D'Effiat, who arrived in London in July. Though it was expected in England that the French would not insist as strongly as the Spaniards that the conditions for Roman Catholics in England be improved, this was not to be the case. The English offered as a model the draft treaty of 1616 for a marriage between Charles and Princess Christine, a document which called for religious toleration only for the princess's household. The French countered with a draft of thirteen articles based on the recent Anglo-Spanish treaty, which promised a generous measure of religious liberty for all English Roman Catholics.[83] The French minister, Charles, marquis de La Vieuville, subsequently suggested that the treatment of English Roman Catholics need not be dealt with in the treaty itself but could be dealt with in a separate letter by the British king, an assurance which he believed would be sufficient to obtain a papal dispensation for the marriage. By the beginning of August this suggestion had provoked Henri-Auguste de Loménie, count of Brienne, the French secretary of state, to contrive the ouster of La Vieuville from his job, a development that naturally upset the English court.[84] Meanwhile in order to show his own willingness to make reasonable concessions on this issue, James agreed in July to review every judgement against Roman Catholics under the penal laws before it was put into effect.

---

[82] Cogswell, *The Blessed Revolution*, pp. 121–127.
[83] Gordon Albion, *Charles I and the Court of Rome: A Study in 17th Century Diplomacy* (Louvain: Bibliothèque de l'Université, 1935), pp. 50–55.
[84] Ibid., p. 57; Philip Yorke, earl of Hardwicke, ed., *Miscellaneous State Papers, from 1501 to 1726*, 2 vols. (London: W. Strahan and T. Cadell, 1778), vol. I, pp. 523–525 (Edward Conway to Carlisle and Kensington, August 12, 1624).

By September Effiat reported that James and the Privy Council had accepted a revised version of La Vieuville's original idea – namely that there should be an *Ecrit particulier*, separate from the treaty, according to which English Roman Catholics would be given the right to practice their faith in secret. Since even a rumor of relaxing the penal laws was likely to provoke vociferous opposition in the English Parliament, the session planned for the autumn of 1624 was postponed. On November 18, in Paris, the French authorities and the two English ambassadors, Carlisle and Kensington (now the earl of Holland), agreed to a statement which said that James would give Louis XIII an *Ecrit particulier*, signed by Charles, the English secretary of state, and himself, in which he would permit all of his Roman Catholic subjects "to enjoy more liberty and freedom, in that which concerns their religion, than he had done by virtue of whatever articles had been accorded them by the treaty of marriage concluded with Spain."[85] The statement continued by saying that James did not wish his Roman Catholic subjects to be "disturbed in their persons and property" by the profession of their religion, providing that they practiced it modestly and rendered obedience as good subjects of their king, who "will not restrain them by any oath contrary to their religion."[86] Less than a month later, on December 12, James ratified the treaty of marriage drawn up in Paris, including an *Ecrit particulier* based on the statement of November 18. All that remained was to secure the papal dispensation.[87]

The difficulties involved in Anglo-French cooperation in military affairs were illustrated by the expedition conducted by the German commander Mansfeld in late 1624. Mansfeld arrived in England in September with assurances from French officials that France would aid him in a campaign in the Palatinate if England would do so. The proposition was that France would meet half of his expenses and supply 3,000 cavalry. England would meet the other half of his expenses and supply 12,000 infantry. The force would rendezvous in northern France and would cross the country to the Palatinate on the Rhine. In late October the Privy Council directed the lord lieutenants of the counties to conscript men for the army; these men were not to be members of the Trained Bands, who might be needed for defense at home. By the end of December untrained, undisciplined, and as yet unpaid soldiers were converging on Dover, the port of embarkation, creating a nuisance almost everywhere they went. By this time James had turned down a request by Louis that the troops be used for the relief of Breda in the Netherlands, which was under siege by Spanish forces on the Dutch border. Eager to avoid a confrontation with Spain, he also forbade

---

[85] Hardwicke, *Miscellaneous State Papers*, vol. I, p. 546.   [86] Ibid., pp. 546–547.
[87] Albion, *Charles I and the Court of Rome*, pp. 62–63; Hardwicke, *Miscellaneous State Papers*, vol. I, p. 547 (Conway to Carlisle and Holland, December 23, 1624).

the troops to cross Spanish territory. Louis, for his part, decided that Mansfeld could not, after all, land in France. Louis was worried about the effect this military operation might have on the papacy, on French relations with other Roman Catholic states, and on his suppression of the forces of Benjamin de Rohan, count of Soubise, the Huguenot nobleman who was leading a revolt near La Rochelle.[88] As a result Mansfeld, after having to keep his men on board ship for several weeks, finally sailed for the United Provinces on January 31, 1625. Half the soldiers disembarked at Walcheren, in Zeeland, while the others were sent to Gertruidenberg, just north of Breda. Because of bad weather, those who were sent to Gertruidenberg had to continue to remain on board ship, where many died of disease. When the remaining soldiers were put ashore there were inadequate provisions for them and many of them perished. Mansfeld's English forces eventually melted away, reduced by illnesses and desertion, without having engaged in any fighting.[89]

Early in February 1625 word reached Paris that the dispensation for the marriage of Henrietta Maria and Charles had been issued in Rome, but with many modifications requested in the treaty. French negotiators pressed for what Carlisle described as

no less than a direct and public toleration, not by connivance, promise, or *escrit secret*, but by a public notification to all the Roman Catholics, and that of all his Majesty's kingdoms whatsoever, confirmed by his Majesty and the Prince his oath, and attested by a public act, whereof a copy to be delivered to the Pope or his Minister, and the same to bind his Majesty and the Prince's successors for ever.[90]

The English, however, refused to make any changes to a treaty Carlisle considered to be "concluded, signed, and sworn by his Majesty."[91] This resolute approach carried weight with the French. By March 10 Carlisle was assured that the marriage would take place in thirty days. But King James had become seriously ill early in March, with the result that the marriage had to be postponed. Because of James's illness and his death later in March, Charles did not go to Paris for the wedding. It was celebrated at the Cathedral of Notre Dame on May 1, with Charles's cousin Claude de Lorraine, duke of Chevreuse, standing in for him. The dispensation had

---

[88] Roger Lockyer, *Buckingham: The Life and Political Career of George Villiers, First Duke of Buckingham, 1592–1628* (London: Longman, 1981), pp. 206–209, 222–227; Victor-L. Tapié, *France in the Age of Louis XIII and Richelieu*, trans. D. M. Lockie (Cambridge: Cambridge University Press, 1984), pp. 122–129; Hardwicke, *Miscellaneous State Papers*, vol. I, pp. 547–553.

[89] Lockyer, *Buckingham*, pp. 228–229; Hardwicke, *Miscellaneous State Papers*, vol. I, pp. 547–553.

[90] Hardwicke, *Miscellaneous State Papers*, vol. I, p. 552 (Carlisle to Buckingham, February 16, 1625).

[91] Ibid., p. 552.

been turned over to Louis after he promised to see that England kept the promises made in the treaty.[92] Henrietta Maria arrived in Dover on June 12 with a numerous company of courtiers from both nations, including the duke of Buckingham, who had been sent by King Charles I to bring his bride back to England. The more lenient treatment of English Roman Catholics provided for in the *Ecrit particulier* brought an improvement for them in the first six months of 1625, but was at variance with Charles's and Buckingham's strategy of seeking support for war in Parliament, where anti-Catholic sentiment was strong. As a result the enforcement of the penal laws against Roman Catholics was soon made more rigorous.[93] The French match did not bring the significant improvement in the condition of English Roman Catholics which the *Ecrit particulier* had eloquently called for.

After enduring fever and convulsions for three weeks, James died on March 27, 1625 at the age of fifty-nine. According to John Williams, bishop of Lincoln and lord keeper of the Great Seal, the king asked, four days before his death, to receive the sacrament of Holy Communion. "Being desir'd to declare his Faith," James repeated the articles of the creed and then added that "hee beleeued them all, as they were receiued and expounded by that part of the Catholique Church which was established here in England."[94] As succinctly as a verse from Proverbs or the Psalms, he thus stated both his commitment to the Church of England and to the larger Church to which particular churches belonged. To a greater degree than either his contemporaries or historians have recognized, his reign in England was dedicated to restoring, in an age of intense religious and political conflict, the visible unity of that "Catholique Church" of which the churches of his realms were a part.[95]

[92] Albion, *Charles I and the Court of Rome*, pp. 74–76.   [93] Ibid., pp. 64, 76, 79, 81.

[94] John Williams, *Great Britains Salomon: A Sermon Preached at the Magnificent Funerall of the Most High and Mighty King, Iames, the Late King of Great Britaine, France, and Ireland, Defender of the Faith, &c., at the Collegiate Church of Saint Peter at Westminster, the Seuenth of May 1625* (London: John Bill, 1625), p. 69.

[95] James saw the sister churches, the Church of Scotland and the Church of Ireland, as part of that "Catholique Church" and believed that those churches, like the Church of England, should exhibit marks of continuity with the past in liturgy and polity. But he did not insist on complete uniformity among the three. Within limits, each was allowed to develop structures and formularies according to its own traditions. See John Morrill, "A British Patriarchy? Ecclesiastical Imperialism under the Early Stuarts," in Anthony Fletcher and Peter Roberts, eds., *Religion, Culture and Society in Early Modern Britain: Essays in Honour of Patrick Collinson* (Cambridge: Cambridge University Press, 1994), pp. 209–237. Neither in Scotland nor Ireland was the Jacobean settlement smooth or entirely successful, since presbyterianism remained strong in Scotland, and most of the Irish, outside the English and Scottish enclaves, did not adhere to the established Church. For Scotland, see Walter Roland Foster, *The Church before the Covenants: The Church of Scotland, 1596–1638* (Edinburgh: Scottish Academic Press, 1975), *passim*, and Maurice Lee, Jr., *Government by Pen: Scotland under James VI and I* (Urbana: University of Illinois Press, 1980), esp. pp. 61–111, 155–194. For Ireland, see T. W. Moody, F. X. Martin, and

Bishop Williams, who preached the sermon at James's funeral at West-minster Abbey on May 7, identified four achievements of the late king which deserved to be remembered. The first was James's care for religion. The bishop singled out James's sponsoring of a translation of the Bible, his affirmation of the polity of the English Church at the Hampton Court Conference, his ending of the practice of leasing church lands to the crown and to courtiers, and his defense of the faith in his numerous books.[96] After dealing with two other achievements, namely the king's even-handed administration of justice through the courts, and his defeat of his enemies in the field in Scotland as well as his defense of his realms, Williams turned to the subject of peace. "None can be honoured of all Europe," he said of James, "but he that held the Ballance of all Europe, and, for the space of twentie yeares at the least, preserued the peace of all Europe."[97] This era of peace, said Williams, had also been remarkably beneficial to James's own realms in learning, commerce, internal security, and expansion overseas:

the Schooles of the Prophets [had been] newly adorned, manufactures at home daily inuented, Trading abroad exceedingly multiplied, the Borders of Scotland peaceably gouerned, the North of Ireland religiously planted, the Nauy Royall magnificently furnished, Virginia, New-found-land, and New-England peopled, the East India well traded, Persia, China, and the Mogor visited, lastly, all the ports of Europe, Afrique, Asia and America to our red Crosses freed, and opened. And they are all the Actions, and true-borne Children of King Iames his Peace.[98]

There was no incentive for a preacher to understate James's achievements on an occasion like this, and some of the items in Williams's catalogue may look more ambiguous or less permanent than he assumed they were. But British educational institutions had flourished, the economy had grown and become more diversified, the border country between England and Scotland had been pacified, the foundations of the British empire had been laid in the New World, and British traders were active in the Levant, Persia, India, West Africa, and the western hemisphere.[99] The "red Crosses" of St. George had entered ports in all the known continents. Williams did not claim that James was personally responsible for all of these developments.

F. J. Byrne, eds., *A New History of Ireland*, 6 vols. to date (Oxford: Clarendon Press, 1976–   ), vol. III, pp. 29–30, 52–65, 137–141, 188–232.

[96] Williams, *Great Britains Salomon*, pp. 46–51.   [97] Ibid., p. 60.

[98] Ibid., pp. 57–58.

[99] See, for example, Lawrence Stone, "The Size and Composition of the Oxford Student Body, 1580–1910," pp. 3–110, esp. pp. 5–6, 12–37, and Victor Morgan, "Cambridge University and 'The Country,' 1560–1640," pp. 183–245, in Stone, ed., *The University in Society*, 2 vols. (Princeton: Princeton University Press, 1974), vol. I; Joan Thirsk, *Economic Policy and Projects: The Development of a Consumer Society in Early Modern England* (Oxford: Clarendon Press, 1978), *passim*; and C. G. A. Clay, *Economic Expansion and Social Change: England, 1500–1700*, 2 vols. (Cambridge: Cambridge University Press, 1984), vol. I, pp. 102–141, vol. II, pp. 1–141.

But he did point out that they had been fostered by the era of peace in the British Isles and in Europe, peace which James had worked long and hard to maintain.

Other contemporaries also celebrated James as a peacemaker. Before the king's death, Joseph Hall, in a sermon delivered before James on September 19, 1624, rejoiced in the peace which had long prevailed in the British Isles and exhorted his hearers to make it the opportunity to extend social justice: "Let there be no grinding of faces, no trampling on the poore (Amos 5. 11), no swallowing of widowes houses, no force, no fraud, no perjury."[100] John Donne, in a sermon on April 26, 1625, during the interval before James's funeral, referred to "that Hand that ballanced his own three Kingdomes so equally that none of them complained of one another, nor of him, and carried the Keyes of all the Christian world, and locked up, and let out Armies in their due season."[101] James's "desire and intension," as Donne later said in a sermon on May 21, 1626, was to be "Peace-maker of all the Christian world" and to silence "all Field-drums."[102]

The most striking tribute to James's role as a peacemaker is the ceiling of the Banqueting House at Whitehall, where Peter Paul Rubens's paintings of James's achievements were installed in 1635. The paintings were commissioned by Charles I in 1629. By this time Charles had determined to make his own reign an era of peace. He and Buckingham had discovered how difficult it was to carry out effective military and naval operations against Spain and how reluctant Parliament could be in its support of their actions. Rubens, who served as an envoy from Spain to negotiate a peace between England and Spain, subsequently devoted one of his three major panels on the ceiling of the Banqueting House to the theme of peace. In this south panel James is shown on his throne making a sweeping gesture, which at once shows his rejection of military triumph as represented by the warrior-god Mars – whom Minerva is pictured as vanquishing – and his protective care of two female figures, representing peace and plenty, who are embracing each other. Minerva embodies that wisdom, backed by the power of Jove's thunderbolt, which can banish war. At the foot of the picture the messenger Mercury leans forward with his caduceus to heal and reconcile the vanquished foes. Two side panels alongside the central painting of James's ascent into heaven depict a new age, such as that described by Isaiah and Virgil, in which winged children, or *putti*, tame wild beasts and

---

[100] Joseph Hall, "The True Peace-Maker: Laid Forth in a Sermon before His Maiestie at Theobalds, September 19, 1624," in *The Works of Joseph Hall, B. of Exceter* (London: Edw. Brewster, 1634), p. 502.

[101] John Donne, *Sermons*, ed. Evelyn M. Simpson and George R. Potter, 10 vols. (Berkeley: University of California Press, 1953–1962), vol. VI, p. 290.

[102] Ibid., vol. VII, p. 166.

produce a cornucopia of the fruits of the earth.[103] The south panel and the two side panels represent that creative and fruitful peace which Williams described in his sermon.

Even James's harshest critics among contemporary writers gave him credit for his ability to preserve peace in his dominions. The history of James's reign written by Sir Anthony Weldon, clerk of the Green Cloth in James's household, includes a character sketch of the king which has influenced – negatively – James's reputation to the present day. In a key passage Weldon wrote: "He was naturally of a timerous disposition . . . His eyes large, ever rowling after any stranger [who] came in his presence . . . his tongue too large for his mouth . . . his skin was as soft as Taffeta Sarsnet, which felt so, because he never washt his hands, only rub'd his finger ends slightly with the wet end of a napkin, his legs were very weake."[104] The impression Weldon conveyed was that James was not only unattractive but timid, indecisive, and lacking in moral fiber. Yet Weldon ended this passage with the comment: "In a word, take him altogether and not in peeces, such a King I wish this Kingdome have never any worse, on the condition, not any better; for he lived in peace, dyed in peace, and left all his Kingdomes in a peaceable condition."[105] This "peaceable condition" must have been seen as a signal achievement when the book was published in 1650, after civil wars had raged in all three kingdoms. The same contrast occurs in the description by the historian Arthur Wilson in 1653. Wilson's treatment of James's physical and psychological attributes recapitulated Weldon's. He also acknowledged James's success in peace-making, though in a highly ambiguous way: "Some Parallel'd him to Tiberius for Dissimulation, yet Peace was maintained by him as in the Time of Augustus; and Peace begot Plenty, and Plenty begot Ease and Wantonness, and Ease and Wantonness begot Poetry, and Poetry swelled to that bulk in his time, that it begot strange Monstrous Satyrs, against the

---

103 The iconography and historical context of the panels cited here are discussed in Per Palme, *Triumph of Peace: A Study of the Whitehall Banqueting House* (London: Thames and Hudson, 1957), pp. 1–7, 78–81, 233–262; Oliver Millar, *Rubens: The Whitehall Ceiling* (London: Oxford University Press, 1958), pp. 1–13, 16–18; D. J. Gordon, *The Renaissance Imagination*, ed. Stephen Orgel (Berkeley: University of California Press, 1980), pp. 3–10, 24–35, 41–42, 45; Roy Strong, *Britannia Triumphans: Inigo Jones, Rubens, and Whitehall Palace* (London: Thames and Hudson, 1980), pp. 7–13, 34–51; Graham Parry, *The Golden Age Restor'd: The Culture of the Stuart Court, 1603–42* (Manchester: Manchester University Press, 1981), pp. 32–37. For the "cult of peace" in Charles I's reign, see R. Malcolm Smuts, *Court Culture and the Origins of a Royalist Tradition in Early Stuart England* (Philadelphia: University of Pennsylvania Press, 1987), pp. 245–270. See also, for Charles's peace policy, Kevin Sharpe, *The Personal Rule of Charles I* (New Haven: Yale University Press, 1992), pp. 65–104.
104 Anthony Weldon, *The Court and Character of King James* (London: John Wright, 1650), p. 178.
105 Ibid., p. 189.

King's own person."[106] Wilson viewed James's era of peace critically, as he did much else in James's reign, yet he saw this king as in the pattern of the first and greatest of the Roman emperors.

If James's peacemaking was widely recognized by contemporary writers, the same can hardly be said of his efforts on behalf of Christian reconciliation and reunion. Joseph Hall did comment briefly on James's concern for the universal Church in his dedication of the first edition of his own *Works* to the king in 1621. Alluding to Atlas's bearing of the world on his shoulders as an image of a king, Hall wrote: "As Kings are to the World, so are good Kings to the Church: None can be so blinde, or envious, as not to grant, that the whole Church of God upon earth, rests her selfe principally (next to her stay above) upon your Majesties Royall supportation."[107] As extravagantly laudatory as this dedication was, Hall's comment about James's concern for the whole Church evidently came with conviction from one whom the king had sent as a delegate to the Synod of Dort.

The most explicit reference to James's ecumenical activities, however, was in a work by the Scottish Bishop William Forbes. In a passage in a work published in 1658, Forbes mentioned James in connection with a discussion of Isaac Casaubon's published response to Cardinal du Perron. Forbes referred to "that most serene and never sufficiently to be praised prince, James VI, who, though he had nothing more at heart than the wish to bring about a pious peace and concord among Christian Churches, never was able to obtain or give effect to what he so greatly desired, in consequence of the morose and quarrelsome dispositions of a number of would-be theologians."[108] Forbes's knowledge and appreciation of James's efforts towards achieving concord among the churches could have come from his reading of Marco Antonio De Dominis and David Pareus, whom he admired, or his acquaintance with Hugo Grotius during his study abroad in the first decade of James's reign in England.

Since James was evidently little remembered in the seventeenth century for his efforts to achieve a religious reunion among Christian churches, it is not surprising that he is little known for those efforts today. King James VI and I has not been given a good press by historians until comparatively recently. A tradition of interpretation stemming from S. R. Gardiner in the late nineteenth century found the king lacking in many significant qualities

---

[106] Arthur Wilson, *The History of Great Britain, Being the Life and Reign of King James the First, Relating to What Passed from His First Access to the Crown Till His Death* (London: Richard Lownds, 1653), pp. 289–290.

[107] Hall, *Works*, sig. A₃ verso.

[108] William Forbes, *Considerationes modestae et pacificae controversiarum de justificatione, purgatorio, invocatione sanctorum, Christo mediatore, et eucharistia*, fourth edition, 2 vols. (Oxford: J. H. Parker, 1850–1856), vol. II, pp. 95–96.

of leadership and character.[109] He has been viewed as cowardly, double-dealing, intolerant, unkingly, and inattentive to the task of governing. A reassessment of James is now under way. This reassessment has already produced a more favorable view of James as the ruler of Scotland.[110] He is

[109] Gardiner, *History of England from the Accession of James I. to the Outbreak of the Civil War, 1603–1642*, vol. I, pp. 48–52, 87–88, 193–194, 232–233, vol. II, pp. 218–223, vol. III, pp. 183–184, 280–281, 325–327, 344–345, 370–372, vol. IV, pp. 268–271, 358–360, 411, vol. V, pp. 64–65, 141–142, 160–161, 170–171, 213–214, 272–274, 290–291, 313–316; G. M. Trevelyan, *England under the Stuarts* (London: Methuen, 1965 – first published, 1904), pp. 28–29, 67–75; Hugh Ross Williamson, *King James I* (London: Duckworth, 1935), pp. 13–20; Clara and Hardy Steeholm, *James I of England: The Wisest Fool in Christendom* (New York: Covici Friede, 1938), pp. 7, 270, 258, 473; Godfrey Davies, "The Character of James VI and I," *Huntington Library Quarterly*, 5 (1941–1942), 33–63; Willson, *King James VI and I*, pp. 14, 47–48, 168, 273, 287, 333, 341, 363, 378, 388, 408, 440–441; William McElwee, *The Wisest Fool in Christendom: The Reign of King James I and VI* (London: Faber and Faber, 1958), pp. 14–15, 90–92, 102–106, 124–126, 262–263, 275–277; and David M. Bergeron, *Royal Family, Royal Lovers: King James of England and Scotland* (Columbia, Mo.: University of Missouri Press, 1991), pp. 2–3, 12, 17, 104, 139, 143, 170–171, 185–186. T. F. Henderson, *James I. and VI.* (Paris and London: Goupil, 1904) treats James favorably as an ecclesiastical and political peacemaker (pp. 101–102, 238–241, 268–270, 300–301). Charles Williams, *James I* (London: Arthur Barker, 1934) writes sympathetically of "The King among the Churches" (pp. 185–199). Suggestions of a fresh view of James's career are found in G. P. V. Akrigg, *Jacobean Pageant: or, The Court of King James I* (Cambridge, Mass.: Harvard University Press, 1962), pp. 5–6, 14, 394–397; David Mathew, *The Jacobean Age* (Port Washington, New York: Kennikat Press, 1971 – first published, 1938), pp. 17–36, and *James I* (London: Eyre and Spottiswoode, 1967), pp. 4–10, and *passim*; and, especially, Robert Ashton, ed., *James I by His Contemporaries* (London: Hutchinson, 1969), pp. xx–xxi, 22–27, 56–61, 86–88, 105–112, 140–146, 168–173, 203–207, 228–230, 252–254.

[110] Reassessments of various aspects of James's reign include Charles H. Carter, *The Secret Diplomacy of the Habsburgs, 1598–1625* (New York: Columbia University Press, 1964), pp. 27, 47–49, 100, 110–113, 241–244; Alan G. R. Smith, "Introduction," in *The Reign of James VI and I* (London: Macmillan, 1973), pp. 1–21; S. J. Houston, *James I* (London: Longman, 1973), pp. 3–9, 56–107; Antonia Fraser, *King James VI of Scotland, I of England* (London: Weidenfeld and Nicolson, 1974), pp. 8–9, 210–214; Marc L. Schwarz, "James I and the Historians: Toward a Reconsideration," *Journal of British Studies*, 13, 2 (May 1974), 114–134; Caroline Bingham, *James I of England* (London: Weidenfeld and Nicolson, 1981), pp. 207–212 and *passim*; Jenny Wormald, "James VI and I: Two Kings or One?" *History*, 68 (June 1983), 187–209; Maurice Lee, Jr., "James I and the Historians: Not a Bad King after All?" *Albion*, 16, 2 (Summer 1984), 151–163; Kenneth Fincham and Peter Lake, "The Ecclesiastical Policy of King James I," *Journal of British Studies*, 24, 2 (April 1985), 169–207; Conrad Russell, "English Parliaments, 1593–1606: One Epoch or Two?" in D. M. Dean and N. L. Jones, eds., *The Parliaments of Elizabethan England* (Oxford: Blackwell, 1990), pp. 191–213; Maurice Lee, Jr., *Great Britain's Solomon: James VI and I in His Three Kingdoms* (Urbana: University of Illinois Press, 1990), pp. 299–301 and *passim*; Linda Levy Peck, ed., *The Mental World of the Jacobean Court* (Cambridge: Cambridge University Press, 1991); and Christopher Durston, *James I* (London: Routledge, 1993), pp. 1–13, 64–66, and *passim*. For treatments of James's reign in Scotland, see Gordon Donaldson, *Scotland: James V to James VII* (Edinburgh: Oliver and Boyd, 1965), pp. 157–219; Maurice Lee, Jr., *Government by Pen: Scotland under James VI and I* (Urbana: University of Illinois Press, 1980), pp. 3–26, and *passim*; Jenny Wormald, *Court, Kirk, and Community: Scotland, 1470–1625* (London: Edward Arnold, 1981),

now seen as having brought an unprecedented political and social peace to his native land following a long civil war and a religious revolution. This study of his ecumenical and irenic activities in a European context is intended to be a part of that reassessment.

James's efforts on behalf of church unity can well look like a fantasy of unrealizable hopes and impracticable plans to a modern observer. Seen from the perspective of the Reformation era, however, they look a good deal more credible. As James recognized, religion was the transcendent ideological force in sixteenth- and early seventeenth-century Europe. During these years religion played a major part in dividing Germany into rival groups of states, creating an independent United Provinces of the Netherlands, driving Mary Queen of Scots from her throne, plunging France into a generation of civil war, and provoking the Bohemians and their neighbors to rebel against their Habsburg overlords. Politically speaking, religion could be deeply divisive, but it could be constructive as well. Roman Catholicism helped to forge the national cultures of Spain, France, and Austria, just as Protestantism did the national cultures of the United Provinces, Scotland, and England. Religious convictions helped to bind together coalitions of states, such as the French Catholic League in the late sixteenth century and the Evangelical Union in the early seventeenth century. What James wanted to do was to harness this powerful ideological force to achieve a stable and lasting peace in Europe. He saw Christendom as fragmented by religious and political conflicts of an increasingly ominous and destructive kind. The universal Church appeared to him to be a series of national or particular churches, most of them directed by temporal authorities; some of them recognized the spiritual jurisdiction of Rome while others did not. From his own experience in Scotland, his reading, and his conversations with theologians, James saw that the Roman Catholic Church and most of the churches that had emerged from the Protestant Reformation – as well as the Orthodox Churches in the East – shared a common foundation of religious beliefs. Where they diverged in doctrine or practice, room for compromise and agreement might be found. On some issues agreement could be reached to accommodate differences. James wanted to reverse the trend which had led to ever wider and more serious divisions, and to build a European peace on the basis of fundamental tenets of faith.

James saw as a principal means of accomplishing this objective the institution of the ecumenical council. Like Richard Hooker and other theologians in Scotland and England, he saw as the model for such a council not the medieval councils of the western Church but the ancient councils in

pp. 111–193; and Rosalind Mitchison, *Lordship to Patronage: Scotland, 1603–1745* (London: Edward Arnold, 1983), pp. 1–21.

which all the great sees were represented, including Antioch, Alexandria, and Constantinople as well as Rome. He saw the monarchs of his time as the political authorities who could convene such an assembly as the emperors had done in ancient times. The bishop of Rome, as the focus of unity and the patriarch of the West, even as president of the council, had a central part to play. Thus James's first attempt to move towards the reunion of Christendom had been to appeal to Pope Clement VIII for a truly ecumenical council. Subsequently the idea of an ecumenical council figured prominently at several stages of James's career – in his appeal to the rulers of Europe in his *Premonition*, in Casaubon's exchanges with du Perron, and in the books of De Dominis and Paolo Sarpi. The conciliar movement of the late fourteenth and early fifteenth centuries had restored the unity of the western Church when the Great Schism had become increasingly intractable. Conciliar theory continued to be supported by many Roman Catholic theologians, especially in France. Henry IV proposed a general or national council to heal the religious divisions of France during his struggle for the French throne. An ecumenical council was the most promising means available for resolving religious disputes on an international scale. But even if an ecumenical council could not be convened, the conciliar idea remained attractive to James. The most detailed plan for achieving a broader Christian union was that by Pierre du Moulin, which James's emissary, David Home, took to the Synod of Tonneins. Du Moulin subsequently sent it to the delegates at the Synod of Dort. It called for two successive councils of Protestant churches, followed by a fresh attempt to reach agreement with the papacy. Conciliarism appealed to James because it called for the same methods of discussion, negotiation, and the reconciliation of differences which he and his diplomatic corps used with remarkable success for over two decades in dealing with international political issues.

James encouraged such intellectuals as Jacques-Auguste de Thou, Jean Hotman, Isaac Casaubon, Hugo Grotius, and Georg Calixtus, all of whom sought to reconcile religious differences among Christians. He brought the cause of religious reunion explicitly and forcefully to the attention of his fellow monarchs and the papacy. As a result of his efforts the Church of England established close relations with the Reformed Churches of France, the Reformed Church of the United Provinces of the Netherlands, and the Greek Orthodox Church. James supported the publication of De Dominis's major theological work and Sarpi's celebrated and controversial history of the Council of Trent. He helped to preserve the stability of the church and the state in the United Provinces on the eve of the expiration of its truce with Spain. In the last years of his reign, he supported the cause of peace in the face of increasingly severe religious and political conflicts at the outbreak of the most destructive war of early modern times. James's vision encompassed both a lasting peace among the European nations and the reuniting of the Church, shattered in the West by the Reformation and the Counter-Reformation. The latter part of his vision remains unrealized, but the ecumenical movement in its many expressions in the twentieth century testifies to its continuing appeal.

BIBLIOGRAPHY

PRIMARY SOURCES

Secondary sources are cited in the footnotes, where bibliographical information is provided.

MANUSCRIPTS

Edinburgh

National Library of Scotland

Advocates MSS. 29.2.6, 29.2.7, 29.2.8, 33.1.1: Letters and papers of James VI (1580–1610)
Wodrow MSS. Quarto XXII: Papers concerning the Reformed Churches in France (1604–1614)

Geneva

Bibliothèque Publique et Universitaire

MSS. Français 421, 422, 423: Letters to and from the Company of Pastors (1612–1620)

London

British Library

Additional MS. 5873: Letter from Venice to Isaac Casaubon (1612)
Additional MS. 24195: Poems and Letter (1611) of King James
Burney MS. 367: Correspondence of Isaac Casaubon (1610–1612)
King's MSS. 121–128: Dépêches de Messire of Christophe de Harlay, comte de Beaumont (1602–1605)
Stowe MSS. 172–176: Papers of Sir Thomas Edmondes (1612–1632)

Lambeth Palace Library

Fairhurst/Laud Papers 3472–3473: Diplomatic and ecclesiastical papers (c. 1611–c. 1629)

Gibson MSS. 930, 941: Diplomatic and ecclesiastical papers (*c.* 1603–*c.* 1621)

Public Record Office

French Transcripts, PRO 31/3/42, 31/3/47 (1610–1615)
Roman Transcripts, PRO 31/9/88 (1604–1610)
State Papers, Domestic, 14/109 (1619), 14/216 (Gunpowder Plot Book, 1604–1605)
State Papers, Flanders, 77/7–9 (1603–1610)
State Papers, France, 78/49–74 (1603–1625)
State Papers, German States, 81/9–10 (1603–1610), 81/15–18 (1617–1620)
State Papers, Holland, 84/64–68 (1603–1606), 84/87–90 (1618–1619)
State Papers, Holy Roman Empire and Hungary, 80/2–5 (1604–1622)
State Papers, Italian States and Rome, 85/3–5 (1603–1625)
State Papers, Miscellaneous, 104/164–165 (King's Letter Book, 1603–1611)
State Papers, Savoy and Sardinia, 92/1 (1577–1613)
State Papers, Spain, 94/9–13 (1603–1607), 94/22–25 (1616–1622)
State Papers, Turkey, 97/11–14 (1625–1629)
State Papers, Venice, 99/2–4 (1599–1607)

Montpellier

Bibliothèque de la Faculté de Théologie Protestante

MS. 16400: Recueil des Actes des Synodes Nationaux des Eglises réformées du royaume de France, 1559–1620

Oxford

Bodleian Library

Smith, MS. 36: Letters and papers relating to the Eastern Churches
Smith MS. 68: Letters of members of the royal family (16th–17th centuries)
Smith MS. 74: Letters of learned men (16th–17th centuries)
Smith MS. 77: Letters relating to James VI and I
Tanner MS. 73: Letters of James VI and I and others
Tanner MS. 74: Letters of learned men (*c.* 1617– *c.* 1619)
Tanner MS. 283, fol. 122: Fragment of Marco Antonio De Dominis's manuscript of *De republica ecclesiastica*
Tanner MS. 290: Letters of public figures (early 17th century)
Tanner MSS. 462–463: De Dominis's manuscript of *De republica ecclesiastica*, Books I, II, VI

Paris

Bibliothèque Nationale

MS. Collection Cinq Cents de Colbert, vol. 466: Papers concerning relations between England and France (1601–1610)
MSS. Collection Dupuy 16, 409, 569, 571, 632, 819, 830: Letters (early 17th century)

MSS. Français Anciens Fonds 4331, 6641, 15976, 15896, 15984, 15985, 23194, 23200, 23298: Letters (late 16th and early 17th centuries)
MS. Nouvelles acquisitions françaises, vol. 5130: Letters (early 17th century)
MS. Nouvelles acquisitions latines, vol. 2456, fols. 99–100: Censure of De Dominis's *De republica ecclesiastica* (1617)

Bibliothèque de l'Arsenal

MS. 3847: Papers relative to the Huguenots (1572–1686)
MS. 4110: Letters and papers (early 17th century)
MS. 4111: Diplomatic and ecclesiastical papers (early 17th century)

Rome

Vatican Secret Archives

MS. Fondo Borghese, ser. I, vol. 118: Reports of the nuncio in Flanders (*c.* 1610)
MS. Fondo Borghese, ser. I, vols. 269–273: Reports of the nuncio in Flanders (1613)
MS. Fondo Borghese, ser. I, vols. 290–302: Miscellaneous documents
MS. Fondo Borghese, ser. I, vol. 308 Bis: Letters of the nuncio in Madrid (1605–1606)
MS. Fondo Borghese, ser. I, vols. 340–344: Miscellaneous documents
MS. Fondo Borghese, ser. I, vol. 512: Letters of bishops of the Holy Roman Empire (1606–1615)
MS. Fondo Borghese, ser. I, vol. 513: Letters to Pope Paul V and Cardinal Borghese (1606)
MS. Fondo Borghese, ser. I, vol. 594: Register of the letters of the nuncio in France (1612–1615)
MS. Fondo Borghese, ser. I, vol. 630, fols. 46–49: Compendium of the life of King James of England (*c.* 1603)
MS. Fondo Borghese, ser. I, vol. 758: Miscellaneous documents
MS. Fondo Borghese, ser. I, vol. 827 Bis: Instructions of the papal secretary to the nuncios (1621–1623)
MS. Fondo Borghese, ser. I, vol. 896: Register of the letters of the papal secretary to the nuncio in France (1613)
MS. Fondo Borghese, ser. I, vol. 897: Register of the letters of the papal secretary to the nuncio in Venice (1609–1611)
MS. Fondo Borghese, ser. I, vol. 898: Register of the letters of the papal secretary to the nuncio in Cologne (1609–1610)
MS. Fondo Borghese, ser. I, vol. 901: Letters of the papal secretary to the nuncio in Switzerland (1609–1613)
MS. Fondo Borghese, ser. I, vol. 902: Register of the letters of the papal secretary to the nuncio in France (1615–1616)
MS. Fondo Borghese, ser. I, vol. 904: Register of the letters of the nuncio in France (1610–1612)
MS. Fondo Borghese, ser. I, vol. 905: Register of the letters of the papal secretary to the nuncio in Venice (1612–1613)
MS. Fondo Borghese, ser. I, vol. 907: Register of the letters of the papal secretary to the nuncio in France (1609–1612)

MS. Fondo Borghese, ser. I, vol. 908: Register of the letters of the papal secretary to the nuncio in Venice (1605–1608)

MS. Fondo Borghese, ser. I, vol. 910: Register of the letters of the papal secretary to the nuncio in Naples (1608–1609)

MS. Fondo Borghese, ser. I, vol. 914: Register of the letters of the papal secretary to the nuncio in Spain (1611–1613)

MS. Fondo Borghese, ser. I, vol. 915: Register of the letters of the nuncio in France (1607–1610)

MS. Fondo Borghese, ser. I, vol. 925: Register of the letters of the papal secretary to the legates in France (1606)

MS. Fondo Borghese, ser. II, vol. 68: Miscellaneous documents

MS. Fondo Borghese, ser. II, vol. 100: Letters of the nuncio in Flanders (1607)

MS. Fondo Borghese, ser. II, vol. 103: Reports of the nuncio in Flanders (1606–1620)

MS. Fondo Borghese, ser. II, vol. 108: Letters of the nuncio in Flanders (1606)

MS. Fondo Borghese, ser. II, vol. 410: Papal briefs (1606)

MS. Fondo Borghese, ser. II, vol. 489: Register of letters of the nuncio in Flanders (1605–1609)

MS. Fondo Borghese, ser. III, vol. 45C: Papers concerning Germany, Poland, Hungary, Flanders (1607–1608)

MS. Fondo Borghese. ser. III, vol. 98, D 3: Letters of the nuncio in Flanders (1603)

MS. Fondo Borghese, ser. III, vol. 110 B, C, D, G: Letters of the nuncio in Flanders (1603–1605)

MS. Fondo Borghese, ser. IV, vol. 122: Papers concerning the Treaty of Flanders (1609)

MS. Fondo Nunziatura Fiandra, vol. 136A: Register of the letters of the papal secretary to the nuncio in Flanders (1605–1609)

MS. Fondo Pio, vol. 167: Register of the letters of the papal secretary to the nuncios in Cologne and Flanders (1605–1609)

MS. Miscellanea Armadio, III, vol. 44: Papers concerning the king of England (1602–1605)

Washington

Folger Shakespeare Library

MS. Bd. w. STC 14344, copy 3: Miscellaneous documents (1621)

MS. G. g. 7: Sir Roger Twysden's Historical Collection (*c.* 1620–1630)

MS. L. a. 548/126/1060: Letters and papers relating to King James

MS. M. b. 27: English State Papers (1587–1620)

MS. V. a. 24: Supporter of King James, "In what lamentable estate, and uppon what unapeasable termes all Europe now stands" (*c.* 1620)

MS. V. a. 121: Constitutional and legal documents (1610–*c.* 1621)

MS. V. a. 205: Speeches of King James to Parliament (1624)

MS. V. a. 339: Joseph Hall's Commonplace Book (*c.* 1650)

MS. V. a. 348: Diplomatic papers and parliamentary speeches (*c.* 1558–1628)

MS. V. b. 132: Letters of Sir Francis Bacon

MS. V. b. 182: Edmund Tilney's Descriptions of European countries and English policies (*c.* 1598–*c.* 1600)

MS. V. b. 207: *Mirabilia huius anni* – views of the military situation in the Palatinate and Bohemia (*c.* 1619)
MS. V. b. 303: Political and parliamentary documents (*c.* 1550–*c.* 1650)
MS. V. b. 303: Speeches delivered in Parliament (1587–1624)
MS. X. d. 150: King James's speech in Parliament (1621)
MS. X. d. 241 (a): Letter of Sir Walter Raleigh to King James (1604)
MS. X. d. 241 (c): Letters of Raleigh to King James (1618)
MS. X. d. 332: Petition of English Roman Catholics to King James (1604?)
MS. Z. e. 1 (15): King James's speech at the opening of Parliament (1621)
MS. Z. e. 1 (19): Articles of Marriage proposed between Prince Charles and the infanta of Spain (1623)
MS. Z. e. 1 (20): King James's speech to Parliament (1624)
MS. Z. e. 1 (21): Notes on Lord Chancellor Williams's speech and King James's reply (1624)

PRINTED SOURCES

Abbot, Robert. *De suprema potestate regia exercitationes habitae in academia Oxoniensi contra Rob. Bellarminum & Francisc. Suarez.* London: Norton, 1616
Akrigg, G. P. V., ed. *Letters of King James VI and I.* Berkeley: University of California Press, 1984
Allen, Ward, ed. *Translating for King James: Being a True Copy of the Only Notes Made by a Translator of King James's Bible, the Authorized Version, as the Final Committee of Review Revised the Translation of Romans through Revelation at Stationers' Hall in London in 1610–1611, Taken by the Reverend John Bois.* Nashville: Vanderbilt University Press, 1969
Allen, Ward and Edward C. Jacobs, eds. *The Coming of the King James Gospels: A Collation of the Translators' Work-in-Progress.* Fayetteville: University of Arkansas Press, 1995
Allen, William. *An Admonition to the Nobility and People of England and Ireland, Concerninge the Present Warres Made for the Execution of His Holines Sentence, by the Highe and Mightie Kinge Catholike of Spaine.* [Antwerp: A. Connicx?] 1588
A Trve, Sincere, and Modest Defence of English Catholiqves That Svffer for their Faith both at Home and Abrode against a False, Seditious and Slaunderous Libel Instituted, the Execvtion of Injustice in England. [Rouen: Fr. Parson's Press,] 1584
Andrewes, Lancelot. *Opuscula quaedam posthuma.* Library of Anglo-Catholic Theology, vol. X. Oxford: J. H. Parker, 1852
Responsio ad Apologiam Cardinalis Bellarmini quam nuper edidit contra Praefationem monitoriam serenissimi ac potentissimi principis Iacobi, Dei gratia Magnae Britanniae, Franciae, & Hiberniae Regis, fidei defensoris, omnibus Christianis monarchis, principibus, atque ordinibus inscriptam. London: Robert Barker, 1610
A Sermon Preached before the Kings Maiestie at Hampton Court Concerning the Right and Power of Calling Assemblies, on Sunday the 28. of September, Anno 1606. London: Robert Barker, 1606
Tortvra Torti: sive, ad Matthaei Torti librvm Responsio, qui nuper editus contra Apologiam serenissimi potentissimiqve principis, Iacobi, Dei gratia, Magna

Britanniae, Franciae, & Hiberniae Regis, pro ivramento fidelitatis. London: Robert Barker, 1609

Ashton, Robert, ed. *James I by His Contemporaries.* London: Hutchinson, 1969

Atterbury, Lewis. *Some Letters Relating to the History of the Council of Trent.* London: W. Hawes, 1705

Aymon, Jean, ed. *Tous les Synodes Nationaux des Eglises Réformées de France.* 2 vols. The Hague: Charles Delo, 1710

Barclay, William. *De potestate papae: an & quatenus in reges & principes seculares ius & imperium habeat.* Ed. John Barclay. [London: Eliot's Court Press,] 1609

De regno et regali potestate, adversus Buchananum, Brutum, Boucherium & reliquos monarchomachos. Paris: G. Chavdière, 1600

Of the Avthoritie of the Pope: Whether and How Farre Forth He Hath Power and Authoritie over Temporall Kings and Princes. London: William Aspley, 1611

Barlow, Thomas. *The Gunpowder–Treason: With a Discourse of the Manner of Its Discovery; and a Perfect Relation of the Proceedings against Those Horrid Conspirators; Wherein Is Contained Their Examinations, Tryals, and Condemnations; Likewise King James's Speech to Both Houses of Parliament on That Occasion.* London: Walter Kettilby, 1679

Barlow, William. *An Answer to a Catholike English-Man (So by Him-selfe Entitvled) Who, without a Name, Passed His Censure vpon the Apology, Made by the Right High and Mightie Prince Iames by the Grace of God King of Great Brittaine, France, and Ireland, &c. for the Oath of Allegeance.* London: Mathew Law, 1609

One of the Foure Sermons Preached before the Kings Maiestie, at Hampton Court in September Last: This Concerning the Antiquitie and Superioritie of Bishops, Sept. 21, 1606. London: Matthew Law, 1606

The Svmme and Svbstance of the Conference, Which It Pleased His Excellent Maiestie to Have with the Lords, Bishops, and Other of His Clergie (at Which the Most of the Lordes of the Councell Were Present) in His Maiesties Priuy–Chamber, at Hampton Court, Ianuary 14, 1603; Whereunto Are Added, Some Copies, (Scattered Abroad,) Vnsauory, and Vntrue. London: Mathew Law, 1604

Barret, William. *Ius regis, sive de absoluto & independenti secularium principum dominio & obsequio eis debito.* [London: N. Oakes,] 1612

Baumgardt, Carola. *Johannes Kepler: Life and Letters.* New York: Philosophical Library, 1951

Bayle, Pierre. *Dictionnaire historique et critique.* 3rd edn. 4 vols. Rotterdam: Michael Bohm, 1720

Becanus, Martin. *The Confutation of Tortura Torti: or, Against the King of Englandes Chaplaine, for That He Hath Negligently Defended His Kings Cause.* [St. Omer: English College Press,] 1610

Controversia anglicana de potestate regis et pontificis, contra Lancelottvm, sacellanum Regis Angliae, qui se Episcopum Eliensem vocat, pro defensione illustrissimi Cardinalis Bellarmini. Mainz: Ioannes Albinus, 1612

Dissidivm anglicanvm de primatv regis, cum brevi praefatione ad Catholicos in Anglia degentes. Mainz: Ioannes Albinus, 1612

Dvellvm Martini Becani, Societatis Iesv theologi cum Gulielmo Tooker. Mainz: Ioannes Albinus, 1612

The English Iarre: or, Disagreement amongst the Ministers of Great Brittaine Concerning the Kinges Supremacy. [St. Omer: English College Press,] 1612

Examen concordiae anglicanae de primatu ecclesiae regio. Mainz: Ioannes Albinus, 1613

Refvtatio Torturae Torti seu contra sacellanum Regis Angliae, quod causam sui regis negligenter egerit. Mainz: Ioannes Albinus, 1610

Serenissimi Iacobi Angliae Regis Apologiae & Monitoriae praefationis ad imperatorem, regis & principes refvtatio. Mainz: Ioannes Albinus, 1610

Bellarmine, Robert. *Apologia Roberti S. R. E. Cardinalis Bellarmini pro responsione sva ad librum Iacobi Magnae Britanniae Regis cuius titulus est Triplici nodo triplex cuneus: in qua apologia refellitur Praefatio monitoria regis eiusdem: accessit eadem ipsa responsio iam tertio recusa qua sub nomine Matthaei Torti anno superiore prodierat*. Rome: Bartholomew Zannetti, 1609. 2nd edn. Rome: Bartholomew Zannetti [St. Omer: English College Press,] 1610

Matthaei Torti, presbyteri & theologi papiensis, responsio ad librvm inscriptvm, Triplici nodo, triplex cuneus, sive apologia pro iuramento fidelitatis. [St. Omer: English College Press,] 1608

Birch, Thomas. *An Historical View of the Negotiations between the Courts of England, France, and Brussels, from the Year 1592 to 1617*. London: A. Millar, 1749

Birch, Thomas, ed. *The Court and Times of Charles the First*. 2 vols. London: Henry Colburn, 1848

Blackwell, George. *His Answeres vpon Sundry His Examinations; Together with His Approbation and Taking of the Oath of Allegeance; And His Letter Written to His Assistants and Brethren, Moouing Them Not Onely to Take the Said Oath but to Aduise All Romish Catholikes So to Doe*. London: Robert Barker, 1607

In Georgivm Blacvellum Angliae archipresbyterum a Clemente Papa Octavo designatum quaestito bipartita: cuius actio prior archipresbyteri iusiurandum de fidelitate praestitum; altera eiusdem iuramenti assertionem contra Cardinalis Bellarmini literas continet. London: J. Norton, 1609

A Large Examination Taken at Lambeth According to His Maiesties Direction, Point by Point, of M. George Blakwell, Made Archpriest of England by Pope Clement 8, vpon Occasion of a Certaine Answere of His, without the Priuitie of the State, to a Letter Lately Sent unto Him for Cardinall Ballarmine Blaming Him for Taking the Oath of Allegeance. London: Robert Barker, 1607

Blondel, David. *Actes avthentiqves des Eglises Reformées de France, Germanie, Grande Bretaigne, Pologne, Hongrie, Païs Bas, &c., touchant la paix & charité fraternelle*. Amsterdam: Jean Blaev, 1655

[Blount, Thomas,] *Calendarium Catholicum: or, An Universall Almanack, 1661, the First after Leap Year, with Memorable Observations*. n. p. 1661

Boderie, Antoine le Fevre de la. *Ambassades de Monsieur de la Boderie en Angleterre, sous le regne d'Henri IV. & la minorité de Louis XIII. depuis les années 1606. jusqu'en 1611*. 5 vols. [Paris,] 1750

The Book of Common Prayer and Administration of the Sacraments and Other Rites and Ceremonies of the Church according to the Use of the Church of England. Oxford: Oxford University Press [c. 1969]

The Book of Common Prayer and Administration of the Sacraments and Other Rites and Ceremonies of the Church, together with the Psalter or Psalms of David, according to the Use of the Episcopal Church. New York: Church Hymnal Corporation, 1979

Boucher, Jean. *Apologie pour Iehan Chastel*. [Paris,] 1595

De ivsta Henrici Tertii abdicatione e Francorum regno, libri qvatvor. Paris: Nicolas Nivelle, 1589

Bowler, Hugh, ed. *London Session Records, 1605–1685*. Publications of the Catholic Record Society, XXXIV. London: Catholic Record Society, 1934

Brandt, Geeraert. *The History of the Reformation and Other Ecclesiastical Transactions in and about the Low-Countries, from the Beginning of the Eighth Century, down to the Famous Synod of Dort*. 4 vols. in 2. London: Timothy Childe, 1720–1723

Bruce, John, ed. *Correspondence of King James VI of Scotland with Sir Robert Cecil and Others in England during the Reign of Queen Elizabeth*. London: Camden Society, 1861

Buchanan, George. *The Powers of the Crown in Scotland [De Jure Regni apud Scotos]*. Ed. and trans. Charles F. Arrowood. Austin: University of Texas Press, 1949

Buckeridge, John. *De potestate papae in rebus temporalibus sive in regibus deponendis usurpata: adversus Robertum Cardinalem Bellarminum, libri duo*. London: Norton, 1614

   A Sermon Preached at Hampton Court before the Kings Maiestie on Tuesday the 23. of September, Anno 1606. London: Robert Barker, 1606

Burhill, Robert. *Contra Martini Becani Iesuitae Moguntini Controversiam anglicanam auctam & recognitam: assertio pro iure regio proque reu^{di} Episcopi Eliensis Responsione ad Apologiam Bellarmini*. London: N. Butter, 1613

   De potestate regia et vsurpatione papali pro Tortva Torti, contra Parallelum Andreae Evdaemonioannis Cydonii Iesuitae responsio. Oxford: Joseph Barnes, 1613

   Pro Tortura Torti contra Martinum Becanum, Iesuitam, Responsio. London: R. Barker, 1611

Burnet, Gilbert. *The Life of William Bedell, D.D., Bishop of Kilmore in Ireland*. London: John Southby, 1685

Burton, Henry. *A Plea to an Appeale: Trauersed Dialogue Wise*. London: W. I., 1626

Calderwood, David. *The History of the Kirk of Scotland*. Ed. Thomas Thomson. 8 vols. Edinburgh: Wodrow Society, 1842–1849

Calendar of State Papers and Manuscripts, Relating to English Affairs, Existing in the Archives and Collections of Venice, and in Other Libraries of Northern Italy. 40 vols. London: PRO, 1864–1947

Calendar of State Papers, Domestic Series, of the Reigns of Edward VI, Mary, Elizabeth, and James I, 1547–1625. 12 vols. London: HMSO, 1856–1872

Calvin, John. *Institutes of the Christian Religion*. Ed. John T. McNeill. 2 vols. Philadelphia: Westminster Press, 1961

   Institutio Christianae religionis, in quatuor libros digesta, Johanne Calvino auctore, in Bohemicam vero Lingvam a Georgio Streyzio versa, et in communem usum omnium latissimae Slavonicae linguae populorum a Johanne Opsimathe edita. Amberg in the Upper Palatinate: Léta Páně, 1615

Camden, William. *Gulielmi Camdeni et illustrium virorum ad G. Camdenum epistolae*. London: Richard Chiswell, 1691

Cameron, Annie and Robert S. Rait, eds. *The Warrender Papers*. 2 vols. Edinburgh: Scottish Historical Society, 1931–1932

Cameron, James K., ed. *First Book of Discipline*. Edinburgh: Saint Andrew Press, 1972 ed. *Letters of John Johnston, c. 1565–1611, and Robert Howie, c. 1565–c. 1645.* Edinburgh: Oliver & Boyd for the University of St. Andrews, 1963

Cardwell, Edward. *A History of Conferences and Other Proceedings Connected with the Revision of the Book of Common Prayer.* 3rd edn. Oxford: Oxford University Press, 1849

Cardwell, Edward, ed. *Documentary Annals of the Reformed Church of England.* 2 vols. Oxford: Oxford University Press, 1844

Synodalia: A Collection of Articles of Religion, Canons, and Proceedings of Convocations in the Province of Canterbury, from the Year 1547 to the Year 1717. 2 vols. Oxford: Oxford University Press, 1842

Carleton, Dudley. *The Letters from and to Sir Dudley Carleton, Knt., during His Embassy in Holland, from January 1615/16 to December 1620.* London, 1780

Carleton, George. *Bp Carletons Testimonie Concerning the Presbyterian Discipline in the Low-Countries and Episcopall Government Here in England.* London: Nath. Butter, 1642.

An Examination of Those Things Wherein the Author of the Late Appeale Holdeth the Doctrines of the Pelagians and Arminians To Be the Doctrines of the Church of England. 2nd edn. London: William Turner, 1626

Iurisdiction Regall, Episcopall, Papall, Wherein Is Declared How the Pope Hath Intruded upon the Iurisdiction of Temporall Princes and of the Church: The Intrusion Is Discovered and the Peculiar and Distinct Iurisdiction to Each Properly Belonging, Recovered. London: I. Norton, 1610

An Oration Made at the Hage before the Prince of Orenge and the Assembly of the High and Mighty Lords, the States Generall of the Vnited Prouinces. London: Ralph Rounthwait, 1619

Carleton, George, John Davenant, Walter Balcanquhall, *et al. A Ioynt Attestation, Avowing That the Discipline of the Church of England Was Not Impeached by the Synode of Dort.* London: R. Mylbourne, 1626

Casaubon, Isaac. *Ad Frontonem Dvcaevm S. J. theologum epistola, in qua de apologia disseritur communi Iesuitarum nomine ante aliquot menses Lutetiae Parisorum edita.* London: Ioannes Norton, 1611

The Answere of Master Isaac Casavbon to the Epistle of the Most Illustrivs and Most Reuerend Cardinall Peron, Translated out of Latin into English, May 18 1612. London: William Aspley, 1612

Antwoort Isaaci Casavbon op den Brief vanden seer Door-luchtighe ende Eerwaerdighen Cardinael Perronius, Gheschreven wt den name ende van weghen den Alder-door-luchtichsten Koninck Iacobus, Koninck van groot-Britanien etc. n. p., 1612

De rebus sacris et ecclesiasticis exercitationes XVI. ad Cardinalis Baronii prolegomena in Annales & primam eorum partem. London: Norton, 1614

Ephemerides, cum praefatione et notis. Ed. John Russell. 2 vols. Oxford: Oxford University Press, 1850

Epistolae, insertis ad easdem responsionibus, quotquot hactenus reperiri potuerunt. Ed. Theodore Janson. 3rd ed. Rotterdam: Caspar Fritsch and Michael Böhm, 1709

Isaaci Casavboni ad Epistolam Illvstr. et Reverendiss. Cardinalis Peronii responsio. London: John Norton, 1612

Isaaci Casavboni ad Frontonem Dvcaevm S. J. theologum epistola, in qua de apologia disseritur communi Iesuitarum nomine ante aliquot menses Lutetiae Parisiorum edita. London: John Norton, 1611

Casaubon, Isaac, ed. *B. Gregorii Nysseni ad Evstathiam, Ambrosiam & Basilissam epistola*. Hanau: Wechel, 1607

Caspar, Max, and Walther von Dyck, eds. *Johannes Kepler in Seinen Briefen*. 2 vols. Munich: R. Oldenbourg, 1930

Cassander, Georg. *De articvlis religionis inter Catholicos et Protestantes controversiis consvltatio*. Cologne: Henricus Aquensis, 1577

Castellani, C., ed. *Lettere inedite di Fra Paolo Sarpi a Simone Contarini, ambasciatore Veneto in Roma, 1615*. Venice: Visentini, 1892

A *Catalogve of the Depvties of the High and Mightie States Generall of the Vnited Prouinces and of the Reuerend and Learned Divines Who Now Are Met in the Nationall Synode Celebrated in the Citie of Dordrecht in Holland, with a Short Narration of the Occasions and Introduction of the Said Synodicall Assembly*. London: Nich. Bourne and Nath. Newberie, 1618

Catechesis ecclesiarum quae in Regno Poloniae & Magno Ducatu Lithuaniae & aliis ad istud regnum pertinentibus provinciis affirmant neminem alium praeter Patrem Domini Nostri Jesu Christi esse illum Unum Deum Israelis, hominem autem illum Jesum Nazarenum, qui ex Virgine natus est, nec alium praeter aut ante ipsum Dei Filium Unigenitum & agnoscunt & confitentur. Rakow, 1609

Cecil, Robert. *An Answere to Certaine Scandalous Papers, Scattered Abroad vnder Colour of a Catholicke Admonition*. London: Robert Barker, 1606

Cecil, William. *The Execution of Iustice in England for Maintenaunce of Publique and Christian Peace, against Certeine Stirrers of Sedition and Adherents to the Traytors and Enemies of the Realme, without Any Persecution of Them for Questions of Religion, as Is Falsely Reported and Published by the Fautors and Fosterers of Their Treasons*. London: [C. Barker,] 1583

Censvra Sacrae Facvltatis Theologiae Coloniensis, in qvatvor priores libros De repvbl. ecclesiastica M. Antonij de Dominis, quondam archiepiscopi Spalatensis. Cologne, 1618

Censvra Sacrae Facvltatis Theologiae Parisiensis, in qvatvor priores libros De republica ecclesiastica, auctore Marco Antonio de Dominis quondam archiepiscopo Spalatensi. Cologne, n. d.

Challoner, Richard. *Memoirs of Missionary Priests*. Rev. edn. Ed. John Hungerford Pollen. London: Burns, Oates and Washbourne, 1924 – originally published, 1741–1742

Chamberlain, John. *The Letters of John Chamberlain*. Ed. Norman Egbert McClure. 2 vols. Philadelphia: American Philosophical Society, 1939

Chambers, David, and Brian Pullan, eds. *Venice: A Documentary History, 1450–1630*. Oxford: Blackwell, 1992

Chamier, Daniel. *Journal de son voyage à la cour de Henri IV en 1607 et sa biographie*. Ed. Charles Read. Paris: La Société de l'Histoire du Protestantisme Français, 1858

Clarendon, Edward Hyde, Earl of. *State Papers*. Ed. R. Scrope and T. Monkhouse. 3 vols. Oxford: Clarendon Press, 1767–1786

Clark, G. N., and W. J. M. Van Eyinga, eds. *The Colonial Conferences between England and the Netherlands in 1613 and 1615*. 2 vols. Leiden: E. J. Brill, 1940–1951

Coeffeteau, Nicolas. *Responce a l'Advertissement adressé par le serenissime Roy de la Grande Bretagne Iacque I. à tous les princes & potentats de la Chrestienté*. Paris: François Hvby, 1610

Coffin, E. M. *Antonius De Dominis, Archbishop of Spalato, Declares the Cause of His Returne out of England.* [St. Omer: English College Press,] 1623

The Collegiat Svffrage of the Divines of Great Britaine, Concerning the Five Articles Controverted in the Low Countries. London: Robert Milbourne, 1629

Collins, Samuel. *Epphata to F. T. or, The Defence of the Right Reverend Father in God, the Lord bishop of Elie, Lord High-Almoner and Privie Counsellour to the Kings Most Excellent Maiestie, Concerning His Answer to Cardinal Bellarmines Apologie.* Cambridge: C. Legg, 1617

Increpatio Andreae Eudaemono–Iohannis Iesuitae de infami Parallelo et renovata assertio Torturae Torti, pro clarissimo domino atque Antistite Eliensi. Cambridge: C. Legge, 1612

Colomesius, Paulus, ed. *S. Clementis epistolae duae ad Corinthios.* London: James Adamson, 1694

The Constitutions and Canons Ecclesiastical and the Thirty-Nine Articles of the Church of England. London: J. G. and F. Rivington, 1833

Cornet, Enrico, ed. *Paolo V. e la Repubblica Veneta: Giornale dal 22. Ottobre 1605–9. Giugno 1607.* Vienna: Tendler, 1859

Cosin, John. *Works.* 5 vols. Oxford: John Henry Parker, 1843–1855

Coton, Pierre. *Institvtion catholique, ou est declarée & confirmée la verite de la foy, contre les heresies et svperstitions de ce temps; diuisee en quatre liures, qui seruent d'antidote aux quatre de l'Institution de Jean Caluin.* Paris: Claude Chappelet, 1610

Covel, William. *A Ivst and Temperate Defence of the Five Books of Ecclesiastical Policie Written by M. Richard Hooker.* London: Clement Knight, 1603

Craigie, James, ed. *The Basilicon Doron of King James VI.* 2 vols. Edinburgh: Scottish Text Society, 1944–1955

ed. *The Poems of James VI of Scotland.* 2 vols. Edinburgh: Scottish Text Society, 1955–1958

Cranmer, Thomas. *Miscellaneous Writings and Letters.* Ed. John Edmund Cox. Cambridge: Cambridge University Press, 1846

Creswell, Joseph. *A Proclamation Pvblished vnder the Names of Iames, King of Great Britanny; With a Briefe & Moderate Answere Thereunto: Whereto Are Added the Penall Statutes Made in the Same Kingdom against Catholikes.* [St. Omer: English College Press,] 1611

De Dominis, Marco Antonio. *Concio habita italice a reverendo patre Marco Antonio De Dominis, archiepiscopo Spalatensi primo die dominico Adventus Anno 1617; Londini in Mercatorum Capella, coram italis ibi commorantibus, & aliis honorificis in illa synaxi & conventu.* Leeuwarden: Ioann Starter, 1618

De pace religionis: epistola ad venerabilem virum Iosephum Hallum, archipresbyterum Vigorniensem. Besançon, 1666

De repvblica ecclesiastica, libri X. London: John Bill, 1617

De repvblica ecclesiastica, pars secvnda, continens libros qvintum et sextvm. London: John Bill, 1620

De repvblica ecclesiastica, pars tertia, continens libros VII. VIII. IX. X. Hanau: L. Hulsius, 1622

De repvblica ecclesiastica, pars tertia, continens libros VII. VIII. IX. X., cum utilissimo Georgii Cassandri tractatu, De officio pii viri circa religionis dissidia. Frankfurt: Joannes Rosa, 1658

Declaration de Marc Antoine de Dominis, archevesque de Spalatro, metropolitain des deux royaumes de Croatie & Dalmatie; sur les raisons qui l'ont meu à se departir de l'Eglise Romaine. Saumur: T. Portau, 1616

Les écueils du naufrage chrestien découverts par la sainte Eglise de Christ à ses bien aymez enfans affin qu'ils s'en puissent esloigner. La Rochelle: J. Hebert, 1618

Erste Evangelische Predigt von Herrn Marco Antonio De Dominis, Erzbischoffen zu Spalato; nach dem er durch Gottes sonderbare schickung vom Bapstumb abgetretten; zu Londen in Engelland, am ersten sontag dess Advents, im Jahr 1617, gehalten; in der Capellen, genennt delli Merciari, welches der italianer Kirchedaselbst ist. [Frankfurt?] 1618

M. Antonius De Dominis, Archbishop of Spalato, Declares the Cause of His Returne out of England. [Trans. E. Coffin.] [St. Omer: English College Press,] 1623

A Manifestation of the Motives, Whereupon the Most Reuerend Father, Marcvs Antonivs De Dominis, Archbishop of Spalato, (in the Territorie of Venice) Vndertooke His Departure Thence: Englished out of His Latine Copy. London: John Bill, 1616

Papatvs Romanvs: liber de origine, progressu, atque extinctione ipsius. London: John Bill, 1617

Predica fatta da Monsr Marc'Antonio De Dominis, Archiv°. di Spalato, la prima domenica dell'Auuento quest'Anno 1617. in Londra nella Capella detta delli Merciari (ch'e la chiesa degl'italiani) ad essa natione italiana. London: John Bill, 1617

The Rockes of Christian Shipwracke, Discouered by the Holy Church of Christ to Her Beloued Children, That They May Keepe Aloofe from Them. London: John Bill, 1618

Scogli del christiano naufragio, quali va scoprendo la santa Chiesa di Christo. [London,] 1618

Scritti giurisdizionalistici inediti. Ed. Antonio Russo. Naples: Luigi Loffredo, 1965

The Second Manifesto of Marcvs Antonivs De Dominis, Archbishop of Spalatro: Wherein for His Better Satisfaction, and the Satisfaction of Others, He Publikely Repenteth, and Recanteth His Former Errors, and Setteth downe the Cause of His Leauing England, and All Protestant Countries, to Returne vnto the Catholicke Romane Church. Trans. M. G. K. Liège: G. Houius, 1623

Sermon de Mre Marc Anthoine de Dominis . . . faict le premier dimanche de l'Advent de l'année 1617, à Londres, en la chappelle des Merciers, qui est l'église des italiens, à eux adressée [sic]. Charenton: Mondière, 1619

A Sermon Preached in Italian, by the Most Reuerend Father, Marc'Antony De Dominus, Archb. of Spalato, the First Sunday in Aduent, anno 1617; in the Mercers Chappel in London, to the Italians in That City, and Many Other Honorable Auditors Then Assembled. London: Iohn Bill, 1617

Steinklippe dess christichen Schiffbruchs, welche die heilige Kirche Christ ihren vielgeliebten Sohnen entdeckt. Frankfurt: Rosen, 1618

Sui reditus ex Anglia consilium exponit. Rome: Apostolic Camera, 1623

Svae profectionis consilivm exponit. London: John Bill, 1616

Verclaringhe van de Motiven ende Oorsaecken daer door de E. heere Marcvs Antonivs de Dominis, Aerts-bischop van Spalaten. The Hague: Hillebrant Jacobsz, 1616

De Thou, Jacques-Auguste. *Choix de lettres françoises inédites.* Paris: Société des Bibliophiles, 1877

Histoire universelle. 11 vols. The Hague: Henri Scheurleer, 1740

Historiarum sui temporis, pars prima. Paris: Mamertus Patissonus, 1604

Donne, John. *Conclaue Ignati: siue, eivs in nvperis inferni commitiis inthronisatio.* [London: William Hall,] 1611

Ignatius His Conclaue: or, His Inthronisation in a Late Election in Hell. London: Richard More, 1611

Pseudo-Martyr: Wherein out of Certaine Propositions and Gradations This Conclusion Is Evicted, That Those Which Are of the Romane Religion in This Kingdome May and Ought To Take the Oath of Allegeance. London: W. Burre, 1610

Sermons. Ed. Evelyn M. Simpson and George R. Potter. 10 vols. Berkeley: University of California Press, 1953–1962

Du Moulin, Peter. "The Authors Life." Prefixed to Pierre du Moulin, *The Novelty of Popery, Opposed to the Antiquity of True Christianity.* London: Francis Tyton, 1662

Du Moulin, Pierre. "Autobiographie de Pierre du Moulin, d'après le manuscript autographe, 1564–1658." *Bulletin de la Société de l'Histoire du Protestantisme Français,* 7 (1858), pp. 170–182, 333–344, 465–477

Copie de la suite ou seconde partie de la lettre de Monsieur du Moulin, Ministre en l'Eglise Reformée à Paris, omise de propos delibere, & par tromperie, en l'edition de Schiedam; ensemble des Ouvertures dudit sieur pour travailler à l'union des églises de la Chrestienté, & à appaiser les differens, &c. The Hague: Hillebrant Iacobssz, 1617

De monarchia temporali Pontificis Romani. London: Norton, 1614

Defense de la foy Catholique contenue au livre de trespuissant & serenissime Roy Iaques I Roy de la Grand' Bretagne & d'Irlande: contre la Response de F. N. Coeffeteau, docteur en theologie & vicaire general des Freres Prescheurs. [Paris?] 1610

A Sermon Preached before the Kings Maiesty at Greenwich the 15. of Iune. 1615. Oxford: Henry Cripps, 1620

Du Perron, Jacques Davy. *Harangve faicte de la part de la Chambre ecclesiastiqve en celle du Tiers estat, sur l'article du serment.* Paris: Antoine Estiene, 1615

A Letter Written from Paris by the Lord Cardinall of Peron to Mons\r Casavbon in England. [St. Omer: English College Press,] 1612

Lettre de Monseignevr le cardinal dv Perron envoyée au sieur Casaubon en Angleterre. Paris: Iean Laqvehay and Iean Bovillette, 1612

An Oration Made on the Part of the Lordes Spiritvall, in the Chamber of the Third Estate (or Communalty) of France, vpon the Oath (Pretended of Allegiance) Exhibited in the Late Generall Assembly of the Three Estates of That Kingdome. [St. Omer: English College Press,] 1616

Répliqve à la response dv serenissime Roy de la Grand Bretagne par l'illvstrissime et reverendissime cardinal du Perron, archeuesque de Sens, primat des Gaules & de Germanie & Grand Aumosnier de France. Paris: Antoine Estiene, 1620

The Reply of the Most Illvstrivos Cardinall of Perron to the Answeare of the Most Excellent king of Great Britain. Douai: M. Bogart, 1630

Duplessis-Mornay, Philippe. *Mémoires et correspondance de Duplessis-Mornay.* 12 vols. Paris: Treuttel and Würtz, 1824–1825

Edmondes, Thomas. *Remonstrances Made by the Kings Maiesties Ambassadovr vnto the French King and the Queene His Mother, Iune Last Past, 1615, Concerning the Marriages with Spaine, as also Certayne Diabolicall Opinions*

Maintayned by Cardinall Perron about the Deposing and Murthering of Kings. London: Nathaniel Butter, 1615

Elton, G. R., ed. *The Tudor Constitution: Documents and Commentary.* 2nd edn. Cambridge: Cambridge University Press, 1982

An Epistle for the Moste Myghty & Redoubted Prince Henry the VIII. London: Thomas Berthelet, 1538

L'estat present des gverres de la Boheme & Allemagne auec le denombrement des troupes qui y sont ariuees tant pour le secours de l'Empereur, que pour le party du Comte Palatine. Trans. J. D. C. Paris, 1620

Eudaemon-Joannes, Andreas. *Ad actionem proditoriam Edouardi Coqui, apologia pro R. P. Henrico Garneto anglo.* Cologne: Joannes Kinckium, 1610

Parallelvs Torti ac tortoris eivs L. Cicestrensis: sive responsio ad Torturam Torti pro illvstr^{mo} Card. Ballarmino. Cologne: Joannes Kinckius, 1611

Featley, Daniel. *Pelagius Redivivus: or, Pelagius Raked Out of the Ashes of Arminius and His Schollers.* London: Robert Mylbourne, 1626

A Second Parallel, Together with a Writ of Error Sued against the Appealer. London: Robert Milbourne, 1626

Field, Nathaniel. *Some Short Memorials Concerning the Life of That Reverend Divine, Doctor Richard Field, Prebendarie of Windsor and Dean of Glocester.* Ed. John Le Neve. London: Henry Clements, 1717

Field, Richard. *The Fifth Booke, Of the Chvrch, Together with an Appendix, Containing a Defense of Such Partes and Passages of the Former Bookes as Have Bene Either Excepted against or Wrested to the Maintenance of Romish Errours.* London: Simon Waterson, 1610

Of the Church, Five Bookes. London: Simon Waterson, 1606

※ Fincham, Kenneth, ed. *Visitation Articles and Injunctions of the Early Stuart Church*, vol. I. London: Church of England Record Society, 1994

The First and Second Prayer Books of Edward VI. London: Dent, 1910

Fitzherbert, Thomas. *A Supplement to the Discussion of M. D. Barlowes Answere to the Iudgment of a Catholic Englishman &c. Interrupted by the Death of the Author F. Robert Persons of the Society of Jesus.* [St. Omer: English College Press,] 1913

※ Floyd, John. *A Svrvey of the Apostasy of Marcvs Antonivs de Dominis, Sometyme Arch-bishop of Spalato.* n. p., 1617

Foley, Henry, ed. *Records of the English Province of the Society of Jesus.* 7 vols. London: Burns and Oates, 1878

Forbes, William. *Considerationes modestae et pacificae controversiarum de justificatione, purgatorio, invocatione sanctorum, Christo mediatore, et eucharistia.* 4th edn. 2 vols. Oxford: J. H. Parker, 1850–1856

Forbes-Leith, William, ed. *Narratives of Scottish Catholics under Mary Stuart and James VI.* London: Thomas Baker, 1889

Fuller, Thomas. *The Church-History of Britain, from the Birth of Jesus Christ untill the Year M.DC.XLVIII.* London: John Williams, 1655

The Church-History of Britain. 6 vols. Oxford: Oxford University Press, 1845

Gardiner, Samuel R., ed. *The Constitutional Documents of the Puritan Revolution, 1625–1660.* Oxford: Clarendon Press, 1906

ed. "The earl of Bristol's Defence of His Negotiations in Spain." In *The Camden Miscellany*, vol. VI. London: Camden Society, 1871, pp. i–xxxix, 1–56

ed. *The Fortescue Papers, Consisting Chiefly of Letters Relating to State Affairs, Collected by John Parker.* Westminster: Camden Society, 1871

ed. *Letters and Other Documents Illustrating the Relations between England and Germany at the Commencement of the Thirty Years' War.* 2 vols. Westminster: Camden Society, 1865–1868

ed. *Narrative of the Spanish Marriage Treaty* [by Francisco de Jesus]. London: Camden Society, 1869

ed. "Two Declarations of Garnet Relating to the Gunpowder Plot." *English Historical Review,* 3 (1888), 510–519

Gerard, John. *The Autobiography of an Elizabethan.* Ed. Philip Caraman. London: Longmans, Green, 1951

Gondomar, Diego Sarmiento de Acuña, Conde de. *Correspondencia oficial.* Ed. Antonio Ballesteros y Beretta. 4 vols. Madrid: Press of the Archives, 1936–1945

Goodman, Godfrey. *The Court of King James the First.* Ed. John S. Brewer. 2 vols. London: Richard Bentley, 1839

Gordon, John. *Anti-Bellarmino-tortor, siue Tortus retortus & Iuliano-papismus.* London: R. Field, 1612

Antitortobellarminvs, siue refutatio calumniarum, mendaciorum et imposturarum laico-Cardinalis Bellarmini contra iura omnium regum et sinceram, illibatamque famam serenissimi, potentissimi piissimique principis Iacobi, Dei Gratia, Magnae Britanniae, Franciae et Hiberniae Regis, fidei Catholicae antiquae defensoris et propugnatoris. London, 1610

Orthodoxo–Iacobus et papapostaticus: siue theses confirmatae testimoniis Graecorum et Latinorum patrum qui vixerunt usque ad millesimum a Christo annum; quibus probatur serenissimum Regem Maximae Britanniae &c. esse Catholicae fidei verum defensorem & propugnatorem. London: F. Kyngston, 1611

Greaves, John. *Miscellaneous Works of Mr. John Greaves, Professor of Astronomy in the University of Oxford.* 2 vols. London: J. Bridley, 1737

Gretser, Jacobus. *Antitortor Bellarminianus Joannes Gordonius Scotus pseudodecanus et capellanus Calvinisticus.* Ingolstadt, 1611

βασιλικον Δωρον, *sive commentarivs exegeticvs in serenissimi Magnae Britanniae Regis Jacobi Praefationem monitoriam et in Apologiam pro iuramento fidelitatis.* Ingolstadt: Adam Sartor, 1610

Grotius, Hugo. *Briefwisseling.* Ed. P. C. Molhuysen, and B. L. Meulenbroek. 13 vols. The Hague: Martinus Nijhoff, 1928 –

De veritate religionis Christianae. Leyden: Johannes Maire, 1628

Meletius sive de iis quae inter Christianos conveniunt epistola. Ed. Guillaume H. M. Posthumus Meyjes. Leiden: E. J. Brill, 1988

Ordinum Hollandiae ac Westfrisiae pietas ab improbissimis multorum calumnijs, praesertim vero a nupera Sibrandi Lvbberti epistola. Leyden: J. Patius, 1612

Sensvs librorvm sex qvos pro veritate religionis Christianae. Leyden: Johannes Maire, 1627

The Truth of the Christian Religion. Ed. John Le Clerk. 13th edn. London: F. C. and J. Rivington, 1809

Via ad pacem ecclesiasticam. Amsterdam: I. Blaev, 1642

Votum pro pace ecclesiastica, contra examen Andrae Riveti & alios irreconciliabiles. n.p., 1642

Hacket, John. *Alter Ecebolius, M. Ant. De Dominis, arch. Spalatensis, pluribus dominis inseruire doctus.* London: John Bill, 1624

Scrinia reserata: A Memorial Offer'd to the Great Deservings of John Williams, D.D. London: Samuel Lowndes, 1693

Hakewill, George. *Scvtum regivm: id est, adversvs omnes regicidas et regicidarvm patronos ab initio mundi vsque ad interitum Phocae Imp. circa annum ab incarnatione domini 610, ecclesiae Catholicae consensus orthodoxus.* London: John Budge, 1612

Hales, John. *Golden Remains of the Ever Memorable Mr Iohn Hales of Eton College.* London: Tim. Garthwait, 1659. 2nd edn. London: Robert Pawlett, 1673

Hall, Joseph. *The Works of Joseph Hall, B. of Exceter.* London: Edw. Brewster, 1634

   The Works of the Right Reverend Joseph Hall, D.D., Bishop of Exeter and Afterwards of Norwich. Ed. Philip Wynter. Rev. edn. 10 vols. Oxford: Oxford University Press, 1863

Hardwicke, Philip Yorke, earl of, ed. *Miscellaneous State Papers, from 1501 to 1726.* 2 vols. London: W. Strahan and T. Cadell, 1778

Harris, Richard. *Concordia anglicana de primatu ecclesiae regio: adversus Becanum de Dissidio anglicano.* London: G. Hall, 1612

   The English Concord: In Answer to Becane's English Iarre, Together with a Reply to Becan's Examen of the English Concord. London: M. Lownes, 1614

Hartsoeker, Christian, ed. *Praestantium ac eruditorum virorum epistolae ecclesiasticae et theologicae.* 3rd edn. Amsterdam: Franciscus Halma, 1704

Hayward, John. *A Reporte of a Discovrse Concerning Svpreme Power in Affaires of Religion: Manifesting That This Power Is a Right of Regalitie, Inseparably Annexed to the Soueraigntie of Euery State.* London: Iohn Hardie, 1606

Hearne, Thomas, ed. *Titi Livii Foro–Juliensis vita Henrici Quinti, Regis Angliae; Accedit sylloge epistolarum a variis Angliae principibus scriptarum.* Oxford: Thomas Hearne, 1716

Henderson, G. D., ed. *Scots Confession, 1560 (Confessio Scoticana) and Negative Confession, 1580 (Confessio Negativa).* Edinburgh: Church of Scotland, 1937

Hessels, J. H., ed. *Ecclesiae Londino–Batavae Archivum.* 3 vols. in 4. Cambridge: Cambridge University Press, 1887–1897

Historical Manuscripts Commission. *Calendar of the Manuscripts of the Most Honourable the Marquess of Salisbury, K.G., Preserved at Hatfield House.* 24 parts. London: HMSO, 1883–1976

The Holy Bible, Conteyning the Old Testament and the New: Newly Translated out of the Originall Tongues and with the Former Translations Diligently Compared and Reuised, by his Maiesties Speciall Cõmandement. London: Robert Barker, 1611

[Home, David.] D. H. *Le contr'assassin, ou response à l'apologie des Jesuites, faite par un pere de la Compagnie de Jesus de Loyola.* n. p., 1612

Hooker, Richard. *Of the Laws of Ecclesiastical Polity.* Gen. ed. W. Speed Hill. The Folger Library Edition of the Works of Richard Hooker. 6 vols. in 7. Cambridge, Mass. Harvard University Press, 1977–1990, and Binghamton, New York: Medieval and Renaissance Texts and Studies, 1993

Hoskins, Anthony. *A Briefe and Cleare Declaration of Sundry Pointes Absolutely Dislyked in the Lately Enacted Oath of Allegiance Proposed to the Catholikes of England.* [St. Omer: English College Press,] 1611

[Hotman, Jean.] *Syllabus aliquot synodorum et colloquiorum, quae auctoritate et mandato caesarum et regum, super negotio religionis ad controversias conciliandas, indicta sunt; doctorum item aliquot ac piorum virorum utriusque religionis, tam Catholicae Romanae, quam Protestantium, libri & epistolae, vel ex iis excerpta.* Orléans [Strasbourg],1628

Ivdicivm Synodi Nationalis, Reformatarvm Ecclesiarvm Belgicarvm Habitae Dordrechti Anno 1618 & 1619. [Dordrecht,] 1619

James VI and I. *An Apologie for the Oath of Allegiance: First Set Forth without a Name, and Now Acknowledged by the Author, the Right High and Mightie Prince, Iames by the Grace of God, King of Great Britaine, France and Ireland, Defender of the Faith, &c.; Together with a Premonition of His Maiesties to All Most Mightie Monarches, Kings, Free Princes, and States of Christendome*. London: Robert Barker, 1609

Apologia pro iuramento fidelitatis: primum quidem ἀνώνυμοσ nunc vero ab ipso auctore, serenissimo ac potentiss. principe, Iacobo, Dei gratia, Magnae Britanniae, Franciae & Hiberniae Rege, fidei defensore, denuo edita; cui praemissa est praefatio monitoria sacratiss. Caesari Rodolpho II., semper augusto, caeterisque Christiani orbis sereniss. ac potentiss. monarchis ac regibus, celsissimisque liberis principibus, rebus publicis atque ordinibus inscripta. London: J. Norton, 1609

βασιλικον Δωρον: Devided into Three Bookes. Edinburgh: R. Waldegrave, 1599

βασιλικον Δωρον: or, His Maiesties Instructions to His Dearest Sonne Henry the Prince. Edinburgh: R. Waldegrave, 1603

A Counter-Blaste to Tobacco. London: R. B., 1604

Daemonologie, in Forme of a Dialogue, Divided into Three Bookes. Edinburgh: Robert Waldegrave, 1597

The Essayes of a Prentise in the Divine Art of Poesie. Edinburgh: Thomas Vautroullier, 1584

Declaration dv serenissime Roy Iaqves I. Roy de la Grand' Bretaigne, France et Irelande, Defenseur de la Foy, povr le droit des rois & independance de leurs couronnes, contre la harangve de l'illvstrissime Cardinal du Perron prononcée en la Chambre du Tiers Estat le XV. de Ianuier 1615. London: John Bill, Printer to the King, 1615

Frvitfvll Meditation, Containing a Plaine and Easie Exposition, or Laying Open of the vii. viii. ix. and x. Verses of the 20. chapter of the Revelation, in Forme and Maner of a Sermon. [First published in Edinburgh, 1588.] In *The Workes of the Most High and Mightie Prince, Iames by the Grace of God, King of Great Britaine, France and Ireland, Defender of the Faith*. Ed. James Montague. London: Robert Barker and John Bill, 1616–1620

God and the King: or, A Dialogue Shewing that Our Soueraigne Lord King Iames, Being Immediate vnder God within His Dominions, Doth Rightfully Claime Whatsoeuer Is Required by the Oath of Allegeance. London: By the King's Command, 1615

His Maiesties Declaration Concerning his Proceedings with the States Generall of the United Provinces of the Low Countreys, in the Cause of D. Conradus Vorstius. London: Robert Barker, 1612

His Maiesties Poeticall Exercises at Vacant Hours. Edinburgh: Robert Waldegrave, 1591

His Maiesties Speach in This Last Session of Parliament, as Neere His Very Words as Could Be Gathered at the Instant; Together with a Discourse of the Maner of the Discouery of This Late Intended Treason. London: Robert Barker, 1605

A Meditation vpon the Lords Prayer: Written by the Kings Maiestie, for the Benefit of All His Subiects, Especially of Such as Follow the Court. [First published, 1619.] In *The Workes of the Most High and Mighty Prince, Iames, by the Grace of God Kinge of Great Britaine, France and Ireland, Defender of the Faith, &c.* Ed. James Montague. London: Robert Barker and John Bill, 1616–1620

A Meditation vppon the xxv. xxvi. xxvii. xxviii. and xxix. Verses of the XV. Chapter of the First Booke of the Chronicles of the Kings. [First published in Edinburgh, 1589.] London: Felix Norton, 1603

A Meditation vpon the 27. 28. 29. Verses of the XXVII. chapter of Saint Matthew: or, A Paterne for a Kings Inavgvration. [First published 1620.] In *The Workes of the Most High and Mightie Prince, Iames, by the Grace of God Kinge of Greate Britaine, France and Ireland, Defender of the Faith, &c.* Ed. James Montague. London: Robert Barker and John Bill, 1616–1620

The Peace-Maker: or, Great Brittaines Blessing, Fram'd for the Continuance of That Mightie Happiness Wherein This Kingdomme Excells Manie Empires. London: Thomas Purfoot, 1619. [First published 1618.]

The Political Works of James I. Ed. Charles H. McIlwain. Cambridge, Mass.: Harvard University Press, 1918

Remonstrance of the Most Gratiovs King Iames I. King of Great Brittaine, France, and Ireland, Defender of the Faith, &c., for the Right of Kings and the Independance of Their Crownes against an Oration of the Most Illustrious Card. of Perron, Pronounced in the Chamber of the Third Estate. Ian. 15. 1615. Cambridge: Cantrell Legge, Printer to the University of Cambridge, 1616

The Trew Law of Free Monarchies: or, The Reciprock and Mvtvall Duetie betwixt a Free King, and His Naturall Subjects. Edinburgh, 1598

Triplici nodo, triplex cuneus: ou Apologie pour le serment de fidelite, que de Roy de la Grand Bretagne veut estre faict par tous ses sujets, contre les deux brefs du Pape Paul cinquième & l'epistre, ou lettre, nagueres envoyee par le Cardinal Ballarmin à G. Blackwel Archiprestre. Leyden, 1608

Triplici nodo, triplex cuneus: sive Apologia pro iuramento fidelitatis, adversus duo brevia P. Pauli Quinti & epistolam Cardinalis Bellarmini ad G. Blackvellum Archipresbyterum nuper scriptam. London: R. Barker, 1607

Triplici nodo, triplex cuneus: or, An Apologie for the Oath of Allegiance, against the Two Breues of Pope Pavlvs Qvintus, and the Late Letter of Cardinal Ballarmine to G. Blackwell the Arch–priest. London: Robert Barker, 1607

☙ *The Workes of the Most High and Mightie Prince, Iames by the Grace of God, King of Great Britaine, France and Ireland, Defender of the Faith, &c.* Ed. James Montague. London: Robert Barker and John Bill, 1616–1620

Jansson, Maija and William B. Bidwell, eds. *Proceedings in Parliament, 1625.* New Haven: Yale University Press, 1987

Jewel, John. *An Apologie, or Aunswer in Defence of the Church of England, Concerning the State of Religion Used in the Same.* London: Reginalde Wolfe, 1562

Johnson, Robert C., Mary Frear Keeler, Maija Jansson Cole, and William B. Bidwell, eds. *Proceedings in Parliament, 1628.* 6 vols. New Haven: Yale University Press, 1977–1983

Jones, Thomas Wharton, ed. *A True Relation of the Life and Death of the Right Reverend Father in God William Bedell, Lord Bishop of Kilmore in Ireland.* Westminster: Camden Society, 1872

Journals of the House of Lords, 19 vols. London, 1767

The Ivdgement of the Synode Holden at Dort, Concerning the Five Articles, As Also Their Sentence Touching Conradvs Vorstivs. London: John Bill, 1619

Kellison, Matthew [John Heigham]. *The Gagge of the Reformed Gospell, Briefly*

Discovering the Errors of Our Time, with the Refutation by Express Textes of Their Owne Approoved English Bible. 2nd edn. [St. Omer: Charles Boscard, 1623.]

Kellison, Matthew. *The Right and Iurisdiction of the Prelate and the Prince: or, A Treatise of Ecclesiasticall and Regall Authoritie.* Douai: P. Auroi, 1617

Kenyon, J. P., ed. *The Stuart Constitution, 1603–1688: Documents and Commentary.* 2nd edn. Cambridge: Cambridge University Press, 1986

Kepler, Johannes. *Gesammelte Werke.* Ed. Walther von Dyck and Max Caspar. 20 vols. Munich: C. H. Beck, 1937 –

"King James and the English Puritans: An Unpublished Document." *Blackwoods Magazine*, 188 (September 1910), 402–413

King, John. *The Fovrth Sermon Preached at Hampton Covrt on Tuesday the Last of Sept. 1606.* Oxford: Joseph Barnes, 1606

Kingdon, Robert M., ed. *The Execution of Justice in England by William Cecil, and A Trve, Sincere, and Modest Defense of English Catholics by William Allen.* Ithaca: Cornell University Press for the Folger Shakespeare Library, 1965

Kinser, Samuel. *The Works of Jacques-Auguste de Thou.* The Hague: Martinus Nijhoff, 1966

Kirk, James, ed. *The Second Book of Discipline.* Edinburgh: Saint Andrew Press, 1980

Laemmer, Hugo, ed. *Meletematum Romanorum mantissa.* Ratisbon: G. J. Manz, 1875

Larkin, James F. and Paul L. Hughes, eds. *Stuart Royal Proclamations.* 2 vols. Oxford: Clarendon Press, 1973–1983

Larking, Lambert B. "Notes of Sir Roger Twysden on the History of the Council of Trent." *Notes and Queries*, second series, 14 (July–December 1857), 122–123

Laud, William. *An Answere to Mr Fishers Relation of a Third Conference betweene a Certaine B. (as He Stiles Him) and Himselfe.* Ed. Richard Baily. London: Adam Islip, 1624

The Works of the Most Reverend Father in God, William Laud, D.D., Sometime Lord Archbishop of Canterbury. 7 vols. Oxford: John Henry Parker, 1857–1860

Law, Thomas Graves, ed. *The Catechism of John Hamilton, Archbishop of St. Andrews, 1552.* Oxford: Clarendon Press, 1884

ed. "Documents Illustrating Catholic Policy in the Reign of James VI." *Miscellany of the Scottish History Society*, vol. I. Edinburgh: Scottish History Society, 1893

Lee, Sidney, ed. *The Autobiography of Edward, Lord Herbert of Cherbury.* 2nd edn. London: Routledge, 1906

Leech, Humphrey. *Dvtifvll and Respective Considerations upon Foure Severall Heads of Proofe and Triall in Matters of Religion.* [St. Omer: English College Press,] 1609

Legrand, Emile, ed. *Bibliographie Hellénique, ou description raisonnée des ouvrages publiés par des Grecs au dix-septième siècle.* 5 vols. Paris: Alphonse Picard, 1894–1903

Lessius, Leonard. *De Antichristo et eius praecursoribus disputatio apologetica gemina qua refutatur Praefatio monitoria falso vt creditur adscripta Magnae Britanniae Regi.* Antwerp: Plantin, 1611

L'Estoile, Pierre de. *Journal de l'Estoile pour le règne de Henri IV.* Ed. Louis-Raymond Lefèvre and André Martin. 3 vols. Paris: Gallimard, 1948–1960

Levi, Eugenia. "King James I. and Fra Paolo Sarpi in 1607." *The Athenaeum*, 4062 (September 2, 1905), 304–305

"King James I. and Fra Paolo Sarpi in the Year 1612." *The Athenaeum*, 3689 (July 9, 1898), 66–67

Lloyd, Charles, ed. *Formularies of Faith, Set Forth by Authority during the Reign of Henry VIII*. Oxford: Oxford University Press, 1856

Loomie, Albert J., ed. *Spain and the Jacobean Catholics*. 2 vols. London: Catholic Record Society, 1973–1978

Mariana, Juan de. *De rege et regis institutione libri III*. Toledo: P. Rodericum, 1599

[Marcelline, George.] *Les trophees dv Roi Iacques I. de la Grande Bretaigne, France, et Ireland*. [London?] A. Elevtheres, 1609

The Triumphs of King Iames the First of Great Brittaine, France, and Ireland, King. [London:] Iohn Budge, 1610

[Marta, Giacomo Antonio.] *The New Man: or, A Svpplication from an Vnknowne Person, a Roman Catholike vnto Iames, the Monarch of Great Brittaine, and from Him to the Emperour, Kings, and Princes of the Christian World, Touching the Causes and Reasons That Will Argue a Necessity of a Generall Councell To Be Forthwith Assembled against Him That Now Vsurps the Papall Chaire vnder the Name of Paul the Fifth*. Trans. William Crashaw. London: George Norton, 1622

Svpplicatio ad imperatorem, reges, principes, svper cavsis generalis concilij convocandi contra Pavlvm Qvintvm. London: Bonham Norton, 1613

Svpplication et reqvette à l'emperevr, aux roys, princes, estats, republiques & magistrats Chrestiens, sur les causes d'assembler un concile general contra Paul Cinquiesme. Trans. Nicolas de Marbais. Leyden: Elzevier, 1613

Meel, J. W. van, ed. *Francisci et Joannis Hotomanorum patris ac filii et clarorum virorum ad eos epistolae*. Amsterdam: G. Gallet, 1700

Melville, James. *The Autobiography and Diary*. Ed. Robert Pitcairn. Edinburgh: Wodrow Society, 1842

Middleton, Thomas. *Works*. Ed. A. H. Bullen. 8 vols. New York: AMS Press, 1964 – originally published, 1885

Montagu, Richard. *Appello Caesarem: A Iust Appeale from Two Uniust Informers*. London: Matthew Lownes, 1625

A Gagg for the New Gospell? No, A New Gagg for an Old Goose, Who Would Needes Vndertake to Stop All Protestant Mouths for Ever, with 276 Places out of Their Owne English Bibles. London: Matthew Lownes and William Barret, 1624

Morris, John, ed. *The Condition of Catholics under James I: Father Gerard's Narrative of the Gunpowder Plot*. 2nd edn. London: Longmans, Green, 1872

Morton, Thomas. *Causa regia, sive de authoritate et dignitate principum Christianorum dissertatio: adversus Rob. Cardinalis Bellarmini tractatum De officio principis Christiani inscriptum, edita*. London: John Bill, 1620

Mundy, John Hine, and Kennerly M. Woody, eds. *The Council of Constance: The Unification of the Church*. Trans. Louise Ropes Loomis. New York: Columbia University Press, 1961

Neile, Richard. *Alter Ecebolius, M. Ant. De Dominis, arch. Spalatensis, pluribus dominis inseruire doctus*. London: John Bill, 1624

M. Ant. De Dñis, Arch-bishop of Spalato, His Shiftings in Religion: A Man for Many Masters. London: John Bill, 1624

Nicholas of Cusa. *The Catholic Concordance.* Ed. and trans. Paul E. Sigmund, Cambridge: Cambridge University Press, 1991

Notestein, Wallace, and Frances Helen Relf, eds. *Commons Debates for 1629.* Minneapolis: University of Minnesota Press, 1921

Overall, John. *Bishop Overall's Convocation–Book, MDCVI., Concerning the Government of God's Catholick Church and the Kingdoms of the Whole World.* London: Walter Kettilby, 1690

Owen, David. *Herod and Pilate Reconciled: or, The Concord of Papist and Pvritan (against Scripture, Fathers, Councels, and Other Orthodoxall Writers) for the Coercion, Deposition, and Killing of Kings.* Cambridge: Cantrell Legge, 1610

Pareus, David. *De pace & unione ecclesiarum evangel. oratio inauguralis habita in solenni Universitatis Heidelbergensis.* Heidelberg: Jonas Rose, 1616

　Irenicum, sive de unione et synodo evangelicorum concilianda liber votivus paci ecclesiae & desideriis pacificorum dicatus. Heidelberg: Jonas Rose, 1615

　Opervm theologicorum partes quatuor. Ed. Philipp Pareus. 3 vols. Frankfurt: Jonas Rose, 1647

Parsons, Robert. *A Conference abovt the Next Succession to the Crowne of Ingland.* [Antwerp: A. Conincx,] 1594 [1595]

[Parsons, Robert.] *The Jesuit's Memorial for the Intended Reformation of England under Their First Popish Prince, Published from the Copy That Was Presented to the Late King James II.* Ed. Edward Gee. London: Richard Chiswell, 1690

　The Ivdgment of a Catholicke English–man, Living in Banishment for His Religion, Written to His Priuate Friend in England, Concerning a Late Booke Set Forth, and Entituled, Triplici nodo, triplex cuneus, or, An Apologie for the Oath of Allegiance. [St. Omer: English College Press,] 1608

Parsons, Robert and Thomas Fitzherbert. *A Discvssion of the Answere of M. William Barlow, D. of Divinity, to the Booke Intituled The Iudgment of a Catholicke Englishman Living in Banishment for His Religion &c. Concerning the Apology of the New Oath of Allegiance.* [St. Omer: English College Press,] 1612

Pollard, Alfred W., ed. *Records of the English Bible: The Documents Relating to the Translation and Publication of the Bible in English, 1525–1611.* London: Oxford University Press, 1911

A Protestation Made for the Mighty and Most Redoubted Kynge of Englande, etc. and His Hole Counsell and Clergie. London: Thomas Berthelet, 1537

Prynne, William. *The Church of Englands Old Antithesis to New Arminianisme.* London, 1629

　God No Imposter nor Deluder: or, An Answer to a Popish and Arminian Cavill. n. p., 1629

　The Perpetuitie of a Regenerate Mans Estate. London: William Jones, 1626

Quick, John, ed. *Synodicon in Gallia Reformata: or, The Acts, Decision, Decrees, and Canons of Those Famous National Councils of the Reformed Churches in France.* 2 vols. London: T. Parkhurst and J. Robinson, 1692

Rees, Thomas, ed. *The Racovian Catechism, with Notes and Illustrations, Translated from the Latin: To Which Is Prefixed a Sketch of the History of Unitarianism in Poland and the Adjacent Countries.* London: Longman, Hurst, Rees, Orme, and Brown, 1818

A Relation Sent from Rome, of the Processe, Sentence, and Execvtion, Done Upon the Body, Picture, and Bookes of Marcvs Antonius De Dominis, Archbishop of Spalato, after His Death. London: John Bill, 1624

Richer, Edmond. *A Treatise of Ecclesiasticall and Politike Power.* London: Iohn Budge, 1612

Robinson, Hastings, ed. *Original Letters Relative to the English Reformation, Written during the Reigns of King Henry VIII, King Edward VI and Queen Mary.* 2 parts. Cambridge: Cambridge University Press, 1846–1847

Robinson, John. *A Defence of the Doctrine Propovnded by the Synode at Dort.* [Leyden,] 1624

Roe, Thomas. *The Negotiations of Sir Thomas Roe in His Embassy to the Ottoman Porte, from the Year 1621 to 1628 Inclusive.* Ed. Samuel Richardson. London: Society for the Encouragement of Learning, 1740

Rossaeus, G. *De ivsta reipvb. Christianae in reges impios et haereticos authoritate.* Paris: Guillaume Bichon, 1590

Rous, Francis. *Testis Veritatis: The Doctrine of King Iames, Our Late Soueraigne of Famous Memory, of the Church of England, of the Catholicke Chvrch, Plainely Shewed To Bee One in the Points of Praedestination, Free–Will, Certaintie of Saluation, with a Discouery of the Grounds both Naturall and Politicke of Arminianisme.* London: W. I., 1626

Rozemond, Keetze, ed. *Cyrille Lucar: Sermons, 1598–1602.* Leiden: E. J. Brill, 1974

Rushworth, John, ed. *Historical Collections.* 7 vols. London: George Thomason, 1659–1701

[Salvard, Jean François, ed.] *Harmonia confessionvm fidei, orthodoxarum, & reformatarum ecclesiarum, quae in praecipuis quibusque Europae regnis, nationibus, & prouinciis, sacram euangelij doctrinam pure profitentur.* Geneva: Petrus Santandrea, 1581

Sandys, Edwin. *A Relation of the State of Religion: And with What Hopes and Policies It Hath Beene Framed, and Is Maintained in the Severall States of These Westerne Parts of the World.* London: Simon Waterson, 1605

Sarpi, Paolo. *Historia del Concilio Tridentino: nella quale si scoprano tutti gl'artificii della corte di Roma, per impedire che né la verità di dogmi si palesasse né la riforma del papato & della chiesa si trattasse, di Pietro Soave Polano.* London: John Bill, 1619

   The Historie of the Covncel of Trent: Containing Eight Bookes, in Which (Besides the Ordinarie Actes of the Councell) Are Declared Many Notable Occurences Which Happened in Christendome during the Space of Fourtie Yeeres and More, and, Particularly, the Practises of the Court of Rome, to Hinder the Reformation of Their Errors, and to Maintain Their Greatness. Trans. Nathanael Brent. London: Robert Barker and Iohn Bill, 1620

   The History of the Quarrels of Pope Paul V. with the State of Venice. London: John Bill, 1626

   Lettere ai gallicani. Ed. Boris Ulianich. Wiesbaden: Franz Steiner, 1961

   Opere. Ed. Gaetano and Luisa Cozzi. Milan–Naples: Ricciardi, 1969

Schaff, Philip, ed. *The Creeds of Christendom.* 3 vols. New York: Harper & Brothers, 1877

Schulcken, Adolph. *Apologia Adolphi Schulckenii Geldriensis, S.S. theologiae apud Ubios doctoris et professoris atque ad D. Martini pastoris pro illustrissimo domino D. Roberto Ballarmino S.R.E. Card. de potestate Romani Pont. temporali.* Cologne, 1613

Scott, Thomas. *Vox populi: or, Newes from Spayne, Translated According to the Spanish Coppie, Which May Serve to Forwarn Both England and the Vnited Provinces How Farr to Trust to Spanish Pretences.* n. p., 1620

Shuckburgh, E. S., ed. *Two Biographies of William Bedell, Bishop of Kilmore, with a Selection of His Letters and an Unpublished Treatise.* Cambridge: Cambridge University Press, 1902

Smith, Logan Pearsall. *The Life and Letters of Sir Henry Wotton.* 2 vols. Oxford: Clarendon Press, 1907

Sollom, M. N., ed. *A Complete Collection of State–Trials and Proceedings for High–Treason and Other Crimes and Misdemeanours.* 6 vols. London: J. Walthoe, 1730

✝ Sommerville, Johann P., ed. *King James VI and I: Political Writings.* Cambridge: Cambridge University Press, 1994

Spottiswoode, John. *The History of the Church of Scotland.* Ed. M. Russell. 3 vols. Edinburgh: Oliver & Boyd, 1851

Suarez, Francisco de. *Defensio fidei Catholicae et apostolicae aduersus anglicanae sectae errores, cum responsione ad Apologiam pro iuramento fidelitatis & Praefationem monitoriam serenissimi Iacobi Angliae Regis; ad serenissimos totius Christiani orbis Catholicos reges ac principes.* Coimbra: Gomez de Loureyro, 1613

Sweet, John. *Monsig.r fate voi, or a Discovery of the Dalmatian Apostata, M. Antonivs De Dominis, and His Bookes.* [St. Omer,] 1617

T. H. *Newes from Rome, Spalato's Doome: or, An Epitome of the Life and Behaviour of M. Antonius de Dominis, First Bishop of Segnia, Afterwards Archbishop of Spalato.* London: Richard Whitaker, 1624

T. W. [Thomas Wilson?] *The Araignment and Execvtion of the Late Traytors, with a Relation of the Other Traytors, Which Were Executed at Worcester, the 27 of Ianuary Last Past.* London: Jeffrey Chorlton, 1606

Tanner, J. R., ed. *Constitutional Documents of the Reign of James I, A.D. 1603–1625, with an Historical Commentary.* Cambridge: Cambridge University Press, 1930

Tesimond, Oswald. *The Gunpowder Plot: The Narrative of Oswald alias Greenway.* Ed. Francis Edwards. London: Folio Society, 1973

Thomson, Richard. *Elenchus refutationis Torturae Torti: pro reverendissimo in Christo patre domino Episcopo Eliense adversus Martinum Becanum Iesuitam.* London: R. Barker, 1611

Thomson, Thomas, ed. *The Historie and Life of King James the Sext.* Edinburgh: Bannatyne Club, 1825

Thomson, Thomas and C. Innes, eds. *The Acts of the Parliaments of Scotland.* 12 vols. Edinburgh: Published by Royal Command, 1814–1875

Tooker, William. *Dvellum siue singvlare certamen cum Martino Becano Iesuita, futiliter refutante Apologiam et Monitoriam praefatione.* London: N. Butter and R. Mab, 1611

Treatise Concernynge Generall Councilles, the Byshoppes of Rome, and the Clergy. London: Thomas Berthelet, 1538

A Trve and Perfect Relation of the Proceedings at the Seuerall Arraignments of the Late Most Barbarous Traitors. London: Robert Barker, 1606

A Trve and Perfect Relation of the Whole Proceedings against the Late Most Barbarous Traitors, Garnet a Iesuite, and His Confederats, Contayning Sundry Speeches Delivered by the Lords Commissioners at Their Arraignments, for the Better Satisfaction of Those That Were Hearers, as Occasion Was Offered; the Earl of Northamptons Speech Hauing Bene Enlarged upon Those Grounds Which Are Set Downe; and Lastly all That Passed at Garnets Execution. London: Robert Barker, 1606

Van der Essen, Léon and Armand Louant, eds. *Correspondance d'Ottavio Mirto Frangipani, premier nonce de Flandre (1596–1606).* 3 vols. Rome: Institute historique belge, 1924–1942

Vitoria, Francisco de. *Political Writings.* Ed. Anthony Pagden and Jeremy Lawrance. Cambridge: Cambridge University Press, 1991

Vossius, Gerardus Joannes. *Gerardi Joan. Vossi et clarorum virorum ad eum epistolae.* Ed. Paulus Colomesius. 2 parts. London: Samuel Smith, 1690

Wadkins, Timothy H. "King James I Meets John Percy, S. J. (25 May 1622): An Unpublished Manuscript from the Religious Controversies Surrounding the Countess of Buckingham's Conversion." *Recusant History,* 19 (1988), 146–154

Walton, Izaak. *Life of Mr. Richard Hooker* [first published, 1665]. In *The Lives of John Donne, Sir Henry Wotton, Richard Hooker, George Herbert & Robert Sanderson.* Ed. George Saintsbury. London: Oxford University Press, 1956

Weldon, Anthony. *The Court and Character of King James.* London: John Wright, 1650

Westcott, Allan F., ed. *New Poems of James I of England.* New York: Columbia University Press, 1911

White, Francis. *A Replie to Iesuit Fishers Answere to Certain Questions Propoūded by His Most Gratious Matie King James.* London: Adam Islip, 1624

Widdrington, Roger [Thomas Preston]. *Apologia Cardinalis Bellarmini pro ivre principvm: aduersus suas ipsius rationes pro auctoritate papali principes seculares in ordine ad bonum spirituale deponendi.* [London: Richard Field,] 1611

　A Cleare, Sincere, and Modest Confutation of the Unsound, Fraudulent, and Intemperate Reply of T. F. Who Is Known To Be Mr. Thomas Fitzherbert, Now an English Iesuite. [London: Edward Griffin,] 1616

Williams, John. *Great Britains Salomon: A Sermon Preached at the Magnificent Funerall of the Most High and Mighty King, Iames, the Late King of Great Britaine, France, Ireland, Defender of the Faith, &c., at the Collegiate Church of Saint Peter at Westminster, the Seuenth of May 1625.* London: John Bill, 1625

Willson, David Harris, ed. *The Parliamentary Diary of Robert Bowyer, 1606–1607.* Minneapolis: University of Minnesota Press, 1931

Wilson, Arthur. *The History of Great Britain, Being the Life and Reign of King James the First, Relating to What Passed from His First Access to the Crown Till His Death.* London: Richard Lownds, 1653

Winwood, Ralph. *Memorials of Affairs of State in the Reigns of Queen Elizabeth and King James I.* Ed. Edmund Sawyer. 3 vols. London: T. Ward, 1725

Wood, Anthony à. *Athenae Oxoniensis: An Exact History of All the Writers and Bishops Who Have Had Their Education in the University of Oxford.* Ed. Philip Bliss. 4 vols. London: F. C. and J. Rivington, 1813–1820 – originally published, 1691

Wotton, Anthony. *A Dangerous Plot Discovered: By a Discourse Wherein Is Proved that Mr. Richard Mountagu in His Two Bookes, the One Called A New Gagg, the Other, A Iust Appeale, Laboureth to Bring in the Faith of Rome and Arminius under the Name and Pretence of the Doctrine and Faith of the Church of England.* London: Nicholas Bourne, 1626

Wotton, Henry. *Letters and Dispatches from Sir Henry Wotton to James the First and His Ministers in the Years MDCXVII–XX*. Ed. George Tomline. London: William Nicol, 1850

Yates, John. *Ibis ad Caesarem: or, A Svbmissive Appearance before Caesar, in Answer to Mr. Mountagues Appeale, in the Points of Arminianisme and Popery, Maintained and Defended by Him, against the Doctrine of the Church of England*. London: R. Mylbourne, 1626.

INDEX

cut

and the Levant 197–8
and the papacy 91, 97, 115–17, 222–3, 224, 226, 230, 246
and Sarpi 116, 223, 246, 247, 250n, 257
and Spain 91, 116, 117
and the Uskok pirates 222
Victor Amadeus, heir to the duchy of Savoy 352
Villeroy, Nicholas de Neufville, seigneur de, secretary of state in France 99, 132, 156, 167, 186
Villiers, Sir Edward, English envoy 307
Vitré, National Synod of 192–3
Vlastos, Jacobos, Greek student at Oxford 206
Vorstius, Conradus, Dutch Protestant theologian 262–3
vows, monastic 214

Wadsworth, James, English Roman Catholic in Spain 323
Walloon churches 264
Walton, Izaak, English writer and biographer 67
Ward, Samuel, master of Sidney Sussex College, Cambridge
on the atonement 271–2
and Dort 264, 265, 271–2, 281, 285
Ward, Samuel, minister (lecturer) in Ipswich 283
Warmington, William, English Roman Catholic writer 103
Watson, Anthony, opponent of Montague 286
Watson, William, English Roman Catholic priest 49
Weldon, Sir Anthony, clerk of the Green Cloth, historical writer 359
Weston, Sir Richard, chancellor of the exchequer, diplomat 311, 312, 313, 318, 337
Whitaker, William, master of St. John's College, Cambridge 107, 189
White, Francis, dean of Carlisle 342, 344
White Mountain, battle of the 305

Whitgift, John, archbishop of Canterbury 44–5, 65
Widdrington, Roger *see* Preston, Thomas
Williams, John, bishop of Lincoln and lord keeper of the Great Seal 206–7, 356, 357–8
Williams, John, principal of Jesus College, Oxford 204
Wilson, Arthur, historian and dramatist 220, 359–60
Winwood, Sir Ralph, English ambassador to the United Provinces, secretary of state 156, 295
Wittenberg University 213
Wood, Anthony à, antiquary and historian 205
Wotton, Sir Henry, English ambassador to Venice 116, 126n, 129, 163n, 223, 232, 246, 301
Wotton of Marley, Edward, Lord, English ambassador extraordinary to France 129
Wren, Matthew, fellow of Pembroke Hall, Cambridge 323–4
Württemberg, duchy of 161
Wyche, Sir Peter, English ambassador to the Ottoman Empire 209

Xanten, Peace of 294

Yates, John, rector of St. Mary's Stiffkey in Norfolk 283, 286
Ynojosa, Juan de Mendoza, marquis de la, Spanish ambassador extraordinary to England 329
York House, conference at 285
Young, Sir George, of Wilkinton 203
Young, John, dean of Winchester 273
Young, Patrick, keeper of the library of James VI and I 202, 204, 219
Young, Peter, James VI's tutor 17

Zabarella, Francesco, conciliarist writer and theologian 57
Zeeland, province of 172

CAMBRIDGE STUDIES IN EARLY MODERN BRITISH HISTORY

George Lawson's 'Politica' and the English Revolution
CONAL CONDREN
Puritans and Roundheads: The Harleys of Brampton Bryan and the Outbreak of the English Civil War
JACQUELINE EALES
An Uncounselled King: Charles I and the Scottish Troubles, 1637–1641
PETER DONALD
Cheap Print and Popular Piety, 1550–1640*
TESSA WATT
The Pursuit of Stability: Social Relations in Elizabethan London
IAN W. ARCHER
Prosecution and Punishment: Petty Crime and the Law in London and Rural Middlesex, c. 1660–1725
ROBERT B. SHOEMAKER
Algernon Sidney and the Restoration Crisis, 1677–1683
JONATHAN SCOTT
Exile and Kingdom: History and Apocalypse in the Puritan Migration to America
AVIHU ZAKAI
The Pillars of Priestcraft Shaken: The Church of England and its Enemies, 1660–1730
J. A. I. CHAMPION
Stewards, Lords and People: The Estate Steward and his World in Later Stuart England
D. R. HAINSWORTH
Civil War and Restoration in the Three Stuart Kingdoms: The Career of Randal MacDonnell, Marquis of Antrim, 1609–1683
JANE H. OHLMEYER
The Family of Love in English Society, 1550–1630
CHRISTOPHER W. MARSH
The Bishops' Wars: Charles I's Campaigns against Scotland, 1638–1640*
MARK FISSEL
John Locke: Resistance, Religion and Responsibility*
JOHN MARSHALL
Constitutional Royalism and the Search for Settlement, c. 1640–1649
DAVID L. SMITH
Intelligence and Espionage in the Reign of Charles II, 1660–1685
ALAN MARSHALL
The Chief Governors: The Rise and Fall of Reform Government in Tudor Ireland, 1536–1588
CIARAN BRADY

*Also published as a paperback